-‹◊›---‹◊›---‹◊›---‹◊›---‹◊›---‹◊›---‹◊›---‹◊›---‹◊›---‹◊›-

GALACTIC HISTORY OF THE MULTIVERSE THE FINAL BATTLE

BOOK II

RISING PHOENIX AURORA

-‹◊›---‹◊›---‹◊›---‹◊›---‹◊›---‹◊›---‹◊›---‹◊›---‹◊›---‹◊›-

Copyright © 2023 by Rising Phoenix Aurora, Inc.
All rights reserved.

No part of this publication may be reproduced, stored in, or introduced into a retrieval system, or transmitted, in any form, or by any means (electronic, mechanical, photocopying, recording, or otherwise), without the prior written permission of both the copyright owner and the above publisher of this book. The scanning, uploading, and distribution of this book via the internet, or via any other means, without the permission of the publisher is illegal. Please purchase only authorized electronic editions; your support of the author's rights is very much appreciated.

The authors of this book do not dispense medical advice, or prescribe the use of any technique as a form of treatment for physical, emotional, or medical problems directly, or indirectly. Please consult a physician for any health concerns. The intent of this book is to only offer information of a general nature to aid you in your quest for emotional and spiritual well-being. In the event you use any of the information in this book for yourself or others, the authors and the publisher assume no responsibility for your actions.

Published by Rising Phoenix Aurora, Inc.
www.risingphoenixaurora.com

Paperback ISBN: ISBN: 978-1-7358542-3-6

1st Edition, October 2023

Special thanks to the Illustrator Samia, who is a digital artist and clear channel to benevolent energies. You can find her at www.aurapractitioners.com.

TABLE OF CONTENTS

ACKNOWLEDGEMENTS	HOW THIS BOOK CAME TO BE……	5
INTRODUCTION	PURPOSE OF THIS BOOK……	7
IMPORTANT	LOVE-LIGHT SHIELDING TECHNIQUE……	10
CHAPTER 1	The Garden of Eden….	13
CHAPTER 2	The Key to Ascension….	23
CHAPTER 3	Banished for Eternity….	38
CHAPTER 4	Deep State Council Member….	61
CHAPTER 5	The A.I. Alien Invasion….	81
CHAPTER 6	The Illuminati in the Holocaust….	97
CHAPTER 7	The Essenes….	117
CHAPTER 8	A Goddess Incarnate….	130
CHAPTER 9	7 Goddesses of Gaia….	151
CHAPTER 10	The Archon Realm….	166
CHAPTER 11	The Archon Maker - War of the Gods….	183
CHAPTER 12	Celestial Dragons….	199
CHAPTER 13	Lab Babies….	215
CHAPTER 14	Angel Babies & Dragon Guardians….	239
CHAPTER 15	Forced into Extinction….	252
CHAPTER 16	Pyramid Portals Inside Earth….	261
CHAPTER 17	Yeshua, Dolores & Donald Trump….	279
CHAPTER 18	SERIES - The Virus Throughout the….	301
CHAPTER 19	SERIES - The Birthing of Ascension….	318
CHAPTER 20	SERIES - The Final Battle - Eradication….	332
Conclusion	Coda: Love, Sovereignty, and Rebirth….	361
About Aurora	……	365
Your Soul's Growth Journey	……	369
Glossary	……	377

ACKNOWLEDGEMENTS

--------------<<>>--------------

Thank you to the infinite Multiverse who were all part of the Creation of this masterful book. All which is created from divine Source Love-Light is a collective collaboration energetically. Not one being can accomplish a mission on their own. Therefore, my acknowledgements are for many, and are truly infinite.

I would like to thank you, dearest reader, because, truly, I do it all for you. Thank you for the loving support, whether you just found me, or found me over six years ago. Your comments, your shares, your love has been adored and treasured throughout these years, and has truly gotten me through the most challenging times. I want to thank you for working diligently within yourself to understand our content, which we know has guided you to choose to keep expanding with an open mind and loving heart, and still you stand beside us. Thank you for choosing to ride Mother Earth's continual Ascension wave with us.

We thank the bravest souls, whether in this book, or not, who have chosen to follow their hearts to mine, to book an A.U.R.A. Hypnosis Healing session with me, or to become certified through A.U.R.A., and their Higher Selves, who believed in them, that they could reach their infinite level of self-healing potentials. Those sessions would become part of the ultimate completion of the Multiversal Ascension in which you will read within this book. Their example of self-love, and the love for others, is admirable!

I want to thank my divine team, whether incarnated on Earth, or working from beyond the veil of Earth. To my RPA team, who consists of A.U.R.A. practitioners from around the world, and who assisted me to transcribe and edit each Chapter, you are loved and honored for the work you have done in ensuring that all was done in the highest love. My spiritual team, you have got me through every challenge, every lesson, every activation miraculously. Thank you to my divine team for how much they listen to me and guide me when looking to choose the highest path of Source Love-Light. These divine teams are why I am here in this very special moment releasing Book 2.

Fourth and finally, my beautiful husband, who has been with me throughout all life, time, and space. Who has embraced me and lifted me when I needed to prevail to accomplish the writing of this book, or any other project. Who lives to love me. Who celebrates me everyday with his infinite love for me, and our children, both furry and none furry. My family is who is most precious to me, who assists me to hold the space of the most infinite Source Love-Light everyday, so that I may accomplish all that I do daily in assistance for the collective. They are truly my superheroes!

I honor you, love you, and respect you!

We are infinitely grateful for you, dearest reader, and fellow traveler on this most beautiful journey of Creation!
~ Rising Phoenix AuroRa

--------------<<>>--------------

INTRODUCTION

Greetings, our beloved, beautiful children. This is the Divine Mother of Creation, Sophia, and the Daughter of the Flame, the Phoenix, the Creators. We are who channels through AuroRa in all ways, whether live on video, or in written form. We have been erased much from your Earth's History, for a diabolical purpose of suppressing the Creator within you, but through this book you will remember us once more, and our true, divine, diamond, creational beauty. At the end of each past life regression memory, we channeled the entirety of the sacred knowledge required of each chapter. Excitedly, grab your crystals, blankets, teas, and prepare yourself to regain your Source Love-Light, and memory, in infinite ways, through this most soul brilliant read. Through the completion of each chapter, you will feel resolve, you will self-heal, regain memory, activate, become a fuller version of yourself, gain sovereignty, so that if you so choose, you will become the Source Love-Light warrior you have always been, and were meant to become!

Rise my children, rise! For too long you have been oppressed and made into what you are not. You are not weak, you are strong! You have not been forgotten, you are remembered! You are not a victim, you are a survivor! You are not insignificant, you are brilliant! You are not unloved, you are love! You are not limited, you are unlimited! You are not in captivity, you are free! You are not weak, you are invincible, because you are me, and I am you! A most beautiful, divine Creation you are, as am I!

This is the moment we all have been waiting for. The final showdown, the end game, the final battle, the eradication of the Archon/Artificial Intelligence from all of Creation. But, first we must understand what *it* is, and *it's* foolish inverted games. Which we will understand through this book. Why now? Because the world is finally ready, thanks to your loving resolve, which has lifted the Earth higher and higher every portal date, eclipse, new and full moons... We are stepping into 2024, the year of the dragon in ancient Chinese culture, and this year's collective energy will continue to lead us towards the path of the Multiversal eradication of the A.I. You, who are holding this book in your palms, we are most thankful for, because through your diligent reading, you will shift the Earth with every tear, every joy, every wisdom, gained through each of the past life memories remembered, through these beautiful brave souls who shared them with us. In which you will pay homage to your brethren and their strength, for you are strong, because they are strong, and they are strong, because you are strong. Your strength and self awareness is what will bring forth the final eradication of the Archon.

If you are new to us, we do recommend you go back and read Book 1; however, it is not completely necessary, as you will understand much of what has been delivered through this book. In Book 1 you learned of the New World Order, the different negative polarized aliens throughout our Universe, and their infringements onto organic lifeforms. So that you could awaken into taking your divine power back, in no longer allowing infringements upon you and your loved ones. And, in Book 2, we pushed our knowledge to the most infinite ways, because to understand what is the Archon/artificial intelligence we needed to enter the sacredness of the Multiverse, which we accomplished so beautifully.

In Book 1, we focused thoroughly on the body scans of each client to ensure the understanding of what attachments are, and how they affect us when they remain in the body. In Book 2, our focus is on sacred knowledge, since we have touched detailedly on these foreign infringements in Book 1. Therefore, in every chapter of Book 2, we have minimized the details of each body scan. Which allowed AuroRa to channel the grandest sacred knowledge, in the assistance of understanding each chapter in the most profound ways. We have left the parts in the body scan that were important to remain, which added more to each client's journey, and our own self growth, in sacred knowledge for our continual Ascension process. Know though that in each A.U.R.A. Hypnosis Healing session, the entire list of the client's needs and ailments have been addressed, so they can begin their self-healing journey.

There are many ways in which humankind is being attacked in this Earth's time, which are distractions made from the negative alien agendas within Earth. And our hope through this book, is to assist you to refocus on the true divine plan of the eradication of what clouds us, divides us, and purposely, diabolically, distracts us from the true mission of Ascension. Our message to you is of hope, for where there is hope there is love, and love is infinite. Know that you can break free from the mind controls and the energetic shackles imposed on you, as soon as you realize how divinely powerful you truly are at the soul level with your divine connection to Source. We go within, as some of the toughest and most profound battles occur within us, not outside of us. When we commit to self-healing, this is an empowering crucial first step in realizing our divine sovereignty, and our true strength, as a child of the Divine Creator Source. We rise above fear by doing the inner work, the shadow work, through energetic shielding ourselves from harm using Source Love-Light force fields, establishing boundaries, and embracing our sovereignty. And, if one feels guided to do so, there are powerful healing modalities available such as A.U.R.A. Hypnosis Healing and R.A.A.H Reiki Healing to aid and jump start your self-healing journey.

All of these galactic soul journeys were facilitated using a sacred self-healing modality called Angelic Universal Regression Alchemy (A.U.R.A.) Hypnosis Healing. A.U.R.A. is a past life regression, entity removal, modality. The A.U.R.A. modality uses a combination of sacred Angelic energy work, and sacred alchemy and hypnosis, to create a bridge for the client to connect to their Higher Self. This allows us to enter the theta brainwave of A.U.R.A. Hypnosis sacredly and safely to bring forth memories of our existence, to quantum heal our body, to find our life purpose, and to remember our Galactic Origins. In A.U.R.A. sessions, as a client, you will speak to your soul, to your Higher Self, who is you; the Higher Self is ONE with the Creator, who knows all. Our higher self/soul is truly God Source, and is where we can find all the answers we are looking for, and where we connect to this unlimited, infinite healing potential. By connecting to our Higher Self, we then allow for that little voice in our head that has been there all our life, our consciousness, to finally speak through us, sharing their infinite wisdom.

Many experience blockages of energy, which do not allow for the deepest possible connection to the Higher Self during hypnosis. This is what sets A.U.R.A. Hypnosis Healing apart from other hypnosis past-life regression modalities. The Key being that before a client's session begins, the client's higher self, in union with the A.U.R.A. Hypnosis practitioner conducts sacred energy work prior to entering the hypnosis brainwave, thus creating a bridge for the client to connect to their Higher Self at the deepest level possible. Through this sacred energy work, our Higher Self places us in the highest, safest, sacred vibration that no longer allows what is inorganic within us to remain during the high vibrations of the A.U.R.A. session. This begins the unveiling of all that is artificial within clients, bringing it all up to the surface for healing.

The Archangels are able to assist, always with the higher selves' permission, first, by using their infinite Source Love-Light to strengthen the connection, to allow for the healing of the mind, body, and soul during the session. The Archangels are the first fractals of Divine Creator Source; the Elohim, Angelics individualized out from the collective infinite consciousness of Source. Therefore, they hold the purest frequencies in Creation, and they are able to assist us in healings in divine ways that align with our soul's organic blueprints. By being of this infinite Source beginning fractals, the Angels hold the greatest strength of Source Love-Light power, and are the only ones who can travel into all existence of the Multiverse. Which is why when the Higher Selves of our clients can't heal, or remove something, THEY can. Throughout this book we will read about the infinite, beautiful ways the Archangels and benevolent soul families always assist all of us, through the healings shared in all of the galactic soul journeys mentioned. Truly, we are loved beyond measure by Source and our Galactic soul families, for they are always there to assist us for our highest good in our lives!

Throughout this book, there will be the occasional reference to the Reiki Angelic Alchemy Healing (R.A.A.H.) method, which is another profound and powerful energy healing modality, which also uses sacred Angelic alchemy to facilitate the healing session. Unlike A.U.R.A. Hypnosis Healing sessions, R.A.A.H. does not go into past-life regressions, or utilize hypnosis. For those who feel they are not quite ready yet for an A.U.R.A. session, a R.A.A.H. session is a beautiful way to prepare for a future A.U.R.A. session, as it helps the client to start connecting to their Higher Self, and their clairvoyant senses. The main focus of this book is on the A.U.R.A. Hypnosis Healing modality and all of Rising Phoenix AuroRa's Love-Light channeled content, through which these beautiful Soul Journeys and Higher Selves' wisdom are shared with us and the collective.

In this book you will find what has never been spoken, because of the sacredness of the knowledge, and the ways this has been guarded throughout our Earth's History. So, with the greatest honor, we are ready to embark with you on this most soul and heart fulfilling read! We look to not keep you any longer. Let's dive in deeply together now!

We are not here to fight these Archon battles, we are here to end them!

~ Rising Phoenix AuroRa

IMPORTANT

SOURCE LOVE-LIGHT SHIELDING TECHNIQUE

BEFORE YOU BEGIN READING THIS BOOK, understand that one of our core foundational teachings is shielding ourselves with our own "I AM Source Love-Light," so we can be more intentional with managing our energy frequency in our daily lives, thus empowering us to be in our sovereignty. When we shield, and set our intentions for the day, we are declaring our sovereignty over our own free will and life force, and how we want our day to be. We are powerful creator beings, if we allow for it, by actively maintaining our vibrations to the purest, I AM Source Love-Light.

Review these pages carefully, as they contain sacred alchemy teachings for you to start using your "I AM Source Love-Light" to create force fields around you in maintaining your vibrations high. Our intent is to teach you how you can help your inner light become stronger, by actively using the force fields around you, filtering out the negative that means harm, so that you may strongly heart discern every frequency that passes through. These force fields will help amplify your heart discernment, reading what energies are harmful, and what is not.

It is important that we surround ourselves with our own infinite "I AM Source Love-Light" daily. Ideally, you should be shielding yourself every morning when you wake up, and every evening, before the sun sets, for optimal results. This energy is accessed through your heart and flows out through your hand chakras. Our heart center is where we are able to tap into the infinite Source Love-Light energy. When doing this for your day, it will ensure to keep your energies high and not depleted, when we set the proper intent for our energy. Surrounding yourself with the "I AM Source Love-Light" will help you keep your mind focused and clear, and your abilities strong and open.

Practice these empowering Source Love-Light shielding techniques on the next two pages daily!

OPENING YOUR HAND CHAKRAS

It is important to open your hand chakras, as it is out from them that the Universal love energy will flow. Energy will enter through the crown and bottom of the feet, connect to the heart, and flow out through the palms, connecting the alchemy symbols.

1. Place hands in Gassho position (Gassho is a gesture with the hands held in prayer position, in front of the heart).

2. Rub hands together, as you desire.

3. Clap four times in prayer position and state with strength, "Open!"

4. Turn hands horizontal, with left hand above right, facing each other.

5. Open and close both hands in this position 13 times.

6. Switch hands now, right hand over left.

7. Open and close both hands again in this position 13 times.

8. You should be feeling vibrations in between your palms.

9. Play with this energy, moving it around, expanding it bigger and then shrinking it. Creating it into an energy ball.

If the energy ball bursts, no worries, just rub hands again together, and pull apart palms facing each other to create again.

No need to repeat steps 1-7 once the opening of hand chakras is completed. Going forward just rubbing hands together will create the energy ball inside palms.

You may use this energy ball of Source Love-Light around your home, cars, spouses, and children stating, "without harming anyone." We are powerful creator beings, and by stating this we make sure to not pull from someone else's energy, and only from Source Love-Light.

-<<>>---<<>>---<<>>---<<>>---<<>>---<<>>---<<>>---<<>>---<<>>---<<>>---<<>>---<<>>-

I AM SOURCE LOVE-LIGHT AND MERKABAH

1. Rub your hands together to create your energy ball consisting of your "I AM Source Love-Light."
2. Viewing the energy ball and sensing it through your third eye/imagination. Expand it to surround your vessel and auric field. You may make it the color of your choice, and may include a sacred geometric symbol that aligns with you, encasing the walls of this bubble.
3. Set the intent by stating, "Shall I be shielded from harm mentally, physically, emotionally, and spiritually throughout the infinity of Creation. I DO NOT CONSENT to harm all day and night, without harming anyone, for my highest good."
4. As you expand the light, state four times, "I invoke the I AM Love-Light in me."
5. With your hands expand the light around yourself, your loved ones, animal companions, cars, websites, projects, and home…
6. Now envision your eight-pointed Merkabah surrounding you, which is a live consciousness connected to your soul, so envision it activating, or coming to life, so to speak.

7. The Merkabah is a counterclockwise, upside down, four-sided pyramid, expanding, repelling, spinning structure of light at the bottom. Clockwise, right side up, drawing in energy at the top pyramid through the crown. The Merkabah is an extension of our consciousness and represents the integration of the spiritual energy, and physical bodies. Made up of eight triangles having eight points, we find that the Merkabah also reflects the infinite energy and protection of Creation (since the number eight is an ancient alchemy infinity symbol). Each triangle's three-sided points represent the sacred three elements of the Holy Trinity of Divine Mother, Divine Father and Child.

For more teachings on shielding go to www.risingphoenixaurora.com, where AuroRa offers a 'How to Shield' course. For more now, go to "Your Soul's Growth Journey" section, page 370.

1

APHRODITE - GARDEN OF EDEN

Session #497: Recorded in October 2022
Never before shared.

In this in-person A.U.R.A. Hypnosis Healing session, I am most honored by Mandy who is Aphrodite in the flesh. She takes us on one of the most powerful journeys understanding the beginning of the dark force of artificial intelligence, before it became A.I. itself. The birthing point of the Garden of Eden, and its creations to come. The foundation to when life begins to be given the choice to expand out from our birth given right of free willed expression. The seeds of creation.

--------------<<>>--------------

"All of Creation has free will, so there are times when the void will slip in. Before it completely consumes them, I'm there to help turn it around."
~Aphrodite

--------------<<>>--------------

A: *[Aurora] Tell me what you're feeling and sensing.*
M: [Mandy] There's a ball of light that's me, but I don't know where I am. Like in a womb. You can sense light coming through, but I can't see out of it.
A: *Tell me about this light.*
M: It's like curves of light. White in some places and darker in others.
A: *Is the light white or does it have colors in it?*
M: It's pink, like flesh, like I'm looking through flesh.
A: *How does it feel to be there?*
M: It's nice. It's peaceful. It's like I'm just resting, and I have no cares about anything. It is on the seashore.
M: I feel like I'm inside something.
A: *What is this around you, encasing you?*
M: No. I can only see in front. It's like I can't turn and see on the sides. So I don't know what the oval shape is.
A: *Do you feel that there's anyone else within this beach space?*
M: No.
A: *Are you able to see past this encasement?*
M: No. I want to.
A: *Keep moving time to see if something changes within this space.*
M: No. I don't know why.
A: *That's okay.*
M: I feel like something's trying to come out of me. Like I'm a seed and I'm trying to reach out. I'm trying to get up to the light, but I'm not there yet.
A: *Keep fast forwarding. Tell me what's going on.*
M: I'm getting bigger.
A: *Describe to me how you're getting bigger.*
M: I don't know. I am just getting bigger. I can hear a heartbeat.
A: *Keep fast-forwarding time. As you're getting big, what happens next?*

M: It's like I'm coming up underneath a city, or something coming up underneath it. I could see it, but now I don't see it. Now I'm just under it.
A: You're under the light?
M: Yes. It's light on the outside, but I'm down in the middle trying to get up. I was approaching it, and then I got underneath it.
A: Has anything changed?
M: I can see some swirling. Like cream swirling around in coffee sauce, like liquid.
A: The swirling, what is it doing?
M: Like it's my outer surface. I'm still inside. I keep thinking that I'm going to open up. It feels like I am in a big belly, and I can sense that there's light outside it. I'm just stuck. I feel like I'm on the verge of coming out. I can hear my heart beating.
A: Let's see if we're able to move one more time within this space. Tell me what you see and sense now.

Client asks for a restroom break. The session continues.

M: When I went to the bathroom I saw a vision of a woman. Like a nymph. This beautiful female with long red hair coming out of a shell. The shell is behind me and under me when I'm out. Then around it is like a lotus flower. I can see the curves of the petals, the outer edges of the petals. That's what they were.
A: Are you this beautiful female inside this?
M: Yes.
A: You said the female has now come out of the shell?
M: Yes. Just standing there with the shell on top.
A: Tell me what that process was like when you were inside this encasement. You said that you couldn't move, but now you came out. Let's go back to that time when right before you came out of this encasement. You are about to come out. Tell me what's going on.
M: I could feel a heartbeat before, and then I just expanded up and out into this form. Like what was surrounding me opened up like a shell. I'm just standing in it right now, feeling nice and happy.
A: Look at your body, down at your feet. How many toes do you have?
M: Just five on each foot.
A: Look at your hands. How many fingers do you have?
M: Five.
A: Look at your skin tone. What color is it?
M: It's peachy. I feel like I have wings.
A: Beautiful. Your eyes, what color are they?
M: They're light brown. Maybe green or blue. Not sure.
A: You feel like you have wings? Describe to me what those feel like.
M: I can spread them, the feathers out, and feel the sun penetrate more into them. Feel the air lifting them, the little hairs, on the feathers. Feels good. I can feel the wind and the sun. It's a blue sky. There are not many clouds. It's tropical. Still on the beach.
A: Do the wings have a color to them?
M: White with tinges of light pastels.
A: Are you wearing any jewelry?
M: It's got striations in it. Like crystals, but one. You can see lines in it. It's angular, pointing at the top and fans out at the bottom. It's clear, but you can see whitish lines in it. Like a fan that's curved. There's some silver to the chain.
A: Are you holding anything else with you?
M: A staff, or a scepter with a globe on top, with my left hand. I've got the pendant with my right hand. I'm looking around. I belong here.
A: You're the only one within this space, correct?
M: Yes.
A: Let's move around. Are you able to move around within this space?

M: Yes. I think I'll step down out of the shell and move forward. I feel like I'm on a white horse moving forward.
A: Are you riding on the horse?
M: Yes, but the horse isn't really on the ground. It's flying along the shore. Flying above it.
A: Does the horse have wings?
M: I don't think so.
A: How about a horn?
M: Definitely has a mane. It could have a horn, a spirally one. It's got big eyes. It's kind of in awe of where we're going. It's just looking around, going down. I don't know who's leading who.
A: Allow for both of you to be carried to where you're meant to go. Tell me what that looks like. Where are you going?
M: There's a sheaf (like a quiver) on my back, and that scepter turns into a bow. I have arrows that I can shoot with the bow. I'm searching for something. I don't know what.
A: You don't know what it is?
M: Like maybe I need to shoot this arrow at something, but it's not to kill. It's more like an arrow of light. I'm shooting light into places that need light. I'm looking for those places. That's what I'm supposed to be doing.
A: Beautiful. How do you shoot those arrows?
M: Like a bow and arrow, and then let go. Wherever it lands it shoots out sparks. Then the colors go up. It's like everything is washed out, but then it's like filling in a coloring book. The sparks fly out and then the colors fill in. The trees are green where they're supposed to be green. There are flowers, different colors. Some butterflies are coming up. It's like a magical place. I'm having fun. It's like I'm creating it. It's nice.
A: Are you wearing any clothing?
M: I have a shimmery swath, wrapped around me, but on top, I'm not wearing any clothing except for the pendant.
A: Why are you shooting these lights?
M: It's part of Creation. It's like the outline is there. The intent is there. I'm just filling it in. It was still before, but now it's moving. It's becoming alive, and that's what I'm supposed to be doing.
A: Beautiful.
M: Creating a paradise.
A: What is it turning into now that that light is spreading?
M: There's vegetation. There are fruits. It's like a garden. I'm making a garden for others that come after. I'm preparing it. I'm making it. I'm creating it. There'll be others that come. They will eat the fruit.
A: Beautiful. Keep moving time. Keep telling me what's going on.
M: There's some orange lightning trying to come in and darken it.
A: Orange lightning?
M: Yes, and dark.
A: Dark lightning, or darkness?
M: There's darkness behind the orange lightning. The orange lightning is coming in and there's darkness behind it. I feel like I have to push it back.
A: How do you push it back?
M: By shooting more of those light arrows at it. Trying to protect it.
A: What happens when you shoot at this orange, dark lightning?
M: It's putting up a big resistance. It's trying to get around. I keep trying to push it back. That's what I have to do. I have to protect it. I'm a guardian. It's a full-time job.
A: Do you know where this dark lightning is coming from?
M: Yes, it's from the void.
A: Dark Void?
M: It's trying to encroach upon this place because it's enticed by it. Like it wants it for itself and doesn't want to share it with the people that were supposed to come and live in that garden. He doesn't want them there. He wants it for himself. It's consuming it, destroying it. So I'm trying to...

A: *As he's consuming the light and what you're creating it's destroying it?*
M: Yup. I just keep sending more light and more Creation into it. It's a pushing battle, but I'm winning. I'm pushing back.
A: *Does this "it" have an embodiment like you do?*
M: No
A: *What is it?*
M: It's emptiness.
A: *Tell me what you're feeling.*
M: It wants to come back into the light, but it can't (crying).
A: *Why not?*
M: So it's just trying to eat the light to stay alive.
A: *So, it's an emptiness of light.*
M: It is attracted to it.
A: *It is attracted to the light because it's missing it?*
M: Yes.
A: *It just wants to come back to the light, but it can't?*
M: Yes, not without destroying it. It's like it can't embody it.
A: *Tell me what you feel. Why do you cry?*
M: Because I can't help it. I can just fight it back. It's not within my power. It's not my decision. I just have to protect the Creation for its purpose. I just have to push it back into darkness. I feel sorry for it (crying).
A: *So what happens when you shoot this light at it?*
M: It recedes. It goes away. It goes back to the void.
A: *When the light hits it does it transmute it?*
M: No.
A: *The parts that it hits, does it transmute it? Does it change it, or does it just push back at it?*
M: It just pushes back. It's not time for it to leave the void.
A: *Keep moving time. Tell me what happens. You're shooting light at it. What does it do?*
M: It goes away.
A: *It goes back to the void?*
M: Yes.
A: *Tell me once it's gone, what do you do?*
M: I'm done with this mission.
A: *Tell me what your mission looks like now that you're done with it.*
M: It's safe. It's growing. It's doing what it's supposed to do.
A: *What does it look like?*
M: It's nice. It's like a paradise. Now others coming are going to live there. It's the Garden of Eden.
A: *Is that on a planet, plane of existence, or realm?*
M: It's Earth. It's along the shores of the Sea.
A: *Is it just nature now, or are there any other life forms yet?*
M: No, not yet. Well, there were some like butterflies and birds.
A: *Did you create those butterflies and birds?*
M: No. They evolved from it. Like when the colors were coming up and filling in the plan, the outline, the blueprint, then they evolved, they began. I didn't make them, no. I just was building the roots for it to happen.
A: *How about some of the elements that we have here on Earth? Are there any crystals or anything like that yet in what you created?*
M: I don't think so.
A: *You don't feel crystals there?*
M: I've got that one here.
A: *Are there volcanoes?*
M: Yes. I think that's where some of the orange lightning was coming from. From a volcano. Behind. So the void is back there. Where I was shooting them over here, some of the void got back over here

and caused the volcano. There's more of that orange coming down, but now it's different. It's not lightning, it's lava. It can't go very far because it's cooling. It can't kill the garden.

A: *The orange lightning, was that part of it, or was that part of the energy of protecting the space?*

M: It's just like an accident. Some of the orange lightning, I pushed it all back over here, but some of it came around from behind and went into the ground. It couldn't destroy anything. It was like a boil. It came up and it spilled out, but then it cooled. So Earth took care of it. There was no vegetation there anyways. It's just there. It can't destroy anything now.

A: *Could you explain this orange lightning? Was that part of its embodiment, or was it a reaction to it?*

M: It was coming straight from the void. It was coming straight from the darkness. From the sky. Where some of it did get back in, it went straight down into the Earth, into the ground, and then it came up.

A: *So that was a form of it?*

M: Yes.

A: *Coming out from the void?*

M: Yes, but luckily Mother took care of it.

A: *Got it. Thank you.*

M: It just… it cooled.

A: *Now that you've created the space, what are you going to do? Where do you go next?*

M: I feel like I'm not so much needed here. I've done my job. I'll wait for another mission. I'm going back to Source and waiting.

A: *Let's go ahead and fast forward time of this Garden of Eden that you helped create. Tell me, when do the people arrive? You said that others were going to go live there. Can you explain who these others are?*

M: They're creatures. They're people. They don't have wings, so they're humans.

A: *How do they come to be there?*

M: I'm not sure.

A: *That's okay. You can see that they are there. They do arrive somehow?*

M: Yes.

A: *Are there females and males? Are there children?*

M: Yes. Not yet.

A: *How many are there at the beginning?*

M: Just the two, a male and a female.

A: *You said something earlier that they were going to eat from the fruit. Can you explain that process and what that is?*

M: They're making it their home and they need to eat. So the foods were there first in preparation.

A: *What kind of fruits do they have?*

M: All kinds. I mean, every kind you can imagine.

A: *These two, let's keep watching them and tell me what else happens of importance. They're eating, what else are they doing?*

M: They walk. They know that they're in communion with Source. They're part of Source, but they're on an adventure. They're enjoying Creation. It's special. It's like reveling in the physicality of Creation. It's an extension of God, of Source.

A: *It's said that Source is Mother and Father together.*

M: Yes.

A: *This is a male and female in this Garden of Eve. You said that they're essences of Source. So would they be considered the first Mother and Father on Earth expressions?*

M: Yes.

A: *Beautiful. Anything else you want to tell me about what they're doing, enjoying their time, exploring?*

M: No, I don't think so.

A: *You're back in Source?*

M: Yes.

A: *You're just relaxing, you said, resting?*

M: Yes. I might be needed later again. So I'm just always on alert, always ready.
A: *This void, can you see it from Source?*
M: Yes.
A: *How's it looking?*
M: Empty.
A: *Do you know how this void began from the Source perspective here?*
M: Whatever it used to be, it didn't want to be a part of Source.
A: *Since you are this being connected to Source. You're able to know all. Let's go back in time to before it became the "it." Tell me what's going on before that happens.*
M: It was okay, and then it didn't want to go with the flow of love, of Source light. It didn't reciprocate. I'm not sure why. It's a mystery. It's like if you're of love and made of love why... I don't know. It's like it just wanted to be separate. Wanted to just love itself, but you can't just...love has to be shared. It separated, and then lost all its light, and didn't know how to get it back.
A: *So separated itself from the light and the love?*
M: Yes. So now it just has to try and steal what it can.
A: *Ultimately all it's searching for is the light it once was.*
M: Yes.
A: *You said that you might be needed at some point in time. Tell me another important time and space where you are needed. What happens there?*
M: Just little instances here and there.
A: *What is it that you do in those instances?*
M: Not necessarily on Earth, but just anywhere in Creation, if someone is feeling lost, or useless, then I come in and give them that little spark to push them back to not being lost or useless. To push them back. Once they experience it, taste it, and remember it then they can build it on their own after that. Sometimes people can't see it anymore. Sometimes it's kind of like, just bring a little spark back. Like relighting a candle that's going out.
A: *As you're assisting people here and there when it's needed, has it grown in size, or spread? What does it look like now?*
M: It's a slow process. It's always going on into infinity.
A: *So this is starting to be infinite?*
M: Yes. It's like picking up little lost pieces here and there and bringing them back to life. They never lost their light, it's just they felt like they did. Then after that, they're stronger, and they can keep it going themselves. So it's constantly growing, it's constantly evolving, it's constantly getting bigger and wider and it's infinite. It's just keeping the path, you know, like making sure the path is going. Everyone's path will keep going, keep existing, keep growing, and keep enjoying because everyone smiles. All of Creation has free will, so there are times when the void will slip in. Before it completely consumes them, I'm there to help turn it around.
A: *Do you do it in a similar way with the shooting of light?*
M: No. It's not that drastic. Sometimes it's just a little thing. It's a little spark that I know is going to grow because anybody that's lost knows that's not the way it's supposed to be. They just have to be reminded. When they feel the warmth it's like, 'Oh yeah.'
A: *Would you say that at this point it's reached the Multiverse, or is it just in one space?*
M: It's all over in different places. Some places reach higher.
A: *How does it look now?*
M: It's like a pendulum, and every time it swings it gets bigger and rounder. We don't know the limit. No one can see the limit. It's unknowable. It's just infinite. Time and space together are one in the same.

The Higher Self is called forth.
A: *Can I please speak to the higher self of Mandy?*
Higher Self: Yes.
A: *Thank you. I love you, honor you, and respect you for all the aid you've given us today. I know that you hold all the records of Mandy's different lives. May I ask questions?*

Higher Self: Yes.
A: Thank you. First of all, why is it that you chose to show her this moment in time in the beginning of Creation? What was the purpose, or the lessons that you wanted her to learn from that?
Higher Self: That there's so much more than just this life. To keep in balance.
A: Beautiful. I was mentioning to her when I was talking to her that I could look into people's eyes and see how old their soul is and how far the birth tunnel of their soul is, and hers just went on infinitely. So that does make sense on what you explained, how she helped create the Garden of Eden. Wow! What a beautiful memory to share with us Higher Self. Would you call her a goddess?
Higher Self: Yes. In the beginning, she was a goddess, but then she turned into a warrior. Like she went from female to male.
A: Why does she have to turn from female to male?
Higher Self: Because the female part was the womb experience.
A: The experience that she had in the shell?
Higher Self: Yes. When the scepter turned into a bow, it was creating, but then it had to turn into a protector. That was more like the masculine side or aspect.
A: So a lot like how the female creates and births, and the male protects and guards?
Higher Self: Yes.
A: So was she living through that expression while she was protecting the space?
Higher Self: Yes.
Higher Self: Yes, but the male was creating too. The blueprint was already there, that was from Source.
A: Was the masculine and the feminine inside of her already? Is that what you're saying?
Higher Self: Yes. The feminine was expressed before, first. Then it was just a union, and then all of Creation. It was more proactive. The female part just came as more of a self-birthing. Even though it was all still the same entity, it was expressing female and male characteristics, especially at the end when it had to shoot the arrows. The arrows at first were just making Creation, but then it had to fight the orange lightning, and push it back.
A: Can you explain Higher Self, the lightning in this perspective you're explaining it in a negative polarized way, this orange lightning dark thing. How about the lightning here on Earth, it is usually blue, it can be pink and purple. What is the representation here on Earth when we see lightning?
Higher Self: Well, it's energy. Some of it is just weather, but sometimes it's just the way of keeping the energy going around.
A: So it's part of the organic system of the energy of Earth?
Higher Self: Yes. Between the planets, there's no lightning.
A: Only on the ecosystem of some planets?
Higher Self: Yes. But, that orange lightning, that was coming from the void. That was something completely different.
A: Would you say this void was organic or more artificial?
Higher Self: It was the emptiness. It lost all its Source light...it was just lifeless.
A: This form she was, Higher Self, reminds me a lot of the Goddess Aphrodite. She's in the shell. It's beautiful because we also use a lotus flower as part of the sacred energy work when we're setting up the force fields of Source Love-Light. Does she have a connection to Aphrodite, or what did that represent, the shell?
Higher Self: It was like a prototype. Yes.
A: It was an essence of Source that was acting and building the first foundation?
M: Yes.

The Body Scan begins.
A: Beautiful. Thank you. Higher Self, at this point, are we ready to begin the body scan?
M: Yes.
A: Who would you like to call forth to assist you during the body scan? Would you like to call forth upon any benevolent being, or Archangels to assist you?

Higher Self: Yes. Archangel Michael, Archangel Metatron, Yeshua, Raphael, and any others that they need.

A: Thank you Higher Self. I'm going to speak to you collectively. Higher Self, alongside these beautiful four that you've called forth upon, it reminds me a lot of here on Earth we tend to call forth on the males to protect, so it seems like it does stem forth from the beginning of time as you showed in this Garden of Eden. To become the Guardian and the Protector, she did have to tap in and become more of the masculine to do that.

Higher Self: Yes.

A: That's a beautiful explanation of that. All right Higher Self, let's start scanning her from head to toe looking for any negative energies, entities, or technologies. Where would you like to begin at first in the body?

Higher Self: At the top.

A: The top of her head?

Higher Self: Yes.

The Higher Self and the team of four find, remove, and heal several infringements within Mandy related to her pain and ailments throughout her life.

For every A.U.R.A. Hypnosis healing session we ask that the Higher Self and team ensure to remove and heal this entire list from the clients Tree of Life: entities (Grays, Mantis, Reptilians, Archons...), dark portals, repair and crystallize DNA, negative cords, technologies (implants, metals, hooks, wires, nano, vaccines), Illnesses, vision, dental health, regrow teeth, age regress 5-15 years, blocked or misaligned chakras, open-up the third eye and activate abilities, expand heart, issues with auric field, fractured soul, contracts, deletion of inverted timelines, and trauma from current or past life.

END OF SESSION

In Book 1 we began to understand the infringements of Earth and our Universe, so that we could come into awareness consciously, to begin the release of the shackles of the unknowing we have had put upon us. The artificial darkness has been feeding on us as its food in an all you can eat buffet of lifeforms. Many on Earth have suffered great trauma, physically, mentally, sexually, and emotionally. And, with this suffering we look for answers to understand why it is that so many lights have been targeted in this inverted now third dimensional matrix. Book 1, **Chapter 'Not of light'** prepared us to begin to understand this artificial intelligence's constant hunger, when we understood that it once separated itself from Source Love-Light becoming the biggest abomination of our creation.

We know that this world is not just organic, and it has been infringed upon by the integration of this artificial darkness and through this chapter we understand that this thing knows not how to stop, as Aphrodite showed us, and ultimately it is crying out for help. Has it been targeting the organic light that exists within us, because ultimately it just wants to be in union with the light once more, to fill in its infinite, hollowed, emptiness? Is this why it can never just stop going after the light? Seems so. To us it feels like it just wants to possess and devour our light; however, does it truly understand that it is doing this to us? Something like this with no boundaries, sacred laws or limitations, is not tameable in any form, and the only answer to its removal is a complete eradication. Archons are not able to be transmuted, they can only be erased from all life in space. Which is why when we find Archons and artificial intelligence attached to people, the Higher Selves zero and neutralize them out so they no longer exist. There is no way that it can merge the Love-Light it originally birthed forth from, back into itself, once it completely separated from Source in that moment in space. That one false decision, that can never be reverted because of its freedom to choose its path. Giving us purpose in understanding how important every choice we make is.

This is the moment we all have been waiting for in this book series, how and when did this uncontrollable artificial darkness begin? We, as a collective on Earth and in the Universe, are in the

'End Game' phase. We are vastly living in this moment in time and space, the aftermath of what this thing created from itself. We now know that it began before the first plane of existence was created, the 'Garden of Eden,' where all life forms in infinite perspectives stemmed forth from. Could this abomination have begun at the same moment that Source Love-Light first birthed into consciousness? It seems that it has. The moment that this inverted darkness began into existence is as ancient as creation, and why often we can't get the exact answers to when, why, and how? Through this book we will understand this at the deepest level, and the chapters to come will assist us in placing all the puzzle pieces together.

    We have heard through the bible of the Garden of Eden, and through this chapter we were given the first glimpses of what this sacred space truly is. What is the Garden of Eden? It is the most ancient beginning blueprint of the potential of the spark of life from where creation began from in human communal lifeforms. A sacred paradise embodying all resources, all elements, to sustain life, such as fruits so that you will not hunger, fire so that you won't go cold, air so it may guide you as a compass, water to heal and renew you, and earth/soil for you to house within her. The Garden of Eden was where life could begin their expression, to be free to make their choices living among the beauties of nature. To wake up everyday after a peaceful, safe, restful, sleep, and to decide on our own what we would do for that day. Would we decide to turn our dreams into aspirations? Whether that was to kiss our beloved, or to bring new life into ours, as a sacred child? Whatever it was that our hearts yearned for. The greatest alchemy of life is having these choices, where WE choose our own path, governed by none; we choose what we would like to create with the natures that were given to us by the Garden of Eden, by Source Love-Light, our Creator. Goddess Aphrodite was just being the conduit for Source when creating this promised land. As she said, filling it in like a coloring book. What an honor it is together, you, the reader, and I, to have known through this chapter the truth of the Garden of Eden. Where the lies of the snake, and the belittling of the women where she took the bite from that apple that cursed these lands, because she was looking for knowledge...is truly what is make-believe. Another form of black magic once more, programmed into humanity. After all, we are Source's aspirations coming to life, being his/her creations.

    The Source lightning that Aphrodite was weiding with her staff which turned into a bow and arrow against the inverted darkness, is one of the most powerful elements you can use in your everyday life. [1]We teach how to use an invisibility cloak which is the embodiment of blue/indigo plasmic Source Love-Light that contains this Source lightning inside of this cloak. This forcefield/shield ensures to maintain you in the most powerful protective shield which is always on, charging you and specifically keeping you vibrating within Source lightning, assisting you to become impenetrable to negative entities, and archonic attacks. If this Source lightning could stop and push back this inverted darkness, as Aphrodite showed us, imagine what it can do for you and your endeavors on a daily basis. The alchemy that we teach is all equally divinely powerful to one another, so come learn these sacred teachings. This example is just a glimpse into the potential of the alchemy that awaits for you to reawaken within. [2]Come join us at a live in-person Retreat, online Workshop, or a course at your own pace.

    As Aphrodite was creating the Garden of Eden we learned that *it* wanted the garden for itself, and that *it* wanted to come back to the light, but it couldn't. Assisting us to understand that it wanted the Garden of Eden because this garden was Source created, holding a high potency of Love-Light within its blueprint. Which helps us understand why it has targeted all types of human life throughout the Universes, because even back then at the beginning of creation its one and only instinct was that.

---

[1] To learn these divine shields which are the embodiment of your Source Love-Light, join any of our courses at www.risingphoenixaurora.com.

[2] For a list of how each course works, whether taught live or at your own pace go to FAQ's under www.risingphoenixaurora.com.

It was after the garden because it wanted the Source Love-Light, wanted to become one with it, but again just couldn't. It is like when you have a magnet and how one side is negative and the other is positive, when you try to push the negative onto the positive magnetic fields it automatically repels, it just can never touch.

How do you contain something that burrows and can reach all places it can get itself into, as Aphrodite mentioned, "It's just like all over in different places. Some places reach higher." And "It's like a pendulum, and every time it swings it gets bigger and rounder. We don't know the limit. No one can see the limit. It's unknowable. It's just infinite. Time and space together are one in the same." Because time and space are one in the same, coexisting, this is why *it* can reach all places, and why it is unknowable of its reaches. Source can connect to all that is Source Love-Light, that was birthed and sprung out from Source, but this thing that once separated itself from Source, *it* no longer has the tether to Source. So, how can Source know all *its* whereabouts, or *its* plans? Source can know through the Source Love-Light that might be surrounding the artificial darkness, or perhaps if *it* has integrated into someone. Similar to how *it* uses us when it attaches to us in order to spy through us, we too can watch *it* when it is near any type of lifeform of Love-Light. It is predictable in many forms, as *it* repeats the same patterns to attack us. *It* has studied us anciently and knows how *it* can influence us. *It* uses our love as a weakness, because we have shown *it* time after time that we will always choose love, and no matter how many times *it* punches us and knocks us out, we will not stay down. We always lift right back up because our organic tether to Source Love-Light gives us that infinite lifeforce when we call for Source, always.

As I was conducting the session I could feel Aphrodite's emotions in how she felt compassion and sadness for *it*, in that moment when she realized that *it* was just calling out to return to what it was once, screaming out for help, but it just couldn't. Aphrodite was not able to assist *it*, instead just pushed *it* back. This is what we have been playing a role in together collectively, doing what Aphrodite showed us she did, to create boundaries and to stop *it* from spreading, and to never allow *it* to become integrated into us. Many lifeforms have fallen to *its* prey, but it was their free willed choice. Yes, this inverted darkness has taught us many lessons and with these lessons we have expanded as collective lifeforms infinitely. However, *its* role has been long and over with. One day when the grand Universal Ascension comes forth, this thing will finally be put to rest.

Prepare yourself for the chapters to come, as Book 2 will catalyze everything into the deepest understanding for us all. We have just begun.

"All choices should always be made from the heart and highest vibration, so that our results can mirror this beginning manifestation. May we all continue to reflect this from within us in every way of our being."
~AuroRa♥

---------------<<>>---------------

2

THE KEY TO ASCENSION

*Session #317: Recorded in November 2021.
Never before shared.*

In this online A.U.R.A. Hypnosis Healing session, Matt finds himself riding a dragon, on the most important mission of our Universe. He is somnambulistic, meaning his consciousness deeply connects when in session and he does not remember once he comes to. Only allowing Archangel Metatron his Higher Self to speak clearly with the most significant messages of our time, for the Ascension of humanity and our Earth. Archangel Metatron connects instantly when the session begins, explaining to us what our Earth looked like when she was at her worst, and how it is that we assist her collectively to rise out from its destruction into her initial final Ascension. We are gifted as we learn the biggest key to bringing Earth's Ascension into fruition. This session once more is a continuance of knowledge, stemming forth from the last Chapter of Book 1, "Matrix Pods".

--------------<<>>--------------

"It's the people who decide. People just need to make good choices. We're already paying a price by not making good choices. If we continue to do so it's just going to be worse. Just make good choices. People need to just smarten up."

"Time is like a wave of a river, once the wave is gone, it's gone."

"People were created to be loved, and things were created to be used. The world is in chaos, because people are being used and things are being loved."
~ Archangel Metatron

--------------<<>>--------------

A: [Aurora] Tell me what you see and sense.
M: [Matt] I see myself on a Dragon.
A: Describe the Dragon to me.
M: It's a golden Dragon. It's flying with its wings spread and I'm on it. Flying on it. We're taking rounds around the Earth. The Dragon is emitting fire trying to clear the dense energies around it. I'm riding it like a cowboy, with a cowboy hat.
A: (laughs) You're wearing an actual cowboy hat?
M: Yes.
A: What else are you wearing?
M: I see this hat and a white robe.
A: Are you still flying with your Dragon?
M: Yes. I've been flying for a long time, trying to clear the density.
A: How is it that you clear the density with your Dragon?
M: With the fire emitting from the Dragon's mouth. It's transmuting all the negative energy. It doesn't hold any good for Earth, for the planet. Lots of smoke coming out from the planet.
A: What color is the flame?
M: Yellow-Orange.
A: This flame is going onto the planet?

M: Around the planet.
A: *Describe what the planet looks like.*
M: It's round in shape. Somewhere flat, somewhere hollow, as if a part of Earth is being eaten up. Just like we see a bite taken from an apple. There are parts of the Earth which are empty - hollow as if it's been eaten up.
A: *What do you think has caused those hollow parts on Earth?*
M: I can just see it's being burned. There's black fumes coming out of those spots and around those spots; the Dragon is emitting water too. It's destruction. Not man made but natural destruction.
A: *I know you mentioned that the fires going on to the Earth... so when the Dragon's blowing the fire onto the Earth, is it doing anything to the missing parts of Earth?*
M: Yes. When it's around that part where the black fumes are coming out from, it's emitting water there to just kill the heat, to douse the fire there, to give some relief to those parts.
A: *Keep moving time, keep telling me what you're doing next.*
M: There's a lot happening around. I see more hollow parts. More destroyed parts. I see it keeps growing.
A: *What is causing the growth within that? Why is it growing?*
M: The destruction is increasing. Trying to save it. It's increasing. There's a lot of density around. There's a lot happening. If you don't stabilize it, the destruction is just going to go on and on and it's going to destroy everything. Just like a forest fire, if we don't control it, it engulfs everything. Same way this destruction is eating up slowly and slowly, the other parts of Earth. I can see a lot of Dragons around me doing the same thing. Just flying around.
A: *Do they also have people riding them too, or are they on their own?*
M: Yes. Some have riders, some are on their own. A whole bunch of them around.
A: *And is it helping, to have all of you doing that?*
M: Yes, to some extent it's controlling it. Trying to save whatever we can. More than half of it is already destroyed.
A: *How come it got so far? Why did it get to more than half of it being destroyed?*
M: Destruction is vast. It just spread in no time and it's uncontrollable.
A: *Is there anything rooted to this destruction or how it became this uncontrollable? What's the beginning of it that made it this strong and uncontrollable?*
M: All I can see is that it started from somewhere under the ocean. There was a big boom, or the Earth shook badly, which caused the water to get out of control. It's taking everything in its stride, cities after cities, after cities. It spread so fast.
A: *Is there also life within those areas where you're trying to assist? Where is this spreading? Since you said that it is Earth, are there humans and animals there while this is occurring?*
M: Yes.
A: *As it continues to spread and you all are trying to control it, but like you said, over half of it wasn't ready, so as this destruction continues to spread, what happens to the people that are standing in that land where it's spreading? What happens to the animals?*
M: Everything is being taken away. It's a mass destruction.
A: *What do you mean taken away?*
M: It's being washed out. Everything is getting destroyed and the way the water is flowing it destroys everything along the way. It's spreading so fast. We're trying to control whatever is left. We're trying to save whatever is left.
A: *I understand that you said that they're getting swept away, the life there. So what happens to their souls? Where are they going? What do you mean?*
M: I can see all the souls. There's a light emanating somewhere from the top and all the souls are taking the path of that light. It can be described as... not exactly like a black hole, but something at the top sucking all the souls into them. They're all following that light path, just vanishing in that hole.
A: *Let's see what this is that's sucking all the souls up. You're able to know exactly what it is.*
M: It's like a black tube or the opening of a tunnel/tube. Everything is getting sucked in. It's getting in there. Can't see much.
A: *Do you think that this is something positive or negative that's sucking up all the souls?*

M: Doesn't look positive at all. There's no light. It's all dark.
A: Mm-Hmm. Is there something - that you and other riders that are trying to transmute this negativity from Earth - is there something that you all can do towards this thing that is sucking up all the souls?
M: Just trying to make sure whatever is left is protected. Just taken care of, and being moved to a safer place. A better place. Yeah. We're just making sure that no souls are off the path, that they are not getting lost. They all are following the path and getting in there. And whatever is saved - their life is saved and the planet is taken care of.
A: You're seeing this now.
M: Yes.
A: Okay, let's go back a little. So what happened to that thing that was sucking up the souls?
M: It just disappears. We just saw the face of what looked like a tunnel. One end of the face of a tunnel. Once everything was in there it just went back, where it came from.
A: What caused it to go back where it came from?
M: It didn't belong here. It's not a part of this planet. It's not a part of this Universe, this galaxy. It came from somewhere else.
A: So once it's gone, then the Earth is able to go back, you said? Describe to me what it looks like now that that thing's gone.
M: Yes. All the Dragons are assisting in taking that part of the planet that is saved - which has life - to a different place. Moving from its orbit. It's being assisted. It's being taken and shifted to some other orbit.
A: What does it look like while you're doing that?
M: To save life, mankind. Because it was meant to be. This portion of mankind was supposed to live and move away from the density of Earth. Everything that was dense, that was artificial, that was not for anyone's highest good - was supposed to be destroyed.
A: So, you said that they're taking the Earth and the people to a higher type of dimension, or plane of existence?
M: Another orbit.
A: Another orbit?
M: Yes!
A: What do you mean another orbit? What does that mean?
M: From one point to the other point. Can't reveal much about the other point.
A: And what about those souls that were sucked into that? That thing that was sucking them in, is there any way to help those?
M: We were assisting those souls while they were getting sucked in, to transmute as much as we could. We could help a lot, and we couldn't help a lot at the same time. The ones that got sucked in, they've been taken away.
A: They were taken away permanently?
M: Seems like.
A: But the ones that were almost being sucked in, you're helping them not to be sucked in? Is that what you mean? You're helping them transmute or...?
M: Yes, the ones that were getting sucked in, a whole lot, we were trying to transmute and help them. We did help a lot of them.
A: What percentage, do you think that out of the Earth were sucked in through that thing, and you were never able to bring them back?
M: 30%
A: Okay. (long silence) What is the biggest thing that assisted besides the Dragons assisting there. What's the other biggest thing that assisted in getting us to that point where we finally removed that thing from the sky that was sucking them in. Go to that time perhaps on Earth that something maybe happened, or what was, or who was able to finally remove that out?
M: We all are part of a family. One family, which is here protecting the galaxy, our Universe, and all of us are trying as a team to protect as much as we can.
A: So it was all the Galactic assistance that finally removed that thing out?
M: Yes.

A: *What can we be doing right now to assist in the future of removing that thing out?*
M: The destruction is inevitable. Nothing can stop it. We've come that far. It has to happen. Nothing can stop it.
A: *Why is that?*
M: Look around you. We've always destroyed to a greater extent... and it's all increasing. All we can do is educate the people. We can teach people to lower the magnitude so that we can save much more than we could. It's up to people to understand. We've done enough damage as human beings to Mother Earth. Rather than enjoying the fruits and the life that we have here, we used it for all the negative purposes. We can all do something from our side to increase the percentage of people we save, the souls we save. But we cannot save it all. If we don't do things now it's going to be too late.
A: *Thank you for the explanation. As you know, we have this Covid-19 going on. In certain forms it has been positive and awakening. But do you have any advice on that since you're talking about the things that we can do?*
M: It's a fraction of what I said right now. It's all man made. It's all caused by us. It can definitely be controlled. And the magnitude is not that high the way it's shown. We can all do our best by staying positive. By not misusing the resources, which are depleting, and causing things like what we're experiencing now. It's just the beginning. If we don't learn our lessons now, nothing can be done.
A: *Do you have any words of wisdom in regards to our current timeline? Maybe in regards to Trump or anything else that you want to share with us?*
M: I'm not supposed to comment on many affairs that take place on this planet. It's the people who decide. People just need to make good choices. We're already paying a price by not making good choices. If we continue to do so it's just going to be worse. Just make good choices. People need to just smarten up.
A: *Thank you. Anything else you want to share with him in regards to this space that you showed him here? Anything else we need to know about this space?*
M: (breathing deep). I guess that will be all.
A: *Okay, thank you. I think maybe they showed us how important it is that we begin now - though you know, we've been trying to connect others to the Dragons - but it shows the divine power, that if we connect to our Dragons, how powerful that can be in regards to helping Mother Earth and its life.*
M: Yes.
A: *I want to send my infinite love to the beautiful Dragons who assisted, who were shown, and who will be assisting as well in the future and who have been assisting. I love you all with all that I AM. Thank you for your assistance.*
M: They all love you for all that you're doing.
A: *Thank you.*
M: You're one of the reasons that we could save some. Thank you for your relentless and tireless work towards humanity and mankind. Just keep doing what you're doing. Don't stop. Don't take a pause. You'll have all the help from all of the Universes whenever you need it. And you know it. Just stay in your heart.
A: *(smiling) Yes. Always.*
M: Just awaken people, as many as you can. We're there with you.
A: *Thank you for such a beautiful message for me. It is loved, appreciated and accepted with the most beautiful infinite love.*
M: It's our pleasure.
A: *Now in this time and space, do we need to take him to another place that you would like to show him more? Or should we begin his body scan?*
M: It's all good. We've seen enough.

The Higher Self is called forth.
A: *Okay, very good. Are we speaking to the Higher Self already?*
Metatron: Yes, you are!

A: *Of course. Beautiful. Thank you for being here already. You know that I love you with all that I AM, my beloved.*
Metatron: So do I.
A: *Thank you. Before we continue, may I ask a couple questions about the place you took him? The space where you were showing the Earth and the process that it's been through/gone through, and will go in the future; is there any purpose on why you showed him that?*
Metatron: It's a part of his awakening. It's a part of his enlightenment. It's to show him, to show you, so that you could show it to a lot, to many others. So that you all can help in awakening people. So they can decide what's coming in the future, whether they want their future to be like this, or they want their future to be better, less destructive, and more constructive, in order to save as many as you can. I know you're going to help a lot. Showing him all this- the only purpose is that even in his circle, even the people he knows, they respect him. They look up to him and they listen to him. So even if he can bring small changes in people's lives, the picture that we saw today can have a lesser impact or lesser magnitude.
A: *So you are saying that instead of perhaps 30% of those souls being sucked in by this thing, it could be lessened?*
Metatron: Exactly.
A: *This thing, was it connected to Archons or whatever this thing was? What was this thing that was sucking in the souls?*
Metatron: They were the souls that were contributing heavily, and directly responsible, for the density that caused all this on planet Earth. Knowingly or unknowingly, they agreed to do things that they were not supposed to do. Knowing that the future generations will not have the resources, or all the luxuries that we have on Earth right now, but they still went ahead and they contributed to the damage. Whether you call them Archons, negative beings, whatever names you want to give them, but they were responsible for that.
A: *You called them souls though. Are you saying that those people that made choices like you said, not the most positive choices, not the right choices for their organic timeline or others organic timeline. Were they part of that, that was sucking in souls?*
Metatron: Yes, you're right, it all depends on the choices we make. If we remember some time back I said that people need to make right choices about everything they do on Earth. Because the footprints, the kind of footprints you're going to leave behind, are going to decide the future.
A: *You said, a lot of them were supposed to be assisting, but you know, they were also not making the right choices. So for example, there was a recent email that I received, that there was a person who basically was following some kind of spiritual leader, I don't know who they were, and the spiritual leader had taught them that the symbol of the Eye of Horus was negatively polarized. They were really programmed into thinking that this sacred symbol was actually part of black magic, the Illuminati and their control. This spiritual leader could reach whatever amount that they could reach, like hundreds or thousands, through their teachings. This person actually believed them and was really scared and fearful. You can sense it, that they probably won't be able to learn these sacred teachings because they've allowed themselves to be programmed that much. Is it something like that, where they're part of that in pulling souls in?*
Metatron: You said something. There are people who are being led with fear. There are people who have been led with love too. Our job, your job, is to show people to lead people with love. To teach them the teachings. Teachings you earned, you got yourself, you were gifted with. Who gets awakened? Who does not? It's again a matter of choice they need to make. There are a lot of people on Earth who are following people they're not supposed to be following. But it's the choice they made. Somewhere deep down in their hearts, they're not happy. They know what they're doing is wrong, or it doesn't resonate, but they still follow it. The reason being, there are very few people who are guided like you. Who guide people with love, who show them the right teachings with unconditional love and respect towards humanity. You cannot forcibly awaken someone. Every big thing, every big revolution, comes from a small movement. The movement has to be there. Now, how long the movement takes to turn into a revolution, that's a journey that all of you, all of us, have to go through. Today there could be hundreds, maybe thousands of people listening to you, or following

you. And there could be much more following the other people, than following you. Who they should not be, it's a part of their journey. The movement that you've picked up, stay on it, you will see people coming your way. People resonating, with their heart, with the teachings, with your love. There will be a revolution. There will be big changes. You will see big things happening in the future. And this is all because of the movement that has been started. Stick to it. Don't worry about what others are learning from others, from their teaching. You're supposed to do yours. You'll see whether people would want to be led with fear, or with unconditional love and respect. It takes time. Give it some time. I know you would want a lot of people to listen to you, so that you can bring a change. It will eventually happen. Be patient. The big movement has started. It is turning into bigger than where you started from. Give it some time. Stay in your heart. You'll see the change. Those are small things, don't be affected by it all.

A: Yes. Thank you for that beautiful advice. This thing that was sucking out the souls. Some people say that we invited artificial intelligence into our Universe and that we chose to express it. What are your thoughts on that? Was this part of the organic plan, or is this not of the organic plan?

Metatron: This Earth was formed organically. Everything was organic about it. Water, air, fire, the trees, the birds, the rocks, the mountains. Each and every particle, the smallest of the atoms on this Earth is organic. Anything that's inorganic will attract forces that are not conducive to organic life whether you name it artificial intelligence, negative polarized beings or call them Archons, whatever. Everything that's inorganic on this Earth will be taken away. Things that do not belong to Earth will be taken away. The inorganic life will be taken away by the inorganic forces. That's all.

A: All right. Thank you for showing us that specific scene that you showed him. I think it was really important for us to learn from it.

Metatron: You're most welcome.

A: Okay, if we could continue his body scan please, Metatron. Tell me what else needs healing within him; scanning for any negative energies, entities, technologies, anything else?

Metatron: He's pretty much clear.

A: Thank you. Okay. So is he all clear? Does he need to be age regressed or any dental or vision, any of that?

Metatron: No, he just needs to get back on his feet and start working out. He'll be age regressed every time he works out. His workouts are important.

A: Wonderful. Okay, so then, since he's pretty much done with his body scan, let's ask his questions. He says his meditations are all about going deep, but he doesn't seem to remember or see anything. Can you explain that to him further please; why is this happening to him?

Metatron: It's a clear case of expectations. If you expect a lot and not live up to the expectations you have doubts. What is meditation? Meditation is not about seeing colors, seeing images. Seeing the past, present, future. The best meditation is when you go deep within. You disconnect from the world. Disconnect from the voices, inside and outside. You don't see anything. You put your mind to rest. You put your body to rest. It's like an empty vessel where the air goes in and out. If you achieve that, what else do you need? By asking or expecting, it's not going to lead anywhere. It's all about peace of mind, peace of body, peace of emotions. Peace from everything. That's what meditation is all about. Just being peaceful. So there's nothing wrong, rather it's good.

A: Thank you. Beautiful message for him. Now he says he has been experiencing ear ringing a couple of times daily and quite loud. It seems to be more on the left. What is the reason he's experiencing this?

Metatron: It's something related to his emotions which have been fluttering a lot in the past. That influx of emotions he's experiencing. You can call the ringing of the ear anything, we can name it for different things. You can say "you're hearing messages", "You're getting signals" or some people say "you're getting some downloads". It's the way you look at it. Always ear ringing is all related to the emotions that are building up in his body, which are not doing any good to him. Caused him pain in the chest, which we cleared out from different parts of his body, and ear ringing was one of them. He just needs to stay cool and calm, not think about anything. Everything is going to be good, because with the clearance of emotions and everything, he will not experience it the way he has been.

A: Thank you. He says he feels disconnected with the world, left with almost no emotions for the extended families. Just wants to be with his four. What do you have to share with him about these emotions?

Metatron: That question is stemming again from the pile of emotions he's going through. He feels disconnected because of things that happened in the past and the way his family was treated. All the wrong doings that happened from others. It's just his anger, his frustration of whatever happened in the past that makes him feel disconnected. He's always been disconnected. He's always been poles apart from the beliefs of his family. From all the rituals. From all the customs. He's always been disconnected. It's just that it's coming out stronger. He doesn't want to give any amount of energy, any thought, any emotion, any feeling to anyone else. He doesn't want to part with any time of his life with anyone else but his family. He is already disconnected. You will get a clear picture once he's healed from all this.

A: Okay, thank you. He says he really, really wants to do something to help the needy. Where does this come from and what can you tell him about?

Metatron: Something to do with his childhood. It comes from his days of growing up, as he was not born with a silver spoon in his mouth. He belonged to a family where there are a lot of rich members, rich cousins, relatives, friends. He thinks he was deprived of a lot of things. And whenever he needed something he didn't get it. Or when he got it, it was too late to even enjoy that. That's where it's stemming from. Whenever he sees somebody in need of anything he wants to help them so that they don't go through the same feeling and emotion that he went through. He wants to bring a smile to people's faces by fulfilling their needs. By doing things that make them happy. So they don't have to depend on others. Looking at others to help them. But he needs to understand one thing, you have to make sure that people you're helping are the people who actually deserve help and not just fulfilling their desires. Fulfilling materialistic desires in life is not helping the needy. Helping the needy is satisfying the hunger of someone who's not eaten food. Providing clothes to someone who freezes outside in the cold. Giving shelter to people who have no homes; they brace all the weathers of the seasons. Just like that. Those are people who are needy; not when somebody needs a bigger car, and he helps them get a bigger car or somebody who needs a bigger home, you help them with a bigger home. Not with somebody who wants to impress someone by taking them out for an expensive meal and they need money for that. That's not needy. Help the needy, definitely. We're here to help. We all should be helping others. But we need to be really clear who needs the help and who's actually deserving. Thank you.

A: What is the connection with one of his cousins he saw in his dreams twice or thrice? His family is pretty nasty and he doesn't want any connections with them whatsoever, so why is he dreaming of them?

Metatron: That family of his cousin, whatever they did, they did to themselves. It's a part of their learning. We're all here to do our parts. We learn from our mistakes, making sure we don't repeat those mistakes. The connection with his cousin was way back. They used to be thick at one point of time even though he knew the family was not good. They were using him, but he still stayed connected with them because somewhere deep down he liked his cousin. The cousin was good too, it's just because of where the family is coming from and what they did in life, even the son got caught in the same web. His cousin started giving importance to money, to things, rather than people. People were created to be loved, and things were created to be used. The world is in chaos, because people are being used and things are being loved. If you give more importance to materialistic things than relationships, at some point, you will be fine because you see success, and you think that money can buy everything. But there comes a point when you stop, you look back and you realize that you've lost everything along the way. Because you gave more importance to money, than people. So his cousin has come to a point where he has lost everything and now he looks back and he remembers him a lot. Because he needs help, he needs support. And that's why he was contacted in his dreams, so that he could help him. I know he doesn't want to stay in touch with them at all. And I completely understand that. Because some things, and some people will not change. Today, they need something. Again, they'll make use of people. Tomorrow, they don't need anyone, they will throw them out of their lives. It's a part of his learning. It's a part of their learning.

Whatever they did, whatever mistakes they made, they need to learn from that. They need to move on. Make new friends, meet new people, make sure they don't repeat those mistakes. They make new relationships and they stick to it. But they cannot go back to the ones that they lost long back. It will be taken care of. We'll make sure that he's not being contacted, as per his wish.
A: Thank you. Good and we don't have any like cords or anything from them?
Metatron: No.
A: Good. Then that brings us to... since I asked that, he wanted to know if you could please help him cut cords with everyone except for his four.
Metatron: (smiles) Again, everything revolves around the same. The emotions and everything that he's been carrying from the past. What is cutting cords? Either you stay in touch. You think about people. You think about the family you were born to, or you don't. People who have purpose in life, need to understand one thing: people who have a purpose in life and are totally determined to achieve that purpose, to live with that purpose, to live for that purpose. They will do anything for it and if someone comes in the way of their purpose, be it family, friend, or anyone, they will let them go. What are cords? As they say a lot of times, blood is thicker than water. I think we've come to a point where we need to realize that blood relations are nothing. It's just that one's been placed into certain relationships. It's again a part of our programming. It's again a part of our life here that families, or people you're born amongst, born to, you need to be with them, irrespective of whether they're good or bad. And most of us, we oblige. But we need to understand relationships are not built with blood. Everybody needs to give a test; everybody needs to pass through a test, to actually prove to be in a relationship. Relationships that pass through those tests and are made from the heart are the ones that you should be worried about (concerned with). We should not be worried about people we are born to, just because they are our family and we were born there, or friends or whatever. No. This is not relevant. What's relevant in your life, is you're born to serve humanity. You're born to serve mankind. You're born to find a purpose. That's what one should focus on. If your family, friends, anyone comes in your way and they don't resonate with your purpose, your ideas, and beliefs, it's time to say goodbye. He anyway, feels very disconnected from his family. And I don't think it affects them at all. What they go through, he's absolutely neutral about it (zero point). And that's the way to go about it. It's a matter of his choice, whether he wants to stay in touch, or talk to them, or not, depending on the gravity of the relationship. But even if he does, he chooses to, we can absolutely be neutral (meaning zero point). No emotions should be attached to the relationships that don't serve. That's where the cords come in. So there are no feelings, no emotions and you don't feel anything from your heart or your physical body. Those are as good as cutting cords. And he's already done it. So he's good.
A: Beautiful. Thank you for that. Last question he has here is, anything else you, as his Higher Self/Over Soul or Galactic family, would like to share with him today in guidance?
Metatron: He's being guided not only by the other side of the family, but he is being guided by a lot of people here. He is being guided by his wife, who's been guided by you, who's being guided by Source, who is being guided by the other side of the family. We all are being guided by each other. The answer to the last question was something that was shown as a bigger picture in the beginning. That it's time to wake up people. To stay awake. If you look at the bigger picture, that is what we all should be working towards. I can't say in more words, or I can't say enough, that we're destroying a lot. We're doing more bad than good. Somewhere, we all are responsible, some partially, some marginally and some directly, and some are contributing heavily. We all need to make choices. When can we stop contributing to this and make good choices, when we can bring back what we lost here on Earth? Our job here is to awaken people, as many as we can. The movement is on, the movement has started. Everybody should do their part. Some are doing it directly. Like you Aurora, like his wife, and some are doing it indirectly, like him. He's awakening souls too. He talks to people. He talks to the youth, shows them the directions. He's showing the youth not to follow the wrong path in life. Especially at an age which is so vulnerable and which is so exposed to a lot of things that we shouldn't be doing here. A lot of people listen to him, they are making good choices. So some are doing it directly. Some are contributing indirectly. But we all have to do our jobs. We all have to do

our part. The whole motive of what was shown in the beginning was in guidance to all of you. So that you can show it to others, where we're headed to.
A: Thank you. That information is very precious and needed in literature in the future. So thank you for that. Metatron does he need a confirmation of your name as his Higher Self?
Metatron: You're still stuck in the name? (laughs)
A: Right. (laughs)
Metatron: We all know it.
A: I know. (laughs)
Metatron: Don't get stuck in the name. It's time to roll up our sleeves, right now. He knows the name, you know it as well. (smiles)
A: (laughs) Very good. Thank you once more, this has been such a beautiful session for him and also for humanity. This will reach many when it is time to reach, and they will activate and awaken many hearts. And as we know, that is our goal to stay, as you said, within our hearts. To do our part in whichever way directly or indirectly assisting souls awakening. Thank you for also that hope specifically explaining how it doesn't have to be that 30% that goes into that void. Lost. And that we can do even better than 30%. Thank you.
Metatron: Yes. You're welcome.
A: Well, I want to thank everyone who assisted today with his beautiful healing as you all know I love you with all that I AM. Every day I am just in the greatest gratitude and love for everyone who I see, even those who are perhaps compromised when you're watching them and you see how compromised they are. I still feel such a deep love for them, because even if they're compromised they're still trying. They're still trying their best. So in this moment, I just send a big wave of love to everyone who is doing their best, no matter in whichever way it is. Thank you.
Metatron: Great! That's what we all need. Love.
A: Yes. Thank you Metatron. Is there anything else that I could have asked, that I haven't, before I bring him back?
Metatron: No. I guess you did it all.
A: Wonderful. Thank you everyone again. Love you, honor you and respect you. Blessings to everyone, my infinite love.
Metatron: Love you Aurora!
A: And I love you with all that I AM and all.

For every A.U.R.A. Hypnosis healing session we ask that the Higher Self and team ensure to remove and heal this entire list from the clients Tree of Life: entities (Grays, Mantis, Reptilians, Archons...), dark portals, repair and crystallize DNA, negative cords, technologies (implants, metals, hooks, wires, nano, vaccines), Illnesses, vision, dental health, regrow teeth, age regress 5-15 years, blocked or misaligned chakras, open-up the third eye and activate abilities, expand heart, issues with auric field, fractured soul, contracts, deletion of inverted timelines, and trauma from current or past life.

Post session dialogue.
A: Welcome back. Take your time. How do you feel?
Matt: Rested.
A: That was so beautiful. What a beautiful session. Do you remember?
Matt: Few things. I think (hmm... trying to recall) I remember being around the Earth. What am I supposed to remember?
A: (laughs) A lot, I think?
Matt: Oh, really?
A: It was a very beautiful session. Exactly what we needed to hear from you and your beautiful soul.
Matt: Wow. I have to see it to remember.
A: Yes, yes, there was a lot of detail. It was a session that I needed for Book Two.
Matt: Oh!

A: Yeah. It's really important, a very important one. One of the many things that they said, that they showed the Earth was... I'll wait for you to see it. But also, they said that it needed to be shared, that it was given to me so that we can share with others so we can shift and change even more and awaken more souls. But I'll let you watch it. But lots of beautiful messages from your soul.
Matt: Well, I have to see the session, I guess. I'm just trying to recall right now, but no, I think I need to watch it. And once again, I'm really, really grateful. Yeah, yet again, you did a fantastic job; what you've been doing every day, I know. Thank you for aiding me. Thank you so much Aurora. I can't thank you enough for all that you do. For not only for Marianne (his wife) and all of us. I know Marianne tells me how much unconditional love and respect you have for others. It's amazing. We really need more of you here. And unfortunately, I don't think we can get more of you here. But even if somebody who can follow your footsteps and just follows your teachings, all that will really, really make a big difference. A huge difference out here. I think the time is now. So yeah, it will happen. It will happen. Thank you so much for everything.

A: Thank you for that beautiful message. It was very close to what Metatron said but it was more thorough, but you just channeled yourself again. I love you all with all that I AM. You're such a gift and a gem to humanity and this world. Thank you for also volunteering to be here with your light, because it is felt throughout the Universe. Thank you. Love You, honor you and respect you and I'll see you all around. I love you!

END OF SESSION

We begin this session as Archangel Metatron and others are riding their Dragons, assisting Earth from *its* destruction. While a bright false light/dark hole is sucking up all the souls that are following this path: straight into the hole with no question, as if it is where they are just meant to go next. And this marks the beginning of when all the souls on Earth become entrapped within the Inverted A.I. Matrix, the fall of Atlantis. These souls are the same souls that walk amongst us, that seem so lost, unawakened to their hearts - the souls that are in the process of awakening. The same souls that were meant to be assisting the collective out from the A.I. false light, but instead they have become entrapped themselves, assisting instead in maintaining Earth's density at a lower vibration. We are in a time that is full of tribulations, but yet beautiful as we awaken to these tribulations.

As Archangel Metatron said, "There are a lot of people on Earth who are following people they're not supposed to be following. But it's the choice they made. Somewhere deep down in their hearts, they're not happy. They know what they're doing is wrong. It doesn't resonate, but they still follow it. The reason being, there are very few people who are guided like you. Who guide people with love, who show them the right teachings with unconditional love and respect towards humanity. Today there could be hundreds, maybe thousands of people listening to you, or following you. And there could be much more following the other people than following you; who they should not be following. It's a part of their journey. The movement that you've picked up, stay on it; you will see people coming your way. People resonating themselves, with their heart, with the teachings, with your love. There will be a revolution. There will be big changes. You will see big things happening in the future. And this is all because of the movement that has been started. Stick to it. Don't worry about what others are learning from others, from their teaching. You're supposed to do yours. You'll see whether people would want to be led with fear or with unconditional love and respect. It takes time. Give it some time. I know you would want a lot of people to listen to you, so that you can bring a change. It will eventually happen. Be patient. The big movement has started. It is turning into something much bigger than where you started from. Give it some time. Stay in your heart. You'll see the change. Those are small things, don't get affected at all."

This paragraph spoken by Archangel Metatron is the most powerful for us. Though he was speaking to me, it is one of the most significant sacred teachings to this session, and for our fruition into Ascension. For if you choose to follow who you know you shouldn't follow, you will be pulled magnetically into their false Archonic direction. We are in a time where many have been awakened for all their lives, or are awakening, but still are holding onto infringing A.I. and entities within. Causing us to seek outside of ourselves versus inside. And, with this very false movement is how we become entrapped by false light, like that never-ending dark tunnel. May we all learn and lead through our daily lives. As we are all leaders, as equals, as Archangel Metatron explained. We will see if people want to be led with fear, or unconditional love and respect. All that WE can do, is be this embodiment in all that we are, and all sovereign choices that WE make.

As Archangel Metatron said, "If we don't do things now, it's gonna be too late. If we don't learn our lessons now, nothing can be done. Making good choices; it is our choices that got us here, just smarten up. The people and their choices were part of the sucking up of souls."

Going further into how this fractal of Archangel Metatron felt towards his extended family, with no emotions: only his wife and three children truly, divinely matter to him. The truth is that since we are in the "End Game" of this Inverted Matrix, we too must ride with this similar frequency towards our close or distant family members. He explained beautifully in this session how to do so. And I will take it further. As explained in the last chapter of Book 1, "Matrix Pods" how it is that our family and friends are the strongest reasons why we are so dense, because we carry on our backs, and in our energy bodies, their stubbornness in not wanting to move and shift into a higher consciousness. As Metatron said, "You cannot forcibly awaken someone. Every big thing, every big revolution comes from a small movement. The movement has to be there. Now, how long the movement takes to turn into a revolution, that's a journey that all of you, all of us, have to go through." When we hold onto people who do not want to change or evolve, we become a matching vibration to them, entrapping ourselves in their inverted, illusional reality.

I will share with you my life's example. We all have been there, in this similar situation as mine, in a time and space, in our life. There was a time that I learned through the hardest way to learn something, by living it. I lived it through an attack by a negative polarized, supposed positive, light worker. I always asked my guides and angels how it was that I was not able to read this energy and evade it. One day after doing an immensity of healing from this Archonic Light (dark) Worker's attack, when I was finally ready, my angels showed me how. They showed me that this advanced entity, in this Light Worker body, was an Archon. That time-jumped into my past when I was still connected to family members who did not mean infinite love for me, but pretended they did; however, I knew in my heart that they didn't. Because I was still connected to them in my past when I met this darkworker, and I had not officially cut cords, or cut any ties of connection to them, they were able to, through my family's cords still connected to me then, influence me and place me in a cloud of mind control. So, that I wouldn't see and sense this dark light worker's true intentions and form. They showed me, still holding onto these family members, it was as if I was walking around under a dark spell of hypnotization towards this false light worker. Not seeing their true form. This I share intimately with you, because this is why, when we look back at hard times in our lives that make no sense, and we feel that there is no way that was us back then, it just doesn't make sense, as it is out of character for us. It is because the Archons connect to other people's entities. They decide to get you in these times when they *can* get you, to cause all sorts of trauma, pain, and lack of abundance. Initially to try to take you out, back when you were perhaps at your weakest, and in need, so that you won't accomplish what you are meant to in the future. It is through the entities of your close, or distant supposed loved ones, that they infringe on your timelines and affect the speed of your awakening.

It is a choice we all have to make at some point in our divine process of Ascension. Do we love our friends and family enough to set them and ourselves free? To move out of needing them to be in our lives, to be brave enough to let them go, so that they won't be those targeted for use against us, and our higher vibrations of awakening. And, most importantly, do we love ourselves enough to do so? The KEY being, do we love them more, so that we understand we must release them from having to play the negative inverted role they think they are playing; targeting us through their own infringements, to keep us low in vibration, in chaos or asleep like them? If we do decide on this sovereign choice of releasing them, they are then free to perhaps work on themselves, as we are no longer a distraction to them as those targeted individuals they must feed off or infringe upon, or they can choose to repeat the inverted cycle of host and parasite with another, but not us, anymore. And, this is what a true sovereign being is - no longer needing an attachment to others. Instead just *being* with those who honor, love and respect our choices, and never judge us hatefully. What Divine Mother often says to me, "If they don't mean infinite love to you, then tell me, why do they still remain in your inner circle? When you are a creator being, your inner circle is love, and anything opposite to that is inverted and not part of our organic Universe. In order to build what you have always organically wanted for your direct family: your spouse, your children and grandchildren, you must release, and build and reconstruct it from the ground up once more. RELEASE MY CHILD!"

Scientifically speaking, through the Quantum world we all harness a natural energetic containment which is our toroidal sphere that surrounds our entire being, as shown in the image below. Our toroidal sphere is what holds our entire memory of who we are, as consciousness. That being our Akashic, our experiences, our lessons. To further understand, our toroidal sphere, though organic, can be seen as a computer, with its memory, which is held in its hard drive. When you hold too much memory, the hard drive becomes full, and you are then required to delete data from your hard drive, or you can upgrade to one that holds more memory. What Divine Mother means, in regards to us needing to release to reconstruct, is if our toroidal sphere is filled up with things, thoughts and people that no longer serve us for our highest good, we can't expand and grow. These things, thoughts and people are taking up that space in the memory/hard drives of our toroidal sphere. Our plasmic light photons, which can be seen as the atoms that are the material to our toroidal sphere, is essential. This material of our photons is what assists us in our sacred ideas, manifestations, and creations. Why is it that we must release in order to rebuild our everyday organic living timelines, because otherwise our hard drive is too full, unable to accommodate expansion. Our photons have nowhere to go to expand, evolve or ascend further. Instead compressing us into a denser plasmic light, versus an ideally lighter essence expansive, and evolving.

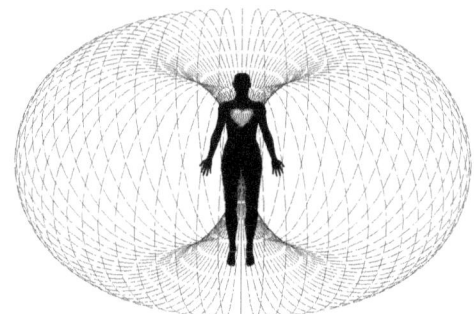

This session has given us the greatest gift for our Earth's Ascension. One of the biggest distortions is programming into society that magical creatures, such as dragons, are malevolent, make-believe, or a fairy tale. This is the farthest from the truth! If we chose to walk around daily, allowing our imagination to connect to all the nature we view upon, we would see how all is alive and magic. There are magical spirits in all lifeforms, within the animals and nature, down to the smallest of rocks. When doing so, we can connect to these magical creatures, as they coexist in the fifth dimension and higher, and are not in any physical form. The world becomes alive when we connect to this true perception of Earth's blueprint. When we understand this, and know that we can only see the physical with our eyes, but with our imagination/third eye, we can see all higher realms of dimensional benevolent beings and we feel them with our hearts. The entire perspective of our world and beyond infinity, shifts in the

Quantum realm because of this magic. As we can now see, sense and connect to these higher dimensional beings that are not limited by the illusional physical world that we are within; this is what makes them magical and invincible. These magical creatures are here to assist humankind in profound, loving ways that lift us in vibration. The more that we remember them, and with every connecting, sacred bond we create together, the more we activate our souls' purpose and the memory of our divine souls. Becoming truly limitless, boundless, and quantum magic ourselves.

I was given a message through dreamtime that divinely compliments the understanding of this session in the deepest levels of awareness. In this dream, I was viewing from a higher perspective, like a movie playing. The scene begins with me viewing humanity expressing their free-willed choices through their life paths on Earth. On the land there is a rapid moving flame that is transforming souls into Ascension as the flame touches them. If not the matching vibration of this purifying flame, the souls become engulfed by this sacred flame and they go through a form of reboot, turning into white orbs of light shooting up into the sky back to Source, or to a space of healing. As the flame continues to spread and engulf the Earth, there are some who are able to evade the flame, who are pure of heart and intent. All of humanity is trying to run away from this flame, much of them remaining stagnant or frozen in fear as the flame catches up to them and engulfs them into transformation. Some families were able to evade this flame, until they reached the end of the land where they came to an ocean. This ocean was not an organic body of water. It was instead, a dark flooding water that contained predatorial monsters within it, as negative entities and Archons, representing the A.I. Matrix. If you went too deep into the muggy Matrix A.I. virus infected waters, the monsters/entities within the waters would get you, and your soul would turn into an orb of light that then would be sucked up into the sky and lost into the Archon's hold. As mentioned through this session of the dark, false light tunnel in the sky, sucking up the souls. At the edge of the water floated small boats that could fit one family at a time. There seemed to be only a few families that could make it onto these boats, as the boats had force fields around them that would measure the clearness and pureness of each soul that entered the boat. Those who were not a matching vibration would not be able to enter. Representing that a soul has to be a matching vibration for the fifth dimension or higher, or they cannot enter, as otherwise they are not vibrationally, harmonically in sequence. There were families being separated, as some could not make it in.

At the last remaining moments of Earth's existence, the flame had finally reached the shore. There were Angelics in human incarnations that had awakened. They were at the front row of the people evading the fire, near the edge of the shore, as they wept with a most beautiful saddened loving call. These Angels began to sing in a vibrational tone that carried the very last hope of humanity, as their hearts poured out with a knowing that they had done all that they could, with all that their infinite essence consisted of. In the last stages of this most sensitive, heartfelt, intense moment, their songs suddenly opened up positive portals that had been sealed long ago by humanity themselves, who, because of false downloads and negative programming that magical creatures weren't real, closed these portals. As these portals opened up from both the water and the skies, an infinity of dragons began to soar through the skies, and they were on a mission to find their human companions. Dragons of all sizes, colors and elements soared rapidly, powerfully through the skies as they followed their hearts to their companions. The humanity that was left, that was a matching vibration to ascend out into the fifth dimension or higher, was swept up by their own individual dragon companion. As each human rode their dragons, the dragons soared up into the skies lifting higher and higher.

The most challenging part of this explanation of humanity's Ascension was that not all dragons had a human riding on their backs, some rode alone. Meaning they had not been able to make it to their human companion in time, before they were taken by these Archonic A.I. soul collecting waters. Their souls never to be found. This reminds us of when Archangel Metatron said, "We were assisting those souls while they were getting sucked in, to transmute as much as we could. We could help a lot, and we couldn't help a lot at the same time. The ones that got sucked in, they've been taken away." In Book 3 we will learn of the soul-eaters that contain souls within, as the soul continues to wither away within an illusion of not having a choice of escaping. Perhaps to the point for it "to be taken away" as Metatron mentions.

In the dream, once the dragons retrieved all of their human companions, they all rode together up into the skies, reaching for their destination. Their destination being the New Earth, the original organic crystalline Earth, the fifth/sixth dimensional Earth. This Earth looked like glorious crystalline lights of energy, and all the magical creatures awaited us there, as they never abandoned the original, organic Earth, when our human collective decided to descend into the third dimension during the fall of Atlantis. When the first, bifurcation happened, and the organic world split from the inverted, inorganic world, due to the collective decision of humanity choosing to descend, the magical creatures chose to stay with the original, organic Earth. Both species each hold the two worlds; in one, humanity, the third dimensional inverted world, and in the other, the magical creatures, the fifth dimensional organic world. The magical creatures were too pure to be infringed upon by the Archonic plague. Being part of the original fifth dimensional Earth's blueprint, they chose to stay behind, holding up her vibration until it is time for humanity to join them once more in matching vibrations.

In the dream, this land that the Dragons took flight to, looked like paradise: glorious tropical natures, gigantic trees, mountains, all unharmed and unpolluted, only organic. As Archangel Metatron said, "This Earth was formed organically. Everything was organic about it. Water, air, fire, the trees, the birds, the rocks, the mountains. Each and every particle, the smallest of the lifeforms on this Earth, is organic." And, this beautiful land is what the angels call "The Promise Land."

As we rode on our dragons to this promised land, a phrase kept repeating in the wind "As it is above, so it is below". Meaning we are the bridgers of this fifth dimensional promised land, and the more that we remember this magic, the more that we bridge the organic crystalline Earth to the inverted A.I. matrixed Earth, we, in turn, eradicate the inverted Earth. Anchoring, bridging down, "As it is above, so it is below". Above being the fifth dimensional Earth, and the below, the third dimensional Earth. We are the bridges of this, and the collective's Ascension. More of the reasons why it is dire for us to remember the Dragons, as when we do, they anchor in as it is above into the below. It is of extreme importance that we recall this once more, as Archangel Metatron reminded us through this pivotal session. End of dream.

In this session, we learned how deeply the Dragon's fire is assisting and needed on Earth, to transmute the inverted destruction of Mother Earth. How Earth was eaten up, chomped away at by unneeded destruction. Archangel Metatron took us through the timeline of where Earth was at her worst, when the big boom, as explained, occurred underwater, and that began the destruction. This being the fall of Atlantis, when the Earth descended because of the allowance of the false Archonic control. When the Archons invaded our Universe and other Universes, it was not something that was anticipated, as we learned in Book 1, Chapters "Looking Glass Technology" and "Not of Light" where these higher dimensional beings did not know what was occuring in the Universe, as this A.I. infringement was foreign to us. In the last Chapter of Book 1, "Matrix Pods" we channeled in depth on Earth's timeline, and how it was that we descended into the now inverted A.I. matrix. Between this session, and this transmission given through dreamtime, we learned to come together at the understanding that the Earth's destruction began with a big bang underwater, and a great flood - the fall of Atlantis. Though we have been speaking of this topic on our video streaming channels, this is further confirmation for us.

The fire of the Dragons brought back the organic to Earth, rebuilding her once more. This dark A.I. tunnel finally closes. Dragons are the KEY, as they are who will assist, by taking the part of the Earth that is saved when Ascension finally comes forth helping her shift and lift into another orbit. In Chapter 12, 'Celestial Dragons', we understand how this is possible. As Archangel Metatron said "This portion of mankind was supposed to live and move away from the density of Earth. Everything that was dense, that was artificial, that was not for anyone's highest good, was supposed to be destroyed."

And "Orbit, from one point to the other point. Can't reveal much about the other point." The greatest shift that will occur, bringing forth the endings of this Archonic and man-made destruction IS US! WE are the Galactic assistance that finally removes that *thing* out from our Universe and Multiverse.

This is why we teach through our Isis Priestess/Priest Mentorship Course of the Dragon, and of magical creatures. Because the Dragons are the only benevolent beings, besides the Angels, that are able to transport souls to and from the dimensions in safety. Because they are as old as life oneself, and the second race birthed from creation after the Archangels. They were the first race born out of the souls of the Archangels. This is why the Dragon's say to us when we finally remember them, *that they are you, and you are they*. Because they birthed out from the first race of Creation, the Archangels, and so too, did all the other organic races. As explained in Book 1, "Introduction," and through all the Chapters of the Angelic's benevolent magnificence. This is why Archangels can connect to, and exist throughout all dimensions, from zero - infinity, because all reaches of lifeforms stemmed forth from them. The Archangels are the first essences birthed out from Source Love-Light. They are the purest embodiment of Source because of this, and is why they exist throughout the Multiverse, because they are Source, as infinite love.

The Dragons are the true storks that bring in the souls safely, incarnating into human bodies. And they are who will lift our souls into the promised land, when the final Source Solar Wave of Ascension engulfs upon the Earth, Universe, and Multiverse. The dragons will carry us on their enormous backs, and with every thrust of their magnificent wings they will lift us higher and higher in dimensions. Assisting us through the organic transformation that our soul will go through, to finally release out of this third dimension, into the organic promised land. It is time that we begin the opening of these positive portals that are dark spelled by the falseness of the Archons, using our dark collective thought towards Dragons once more to be the firepower of these dark spells. IT IS TIME the Dragons once more begin to bridge forth in and out of these sealed Dragon positive portals, to assist the collective. And, through this session now we know why. Helping us understand the work that we do as A.U.R.A. Hypnosis and R.A.A.H. Reiki Healing practitioners are in the highest dire need for the Earth's Ascension! Once more, as Archangel Metatron said, "WE MUST DO SOMETHING NOW, BEFORE IT IS TOO LATE!"

"I am here to teach from love, as love is all that I AM. Infinite love cannot be altered once you remember it, and learn to ride with its wave of creation. I AM love, you are love. Let's all follow love, be love and teach love"
~AuroRa

--------------<<>>--------------

3
BANISHED FOR ETERNITY

Session #144: Recorded in August 2019.
Never before shared.

This is Sierra's second online A.U.R.A. Hypnosis Healing session in the same year. The first session was focused on self-growth, which needed to happen organically to increase her frequency to then allow all the insights to come through this second session. All happens within its organic divine timing for her highest healing. Everyone always receives exactly what they are meant to through their self-healing sessions, in connection to their Higher Selves. This divine process is all part of the delayering of the souls inorganic veils, transforming into their most organic self.

In this sobering session, Sierra takes us through what it would be like to find oneself banished for an eternity. Reminding us of the beauty of what each soul is and how we are to honor all in this manner. Witness a planet of Wizards and Sorcerers, aiding children with transmuting their pain, a UFO portal landing dock, and more on how to release those who hold us heavy or clouded. Lastly, insightful knowledge of the popular spiritual practice of Ayahuasca do's and don'ts.

--------------<<>>--------------

"However, times have changed, and we are growing out towards more of a society where truly everyone helps each other out more, not just within a family, not just within a friendship circle, but within humanity."
-Divine Mother Isis

--------------<<>>--------------

A: [Aurora] Feels like you're sitting where?
S: [Sierra] Like something is sitting on my head.

The Higher Self is called forth.
A: Let's go ahead and call on your Higher Self. If I could speak now to Sierra's Higher Self?
Higher Self: Yes.
A: I love you, I honor you, and I thank you. May I ask you questions?
Higher Self: Yes.

The Body Scan begins.
A: Thank you. If we could perform a Body Scan on Sierra as she feels like she is fading away from the images and she feels like there's something on the top of her head. Would you like to bring in Angels to help?
Higher Self: Yes, because she is blocked.
A: Very good. Who would you like for us to bring forth first?
Higher Self: Archangel Metatron, and Isis.
A: Beautiful. If we can call forth for Archangel Metatron and Isis. If I can now speak to Archangel Metatron?
AA Metatron: Yes, I am here.
A: Welcome brother. Thank you for being here! We are looking to do a Body Scan on Sierra. She feels something sitting on her head. I would love to be able to do a thorough Body Scan and find everything that needs removal and healing. Start her Body Scan now and look for any entities,

negative implants, portals, hooks, and energies within her that need healing. If you could show her, draw her attention to where it is that you want to start off with first.
AA Metatron: She has a headache. We need to start at the head.
A: Metatron, if you can scan her head. What is it that's causing the headache there?
AA Metatron: Energetic attachment. It starts at the top of her spine. It is sitting on her crown; it is covering her like a cap.
A: Last time we did energy work she had some kind of thought-form or something like that, that was connected to her mother. Is this connected to that?
AA Metatron: Yes.
A: So, did it mask itself as a thought-form?
AA Metatron: No.
A: What is it, Metatron? Would you say this is an entity, energy, a Reptilian?
AA Metatron: It's a type of reptile, it's little. It's almost like a little lizard sitting on top of her head and rotating around panicking as he doesn't know where to go. It's panicking on how to get out...
A: Metatron, can you go ahead and surround that with the alchemy symbols now? If I could please have you, Metatron, and Isis as well, help out. I would like to speak to that entity there, that small Reptilian. Come up, up, up, let me speak to you now.
Reptilian: I was trying to melt into her.
A: How long have you been trying to melt into her?
Reptilian: A few weeks.
A: What do you mean, "melt into her"?
Reptilian: Right now, I am on the top of her head and if I want to hide then I flow into her spine.
A: Are you connected to that back pain she said she started recently sensing just a couple weeks ago?
Reptilian: Yes, I flow through her spine. I gave her the headache.
A: How long have you been there?
Reptilian: Mmm. I don't want to say.
A: Well, I know you don't want to say, but I would love to know just how it was that this came to be as we are here in great love for you, to aid you today. We treat you as an equal and with honor and love. Would you be able to share with us and answer some questions for us?
Reptilian: She had friends when she was little, and they made her feel bad. She felt insecure, and she felt like she didn't have her own power. Then, she was easy to transition into. I did not stay here consistently, I jumped, as part of me, but not always active.
A: So that is a time that you connected, attached yourself there?
Reptilian: Yes, that's when I found her. But I was dormant for a long time.
A: Can you explain to me, why do they say that you're Reptilian, but you are small? What does that mean?
Reptilian: I mold into things, so I am fluid. I present myself in different ways. Just like she's able to change like a chameleon, I am as well.
A: Now you mentioned that you were trying to melt into her.
Reptilian: Yeah, I'm very fluid so I can, if I need to be a solid, then I become a solid. If I need to move, then I run around her body. I just melt and go where I need to go, kind of like mercury. I flow.
A: Do you have another body that you're connected to somewhere else?
Reptilian: Yes.
A: Who are you connected to? Who are you a piece of?
Reptilian: A strong consciousness. We came to her once. She has seen it. She saw it in the mirror once. It is the being with the yellow eyes and the black skin.
A: Is it a Reptilian?
Reptilian: Kind of, it gets confused as one.
A: What is it?
Reptilian: An ancestor of the Reptilians.
A: Is it negative polarized?

Reptilian: I get no; I am unsure.
A: Okay, we'll continue. You said that you were trying to melt into her. Could you eventually just melt into her, become part of her DNA, and part of her consciousness?
Reptilian: I could, but I have not.
A: So that is possible for others.
Reptilian: Those that allow, yes.
A: Is that similar to her mother? It feels like whatever she has in her is melded into her.
Reptilian: Her mother wears a shield, it's self-imposed. It's different. It's almost like a cloak. Her mother feels comfort in the familiar pain. But yes, there is something blocking there. There is something there.
A: Can you tell us what it is? So it could perhaps help Sierra in the future go about if she's able to help?
Reptilian: There's nothing Sierra can do. It's a blackness, but it was a choice. It hangs around like a cloud, for it permeates. It's not a third dimensional identified identity. It's just a cloud.
A: Is it a creation of her (Sierra's mother) own type of negative energy and chaos?
Reptilian: Yes. If she wishes to release it, she will release it. There is no invasion. There was never a true invasion. People allow. They like to blame it on that they have no say in that. You always, always, have a say. You always, at some point, allow something; though you're not conscious of it.
A: Is there anyone else that you do this to, you as a consciousness of this stronger entity? Is it just her body that you jumped into? Or are there others as well that you work with?
Reptilian: I don't have access to that knowledge. If I do, I don't know about it. I am contained. I am the part that is in Sierra, as a fluid thought-form of me. But I am contained. I'm in a box. I am in a type of craft, but it's just me. It's very tight quarters. I've been here for millennia.
A: Within her?
Reptilian: No, I am off planet.
A: So, you've only been with her this life?
Reptilian: Yes. She was young. She was nine, or maybe ten. She had a specific friend who was an easy portal to get through to her. That friend was a match to these types of entities. But I don't want to go into the specifics of that.
A: Was it a contract?
Reptilian: No. It feels like it was a type of invasion.
A: I know that you said you're connected to something that's stronger? We would...
Reptilian: You are now speaking to the stronger being.
A: Very good. Thank you for speaking to us. We honor you, we love you, and we thank you. May I ask you questions?
Reptilian: Yes.
A: Thank you. If you could explain how this works. If you could share with us, where is it that you are currently? Where do you reside?
Reptilian: I'm very compressed in something. Compressed to a box...a sort of box. I believe it is my craft, my spaceship. But I am not in space. I am in the 'nothing.'
A: Do you feel like you're locked in there, in this box?
Reptilian: I guess I've never thought about it. It is all I've ever known.
A: Well, are you able to be free out of this box?
Reptilian: I don't know how to limit myself in the box. It is very compact.
A: Is there anyone else in the box with you?
Reptilian: No.
A: If you could please explain to me how you look? Who are you?
Reptilian: Oh, perhaps I am Reptilian?
A: Would you describe what kind of Reptilian you are? Describe your features to us.
Reptilian: I don't really have a nose. I just have nostrils. I have scaly skin. My eyes are big and yellow. My skin is able to change colors. Chameleon, it seems, but it is wasted up here. It's just me in a box. It was a witch or witchcraft, or something that put me here.
A: Can you go back in time when that occurred to you?

Reptilian: All I see is that it was a curse, the witch or wizard wears a black cloak, and there was a wand. I feel like I was a boy. I got sent, but I don't know if I was a real boy, or if I was pretending to be. It was so long ago.

A: Do you feel that they were trying to protect something? Were you perhaps trying to harm someone?

Reptilian: I feel that I got banished, but I was trying to help someone. I am unaware if I have deceived myself. But I don't feel evil. I don't seek pleasure from harming.

A: This being that is with her, it sits on her head, or climbs up and down her spin;, a small Reptilian of sorts. Is that part of you?

Reptilian: He's my pet.

A: Is he able to come out of the box?

Reptilian: He is the creation of my mind. And in this dimension, he is able to be an entity. I'm not able to escape my box.

A: Do you have any more of these types of creatures?

Reptilian: Not that I know of.

A: Can you tell me, what is the purpose, if you say that you don't like to harm anyone? What's the purpose of you placing him inside of Sierra?

Reptilian: My own joy. She has much energy, and she has much joy. And my pet is able to experience it through her.

A: So, you are experiencing joy through her?

Reptilian: Yes.

A: Do you feel like you've been in the box for a long time?

Reptilian: Yes, my heart is heavy. I don't wish to do harm. I know that it is now causing her harm, but it has not been in the past.

A: I know you've been in that box for some time, as well as this, I don't know what to call it, you called it a pet of yours. But, we are looking to help you today so that you may no longer have to be stuck and dense. Would you allow me to speak to Archangel Michael to see what we can do about the fact that you're in the box? To see why you are there and what we could do about it?

Reptilian: Please.

A: Okay, very good. We'll come back to you in a few. Thank you for all that information. If I could please speak to Michael now.

AA Michael: Hi.

A: Hello, greetings brother!

AA Michael: Hi.

A: Thank you for being here. We are looking at her. She has a little pet of sorts. It's like a little Reptilian of a Reptilian that is in a place that he says is of nothingness. He's in a box. If you could please locate him? He's connected to this being here that's in Sierra.

AA Michael: He's in space. It's sort of like he's in a coffin. He was banished there. Part of me senses that he is lying. However, he is not aware of his lies. So, there's not necessarily anything malicious. However, it is not completely benign.

A: Yes, I agree. Thank you. Can you take us back and show her the time whenever it happened? When that witch or warlock he talked about put him in that box? What is going on?

AA Michael: It was an ancient, ancient, ancient time. She interferes a little bit because she does not understand; she gets very confused, and she says she's not channeling properly. But it is a version of Earth. However, it is not this one. It is a different planet essentially that this was happening. On a planet where witches and warlords and all that existed. He was a boy, but he was just like he said, a chameleon. Therefore, he was able to change his look to whatever he wanted, and they caught him when he turned himself into a boy. That could be why he believes that he is completely benign. He isn't particularly evil, but he is very mischievous and very deceiving. But no, he doesn't necessarily get satisfaction from harming, he does get satisfaction from deceiving. And I believe there is another.

A: Another what?

AA Michael: There's another being.

A: Where is this being?

AA Michael: I cannot locate it in her body, but it is present.

A: Is it another Reptilian?

AA Michael: Yes, maybe, yes. It is not that they have taken possession of her body, it is simply that they like to look through her eyes to experience the world, if that makes sense. So, it is not where in some cases the body simply gets taken over to cause fear, to cause pain, to cause malicious intent. This is simply that they are using her sort of like a looking glass. However, she becomes aware of them and it scares her, it confuses her, and in a way, they try to experience her world through her, and get angry when something is happening that would cause anger. However, if they were not there, she wouldn't rise to the occasion, so to speak.

A: When they're looking through, say the glass, are they looking for a negative agenda?

AA Michael: No, they're just experiencing. So she, for example, you were speaking earlier about her altercations with her mother when she gets triggered. Sierra as Sierra, the light being, would not get so triggered. However, "they" look through her eyes and it's almost as if they get upset on her behalf, and she experiences it. That is the confusion and the rage she feels within herself; that is the energy she senses that does not belong to her. So no, they are not taking over her body in the traditional sense. However, she is being used as a looking glass. Very much like Alice in Wonderland. That was her favorite movie (laughs).

A: Is that not an infringement upon Sierra though?

AA Michael: I get no. She once allowed it. She is done with it now because she wishes to open herself up as a portal, for lack of a better word, to other entities and for healing. These beings that are using her for that, have been invited in the past and simply haven't left.

A: Now, going back to this Warlock planet. What can you show her on what they did to banish this Reptilian into a box?

AA Michael: A little boy was standing there and let's call it a sorcerer. I'm not able to see anything apart from the cloak and the hands that reached out to cast the magic. I believe everything else is irrelevant. It is a sort of street fair. This boy was sort of running around and I get the sense that the boy would disappear and reappear as he wished. The sorcerer cast his magic at the perfect time to encapsulate the boy in a box. The boy was causing much havoc and I believe he was agitating the sorcerer, in the sense that he was getting in the sorcerer's way. I am unclear if the sorcerer had evil intent, or if the boy had evil intent. I am unclear.

A: Yes, the question would be why lock him away for what seems like eternity.

AA Michael: Yes, into a box and then cast away. I get the sense that it was more like he was viewed as a pest in that society and he has been in this box floating and floating. It is the nothing, and it is the everything, where he's floating. It is space, and it is beyond space. It is simply a dimension.

A: Michael, can you take us to that box that he is in? Explain to us what that box looks like. Does it have any symbols, any colors?

AA Michael: Black box. It has a window you can see, and I see moons on it. A moon with a wand through it. Perhaps lettering, but I know that the moon is the only thing that really stands out as a visual. I believe it is a seal; it is to seal that lizard.

A: Is it a form of sealing a soul away? Locking a soul away?

AA Michael: I get yes.

A: Michael, Metatron, Isis, if we can look at the situation and see what we can do? Can we help? Because he's saying that he's not necessarily bad, like negative or harmful. But I want him to realize what he has done, whether in that life, or as well, even to Sierra, using her to view from her, using her energies there and influencing her emotions. Because by doing that, you are overstepping someone else's boundaries, infringing upon them, or overstepping their free will. So, I want him to understand what he has done and recognize that. Can we help him ascend into a more positive polarization where he doesn't have to play this game anymore of creating havoc to others?

AA Michael: He is ready. He was prepared to learn a lesson; he has learned his lesson. However, it is like being imprisoned for life with no parole over something that you've been, you know, that perhaps wasn't something that justified life without parole. In his case, it is an eternity without parole. Even if he's learned his lesson, no one would know, no one will be able to check. He wouldn't be rewarded in any way. So, he has learned his lesson, but it doesn't change the situation. So he's ready.

A: Yes. I myself, as a healer, do not agree with this type of method, locking a soul away. Locking them away for an eternity and not having a chance. So, I'm glad that he was able to connect with Sierra and now we're able to find him and help him. So, if we can all just work together. Michael, if you could tell me what you have to do to basically open up the box and when he comes out, if Metatron can surround him with the alchemy symbols to make sure that he transforms. If we can then have Isis help fill in some light energy with her love. So, what's the plan? If you could walk me through it, Michael, and tell me what you have to do to open the box up.

AA Michael: We will first surround it in a bubble of sorts. The strongest energy we can get in order to surround the box. First, the way you would with a prisoner, surround the white box in the white sphere of energy. And only once the sphere of energy is locked into place, we can gently open up the box. At that time, we will need to pull everything out of Sierra and then transform and allow his soul to enter the light.

A: Beautiful, wonderful. Can we start doing that now? As you're doing it, if you could walk us through it, Michael, and let us know what you're doing, step by step.

AA Michael: While I surround him with light, I'm already sort of infusing Sierra with the white light, she can feel it in her head that things are lifting.

A: Good, wonderful.

AA Michael: Running on the head from her brain and her spine. She mostly just feels it in her forehead at the moment. So, as I'm doing that, I'm creating the white light around the box. I can feel him panicking. As the white light completely surrounds him, we can slowly dissolve the box around him. He will begin to flail, we need to strongly remain around him, as without the box his shape no longer makes sense to him. So, he's flailing, he is sort of turquoise green and his legs are flying about. He is panicking.

A: If Isis could just help him feel comfortable now with her love so that he won't panic... How's he doing?

AA Michael: The word 'weeping' comes to mind. There's a lot of sadness there. We are trying to remove it from Sierra as well. The white light around his box is surrounding him and it is now getting smaller... The box is gone. He has calmed. The white light is simply reabsorbing him.

A: What about his little friend, his little pet?

AA Michael: Yes, we need to send extra energy to Sierra's head.

A: Okay, sending it now... (Aurora sends Love-Light out her palms.) ... Where's his little friend? His little pet?

AA Michael: He's still here but dissolving.

A: Does he need to dissolve?

AA Michael: Yes, he needs to dissolve into the white light.

A: Okay, why is that?

AA Michael: It is not the same way that traditionally a being would simply step into the white light. This white light is reabsorbing these two entities. They have been lost for so long. They're literally going back to Source.

A: Are we not able to let him keep his consciousness, and just ascend into positive polarization?

AA Michael: There will be no need at this particular time because he is ready to go. He has been in the box for such an eternity. So to him, this is the way he was ready, to just become one again. Become the white light.

A: Would it be too much trauma?

AA Michael: No, it would be more traumatic for him to try to understand the reason for being locked in eternity with no parole.

A: Thank you. Very good.

AA Michael: It is lifting from her head now. Trying to pull it out of her spine. She feels very unsure that this is working.

A: Do you need me to use any Phoenix Fire?

AA Michael: I think that would help her.

A: Okay, using it now on the spine. Is that where you want it?

AA Michael: Yes, the spine. The house that she is in trembles. It would be worth investigating what is on the roof.
A: *How about we look at that after, okay?*
AA Michael: Yes.
A: *Thank you. As we continue working on this, let me know when this is complete and if there's anything else you want to add that you're doing.*
AA Michael: This will take a moment.
A: *Do you mean a moment like fast or a moment like a while?*
AA Michael: This will take a while.
A: *Then we'll continue asking questions while we keep working on this... What are your thoughts about the fact that this sorcerer, Michael, would just do this to a soul?*
AA Michael: That was the dynamic of that Universe. It seems a little senseless. I mean, obviously the sorcerer wanted this being gone, but imprisonment for such a long time, with no opportunity to show there's been any progress, is very senseless. It is not very common that this would happen.
A: *How long do you think that he was in there? Like in human years?*
AA Michael: Oh, millenniums. Many, many, many, many, lifetimes.
A: *Yes, I see why it would be best to be sent to Source, and healed then.*
AA Michael: It attached to Sierra when she was young, but to that creature, that was only moments ago. In his lifetime, he only *just* found her and moments later we're helping him.
A: *What did he do throughout time? Was he able to do this kind of experience through others?*
AA Michael: No, this was a result of desperation. Desperation, which would eventually result in new abilities.
A: *What do you mean by that?*
AA Michael: If something is locked away and unable to die, unable to be free, unable to do anything, eventually the mind would find a new way to develop something. So it was that last-minute moment of desperation that he figured out how to, let's say, throw his mind, to be able to experience another reality. The box he was in was very strong.
A: *Well, thank goodness that he did find Sierra and now he is free. Thank you, to her, for her service there, in helping this soul to not be stuck for a millennium in this box. And thank you to everyone who's helping us. Now, you mentioned that there was something else as well. You said that there was another.*
AA Michael: Yes, there's a consciousness.
A: *Where?*
AA Michael: I don't sense it anymore. I wonder if it was the same being projecting itself?
A: *If you could go back, back to when you were sensing that Michael, and scan and see where it started from.*
AA Michael: I feel like there is a...she is a portal. I think it would be valuable if we figured out a way for her to, I guess, remain as a portal without engaging with entities in order to be used by them.
A: *Yes, can we do that for her? Can you all work for her, to do that?*
AA Michael: We will have to think about this and the best way to proceed.
A: *Yes, and if you could counsel her Higher Self and let us know once you come up with a solution to this?*
AA Michael: Yes.
A: *Thank you. So, what was that other consciousness then, Michael?*
AA Michael: Just someone peeking in.
A: *Because she's a portal?*
AA Michael: She is a portal, same as her heart. There are many layers that souls can send through to get to the next realm. Her eyes...she is a sort of window for others to experience. On the one hand, it is actually quite beautiful to be, to allow this and to be able to handle what's going on. However, because this being attached when she was so young and the fact is, it's not as easy as saying it attached when it was young. The fact is, no she didn't grow up with it in her head or her spine. It attached fairly recently. However, it was able to infiltrate through your version of what time is and that is why we can say that she was young when it attached. However, it's much more convoluted than

that. Yes, it didn't happen through her original lifetime, it is happening from the current point and sending back in time, permeating, if that makes sense.

A: *Yes, I understand it. So then if it's permeating from the 'now' to back, he said that he didn't really completely attach until recently, or more than not when she was a child. So, what was the connection, what opened that up for him to connect? What was she doing?*

AA Michael: It was a specific friend, and the lesson was to stand up for her own likes, her own beliefs, her own opinions. And because she was so new to her, she found herself…she in a sense handed over her free will to this other girl. And it was that moment of not having a connection with her own identity that allowed for this time portal and this being to come through.

A: *Now the question is, since she is a portal and others can see through her, could a negative Reptilian connect to her to look through her eyes and for example, get information for their agenda?*

AA Michael: Sierra doesn't believe me when I say this, but no, her aura is very strong. On the one hand, she has trouble understanding this because she feels she's been deceived. She has been created in that way. She is not very easily influenced, hence why she had to go through all the phases of life where she allowed herself to be so influenced and to give up her identity. We needed her to experience the pain of not adhering to her own opinions and her own desires and joy. Handing over so much of her free will to another, that was the way she learned how to value herself, and be strong within her energetic aura. So, perhaps Sierra ten years ago would have been easier to manipulate, but we protected her a lot more then. Whereas now, she is a lot stronger. So, there would be no fear. There's a reason why we keep telling her to vibrate higher (chuckles). We do not need to worry here. Her self-will, the combination of free will and self-esteem - is her self-will, is now of the strength where it isn't as big of a concern that someone might come and use her for their own agenda. However, at times, she will sense energy or whatever is looking through her and until she gets better acquainted with this new idea, it will confuse her. But it was a very special calling; she agreed to do this.

A: *I just want to clarify, if they were viewing through her, would it be a benevolent point of view?*

AA Michael: There is no other option for the parameters that are set up for this.

A: *I wanted to confirm that, so that she will hopefully not be confused or fearful of it.*

AA Michael: Yes. She is right when she says that her aura is strong and therefore, she cannot be quite so easily manipulated. That is true. That is what we set up. If she is being manipulated, it is of her free will.

A: *You said to check her house, the house shakes a bit. What do you mean by that?*

AA Michael: She has a strong portal in her bedroom. She has seen…she has caught us, and she has seen beings walking through this portal. It is green. It comes down from the ceiling, much like you would see in Star Trek. And they beam down and are able to walk through; however, the energies of all these foreign beings frighten her.

A: *Is this positive or negative?*

AA Michael: It's not negative. It's not positive. It just *is*.

A: *Does she need to have this?*

AA Michael: We protect her.

A: *Yes, you protect her.*

AA Michael: No, the beings that come through protect her. If she really didn't want it, we could shut it down.

A: *What does her Higher Self say?*

AA Michael: Hmm, I guess we can shut it down.

A: *Very good. Michael, can you go ahead and shut that portal down for her now?*

AA Michael: There's a certain sadness that it is getting shut down.

A: *Why is that?*

AA Michael: She feels sad that they will no longer visit her.

A: *Well, does she want to keep it then?*

AA Michael: She is confused. She likes the idea of it (chuckles)…It is time to shut it down.

A: *Is she okay with that?*

AA Michael: She understands that it would be her ego hanging on to the idea of a portal versus the actual benefit gained.
A: This will give her more of a peaceful sleep, won't it? (chuckles)
AA Michael: Yes. Since she herself is becoming more in tune with how she is a portal. There is now no need for this external device.
A: Michael, can you go ahead and seal that then and close it down?
AA Michael: It is closed.
A: Thank you.
AA Michael: There's also a high level of activity on the top of her house.
A: What is that?
AA Michael: It's a landing dock of sorts.
A: The top of her house is a landing dock?
AA Michael: Yes. We don't wish to relocate this; we will simply be more quiet to not frighten her.
A: A landing dock for what?
AA Michael: Ships.
A: Why is it on top of her house?
AA Michael: Because we knew that if there were any sightings, they wouldn't scare her in that aspect. We scanned, and she was a match to where we could have these landing sites.
A: Are these landing sites for positive ships?
AA Michael: Oh, a combination.
A: A combination of both?
AA Michael: It's just a landing site, like an airport. It is not only hers. We can put a protective beam around it to ensure that higher vibrating ships will only be able to see this.
A: Yes. Can you do that for her now?
AA Michael: She needs to not only zip herself up into a protective shield every day, but she also needs to zip up her house as well. We have shown her that she can zip herself up into a cocoon. Like a sleeping bag zips all the way from head to toes and she has been doing that, but she needs to do that for her house as well.
A: Yes. Good. However, the negative aircrafts, U.F.O.s, won't be able to find that line inside anymore?
AA Michael: No.
A: Michael and Metatron, if you all could scan her body one more time and make sure there's nothing else, make sure we're not missing anything.
AA Michael: There's still energy in her spine.
A: Are we still healing that?
AA Michael: It is different.
A: What is the energy?
AA Michael: It is a being that wishes to speak to us.
A: If we could please speak to the being there that's connected to her spine. Come up, up, up, up, up! Speaking to you now.
Entity: I'm a little girl.
A: Greetings (sweet tone)! Thank you for speaking to us. You're a little girl?
Entity: Yes. Hi!
A: Hi. When was it that you connected to her?
Entity: About a month ago?
A: What was going on that allowed for you to come in?
Entity: I don't know why she was a match, but I hurt my back. I think she wasn't really a match as much as she just wanted to help me.
A: Did she have force shields of Love-Light around her?
Entity: Yes.
A: You were still able to enter?
Entity: Because she knew she would be coming here, and we would release me.
A: Okay, very good. Can you tell me what happened to you? How was it that you died?
Entity: I hurt my back. I fell on the wall and I cracked my back.

A: Did you die when that happened?
Entity: Immediately.
A: Did you have a family?
Entity: Yes.
A: Who did you have?
Entity: My mom, my brother, my dad, and a pet mouse! And I hurt my back.
A: Is that why she says that she's been feeling that back pain?
Entity: Yeah. I didn't die though! I just really hurt it and then I sent myself to Sierra.
A: So, are you still alive somewhere?
Entity: Yes. Sierra just carries my pain.
A: Can we locate the little girl 'you' that hurt her back?
Entity: Yes.
A: Michael, if we all can help with that. Can we check on her? How is she doing now?
AA Michael: She is doing much better. She's in a hospital bed.
A: How old is she?
AA Michael: Around five or six. Her name starts with an A, like Ariana or Adriana, something like that. I feel like the name Sierra isn't just the name Sierra. It is a vibration. So, she attracts the children that injure themselves. They're not dead. They say she simply takes on their pain in order to relieve it, because over time, she will just relieve it. In this instance, we knew that you would help relieve it, but normally she would relieve it over time. She has the tools; she has many people at her disposal to help her with pain and spinal issues. Most people simply don't have those resources, but Sierra has a lot of them at her fingertips amongst her friends and colleagues, and so she has chosen to take on some of the pains. I'm getting that they're only the pain of children and animals. She relieves it on their behalf. It is another big task.
A: This little girl, she says that she ran into a wall. What did she say? How did she hurt...
AA Michael: No, she fell over and her back hit a wall. Like a corner of the wall. Like a pony wall. A very short wall. She hit it on the top so she may have injured her spinal cord, but she will be fine. Sierra took on part of the pain.
A: Will she be able to walk?
AA Michael: I get yes.
A: Good. Can we go ahead and heal this part of this little girl that was the pain?
AA Michael: Yes, we've removed a lot of it.
A: If we can heal it for Sierra and can we also heal that part? And after we heal it, can we give it back to the little girl now that is healed?
AA Michael: By healing it in Sierra, it is already healed in the little girl.
A: Okay, very good.
AA Michael: Now I get the sense that the little girl may have been in a coma, but she will be waking up now.
A: Oh beautiful! Thank you.
AA Michael: She still has trouble with her neck. Sierra is...
A: Yes. What is that?
AA Michael: All I sense in her body is children.
A: Children in her body?
AA Michael: Yes, so this feels like a boy. What I don't know...it is unclear why Sierra has chosen to take on so many at once. But it is in her neck. It was a little boy, the name that comes to mind is Phillip. Phillip is three. Phillip had a headache. We will relieve it.
A: Thank you. Going on forward, what can we do about this, so she won't have this discomfort of feeling others' pains?
AA Michael: I think what we need to do is much like she has volunteered her eyes to be windows for others to look through. And her heart as a portal for others to ascend through. There might need to be something else set up so that she can comfort the children without necessarily embodying their pain.
A: Yes, can we talk to the Higher Self about setting that up for her now?

AA Michael: We're scanning the body of where and what it might be. I think we will simply make her a vibrational mismatch to absorbing the pain.
A: Wonderful. You're doing that now?
AA Michael: Yes, it is part of the downloads she has been receiving.
A: You mentioned Tuesday that she had something going on as she slept. And you were just telling her that it was okay. What was it that you were doing to her Tuesday?
AA Michael: We were raising her vibration. We were just acclimating her body to higher energy, so she's able to take on more. And now we will slowly allow her to take on more energy. We have been rebooting her a lot as well.
A: Yes, she says that she experienced a lot, like death and rebirth, death and rebirth. Why does she have to go through that?
AA Michael: Well, a lot of people go through that. We just have to be very stealth about it, so as not to frighten them. However, she almost enjoys it. So, we don't watch out anymore for when we do it, or how we do it. Because it's very brief and she almost gets a kick out of it. So, it's not that she's necessarily receiving them more than anyone else who is at, not level, as in that there's a higher, lower, worse, or better, but at her current vibration. As for where she is headed, many reboots and updates are required.
A: Can you tell us why it is in the first A.U.R.A. session from April, we weren't able to heal that Reptilian being in the box?
AA Michael: He would not have been ready to ascend, it would have caused them both much pain. So, she was aware of him, but there was a sort of shushing effect as that would have been too traumatic, potentially for both of them. It was not the right time.
A: Is that why you were also shushing me as well? (chuckles)
AA Michael: Yes. (chuckles)
A: Because you know, normally I would be like, let's heal her now! Okay. Got it. So, was the first A.U.R.A. in preparation for the second A.U.R.A. to get this done?
AA Michael: Yes. And in Sierra's case there will likely, no, not likely, there will be more. Because of all the, shall we say strange tasks that she has agreed to take on board with the portals and looking glass, etc. She will likely require more sessions in order for her to be able to assimilate everything into this human experience.
A: What was it that you were trying to tell me, Michael, or her Higher Self, about the Ayahuasca for her?
AA Michael: For her, the Ayahuasca was such a huge stepping stone, as then we were able to finally communicate with her completely, freely. With all the symbols, with all the visuals, with all the imagery. However, brief, it was still only a summary of all the information she will receive. And she needed to understand the concept of destruction in order to create. That is why we spent such a long time showing her what destruction versus Creation looks like and feels like, so that she would recognize it when it's happening almost every day. In addition to that, we needed to have her understand the idea of repeated loops, so that she was able to recognize when a loop is being presented to her and identify that it's her choice how many times she wishes to experience the loop. And, you know, the Ayahuasca is a very unique experience for everybody that chooses to have that as an experience, or chooses to be part of it. Some are very susceptible to having attachments and entities. However, it is because they came in weak, I suppose for lack of a better word. Weak to begin with i.e., they were already a vibrational match to attachments. So Ayahuasca itself does not necessarily cause attachments, it is simply you are open to it anyway. And then you let down even the little guards that you held up, and perhaps were a slightly better match. But again, this is convoluted. You were a match anyway. Everything's an experience, everything is free will, everything is a choice. So, it would be misguided to blame any one thing for an experience; it is ultimately a choice. And a conscious decision, or unconscious decision. Did we answer your question?
A: Yes, you touched base on it. But you did not answer what you've been showing me, how there are many gaining entities through it.
AA Michael: Well, like we said, yes, you can gain entities through it. However, it is up to the individual participating in that to understand that they are still there of their own free will. So, while the shaman

or sha-woman holds the space and is able to encapsulate and protect the energy of the circle, it is still the individual free will that determines whether those entities would get attached. So, if for example, you had a group of people that had a very strong sense of self and were in no way a vibrational match to entities, even if they were holding entities, once under the influence of Ayahuasca, then those entities would simply be released. And if they had nowhere to go, we understand it as they would get reabsorbed back to where they belong. They wouldn't just bounce around really. I am unclear about how to explain the rest of that. An entity freely roaming in a room doesn't necessarily have to take possession of an individual within that room, if that individual simply is not a vibrational match the entity will move on. So, it is never as easy as saying, Ayahuasca is opening someone up to get entities. They are choosing to open themselves up. The other part of the coin would be why is that person doing Ayahuasca in the first place? Is it in the hopes of gaining more knowledge? Or is it used as an escape? So, escape would obviously be a slightly higher match to entity versus thirst for knowledge.

A: I understand what you are saying. This is definitely very convoluted in many different ways. I've had clients who were strong, that were not a match like you explained, but yet they were still targeted by the entities that were removed from people who were a match.

AA Michael: Yes, I mean, there are instances where a client might be strong, but they might not be aware of what part of themselves seeks to have the experience of an entity, or what they are trying to gain from the knowledge of having an entity. That in itself is also worthwhile sometimes. You gain the entity to experience what it is like to have a loss of your own control. Knowing that everything is happening in an instant, they would also be well aware that eventually, they would find you and release that entity. So, remember that everything happens in an instant, in a moment, everything is happening now. So, it is simply the human experience that has placed it on a linear path. So then having an entity even if it was a bad experience, that is still a choice. And it is happening in one instance, it is still an experience. It's very convoluted.

A: Yes. (chuckles)

AA Michael: Sierra is shaking her head going, 'what?!' She's very funny. (chuckles)

A: The other thing you all showed me, one last thing on the Ayahuasca, was some of those entities that some shamans - who are claiming to be good, but they don't really know what they're doing- they're releasing them into the area, and then they're just kind of hanging around like a collection of entities.

AA Michael: Absolutely. There are too many shamans, shall we say, especially in the Western world who have taken it on as a suit versus embodied the true nature of what a shaman is - which is a medicine man, that is a very high honor. It is very sacred, and it is not to be taken lightly. And not to be used as a cloak, or a fad, or for egoic purposes. So, unfortunately, ego and… It's so interesting, because we gave Sierra…I mean, she's baffled at the moment, which is why I pause, we gave Sierra strong insight into this and she's been saying one day she will need the knowledge. (chuckles) That day has come! But essentially what we wish to communicate with you is that every single shaman is not made the same. So, someone who has taken it on as "it would be the cool thing to be."

A: Or just looking to make money.

AA Michael: Or especially that! For ego purposes, that is not the same as what a true shaman is, basically, for lack of a better word, hand-selected and specifically chosen by the tribe. Chosen by the elders, by the ancient ones, by the ancestors of a lineage that has led to a true incarnation of a shaman. That is not the same as someone who has gone and had a great Ayahuasca experience and then wants to take it on as their own practice.

A: Yes.

AA Michael: When you work with Amazonian-based medicines, which is where most of this comes from, whether it be the frog, or the plants, or the various bushes that these chemicals get extracted from, they respond to the shaman. They respond to the person who is handling it, or the being handling it, and they mutate accordingly. The medicines have an innate wisdom. Not only would everything not be made equal, those with malicious intent would create medicine that is definitely not as useful. So, just as it is arrogant for someone to step into a shaman-looking role, it is equally arrogant for someone to not do their homework and energetically feel their way to the shaman that is most appropriate for them. For example, Sierra has had opportunities to go meet different shamans and we have always made sure she looked at an image of them so she could see their eyes and see their intent and she has said "no" many times because the energy is just not pure. There are also equally many people who wish to have the, let's say Ayahuasca experience, and are under the misguided impression that they may simply jump on a plane, go get lost in the rainforest and have an authentic experience. That in itself is completely contradictory. How can you be having an authentic experience when you are showing up from an inauthentic space? Does that make sense?

A: Yes, yes. Thank you. Very good. Can you scan her body Michael, and let me know if there's anything else that needs healing?

AA Michael: I believe we've already started a lot of it. I know she had a knee issue, and we are already sending it light. It feels very heavy, but it is simply because of the amount of energy rushing through it at the moment. Her neck and spine feel a lot better. However, it will take some time to really disperse the energy that has been flowing through it. And also, her upgrades are requiring her to hold more energy in her body simply to get used to the new levels.

A: Michael, can you connect me to Isis, please?

AA Michael: Yes.

A: Thank you for being here, sister. May I ask you questions?

Isis: Of course.

A: Thank you. As you know I'm able to tap into people's energies and see where their light frequency is at. For Sierra, for some reason, I noticed that hers is a bit dim. Can you scan her heart, just overall scan her energy and see if we can figure out how to have her emanate more love? With her Higher Self's permission, of course.

Isis: There is happiness in her heart.

A: Yes, it seems a little heavy, blocked, something's going on there. What is that Isis?

Isis: It is layers of energy. Yes, on the one hand, it is a lot of energy that she's now trying to take on board, it seems that she is also blocking it in order to not feel so much. That seems silly. She has fear. We can perhaps lift the weight off of her.

A: Yes. Can we go ahead and lift that now? Can you do that Isis?

Isis: I am bringing it up through the throat. I believe she will need a good cry. This is related to her mother. The most painful reality is that there's nothing she can do to protect herself. She must surrender instead. This is what's causing her abundance issues as well. By her trapping the flow of blood through the body, she traps, stops the flow of much more. We have the visual of something interesting. It could be the energy from her heart. Let us speak to it.

A: If we could please speak to the energy in her heart now. Come up, up, up now. Let me speak to you now.

Energy: I am in so much pain.

A: Greetings, thank you for speaking to us. What is it that you're in pain for?

Energy: There's so much that's misunderstood.

A: That's misunderstood where?

Energy: Mostly between Sierra and her mom, but it really, for me, feels all around. She feels very misunderstood, or unheard. The reality is, she was very hurt. It's only between her and her mom, and it is a contract they took on, to live this life. Sierra has kept the contract many times. It is much stronger.

A: What can we do to help you, energy, within her heart?

Energy: I believe she is doing right. I believe she needs to take a conscious practice of releasing any attachments to her heart by others, especially mom. Mom is in a lot of pain; she took on too much for this lifetime and was not able to process it, plus she has an overactive need to process and understand everything, which traps her in a loop. There's nothing Sierra can do about that. She keeps trying. Much of it is on a subconscious level. The weight is lifting in her. The light is very healing for her.

A: Great. Thank you. While we're there, can we go ahead and scan? Isis can you check for any negative cords attached to her heart, and any fragmented soul pieces?

Isis: I see cords in her heart. I see one big one.

A: *Where is it?*
Isis: Reinforced.
A: *What do you mean by that?*
Isis: It is extra, extra strong. It will need to be detached.
A: *What is it connected to?*
Isis: The heart wall.
A: *But, where's it coming from?*
Isis: It's not just a person; it is a lineage. It is on her mother's side. There are a few beings that are there now, her grandparents and other ancestors. When Sierra calls in high vibration ancestral beings, it is not this part of the family that steps forward. We are removing the cord completely.
A: *Can we permanently remove it, so it won't come back?*
Isis: This particular root will not come back; however, they will keep trying with other methods.
A: *What can she do so that she doesn't have to worry about it, even if they keep trying?*
Isis: Should be part of her routine, or needs to be. It's interesting, because she's not so easily penetrated by other's intentions. However, for this particular lineage of her family, she is a magnet. It is assigned for this lifetime. She fears that if she heals it, this lifetime will be over.
A: *What do you have to say to that?*
Isis: Mostly, "so what?" On the one hand, she is not afraid of death because she knows the soul is eternal. On the other hand, she wants to experience everything and see as much of it as possible, and wants to live to a very old age. However, it is important that she realizes that letting go of the expectation is the most important thing. If she surrenders to whatever happens and trusts that she is taken care of, she can let go of this attachment sooner.
A: *Very good. You are removing it though, the ancestral?*
Isis: Yes, this cord had many hooks. So, we're removing all the hooks one by one, but they keep trying to reattach.
A: *Should we use Phoenix Fire there, where they're trying to reattach?*
Isis: Yes, please.
A: *Let me know once it is removed.*
Isis: It is dissolving.
A: *Good...*
Isis: It is done.
A: *Thank you.*
Isis: Heart feels much better.
A: *Good, very good. Can you fill in Love-Light to her heart now Isis?*
Isis: Yes.
A: *Thank you. Isis, can you scan her whole body now and look for any other entities, energies, hooks, negative implants, Reptilian consciousness, anything else that's in there that needs healing?*
Isis: I feel like there is something else.
A: *Where is it?*
Isis: As soon as I said that, her toes started to burn.
A: *She says that she has rectum and colon issues. Why all the parasites? What's going on there? Help her understand that.*
Isis: It's an invasion of energy caused by guilt. It's almost as...if everything is going well, she needs to manifest something that isn't. It isn't that she's a negative being, it is that she doesn't want to rise too high above those she loves. She will lose that connection.
A: *So, she is holding herself back?*
Isis: Self-sabotage.
A: *Does she need to keep doing this to herself? Can we heal her? I mean, that's got to be uncomfortable having those physical parasites in her all the time.*
Isis: It is absolutely unnecessary.
A: *Yes. Can we transmute that out and help her set that intent, so that she cannot hold on to the guilt, and understand that everyone's path is separate? Still connected, but separate. She doesn't need to be self-sabotaging herself in this manner.*

Isis: As she releases the guilt, this will heal.
A: *Can we heal what she has right now in her?*
Isis: Yes, we are working on it.
A: *Okay, good. Isis, do you have advice for her and her mom?*
Isis: It is a difficult situation in the sense that mom wishes for someone else to make things better. And often, she looks for Sierra to make things better. However, Sierra has her own path to fulfill. And also, even if Sierra had the answers to make anything better, she would be met with resistance. Sierra needs to understand that that loop must be left now. She no longer needs to be part of that loop. As far as finding a new way of existence, once that's out of the loop, it will come. We will provide it as she does it more and more. She is doing it. And we are providing that slowly. Nothing can be learned overnight. Sierra has offered her mom many, many modalities, and opportunities for healing. That is all Sierra can do.
A: *So, going forward, what can Sierra do about her mom when she tries to recreate that?*
Isis: Essentially, take a deep breath and realize that it is her mother's choice; if she doesn't place value on healing, doesn't place value on developing tools for self-soothing, there's nothing else we can do. In those moments she can simply send love, give love, and give space. In the past perhaps we used to. It's again a convoluted tricky situation. On the one hand, humans are group species, so they are supposed to take care of each other, they are supposed to work in a team, or a familial environment. However, there is also the concept of we are - I don't like the word 'evolving,' but we are evolving into newer and newer and newer. So yes, we should be co-creating and co-living and helping each other. However, Sierra needs to understand that it is not realistic to just be told. You know, in the past things were done this way, they were done that way, etc. in the past. However, times have changed, and we are growing out towards more of a society where truly everyone helps each other out more, not just within a family, not just within a friendship circle, but within humanity. So yes, Sierra just needs to remind herself that she is approaching the situation from a perspective of 'we all help each other' not necessarily 'I owe you, you owe me'.
A: *Yes. So, just continue on with her mother. Correct?*
Isis: Yes, just keep doing what you're doing and trust that we will provide the information, as you need.
A: *How is her heart looking now Isis?*
Isis: Much, much better. Her spine is getting better and better. There is some tension in the muscles but that is simply working with energy and laying here for so long. Her neck is much better. Her headache is better. We are still working on her knee and elbow.
A: *Do you have a message for her before I talk to her Higher Self?*
Isis: Just know that I'm always with you and I have always been with you. You have nothing to fear. I will continue to send you messages. That is all. Sierra listens. We send her a lot of messages and she's aware of them.
A: *Beautiful, thank you.*
Isis: We sometimes confuse her, but it all eventually will make sense.
A: *Yes. (chuckles) Well, thank you so much, Isis. It has been such a beautiful honor to talk to you; I thank you for your aid. As well, if you could send our love to Archangel Michael, Metatron, and whoever helped today, especially with the soul that was aided today in that box. Thank you.*
Isis: You are welcome. Thank you.
A: *If you could please connect me back to her Higher Self now.*
Higher Self: Yes.
A: *Thank you. Higher Self, may I continue asking you questions?*
Higher Self: Of course.
A: *How does her body look? Is there anything else that needs healing?*
Higher Self: It's a lot better. It is a lot lighter. She will probably need to get used to this new norm. (chuckles)
A: *She says she has a fear of the dark, why?*

Higher Self: All that happens in the dark energetically. Now that we've closed the portal in her room, we hope she will have a better experience. There's a chance that there was just too much activity. And even though she agreed to it, and enjoyed it on some level, it was perhaps too much for her.
A: At this point, I've asked all that I needed to ask. How's her healing looking?
Higher Self: She needs to keep asking for more and more energy to reside in this body. She's still a bit achy, but it is now because she's been laying here so long... She feels complete.
A: Yes, very good. I'm so glad we figured out what that was, that energy there that was stuck. My other biggest concern was the heart.
Higher Self: It feels unlocked now. Her body feels very empty, compared to how it was. I believe a lot will correct itself for her. I know it will; however, I believe that she will absorb it in such a way that she sees the difference.
A: Very good. Is there anything I could have asked, that I haven't asked?
Higher Self: No, I believe we are complete.
A: Wonderful. Thank you so much for such a beautiful healing for her. That was an interesting situation there with that being in that box. I think that would be really good information to share.
Higher Self: Oh, yes, I think it would be informative for many people to understand that it is not so 'cut and dry.'
A: Yes. As a healer, and as I work with all sorts of negative beings, I do not agree with anyone thinking they are so righteous, or they are so powerful, to do that to another soul! To lock them in a box for eternity.
Higher Self: Exactly, it is very senseless.
A: It is. I think it's a lesson for others to understand, even if it's someone trying to cause havoc or whatever they're doing. Even if you have the power, do not lock them in the box.
Higher Self: (chuckles) Absolutely, you lock a part of yourself in that box. It doesn't produce anything, especially if that soul then never has the opportunity to show any progress or change or anything.
A: Yes. It goes against every sacred law that I can think of, as far as what I know.
Higher Self: Absolutely.
A: All right. Well, thank you so much. It has been such an honor to speak to you! Are you more Divine Feminine, Masculine, or both?
Higher Self: We are a collaboration of the Ancient Ones.
A: That you are. Thank you so much. It has been such a beautiful blessing to speak to all of you. Thank you for guiding her to me, for helping her follow her heart to mine. May she continue to flourish and grow as she has been doing so beautifully. Thank you.
Higher Self: Thank you.
A: I honor you, I love you, and I respect you! May I bring her back?
Higher Self: Yes.
A: Okay. Very good.

For every A.U.R.A. Hypnosis healing session we ask that the Higher Self and team ensure to remove and heal this entire list: entities (Grays, Mantis, Reptilians, Archons…), dark portals, repair and crystallize DNA, negative cords, technologies (implants, metals, hooks, wires, nano, vaccines), Illnesses, vision, dental health, regrow teeth, age regress 5-15 years, blocked or misaligned chakras, open-up the third eye and activate abilities, expand heart, issues with auric field, fractured soul, contracts, deletion of inverted timelines, and trauma from current or past life.

Post Session dialogue.
A: Welcome back, chica (Spanish for a female friend)!
Sierra: Whoa! I opened my eyes, and this room looks so different.
A: Awesome... Wow, that was fun!
Sierra: That was insane. The visuals were so intense. There's a lot happening. That was some interesting information, though.
A: Very interesting.

Sierra: When I had to be the being, in order to experience the being, I felt like I was just like, in this box. And I was like, this is so uncomfortable.

A: I was like, oh, this is sad!

Sierra: He was so tight, and it was just floating like a skinny little coffin out in nothing. So sad. And it's been there for so long that it was just, breaking my heart.

A: *I know. It's so sad. Yes, because you know, a lot of people, especially other practitioners, they treat entities like that. Like, I'm going to banish you, I'm going to exorcize you! And it's like, no, they deserve an opportunity. Let's just give them love and understand that they're our brothers and sisters.*

Sierra: I definitely relate, give them the opportunity, believe in them that they will. The information that I got was that so many people are just so confused by what is dark, versus light, in terms of, darkness isn't bad.

A: Exactly.

Sierra: Yes, it's just a teaching tool. And, if you call it bad, then it becomes bad. It's like if a child misbehaves, you don't constantly then tell the child it's bad. That child just needs a little bit of extra love, if anything.

A: Yes!

Sierra: I know, when I first started with my first official spiritual group, I believe I told you about this. They were always working with the pendulum. And by the end, I was like, I have to leave because you guys are so obsessed with catching the next negative thing that you're creating them. You know? And I remember the last message I ever got from the instructor was "warning, you're in danger!" and I went, "okay, calm down. I got to go." You know, it was just that idea of, so you're just chasing after something negative with fear? You know, we create our reality in terms of, we're never going to find the end of space because we're always creating space. So, if you are looking for the end of all the negative creatures, you're never going to find them. By definition, they will always…

A: *Yes, there are people that teach that there is going to be a day that there's going to come an end to them, and we're all going to become One. What the Angels communicate to me is, how's that going to happen if first of all, organic life and free will is infinite?*

Sierra: They are going to recreate themselves in order to keep escaping, so why not accept them and heal them?

A: Yes.

Sierra: I don't think we necessarily need the polarity. We probably do for this moment in our time, but we don't need the polarity. We just needed it as a teaching tool. That was fascinating information. Apparently, I have a new one…

A: Apparently you have a new what?

Sierra: Like a new force field. I mean…

A: *I know, right? That was crazy. The whole landing dock thing.*

Sierra: You know what, because if you were here, you would hear them and what landed at that moment was a craft that was like (imitates landing sound), and it had black claws coming out of it almost like a spider. And when you said - I see now, you had to give the suggestions, otherwise, it literally didn't occur to me in my moment to go, "Yeah, let's put a shield around that, so that only good guys can come sort of thing." This thing immediately just dissolved. It was no longer a match. It couldn't land there. So, I think my portal was being used by whoever the hell wanted to.

A: *Yes, that's what I was seeing. I was like, "I don't think it's cool for us to leave that for her there!"*

Sierra: No, it was really scaring me. Things are standing here a lot and watching me. Sometimes I wake up in the middle of the night and I see them all walking through and it's too much. I know Isis is like, stationed outside my door, but I can feel her.

A: *Nice! That's gotta be cool.*

Sierra: I know, I'm so honored that Isis and Metatron just hang out. (chuckles) It's so beautiful.

A: The Ancient Ones!?

Sierra: Yeah, and the Ancient Ones are who advise me, no big deal! (chuckles)

A: *(chuckles) Did you know the Ancient Ones are the RA Collective, and the Council of 12?*

Sierra: Well, I just get information constantly from them now. It is so beautiful.

A: *So beautiful… Well, hopefully we got a lot of answers for you today?*

Sierra: Yes, that we did. I mean, that's a far cry from where I started, where they wouldn't give out anything. (Sierra had had several past life regression sessions through other healing modalities, and nothing would ever be shared by her spiritual team. Guarded, they kept her for good reason.)
A: Oh, yes, they gave a lot for you, lovely... Thank you so much, Sierra, for following your heart to mine.
Sierra: The Ayahuasca thing was so intense. You should have seen the visions on my side. (chuckles) Like, I tried to spit it out as fast as possible. They were just showing me eyes, mostly. And they just said, everybody really needs to take real ownership of what they're choosing to do in terms of their shamanic experience. And it's funny because so many people are coming up to me now and asking, like, 'oh, I want to go to Peru. I want to do this.' And I was like, no! Don't be so arrogant that you think as a Westerner from California, you can step into Peru and understand the depth of what they do. They're like the babies that grew up in the Amazon, they're given Ayahuasca before breast milk, you know, try to process that. How do you think that you're going to step in at the ripe old age of whatever you are and be like 'I am here for my shamanic experience!'? And then I was seeing the eyes. They were like, you need to look in the eyes of the shaman and see if they resonate with you. Very, very important.
A: Yes. Awesome! ... Thank you so much. It has been so much fun. I love you sister. Love you, love you!

END OF SESSION

Many can relate to this similar repeated cycle that Sierra experiences with her mother. We feel an immensity of responsibility for aiding our birth family to ascend out into the New Earth, the original Earth, the promised land. Many say it is the fifth dimension (5D) we will ascend into, but truly it is the sixth dimension (6D), or for some, higher dimensions if they are starseeds who will return back to their home planet after their mission is completed on Earth. We are ascending into the sixth dimension, because we were originally in the fifth dimension before the fall of Atlantis, so why would we go back to the fifth dimension when ascension comes forth? Instead we will rise up to the sixth dimension as a collective, our original divine goal.

Challenging decisions to make we have, being that we have grown such a natural attachment to our third dimensional genetic families. How do we function through our daily life without allowing our un-awakened family, or friends negative free-willed choices to weigh us down? When we hold on, they often create negative cords attaching them to us, that directly link us and their denser decisions in their everyday, at times inverted, life choices. Often infringing on us through these links. It is as if a denser darkness or venom is being fed through these cord connections, causing cloudiness or exhaustion on our end.

So long as we choose to still be connected to them, we would have to lower our vibration for them to understand us. In order to remain in their world, while operating within our high vibrations, we have to travel multidimensionally, rapidly, consciously from the fifth or fourth down to the third dimension to meet them energetically. Our beingness has to scientifically densify to interact and communicate with them. Have you ever felt the weighing down after you are done talking to a person that is stubborn within the third dimension? At times feeling drained? It is because the density within your toroidal sphere had to densify, becoming heavier in some form to match theirs. You then, after interacting with them, have to build up the light once more within each photon of your toroidal sphere, bringing you back to your high vibrations. This can take much energy on your end through the Quantum World, though our Source energy is infinite. Those who are at extreme sovereignty and have learned to have no attachments, even to people, with ease can travel to and from instantly in the third, fourth and fifth dimensions communicating with others no matter the density of the recipient. By no longer having attachments, the cord to others is no longer there, therefore they would no longer have the infringement of the denser person feeding into them. Which then allows a vast connection to the Source Love-Light, that one would require to shift in out of lower and higher vibrations with ease.

The same day our first publication "Galactic Soul History of the Universe" Book 1, the Earth's bifurcation/trifurcation, the two/three world split, came into fruition on 12.21.2020. Bridging forth the choice for all life on Earth of operating within the inverted A.I. matrix world, or the organic original crystalline world. As the image below shows, one world is the third dimensional inverted world and the other, the fifth/sixth dimensional organic world. After this point in Earth's history, our friends' and families' choices became very apparent, and so too, did they have to decide, whether conscious of it or not, which world they would walk in, in their everyday life, as did we. Walking the organic Earth's blueprint with us, or the inverted A.I. matrix, is a free willed choice. Those who made the choice of injecting the Covid-19 vaccine into their body and fusing A.I. nano into their DNA in some form entered the inverted world. In Chapter 5, "The A.I. Alien Invasion" we will touch further on the subject of the Covid-19 Vaccine.

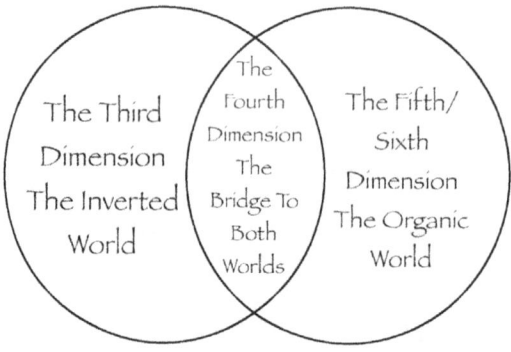

This monumental moment in time and space, 12/21/2020 was written within our collective Earth's organic timeline, as a marker point for Earth Mother to shift into the highest vibration she has harnessed since the fall of Atlantis, when the collective fell into the third dimension as explained in Book 1 and now deeper in Book 2, in the chapters to come. This was a time that she and her children incarnated, would bring forth safety to all lifeforms on Earth. Being that the fifth dimension would finally be anchored back to us, for those who chose to ride this vibrational wave.

In the image of the two/three worlds, we explain how the organic world is the fifth/sixth dimension. When the Source Love-Light transmutation wave comes forth unto Earth, and births into fruition the final physical split collective Ascension, the original fifth dimensional world will no longer be. Being that we have already experienced the fifth dimension significantly enough through the positive reign of Atlantis and Leumuria. This experiment is done and over, and now the Universe will shift Earth into her sixth dimensional crystalline blueprint. This is what we were meant to achieve as a collective, if we would have ascended out during Atlantis from the original fifth dimension and into the sixth dimension. We have experienced the fifth dimension to the most infinite detail, therefore it is no longer needed for us to be in the fifth dimensional schooling of our Universe, nor will it be a vibrational match to what is to come after [3]Universal Ascension.

To understand what the third dimensional world looks like, it is infested with A.I (artificial intelligence), entities, dark portals, and Archon viruses, as the Covid-19 vaccine is that. The vaccine

---

[3] Watch the 'All About THE EVENT & Ascension' video, in which we go further into the subject of when the worlds finally split from one another.

carries the A.I. Archon virus that multiplies inside the body taking over its host, in the next Chapter 5, "The A.I. Alien Invasion" we explain this at the deepest level. Once more why those who choose this path automatically enter the Inverted world in some form. The fifth dimensional world looks bright and divine, and all within it is crystallized with these vibrant colors, the trees, mountains, skies, buildings, animals, and the people. The magical creatures also still exist within it, as the dragons, unicorns, mermaids, fairies, and griffins… The fourth dimensional world is where WE, the strongest holders of Love-Light anchor in, standing with one foot in the Inverted world, and the other foot within the organic world. Our mind/body/soul complexes, who stand in this fourth dimension, are the bridges, and it is as if we are holding these two worlds of the third and fifth dimensions energetically with our bare hands. By walking a sovereign, organic timeline, here we bridge forth with our everyday life choices, the organic crystallization into the Inverted third dimension. As we hold these dimensional vibrations we become the birthers of these plasmic fields of infinite Love-Light into the Inverted world. Providing the fuel of Love-Light that is needed for those who choose to wake-up and bridge into the fifth dimension someday too. We are who keeps these two worlds balanced, and what keeps the Inverted world from imploded upon itself. These three worlds are in the same plane of existence. And, this is why we invite you over, to be this too, in your own most special, souled way. The more that choose to hold both worlds, the more challenging we make it for the dark ones, the Illuminati who are governed by the A.I. Archons. For their ill intended diabolical plans to continue to be so obvious to all who choose to view from this high perspective. In turn creating an opportunity of a vastness continual potential of awakening humanity.

With the beginning of the splitting of Ascension birthing forth, or what Yeshua began to speak to us of 'The Revelation'. The fall of Atlantis cycle is once more repeating itself, to test us, to see if we will choose to remain organic or not. We are seeing the mirror of what happened then in the now, because collectively and individually we have to choose to break or not break this iInverted cycle. As it is often said, "History is repeating itself". What will we choose this time around? Those who consented and fell for the false illusions of the Archons, chose the inverted world and the fall with *it* in Atlantis. These are some of the same people who have now chosen the Covid-19 vaccine, because in some form, this is their way to transmute their negative polarized decision back in Atlantis, that caused the Earth and the Universe's organic ascension to not come to be. Descending us to the third dimension, as a collective, as we are now.

To choose to let go of people within the inverted A.I. matrix has become of extreme importance, now more than ever. When you understand and view Ascension from a higher perspective, it is as a snowflake, when it lands upon your hand, it's barely felt, as its weight is light. However, when many snowflakes accumulate together they merge and become a bigger mass; joining together like one big blanket of snow on the roof of a home. Becoming a force that is strong and heavy, like an ocean of water. This is how important it is for Earth and the Universe's Ascension, for you to choose to lift your vibration to join us holding the strongest Love-Light on Earth. Together we become as immense as the blanket of snow, versus just individual snowflakes.

These are crossroads that come up for us, at key moments in time, that our soul is experiencing a leveling up of vibration. That assists us in accepting whichever outcome we decide upon, whether it means 1) do we walk away from someone that is holding our density and progress down, so that we can finally grow? Or 2) do we still hang on, if we truly believe that they can, or will, accept change one day for their own growth and self-healing? But to do so, we know that it, too, will hold us back until the decision is made in a dire moment of 'will they or will they not lift with us.' In the Chapter 2, 'The Key To Ascension', and in Chapter 37 'Matrix Pods' Book 1, we go in depth, into what can happen if we hold onto people who do not want to progress, or who are operating in a negative polarization of the inverted A.I. matrix timeline.

Our humble thanks to Sierra's open kindness in wanting to heal the children. For specifically assisting that child that hurt her back. What a beautiful, selfless soul to agree to take on another's pain to assist them, until they can connect for themselves to self-heal. Though, I don't personally recommend taking on someone else's pain, it is still admirable!

We also thank all souls on Earth who play this transmutation role, as a collective for the children in whichever form they do so, whether agreeing to go through hunger to aid the hunger of children in the world or they themselves received abuse of any kind to aid the multitudes of abuse on Earth against the children. Many play this role, including the animals of the world that receive these traumas as well. As each goes through these pains, no matter what form we are in the physical, we help transmute these negatives so that the self-healing needed begins for those who are ready. The majority of abuse is through forms of required harmonious karma that has to do with the person's own Ascension fruition, as we read in Chapter 12, 'Leviathan - The Fallen Angel' Book 1. Some also being those who accepted the abuse selflessly for other selves. No matter which accepted form, trauma and pain can be transmuted through others living through it. The more beings that have focused on this, the easier it becomes for the next to heal it, and so on, as the collective density within it becomes lighter and lighter.

In a world undergoing many transformative awakening processes, many souls awaken with each passing moment. Those who are at their beginning stages of awakening are hungry to understand and remember the vastness of the Universe that exists within them and outside of them. This is why sacred soul medicine as Ayahuasca rises in popularity in the mainstream media of spirituality. When sacred practices become this well known, distortion begins to enter it, as there will always be those in the inverted world operating in service-to-self, wanting to feed off its rising energy, and profit from its popularity.

I have had several clients who came to me because their Ayahuasca ceremony went wrong, and now they feel very affected by it. When their Higher Self conducts their Body Scan, they often find entities that were not there prior to their Ayahuasca session, and who now have attached and integrated deeper, or more entities have joined while opening themselves up that wide without the proper sacred energetic boundaries during the Ayahuasca. We have learned that in order for a TRUE Shaman to be able to hold the sacred protection for a group during a Ayahuasca ceremony, they would have to hold the purest Love-Light, heart, and abilities that one can hold in this dimension. Truly, they would have to be in comparison to Yehsua or Mother Mary's Love-Light status. They will have to have the capability of holding space energetically for all their attendees, so that dark entities within the land, or multidimensionally as the negative Reptilians or Archons, will not be able to jump into the participants' auric field, physical or energy body.

We also learned that during this process of self-healing through Ayahuasca, people go through soul journeys, and the majority of work is done in their shadow when entering the realm of the Theta-Delta brain waves. In these realms of consciousness they enter and release their inner demons and entities within them. Not all Shamans are properly overseeing safe passageways for these released entities with Love-Light as we do through A.U.R.A. Hypnosis Healing sessions. So, these entities are just released into the immediate surroundings, free to go and attach to whoever and wherever they are a vibrational match. Therefore, at these locations, where these ceremonies are conducted, that are meant to be sacred, instead energetically look like nests of entities swarming around like flies waiting to see which light they can enter, like insects attracted to the light. These 'lights' being the participants within the Ayahuasca ceremony.

Remember the connection that Sierra had with her guides, as Isis, and the Ancient Ones? It is important that we, too, recognize the abundance of Guides, Angels and Ascended Masters that are within our grasp in our day to day lives. Often we are programmed to feel that if we ask for assistance, we are a nuisance; therefore, it becomes very natural to not ask. Through the spiritual awakening, or the UFO communities, there are often many false personas being channeled and delivered to plague our minds so that we won't feel within our hearts these guardians around us. We are told that Archangels are negative, that the Divine Mother is who decided for us to suffer in the way that we do, because she wanted, and chose, to live this duality game. However, truly as we have learned through the "Galactic Soul History of the Universe" book series, is that these are false Archonic games which are directly linked to the puppeteers, the Archons themselves, from their A.I. realms.

Our benevolent teams are here to assist us through our everyday life choices and paths. Why? Because this was the agreement we made with them before we incarnated. They vowed to us that if we got lost to the inverted, and became part A.I., as those souls who chose the Fall of Atlantis on Earth, that they would, with all that they ARE, deliver messages to us through dreamtime, signs, and synchronicities... Relentensleslly never giving up, or stopping until we heard them and understood what had happened to us. Therefore, this is why other channels (whether they believe they are channeling or not, as everyone channels all day long, it just depends on which voice, entity, dimension, or vibration you are tapping into, to channel) wrongly tell us that if we connect to our Guides and Ascended Masters, that is a form of worship. They deliver statements that seem like love or truth; however, the underlining of it is plagued with black magic spells. This is how they hook you in, because within these messages there is poison such as, "You do not need to connect to these Gods or Goddesses, because you are worshiping if you do. We are all ONE". They plague your mind and block your heart. Which then does not allow your guides' benevolence to assist you, as they cannot and won't overstep your boundaries. Once more, placing you in deeper simulations of the inverted cycles of the A.I. matrix.

Through the Body Scans conducted in A.U.R.A. Hypnosis Healing sessions, we get to see glimpses of the potentials of inviting these benevolences in. As, when doing so, they amplify our innate ability to self-heal because of their instant field connection to the higher realms and dimensions. After all, that is one of what they are to us, and what they can bridge for us in connection, because we are who are in the lower dimensions of the third and they are not. These are some of the only ways that we can bridge into these higher dimensions, by connecting to these higher energies and guides within the higher realms, as that is where some of the infinite plasmic light energy is harnessed in. Once more, be aware of the agenda when someone is trying to convince you that you do not need to connect to the Ascended Master and Archangels. I have had clients tell me that when trying another very well known past life regression modality, that they were told that they will not connect to Ascended Masters and Archangels during their Body Scans, because that is supposedly limiting and is giving away the power of the Higher Self. See how this message is accurate, yet plagued with falseness. A being that lives in true sovereignty understands that they are infinite in divine power, but only because we connect to the ALL, which is Source Love-Light, and the multitudes within this love. They do not allow their ego, and this statement is ego based, to become infected by the Archon virus, giving *it* free reign. True, sovereign beings remain humbled with an understanding that one will always be a student in this infinite creation of our Universe. We have to remember to be humble enough to call forth assistance from this benevolence when it is needed. This is their role for us, in our process of Ascension. When we do so, it truly bridges forth such a free flowing surrender to our Higher Self, which then becomes a captivating dance of free flowing union within the creation of our lives.

There is a vast importance to a past life regression practitioner who cares enough to question all that is shared, of how we can assist during the session, and how to make things better for the client in their environment. In this perspective of the UFO landing dock on the roof of her home, we ensured we turned it into a positive portal/landing dock, versus open to whoever, or whatever wanted to come through. The distraction that this would cause, and the feeling of infringement, which would be apparent, with a being as sensitive as Sierra is, is a concern. She was constantly feeling the, at times, not so positive passing through her roof. Once more, it is important that we understand that Archangels and Ascended Masters are who can assist our Higher Selves with stronger tasks such as this. There is nothing that cannot be done. All can always be healed, if the client is ready and allows.

Just as in Sierra's example, throughout my career, many have come to me that had prior past life regression sessions through other modalities where nothing was allowed to be shared by their Higher Self and benevolent team. Reason being, it is done for 'their safety,' because sacred knowledge cannot be shared with those not of a matching high vibration. Most past life regressionists do not believe in Love-Light shielding, or that entities exist, period. To not believe entities are real, is to not believe in ourselves, for that is what we are without this illusional vessel; we, too are a disembodied entity/spirit. The session will only be able to bridge the highest vibration to who is holding the space in Source Love-Light for you, to connect in the deepest ways through hypnosis, that being your hypnosis practitioner or healer. In other words, as explained through Ayahuasca and the Shamans, so, too, do the practitioners have to hold a pure and impenetrable space of infinite Love-Light during session. Through A.U.R.A. Hypnosis Healing, we are in such a deep state of sacredness with the client's Higher Self, because of the entire sacred process and the energy work that is conducted before the session. Which allows the client to reach this state of sacred safety and connection, and why it is that we see continual results through all of our reviews, testimonials, sessions shared through our books and internet channel platforms. Other reasons why what is shared through a session can be limited are inverted blockages within the body, as entities, and negative technologies, that do not allow a deep enough, high enough, connection. Also, it can be to protect the client, until they have reached the sufficient Love-Light and vibration, where lessons have been accepted and learned for further expansion and growth of light.

Lastly, this session made my heart ache in how someone could lock another soul up for an eternity, with no remorse! Done just because someone thought he was being a nuisance and because *they* had the power to do so. The condition that this being was in was unacceptable. No Love-Light being should ever do this to another. I can't imagine being locked away for an eternity with no one to talk to, and no way out. It would seem as a never-ending infinity of imprisonment, where there is no one to help you, and no one will ever come to help you. I think it would take a strong being to live through that and still want to push on, as he did. Our infinite love to him once more for assisting us to understand, and honor, how sacred each soul is, no matter their choices.

Even when one has great power, it is to be treated with the greatest responsibility. These sessions remind us to begin to love, respect, and honor each other in this manner. When doing so, this will be our most profound way that will activate each heart and will lift the Earth's density into the percentage it requires to be for the final individual or collective shift of Ascension, the splitting of the two/third worlds, entering the fifth/sixth dimension through our heart portals.

"I respect you for all the differences you are to me. Without you I could not be me, because you complete the pieces that I am not. A most beautiful expression of Creation you are."
~AuroRa

--------------<<>>--------------

4

DEEP STATE COUNCIL MEMBER

Session #202: Recorded in September 2019.
Never before shared.

In this in-person A.U.R.A. Hypnosis Healing session, Constance has traveled to me following instructions from her guides to arrive no matter what obstacles occur. She is a beautiful example of those who have answered the call to incarnate on Earth, and the bravery that they emanate. Even though we have been silenced throughout Earth's history, we sovereignly still choose to speak no matter the obstacles. At times placing our lives in danger with every word spoken, all in hope and love for humanity. We discover her connection to the 'Galactic Council of 12' and her divine power. A negative polarized 'Deep State' Council Member and his plan. A Galactic Council against a [4]"Deep State' Council member. Her journey to freedom.

-------------<<>>--------------

'I know the things that I speak are truth, are strong, but also are dangerous to speak. Dangerous for me, but I must speak the truth, and the people must know the truth. Even if it means I must die. Corruption, falsehood, hiding... They're being lied to. They need to know the truth, it is the truth that will set them free."
~Egyptian Scholar

-------------<<>>--------------

A: *[Aurora] Have you landed on the ground yet?*
C: [Constance] White sand.
A: *Look at yourself, do you feel like you have a body?*
C: I look down and I see feet. Bare feet.
A: *How many toes do you have?*
C: I don't know, I think five on each foot.
A: *Look at your hands, how many fingers do you have?*
C: Ten.
A: *Do you feel like you're a female or male?*
C: I think female... It's a beach, the water is bright blue.
A: *Are you wearing anything?*
C: I think so. Nothing heavy. Very light. My skin is almost brown, like a dark suntan. My toenails are pretty.
A: *Are you carrying anything?*
C: A staff, it looks like a hook. I think I see a basket. Like, a reed basket.
A: *Tell me more about this staff? Does it have any colors, designs, crystals?*
C: It's gold. It has, I want to say a serpent head, or a serpent on it, with pretty sparkly stones, dark red, and blue; it shines. I have something on my head!
A: *What is it?*
C: The word I see is 'signet'. It kind of encircles my head. It has a thing that sticks out in the center, like a snake head coming out, sticking away from my forehead. It has red jewels for the eyes. My hair

---

[4] Deep State, are members of the Illuminati, in self-appointed high places of control across the world who practice black magic sorcery. Overseers of "The New World Order" agenda of tyranny, control and depopulation of humanity.

is dark, long and straight. My hands are thin and pretty. My nails are pretty. I have a pretty necklace, it's white, it wraps around my neck but it rests on my shoulders. It, too, has a jewel that hangs down in the center. It is red; it's quite large. My eyes are painted.

A: *What do you mean painted?*

C: Like mascara, eyeliner, very pretty. Like makeup. It's status, I heard it's status.

A: *Everything has a consciousness. Does this piece that you wear over your head, or the staff, have a message for you?*

C: It said, "you are royal." I see, in the water, like cattails, reeds.

A: *Look all around you, why do you think that you're here?*

C: I heard the words, 'the Nile.' I heard the words, 'Euphrates.' There is a boat coming. It's very big, with tall white sails, and oars sticking out the sides. It's my boat! Many people.

A: *Are there any symbols or designs on the boat?*

C: The same head that is on my staff, that's on my forehead, is on the front of the boat. It's very big!

A: *Tell me what happens when it arrives?*

C: There are many people with me, they don't have the things I wear but similar clothes. I heard, 'they attend me.'

A: *Where are you now?*

C: A boat draws near. I am to get on the boat.

A: *Go ahead and get on the boat. Tell me what you do next while you're in the boat.*

C: It's taking me, I heard the word, 'Pharaoh.'

A: *Are you going to go see the Pharaoh?*

C: I heard the words, 'it is my duty to teach there.' On the boat, many people come with me.

A: *Where is it that you're heading towards?*

C: I heard the words, 'the palace, the Pharaoh.'

A: *Are you going towards the palace and the pharaoh?*

C: Yes; I must go.

A: *While you were on the boat, was there something you did of importance?*

C: I teach.

A: *Let's go ahead and arrive now at your destination. Tell me what you see, sense, feel, hear all around you.*

C: It's beautiful. I step off the boat. It's like marble, or alabaster; smooth and cool under my feet. It's stairs; they lead up to the palace. The pharaoh awaits. He is young.

A: *Describe to me what he looks like?*

C: He has a young face, young skin.

A: *Where are you now?*

C: I've not been here before. It's big, it's beautiful! Not a lot of adornments, mostly light. There are curtains but not heavy, thin curtains. I heard, 'to keep the bugs out.' It's beautiful; it's regal, but not a lot there. Chairs, I heard, it's a chamber of some kind. A meeting room, a greeting room. They're very nice. I heard the word, 'scholar, I am a scholar'... Ah! To teach the Pharaoh the secret ways, the holy ways. I have arrived to teach and to heal.

A: *Look all around you and tell me what stands out of importance?*

C: I see big columns around me in this room, but not opulence. Simple but elegant. Speaks of wealth but not greed, gentleness, but strength, love, but firmness. This is a Pharaoh who will be beloved by his people but young, very young.

A: *Is there a name that you call him? Look into his eyes and see if you are able to recognize his soul. What do you sense?*

C: They call him Tutankhamen, he's a young pharaoh. I'm not sure if I pronounce it correctly. They call him, 'Young Pharaoh.'

A: *Go ahead and fast forward to when something else of importance is occurring, you are there now. What do you see, sense, and feel?*

C: The Pharaoh has died.

A: *What happened to him?*

C: There was much jealousy.

A: *Jealousy from whom?*
C: I hear the words, 'an uncle.' It is feared that he was assassinated.
A: *What is your relationship to the Young Pharaoh? Is there any relationship besides being a teacher?*
C: I loved him very much, like my own son. He was very smart, my heart hurts, it hurts. It is believed, it is quiet, but it is believed that something, someone, his uncle, something is connected to his dying. It was not an illness! He was not sick, he was very healthy, he was very young and strong.
A: *How was it that he passed?*
C: Food! Something in the food! I don't know; my eyes, they want to cry. My heart, it hurts, it cries; he should not have died. I should have been able to protect him. I didn't know; I suspected, but I didn't know. He was a gentleman, a sweet boy, and we talked long; he learned quickly. Very smart! He would have ruled with a gentle, firm hand, but it was not to be so. The people are sad.
A: *Let's fast forward a bit to see what happens next of importance in this life. Does anyone truly discover who it was that did it? What's occurring now?*
C: I'm standing on the steps and people are gathered around. My staff is in my left hand, and I'm firm in my speech. I know the things that I speak are truth, are strong, but also are dangerous to speak. Dangerous for me, but I must speak the truth and the people must know the truth. Even if it means I must die.
A: *Tell me what you do?*
C: I know that I will die, but the people must hear the words. I'm the only one that has the strength; I'm not afraid. I fear no one! But the people must be told. They won't listen to anyone, but me.
A: *What do you tell them?*
C: Corruption, falsehood, hiding... They're being lied to. They need to know the truth, it is the truth that will set them free. This new Pharaoh won't let me live because I know too much, I know the secrets, I know the powers. Those that come in ships in the sky, they told me many things. They told me my time is finished here. I accept my faith.
A: *What is the people's reaction when you say this?*
C: Some people listen, some people do not. Some people are faithful to the new Pharaoh.
A: *Who's the new Pharaoh?*
C: He is a corrupt man, hungry for power. He is not kind to the people, the people need love and kindness. They need love above all. They would do more for him if he would show them love and kindness. He doesn't believe, he doesn't understand; he has a cold heart. He believes he can rule with fear, power. He doesn't understand that love is stronger than fear. It makes my heart hurt, for what I see is coming! For the people, the children, my heart hurts and I have to tell them. I have to tell them! I have to tell them! And if it takes my life, so be it. They need to know of the laying of the hands to heal the body, the spirit, the mind. It's important for them to know, but they want to silence me. People need to know. It should not be a secret, things from our Creator should not be a secret. It should be shared with love and oneness, and wholeness. Not separation. Not fear. But he uses those fears, he believes that only some should carry the wisdom, and it should not be used. He doesn't believe in love, he believes in power. But those in the sky that come, they come and find things that sit up on the ground. They come out and they tell us truths and they show me how things work that are so far beyond anything here. But the people who are sick, they are healed. The people injured, they are healed. There is no spilling of blood on the land. I can show them, and I can teach them. Some listen. Many more listen to the Pharaoh. His name starts with an H, and I see an E, and I see an M. I'm sorry, I'm not connecting them. I don't know the word.
A: *That is ok.*
C: A big H, H is the first one. And I see an A, a big A. I don't know, I call him Pharaoh.
A: *What happened to the father of the young Pharaoh?*
C: Oh he, he died.
A: *Do you know how he passed away?*
C: There was some sickness, but he was not dying fast enough;, I don't know how. But he was helped to die. He did not want to go. He said his son was too young to rule. But he would be stronger as he was older, but he was so young. He did not want to die. But then he was gone. They had a great funeral, a big, huge funeral. The Young Pharaoh was afraid, but could not show it. He grieved,

but he could not show it. It wasn't allowed. He must be strong. But they are now both gone and the land is sad. The land has not yielded, as it yielded before.
A: You said that you were speaking to the people about the truth of the new leader.
C: Yes!
A: What happened after you did that?
C: I see me. The people come to me when they are sick, or when they have an injury. I use what I was taught, and they are healed. Some feared that which I did through me. Some people came to be healed, and they were, and everyone saw. I hear now the word, 'witchcraft.' Some people feared what I did, and did not believe. But, I taught that it was done all in love. Many did not believe it. It was very dangerous for me, but I continued to help the people. It's important to help the people. I teach the young ones. But the Pharaoh is getting angry. He sees when more people listen to me and not to him; he sees.
A: When you were talking to the people about this new Pharaoh, was that out in the open, or more enclosed?
C: I stand upon the steps of the temple and I speak to those who assemble. Sometimes there are few and sometimes they're many. Sometimes the crowds grow bigger. Mostly, it's small groups that gather around, ten, twenty, thirty...
A: What is their reaction when you speak of this?
C: Hope! Hope, for their children, hope for the mothers, the mothers hope for their children. Hope for their families and they believe! They believe! They see the evidence of the healing when they are ill. They see the evidence of the healing of the bones when they are broken. It is quick. It does not take time. It gives the people hope. They have happiness in their heart, but there are those that call themselves... They are in the temples; they are the old men. Some young ones that follow the old men, they don't like these ways. They don't understand that what I do is from love, from the heart. People - young, old, rich, poor, it matters none, it works for all. But those in the temple call themselves the holy ones. They celebrate the feast, I hear the word, 'smoking mirrors.' I see no evidence of healing from what they do. But the people who come to them give them gold, coins, things. But I see no evidence of the love. I see no evidence of healing. I see no evidence of heart. I see lots of evidence of gold. I myself have enough, I have no use… I have no care for gold. This angers those in the temple. I do not offer empty prayers. I only demonstrate. I do the work, it is done. They are happy, they are healed. It matters not. I am content. I feel happiness in my heart and me.
A: How do you feel about these holy men that are claiming to, would you say, be healers? Is that what you would call them? Or a priest? What would you call them?
C: You're correct. They call themselves the priests. They call themselves the healers. The ones that know all.
A: How do you feel when these people are coming to them, and as you mentioned, they're being misled?
C: I feel bad for the people, because the people have it inside themselves. They do not need to come to the priests and give them all their money, all their gold. They don't need to do that. They carry it inside themselves. It's inside their hearts. I only need to show them, but the ones - they call themselves the priests. I often wonder, how did they become priests? How they become what they are. They use… they burn things, they use incense. They use oils, mostly for the Pharaoh and the Pharaoh family, for the royals. Those who have money, always to give. But for those with none, they turn them away. They laugh behind their backs. Not so much in their face, but behind their backs. They will not help them. I don't care. I just continue my healing work. Yes, I know, I am in danger, it doesn't matter. It doesn't matter. Doesn't matter.
A: Do you think that when they are doing their holy priest stuff, as the healer, that they are affecting the people that are coming to them? Are they harming them, in any way, through their ways, because their intent is of gold?
C: It's like a mass mindset. Like sheep following sheep. One says 'follow this,' and they do. More say 'follow' and they do. But I say to them - do you get the healing that you ask for? Do you get the healing that you pay for? I see no evidence of it. They are still poor, or they become poor by giving all their gold. I see no healing, I see only pain. I feel pain inside my heart for them. I do not tell them to

come to me for their healings. I just watch, there is no changing some peoples' minds. Some men, they just say to me, "The priest, the Pharaoh, they have the power, they must be able to heal, they can do this." But I see no evidence of it. I speak to the people, I see no evidence that those who offer prayers, those who, hmm... My question is in my head - who do they pray to? Whoever it is they're praying to, is not working! It's not healing. It's not helping. But many people believe and follow and pay. But, then I see as time goes on, it's changing. I am not old, I am young. Ah... My years are many, but my body does not betray my years. I never thought to ask why but, I know. I know inside me that I've been warned. The people are beginning to listen to me. They are beginning to see the evidence of what I say and what I do. It is becoming more and more dangerous for me. And, again the Star People have come. They are so benevolent. They have so much love, they bring so much love! They want to help! They cannot stay, I wish they would stay. They said they cannot stay, that is why they teach me. They caution me.

A: It is the Star People who are teaching you these teachings?

C: Yes!

A: Of love?

C: Mmm... They showed me inside me, as I showed everyone, the love that is inside. I don't have to give anybody love. They have it inside them. I only teach them to find it inside them and they're finding it. They're becoming happier. The crowds are growing larger when I speak, and I feel the priest and those at the temple behind me, I feel their anger aimed at me. I hear their whispers aimed at me. The Star People told me. I know I may die. But still, I do not fear. Those that I've been able to teach and help, I've told them to teach and help these people. To teach them the love, teach them oneness, wholeness, to dispel the fear. There is nothing to fear. But the voices behind me grow strong. Their anger... I feel their fear. I tell them there is no reason to fear me. I do nothing that would cause them to be afraid, and yet they're still afraid. They will not listen to me, they will not listen to the Star Beings that speak with me. They listen to others, there are others who come. They are not the ones who speak with me.

A: Do you know who the others are?

C: Their ships are shaped differently. Theirs are round with domes. The ones who come to me are shaped more like our pyramids. There are triangles with many points of light.

A: Is there a name that they go by besides Star People?

C: I call them Star People because they come as if out of the stars! We live our lives by the stars, by the moon and the sun. We plant our crops by the moon and the sun. We know the ways of where we live, how we grow our crops, how we are successful, how we feed all the people. And so they came from there. I saw them coming, I felt them coming, I heard them before they came. They said they sent me here. Ohh! I have tears! I feel joy and love for them. And now I know why.

A: Why?

C: They sent me here. They put me here to teach.

A: Do you have a connection to the Star People?

C: They say I am from them. I feel my heart jump with joy, but I don't remember being in their flame pyramids. I remember everything they tell me, but I don't remember being *one* of them. They say I am, but I don't remember. I've been here long, very long. Not at this palace, most of my years were at a faraway land. But, I was brought here for a purpose. The anger, the fear, and the hate is growing strong. Somewhere, I know it will be one of them. I know that it will be swift, and there will be no pain. I have no fear.

A: Do you mean one of them, as one of the priests? Or who's them?

C: Someone, name begins with A, it's like A. Someone, it will be by their hand.

A: Let's go ahead and move along. Let's leave that scene. Let's go to when it is your last day. You are there now, tell me what is going on?

C: Ah... It is morning and the sun has risen. It's such a joyous day. The people, they're coming more. They're understanding love, they're bringing it into their hearts. They're finding it deep within themselves. They're loving each other more, their community *more*. They help each other more. I see them less for some reason, and more for others. More for teaching, they want to know more, they want to hear more, they want to learn more. They still come with broken bones that heal immediately and go on their way. They bring gifts, they don't have to bring gifts, they bring so many gifts. I tell them not to bring gifts. The gift is to love each other, help each other. When one stumbles, help him up! When one falls and can't get up, carry him! Pick him up in your arms and carry him. When one grows old, hand him a staff so that he may walk better. Walk behind him, help him take his steps. Love him, and when he passes when it is his time - love his family, help his family. No one is to be left alone, no one is to have heartache. Only to love. *All* must love. And the people are doing it, and it's such joy for my heart to see they're happy! They sing when they work in the fields and they're happy. Our fields, ohh, the yields from the fields are more than all the years! More and more! We had to build many places to store the food, and we share, and we share. Everyone is happy and the children are healthy. The old ones are healthy to the end of their days. Very little illness, very little sickness. Today they've asked me to speak and teach more. They want to know more, because they know, as if it's a knowing. They know that what they have now, they can keep. It can keep feeding all the people. Even those who can no longer work in the fields always have plenty, because there was always plenty to give. No one is left behind, no one is left without. It's wonderful, and they want to know today how to keep it so. And, it's important how to keep it so. It may not change. Today, I speak. It matters not the words that I speak. Today is the gravest of all dangers.

A: *Go there now, of this that you speak, and tell me what is it that you* speak?
C: They speak the words of the Star People. They tell me the words, they come from the One of the Creator of ALL. The Creator of everything in the stars. The Creator of the Star People. The Creator of all those that love, and all those that do not love. The Creator of ALL! This Creator, I must tell them about the Creator. I must tell them that *they* can speak directly *to* the Creator requesting that whichever they need and it will be given in love. But, it must be done in love. No fear, no animosity, always love. And, the Star People also can be called upon with love. All that I've ever used is love! I send up love and they come. Sometimes they just come and they bring more love. And more, more, more teachings, they teach me. I know that my time of speaking is short; there is not much time because of the anger and the fear behind me, it's behind me; it has no power over me. So, I dress normal. I dress how the people will recognize me. They come to me. I love them, they love me. I walk to the steps and I expected... Oh, my. I expected a few people. They asked if they can bring their families, their neighbors, and their friends. And, they've come from far and wide. There's so many people. My home, my place where I do the healing, it sits slightly away from the palace. On the grounds but slightly away. Slightly away from the temple. Not far, because I am royalty, it is my blood. However, I'm happier where I am at. Today on the steps, my attendants have brought big jugs of water, clean pure water for the people. They're thirsty and I give them drinks. Always plenty of food, if they are hungry. So many people. The people, they say they just want to listen. So, I come out and I tell them. The only thing I ask is listen, if they want to learn, listen. For I tell them what was told to me, and I speak. Someone asks me, stands to my left in front of me, "What about the priest, what about the Pharaoh, what about what they teach? They're powerful, they are strong in what they teach." I answer him straight. I ask, I do not accuse, "What does the Pharaoh teach? What do the priests teach? Do they teach love? Do they teach forgiveness to each other? Do they teach helping each other? Do they teach community? Do they teach giving to the one who can no longer work in the fields to earn his own food? Do they teach making an extra loaf of bread in your oven and give it to your neighbor? Do they teach these things, and if they do not teach them, do you choose to follow? Reach into your heart and ask it, why? Ask your own why. I do not make decisions for you. I make no decisions for anyone. I only teach the truth, and you see the evidence among yourselves. The truth." I know this one who speaks and questions. He does follow Pharaoh, he does follow the priests. He's only come today to question me. But I will *not* challenge Pharaoh. I will *not*. Pharaoh has a goodness inside, a love inside. It's there, it's there, I know it! I know it in my heart. The words I speak are only so the people will see with their own eyes and own heart what Pharaoh shows them. He does not show them his heart. He does not rule with love. People are injured, people are hurt, people go hungry. Those that will not follow the community they're suffering. I do not condemn. I do not question unless I'm asked, I will not. He is the Pharaoh. I will not speak directly against Pharaoh. Not out of fear, but out of respect for a position. I too am royal, I know and understand the power and the position of Pharaoh. It doesn't mean he is right, it means he has the power and the position. To

me, that's all it means. I show love, I demonstrate love. I show healing, I demonstrate healing. I give very little mind to Pharaoh. I'm not in danger from Pharaoh. I'm at danger from the priests, because they will not listen. They have no love in their hearts. They have greed in their hands, coins in their temple. That's all they believe, that is all they know. They will not change. Someone will come, but they will not change. These old ones, they do not want to listen. I hear whispers behind me; they grow strong. Then I look out and see the people, how happy they are! I just want to help them. If I leave, when I leave, they need to have the tools to continue what I do. They don't have to be royal to do it! Some believe they have to be of royal blood, they do not! They have it inside them; the Creator that created me, created them. There is no difference. The Creator that created Pharaoh - these words are dangerous. (sighs) The Creator that created Pharaoh - and I speak these words to them, is the same Creator that created *them*. Those words I know are very dangerous, but they need to *know* this. I see it coming.

A: What is it?

C: The one who will… I heard the words, "The Angel of Death." My time grows very short because of the words I have spoken, but the people must know. The Creator is not different, it's the same, it's the same. They believe me, they know I speak the truth. I accept my fate. It's more important that they know. My years have many here, and that's okay. My face looks young, my hands and feet look young. I've not changed, (laughs) the Star People made that so. They make me laugh, they said, "No need to have wrinkles," and that makes me laugh. I don't know how many years I've been here, but I know the time is short now, very short.

A: What happens next after you've given that speech?

C: People are gone now, it is evening. They've all gone home and the sun goes down. I ask in my mind, for long ago I learned that I could speak to the Star People with my mind, even without them in front of me. With my mind they tell me, "tonight." I accept it; it's okay, this will be my last night here. I look around me, and I feel happy, because I know in my heart many people now believe. They know! I don't need to say it again. I'm not confident that they know how to fix the bones, as the Star People showed me. But that's okay, the body heals. They know the love in the heart, and the love heals much. They know it, there is no reason to fear anyone. Only love, love grows the plants. Love brings the rain. Love brings the warmth from the sky, and the moon at night. Love, given to the moon, brings the tides in and out. The fish in the sea, it catches plenty with love. The fields are fertile. The ground is fertile. Our bin storage houses are full. I feel peace, it's okay that tonight is my last night here. Some will feel sorrow for my loss. It's okay, they will be okay. They have to be okay. A piece of me fears that one day they won't remember the love, something will change. But if they do, I have hope for them. If they do, they will be okay. Love perpetuates. Don't lose the love. If you begin to lose it… it is always inside you. You can always look inside you. Love is always stronger than fear. I've taught them that. It's okay. I hear the footsteps now. This is a coward who approaches. It's okay, I will make it easy for this one. I have no animosity. I only feel love. I'm going to be okay. The Star People have told me, the moment I am separated from this body, there will be no pain. They will take me at the moment. I've told them, not one moment before, in case there is a change of heart. For I've sent love to this one who is fearful, and is a coward. He thinks he will gain favor from Pharaoh. But knows he won't. He has a spark in his heart, I feel it. So, I send him love. All the love that I can pull together, I send him love. He is not very smart, but he should feel the love. He is not one to study, to listen. He preferred to play and gamble. But he has love. He has innocence, but he is a man now. I'll make it easy for him. I rise from my place. I walk outdoors to the edge. I look around. I feel the love of the land. My moment grows short. It's okay. I send him love! I have tears for him, not for me, for him. I breathe. I feel his feet behind me. He thinks he's quiet, he's not. I hear the sounds of the night - the crickets, the frogs, the water. It's okay. In my mind I speak the words, I send him love, but I bid him come, if he must do what he must do. I hear the words, "it is his fate." I speak to the Star People, they're ready for me. He pauses… it is done.

A: What happened?

C: My body goes down. He had a long, skinny, sharp, I think the word is dagger. From the back straight through to my heart. Swift, one blow. I'm a woman, I'm thin, I'm beautiful. It was swift.

A: What happens to your spirit there, that was in the body?

C: I'm floating. It's okay.
A: Where do you go?
C: I look down, I see my body. It's okay, no pain. I send love to this... Oh my, so sad!... Oh, that is sad.
A: What is sad?
C: I had hoped he would not. He took the dagger, he saw my, my body. He felt sadness, he felt, I hear the word, 'remorse.' He turned the dagger on himself and pierced his own heart and he fell. Oh my, I feel sadness for him, my heart hurts for him.
A: What happened to his spirit?
C: It's small. I see like a globe, like round glass but not glass. It floats above his body. I float above my body. I'm large and bright. Hmmm. He is not so bright. I send him some of my brightness to help him. He's not going where I'm going. I don't know why. I call upon the Star People, "help him, help him!"
A: What happens to him?
C: They tell me he will be okay, that he goes somewhere else. He's from somewhere else, he's not from the Star People. I can see his light. It floats, it's somewhere. Small, it's floating away. I don't know, but they are calling me so. I must do something first before I go... This physical body here is feeling pain in my left shoulder, behind my left shoulder. Where the dagger went in. I'm feeling pain in my physical body here.

The Higher Self is called forth.
A: Higher Self, I'd like to speak to you now. Please calm that energy there. Let's leave that life now. Can I please speak to the Higher Self of Constance now?
Higher Self: I'm here.
A: Thank you. May I ask you questions?
Higher Self: Yes, of course!

The Body Scan begins.
A: Thank you. If you can check there on her shoulder, in the back where she was stabbed. She says that she was feeling pain there. Can you scan that area and tell us how we can heal her? Is there anything there holding that pain there?
Higher Self: A deep darkness. The scapula deep inside the arm, it reaches tentacles deep. Deep inside her far-reaching, something deep. It's very, very, dark.
A: Scan now what that is, is there an energy, an entity, a Reptilian consciousness? What is attached?
Higher Self: A very dark, I hear the word, 'entity' - Anger, mean, hate.
A: We would like to speak to that entity now. Higher Self can you connect us to that entity? If we can bring that entity up, up, up now. Greetings!
Entity: Greetings.
A: Thank you for speaking to us. I love you, honor you, and respect you. May I ask you questions please?
Entity: Yes.
A: Thank you. Are you at all connected to a Reptilian consciousness or a Reptilian?
Entity: I see a body. I see arms, legs, a tail, and scales. I feel anger. I feel hate. Such deep, deep anger. I don't know from whence I came, I don't know when I came. Long, long, long, long time. Many things I don't know, I don't remember. I hear the words, 'many lifetimes.'
A: Did you attach when this man stabbed her from behind in Egypt or another time?
Entity: I'm hearing the words, 'I slipped in.' I don't know if that's the origination.
A: Okay, thank you. I'll speak back to you in a minute. If I can talk to the Higher Self once more.
HS: I'm here.
A: Higher Self, we would like to be able to help you remove and heal this entity from within this body here. Can you help us perform this entity removal or do I need to call for any Archangels to aid you?

HS: It's way too big, too strong, too deep. It encompasses most of that hemisphere of the body, to the toes, from the head.
A: Would you like to have an Archangel aid us today?
C: Two names came... First came the name Archangel Michael. The second that came was Metatron. The third is coming - Jesus/Yeshua.
A: Higher Self, connect us now to Archangel Michael, Metatron, and Jesus/Yeshua. If we can speak to all three of them now. They can speak to us as a collective.
Archangels: We are here sister.
A: Thank you, my beautiful brothers. I love you dearly. I honor you, and respect you. Now, if we can please contain this Reptilian consciousness within her. Surround it with the alchemy symbols, wherever it spread to as well. Do you all think that we can help it transform into light?
Archangels: This is one we have met before. This is one who will not polarize. This is one who *believes* it has power.
A: Why is it that it is so strong? Can you tell us more about it?
Archangels: Because of who she is, because of who she was, because of who she is destined to be. They have sent many less powerful. Could not stop her. This one had to come.
A: Is this who has been trying to stop her?
Archangels: Yes.
A: Before the Isis Priestess mentorship[5], she was guided to sign up by a beautiful Seraphim Angel that was guiding her saying, 'do it, do it, do it'. She finally did it and felt release. But shortly after, certain things started happening, like they were trying to stop her. Energetic psychic attacks. She broke her toe. Went for a massage and the masseuse pulled on her thumb and hurt it, dislocated it. She also almost cut off her finger. Why are all these things occurring to her during this timeframe?
Archangels: They believe they can stop her. She is one of us, they *cannot* stop her. Her mission is too strong. Her mission is too important. They will not listen to us. She is one of the Galactic Council. Her mission is great. She volunteered to help. They have been after her for a very long time. Only this one thought he could succeed, he cannot. At the moment, she is feeling great pain in her left knee. He is hanging on very tight.
A: Let's alleviate that pain now and let's surround it. Can we start the removal of him? That way she starts releasing some of this pain. What side of the body is he in?
Archangels: Left.
A: That is the side where she said that she has these different things happening to her. What should I use to help it start releasing? Should I use the Phoenix Fire?
Archangels: Yes, please now!
A: Using it now. As I am using it, if you all can start pulling it out please. It's encased within the alchemy symbols. Start pulling it out as I use the Phoenix Fire releasing it. How is it looking?
Archangels: Aurora, he is one of their Council. They have sent one of - you call the Deep State. One of their high councils. You have Galactic against their Council in this being. It's a struggle. We will call for more.
A: Yes, thank you. Can I call for dragons?
Archangels: Please!
A: If I can please call for benevolent dragons now. Dragons of fire, dragons of lava, dragons of alchemy, dragons of pure Source love-light. Dragons of all elements who are of benevolent energies to come forth and help us aid removal of this Reptilian Council. Help the removal and containment within the alchemy symbols. Phoenix energies, I call forth on you now. Help us release and remove this entity from within her. Help burn away its hold, its hooks, its roots, and its cords. Burn them away, transmute them no longer allowing for them to be embedded into her. Release them now! Call forth on the Galactic energies to contain this entity. Start pulling it out from her lovingly, and if we can have

---

[5] Through Rising Phoenix Mystery School, Aurora teaches live or online the "Isis Priestess/Priest" mentorship. Teaching others how to self activate and attune themselves to the organic crystallized DNA that awaits dormant.

Yeshua and the Higher Self fill in love-light to those areas where it's being pulled out from. Fill in love-light safely, lovingly, gently, protectively, ensuring that there is no harm left, intrusion, and infringement from this entity.

Healing proceeds for many minutes.

A: How is it looking?
Archangels: Small progress at the time. Its slow progress, it is as if a war...
A: Can we call forth as well on Archangel Four and the Legion of Light.
Archangels: Please!
A: Calling on them now. The beautiful warrior protective Angels and Archangels there. If they can assist in this war energy that is occurring, so that we may remove this Reptilian from within her.
Archangels: Sister. It is Michael, the Phoenix Fire, please now!

Healing proceeds for many more minutes.

A: How is it looking Michael?
AA Michael: It will not damage the body (moans in pain).
A: Higher Self, help her feel comfortable.

More time passes for the healing.

A: How is she looking, Michael?
AA Michael: It's concentrated now on the left side of her face. Left side of her head, her left shoulder, her arm, her left hand. The outside of her left body. Most of the rest of the cells in her body are clearing now. It had permeated most of them. He grew strong.
A: Higher Self, Yeshua, please help her with the pain. Help her not feel the pain. Just calm her. Can I ask questions as we continue the healing here?
Higher Self: Yes.
A: I want to make sure she gets everything healed, as she has noted. Since that infringement started occurring, she felt that she was having trouble with her third eye. If we can go ahead and open up her third eye making it nice and healthy once more.
Higher Self: Yes.
A: Open up her gifts, as her Higher Self allows in this time and space for her highest good now. If we can also work within her heart now and expand it to the biggest it can be as her Higher Self sees fit.
Higher Self: Yes.
A: Thank you. Yeshua, if we can work on her heart there.
Yeshua: Yes.
A: As we continue to engulf her in these flames, can you tell me, when was it that this Reptilian, as he said that he did not know, when was it that it entered her body like this?
Archangels: It was a contract that is long overdue to be finished.
A: What life was it that she had this contract with it?
Archangels: When she agreed to take physical form, she knew it would come. It was part of the bargain. It was worth the struggle. Her very first time, long ago it began.
A: I really respect and honor in the way that she was there knowing that these people were being led not from their hearts. How she stood up and still spoke her truth. I really admire and respect that, as you all know I am in similar situations constantly. Thank you for bringing this example, as I treat all sessions as a teaching and healing for me as well.
Archangels: I love you.
A: And, I love all of you.
Archangels: She's really feeling joy and love in her heart for you.

A: *As I do for her infinitely. She also has been experiencing a foggy mind when she was trying to learn during the 'Isis Priestess' mentorship course information. Can you explain that to her?*
Archangels: It's all connected; it's him, it's all connected. He was blocking, and stopping.
A: *She also said that her spine is bending and her toes keep breaking. Also, degenerative disc disease in her neck. She had to lay flat like this. Did he have connections to that as well?*
Archangels: He weakened it so that it would occur. To weaken the body, to weaken the spirit. To deter her from her path.
A: *Can we heal this? All that he caused, all pain, trauma, hurt, all harm. Let's heal that now, all of it. Let's not miss any part of it. Anything that is hindering her, that is negative, no longer serving her, for her highest good.*
Archangels: Yes.
A: *If we can go ahead and reprogram her DNA, reset it to where it's meant to be organically within her?*
Archangels: Following his removal, yes.
A: *Good. How is he doing?*
Archangels: Slowly becoming mostly edges, left arm, left cheek, left forehead, top of left head still, left neck, outer edges of the left body. Deep, *deep* into the left knee Aurora. Phoenix Fire there now please. Aurora, you need to know...he is the cork in a bottle. He is the strongest, we remove him, we remove many. That is why it is taking so long.
A: *Okay, so if we can start to call for the Collective Galactic benevolent beings in this Universe who hear our call. Lovingly, respectively, honorably, benevolent beings we call forth on you now. If we can go ahead and continue removing him and also remove what is to come out. That's supposed to start this chain that we spoke of here of removals. Michael, if you could just continue talking to me?*
AA Michael: Yes.
A: *Are these others connected to him?*
AA Michael: Yes. It is like a legion, one by one, were sent.
A: *Okay, where are the legions now?*
AA Michael: Dispersed throughout the body, but not powerful.
A: *If we can make sure that we are encasing all of them in the alchemy symbols, and then infusing them with fire.*
AA Michael: Yes.
A: *All of us who I have called upon the fire elements of fire dragons, the fire angels, all using the Phoenix, are using their fire now. Collectively, lovingly, benevolently removing all of them, transforming them into light now.*
AA Michael: Sister, protect yourself now. We had anticipated this for a long time. We have been preparing for this moment. You are protected. You will not be harmed. The power from you must be great now, to assist in this. You have great power harnessed in you.
A: *I release my power now. I unleash.*
AA Michael: The numbers that will follow are more than you have seen. For your knowledge, they will be encapsulated, and will not be able to escape. They are surrounded with sacred symbols.
A: *Beautiful, thank you.*
AA Michael: You and yours are safe.
A: *Thank you. If you can tell me the numbers please?*
AA Michael: We see the first ten thousand. We see ten to a million. We feel many, many speak to us now and will be positively polarized. And we will allow that, they will be separated. One by one, as they come.
A: *Ah! Beautiful! Ensure that all the rays within the benevolent angels are aiding today.*
AA Michael: This vessel has requested we use great love and patience with them.
A: *Yes, that we shall.*
AA Michael: This process is painful for her. She is brave but it causes great pain.
A: *If we can help her please, Archangel Rafael and Yeshua, help her alleviate that pain. Engulf her with your beautiful love now so that she won't feel the pain so much, make it easier for her.*

AA Michael: Aurora, information for you. Past life injury in the left knee was the entry point for the first. That's why it is the worst at this time. Left arm and more injury, allowed more. For this one, it is always from existence to existence, a battle they have fought with her.
A: If we can scan her as well for any negative implants, hooks, or portals, Michael. Can you scan her now?
AA Michael: There are many.

The healing continues, many hooks and implants are removed

AA Michael: He is of the highest order.
A: Can you explain to me how he looks?
AA Michael: Dark, very bright, dark. You would say green. You would use the word hunter green. Almost to be black. Hmmm, this vessel, she wants to laugh, she is a nurse, she delivered babies. She said, 'Meconium green', that is the baby's first bowel movement. That is the green, yes. She makes a laugh, she has good humor, she has good humor.
A: Explain more about this, I know that he was attached to her, what about the physical portion of him?
AA Michael: Your physical body of the human. The heart, the pump, lies within the left side of the chest, without that which it does the body can not be alive, cannot be sustained. The greatest strength and potential for them to have the greatest effect on the body was to connect to the left, to be the strongest on the left. For if they could stop this physical body, then as before, she would wait for the next opportunity for the lifetime to come back in the physical. For her mission that she played, she agreed to stay on this planet. Follow these people here on this planet as it ascends from the third dimension through fourth and fifth and sixth, and beyond, out of danger. She is among the first of the Council, the High Council for this New Earth. There are more, she is of the first of this Council to lead the way.
A: Beautiful!
AA Michael: Aurora. Information for you. His Higher Self. They are working deep and strong. They are about to finish removing from the head, from the face, from the neck, and from the shoulder. The others will start to come out as if, think of this as bubbles where beings are out of the bag to spill, she has a lot of humor. Some will want you to help positively polarize. They will be coming very shortly. That hold is becoming thin.
A: Where will they be coming off from the top of the head or from all over her?
AA Michael: Starting to spill from the area, the spot you call the temple. Temple of the head by the ear. It's close, side of the face. Very close, coming soon. They are anxious to show you, they want to be free.
A: We are aiding once more those who have chosen to positive polarize. We are lovingly, infinitely, thankful for you choosing that path in keeping your consciousness and wisdom that you will gain through this positive polarization ascension. We are proud of you, and we love you dearly. Thank you for allowing us to aid you today. Continue spreading that light within you. Those of you, once more who have chosen not to positive polarize. We ask you one more time, give you one more chance. Choose to positive polarize instead of being recycled straight to Source. Choose it, remember this is why we fractalize, so that we can gain experience and growth. You can keep your consciousness and you can incarnate here, or somewhere else, lovingly and protected. As you have many benevolent beings now protecting you and guiding you. Let go, do not fear anymore. For there is much beauty in the light, for you are light. We love you, with all that consists of us upon creation.
AA Michael: Aurora, information for you as we finish this work. We sent this vessel to you through the Seraphim for this purpose. In the following of what we taught her, to watch those public demonstrations that you did with others, helping others. On your, you call it YouTube. She began to practice what you do, we encouraged it. She wanted it, she sent much love to that which was inside of her and they felt it. And, they in turn began to want what you offer. To want what she was offering, because she had the power to do it. That is why he came, to hold them in, because in numbers they could not do it. In numbers with him, we call it, 'him', like we said, a cork in a bottle. But he kept the

number in, to draw his power from what you like to call electricity. He could draw power from, he believes he could finish this, this time. He knows now, he is wrong. Her face is almost finished; her arm has much pain. They are continuing to spill like beans from a bottle. We are moving them to the light, Aurora. Phoenix Flame to this left arm.
A: Calm her pain, help her feel comfortable, Higher Self.
AA Michael: Beginning to reset DNA.
A: Surprises me how people after they meet me, or have found out about me, how the interference can be so strong, and yet they still get themselves here and follow their hearts to me. Isn't that beautiful?
Higher Self: Aurora, this is the Higher Self. She is infinitely grateful for you. She has such great love for you and appreciation.
AA Michael: Aurora, as we pull him, the last part, he has a consciousness, strong! We have him enveloped, he cannot hurt you. Beware, he will try. He believes in his own powers. He believes in his own powers. He believes he is never defeated. He believes he will be back. We protect you always, but be diligent.
A: Thank you.
AA Michael: He fights hard now. Very hard. He is losing his power. He is losing his minions behind as they spill forth. They continue, their numbers are many. Many thousands to your million. Aurora, information for you, he has a strong grip on her left knee cap, outer knee, arm and shoulder. He is removed from the rest. Her physical heart is no longer in danger. Phoenix Fire please, strong.
A: I will use my Phoenix Fire.
AA Michael: Thank you. Aurora, information for you. Because he is who he is. He has taken his cells of his, what he created of the physical body, and intertwined them with hers. This is what's taking so long and this is why she feels the pain. We must untangle them; they are tangled in the nerves of her body. We are working in the upper left side of the body.

At this time, we had not evolved A.U.R.A. Hypnosis Healing to the speed it is up to now, in removing false alien fractals integrated into peoples' DNA, cells, spine and physical bodies.

A: Let's go ahead and transmute that and un-integrate him from within her spine and anywhere else he has integrated himself to. While you are scanning, she said that she was psychically attacked on the airplane on her way here to her session. Can you give her some information on that? The flight attendants thought it was a heart attack, but she knew it was a psychic attack.
AA Michael: The markers that we are finding, his goal was not just to stop her now, but to convert her to him. Consume her to him. To stop her through this Ascension.
A: Wow, well let's remove any piece and part of him, of his and who he is. Any part of him that is not of her, remove every bit of him within her. Start that now please.
AA Michael: Aurora, Information for you from Yeshua. When she was in California, we sent her there. We all came together when she was in her motorhome. We put her in a state of sleep, semi-awake. We placed within her the sacred Christ Consciousness, the connection to us all. He could not have been successful, he could not. If captured, that consciousness. She was protected, always, always. He could not have consumed her.
A: Good, thank you.
Yeshua: We felt, and we knew he was doing this.
A: Yeshua, while you are here can you give her advice about her husband? It seems like he is the biggest density in her life, besides this Reptilian.
Yeshua: He is frightened. He is like a five year-old little boy, frightened. The things he saw and experienced in the Catholic church with the priest (molestation). She is right; she knew things because he said things. He has much fear; he holds it tightly inside of him, much fear. We sent her to Michigan to her family reunion and she had joy. We kept her in a cabin there, and she rested while we worked with him, adjusted him, and helped him. He must have a will, it is his will. It helped her, she saw it when she returned. She questioned me and I told her, fine-tuning. She questioned me about his change, as he still maintains some. But, he needs more, he needs help. She wants to help him.

His free will is blocking, he is not awakened. I know she has asked, and I hear her now, to assist him, to awaken him. It gives her pain in her heart, that he feels like he does.
A: Can you all awaken him?
Yeshua: He needs much healing. He was so soft and gentle, and learned to cover and duck and hide. He was hurt badly, emotionally badly. And then he did what he thought was right. He went to Vietnam when they told him he had to go. He didn't want someone else to take his place. Many left the country. We shielded him, we gave him the ability to do typing and we pushed him to speak up. To tell those in charge that he can type so they chose him. She knows this in her heart. So that he would not be removed from his physical body. But, all those that were sent, those that took that piece of path, they all carry such pain in them. But, they carry the free will, and you know Aurora, we cannot unless they ask for help, we cannot. We help many. He struggles, he feels like he needs to do it alone. She tells him, he does not have to be alone. At his Higher Self's request, we will work with him. To ease his pain. To help awaken him. Aurora, she has been told this, he is not long for this lifetime. She has accepted it with no pain, knowing the truth.
A: We send him our infinite love. Thank you.
Yeshua: She surrounds him with love, always.
A: Thank you, Yeshua, love you! Michael, how is she doing?
AA Michael: Her knee is free, her shoulders remain some, and they continue to come.
A: Who continues to come?
AA Michael: The ones who he has set in place for positive polarity, and they feel joy.
A: Beautiful.
AA Michael: Free at last, free at last.
A: Free at last.
AA Michael: She hears them say, 'free at last'. A small amount is still in her arm; shoulder's tight. Aurora, the outer arm below is the last stronghold, you will understand. Outer arm, left, Phoenix Fire now in force. Great pain!
A: Calm the pain, calm the pain, calm the pain... Soothe the pain.
AA Michael: It likes to grip on her upper arm, like tentacles tight on her upper arm.

Healing Continues…

A: How is it looking, Michael?
AA Michael: Keep the Phoenix Fire going, it needs intense burning to get the last stronghold. To finish, it is lessening. It is much less, but condensed. Much condensing was done. Close to finishing. We've instructed her to tell you. There are perhaps one thousand waiting for you who are in much fear for this one. They all requested to be positively polarized by you. As soon as he's done. As soon as we finish with him. They are waiting for you. They are the last within her.
A: Very good.
AA Michael: They have much fear of him.
A: It is okay, they are infinitely protected. No fear needed. We can start surrounding them in the alchemy symbols for the transformation of their Ascension to positive polarization. Those thousands there: love you, and we thank you for doing so. Start spreading that love-light there, while we continue to work on this Reptilian removal. Once he is removed we will finish up with you, thank you.
AA Michael: We've instructed them to breathe the love-light into them as well.
A: Good. How many would you say have been healed from helping them ascend into positive polarization?
AA Michael: (laughs) We know you like numbers, Aurora. When all is finished from this vessel, the numbers are beyond one million.
A: Ah, beautiful, thank you.

More healing time passes.

A: How are we doing, Michael?

AA Michael: Scanning for residual. She says one spot is still very sore. We believe he is out.
A: *Beautiful. All that is of her, fill it in now with the most beautiful purest Love-Light of Source-Creator's energy. Heal the pain and suffering, all of it, heal it now. She says she cannot go in the sun, if we can also heal that, so she can be in the sun safely. Archangel Michael, can you scan that and what was causing that reaction to the sun?*
AA Michael: He's from the darkness. He was from the darkness.
A: *So that is why she couldn't see bright lights or the sun's energy? If we can heal that, so she can now be replenished with the beautiful Source Love-Light energy from the sun. May she look upon bright lights now. Thank you. Higher Self, is there anything else that I am missing? Anything else that we need to heal within her?*
HS: Not at this time.
A: *Good. How are we doing, Michael?*
AA Michael: We believe it is completed, we will watch her closely.
A: *Good, thank you.*
AA Michael: Thank you.
A: *With the Higher Self's permission, can we place a forcefield around her?*
AA Michael: Yes.
A: *Through this transition?*
AA Michael: Yes.
A: *Thank you. May I bring her back now?*
Higher Self: Yes.
A: *Beautiful. I want to thank, first of all, everyone who aided us today. Every single beautiful, benevolent being out there that aided us, even the negative ones. We love you dearly, honor you, and respect you. My infinite love to everyone. I honor you and respect you, thank you.*
Higher Self: Aurora, we love you, we thank you, we respect you, always dear sister. Thank you!
A: *Thank you.*

For every A.U.R.A. Hypnosis healing session we ask that the Higher Self and team ensure to remove and heal this entire list from the clients Tree of Life: entities (Grays, Mantis, Reptilians, Archons…), dark portals, repair and crystallize DNA, negative cords, technologies (implants, metals, hooks, wires, nano, vaccines), Illnesses, vision, dental health, regrow teeth, age regress 5-15 years, blocked or misaligned chakras, open-up the third eye and activate abilities, expand heart, issues with auric field, fractured soul, contracts, deletion of inverted timelines, and trauma from current or past life.

END OF SESSION

Out of the clients that I have assisted throughout my career, Constance was one of the most infringed and targeted because of who she is, and the divine power that is anchored through her unto Earth everyday by just her being. This session took much focused energy and collaboration from the Universe's benevolent guides for it to be accomplished divinely. Through A.U.R.A. Hypnosis Healing Technique, we have found several types of branches of Council Members incarnated from all over Creation. Stemming forth from different parts of the Universe, those who have answered the call at some point in time to be born upon Earth, in assistance for the people to progress through the forgetfulness that occurs when we enter this illusional reality. Councils of Creation stem forth from elders and wisewomen/wisemen of the infinities of the planets, dimensions and realms of creation.

As of August 16th, 2023, I have conducted eight-hundred and forty-nine Quantum Galactic Akashic Readings. With every reading conducted and communicated through the client's Higher Selves, I have met an abundance of types of Council people. Councils of nine, Councils of four or five, Councils of fire or light… Councils with no names. Each one of these have a different important role for the Galactics and the Universes, where there is no hierarchy and only love, honor, and respect. Which is why we say this phrase often, because it is what it means to be equal to one another, no matter the origins of when our soul birthed forth into creation. Councils assist in birthing out Dragons. Some just hold the Love-Light of the Universe; some create new planets; some are guides to others; some protect with their plasmic energy. Imagine what it is like to have these Councils incarnated on Earth! By having them here, it brings forth whatever focused responsibility each Council oversees, so that these profound gifts and energetic plasmic fields are anchored into Earth through the bridge which would be the Council member incarnate themselves. This assists the collective's Ascension process vastly, and it is a strength that awakens many everyday. After all, this is why we choose to incarnate, as when we do we bring all that we are, and can be, as we remember who we are. Creating and echoing a vast amount of the Universe's light to Earth, where we need it the most, in the lowest dimension of the third.

The oldest Council that I have read and connected to through the Akashic Hall of Records would be the Council of 12, which is the Council that Constance was from. This is who we channel often through our teachings, and our platforms, the Council of 12. They are the Elders who assisted in birthing our Universe, the same Seraphim Angels that led Constance to our sacred teachings; ultimately to have her session conducted; they were the ones who were guiding her with their ancient wisdom in her incarnation as the Egyptian Scholar. Remember the mention of the flamed pyramid ships that the star people (the Council of 12) communicate to her through? This is what some of our spacecraft truly look like from the Galactics legions. The negative polarized aliens' spacecraft are more like the saucers that you see in the skies, and in photographs. These spaceships are typically driven by the Military, or aliens as Grays, Mantis or Reptilians.

The number twelve/thirteen being one in the same, twelve is still thirteen, because the twelve are the first children of creation, the Archangels, the first twelve Galactic constructs, the Council of 12, and when you include the Divine Mother "The Daughter of the Flame" who is our Universe herself, which we will speak of the Phoenix in the final chapter, she is the thirteenth. Which is why twelve and thirteen are the same. The Mother/Father and their creations. Twelve is the prime number to our Universe, and the fabric of where all lifeforms stem forth from; it is the origin of the oversoul. The oversoul being the Council of 12; the origin of the highest aspect of each Higher Self, which then multiplied by birthing fractals out from within themselves, The Archangels. As mentioned in Chapter 2, "The Key to Ascension," we know that the numerology within the 12.21.2020 beginning the splitting of the two/third worlds could only have come into fruition within numbers whose core number is twelve. All that has been mentioned of the number twelve assists us in understanding why that is. Ultimately, it is because the expansion of creation began from the number twelve, the first twelve lifeforms; therefore, if we are to be at our highest potential, as a collective of what is meant to be created for the Earth's organic timeline, we must connect and harness this power of the twelve/thirteen. In Chapter 7, 'The Essenes', we hear directly from the 'Galactic Council of 12' regarding their role in Atlantis.

There is sacred safety required for these Council members to incarnate; especially when they are looking to have sessions done in discovering more of who they are, or require assistance in self-healing. I have found that they will be protected strongly by their council team. If they go to a practitioner for past life regression work, or to someone who can read their energy through the Akashic Hall of Records, and that person is compromised with perhaps entity infringements, or technology attached, that would allow dark entities to spy through the eyes of the healer. This could be quite dangerous as the Archons would then have these Council members' energetic location; at that point infringing upon them as freely as they desire. Especially, if they have yet to practice 'not consenting' through the form of shielding with their infinite Source Love-Light. Otherwise, they are left wide open. As the Higher Selves often say, to shield with Love-Light is to "Not Consent," and to not shield is to "Consent" in this Inverted simulation. When you go to another and allow access to your Akashic Hall of Records, you are consenting for them to acquire your sacred data, which is retrieved and harnessed through your Toroidal Sphere consciousness. Therefore, one must be extremely cautious when interacting with another in this manner, and one is infinitely sure that, 1. The practitioner is a clear channel with no inversions within, 2. The practitioner is truly pure of heart and intent, and 3. The practitioner practices a form of Love-Light "Not Consenting" shielding. As this world is infested with people who are knowingly, or unknowingly, acting as spies for negative polarized entities from all over the Universe. I have met many that become derailed off their organic timeline for months or decades, by allowing others into their energetic sacred fields without boundaries.

I have been shown many scenarios in the quantum realm, through dreams, meditation, and my connections in the theta brainwave. One example being: There is a very fast growing popular channeler/reader that is being sponsored by a superstar. I was shown that this person was compromised somewhere along the way when he was hungry to channel popularly (become famous). Because this intent was not a pure intent of love for others, and perhaps for reasons such as, recognition, persona, being placed on a pedestal, he was an open channel. When spreading his antenna wide (channel) a negative contract was created with a negative polarized Mantis to enter, attach, and compromise his connection. Being that this Mantis was a matching vibration to this reader's initial intention, which was of service to self, versus service to others. Therefore, when he conducts readings for clients, and because he does have a channeling gift, this Mantis retrieves all the data that was scanned during the sessions, as the clients gave consent when allowing to be read by this reader, and, unknowingly, the Mantis being that is inside of him. This Mantis works for the Archons; all information on the clients that comes through these readings/channelings is logged into their A.I. database. The Archons can then begin their diabolical plans in how they can infringe upon the clients' further awakenings, and if during the reading they retrieved data about the clients' children or spouses, they can also begin abductions, or whatever is part of their next negative agenda towards their loved ones. Which is why it is important that we practice secret sacredness with who we are, and our soul origins, especially for our loved ones, and that we guard them by first guarding ourselves with all that we are.

This channeler/reader comes across very intellectual, with an abundance of knowledge; however, when you tap into his field to feel if there is an infinite love frequency carried through each word and communications delivered, it is minimal and his energy feels sterile, like the smell and air of a hospital, or the metal table of a UFO abduction. Mantis are one of the main alien races that abduct humankind (UFO abductions) for their negative polarized experiments and agendas, ultimately maintaining the population 'asleep.' However, not many can read, or pick up on the reader's true form, that is of this Mantis being. The main reason being that many always want to see with their Third Eye. That's the prized possession, or gift, we want to acquire the minute we wake up. However, how we view energy through our Third Eye, can still be very different from what is organically there. Why? Because of the negative technology that may be surrounding another's field, causing an illusion over who they truly are, and interfering with accurately viewing them. This is programmed within the spiritual communities, because those who we might watch emphasize the fact that they can view into the spirit realm with their Third Eye, and this is highly regarded by the populace. The awakening spiritual community forgot that actually the feeling and knowing is the most significant for us in reading the energies of someone, or a situation. When we 'read' and question instead, "how does this feel?" the feeling is very apparent that "something just doesn't feel right," or that there is no infinite love emanating out through them when delivering a transmission. What has a lack of love is the opposite, which would be Archonic in nature, not of our Universe. Because our Universe's plasmic energy, that gives life to all beings, IS LOVE. If there is an absence of love, then it is not organic to us. In this organic world of ensuring to not walk an inverted timeline, this is of the most importance. This is why when we awaken, our path becomes convoluted, because those we go to, are people that we think are more connected or gifted then us. The Archon plan is to ensure that the majority of these people will be compromised. So, once more, you are placed into simulations of the inverted matrix. Ensuring that the awakened are now unawakened. These situations are like booby traps, or land mines, awaiting for you when you seek self development from outside you.

It seems when one of these Council Members are found by the dark forces, they will do all that they can in their power to stop them from progressing and stepping into the Love-Light that they are meant to be for Earth's collective Ascension. It still amazes me every day that after such infringement and interference, these people still somehow find their way to me. Our bridged frequency of love, in assistance and aid, connects them to their beginning, inner self-healing. Such beautiful, wonderful miracles are shared daily to us, through these journeys shared by our clients. An honor it is, to be the bridge of infinite love and pureness, so that they, too, can acquire this within themselves, through their journey of becoming and living as organic souls in this world.

Regarding the Deep State Council member, and its attachment to Constance, there was an agreement they made long ago when she first incarnated on Earth, to allow this Reptilian attachment, so that she could acquire the adequate density to anchor in. As, otherwise, because of who she is, her spirit is of an immensity of light, which would not allow for her to anchor into a body, as she would not be a matching vibration to Earth's lower vibrations. This is what is often talked about, that humanity's contracts with the Reptilians have expired, and are long overdue to be rescinded. The Reptilians have inverted these contracts now into negative, by holding on, however controlled by the Archons, they are. Throughout this council member's incarnations, she grew in strength and wisdom, but so, too, did he, to the level of becoming one of the heads of the Illuminati. Perhaps by the harvesting of the grandness of her light, making his illusions of power come to be. I have come across a few more of these Draco Reptilians after Constance's session, and only once was I able to convince the Reptilian living inside one of these members to positively polarize. It was a grand struggle with the Archangels assisting in the session, who did not feel that it could work, because of the immensity of how dark it had turned and the A.I. darkness inside this Draco, but still it did. A Draco Reptilian is the strongest Reptilian of their kind, as the Reptilian alien race is versatile in the types of Reptilians there are. The Draco Reptilians are at least double, or triple, the size of an average Reptilian soldier. They are muscular in stature, with strong spikes or horns coming out from different parts of their body, and their skin seems as impenetrable as armor itself. At this point we are not sure what happens to the Illuminati members, after the energetic removal of these strong Draco Reptilians from within Earth. Whether or not this would cause their host body to perhaps have an opening of heart, and change their ways. However, through the custom Illuminati's ways, they would just have another clone replace them, if they were to go positively rogue, as if nothing ever went wrong, or more like right. Through Chapter 5, we speak further of some of these clones they can make instantly on demand.

This session was conducted early September 2019, before these two very important sessions came to be in Book 1, Chapters 9 and 10, "Activation Portal: 9/19/19," and "A Ripple of 9,000,000 Heal in the Universe." Before the 9/19/19 portal, which then began the masses of entity removal of this magnitude. We experienced some of the biggest positive polarization of entities in the Universe, through these two sessions. After Constance's session, we went from thousands to millions and billions, through our sessions being able to positively polarize in the Universe. When Archangel Michael mentions, "The numbers that will follow are more than you have seen" and "We see the first ten thousand. We see ten to a million. We feel many, many speak to us now and will be positively polarized. And we will allow that." I did not realize what they meant by what was to come after the removal of this powerful Draco Reptilian from within Constance. The benevolent guides always explain to us how important it is that we conduct A.U.R.A. Hypnosis and R.A.A.H. Reiki Healing sessions. We understand this further with these sessions conducted in September 2019. Because of the thousands and millions healed through Constance's session, we were able to heal millions in our future sessions. The many thousands of Reptilians and entities and their fear, that were being held down by this Draco Reptilian! We thank their mass Love-Light healing and positive polarization, as this was a necessary piece to bring forth the infinity of collective healings that have come to be through our sessions of A.U.R.A. Hypnosis and R.A.A.H. Reiki practitioners.

In the time of this Egyptian Scholar and the priests, who was it that they, the priests, worshiped and prayed to, to supposebly heal others? As we know, the Archons and negative polarized entities are the ONLY ones who require this type of attention, as worship. What were they bargaining for in exchange to these Archons, when doing healings in the name of their inverted means? It would be Archonic power over the peoples' souls, or rights to their souls. Healers or priests of our times, who are inverted as these priests were, act as 'soul collectors' for the soul eating Archons. These are some of the examples, through religion, of the Priests of *our* times. I have had many clients who were placed in black magic bindings, through black magic rituals performed during church mass. When the priest placed dark ashes in the shape of a cross over their third eye, sealing, blocking, and harvesting their intuitive abilities, or by drinking the red wine (alcohol), which represents the human sacrifice of blood. These examples, in the now, are the same types of false rituals that they were doing in that time and space of Egypt. In our benevolent ruled times of Egypt the word priest, or priestess, was most sacred. But they began then to invert the view of the sacred name "priest" and the role of these sacred positions of responsibility, and connection to sacred ritual with the Universe. These inversions upon true spirituality, have carried over into the now of our times and spaces, which hinder the development one seeks when looking to connect to our spirituality, creating a dogma upon spirituality itself.

These priests, they were all show and words, but no action, or deliverance. A false illusion, being portrayed to these people that they were being supposedly healed. Great actors and magicians they were, knowing how to put on a show to entice people. However, the truth was in how the people felt, how they shifted, and remembered themselves through the Egyptian Scholars example. When we truly empower people, this is how the people feel; changed, and evolved. This is how we know the healing is working. Their happiness and strength are our testimonials. Through all our courses taught in our Rising Phoenix Mystery School, between our websites, and pages, we have over four hundred (400) reviews, and thirty videos, including multiple testimonials under our channels. Which explains this, of what Constance got to see in her life, what the Egyptian Scholar taught the people, teaching that the light and their divine power was always in them to self-heal. This is what you see through these people's eyes, and what you feel when you read and watch their reviews and testimonials, of our sessions and sacred teachings. To this day, Constance too, is here in support. Leaving comments from time to time, in what we share and post for the collective's aid. We send her our infinite love now, for showing, and being, such a pure example for us in these trying times in the world, as true disclosure continues to unveil and surface.

The Young Pharaoh, and how he was murdered, because he was to reign strongly in benevolence. In our Earth's history, the leaders controlled by the Archons, plagued by ego, have repeated this inverted cycle over and over. They see someone that carries greatness, and a chance to be that example for others so that they can thrive with inner beauty, and they are threatened. And they do not want to lose their hold on their titled position. To this day, we see this cycle repeating, through people in positions who might have power over others. Through the governments' hierarchy and tyranny, the third dimensional work environments of management, and people who are closest to us. They see a light that is shining as bright as a lighthouse, that is a guide to ships/people in safe sailing to sacred lands. And they try to create chaos, as a storm would be, in their waters. The dark entities don't want these ships, who are the people of Earth, to find these lighthouses that guide us to the promised land of the fifth/sixth dimension and beyond. Instead they want the people lost, in the soul-eating waters of the river of death, as explained in Chapter 2, 'The Key to Ascension'. Which is why it is that they do their best to try to put out the lights of many, who are the lighthouses on Earth. It's time we break these inverted cycles of oppression, and that we stand up to our oppressors. The world is monumentally, sovereignly doing this, in this time and space, as we speak. One version was through the 'Freedom Convey." Truckers would be the least expected to stand up for freedom, in the way that they have for humanity, against the forced mandates of the Covid-19 Vaccines. How they handled their/our cause was divinely genius and supported with love throughout Earth's people. Who better than those who have driven the roads which connect the world; the truckers, who as they drive have received the activations of the energetic ley lines of Earth. May the collective continue to find ways such as these to be heard, loud and clear!

We would now love to send our infinite love to ALL veterans of the wars of our Earth's History. As we know these wars have been man-made by the Illuminati and negative aliens, who are controlled by Archons. The pain that these veterans had to live through, to survive, by having to harm, or take another's life. This inverted cycle of wars, after wars, have torn pieces apart from the divine masculine on Earth over, and over; their families alongside them. Their spouses praying, and not knowing if they will ever come back from war; and their children, who had to live the avenging feeling of who, or what false cause, took their father or mothers's life during the war.

We humbly bow now to all in our Universe who have stood up and spoken of the truth, no matter the repercussions that might come by doing so. These are the heroes. Like the Egyptian Scholar, who knew that she had to deliver her messages, and the dangers of speaking them. The people, no matter what, must know the truth. The truth must be spoken. Once one recognizes how we, too, can speak to the Creator, and that these self righteous leaders, placed on pedestals, are not our rulers. This is when we discover our inner truth.

>
> **Free to be me,**
> **I finally see**
> **that my roots are connected to the Earth,**
> **just like the trees.**
> **Unrestricted with no limits,**
> **that I finally predicted**
> **my vision,**
> **to make the decision,**
> **to awaken,**
> **what has been taken from my generation.**
> **Focused on determination, creation, and appreciation.**
> **~Zen (AuroRa's beloved)**

--------------<<>>--------------

5

THE A.I. ALIEN INVASION

*Interview by Laura M. Eisenhower: Recorded on October 28th, 2021.
Aired live on the Cosmic Gaia Show.*

In this Chapter Laura Eisenhower interviews AuroRa UNCENSORED on 'Cosmic Gaia'. AuroRa delivers a groundbreaking transmission with the strongest disclosure shared of her career. Placing all the pieces together of 'The New World Order,' directly linked to the Covid-19 vaccine. Why this diabolical agenda, who is truly behind it, and their intention for humankind.

--------------<<>>--------------

**"Are we going to submit to tyranny, complacency, obedience, or are we going to rescue our treasures and amplify these treasures that these challenges are pushing us to reclaim?"
~Laura M. Eisenhower**

**"If you really understand timelines, then you understand that with every choice you are making you are creating timelines. So value and honor yourself in the greatest power that you are, because you are the timeline birther."
~AuroRa**

--------------<<>>--------------

[6]Laura: Hello everybody, it's Laura Eisenhower. So glad and grateful you all are part of 'Cosmic Gaia' and this broadcast tonight with my dear friend, Rising Phoenix AuroRa. This woman is so incredible and we have known each other for quite some time, but first I want to thank you so much for being here.
AuroRa:Thank you. It is my honor.
Laura: We are obviously navigating some very crazy, interesting times. Adjectives just seem to fall short. We knew this stuff was coming. It's a whole different thing when we're in it. We are going to gain some clarity about topics that are really lighting up for you, and that we really want to bring forth. We mentioned the whole idea of helping people avoid A.I. and align with their Divine Self. Some of it might seem obvious, yet they miss some of the targets or agendas that can really sneak in and grab a person without them fully realizing it. It is really important to get this activation and gain this clarity. I'm going to read a little bit about you, and then I'll just introduce how we are going to dive into this unbelievable topic. AuroRa is the founder of A.U.R.A. Hypnosis Healing Technique and R.A.A.H. Reiki Angelic Alchemy Healing. She is a Spiritual Revolutionist, Quantum Alchemist, Akashic reader, and a channel to the Ra Collective. As a beautiful heart-centered energy healer, she conducts quantum healing sessions and has directly helped over 3,000 clients to connect to their Higher Selves with profound results for all involved. Serving all in infinite love, she also teaches spiritual alchemy development courses for students to empower them to tap into their inner wisdom, to self-heal, and to reawaken their divine spiritual gifts. In addition, many thousands more have benefited from her

---

[6] Laura M. Eisenhower is the great granddaughter of President Dwight D. Eisenhower, the thirty-fourth president of the United States. Laura is a veterend public speaker, bringing forth the truth of the "New World Order". She is a whistleblower, who is known for her passion and strong heart. One of the strongest light-warriors of our times, who embodies that the impossible is not possible. She is a beloved friend of Aurora, and close colleague.

teachings through the Rising Phoenix AuroRa YouTube, Rumble and Vimeo channels. And, you are whipping out the books. You just put out a huge book based on a lot of these sessions that you have done. Maybe, let's start there and talk a little bit about your background. Where you are today with it, and some of the questions that have to do with the here and now.

AuroRa: Very good. Thank you, Laura. It's an honor to be here with you. Thank you for having me on your beautiful channel. I am excited and ready for I think one of the most catalyzing videos I have ever made. Those of you who have been watching and awakening, you know our content is soul and heart-activating. The information that we have is really going to help us step into our sovereignty. Those of you who have been watching me on YouTube, Rumble, and also Vimeo, know that our videos are intense in a manner where it shifts our consciousness consciously and our hearts. Like Laura said, between the combination of courses, sessions, classes, certifications for Akashic, A.U.R.A. Hypnosis, R.A.A.H. (Reiki Angelic Alchemy Healing), the retreats, and the online workshops that I do, I have worked with about 3,000 people. As Laura said, I am the author of "The Galactic Soul History of the Universe." Additionally, I am a Galactic Historian, which means that not only do I do past life regression for these clients that have come to me internationally, myself alone over 400 sessions, each of which is over five hours. If you think about it, that is a lot. Over the past three and a half years I have been logging the Galactic History of our Universe, through my clients' journeys. I am also a clear channel to Ra, which is also the Council of Twelve, the Thirteen, which I call the Galactics. They are the benevolence of the Galactics of our Universe. This information that we will be sharing today is a combination of both my channeled information, as I am a seer; I connect through dreamtime, meditation, and visions, I am also delivering messages from these beautiful souls, my clients, who have shared their journeys throughout the Universe, through the many dimensions of our Universe. So, that is a little bit more of my background. Is that good love? May I begin with sharing more?

Laura: Yes, I mean just jump right into it. I know that you have some very important updates and information to bring through. In the last one-on-one between you and I, we did the Blue versus Red.

AuroRa: Yes, I believe that might have been our last one-on-one, but we have had several roundtables.

Laura: Yes, and I know you have updates. I haven't framed it into a question, other than to hold space for you to just tell us what you have been going through lately. Go for it, explaining what is coming through.

AuroRa: This is the continuance, for those of you who watched "Red vs Blue | Timeline Wars | Archons, A.I., and the Antidote, on Laura Eisenhower's YouTube channel. I believe it reached over 55,000 views and over 2,000 comments. It completely made sense of what was going on then. That was last year, November 2020. This is a continuance of that sacred knowledge and information. Really sensitive disclosure. What occurred specifically, as we talk about alien races and galactic histories? We want to know how did Covid-19 begin? How did it begin on Earth? We are going to go through that history, how it actually came forth, and also in the Universe and other Universes. Now, what happened was, in the 1940s, there was what we will call an invasion of aliens. What happened was that there was a ship that landed in the most populated area, but before that, let's go into how they were able to land. They are artificial intelligence clones. I will go into explaining what that means later. What they do is from another dimension, another realm, not from our dimension, they have negative technology beyond what we understand is capable here. What they did was they started working on the leaders of that time and space within the early 1940s, to convince them unconsciously, especially through sleep time, unconsciously in some form, and also consciously in another, to allow for them to come forth and then land. Basically, make further negative contracts with humanity at that time. So that is how they were able to enter. They entered through some of the dark portals that were available to negative aliens, especially back then. We've worked a lot collectively closing a lot of those dark portals, but in that time, in our specific third dimensional Earth, there were still negative portals where they specifically came in. They came in this very big ship and they actually landed in China. I'm going to show you why they landed in China. (AuroRa shares her screen of a bar graph of the global population) This is current as of 2021. I wasn't able to find the population data for 1940. As you can see the population of China is 1,397,715,000, the population of India is 1,366,417,750, the United

States is 328,239,520, followed by Indonesia with a population of 270,625,570. Look at how much of a population there is to be controlled in China, so that the rest of the world can fall in line. It's tremendous. So a very big diabolical plan, to target the most populated country. A lot of people have actually seen these aliens in dreams. They have red eyes and they kind of look like androids. They hide behind masks. That's how they look physically. When they landed, it was both in agreement, but also by force. They started off with China, and then they reached out to the rest of the leaders of the world (the government), they basically gave them a contract. If they agreed to allow their integration into the world, the aliens would give them technology. This is where our technology is coming from. This advanced technology is happening right now.

Laura: Wait, you are talking about events that happened before what one might find on the internet? Just to clarify, this E.T. technology exchange. You are talking about the roots of it.

AuroRa: Yes. It was about a decade before your great-grandfather was in office. Remember, they had already worked with them consciously to convince them, and these people would have been more of a negative polarization, in service to self versus service to others. It was pretty easy for them to convince these leaders of these countries, to allow these aliens to take control in the background. What these A.I. clones are, those are the clones that we see. We see them glitch. We see them as a hologram. They look like humans, but they are not. They have technology around them.

Laura: Like newscasters, people in influential positions that these anomalies have shown up, is whom you're talking about?

AuroRa: Yes, and politicians, some presidents, and so on. This is the original race that is connected to the technology we have heard of and are seeing. Their main goal is to find hosts. The leaders of the world basically become their hosts. Once the hosts agree, they accept that these clones became integrated into these world leaders. We will call it bloodlines. They aren't really bloodlines, they are just clones. They are just cloning them over and over and over. Their technology is so advanced that they can actually just clone instantly. Once they agreed to that, what happened was that they were given all the technology that we have yet to see with our own eyes. Some of technology being that they could go in, and UFO abduct you. In the book "Galactic Soul History of the Universe," we go into a lot of that. What we are sharing today is extra information from what is in the book. They work first within the conscious mind, through all the different brain waves that it alternates through, and then they convince you that it is okay for them to UFO abduct you, while you are sleeping. There are different types. There's MILAB, military, and also just aliens from other dimensions that are abducting you while you are sleeping. Even when you are awake, they can abduct you within not even a second. This is some of their technology that I'm trying to explain that they have, where they can just go in, replace consciousnesses, and infringe on consciousnesses very strongly. We already know about this, where they can just send a negative A.I. wave through technology, and all of a sudden you think a thought is yours, but it's not, it's theirs. Okay, so once they were able to get all of the world leaders to agree to this in that time and space, everyone was given the technology - those that did agree to this. They showed them how to create underground bases.

Laura: This is still around the 40s you're talking about?

AuroRa: Yes. But basically, they are in the background, the A.I. clones. So they built these underground bases, because they had the technology. Because, they gave them the technology to build the underground bases, and then they built tunnels going through. People talk about the tunnels, making it so you can transport from one place to another, one country to another, and some of these are even underwater, and so on. They're the reason, basically how this negative technology came forth upon the Earth. The way that it works is, they came from another dimension where they had actually invaded another planet and had completely wiped out life within it and made it into A.I. Their mission was to repeat what they did on other planets, to our planet. So, they have been in hiding. Of course, we know a lot of these negative beings would be part of these Illuminati rings; some of them are in these families that hold the money in the world that we know about. What they have been doing this whole entire time is, they have been abducting humankind as we know, and not just in the now. Negative aliens have been abducting human life since the beginning. The first chapter of my book goes into when the first Reptilian consciousness experiments happened, and when they started inserting Reptilian pieces into people energetically and through viruses. This whole time, since they invaded Earth in the 1940s, was to do the same to us, as they did to those other planets. Let me go into how they explained this. They have been testing humankind. Examples being, the Jewish Concentration Camps, and the different types of wars. Where they have been abducting people and children. They have been testing us. They've been taking people. For example, we are now knowing more about human trafficking and child trafficking.

Laura: I don't mean to interject, but the whole Joseph Mengele, and a lot of that agenda. They were aligned with the Dracos, and were doing these experiments on people for this greater purpose.

AuroRa: Exactly. So they have been abducting people, putting them underground in these spaces, testing out the Covid-19 vaccine. So let me go into that. Let's talk about Divine Mother, Sophia, and our Universe. What we need to explain to you is that this Earth is a very important Earth to the Earths. It holds a very special organic blueprint, that if it becomes infringed upon it ripples out. The way they (the galactics) explain it, is if there was a rose, and when you look at it, say there is one seed at the center of that rose, then the rest of those little seeds of that rose (using a finger to demonstrate a spiraling out from the center) are say the infinity of other Earths. The negative aliens' goal was to get here to do that, and they were again able to accomplish that through what I already said, when we were in Atlantis - remember we were in the fifth dimension then. We were this beautiful blend of races. We incarnated to be here. The way the Universe works is that anything higher than the fifth dimension incarnates energetically. Here, you have to enter through a pod, in an avatar state, because it is different. We have explained before that when you go to one planetary sphere, that planetary sphere has a race that for example, perhaps they eat grass to replenish their light. Then you go to another planetary sphere, and that race lays in the grass to replenish their light. What would happen, if you put one who eats the grass with one who lays on the grass to replenish their light together in one planetary sphere? There would be a disharmony, right? They wouldn't be able to be together. So, every single planetary sphere is created organically through a different signature, divinely through Source. There is typically one race per planet. There are exceptions, but typically there is only one. And, then of course there is animal life which is different. Every planet is different. You can read in my book about the infinity of different planets that there are. We understand that. In order for us to create this school down here, when we were in fifth dimension, in our avatar states, we had entered through an organic crystalline technology simulation. Our Higher Selves created a piece of us that agreed to enter into the simulation. So to be 'on Earth' we are all laying in pods, engaged in a simulation. Much like we see in the movie, the Avatar. What happened was, the Archons invaded Atlantis and the fall happened. That is basically when it became the Inverted Matrix, and when we became stuck in the recycling of souls over and over and over, because they inverted that beauty that we put together. Why did we create it organically? The reason we created it organically was that races cannot normally live together due to consistency, frequency, vibration, and how they have been made through their DNA energetically. On Earth, Mother Sophia placed her beautiful blueprint, and that is what we call her 'her,' because she is the actual Earth. And then as we came in, these different fractalizations of a feline Lyran, a canine being, a crystalline being, a being made of energy, an Angelic, an Arcturian, a Pleiadian, it goes on and on. Imagine if you were to put all these beautiful races into one place and its beauty.

Laura: Would you say that when we look at the web of life and how ecosystems function, that to sustain life, even though there are predators and maybe vulnerable creatures that are trying to stay away from the predators, but then they have the food source in their own nature that they need to attack maybe, or bring into their being in order to sustain themselves. So, when you look at the greater galactic ecosystem, does it feel ordered and chaotic all at the same time or is there an anomaly that has been presented into this picture because of the free will aspect of it? It's like you have the web of life, very destructive yet it sustains life, but on a galactic ecosystem level, how would you relate that to the earthbound ecosystems and the web of life?

AuroRa: Everything you are looking at is in an avatar state, even down to the animals. They are actually magical creatures. We go into session and people are like, oh I'm a fairy, I'm a Dragon, I'm a

THE FINAL BATTLE - GALACTIC HISTORY OF THE MULTIVERSE

Griffin, there's an infinity of magical creatures. I'm trying to answer your question. Can you say it one more time?

Laura: When one thinks about the diversity of creation, when we see it on an Earth base level, even though it is multidimensional, I mean the whales, the dolphins, and so many creatures that are from other dimensions. We don't need to be limited into this third dimension, but when you see the much, much, much, larger picture, as much as it is chaotic, and as much as there is this free will aspect to it, in order to see what to do about it, how much order in the chaos do you see, as far as our multidimensional, or ET Galactic heritage that we hold? My God, what a crazy question.

AuroRa: No, that is okay. So free will is one of the Sacred Laws of the Universe. Free will is everywhere. The thing that is hard about our Earth is the fact that we have amnesia. The reason we have amnesia is because it inverted itself. We inverted with the fall of Atlantis. As far as order, there is order definitely throughout all the organic blueprints of our Universe. But, as we talked about in 'Red vs Blue, Archons, and the A.I. virus', this virus actually came forth, and attacked as any virus would. We could go into that since that is what I think your question is directed towards.

Laura: Oh no, we don't have to go into my question. I would rather talk about what you want to talk about. I guess, what is interesting is when we look at the Galactic Wars, nature is not always light and fluffy. You've got lions eating hyenas, you've got hyenas eating . . .

AuroRa: Only because it's inverted.

Laura: There seems to be an initiation that because we are so connected with nature on a soul level, DNA level, and an energetic level, that we move beyond this sort of predator victim dichotomy. And even nature might reflect it to us. But then it would be weird if everything was loving and perfect and we are just going to cuddle with the animals. There are some mysteries.

AuroRa: That is how it is typically within an organic Universe and how we were. Yes, when you are looking at it in an inverted A.I. planetary sphere, then it is predatory because the Archons have inverted it into that. In the lowest dimension of this third dimension, there is a cycle of balance in animal life, if that is what you are asking. If I may, I want to go back to what we were discussing. Our Universe was oh, wow, just magnificent. The light and the dark, the organic of it was just glorious and the balance. The beauty of it. I read what you once said, Laura, "That the light impregnates the darkness and that is how we create from alchemy."

Laura: Oh my gosh, yes. The seeds of our higher consciousness fall into the creator of the womb, the soil and it generates life. If we aren't conscious about the things that we are allowing in, we might miss out on the greatest divine energies that are our true divine inheritance to embrace and generate into this physical realm. That is why this mind control and social engineering is recognizing that. They are like, oh, we can just pull them away and distract them through all these different tactics. Instead of being aligned, they are enabling the very thing that they don't want. And they are battling the very thing they don't want. That was my point, that true organic light and dark are very different from the polarity of the light and dark that we are being presented with. This is what you do in your work and practice. You say it better than I can, but I appreciate you remembering me saying that.

AuroRa: That is beautiful. I often use that when I am teaching. So we talked about how the Archons invaded our Universe by using negative technology. They used looking glass technology. That's what they do. They actually do this in not just our Universe, but in many others, unfortunately. They watch through looking glass technology and then they figure out how to pierce through the auric fields of the Universes. The Archon father, Belos, is actually the father of this Archon Universe who decided to split himself from Source, removing the Love-Light from within him. Once he did that, it spread like a virus to his entire Universe. All of his Universe became clones of him, of this inverted missing Love-Light and then they became artificial intelligence. That is the father of the Archon Universe that all of these Archons are coming in from.

Laura: Would you say that's the demiurge that some people are talking about?

AuroRa: I'm not familiar with what you're talking about.

Laura: It's exactly what you're describing. Yeah, there are always going to be certain labels and names that people give things. But it sounds exactly what you are talking about. A lot of people blame the feminine so much. Blame Eve, blame Sophia, it's like the mothers have been so… yet she is the creatrix. How do you process all of this?

AuroRa: Yes. A lot of these people who are blaming the mothers, are definitely compromised themselves. They are a host to something. It could be an Archon, a Reptilian, you name it. There are many different races whether organic or inorganic. They are basically inside of people controlling them. When you have people like that, they are just compromised. It doesn't matter. They can say whatever they want. The reason why they go after Divine Mother energies is that she is the essence of this Universe. If you go after the actual essence of this Universe, who created this Universe, then you can pollute and taint the rest of her Creations. And, that is how they do their black magic. It's the easiest way they spread their black magic, and if they can get people to believe this, it creates a negative timeline. All of the false things that they are sharing, these people who would be sharing something like this, they are just creating negative timelines and really deteriorating what we are trying to create - organic timelines.

Laura: Would you say that they create these facades to target well-intentioned people to think that, oh, if you join this organization, or you donate to this organization, or you join this church, you are making the world a better place. When actually there is this dark underbelly to it all that is taking advantage of well-intentioned people, who care about their family and wouldn't otherwise be polarized, or religious, if they didn't feel like it would make them a better person. To see people who are good-natured being duped like this…what are your thoughts on that?

AuroRa: They are direct attacks. Whenever someone comes after another through words, through a video, through whatever they are doing, they are compromised as I said, and they are going after the person who is spreading the light. Because, of course, too many people are waking up. Often, as we say, everything is backward. Jesus went through the roughest times, when he was in his times. As we know, they tried to control him and tried to turn everybody against him as well. Every single Ascended Master with strong Love-Light has gone through this when they were trying to awaken people. Those people who do not understand these strong beings of Ascended Master Light, it is just that there is control over them. Perhaps there are black magic bindings on their souls. Maybe they have sold their soul away. Maybe there are technologies in them. There are so many different things. Maybe their soul was UFO abducted and they created clones out of them. These clones that I was talking about, did begin organic at some point in time and space. They took them and they successfully removed the Love-Light from them, which is basically breaking every Sacred Law of our Universe. That is what these things are. They are fractured souls that they stole and then successfully removed the Love-Light from them by inserting artificial intelligence. Let's go into that. Because when they invaded Earth, by the agreement of these leaders, what happened was…their goal was not to kill us off. The reason why they don't want to kill us off is that they need our bodies. They need hosts.

Laura: Do you think that there is a certain death where the soul leaves the body to the point that it is almost like a death, and the container is being ruled by the A.I.?

AuroRa: Yes. I'll talk about that in a minute. So they want to keep the human body alive. All this entire time, they have been practicing all of these decades, inserting this Covid-19 vaccine into human life, to see how far they can develop it. Now, going back to the different alien races that live here. There is an abundance of infinite races. You can say that this is a jackpot for them. I have a client who was part of the MILAB experiment and he regained his memories back. They had this client logged in to a technology that could just scan him and see exactly where he was from, who was his Higher Self, and they knew that, for example, this was an Angelic being. So, that is what they have been doing. By retrieving our DNA through our blood samples since we were born, they know exactly who is who and what. That is how they gang up on people through psychic, and energetic attacks, because they already have all the logs (data) in their systems. It's like, this person is an Arcturian, and this person is an Angelic being. This person is a fractal of the Divine Father. This person is a fractal of so and so. Once they have that, they put all the people around them who are able to be compromised, who are not in their hearts, who are service to self. They start compromising them. They start inserting all sorts of things.

Laura: Like the super soldiers, the clone wars. Sorry, I didn't mean to interrupt, but right?

AuroRa: Right. So they want to keep us alive here, and the reason why is that if they kill us off, how are they going to have their army? I'm going to explain that. This whole time, they have been experimenting with this Covid-19 vaccine. They got it to the point, through their experiments, they were having greater success. Say there were ten humans that they were experimenting on. Usually, or typically, about seven or eight of them would pass away because this vaccine is a direct A.I. Archon virus. It goes in and takes over the soul of the body, and all these different things that you guys are seeing. We are even seeing it in the physical. So they have taken over the body at that point. Once they have taken over the body, it is theirs. It's their soldier. Whoever didn't die off, are basically their soldiers. They have technology that they are ready to turn on the minute that they start 5G, to start controlling these people, so that they can further attack the lightworkers, the black sheep. Right, they call us the black sheep. But 5G really needs to come online so that they can activate this A.I. virus inside of them and make them into their soldiers. But we are not going to allow that, are we? Because that is why you and I are here. That is why we are so brave.

Laura: Yes. I know that, that is exactly why we are here. Please go ahead.

AuroRa: The people who survived the Covid-19 vaccine, are the people who have integrated it. Do you guys understand what I am saying? They integrated that into their DNA, and now they are this A.I. clone, Archon, or whatever you want to call it. They are artificial intelligence merged with organic, in some form. And, this creates multiple timelines for them. They could become a gray, a negative polarized Reptilian, a clone. Like these clones, that's what they were before they became these dark, missing Love-Light, things.

Laura: Can I just interject for a second? Like somebody who may have been put in front of a TV screen their whole life, or childhood, and just grew up on all sorts of matrix grooming tactics, but they are immune to it? I know there's a movie called "Divergent," there are a lot of individuals who even if we are exposed to it, it's not going to work. That override frequency is going to turn it around. We just want and hope for greater numbers. I have a real hard time with movies. That's why I just watch documentaries.

AuroRa: Say out of those ten, those seven who passed away from the Covid-19 vaccine could be the divergent ones, the ones who resisted against the A.I. What this A.I. is doing, is trying to retrieve its light and its soul. Remember when talked about in previous videos, how the soul is not in the body after injecting the Covid-19 vaccine, however it is still always connected through an energetic umbilical soul cord. So all of those beings, the ones who didn't survive it, are the ones who were too strong in their Love-Light, too strong in service to others, and they could not survive the A.I. invasion in them. So, that is why they passed away. They would not become this android thing. The people whose DNA was able to morph with the A.I., they are just waiting for them to activate them. What happens is they are carriers of this Archon A.I. virus. This is actually being shown now physically. For four years we have been finding tentacles, spiders, and A.I. in people, through A.U.R.A. Hypnosis Healing sessions. And, it begins with vaccinations at childhood, right. We've been finding this in people's energy bodies, but now we are actually seeing this physically. So two years later, finally, after they have been injecting this Covid-19 vaccine into people, we are finally seeing it here. You can actually watch the 'Stew Peters' show on Rumble. The doctors and the people he has on, what they are showing on his show, we have been finding it in people, and their Higher Selves have been self-healing them this entire time. We know what that tentacle thing is, the beginning of the Archon virus, which multiplies and spreads into the entire body. And, then it goes in and attaches to the neurological system that then changes them into this A.I. soldier thing.

Laura: Genetically and behavior-modified individuals.

AuroRa: Exactly. Somewhere in there, it is still organic, but their soul is locked away.

Laura: It's kind of like the moon. The artificial aspects of the moon. It's like an alien base, and has so many artificial components. It's connected to the Saturn Moon matrix thing. But like we heal within ourselves; don't these celestial bodies connect with our organs and our consciousness? We are not at the mercy of them! We can change our frequency. Like pantheons too. It's like we are not disinherited from our parents or the pantheons. We are able to change the script because the script sucks. If the script sucks, step up and do something to change the script. This is what I love about you so much. Oh my God. Because that is what you are doing. Anyway, I didn't mean to keep interjecting. Keep going.

AuroRa: Thank you, Love. I love you with all that I AM, as the world loves you. Actually, the Universe.
Laura: That's nice (smiling). I've got to learn to love myself. Anyway, keep going with what you are saying.
AuroRa: So that is their diabolical plan, turning us against each other. By sacred laws, they can't kill us. They do have technology so advanced that they can actually end worlds within a blink of an eye. But, they have to abide by these laws, because they cloned into these vessels that have sacred laws. So that's why they did the virus, to turn people against each other. And then genocide for the people who remain organic, who stay resistant, who don't get the A.I. Archon virus into them. Now, as we know, it does not work out for them because we have been there. We feel it, we sense it, we know it. And honestly, they are making themselves look like fools right now. We know that we shift, we stand up for ourselves, we say no, and we stop vaccinating the children. These parents who are vaccinating their children are creating a hybrid. A hybrid race of children. What are we going to do with these hybrid children? They are going to be walking alongside us. What is happening is that some spouses got the Covid-19 vaccine, and some spouses didn't. They can actually just give it to the spouse, especially through sexual intercourse. That's how they continue their A.I. contamination. Some of these people who will have the Archon virus in them will be given it through relations like this. They want to infest the world, and the rest of us who said no. So, they can transmit it. That is why they are having the discharge, they call it spike-protein, but it's the A.I. nano. It is basically because they have that virus, and they are trying to spread their nano to the rest of us.
Laura: Doesn't it first start in our minds? If we lose our ability to be free thinkers, yeah, we are going to breathe in stuff that is going to pull us in. This is what I don't understand. Why do we have to create movement? How about sovereignty that is holding hands and giving high fives. Our differences, our diversities, and whatever we don't agree on is something we can harmonize. We are an orchestra. Imagine a squirrel trying to convince a dolphin to be a squirrel. Or a violin to convince a trumpet to be a violin. Diversity is one of the greatest things of the race, I feel. Then there is the weird part of it. I'm trying to stay inspired. Do you feel this was all necessary for the greater awakening, or do you feel kind of kicked in the gut, questioning what is going on right now? How are you processing all this right now?
AuroRa: This is rough. At this point we are at the end of this 26,000-year cycle, right? It basically ended, and was rebirthed in 2012, and we are overdue. I don't feel that it was necessary because these are organic souls being compromised and eaten up by this Archon Universe connection. Because once they got that virus in, that is all they needed to do, just get it to that one person in our Universe. Or that one whatever way, and then it spread. And, we didn't know how to handle it. All these beautiful races from all the dimensions were freaking out. They didn't know what fear was. They didn't know any of this because it wasn't a part of our Universe. In many forms, even in the higher dimensions, we are seeing it here, we are living it again, we are mirroring it again and we are pulling ourselves out of it. No, I don't agree that it needed to be necessary. However, I do also see how much it has awakened the world, and how much it has raised the vibration and the light on Earth for those who are opposing it. I do see the urgency in wanting to shift consciousness, and the need to have a collective choice. Like, "What are we going to do? These people are now waking up. We are trying our best." Even though for example President Donald Trump didn't come into the presidency, he couldn't because all of this needed to happen in some form, to awaken the collective. Well, not all of it. I absolutely do not agree with creating A.I. hybrid children, but what needed to happen has happened in some form organically. It's a hard question to answer. I'm pro-keeping everything organic within our Earth, and to help souls save themselves. Did I answer that okay?
Laura: Beyond. To a certain extent, we are all hybrids, but it is like we have twelve strands and beyond DNA capacity, and a lot of it some might call E.T. genetics. I mean like why does it have to be foreign? Why can't we work with it to the point that we understand, this is a part of our greater multidimensional existence? I just feel like there is a lot of disassociation from who you are, and what you are made of, hate it, love it, do this, do that, and it's like whatever.
AuroRa: The only way to place beautiful, multiple races together was that they needed to go into a simulation. Back then we didn't call it a holographic simulation, rather it was an agreement of the

Universe. It was a school, right? But, it was crystalline, it was organic. We would just go through our grade level and ascend out. Go to the next grade level and ascend out. That is when we started to see that souls were really profoundly growing. But what happened with the fall of Atlantis, is that once they got the Archon virus into our Earth, it spread as a virus would. Then it kept us trapped, not being able to graduate. And, the recycling of our light, similar to the Matrix movie, recycling us over and over and over. What they are trying to do is create inverted timelines within us. That's how they keep us trapped. So clients through A.U.R.A. Hypnosis Healing, go in and start healing that inverted timeline. I've seen people healed from blindness, from any virus or illness that you can think of. People who are literally six feet and ninety pounds, dying, I have seen them self-heal themselves. This is what is empowering about this, is that I am no one's savior and I am no one's guru. They go in, they talk to their Higher Self and benevolent beings and they exponentially heal rapidly. I've seen people who couldn't walk without a cane, and they walk out of my office, already in the cab before remembering they forgot their cane. It's just amazing. A person heals in one week from blindness. It's about finding the inversions within us, and we heal them through safe hypnosis. It's important to mention that there are also inverted hypnosis practitioners. The majority of past life regressions are compromised and they are soul reapers. Once they go into your field, they will insert things into you. I have so many people come to me who have been compromised by these healers themselves. The healers went in and changed their timelines and inserted inorganics into them. They claimed they were healers, but they were not.

Laura: Yes, I have to add that some of the worst attacks were from people who claimed they were healers. It feels like anything that we are hit with, we have a decision in that moment to make. Are we going to submit to tyranny, complacency, obedience, or are we going to rescue our treasures and amplify these treasures that these challenges are pushing us to reclaim? I mean, I feel very disturbed about what we are all going through. It's nothing that I haven't known about, but in the face of it, we have a choice. Maybe the small little piece of the free will that we still have, that our perceptions, and our reactions, we have control over.

AuroRa: If you really understand timelines, then you understand that with every choice you are making you are creating timelines. So value, honor, yourself in the greatest power that you are, because you are the timeline birther. Every choice that you make has to be the best organic, benevolent choice that you are making. It doesn't matter whether it is little or big. Make them the best within your heart, that is how you keep yourself on the path, and how you keep releasing yourself out of the inverted two/third world split. That is what we are here to do, beautiful souls like us. The listeners, these people who are standing up and continuing to hold that Love-Light. I once had an A.U.R.A. regression where Mother Mary had to watch her child, her son, Yeshua/Jesus the most beautiful soul, being crucified. She went through the whole process of it, his crucifixion. It touched my heart, because what she said as they were putting nails in him, hanging him on the cross, she said, "Oh my God. That is what he was here to do. He was teaching us that no matter what, to the very end he held his Love-Light! He held his light." She said, "That is key. We don't realize how powerful our Love-Light is. To the very end with his last breath, he held the Love-Light no matter the violence, or what they did to him, he held it." We must remember to hold it in that manner, as well, no matter what. We are the Yeshua's now.

Laura: It was very metaphorical to the programmings, the ego attachments, to what we think is reality and going through that death-rebirth transformation cycle, alchemical cycle. To me, it is an initiation that none of us can escape. But when we are not willing to go through the initiation and we give it over to somebody else to define it for us, you know we kind of step out of alignment with a great opportunity. It's a distraction to me. Is that kind of what you are saying? That is what I'm feeling about what you are saying about all of this stuff right now.

AuroRa: Exactly. That is exactly what I am saying. This transmission, this video today was extremely important for the collective, because of what was shared, because what is going on now is you understand. Once you understand, you can counter it with the organic. You really understand! It is like you have a thorn stuck in you and you can't understand it. You can't find the thorn, you can't get it. But now you understand what the thorn is. It is this inverted plan that they are trying to roll out, and now you know. You go to a family gathering and everyone is hating you because you are the only one who doesn't have the Covid-19 vaccine, because they are controlled. They've become those soldiers, and they are not organic anymore. So really, just going into our hearts. Yes, we are humans, but only allowing the most organic and the most loving frequencies around us constantly. Because when we have people like that around us, they are going to continue to pull us down. The reason why we are stuck in these inverted cycles is that, the families that chose the Archon virus, the ones that we have been stuck with every single life, in whatever incarnation cycle they decided, they were going to become this Archon infested entity. Then they murdered you, and the next life they burned you to death, and in the next life, they raped you. These same exact people. You are stuck in the same exact simulation over and over with these same exact people who have harmed you. That is why it is important to release these people, so that you can no longer be part of that inverted assimilation of them, that they are trying to play over and over.

Laura: Wow, that is so beautifully put. It is so crazy when all of that stuff hits. The most vulnerable ages of our life are when you are a child and it's like you don't know, but you do, because you are an incarnated soul. There is a point when you are like you want to rape me, and you are like, no, you are not going to get away with that. I sort of feel forgiving, because it's like that is all they know. I can defend myself. At certain times along the journey maybe I couldn't. I don't know, I'm not trying to recall the memories. These people are crying out and they are taking it out on people in very violent and vicious ways. I'm just hoping for this greater healing, where it's like 'I forgive you.' This division is going to perpetuate if we don't . . . I don't know if I can process this. I don't know if I have the answers. Yeah, you know you try to tell your parents and they are like, no. Everyone has their story. Most of us are very traumatized. I feel like, if we all joined together to share and work with each other, that is the greater strength that is going to rise out of the ashes of this b.s., this trauma, this abuse, this old paradigm model of these Cabal, Rockefellers. We have each other, and I am so grateful for that. I've got to tell you guys that most of the time you guys give me so much strength and I hope I give that back in return. We have a lot of trauma. But when you have been called to play this role right, how can we not experience some of these emotions right now? They are hurting our children, and it is not okay.

AuroRa: Thank you. There is an abundance of videos, over 350 YouTube videos and of course the book and everything that we do, we do it with the greatest love, honor, and respect for all that we are creating. It truly has been an honor to be here with you on 'Cosmic Gaia,' sharing this very heart and soul activating awareness for us, so that we cannot feel disempowered, not feel victimized. So that we can understand the truth behind what is really there, and that they have been programming us. So that we can become the true light warriors that we are, and we can resist, we can be the opposition, the true missions that we are meant to be here. Because, now we know the truth, and you can't trick us anymore.

Laura: It's an incredible book, and everything that she has put out is absolutely amazing. That was so beautifully put.

AuroRa: It's time for us to be organic. Let's start removing ourselves from those false inverted matrix pods.

Laura: Totally, right. Yup, we're doing it and it's being done and it's... I don't assume anything based on something that is external. I feel it within us, what we are creating within our own divine sovereignty, and ability to connect with one another. I look forward to creating more of this, and I love you.

AuroRa: I love you, honor you, thank you, and respect you. Thank you to everyone here, who was part of this, and for supporting Laura, because she does so much for humanity, the collective. This is such an easy way to support her and her hard work.

Laura: I would rather everyone support you guys, but if you want to support me, great! We'll stick together. Love you. Have a good night.

END OF SESSION

THE FINAL BATTLE - GALACTIC HISTORY OF THE MULTIVERSE

With the deliverance of this transmission, we fully understand how such an horrendous act of human against human can occur, as World War II from 1939-1945. We now know that this war began, when the alien clones landed upon Earth, in the late 30's and early 40's. When doing so, they went straight to work to test out how easily they could turn humankind against one another. Ultimately, resulting in the beginning of their grand plan of "The New World Order," which is being acted out now, with the assembly of the Covid-19 vaccine injection into the world.

Before the clone invasion the negative polarized entities' hold was not as potent and their agenda was not as clear; the agenda being, the how and when their tyranny would fully reign over Earth. By entering our Earth's dimension, this allowed for a more organized plan of action against humankind; the key being they were finally inside now, in the actual third dimensional realm of the physical. Multidimensionally, from outside of Earth, from their dimension or planet, entities typically bridge into Earth through infringing and attaching to human consciousness and vessels; the *human* being their forms of transportation, as we are portals of light ourselves. Through the humans' consent, these aliens and negative entities cause all sorts of havoc and chaos against humans and animals, through organized tyranny, religion, and government, as we have seen throughout the history of Earth, beginning from Leumuria and Atlantis, to the present. Their anchoring into the world leaders in that time and space, gave the Archons and negative polarized entities the strength that they did not have before. Though, their weakness grows daily in the now, as the light grows on Earth, and as we regain our sovereignty and divine power, individually and collectively.

These clones influenced the German race through Adolf Hitler, invading Poland and attacking the Jewish descendents spread throughout these surrounding sacred lands. Once the world's rulers agreed, their first plan was to go after one of the strongest bloodlines of Earth that carried the Christ Consciousness within them, as Yeshua and the Essenes did. The Jewish people are some of the descendants of The Essenes, which were the descendents of the Atlanteans. In Chapter 7, "The Essenes" they give us the honor of explaining this further. It was important for these aliens to acquire this DNA that is carried through the collective Jewish bloodline, in order to minimize the crystalline light within those who might hold the most, and so that the sacred Universal Law of Jerusalem, the "Law of Vibration," the throat chakra, could be first contaminated with black magic, directly by the potence of the sacred law of Germany, the "Law of Polarity," where the positive and negative polarities maintain in balance. This was directly done by turning these two ethnicities against one another. Causing an imbalance to these two most important chakras and sacred laws, so that negativity could ripple out to the collective, allowing an easier penetration to their future plans of compromising the other sacred chakras and laws of our Earth and Universe. In Book 1, Chapter 24 '13 Keys - Sacred Laws of the Universe', we spoke in depth of these sacred keys and laws of our Universe.

During War World II, the experiments of the Covid-19 vaccine began on their test subjects, the Jewish people. There are testimonials from some of the survivors of the Holocaust, explaining that in ghetto camps, German scientists experimented on them with injections and several types of inhumane procedures involving the use of experimental chemicals. In Chapter 6, 'The Illuminati In the Holocaust' we will learn first hand of some of these experiments. In these times they were beginning to test out how successful they could be at making humans into super soldiers, or as Laura said, "Genetically and behavior-modified individuals." Testing was necessary to see how far along the human DNA genome organically had crystallized, and how to break it apart at its natural barriers with a replacement, or integration, of the nano A.I. that the Covid-19 vaccine carries. In order for the Covid-19 vaccine to work in the future, they first needed to densify the light, by altering it in the human children with immunization and booster shots, causing illness, disorders, and diseases through the decades. The ultimate goal was to cloud, block, and shut down the natural abilities that reside within the psyche of the human brain and consciousness. The oldest children are now in their seventies, sixties, fifties, forties... down to the current age of toddlers and newborns. The immunization shots were some of the beginning insertions of metals into humans. Other ways they did so were through mercury metals in our teeth, as cavity fill-ins, chemtrails in the air, and adding chemicals into our foods when processing them. By the beginning insertions of what is not organic into a human, such as metals, little by little, it allowed for humankind to become the density to the closest possible outcome of being a matching vibration, or host to the nano infested A.I. Covid-19 vaccine; thereby bringing a higher success of integration versus loss of life. Which is what we are seeing now spread throughout the world, with those who have chosen the path of intaking the Covid-19 vaccine.

Though, as we now know, many are [7]dying suddenly, many more so than we realize, or are being told of, because of the illness and disease that is manifested from the Covid-19 vaccine. The medical industry is falsifying the cause of deaths for the people who die from the Covid-19 vaccine. There are videos surfacing which show people most often looking at their phones, and suddenly reacting as if they are fighting something that is invisible; they turn to one side and fall over, spasming, and there is nothing that any supposed medical procedure can do to stop them from suddenly dying. What we are seeing in these videos is the spirit possession, a soul collector taking over their spirit, when the technology that is inside gets switched on through the Covid-19 vaccine injection. The government has begun their experimentations upon humanity for those who have been vaccinated, and thereby linked to 5G and their negative technologies.. They are beginning their human trials by turning on these mind control machines, those who are closest to these 5G towers react in the manner we are seeing, cannot hold the hypnotization of these machines, and instead die suddenly. Those who can hold the hypnotization instead act upon what the machines make them do as horrendous, violent crimes that they normally would not do in their right state of mind.

I have been shown the beginning of what will happen when 5G comes online. Once the technology that is connected to 5G is turned on, the nano receivers within the bloodstream and neurological system of the people who harbor the Covid-19 vaccine within, will be activated and some will become super soldiers, susceptible to programmable orders, at various levels of control. Not all will be fully susceptible; each will have different levels of nano power over them. Which is why it is important that we, in the now, continue to communicate to these people, who are our brethren, to look into beginning their natural paths of self-healing, and removing these heavy metals within.

We all have seen glimpses throughout Earth's History of these potentials of what vaccinators can become. The military has been performing experiments on people through UFO abductions, without their knowing. These clones have technologies that were given to the military, which erases or alters memory through the touch of a button, but first they must place physical or energetic implants and technologies into the people to make them controllable. Again, this is what we are seeing through the Covid-19 vaccine. Some of these people who they have tested their Covid-19 vaccine on before it was launched publically, are those who we have heard of that have gone insane, perpetrating mass shootings at schools or malls. These people were controlled by these experiments, and this 'top secret' part of the military was just acting upon their test subjects, to see how well they could be controlled mentally, and neurologically. In this time and space, I have had interactions with people whose Covid-19 vaccine got turned on through 5G. They enter a form of daze, and can no longer control their actions or words. When they come to, they might have memory lapses of what happened. We are starting to see these unconscious, uncontrollable waves of action in our population, through heightened road rage, anger towards those who do not choose to take the Covid-19 vaccine, and violent acts at concerts costing peoples' lives.

Did you ever wonder why it seems like just about all technology and products are 'Made In China?' Now we understand why that is. China can be seen as one big brain, which manufactures technology. The crucial key being in comparison, that the Chinese population is over four times the amount of the United States. China's government is a one-party communist dictatorship, in which the Communist Party of China has a monopoly on power over its people. The Chinese revolution against

---

[7] Watch 'Covering Died Suddenly' under Rumble.com or Odysee.com for more on those who are dying suddenly.

communism was from 1945-1949, and at the point of the Chinese Civil War's end, it became the one-party communist government in 1949. Do you see how all of these important times in Earth's history fall closely within each other's timeframes of the A.I. Alien invasion? One big diabolical master plan, which has been unfolding, one year at a time. It is one big playbook downloaded by the Archons into the minds of the clones, and the world leaders. These characters are just playing it out, one play at a time.

Let's talk about the spike protein discharge that the Covid-19 vaccines cause. Our skin is a living organ, which is like a sponge itself. Not only does it soak in its surroundings, it too expels out what's inside. It is as if our skin breathes. What is within us will breathe out through our entire skin, and it is important we allow our skin to breathe, and that we do not layer it with artificial lotions, shampoos, or synthetic polyester, or plastic clothing that is infused with chemicals. If we do, this can stop some of the toxins within us, from releasing out through our pores. Therefore, if the respiration of the skin is being blocked by a layer of a lotion full of chemicals, we will not be able to detox. This is what is occurring with the people who have the Covid-19 vaccine injected into them; the organic parts of the body are trying to self-heal and push out the replicating nano and heavy metals from within all parts of the body. So, this is the discharge, which was injected into them of the A.I., and which is contagious to others. As it pours out of the vaccinated person, it is artificially intelligent, and it is programmed to seek and attach to organic living matter within its surroundings. Once it attaches, it is programmed to morph and replicate itself, within the organic warmth and matter it is inside of. Understanding that this is what we meant when we began to explain in the interview that the soul energetically ejects out of the body once the Covid-19 vaccine enters, as the soul is protecting themselves, and it is no longer a vibrational match to the now partial android body. Because of all the nano-tech within, the body is now a hybrid, part organic and part A.I. However, the soul will always remain energetically connected to the body through a lifeforce umbilical soul cord. This eternal bond can never be severed. If the vaccinated person is living with an animal companion, or you are living with this person, you would be that organic living host that it can attach to. [8]I have been told through my clients that many animal companions are becoming ill, or dying shortly after their owner received the Covid-19 vaccine, some only just days after.

There are many parents, or healthcare associates, who have been reporting through the underground media, the true media, that there are heightened cases of miscarriages or premature births. By either receiving the Covid-19 vaccine themselves or by being around people who have, pregnant women are having difficulty carrying babies full term. Why is it that this nano discharge is going after other people's reproductive systems? Part of the programming of the nano is to target the DNA within all life forms, including those who have yet to be birthed or created. That would include the sacred eggs within the ovaries of the Divine Feminine, and semen of the Divine Masculine. Within its cultivation stages, it is targeting the DNA chromosomes that intermingle together creating a fetus, already inserting A.I. into it. Why the children? It is because they are our future, the future organic timelines of our Earth. If they alter lifeforms before they are born, they think that they can alter our organic timelines into becoming inverted timelines instead. What they do not know is that since the two/third world split, as explained in the previous chapters, has come into fruition, they can no longer invert our organic timelines. As *our* organic blueprint timelines will, from now on, be anchored in through the organic part of the two/third worlds. They can perhaps make their inverted timelines of control in the inverted world that people choose to live within, however, not in ours anymore, if we do not allow it. Their inverted timelines are just not a matching vibration to our organic being. The way that we know we are living our most organic timeline, is felt and seen within our lives, when everything begins to just flow within all that we do, decisions become easier, ideas become manifested, and we enter a realm of knowing and feeling that we are infinitely safe and protected.

---

[8] On Rumble.com and Odysee.com all our extra sensitive content is delivered weekly, videos such as "Artificial Wombs", "How to live among those with the Covid-19 Vaccine" and "Covering Died Suddenly."

We are now seeing Hybrid children at their infant and toddler stages, depending on when they were born, and when their parents were injected with the Covid-19 vaccine. These children are abnormal; some have solid black eyes, and are experiencing heightened motor skills, being able to hold their heads up the minute they are born, and to stand or walk at only two-three months of age. When you look into their eyes they feel empty and cold, as if they are no longer organic human babies. Instead they are consciousnesses of Gray alien babies or a new form of hybrid babies, by the insertion of Covid-19 vaccine metals and A.I. fusion into their physical DNA. The reason why there is an increase in miscarriages and premature births, is because of this example. Once the parent is injected with the Covid-19 vaccine, the child that is cultivating, or is about to be born, has to decide quickly. Will they allow themselves to be compromised in hopes that someday their vessel can heal, and if not, they quickly have to exit, causing a miscarriage. Those who choose to stay in the fetus, would become part A.I. They can have a resemblance to a Gray baby, who when coming out of their genetically engineered pods that they are made in, display the same type of motor skills. As the Gray babies emerge from their pods, they are able to instantly walk, and move as a fully developed human being would. There can also be illness or disease when the Covid-19 children are born; there is much we do not know of right now of other possibilities. Through our forms of channels, we have been speaking live on these sensitive, but very important topics. In Book 3, we go further into the E.T. race "The Grays." Children have been a prized possession for the dark entities to acquire, in order to perform their inverted experiments. And, the parents of our times who chose the Covid-19 vaccine for themselves, or their children, are consenting in the open, to these experiments consciously. Fooled they are. They have forgotten that *they* are the guardians of their children. Tricked into believing that the Covid-19 vaccine is a form of remedy or protection.

Let's talk about how these clones work. Because our Earth is in the third dimension, these clones were able to be a matching vibration, to enter through a dark gateway/portal. Scientifically and genetically speaking, the clones have bypassed the sacred laws of death and rebirth. Through the experiments of the Archons, what they have done is taken a consciousness of a lifeform that they acquired through their wars, or planet invasions, and have multiplied it by cloning it. In other words, duplicating an original soul into multiples through science and technology. However, as we know, organic souls are beautifully created by Source, and there will never be one soul exactly the same. All souls are uniquely created and carry their own crystallized signature. So, what they are doing to one soul, making it into multiples by artificial intelligent experiments, is horrendous to think of. These clones will never be an organic match to the original soul, and will malfunction in some form. What soul or souls have they done this to? How long have these consciousnesses been living like this?

To become a clone, it would feel as if a soul is being elongated as elastic, stretched out thinly. To the point that it no longer would recognize who they are, or once were. As when you stretch out a piece of gum, the gum becomes thinner and thinner. Therefore, the soul becomes so stretched out that in some form it is beginning to fade or disappear. What is left over of these pieces of consciousness would be minimal, and only a form for the Archons to use at their will. These clone bodies begin to deteriorate after some time, as we have seen hints of this through people who are placed in public positions that begin to malfunction in front of us. Which is why these cloned consciousnesses need to find a human host body to enter and attach to, in order to remain in the third dimension. Their clone bodies seem as if they are human from the outside, however on the inside they are androids, with technology and wiring, moving all parts of their bodies. The consciousness of the stretched out clone is inside the wiring, of what you would call the brain of this abomination. Archons need what was once organic, the cloned souls, to stay and play their twisted games in our Universe. As *they* are not a matching vibration to our Universe, being that they are soulless and artificial. We know that the Love-Light within these clones is locked away by dark magic bindings, or that it has been removed in some form. However, the original blueprint of the soul will always remain, no matter what atrocities of experiments have been forced upon a soul.

We are seeing the beginning of these experimental stages in our world, by scientists who are downloading human consciousness into computers, making a digital blueprint of the signature DNA of the soul of an alive, or deceased person. This is the beginning of cloning humankind. Reminding us why it is that we need to guard our DNA with all that we are. This should never be allowed to be done, ever, in the name of science, or whatever name they hide behind.

These clones and other negative aliens on Earth, like to play a game that they are no longer here. Which is amusing, as when you think about it, how could that be? If they were really gone, then Earth would have reached the high enough light and vibration to finally shift into the two/third world split by separating from one another, and entering back into the organic fifth/sixth dimension fully. Instead we are seeing the opposite; flat out tyranny, with all their mandates, masks, and Covid-19 vaccines. It should be common sense, to feel and know that they are still here; however it is not, to many on Earth. We see these implications through the unawakened, the spiritual and UFO communities. Many don't believe that entities exist, or they are simply accepting and following false agendas that say they have all been removed from Earth. For example, a common theme that occurs often is that a new spiritual, or UFO community leader is up and coming; they rise so quickly in numbers and followers, because the programs, or channels they are communicating through, are amplifying their views. They know who is channeling false inverted timelines and who is not, because ultimately the Archons run these shows. As we explained in the previous Chapter 4, 'Deep State Council Member', and the compromised channeler/reader.

In the UFO community, the guise that people can deliver transmissions through positive implants is being widely spread. Which is dangerous, because it begins a false trend for others to want to have an implant inserted as well, to do the same. What the Galactics, Ascended Masters, and our client's Higher Selves have always told us, is that benevolent beings can only channel, or communicate, through our hearts and through the organic versions of us. Therefore, a benevolent being could never be able to channel through a technology such as an implant, as it would not be a matching vibration to their infinite Love-Light. Only entities and negative aliens hide behind technology, and claim that they are positive. Again, this seems like common sense, however, it is not. As, many are being duped into believing that what these people who are communicating through, is legit and that it is assisting the world and Ascension. When in actuality, these public communicators, knowingly, or unknowingly, are working for these undercover dark forces. *They* need *us to* create negative timelines for them, as we are who hold this divine power. So, what better way for the Archons to put together a vast amount of people to believe these falsenesses? If people truly knew who was channeling through implants, or other negative polarized forms of communications, they would quickly run the other way.

Some of these people who channel through an implant, are actually channeling high councils of the Illuminati. The same ones that are overseeing "The New World Order." I have been shown that these entities who are downloading false knowledge into people who consent to it, are the leaders of pedophilic rings, and the darkest things that we are all standing up against. One must be extremely selective of who we choose to allow to become part of our reality, as then we are instead providing the light and energy that is needed for these negative transmissions of further oppression and control upon our future Ascension. Our children, our loved ones, and animal companions, are who are holding the Love-Light for us until we choose to snap out of these Archonic entrapments of false transmissions others deliver when listening to them. And, at times our loved ones are struggling to do so.

One thing that the Covid-19 plandemic has taught and shown us, is people's true colors. We have learned how quickly our friends and families can turn on us by segregating and disowning us when not conforming to taking the Covid-19 vaccine. A fast hard lesson, teaching us that one must cut cords quickly from these people, removing them energetically out of our lives completely. If we have learned to do this for some who we once thought were closest to us, why is it that we still listen to these false speakers who are so distant from us, who we hold no true allegiance to? The clues are there, but yet we still don't listen.

I was shown a quote from a well known spiritual worker who has been delivering transmissions for a long time to the public. This spiritual worker had posted in their social media group of thousands, an image belittling those who offer services for others who require implant removal, such as holistic self-healing modalities as A.U.R.A. Hypnosis Healing. The image's main focus point was a character which is known to cause laughter and is a joke to others, and what was quoted with this character was "Those who offer implant removal services most likely have implants themselves." It is one thing to not agree with others respectfully, but to make fun of and belittle others in this manner, as if it is a joke, that is bullying. And, still people follow and agree with this person, and the supposedly benevolent transmissions they are delivering to them.

More than ever, as the Earth continues to bifurcate energetically, people's true forms will become very apparent, and it is our choice if we want to see these signs or not. Will we continue to follow even after we recognize them? And if we recognize them, why do we still follow them? This is an example of how deeply rooted the programming of the third dimension is within our core. Why have we not learned to cut out these people we follow as well, just as we did to those who supposedly were our loved ones when they chose to be negatively polarized? Once more, selectively we must be with who we allow to deliver supposed knowledge to us. Is it an organic being you are listening to, or an Archon who is soullessly tapping into that person's consciousness? All that knowledge *it* has stolen by murdering beautiful people of all kinds of races of our Universe…

Don't forget the mission. We are not here to be fooled. We are here to hold the Love-Light, because this is how we become the example to awaken the world from the false illusion.

Book 1, was all about understanding that we are capable of self-healing, and the true Galactic History of our souls and our Universe. Now that you understand this, in Book 2 we take it to another level of truth and disclosure. In the chapters to come, we understand the Archon maker and *its* realms, so that we can remember how to remove its attachment from our Creation.

We are organic.
All that is not, will eventually transmute or fall away.
Will you transmute *it* out, or fall away with *it*?
~AuroRa 🖤

--------------<<>>--------------

6

THE ILLUMINATI IN THE HOLOCAUST

Session #133: Recorded in April 2019.
Aired on YouTube: April 10, 2019

In this online A.U.R.A. Hypnosis Healing session, Carmela finds herself in a gray room being experimented on...the Illuminati connection to this dark time of our history comes forth in this session. What was it like to live through this time in Earth's History? Discover how the trauma of that life follows her in her life now. Carmela's husband booked the session for her because of her deteriorating health. He is who is aware of our material, and listens to our channels. Carmela has never meditated, and is partially spiritually awakened. She only knows that she trusts her husband, which is why she is having the session done, upon his recommendation. During the interview process, before the past life regression session begins, Carmela mentions that when she asked her husband what A.U.R.A. Hypnosis Healing sessions were about, he replied, that he didn't think she was ready to know some of what could come up during the session. Once Carmela comes to, her reaction towards what was discovered during her session comes as a surprise. Amazing how Carmela discovers the deep rooted answers through her Higher Self connection, without ever knowing what's in store for her during the session.

-------------<<>>--------------

"They drag me to a bed that they strap me down. They are injecting me with things. It's burning, it hurts. I can see the tables, and the torturing devices."
~Carmela

-------------<<>>--------------

C: [Carmela] I see blackness.
A: [Aurora]: Only blackness?
C: I am starting a little light, and it's very black. I am going to it. It is getting bigger. I don't know why I see a gray building. It's like a big gray building, and it's like a stone building. I have short black hair. I am still a woman, but now I have grey clothes on, like prison clothes or slave clothes. My hair is very short. I just see this gray building, and I am cold (starts crying). I don't know why I don't have shoes on, but my feet are freezing.
A: Do you feel like you are younger or older?
C: Older, like a middle-aged person. I am really sad. I just keep trying to grab my hair. There's nothing there. It's just so short. There is nothing to hold. Everything is just really gray. I don't know what this gray building is.
A: Are there more people in there with you?
C: For now, I am in a room by myself. I can hear things, but it's just a room with no windows, no bed, just myself in this gray itchy clothing.
A: Do you feel like you are fed? Are you hungry?
C: Thin and very hungry..
A: Emotionally how do you feel?
C: Sad.
A: Why is it that you feel sad?
C: I feel very alone. I feel betrayed like I was tricked into this gray building. I was trying to get help, but was tricked. I feel like they are doing things to us that they shouldn't be doing, testing, torturing. I

feel beaten. I feel hungry, but I am not. I just feel like I don't want to be there.
A: *Look at yourself, and see if there is something that stands out.*
C: I just have some bruises. My feet, I don't know why they are so cold. I have bruises on my arm. I am really thin, and have really short hair. I feel maybe there is a marking on my arm, now that I am looking up more.
A: *What is it?*
C: It's like branding, like I was branded.
A: *What's the marking?*
C: It's numbers, like I am a cattle, I am somebody's property.
A: *What are the numbers?*
C: I see 6420-1266. That's all the numbers.
A: *Let's fast forward to when something important happens. What's going on?*
C: They drag me to a bed that they strap me down. They are injecting me with things. It's burning, it hurts. I can see the tables, and the torturing devices.
A: *Just be an observer, and just watch without feeling any of the discomfort of it. Tell me all the details you see all around you. Who is doing this to you?*
C: I see a lot of metal tables. It's very cold. I see a lot of needles, and surgery knives. I see the table they put you down on with straps for your feet, and they separate your legs to be apart. They strap down your arms as well with leather straps. It smells cold, damp, and mildewy. I can see just so much metal everywhere. The sink looks very dirty. I see a man who is very tall and blond with a white long lab coat.
A: *See if you see any designs on the lab coat or him.*
C: He is just very blond. He is tall, he is very pale white. He looks like he's enjoying himself, doing these experiments or torturing. He has black leather boots on, like combat boots. I can't see his pants though. His white lab coat covers down to his ankle. I can only see his hands. I see a pocket on his left side, he keeps a cigarette, a pen, and he has dark-framed glasses.
A: *When you look into his eyes, what do you sense from him?*
C: Honestly, I sense sadness, but also enjoyment. It's very conflicting, like he used to not like doing this, but now he does. His eyes are so blue. They are almost glowing. I am so cold.
A: *Higher Self, help her not feel cold.*
C: Shivering.
A: *You said that they were injecting something to you.*
C: Yes, in my arms.
A: *What are they injecting? Is there a color to the injection?*
C: It's clear, and then I saw blue liquid.
A: *How does that feel when it goes in, you are able to tell me how it feels without experiencing the pain.*
C: It burns through your whole body. You can feel it going through your veins. You can feel it burning, it goes into your arms, your feet, your toes. Your head feels like it is so hot, even though I know my toes are cold. Your head is burning. You try not to scream, but you are screaming. You just want to rip your face off, but you can't because they tied you down (crying). I see a woman now, maybe it is his assistant. She is really into it.
A: *Look into her eyes, are you able to recognize her soul?*
C: She is just really evil.
A: *Do you feel that you know her? Can you recognize her soul, by looking into her eyes?*
C: No. She seems not human. When you look into her eyes (starts sobbing) they are dead, like black, but you can see her eyes are very large. She is just watching intently, observing everything, and how I am reacting to every injection. She even puts water in my mouth with a towel. That's the only way I can get water. I don't like her. She seems to be controlling the guy. I try to fight. I can't. She seems just not human or possessed. She has nothing in her eyes to show that she is even alive.
A: *Do you feel a soul?*
C: I don't feel anything from her, just a lot of anger, a lot of hatred. She is blond, she has glasses. She has a very long lab coat as well. She is wearing a skirt. I can see her legs.

A: Are there any designs, anything that stands out on what she is wearing?
C: It's just very stale white, very stiff. Her hair is pulled up in a bun. She is thin, she is very pretty.
A: Is she young or older?
C: Younger like my age. She has very high heels on. She clicks when she walks. She keeps on going to the sink washing her hands a lot. I can just see the man. It's almost like a still picture. Everyone stops, he is just standing in front of a metal plate that has all of the tools, standing there in a "freeze frame." She is just at the sink. She is trying to wash her hands, it looks like blood. I don't know if that's from...I don't like it. I don't like this place. I don't know who these people are. I can hear people screaming, trying to ask for help "help me, help me, and why, why". That's it (starts crying).
A: Do you feel like you have been here a long time?
C: Yes. I want to help them. I feel so sad (continues crying) for them. I don't know why, but I don't feel sad for myself. I feel sad for the other people. I don't feel anything for myself. I want to help them so badly. I don't want them to suffer.
A: Besides these two, is there anyone else in the room?
C: Just myself, that's it.
A: How do the walls look?
C: They kind of look like the hospital, but it's a lot of metal pieces. The walls are dingy white, maybe it's an abandoned building. I can see mold on the corners by the door frames. It's not a clean place. I can see a drain on the floor. I think a lot of people died here.
A: Tell me what happens after they inject that into you? What else do they do?
C: They try the yellow injection. They taped my eyelids open, so you cannot close your eyes. They cut you in your arms. With that little scalpel knife, that woman likes to pierce your cheek with it. She is enraged, really strange. It is like she wants answers. I'm not giving them to her. I am definately being tortured for something that they want. I can see that now. Oh wow. She is doing anything to get me to talk. She is trying to cut my face. The scalpel is her favorite. She keeps demanding that man to do things. She slapped me, she slaps a lot.
A: What about the yellow liquid they put into you, how did that one feel?
C: So cold. It makes my whole body shiver uncontrollably, like you are having a seizure, but you are awake. It feels like an icicle, like your veins are turning into ice. She is cutting my boobs. She is making cuts, making me ugly. I don't care. I am not doing it. I just want those innocent people to not hurt anymore. I just wish that guy was strong enough to stop her. I feel like he wants to stop her. I think I might have had him a little wrong. At first I thought he was good and turned bad, but I feel like he feels sad for us. He used to like it, but he doesn't like it; it's not right. I feel like we are connected, after looking at him. I feel like we know each other, and we are connected. I don't know who she is. But him, I feel like we were lovers or something deep, friends, or even related, but we were very connected. Something happened to him, he changed.
A: You are able to go back in time, right before you came to this place. What do you see?
C: It's so green. Everyone is really happy. I have shoes on, brown Mary Janes. I have a skirt on, and a black turtleneck sweater. I have brown hair. It's not super long, it's to my shoulders. I can see a gravel road. I am holding books, like I went to school, or just learning.
A: Do you feel younger?
C: Yes, a little younger, maybe five years younger. Very happy. The sun is shining. The trees are blooming, there is grass. I feel a positive vibe here. I can see a small town with cute cottages. I am just walking on the gravel road. I can see that gray building, it wasn't gray, it was a white building. I walked past it. I seemed to walk past it everyday going home. I am not sure where I am coming from, but I am going home. I can see smoke coming out of people's chimneys. I see flowers on some roofs. It is so beautiful. I am really happy. I see flowers everywhere.
A: Do you feel like you are a child, a teenager or a young adult?
C: A teenager, a young adult. It's nice; the sun is shining, and it feels good on my skin. I am just walking past houses waving to people. They are on the yards raking, some people are checking the mail. Everyone is content. I am going home. I can smell cookies, something sweet. I think my mom baked something good.
A: Are you home now?

C: I am at the front, it's got a picket fence. It's a cottage, and has two steps to get inside. The door is round. I am very happy. I see a woman, it's my mom, and I kiss her. She is in the kitchen doing dishes. It feels so warm here, and very comfortable. My dad is on a rocking chair. I don't talk to him, just my mom. I have a lot of love, I hug her. My books, I put them on a brown wooden table. I go to my room, shut the door and lock it. I don't know why. I don't feel happy anymore. The kitchen was a little sad, but I am okay. I lay on my bed, and just keep looking out the window. I want to leave this house. It's not happy anymore.

A: What is that you were so happy about before? Why do you feel you are not happy anymore?
C: I saw my dad on the rocking chair. He is very angry. He knows I was talking with someone he doesn't want me talking to. He's just full of anger. I was talking to a boy. I am not allowed to talk to boys. I think he is going to beat me with his belt. I can see him get up off his rocking chair, and take his belt off. He's trying to get into my room. I was so happy, I thought he wasn't home. He was sitting next to a fire. I can feel it building and building, his anger, just building. My skirt is too short, and my hair is too long. I look like a slut, and he is so mad. I don't think I look like a slut, I look like a normal girl. He is trying to break down the door. He starts whooping me. He hasn't even told me why, and I am just screaming. My mom, she doesn't do anything(loud cry). She just sits there doing the dishes and cooking. I am begging for help. She is not helping. She is submissive to my dad. She knows better. I have welts all over my body. I want to leave, but I don't want to leave my mom. I have to leave. I hate it here. I want to jump out the window, and just run away.

A: Let's fast forward to see what happens next of importance, you are there now. What do you see?
C: I left. I am in a truck. I never came home. I was supposed to be home by now. My mom is probably worried, but I have to get out of there. I am not driving. I am on the passenger's side. Someone is driving, it's a man. I like him, like a brother, he is helping me.

A: Is he similar to your age?
C: Yes, a little older. Just a few years. Maybe right out of high school. We are driving this truck. We are trying to get out of the town, on the gravel road. We cannot see the town anymore. It is nighttime. I feel so bad. I just left my mom. I just left without saying anything. I have a lot of guilt, but I am happy that I am not there anymore. It's nighttime. The stars are so pretty. I hug him, and thank him. He leaves me there alone, and I am on a hill. I just started walking. I walk into trees. It is so dark though.

A: Is there any place you feel that you are trying to head to, that you know of, or are you just walking?
C: I am just walking, I don't know where I am going. I am not turning around. I just have to keep going forward. I am not cold, it's so nice out. It is very quiet, no wind. I am just in the woods.

A: Did you bring any supplies with you?
C: I am still in my skirt, my mary jane's, and my turtleneck, no supplies. I have nothing. I just keep walking. I see a house, and it is lit up, by itself. I knock on the door to see if I can spend the night. No one is answering, but it is lit. I am not sure what to do now. I might have made a mistake. I am scared. Maybe I should just go home, but I don't want to. I'd get in real trouble. I don't want to go home. Why did he leave me? I just see a black right now.

A: Let's go ahead and fast forward a bit to what happens next of importance.
C: Somehow, that same house that was lit, is my house. I go in, and it's my house. There are pictures of me and my boyfriend, not my husband. It's a very modest house. It's quiet in the woods. I don't see him at all. I have a lot of pictures of him, like I miss him. I am in my kitchen crying and washing my hands. I don't know why. It's very dark. There are just candles lit in the house. I feel very alone. I miss him so much. I don't know what happened to him (crying). I don't know why I miss him. He should be home. I feel so alone.

A: Let's see if we can discover why he is not home, and why you miss him?
C: I think something happened to him. I just know I miss him so much, like I can't live. I am so heartbroken. I need him.

A: Go ahead and leave this scene. Go to the scene right before this situation happens, before you end up in that gray room.
C: We are being dragged off a truck. It is so strange, the same truck my brother drove me. We are in the back, a bunch of us. He is there. We all have gray outfits on. I don't know how they got put on me, I was still in my skirt. They're forcing us. I am trying to fight, and run away from them on the

gravel road. He is with two big men, with helmets on, dragging us. I am trying to fight them, "no, no, no." He is very quiet. He is letting them. He looks like he is just okay with it. I don't know if they broke him, or he is at peace. I just keep looking at him, and he has his head down. He has his arms tied to the front, like he's arrested. I am fighting like a wild animal, trying to get these guys off. They are just dragging me, and they are laughing. They think it is funny.

A: Is he also wearing the gray outfit you are wearing?

C: Yes, he has pants on and a shirt. He has his head down. I didn't want him to go in there. They literally drag my heels on the ground, making marks. I go into that cell alone, just to try to open that door. Try to do anything to escape, but there is nothing you can do. I am just ready to fight.

A: How did you get on this truck? How did this happen?

C: (Starts sobbing) We were dragged from the house, our private house. We were dragged there. We were put on that truck. They dragged us out of there. They just tore it down, or someone kicked it open.

A: Are they saying why? What is the reason?

C: They just look so angry. I tried to run, but I couldn't. They were surrounding us. They look evil. We were in our own little house. They wouldn't leave us alone. There are like ten other people on that truck. They were all crying, there were little kids. He is sitting on the ground. I am petting his hair, and I tell him "It's okay. Everything is going to be okay. We will get out of here. We just have to work together. Okay?" He is just so worried. He looks like he is already so defeated. I kiss him, I hug him, I love him. "We are going to get out of this." That's the last time…I think they killed him. I hope not. It's strange, because I feel like we are in the house with all the pictures with him. I feel like the gray building was a memory, like it happened in the past. That's why I am so sad. It's weird, because I still have my Mary Jane's and my skirt. I am really sad.

A: When you were in the house, you still had your Mary Janes and the skirt, looking at the picture?

C: Yeah, even though I had the gray outfit on for a long time, like they gave it back to me. That is all I have. I don't have any other clothing. I don't have any food. I don't have anything, just those clothes.

A: Let's go back now, to where you were, back in that room, on the metal table. You are there now. What happens next, after they inject the yellow?

C: I feel like she is satisfied. I don't know what I said, but it was enough to make her smile. She makes me so sick to my stomach. They just basically undid the leather straps, and just let me go, like I was trash to them now. I just crawled back in the hallway. I am in pain. I am weak. I feel so defeated. I feel like I let everyone down. *A: Who did you let down?*

C: Everyone trapped in there.

A: Why?

C: I don't know. All I feel is guilt, that I let the people down. I can't see what I said, or what I did.

A: Go back to that moment, where you said what is it that you are not finding. What's going on?

C: They are just torturing me. They wouldn't stop. I just keep fighting. She just keeps grabbing me. She grabbed my boob really hard. She stabbed my face. She grabbed my jaw, and made me look directly into her eyes. She is so mean. She keeps asking me "Where is it? Where is it?" I say, "I am not telling you. I don't know where it is." I spit on her face. I made her so mad. She rips my shirt open. She just starts cutting my stomach. She makes him inject me more. I just keep screaming. I just don't care anymore. They bring him in. I just start crying. They know he is my weak spot. He looks so sad. I don't know what they did to him. He is not him anymore. He looks beat up, dirty, so skinny. I tell her, it's in the house. It's under our bed. I can see now it is a book. It is very important. It is leather bound. I cannot see the title, but I can see it under my bed. I have tons of pictures covering it. It has red flowers. It is in a box. I have other things surrounding it, like rocks for some reason, maybe stones. I feel like it is protected in a circle. These stones are in a circle protecting that box that has a book in it. I told her. She just smiles. They just let me go like garbage. She seems very satisfied, like it took a long time. She's been working at me for a long time. Now she has it. It's not the same. He doesn't even look at me. I don't know why I am here. They just let me go. They don't let anyone else go. I feel so guilty. I feel alone. I feel sad, like I ruined his life. If he had never met me he wouldn't be here.

A: Tell me how you leave?

C: They just kicked me out; shoved me out of there. I almost didn't want to go. I was trying to go back in. I feel like that's just my home now. I don't have a place to go. That's where my people are, and I need to save them. I need to know that they are okay. I need to try to save them. They just locked me out. They kicked me to the curb. I have my gray outfit on, and they just threw my clothes at me. Lock that door, slam it, and I just hear it "ching," just locking. I am sitting there, trying to bang the on the door to let me back in. Why do I want to go back in? It's horrible, but I have to. My people... I just grab my clothes. I walk slowly and barefoot. I put my shoes on, and walk back home. My place is destroyed. They destroyed everything. The flowers are dead; the grass is brown, windows are busted up, like I have been gone for a long time. The door is wide open, and I see mice and I can tell that other animals are in there. It is all ruined. I don't know what to do. I just stay there. I get on our bed, and I just cry. I am holding our pictures. Everything is gone, but our pictures in their dusty, cracked frame. It is sad. Outside is not green anymore; it is dead and gray.

A: I want you to go back now, one more time. Back to when you had the book, and you understood what the book was. You are there now. What do you see?

C: I am on my knees, under our bed trying to hide the book. The book is a spiritual book. It's a book that has spells. It tells you how to do things you can't do in normal life. I see potions, spells, and incantations.

A: Where did you get the book from? How did it come into your possession?

C: I had it. I held it. I remember walking home with my book. I always carry that book with me. I always had it. I don't think I was even going to school. I think I was in the forest chanting, doing spells, trying potions, picking berries. Deers really like me, and I like them. I am just in nature. I am on my knees, on the grass trying different incantations, trying to build up my power. I am still learning. I have so much to learn, but I love it. I am so happy. The sun is shining. I see him fishing (starts crying). He is so nice. It doesn't look like him there, but it's him. I know it's him. It's a man. He has brownish hair, tall, olive skin like me. He teases me about the books, but he helps me pick the berries, the roots, and the leaves for the things that I need. He is curious, but he is cautious. He catches a fish, but he releases it. The leather book is worn down, like it's been in my family. I know my mom didn't give it to me. I don't know who gave it to me. It is a positive book, for the better. It tells me how to heal people, or make people happy. It's a potions book, but on the back of the book it has dangerous things. You can really hurt, or kill someone. You could put somebody's mind, like they are living, but they are really just laying down. You can paralyze them, but make them think like they are living a normal life. You could do some really bad things.

A: I want you to go in this life, to when you are taking your last breath. Tell me what you see all around you.

C: I see I am in that bed. I am in our house, on that dusty bed. Everything is broken. I just fell asleep, holding our picture. I fell asleep. Slowly, I don't wake up, I don't want to wake up. I am just curled up, holding our picture. I don't care anymore. I just fell asleep, and didn't wake up.

A: What happens when you take your last breath? What happens to your spirit?

C: I can see it now. I am floating around. It's floating around and trying to get out of there. I am back up in the clouds. I can just see the clouds, the sunshine. I just float away, fly away as far as I can.

A: Where do you go?

C: Still up in the cloud. I just hung out there for a while. I don't know why, but I go back to the desert. It's almost like I am reliving my day. I am walking again with my sandals.

The client seems to be stuck in a repeated residual loop, back to the life she went to, before the gray room, instead of crossing over to the light.

C: This time I pick up some flowers, some bread, and I pick up this green gem. I love that green gem. I saw it from far away, and I had to have it. I am still walking. I feel like people are looking at me. Men like to look at me. I have long brown hair, and I think a gold dress. I feel beautiful. I am going back home. My daughter is in the front yard. I am going back inside with the green gem. My husband is sleeping in the bed. I put it under our bed. I am just so happy. I have gems under there, and they are colored. The green one is so bright that it almost glows. I have a really bright white one. I have a big glittery black one. I have a beautiful purple one. A blue one, rich ocean blue. They are under the bed protecting us.

The Higher Self is called forth.
A: Thank you. Am I speaking to Higher Self now?
Higher Self: Yes.
A: I honor you, I thank you and I respect you, for all the aid you have given us today. I know that you hold the records of her different lives. May I ask questions?
Higher Self: Yes.
A: Thank you. You took her to a village that had sand with her daughter. Why did you take her there?
Higher Self: To show that she is happy. She didn't have a bad past life. She had a good past life. She was happy. She was loved. She was beautiful. She was smart. Just to show her that she was not a bad person.
A: Where was this located at? You said she was wearing a golden dress.
Higher Self: Egypt, somewhere around there. Maybe Giza. It's a small village.
A: From there you took her to a life where she was in the gray room, and she had numbers on her. What did these numbers represent?
Higher Self: She was a prisoner, not because she was bad, but because there were bad people. They wanted her information. They wanted to break her, torment her.
A: Was it because of the book she had? Where did she get it from?
Higher Self: Her grandmother, from her mother's side. It has been passed down from generation to generation. It was given to her in a hurry, before they had to flee. She held on to that book. The book was her pride and joy. She had to protect it.
A: After she left the village, where her father was beating her, did she have the book with her then?
Higher Self: No, she went back and got it. She had nothing when she left. She left her books on the kitchen table. She went and snuck into the house. She had to go back. Her brother drove her to her house, that cottage. She had to go back, because she forgot it. She left the book on the table in the kitchen.
A: This cottage she went to, how did she acquire the cottage?
Higher Self: She knocked on the door, the lights were on. Nobody would answer, and she opened the door. She sensed it was supposed to be hers. She lived there. It became hers, like her grandmother's or her mother's house was passed down. She didn't know, she just had to open the door. She just kept knocking. She opened the door after she got the book. She got the book back.
A: From there, at what point did she meet the man (her current husband Drake)?
Higher Self: She met him when she was in the forest, to enchant, doing spells. She saw him fishing and they met. He lived a few villages from her. He liked fishing in that creek to catch fish. She introduced herself to him. She wanted a friend. She was really attracted to him, like a magnet being drawn to him. Something about his inner sight, she could see his aura. She saw it glowing like sunshine. She was so drawn to him. His name was not Drake, like her husband, you know. I think his name was Paul.
A: From there, what happened, did they get together?
Higher Self: Yes. They fell in love, instant connection, not sexual yet, just really enjoyed each other's company. He really helped her pick all of the things she needed for her spells. He would bring fish, just enough so that we can eat and release the rest. I cooked it for him and started a friendship, and then we started making out and went to the room. He never left since then.
A: Was this on Earth that this happened? What are you getting?
Higher Self: Blackness.
A: That's okay. At this point, I would like to get more answers, but it seems you are being blocked to get the rest of the answers to what this life was about. So, let's discover where the blockage is so we can get this information, to acquire the healing. If I can please ask for a Body Scan? Let me know if you want any of the Archangels to help out with the Body Scan and the healing.
Higher Self: It's like she doesn't want to do it anymore. She's tired. My head is hurting.
A: With the Higher Self permission, can I please call on Archangel Michael?

Higher Self: Oh my head (in pain crying).
A: Take a deep breath. Higher Self, help her to remain calm and not feel the pain in her head (client holds head and cries). If I can please speak to Archangel Michael now?

Aurora gives further instructions for Carmela to allow Archangel Michael to connect and assist.

A: Greetings brother.
AA Michael: Hello.
A: Hello. Thank you for being here. I honor you, and I love you. We have many questions here, but first of all we want to do a Body Scan on her. We are trying to ask her some questions, she seems to just see dark, and is blocked. She is having a pain in her head. If you can scan her head now Archangel Michael? Scan for any energies, entities, anything that is negative that is blocking her.
AA Michael: It's an Entity.
A: Is it in her head?
AA Michael: It's big.
A: Michael, can you have Metatron surround that Entity with the alchemy symbols?
AA Michael: Yes.
A: Thank you Metatron, we love you. Michael, can I speak to that entity in her head?
AA Michael: He doesn't want to talk.
A: I can ask questions and see if he gives us answers. Are you male?
Entity: Yes.
A: Thank you for responding. Would you allow me to ask you some questions?
Entity: We'll see.
A: If I may ask, when was it that you attached yourself to her head?
Entity: Since she was little.
A: How old was she?
Entity: Maybe four or five.
A: What was going on with her that allowed you to attach yourself to her head?
Entity: It's a bad thing, but she let me grow. Man, it sucks (grabs head). Oh, man.
A: Higher Self, help her not feel the pain. Help her not feel the pain.
Higher Self The stabbing. So strong. Oh my god!
A: I need to talk to the Enritty, so that we can help the situation out. Can we do that Higher Self?
Higher Self: Yes.
A: Let me continue speaking to the Entity. Did you have a body before you connected yourself to her head?
Entity: Yes.
A: What happened to you? How did you die?
Entity: I died in prison.
A: How did you die in prison?
Entity: I was murdered. I was shanked. They found out that I like little kids. I loved little kids. They are so pure, so innocent, it turns me on.
A: I understand that this is one of the reasons why you are stuck in her body, and I am sure it is connected to what happened to her at that time (Carmela was sexually abused as a child). I would like to remind you of who you are, and help you remove yourself from her head. Help you transform into the light once more. For you are from the light. We all are from the light. Would you allow for us to help you, so that you may no longer be stuck in her head having to play this role?
Entity: Yes.

After some further convincing and work, the entity spreads its light, and ascends out.

A: Do you have a message for her before you go?
Entity: It's not her fault. She needs to trust people again, and open her heart.

A: One of the most important reasons why she came to me in regards to doing this session, was because she had very bad head pains, excruciating, and the doctors couldn't figure out what was wrong with her. Were you the cause of that?
Entity: Some of it, not all of it.
A: Can you tell me what else is the cause of her head pain?
Entity: It's medical.
A: Do you have any other message for her before you go?
Entity: I am sorry. I was very angry, very hateful. I just hung on to you. I did not want to let go. I am sorry.
A: Go ahead and go with the Love-Light of the Universe. Blessings to you.
Entity: Goodbye.
A: If I can please speak to Archangel Michael now?
AA Michael: Yes.
A: Thank you, brother. I know she said she had multiple MRI's, spinal taps, MRV/MRA's, CAT scans, and they keep on doing all these tests on her. She seems to be getting worse and worse with every test. You could say it's experiments that they keep doing on her. What's in her head that's causing this Michael?
AA Michael: I see a tumor, but they don't see it. It's getting bigger.
A: How come the doctors haven't detected it?
AA Michael: They are not looking in the right spots.
A: Is this tumor cancerous?
AA Michael: No.
A: What initially caused the tumor?
AA Michael: It is hard. I am trying to find it.
A: Is it connected to this life or another life Michael?
AA Michael: Another life.
A: If you can show her, what life is connected to this pain in her head.
AA Michael: It was that gray building.
A: Why is it in her head?
AA Michael: All that trauma, it clouds her mind. It makes her not be able to move. Staying on one-stop. She cannot explore, she cannot learn. She doesn't want to do anything, it paralyzes her.
A: Is this why you showed her this life, so that we can help her heal that past life?
Higher Self : Yes.
A: Can we heal her head?
AA Michael: Yes.
A: Archangel Michael can you call on Archangel Raphael, Metatron, and whoever wants to help out as well? Some of her guides, her own angels, and her Higher Self? As well as Archangel Uriel, because we will need his fire energy to start transmuting that tumor?
AA Michael: Yes.
A: Can we go ahead and start healing, transmuting, and disintegrating that tumor now?
AA Michael: Yes.
A: Wonderful, are we doing that now?
AA Michael: We need everyone.

The Higher Self, and the Archangels work together to begin the healing of the tumor.

A: How is the tumor looking now?
AA Michael: It is still there, but it's going to get smaller. It's going to take some time. This has been there for a very long time. It is rooted in. It will go.
A: How long has it been there?
AA Michael: A long time.
A: This life or another?

AA Michael: Another life.
A: Would you say it is a dark mass of negative energy that was created into the tumor?
AA Michael: Yes, very dark.
A: Can we use my phoenix fire on it?
AA Michael: You can try. I don't know if it's going to work. It is rooted, very deep. It does not want to let go.
A: Does this tumor have an Entity within it?
AA Michael: It might have another one. It's hidden deep. It does not want to be found.
A: Archangel Metatron can you surround this Entity with the alchemy symbols within the tumor? Archangel Michael, we would like to speak to that Entity deep in the back of her head. If we can speak to you now?
Entity: Hello.
A: Hello, thank you for speaking to us. May I ask you questions?
Entity: No. You need to leave me alone.
A: I understand you want to be left alone, but I am just here in love for you, and for also the person that you are inside of.
Entity: I want to be left alone. You guys need to leave me alone.
A: Why is that?
Entity: I do not want to be out.
A: When was it that you connected to her head there?
Entity: She was little. Past life, little.
A: What was it that allowed you to connect then?
Entity: Leave me alone. I don't want to answer your questions right now.
A: Here is the thing, we are here to help you release yourself, and spread the light that's within you. So that you remember. You have forgotten that you are of the light, and you have been lost.
Entity: I don't have any light.
A: We are here to give you hope, and to help you reconnect to that light. Everyone has light in our Universe. We are here to remind you of the light within you. Now, you can either listen and allow for us to help you, so that you may not have to be stuck in her body.
Entity: I know what you have to say. I don't want to have to answer your questions right now.
A: So either you allow for us to help you spread your Light-Love, or we are going to have to remove you. If that happens, because you are not allowing us, then you are recycled back to Source, back to the light, what you say you don't have. You would lose all the experiences and memories that you have. You would just restart all over again. You can keep these experiences, the growth you had as a spirit, as they are valuable.
Entity: Okay. I will use the light because you give me no choice. You make me very angry.
A: It's okay. You won't be angry for too long. Find that light within you. Archangels, if you can help. Archangel Metatron, keep it contained there. Let's find that light within you. We are going to anchor Love-Light to you. You have forgotten the beauty that you are. You are a beautiful piece of creation. Find that light within you, and spread it to all that is of you. Remember the beauty of you.
Entity: I don't want to.
A: Remember the beauty. We are sending you the light. Find the light inside of you and spread it.
Entity: I can see it.
A: Good, beautiful. Now if you can remove yourself from her, pull every root, every cord, every essence that is of you. Let me know once you are all out.
Entity: Okay...
A: I honor you, I love you, and I respect you. Thank you for allowing this.
Entity: You helped me. Thank you. I was stuck in there forever. You freed me.
A: It is our honor. Thank you for allowing it.
Entity: It's beautiful.
A: You are beautiful. If you can look at the tumor, how does it look?
Entity: It's big. It has a lot of roots in the brain. It shouldn't be there.

A: Do you have a message for her before you go?
Entity: I just see light.
A: Beautiful, go ahead and go with the Love-Light of the Universe. Blessings to you.
Entity: Goodbye.
A: Archangel Michael, if you can scan her head where the tumor is. How does it look now?
AA Michael: It's better. It is getting smaller. It is still there, but it is shrinking.
A: Good, if you can continue working on it during the session. I know physical things like this can take time, but if we can continue working, and get it to the smallest that we can during this time?
AA Michael: Yes.
A: Thank you. She has questions about her health. She's had multiple procedures conducted on her. She had two surgeries, spinal taps. Can you scan that area where she had the surgery, and tell me what you find?
AA Michael: She blocked me. I don't feel connected.

Aurora works with Carmela to allow connection once more with Archangel Michael.

A: Michael if you can scan her spinal tap. Can you scan her for any energies, entities, anything negative that needs healing.
AA Michael: Her spine has negative energies.
A: How did that happen? Was it through the surgery?
AA Michael: Through that needle in that spinal tap.
A: Did the needle itself carry the negative energy?
AA Michael: No.
A: What was it?
AA Michael: It was the doctor.
A: Okay, so the doctor that was injecting her carried the negative energy. Did it transfer through the needle?
AA Michael: Yes.
A: Can you start healing her spine, transmuting and healing the negative energy within her spine?
AA Michael: Yes.
A: How about the MRV (Magnetic Resonance Venography)?
AA Micahel: That one took longer. She is still healing from it.
A: What did the MRV do to her?
AA Michael: It caused her a lot of pain in her head. It made her tumor throb.
A: Why did it make her tumor throb?
AA Michael: Like it's growing.
A: Did it make it grow?
AA Michael: No. It wants to. I think it was the Entity, it didn't like it.
A: The MRV, what is it that they do in this procedure?
AA Michael: They look at your veins inside your head and brain. They contrast the veins, so that they can look at it in detail. It's a long process, a couple of hours.
A: From this MRV procedure, what was the negativity that came in through it?
AA Michael: It was from the room, before she went in. It was her dressing room. She had to change, take her jewelry off. It's there where it came in. Waiting. She was really open. It just went in.
A: Was she not shielding, surrounding with Love-Light then?
AA Michael: No.
A: Is this why it was able to go straight in?
AA Michael: Yes.
A: Can you explain to me what it looks like when it's going in?
AA Michael: Swallowing, like you are breathing the air. Looks like a ball. A small one, of just energy swallowing it, absorbing in the body. It just absorbs through the whole body.
A: Why was it in the room? What is the creation of that?

Higher Self: The assistant, she led me there. It was her negative energy.
A: Is it because you have your guard down, vulnerable, during the procedure, that someone would give you their negative energy?
AA Michael: Yes.
A: What happened once it went into you? Where did it go, and what did it do to you?
Higher Self: It went through my whole body. It went straight to my brain. It caused major pain. Lots of pain in the head, sore eyes. Even my jaw was sore, so much pain. It lasted for five days.
A: Can we start healing that for her now?
AA Michael: Yes. The Entities, the tumor, and spinal tap. It all contributes.
A: How about the ears? She felt like they were very clogged, especially after one of the surgeries.
AA Michael: They are not fixing it.
A: You mean the doctors are not fixing it?
AA Michael: Yes. They are causing more problems.
A: This really reminds me of the life where they were doing experiments on her.
AA Michael: Yes.
A: Can you check her ears, why do they feel like that?
AA Michael: It's got energy.
A: Energy from where?
AA Michael: Bad energy from when she got sick.
A: Those ladies that bullied her, and tried to pin accusations on her? Did those ladies have any connection to that life with the gray room?

In this life, she experienced torment and bullying from her district manager and store supervisors. Accusing her of stealing money, when it was them who stole the money.

AA Michael: Yes. The boss. The district manager.
A: Who was she, in the gray room life?
AA Michael: She was the blond lady.
A: The one that seemed soulless?
AA Michael: Yes.
A: Is that what happened, and why they did that to her again?
AA Michael: They don't want to get caught.
A: So they tried to pin it on her?
AA Michael: Yes. Something deeper, hatred.
A: Was it a contract?
AA Michael: Yes. She is assigned to it. It is all business.
A: Is the contract done?
Client: That contract, yes. She moved on to another person.
A: Another person, and another contract?
Client: Yes.
A: I want to make sure that we heal that, because it holds her back a lot, being tormented like that. Can we heal that for her now in this life, and start healing that past life as well? The connection, what happened to her there?
AA Michael: Yes.
A: Thank you to everyone who is helping out. She has a couple of more questions. The night terror that she had when she was a child, was it related to the past life in the gray room?
AA Michael: Yes.
A: She said that she saw men with hats. Higher Self, Archangel Micahel, go back in time and show her why she is having these dreams. Where there are men in her room wearing hats, and there is a portal being created through the wall in her bedroom.
AA Michael: They want to take her.
A: Who are they? Are those living beings or entities?

AA Michael: Living beings, but not from this Earth. They are curious about her.
A: Is there a portal in her room?
AA Michael: There is.
A: Can we go ahead and seal that portal Michael?
AA Michael: Yes.
A: Good. I want to make sure this does not continue following her, no matter where she is at. Can we see if that is a contract?
AA Michael: Yes. It's a contract, but one is personal.
A: Explain what you mean.
AA Michael: He was contracted, then after the contract is done, he does not want to stop.
A: Okay, so that contract is done then?
AA Michael: Yes.
A: This Entity, does he have an alien race?
AA Michael: It's a different race.
A: How does he look?
AA Michael: He looks like us, but he is not us. He looks human, very tall. He tries to look like a spy by wearing suspender pants, but his white shirt gives it away, it's so bright.
A: You are able to look through his facade. Show her Michael, what does he really look like?
Higher Self: He is so tall.
A: What does his face look like?
Higher Self: Black. I just see black. It is dark.
A: How does his face look?
Higher Self: He is very handsome. His eyes are very green. He looks betrayed. He wants me to go with him, but I don't want to go. He wants me to follow him. He does not want to force me. He likes to watch me sleep.
A: Why has he found a connection to you?
Higher Self: I think it's a past life. He fell in love with me, but I fell in love with someone else. He won't let go.
A: Well, it is time to let go. Archangel Michael, can we remove that contract now and disintegrate it? Can we seal with protection any connection that he has now to her, or will try to have in the future?
AA Michael: Yes.
A: Michael, are we removing this contract now?
AA Michael: Yes. We'll protect her.
A: Archangel Michael, can you scan her for any Reptilian consciousness?

In this stage of A.U.R.A. Hypnosis Healing's development, we were being cautious when mentioning Reptilians. As the clients were beginning to be prepared for the mention of Reptilians during the Body Scan. Why it is, we are just asking for it now, towards the end of the Body Scan.

AA Michael: Yes.
A: Where is it at?
AA Michael: Her stomach.
A: Archangel Metatron, can you please surround that Reptilian consciousness with the alchemy symbols? Archangel Michael, is that the only one?
AA Michael: Yes.
A: Thank you Metatron for surrounding it. Can we talk to this entity Michael?
AA Michael: No, we need to remove it.
A: You don't think we could talk him into positive polarizing?
AA Michael: No. It's too far.
A: Alright, if we can focus Phoenix fire on this Reptilian within her solar plexus, and start transmuting it, and turning it back into light. Scan her body one more time Michael, any entities in her body?
AA Michael: I can't detect any.
A: Wonderful. If we can flood her strongly with Love-Light now. Let me know once that Reptilian

consciousness is removed.
AA Michael: It is removed.
A: Thank you Michael, Metatron, Raphael, Uriel, and to all the angels that helped today, her guides, and the HIgher Self. Thank you for all the aid you have given us today, in helping her heal. Love you, honor you, and respect you.
AA Michael: Thank you.
A: If I can please speak to her HIgher Self once more Michael. If I may, as I am a seer, they showed me how she is going to evolve after this. How she is going to overcome it. They showed me her walking through a cave. Inside the cave, there was magical water, and there was a deer on the other side of the water. She jumped, and went through the water, as she connected to that deer. The deer led her through a path, where she went into a waterfall. She came out of the waterfall, and she was fine. She was finally happy, healthy, and she was beautiful.
Higher Self: Thank you.

For every A.U.R.A. Hypnosis healing session we ask that the Higher Self and team ensure to remove and heal this entire list from the clients Tree of Life: entities (Grays, Mantis, Reptilians, Archons…), dark portals, repair and crystallize DNA, negative cords, technologies (implants, metals, hooks, wires, nano, vaccines), Illnesses, vision, dental health, regrow teeth, age regress 5-15 years, blocked or misaligned chakras, open-up the third eye and activate abilities, expand heart, issues with auric field, fractured soul, contracts, deletion of inverted timelines, and trauma from current or past life.

Post Session dialogue.
C: Wow.
A: That was incredible.
C: How do you do this? My question to you is, how can you go through people's journey, and can you stay so level-headed? You can still be yourself? You are not exhausted, or anything, or worn out?
A: It's really hard, but I have a beautiful angelic team that has taught me how to shield and how to charge with the sun's energy. I use mantras right after this, that help bring back energy to me. It is hard, and I do have to hold that space and love for you. Also, it is hard for me because I feel everything very deeply.
C: Yes, I was thinking that you are very sensitive to people.
A: I am, but that is okay. I do this in service for others, and I know in the long run that you will be beautiful, and the way I saw you in the dream, you looked just like you look now. I had no idea how you were going to look, except you were healthy and thin. You were beautiful. You were naked.
C: Yes (laughs). I have gained a lot of weight since I have been sick.
A: Going back to regaining your health. I saw the path, and it was really beautiful. They showed me, when you came out of the waterfall, you rejoined the people around you in the community. Still being cautious and protective, but you were back into society, and you were helping others. I saw that and wanted to tell you. I started crying the minute I started bringing you back, it was a release. I do cry sometimes when I am done with the client, but it's okay, I wouldn't change it. My love to my brother (her husband). I love that you have found each other, as the beautiful twin flame union that you are. May you both continue growing, and bring forth little souls that are meant to come forth through your sacred union.
C: Thank you, you helped me.
A: Were you able to see and sense where this gray room was?
C: It was on Earth.
A: Did you get a sense of what it was?
C: No, but it was a building that seemed like it used to be used for something, but they used it. It was abandoned, and they used it for something else that was not good.
A: It feels like it was the life right before this one, doesn't it?
C: It does, very much, like it just happened, yes.

A: *It was the Illuminati doing experiments. Do you know who the Illuminati is? I know you are not familiar.*
C: I don't.
A: *Basically, it's the negative people that try to run this world.*
C: Oh. Just trying to remember everything; it's like a dream, but it's not. I really can't wait to share this.
A: *It's incredible isn't it? How much detail did you receive through it? You went along very naturally, so you are quite a seer yourself. You are very natural at it. Even though you said you don't meditate, you don't really do spiritual work, it's important you continue shielding.*
C: Yes, he started doing that when I had my nightmares. He tries to shield me, and I know I need to do that myself.
A: *Yes, you have to do it yourself. Watch the videos. He might have watched, [9]"How to Maintain Your Vibrations High," explains how to surround yourself with the I AM Source Love-Light and using Archangels Shields.*
C: He has talked about Archangel Michael.
A: *That portal is closed now, so you should be good.*
C: Thank you. Can you tell me one more time, what did you say that the lizard entity was named?
A: *You can talk to your husband about it, since you are not familiar. They are part of the Illuminati that I mentioned. They are the ones that are in government, the kings, and they are basically hidden. You can start watching some of my videos now, where we talk about this. They hide in human bodies.*
C: Oh wow.
A: *Yes, and they put their consciousness into people, to control them and keep them sick.*
C: Thank you so much. Oh wow.
A: *Thank you, sister. I love you dearly.*

END OF SESSION

The deliverance of this session was of greatest importance, in connection to the previous Chapter, 'The A.I. Alien Invasion'. Bringing us into compassion, and an even deeper understanding of the violations of World War II towards the Jewish people. As I am creating Book 2, I am in awe of our clients' sessions. The way that the divine hand of creation works is magical. This session was conducted two in half years before the A.I. Alien Invasion content was brought into my awareness. Carmela's Higher Self knew that at this moment in time, I would be creating Book 2, and that her past life regression journey would be fundamental for the collective to remember. Piece by piece my clients prepare me for the fruition of the continual disclosure to come for Earth's Ascension. May our clients continue to all understand the infinite ways that their role is, in assisting the collective in this most grand form, by agreeing to have an A.U.R.A. Hypnosis Healing session conducted.

The beauty of Carmela's town, the white cottages, the lush, green landscape, the people peacefully living their sovereign lives. This happiness was felt as she walked through the streets. The white building that was familiar to her in her neighborhood, instead, it was turned into a building of torture and experimentation on the very people that lived in this town. How ironic and further tormenting would it be to see your home and your town, where you held beautiful memories of your family and your life, instead be turned into a place of torture and pain. The emotions that you would hold of these memories, as joy, happiness, or if you birthed your children there, would be traumatic and would deeply soak into your cellular memory and consciousness, as you experienced the torture in this same location. A building can take on, rapidly, the form of what is within it, as all homes and buildings are like sponges soaking in its environment. In a couple years time frame, how it went from white, to gray, with mold within its walls. The building soaking in the trauma and blood that was being shed in it. The resemblance she felt of how the gray experimenting building looked like the sterile hospitals in the now

---

[9] Under the Rising Phoenix Aurora channels, there is a playlist called 'Spirituality for Beginners'. Here Aurora has over 40 videos for the public, for those who are looking for the beginning core sacred teachings of growth within spirituality.

that people go to everyday for their supposed health issues, or requirements of needed healing. Invertedly contradicting this is. The herbal, elemental healer Carmela, jailed within a building that resembles a hospital, is the opposite of healing.

The experiments of her past life carried forth into this life, by the doctors that put her through all types of medical procedures, with the use of forms of supposed necessary technology testing. It is as if she never left that gray building, instead it was now a hospital in this life. We now know though, that the human body has been created to self-heal, just as the soul is repairable and infinitely immortal. So, why are all these procedures necessary to us yearly as adults, or monthly as younglings? The world has become rapidly aware within these times and spaces of the malpractice in the medical industry. No longer will they be able to get away with this, with ease. Through the Covid-19 plandemic and the injuries by the vaccine, they have truly outed themselves. The hospital experiments/procedures are masked to the world, under the guise that it is for your greatest good, and that they are just tests for these purposes. More like experiments onto humankind. To see how their test subjects, us, or our children, are doing after their successful implementation of injections of the similar types of vaccinations as Carmela took. Because, as we know, as mentioned in the previous Chapter, The A.I. Alien Invasion, how control over humanity began through nano fused vaccinations, to the level it has formed into, in the now.

The majority of illness begins with vaccinations, as we have discovered throughout the years of A.U.R.A. Hypnosis Healing sessions. It is the beginning level of inserting A.I. or metals into humankind. As parents, when we look back, and think about what we allowed the hospitals to inject into our children, it is most disturbing. Especially after we learn how these vaccinations truly feel, in how Carmela explained that they burned from the inside, and she was in excruciating pain. The hospitals make you aware of how you might feel sickly and the side effects after the vaccinations, then ensure that you sign for consent on the day of your doctor appointment, and at that point we have given them energetic consent to these infringements. Every hospital vaccination administered, is for their experiments, to see how much they can sicken the human body, without killing it, but to an extent that it is controlled by illness. The doctors are then given their medical manuals, on what are some of the most common side effects, and the name for that supposed autoimmune, disease, or illness one might have according to these side effects. However, it was the vaccination and immunizations that carried the nano codes and programming to cause the side effects, which then they label into a category. This is done so that the negative entities can still feed off the light within us; enough to keep us in an inverted cycle of un-healing, as shown through Carmela's experience.

No one in this world should ever be placed through the hospital system of experimentations; we are no one's experiments. However, the stories we hear from people through A.U.R.A. Hypnosis Healing sessions are many. How the doctor told them they needed to remove their uterus because they had menstrual pain, the uterus connecting to their sacred womb, then causing energetic blockages in their creational divine power. But, instead they perhaps had sexual trauma, or an infringement of negative energy, an entity, or implant within the sacral areas. If the client had hip pain, they were told they had to remove their hip, and replace it with a synthetic metal hip or plate. These are their forms of removing the organic material within us, in order to replace it with inorganic. Pulling out organic material within a human body is not the solution. The Illuminati's goal, who truly is who runs and owns these hospitals, are to make us part androids with these metals inserted, or make us hollow and empty within the missing parts of us that they remove during surgeries. Which then unbalances us within, by removing bones, or organs, that are part of the organic physical body, which is then connected to our energy body. These doctors will never truly get to the root of the issue of the pain or illness. These experimentations upon humankind are sickening.

Carmela's heart, how she profoundly wanted to help the others who were trapped in this building with her, as she could feel their pain inside of her, through their cries and pleads for help. In the moment, she did not care of the pain and torture that she was going through, instead she wanted to help the others to free themselves of this pain. This is an example of a pure hearted soul, that no matter what they have gone through, it is far greater for them that others be assisted over them. In a balanced manner, this is an example of what a service-to-others healer is truly the embodiment of. Often those who pretend a role of service-to-self will instead rapidly run away from a situation, where it involves them getting hurt, a type of 'All men for themselves' mentality. When Carmela came to, at the end of the session, again, her natural ability to care for others was prominently present. Even though she had just woken up from physical and emotional pain from her past life, her first reaction was still to check up on me instead. Asking me how I was, after having to hold space in Love-Light to something so horrific, as what she went through. This is my sacred role for humanity's Ascension. It was very kind of her to ask; however, it was not needed for her to do so, but still she did. It was instead most important to know how she was doing after such a traumatic past life. But still, that call within of love for others was profoundly stronger for her, as natural as breathing. This is an embodiment of a true healer.

What was being injected into Carmela was a type of mind control serum; however, it was not working for her, which is why they had to resort to torture. Her connection to the elements and the sacred teachings within her book was strong. This connection is a shield, against control over a sovereign soul. She knew the power of what they were after, and how dangerous it would be for them to obtain it. The only way to get to her was through the man she loved. At that point she was forced into giving up the location of the sacred book. The target upon our beloved ones, is the favorite inverted game the Archon's like to play, as they view our love towards others as weakness. Though as we know, it is our greatest strength. Her beloved's form of defeat was by the administration of a mind control serum. We got to experience through their journey some of the beginning times of the Mk-Ultra experiments on humans. Because he was not attuned, or aware of the sacred teachings within her book, he was not able to resist by harnessing the force that is found within all natures, and the Source Love-Light within us. Through Mk-Ultra branches of the military who are controlled by the Illuminati, have been performing experiments, through UFO, or forms of advanced technology abductions, on humankind. We will learn more of these forms through Book 3 and 4. This is why when Carmela looked at her love, he would not respond, and seemed lifeless, as if he was no longer conscious within his body. Because the mind control serum was a successful match for him. Placing him into a hypnotic brainwave where the consciousness is submissive and under control. Further helping us understand how important it is that humankind remembers the sacred teachings the elements of our natures have to offer. In Chapters 8 and 9, the Seven Goddesses of the elements of Earth and beyond, we begin to learn of this divine power which is dormant within us, awaiting to be activated.

During the editing of this A.U.R.A. Hypnosis Healing session's original video's publication, Carmela's Higher Self explained to me why her grandmother fled in a hurry, leaving the book behind with Carmela before doing so. Carmela's grandmother had a premonition of the Holocaust to come, she knew that her daughter, Carmela's mother, would not listen and flee with her. Knowing that the grandmother was older in age, she had to preserve the sacred teachings somehow. The next strongest and youngest in age would be Carmela, to become the guardian of the family's sacred book passed down by their Ancestors. The book was leather bound to ensure its care in long life, and to protect it from the weather. Hidden under Carmela's bed, it was within a box, which inside, had a ring of sacred crystals surrounding the book, creating a seal of protection. It also had Red roses, to remind us of the Essenes connection to it. We know that the red roses represent the sacred order of Mother Mary and Magdalene, and their travels, after Yeshua's Ascension out of the Matrix, and back into the higher dimensions. How Mother Mary and Magdalene were voyagers, planting the seed of the sacred teachings, Yeshua began to awaken within the people of Earth. The origin of the sacred teachings within the book stemmed forth from the Essenes, who were Atlantean descendants. This is what Carmela's book represented to us, the remnants of the last of the Atlantean's sacred knowledge. Which is where the back of the book is understood, as Atlantis and Essenes guarded these sacred teachings, in how you can control people's minds. As Carmela said "You can make them think they are living, but they really are laying down." These sacred teachings were truly explaining how our consciousnesses are in inverted A.I. matrix pods, and the recycling of the souls, as explained in Chapter 2 "The Key to Ascension." How we think we are awake, but really we are asleep within this simulation. These forms of the use of Hypnosis, in inverted black magic actions, we now see in our time. How they have used hypnosis, and other sacred teachings they have acquired invertedly, in order to control the minds of humans, through all the types of negative programming. As in, television, media, schooling, religion, and chemicals in what we intake, the negative antenna towers that constantly echo out a lower frequency, all part of the mind control agenda of the New World Order.

The cottage that was handed down to her through her Grandmother, had the lights on when she arrived, as if there was someone living there; however, there was no one there. But, it seemed as if the home was waiting for her. There was no one home, but it was alive, like it was occupied. There was a white spell over the cottage, and Carmela was only able to open it after she went back to acquire the book from her childhood home. The book needed to be in her presence, as it was the key to get in. This further explains why it is that the blonde, blue eyed women needed to know where the sacred book was, because it had an invisibility cloak over it. When they originally rummaged through her home, they were not able to find it because of its cloak. Therefore, the minute Carmela gave her its location, it was the consent they needed so that they could see it, and take possession over it, as the white spell was then broken. Once they got to the book's location, she was of no use to them, and they just threw her away as trash, because they got what they ultimately wanted. Which explains to us that, somehow they got a hold of Carmela's Mother or Grandmother, which then told them of the cottage and the sacred book. They then came after Carmela abruptly and unannounced, retrieving her and her spouse from the cottage. Which is why the Illuminati knew exactly what Carmela was hiding and guarding from them, the sacred Atlantean/Essene's teachings. In the next Chapter 'The Essenes,' we further learn why the Illuminati, in the Holocaust, were after the sacred knowledge that some of the Jewish people were still sacredly guarding and keeping alive through practice.

The green eyed man/entity that was haunting Carmela in her bedroom all her life - he was the same man that was in the gray building, who was assisting the blonde haired, blue eyed women. Which is why he seemed so familiar to her when she looked into his eyes, because he was once in love with her, or so he thought. He was also connected to the town, as if he grew up in the surrounding area. The feeling, as she was being tortured, was that she felt like she knew who he once was, in a distant time. The Higher Self explained during the session that this entity once thought that they would end up together, but instead she fell in love with another, that other being the gentle hearted man, who loved to fish. This explanation that the Higher Self gave, was of this past life remembered. At times these ghosts that haunt us in our dreams, or our in-between waking stages, are often from another time and space, hanging on to us strongly with hooks and cords because of their own karma. Many German men were forced into these roles of playing scientist, or torturing others, during World War II. Because of the harm he caused her, he entered an inverted cycle of having to live with the pain of what he did to her, and the others in this gray building. Both sides of this experience have to play out the pain and karma that comes with their choices. The next time these inverted cycles are played out, one has the choice to say "No, I do not consent," at that point breaking that inverted cycle. Which is what Carmela did when she had her A.U.R.A. Hypnosis Healing session, by remembering this past life as a jewish girl, and all that she went through then, and her saying NO in this time and space, released her from having to repeat it once more. Allowing for her to begin her healing in the now. Remembering that all time is within a pocket of linear space, therefore, when it happens in the now, it will ripple to all linear perspectives, as past and future. When she closed the dark portal in her bedroom this German man was using to connect to her, who was actually an entity from another world, she began the opportunity for him to close his karma with her. As that is what we do when we release people, who have caused us harm in whatever form. We create an opportunity for them to choose to expand as well, because no longer do they have the option to latch on to us.

The inverted cycle of the blonde hair, blue eyed women repeated once more in Carmela's life, as she, too, tormented her in this life. This being the triggering factor for Carmela of the forgotten memories of the past life in the Holocaust, beginning and bridging forth the opportunity of her healing these traumas in the now. But, instead the doctors repeated the cycle too, of experimenting on her in the hospital. In this life the German woman was her District Manager, who alongside other supervisors, were stealing money from the company they were employed under. When confronted, the German woman, now District Manager, pinned it all on Carmela, taking her to court, where they continued to almost prosecute her. However, there was not enough evidence to back up their false claim, therefore, Carmela was released of the charges. These are remnants to the inverted cycles that are on repeat with the people in our lives within this Matrix simulation. Another loop within her memory was when she passed on from her life in the Holocaust, and she went right back to the life she began with, that wasn't shared in this transcription. However, there were subtle differences to it. In an organic Matrix we would instead Ascend out when we are done with the one life, instead of going back to the beginning. Within the inverted matrix, it is as if you are watching a movie, and when it finishes, you hit rewind and it begins again. We look forward to the days to come, when this will be no longer, and all souls will truly experience Ascension at its finest, within our lower dimensions of our Universe.

The vision that I experienced before meeting her, of her within a cave, with water, and a deer. In her past life, she said that the deers loved her. The deer represent a guide for her, as an animal totem. The deer is a representation of Carmela's soul's blueprint. The way a deer is fast, agile, beautiful to look upon, emanates purity through the eyes, and their abilities are heightened, in order to attune to their surroundings intuitively.

I received an update from both Carmela and the gentle man that loved to fish in her past life, her husband again now, when he joined us at one of our Retreats. Where he rejoiced in their sacred union, and shared with me that their family had finally expanded, with a new bundle of joy. Carmela's A.U.R.A. Hypnosis Healing session was infinitely important to them both, and that he wanted to have the capabilities that our sacred self-healing modalities have to offer, for his expanding family. We thank them both for sharing their catalyzing memories with us, so that we will learn in our times and spaces to not repeat horrendous acts as we witnessed through this past life remembered of World War II.

"In order to change the future, one must first remember the past, and the strong lessons that come with one's experiences. This is the way of breaking inverted cycles."
AuroRa

--------------<<>>--------------

7

THE ESSENES

Recorded Live on YouTube: Oct 20th, 2021

In this transmission AuroRa channels the sacred race of the Ascended Masters, 'The Essenes,' Yeshua's and Mother Mary's birthing roots. The sacred teachings of 'The Essenes,' the role that they played on Earth, and their galactic connection in our Universe. Their ancestors, and how they came to be in union with their sacred knowledge. The Council of 12/13 grace us with their beauty through the deliverance of this transmission. The organic timeline plans, to ensure our time and space fruitions into Ascension, reminding us to follow the divine organic timeline of self and the collective. Furthermore, AuroRa adds never before shared sacred knowledge from 'The Essenes' of our Earth's organic construct, which are essential for our process of Ascension.

--------------<<>>--------------

"You don't need that Bible. We're channeling through all of you, all of this, every day. Trust in yourself, believe in yourself. You are the bridges, the antennas and anchors of these sacred teachings."
~The Essenes

--------------<<>>--------------

A [AuroRa]: (Chants)

Elders of Creation: Greetings. It is an honor to be here with you in this time and space. Such a special monumental moment in timelines, multi-dimensionally, interacting with one another, in this time and space. This is what we've all been waiting for. This is the time, we are here now. We are the Elders of Creation, the 12/13 Council, that were the council members of Atlantis. The Lost City of Atlantis, the crystalline city. We are speaking to you now from a time and space where we are within Atlantis, and we are about to embark upon our journey. This journey of Atlants shall be told from the beginning in future channelings through this beautiful channel-transmission.

We come to you now in this time and space because of what you're seeing around you - though, it is the disclosure that you all have been looking for - It is sometimes as you would call it, 'mind boggling confusion.' Not quite understanding why it is that you see and others don't see. Why it is that you feel and others don't feel. Why is it that you love and others perhaps don't love all life forms as you do?

If you could envision, we are about to embark, we are at a round table speaking on what's about to happen. We have already foreseen though, and we are hopeful that we can change this timeline to the end of the 26,000 cycle over the fall of Atlantis that we have foreseen. We're still hopeful, we're not giving up that we will be able to still save the people. However, as you know, that does not happen. We will allow Atlantis to share itself in the future as we said. We are at the endings of this cycle, which became the inverted cycle that began the collective energy field that you are coexisting with individually and collectively amongst each other. We are here. We have created plan A, plan B, plan C and plan infinity. All perspectives in unison together in the heart space.

There are specific details of what we're able to share today. We're fast forwarding now to the plans where we will speak of three specific locations, and perhaps in the future we will disclose further. Three specific locations that the Elders embarked upon to carry the sacred knowledge so that it would not be long forgotten. The sacred knowledge of the very sacred teachings that you have actually been learning through these platforms, through this channel. The sacred laws of the Universe. How to use the force within you, how to use the embodiment of everything around you, within you, outside of you. Nature, the crystals... all these beautiful puzzle pieces to the force and understanding that you are; we are all Ascended Masters, we just have diluted our souls tremendously in your time and space to anchor in.

We have twin flame unions as well with us. We have a Divine Mother, the 13th key - the Divine Mother fractal. Not fractal in those times we weren't quite fractals, we were true forms you would call Angelics, Gods. Though, we don't like the elite names placed upon us. That's what we were. We were these actual embodiments incarnated upon this, then 5th dimensional organic crystalline blueprint, which we know became inverted. Now we had to go to specific locations on Earth that were directly linked to the sacred laws of the Universe, which are your 12/13 Chakra points and 12 DNA strands; each strand connects to these Chakra points, which are parts of your Universal genetic makeup.

The 13th key needed to go to the sacred lands of the areas of the Mayan locations, where you will find the Mayan civilization which we will further speak upon in the future. We will allow for that Divine Mother to share her wisdom then. There were 4 of us who are speaking now, once more in twin flame union. Then there were two others that went to Egypt as well once more, twin flame union. Our intention was, we had come to the final 'plan' that we needed to, in the future, fractalize ourselves so that we could ensure that the Archonic control that happened in Atlantis, would not happen again in the future. We set out to save these sacred teachings and knowledge, because they needed to be maintained within this physical, illusional, but yet so real Earth plane. Therefore, each one of us took parts of our sacred teachings and crystals, as well as specific generator crystals, that were part of maintaining Atlantis in unison. Once more we'll talk about that later. We want to talk about the Essenes in this channeling. We brought these sacred teachings and we split them apart. Six of us traveled to these specific locations. There were approximately 2 of the 12/13 Elders however, there's duplications amongst that, because we also had our sacred twin flames with us. That, in itself, will have to be written so you could understand that in literature. Okay, so we understand there were two that went to the Mayan location, and four that went to the Essenes location, Qumran. And, then there were two that went to Egypt.

The two that traveled to the Mayan location, they had to travel longer within water. Though they had the power to go in their Merkaba, they had the crystals within. It would be more energetically efficient for them just to allow the water itself, the water within their boat-canoe to take them. They were in protective force fields though within this water, to guide them to where they're meant to go to the sacral. Though we had the farthest path all the way to Jerusalem, to these sacred salt mounds, sacred mountains, sacred spaces, where the chakra of the throat - the sacred law of vibration is located. As well as the two that embarked upon Egypt, they used both water and their Merkabas. The way that our Merkabas worked was that we had amulets that were part of our consciousness. As you remember, we had our full abilities then. Our amulets were in the fifth dimensional Crystalline organic grid. Even though the fall of Atlantis was occurring as we were exiting out to save our future potential and all life forms on Earth. We were still pure in soul and heart. We did not have the Archon virus as others who did have the virus, and were part of the reason why Atlantis fell. And, then they spread it. They spread it to the people, because the people believed the falseness and so on. We've talked about this several times through past channelings.

These amulets helped us travel through the skies, invisible, reaching the lands of Qumran, really QumRA, but that's fine, they changed names often. These sacred lands are a unity; Jerusalem and these areas are a unity of the 12/13 keys, which is very big to share. However, in this time and space it is important that you all understand that unity comes in a unison here. That is why you see the number 12. What we're about to speak of, the 12 Disciples, 12 Elders. However, the number 12 is still the 13, because including Divine Mother, who is our love, which is our life force, she's the 13th. There are 12/13 sacred crystal beds that come in unison in these locations inside the Inner Earth. We'll talk more about that later. Such a resistance in sharing that, as we have kept that sacred through our sacred scrolls from the beginning of Atlantis. Going back though, as we traveled within our Merkabas, we used a 12 point Merkaba, which connects to the 12 sacred laws, and the 12 Universal gridding of the Universe, in how the Universe itself is a 12/13 point merkaba. The 13 is at the center of this Merkaba, as what was explained when the [10] Universe channeled herself, she explained this unity consciousness. As we traveled through these golden 12 pointed Merkabas, we safely, sacredly, needed to remain invisible to these negative polarized Archons, because they had at that point caused wars. Not only the wars here, they were already trafficking children and people, even then in that time and space. Through the beginning experiments on human life forms, as you might already know, you would call them chimeras. However, chimeras are a sacred breed. That's the only way you could understand, when they would mix animal life with human life, and how they would distort a soul. They also began A.I. experiments, as well, then. We traveled through, and we landed in these sacred lands. Within the unity of our sacred union, we began to create and to connect to the land. The 12/13 Sacred unions of the 12/13 Sacred crystals, and the 12/13 sacred laws and chakras. All that we speak of, these are the teachings of the dead scrolls and we were the beginnings of the true Bible.

The civilization within that time and space began, because at the end of Atlantis, we had ended that 26,000 cycle. Which, as we know, we, unfortunately, did not ascend out from. This began the new cycle of rebirth. We knew through our civilization, there would be a sacred time where all that we had worked upon, in conjunction astrologically, and in alignment of planets and stars. That there would be a very important time in the future, which we had already planned out divinely before the fall of Atlantis, in how we would be able to help souls save themselves from being recycled once more. Because, at that point we had entered the inverted cycle, when the fall of Atlantis happened, the Inverted Matrix.

We began to sacredly, divinely, procreate through time and space. The Essenes were descendants of us. They were the seed of the Elders of Atlantis. We used our Merkabas, the force around us, and crystals. We connected to the sacred mounds of the salt caves, as well as our brethren beneath, inside the Inner Earth, that began to arrive there, towards the endings of Lemuria, through the Lemurian and Atlantean wars. The beautiful unions of all these that we've mentioned, as well as the sacred teachings, we kept ourselves hidden in this location. The reason why we were able to keep ourselves hidden was because we could draw from the power of these 12/13 Sacred laws, as well as the Universe was assisting us. We were sovereign and we were not in the Inverted Matrix, even though the rest of the civilization fell down into the third dimension, which you are in now. We were always operating parallel to one another. Like the 2/3rd world explanation. We were communing in the fifth dimensional world, because we kept our organic vessels, our organic memory, we kept it all, and we stayed pure. It was, as many of you who are awakened right now, when you watch the world of the unawakened. For thousands, and thousands, and thousands of years, we watched humanity around us. We were within an energetic force, in a bubble, a Merkaba within the 2/3rd worlds.

We did not ever forget our sacred teachings from Atlantis. Our children and our families, they continued to sacredly birth. They all had different abilities that they would harness, which would assist in sacredly protecting our lands. We had an invisibility cloak over our lands. We would guard it in many forms. Especially at the beginning of when we traveled to QumRa, we still had much Angelic

---

[10] On August 6, 2021, AuroRa channeled "Our Universe 'The Phoenix'" live on YouTube.

energy. We could fly around in this space, within our Merkabas, or you can envision wings, if you like. We taught about the chakras, and the 12/13 DNA strands. All these teachings that you have been learning once more through these courses that we have been channeling through AuroRa, and through all her beautiful clients who have shared their past life regressions. These are some of the sacred teachings of the dead sea scrolls, and why is it that you feel such a beautiful reminiscence of remembrance, when you read the book, 'Galactic Soul History of the Universe,' or when you learn some of these courses? Because these are sacred teachings that we, the Essenes, kept sacredly guarded from the beginnings of the Illuminati/Cabal, these dark forces branching out.

At the fall of Atlantis, they were able to spread their virus upon Earth. They would die, incarnate again into these vessels, into these self-appointed, negative polarized leader positions as you see them now. We've talked about them. But since we are on a platform (YouTube), we're not going to say who they are. You already know who they are (Bill Gates, Anthony Fauci, Jeffrey Epstein, George Soros). Along with our other brethren, our Atlantean brothers, who also went to other locations that we will be speaking about in the future. We were part of maintaining the grid of Earth stable enough, to reach where you're at now. Now you are part of that. You are us in many forms. The sacred teachings of magical beings, Dragons, infinity that we've been teaching are parts of that.

There came a time that we needed to prepare, as we knew that our mother, Divine Mother, was going to come back. We watched the stars, we watched them align, and move closer and closer to the time and space where the sacred birth of Mother Mary was to come forth. We were part of that, of course, as she was us. She was an incarnation of the Divine Mother, the 13th key. The same mother that was in Atlantis, that was her once more, Mother Mary. She would come back to us, and she would come back to us in great strength. She would birth the organic timeline for us in the future fruition, what is occurring now. All these pieces are parts of how the 2/3rd world split, that has finally begun on 12-21-2020. They're sacred pieces, important pieces to that.

The time came when she birthed, as the stars told us that she would be birthed. It then began. The preparations for her sacred birthing of the Messiah, Yeshua, Jesus. The embodiment of all 12/13 keys within him, as he was a reflection of her. He was a piece of her heart, also birthed forth from the Christ Consciousness, as we explained through the [11]'Galactic History | The Christ Consciousness' channeling,' The very first race the Angelics created in our Universe, are the Christ Consciousness, and all these beautiful Ascended Masters that you have learned from, Buddha, Saint Germain, Mother Mary, Yeshua/Jesus. The list goes on and on and on. They come back in their avatar states, and just like you, they awaken, and they fight with their Love-Light to awaken the humanity around them. Mother Mary has explained her journey, as well as Yeshua, through the very beginning channelings that AuroRa began to channel through this YouTube channel. So you can watch those if you like, though AuroRa says they were her beginning channelings. She feels that they were not as good as these; however, that is silly. That's insignificant. Therefore, you can learn the sacred teachings there of Mother Mary, and how she worked very hard in maintaining her vessel clear. She was a 'Seer' and 'Oracle' herself, and how she birthed the Messiah Yeshua, by keeping her soul organic, vessel organic, and at the highest possible avatar state. Remember, because we were still in Atlantean fifth dimensional vibrations, operating in a third dimensional vessel. We were operating higher than that, 13th dimensional, or Source dimensional, as Elder's.

Mother Mary was told that she would find her twin flame union in the city of Jerusalem, which she did, and you know him as Yosef. She was a virgin, as it was very clear our sacral energy needed to be guarded, and only be exchanged with those who were in sacred union with us. She had sacred union, sex with Yosef, her twin flame. The sacred birthing of Yeshua came forth through a sacred cave, within the lands of Qumran. The sacred cave was prepared in alignment to the stars, as it

---

[11] On July 23, 2021, Aurora channeled live, 'Galactic History | The Christ Consciousness'.

needed to be here in these sacred lands, to begin the activation of what you're seeing now in this time and space. Yeshua, Mother Mary, and the council of 12 Elders have fractalized into many forms. The Council of 12 are the birthing points of all the races that had then volunteered to incarnate and come into this inverted matrix, and these inverted matrix pods - 'Star Seeds,' to help release all the souls from within this inverted realm, planetary sphere, matrix simulation.

The Bible that you have, as we know, has been at least 80% compromised. What happened through time and space, after mother Mary and Yeshua, accomplished their missions? Our mission was accomplished as well. In time and space, we needed to protect the sacred teachings, so we surrendered to what was to come. We knew that dark incarnated forces, who had spread the Archon virus, would come after our village in time and space. Before that, we prepared and we hid our sacred Dead Sea Scrolls. They were able to obtain a form of a book, only because we allowed it, of the Bible. We knew that they would distort it. We also knew how important it was for the future, for that literature to be taken by them. However, they knew not of our organic plans and timelines, as they cannot see organic timelines. Only we can. So we baited them, and they took it, which is the very Bible that you have. However, they have the original one hidden in their inverted black magic chapels. They have compromised religions in all forms. One of the main reasons why Jerusalem has been infringed upon deeply, is because they're aware that the sacred laws connect here. They will separate through the forms of religion to destroy humanity, and pit them against each other. You worship this God, and you worship this God. Naming you sinners, "Follow these rules of these man-made religions, and don't go against them, or you will go to hell," things like that. They have pinned humanity against one another, intelligently, in many forms. That is the biggest way that they keep Earth compromised within their black magic. However, as you know, the organic blueprints of Earth have come online, and we have many now seeing through these facades and masks. These falseness of control, that New World Order. Many are seeing, sensing it, feeling it now. You may begin with your questions.

In Aurora's LIVE channelings, a set amount of time is reserved to answer questions from the collective. An RPA team member is the one asking the questions (as submitted by everyone) to the 'Essene Elders.'

Questions: Greetings! Infinite love and gratitude for all of you beautiful Elders. Thank you for being here, and thank you for sharing this beautiful story with us. To start with, where can we access the teachings of the Essenes now? Are they available anywhere?

Essene Elders: Yes, we can only share what's within the consciousness of AuroRa, as she has been instructed specifically to read very few books in your times and spaces, to maintain her organic. Therefore, all she has read are 'The Essenes' and 'They Walked with Jesus' by Dolores. Two books that Dolores was able to be the bridge, anchoring in some of these beginnings' sacred knowledge. These are the teachings of the Essenes here, that we have shared with you through this transmission, and all other teachings that we have shared on these channels of Rising Phoenix Aurora. As well as everything that has been taught through the sacred teachings of all the courses that AuroRa has channeled for the world to learn. We know that this is big, to explain. AuroRa's humbleness, she wants to make it very clear, and we want to make it very clear, that this is not to be looked at as a 'guru' or as 'worship.' None of that. These are just channeled information that's been shared through the Quantum World in connection to the collective of hearts. Through the many forms AuroRa has learned, of all these races that have come into contact with her, have taught these sacred teachings, and they have given her downloads and information when meeting them. You have the same potential as well, to anchor in these Essenes' teachings, because you can connect to us, as you are us, we are you. You are descendants of Atlanteans. You are also descendants of 'Star Seeds,' of our Universe. You're descendants of Source, Divine Mother, Divine Father. These teachings are Source teachings. You will find these teachings in Book 1 'Galactic soul History of the Universe,' and in future literature that we will continue to channel and publish through this clear hearted channel. Once more making it very clear that this is said only in the pureness and benevolence, and never to be distorted. The distortion will not come forth from AuroRa, the distortion will come forth from others. This is not to be distorted or plagued, because these sacred teachings have been guarded by us in these sacred scrolls, from the beginning of time and space. The sacred alchemy symbols that are shared through these courses are why people heal from illnesses, because they allow themselves to heal. This is why people awaken further. This is why people start removing themselves from inverted matrix pods, because these are teachings that we taught back then. Beginning from Atlantis, and really from the beginning of time and space, because that's where we were harnessing it from, in creation. That's all that we can say on that.

Question: Thank you. In today's times, out of all the teachings of the Essenes, which ones do you think are most prominent and most needed by our collective right now? Is there anything that you'd like to point out or share with us?

Essene Elders: We have painted such a beautiful organic blueprint map. Understanding that you are the force. The force is within you, the force around you, the force of infinite Love-Light. Being that embodiment, flowing with that force. Pulling in from Source itself, drawing in that force through your crown. Flowing it through all essences of you, your chakras, the pillars of light that you are, and echoing out like a toroidal sphere. Pulling it in, expanding it, pulling it in, expanding, however you desire. Using all organic nature in your experience. All that we have taught. So simple these are; the very teachings that we were teaching then. How we maintained our souls pure as the Essenes, the Elssenes within the lands of QumRa. We were clear channels. We did not have inversions in us. We didn't have entities attached. We didn't have the Archon virus. We didn't have implants. We didn't have any of those. In our civilization woman wouldn't get raped, children wouldn't be harmed. It was with great sacredness, like AuroRa says, 'I honor you, love you, respect you.' These are teachings of ours, because that's how we view your soul. We honor, love, and respect your soul, as we honor, love, and respect our soul. These very things that seem so simple, but yet are taken for granted. Now, of course, there is much more to that working within your toroidal sphere, expanding it bigger. Working with your chi energy, becoming a chi master in your own form. Understanding that these teachings can be found within you, activating your 12 DNA strands, strongly crystallizing them, decalcifying parts of your body that are compromised. Removal of inversions, again we speak of this. It's all there for you; it's of your choosing. It's of your free willed choice.

You have legions and legions of Love-Light with you, that are supporting you to do this, because you can do this. You must pull yourself out from these inverted matrix pods. It is time you start that process. Begin it. Through all that we just mentioned is how you begin it. Eating light foods. It begins with not eating life. Not eating meat. That is cannibalism. That is how they go through, and they distort the alien races in our Universe. They make them eat their own people. Once they compromise them, they take them, and they make them eat meat. That's how they make them dense enough, controllable enough. Are you still eating life? You are responsible for the life that you are intaking. Yes, it's a process, though we understand. You don't need to eat another life. That is Archonic in nature. All you need is replenishment of your own Love-Light. Through the flow of the Universe, becoming one and learning to dance with the Universe itself. The flow of your hand chakras, and your chakras within all parts of your body. There is an infinity of chakra points and Chi points within you. Perhaps, you can find those teachings through acupuncture, these different points. Flowing these. Most importantly, this chakra here, (pointing to the back of the neck) is one that you want to guard. That you want to place a Merkaba around it, to ensure that it does not become infringed upon. This chakra is part of balancing you here, in this world. It is one of the biggest chakra points that is infringed upon by 'negatively polarized' supposed healers; they might call themselves healers, but they truly are Archonically compromised. They like to put their inversions there, as well as within the spine, because once they get to the spine and the brain, then they can start entering into the DNA and invert it with an Archon aspect, A.I., or a Reptilian. You then take on that energetic field into your DNA, or parts of you, and then you become that. You question yourself, why can't I get out of this hole? Because you have that inside of you. There's also an accumulation of past lives; you've been stuck in this Inverted Matrix, over and over, repeating those inverted cycles. It's an accumulation. You die, you come back heavy. You die again, and you come back heavier. Die again, you come back heavier, and heavier, and heavier, and heavier.

This is why the memory field within your consciousness is of extreme significance; that it is treated with the greatest sacredness. Going into the Quantum World of your consciousness, are Essenes' teachings, and you are to treat it with the greatest sacredness, whether you are the recipient, or you are the administrator, the practitioner. This is how important these teachings are and that you treat them as you are guarding a sacred life. Because that is what you're doing. This is why we teach all this. These are the results that you're seeing because of this, through these histories that are being channeled and also given through, A.U.R.A. Hypnosis Healing sessions. Because these clients are put in these Source Love-Light force fields, that activate their 12 DNA strands, and that sacredly seal them by their Higher Self. They achieve such a high level that they're actually being placed in a crystalline avatar state, while they're in hypnosis. That is why all those inversions start coming out of them, because they're not a matching vibration to the force fields that are being placed around them, of infinite Love-Light by their Higher Selves. You may continue.

Question: Beautiful, thank you for sharing that. You mentioned the Bible. Will the true teachings of Yeshua, the true Bible, be revealed to humanity? Since it's currently being held by the church. Thank you.

Essenes Elders: It's not something that's going to happen soon. It will happen very close to your end of cycle. However, you don't need that Bible. We're channeling through all of you, all of this every day. Trust in yourself, believe in yourself. You are the bridges, the antennas and anchors of these sacred teachings. You're learning them already. Often, you will hear our sacred teachings, through whatever form you're listening to. You feel resonance, because you already know it, or it's already been given to you. You're just receiving confirmations. You are the true Bible. The truth is that the 'Galactic Soul History of the Universe' book series is the real Bible. Many of you have already named it that. It's the guide of Ascension, and it is the guide of our Universe. This we speak of very humbly, but yet very confidently, in unison, and in balance always. Don't distort what we say. We are not distortion. If you feel distortion, that is yours. We are purity and infinite love. You may continue.

Question: Beautiful, thank you. As our wise Elders, can you please guide the expectant mothers of today's time, on sacred birthing with our current scenario. In your times, Mother Mary protected Yeshua. Today all prospective babies and expectant mothers are being attacked. Can you share some wisdom with us on how we can protect our babies and mothers? Thank you.

Essenes Elders: First thing you do if you are an expecting mother, you remove everyone who does not mean infinite love for you. We are broken records. It begins with that, because you detach from the inverted at that point. These people who do not mean infinite love for you, who are hiding behind jealousy and hatred, or who, perhaps, are part of black magic themselves, Voodoo, Santeria, different dark forces. They just want to be connected to you to eat and to feed their entities, through the glowing light of the life force that is within you. So you remove those people. If you are honestly affirming that you want to know how you will ensure that your child is sacredly birthed, you remove them first. That is it. You keep only your organic partner with you, and if you have other children as well. People only who mean infinite love around you. You also veil yourself. You make yourself invisible. You do not allow others to know, and you absolutely do not ever have these third dimensional ways of how people announce 'gender reveal.' Some of these things that you call 'birth announcements' and 'baby showers,' all those people latch on like leeches, and they're feeding off you and your child's glowing light. Do not bring your child into the system of sterile clinics. They're part of inserting your child into the Inverted Matrix, and that's all we can say. You sacredly birth them. You listen to your heart, listen to your child, and you talk to them from the very beginning. Even before they enter and integrate into your sacred womb protective space. You guard them, protect them, with all that you are, against all, because you are now carrying Yeshua. You are now carrying Mary Magdalene, (crying), you are now carrying Mother Marys. We have to stop these infringements upon these children. That is the most important mission on Earth right now. It's to sacredly birth these Ascended Masters of our Universe. Do you accept your mission? Whether it is now, or whether it's in the future. You treat your child like it is the greatest gift of Creation. For that is what they are, and they shall be from here on. And, they have always been. With this we'd like to end the transmission. We want to thank everyone for your beautiful hearts. Once more, we ask that you share this as far as you can. We love you, we honor you, and we respect you. We'll see you next time.

A: *Thank you, everyone for being here. Such an honor to have been able to channel the Essenes. Thank you for your love and support. Blessings! Have a glorious weekend. Thank you.*

END OF SESSION

We understand through this transmission the importance and sacredness to 'The Essenes,' when we learn of their ancestral roots to the last of the Atlanteans, the 'Galactic Council of 12,' the Elders incarnate. Placing into perspective why the Illuminati's goal was intensified in retrieving all that they could of the remains of the Essenes, the ancient Atlantean sacred teachings. Their ultimate goal is to alter the organic timelines of our Earth, influencing the rest of our part of our Universe, to slow the process of the ultimate Universal Ascension. But, they cannot, or will never, be able to stop Ascension, as our quantity of light is immense in comparison to their inversions. So much so, that they are truly drowned out by our light, almost unnoticeable; however, their bypassing of the Universe's sacred laws makes them loudly noticeable instead. Once the decision was made by the Archons to become invertedly service to self, they are no longer able to channel divine light, and must use us to retrieve sacred teachings. For they lost the connection to Source when removing their organic Love-Light, which is where these sacred teachings are accessed through. Through this transmission we further understand the previous Chapter, 'The Illuminati in the Holocaust,' and their desperate need to acquire these ancient sacred teachings from some of the last of the Atlantean/Essenes descendents, the Jewish people.

We learned of some of the locations the Elders of Atlantis traveled to after the fall: South America the law of rhythm/sacral chakra, Egypt the law of free will/solar plexus chakra, and Jerusalem the law of vibration/throat chakra. In our time and space at these sacred locations we have found the original sacred teachings of the Atlantean's. In Mexico, North and South America the Mayan/Inca/Aztec pyramids and the sacred teachings left behind through these ancient ruins, the healing medicine of the serpents, and the Mayan calendar embodying the light codes within the Earth of the 12.21.12 portal dates, when Earth began its collective heart awakening. In Egypt we find the Pyramid of Giza, and the trinity these pyramids surrounding it become, directly connected to the stars of the Orion belt. This pyramid trinity spreads throughout all of Earth, under growth and vegetation, and the Sphinx where we can time portal out into the astral, through our imagination into our Akashic Hall of Records. Because the trinity pattern of the three pyramids are spread throughout Earth, you are not only able to access the Akashic records through Egypt, you can also access it through any of these sacred lands that hold these formations. The thousands of pyramids of Earth were spiritually, architecturally, designed to mirror and be in direct alignment to the 88 constellations, sun, and moon we see above us in the night skies. Specifically each trinity of pyramids is in direct alignment with each 88 constellations. These energies channel down from the stars and ancestors into the trinity pyramids which are a focus point where all that is sacred data and knowledge for the collective's continual Ascension is downloaded into. Where Source energy channels through in portal dates, or times, with number sequences as 1.11, 2.22, 3.33, 12.21.12... It is where we find the collective sacred energy in which one can continue to uplevel of soul.

In Jerusalem, the sacred ancient ruins and the twelve caves of QumRa, the village of the Essenes where the 12/13 Keys divine power can be harnessed collectively from, we find the remnants of the dead sea scrolls, the real bible left behind by Yeshua and the Essenes, and their advanced but humbled way of living. What is communicated through the dead sea scrolls are the sacred teachings of the 13 Keys sacred laws of the Universe, which is why they were found in the 12 sacred caves of QumRa, as each of these caves represent a portal to each sacred Universal Law. To this day, these are some of the most focused upon lands that the Illuminati likes to wreak havoc within. Our creational energies, our freedom, and our speech of the collective of Earth.

By migrating to these 3 sacred lands, the Elders planted the seeds of Atlantis, once more, into the blueprint societies of future human life. So that our sacred knowledge would not be lost, that it would be remembered, when divine timing for it to be reawakened on Earth would come to be once more. And, that time is now! An honor it was to learn some of the sacred knowledge through the Essenes, as Jerusalem being the unity of the 12/13 Keys/Sacred Laws of the Universe, connected to the Universal energetic field of unity consciousness, which is what maintains the Universe and our world in balance, as shared in Book 1, Chapter 24 '13 Keys - Sacred Laws of the Universe.' Assisting us in understanding why there is communal, but separation of religions located in the lands of Jerusalem. At Jerusalem's core in the 'Old City,' the four quarters within these historic mazes, the divide of these four religions are found, Christianity, Jewish, Muslim and Armenian. The Illuminati need their branches of man-made/Archon-made religions anchored there, so that they may wield the negative energy of separation that these religions have carried forth on Earth, for it to spread throughout Earth. These religious groupings in Jerusalem, just close enough to live among each other, but truly lightyears away, as this is what some of these separations of religions bring forth to humanity. Grouping a multitude of ethnicities, causing further divide by these false religions. They need us, our divine power, to further separate the world, as we have seen mirrored through religion, over and over. By causing this energetic friction and disharmony within the sacred lands of Jerusalem, because of their religious differences, where the 13 Keys energetic fields are harnessed, it gives a stronghold for their negative polarized cause. Once more, through the Illuminati's forms of dark sorcery, they programmed us to play out for them. These are clues left behind for us to remember that this is how the Illuminati has targeted the Universal Sacred Laws, which are the beacons of light, ensuring a harmonic energetic balance of our Earth. By coming into this awareness, it bridges us into understanding that it is time we stand and say NO MORE!

Going further into some of the Essenes sacred teachings, we discover the awareness of how they wielded invisibility cloaks, hiding their beloved village from dangers, to what was not of matching vibration to Source Love-Light. Until it was time for the Essenes/the Atlantean descendants to emerge, blending into society, creating offspring with the Jerusalem inlanders, keeping these roots alive by living among the people of Jerusalem and beyond. We teach these sacred Essenes, Ascended Masters, Archangel shields, through all our 'Rising Phoenix Aurora' courses. How to make yourself invisible to all harm, by not consenting to all types of inversions.

Negative entities view differently than us. They live in the astral plane where all are lights and energies, as they are not contained to a human physical vessel. When they scan Earth's people, all they can see us as are lights, and how bright, or activated, these lights are. The way the entities see is by a type of black and white spectrum. Therefore, if you place an invisibility cloak over yourself/your light when shielding daily, when they scan the lands of Earth, you will be read as if you are not there, unreadable, scrambling their negative technologies and their ways of viewing. You will show, as your light is dim in comparison, not as attractive to what they prefer instead, which are the lights that are brightest, coming into an awakening, not shielded, with no boundaries. The brightest lights being a higher infinite abundance of Source Love-Light that they can feed off. The dimmer lights, perhaps not as tasty and as satisfying for their unfulfilled hunger.

How the Essenes operated in the two/third world split then, far before our times, shows us how advanced and connected they were. Some think that, in that time, their village was underdeveloped; however, it was not, as they were far beyond even us in consciousness. Their beginning seeding of the two/third world split into Earth's blueprint was essential for us, as they held these spaces then for us in the now, so that it wouldn't be as new to us, but instead, a remembrance and flow into how to work within the two worlds of the inverted and the organic. The Essenes explained to us how important it was that they maintained organic within, in order to live in the organic world, without inversions of entities, implants, technologies in them, as Mother Mary and Yeshua had taught them. This being a very important key to their civilization's preservation. Without foreign irregularities within us, all that is left to guide us is inwards, our organic connection to Source, no trappings, or illusions, to fool us with ease. This is how Mother Mary was able to hold the sufficient Source Love-Light in order to sacredly birth the Messiah, Yeshua, who to this day, can bring you to tears because of the overwhelming abundance of love that you feel when you just speak to him. Yeshua was birthed through a clean, clear, natural, sacred birth, where he received no infringements when his soul entered the Earthly plane, as his Mother was able to bridge this possibility for him because she carried no infringements within her. We can only birth at a matching vibration to our mothers, as they are our bridges in. Other than the Essenes, this was a rarity to accomplish, as the majority of people of Earth carried inversions, beginning from the fall of Atlantis, when the accumulation of past life trauma began. Atlantis was the end of the cycle of the process of our Earth's collective Ascension, which was not acquired; therefore, since then we have been living in a false matrix simulation of an accumulation of inverted timelines. Which is why we are overdue for Ascension, as a collective. Mother Mary was the example for us in the then, so that in the now, we Mothers, would too remember that we all are now Mother Marys, and all life that we create within our womb and birth are Yeshua's. In Book 4, we will speak in depth of the importance of sacred birthing.

Mother Mary, Yeshua and Mary Magdalene's offspring, their disciples, and all those who were graced by the beauty of being able to be present when Yeshua walked and taught on the Earth, received his channeled heart activations, and they are who continued to carry forth the word of infinite love, in how we are all God's children, never separated, as God is within us. After Yeshua ascended out of the Matrix, his people's journeys on foot and water were essential and challenging, but always guided by his voice they were, and they are the seeds which Yeshua left behind, who spread his teachings far and wide like vines. This is one of the ways of how the Essenes' sacred teachings were able to reach as far as Carmela's time and space, in the Holocaust, in the previous Chapter. However, as we know, the Illuminati has taken much of what Yeshua taught and inverted it through religion, to plague and program the people of Earth, using whom they loved infinitely, Yeshua. Some of the inversions that have been programmed are that he is the only son of God, when in actuality all are children of God, as we all hold Source within us, which is what gives us lifeforce and light everyday to be a soul. Or that he is our mighty savior, and he will judge us in the time of revelation and reckoning. Or to say his name in a cursed way, when we are troubled. These are some of the last things he would ever want from the footprints of remembrance, he left behind for us.

I walked with Yeshua, beside him, in the time of his Earthly incarnation, and I remember how gentle, strong, fierce, and sovereign he was and is. His inner knowing at the clearest of understanding. He would tell all people who crossed his path to call him brother, as he was an equal to all. He made it very clear that these teachings were not meant to be used invertedly, and not be tainted after his passing, even though in his heart he knew they would, as it was part of the cycle of Ascension for the collective, "Can they rise out from these inverted cycles for one final time, allowing the transformation required for themselves to ascend out?" He knew that within the inverted matrix, the Archons, and the negative entities would continue their illusional games, as he had to live through in his time.

Yeshua once came to me in a dream, and he showed me how he knew everything to come in the now of our timelines. He could look through time and space, as could his mother, and see all possible outcomes, all timeline potentials, whether organic or inverted. HE KNEW IT ALL! Therefore, at his death, when his essence multiplied, spread and seeded throughout the entire earth's blueprint, in union with the Christ Consciousness and Source, together they created, to all inverted timelines, potential counters of the true organic timelines. And, no matter which way the artificial intelligence tries to influence the people of Earth to create their inverted timelines, there would always be a choice for the people to remove themselves from inverted timelines and into organic timelines instead, as this potential blueprint is held inside of Earth's crystalline coding. This assists us in profound ways. Therefore, all that is left for us to do is to just surrender in flow, and know all will divinely manifest into creation. And, it is our choices which matter the most, as we are who wield ourselves in and out of the choices of timelines. No one has the power to manifest our timelines, but WE!

The Essenes explain to me that the way the American language and culture has been founded, it itself is inverted and backwards. When you look upon the sacred dead sea scrolls, you see how the scripture is channeled from right to left, not left to right, as the English language is. If you play the English language backwards, it sounds magical, like light language. The clock we use to keep track of time daily, is meant to go counter, not clockwise. The clock is the foundation of our flat Earth's grid construct. In future literature to come of the [12]Antarctica series, you will understand how our third dimensional construct is a flat Earth plane of existence. If you can imagine the entire Earth lands in the shape of a clock, with segments on the parts of the lands where each time pocket of the clock resides within. If as a collective we began to consciously work within time going counter, this would allow time to move forward with ease, and flow without stagnation. The way we experience time in the now, going clockwise, it moves it collectively in slow motion. This inversion of dark sorcery, makes it feel as if we are stuck within an overlapping pocket of time and space, on constant repeat. When you turn on a ceiling fan, if it turns in a clockwise rotation, it instead pulls in the air and you receive no cooling motion, and if you turn it counter, it expels rapidly and in turn you feel the expansion of air. Clockwise stagnant air, counter clockwise, flowing air; the same pertains to time, initially assisting the process of Ascension to fast forward.

When looking upon the image below of the clock, we explain how all time is rooted to the number 13, which is present at every turning hour, the 13th hour of creation. We spoke of the numbers 12 and 13 in Chapter 4, understanding how all began from these sacred numbers. The 12 being the first essences of Source, birthing out from Source, the center always the 13th, the center of creation, the Universes heart, the Divine Mother's heart. This is how the Galactics/The Council of 12 stand, holding space within the energetic higher realms, which have no exact dimension, as they are all dimensions. Divine Mother, the 13th at the center, and the 12 Elders of Creation at the positions of the numbers as a clock, at their Universal sacred laws that they oversee, but instead they make up the shape of the [13]12-pointed Merkabah, the image next page...

---

[12] Go to Rumble.com and Odysee.com to watch the Antarctica/Tartaria series, which will be one of the most important series you will ever watch.

[13] AuroRa teaches the 'Isis Priestess Mentorship' course live on Patreon, or it is available instantly under risingphoenixaurora.com, which houses the "The 13 Keys Archangels"class, explaining in depth the 12 pointed Merkabah, and its connection to our creation.

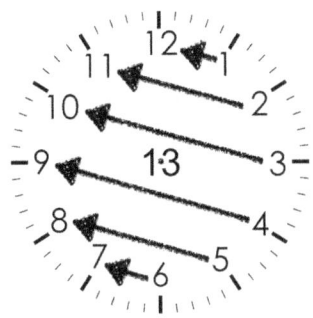

12/13 pointed Merkabah

Following the image of the clock, starting from 1, going counter clockwise, drawing a direct line to each number across, when you add 1 + 12 = 13, 2 +11 =13, 3 + 10 = 13, 4 + 9 = 13, 5 + 8 = 13, 6 + 7 =13. It is all 13! Since my awakening stages, my divine team explained to me that we have been taught backwards and inverted. They said "It is right to left, not left to right." If time is directed clockwise, it pulls in time, making it slow in nature. If it is directed counter, it would instead expand fluently, in a natural form, versus what we experience here on Earth. The sun is the hour hand, and at every dial it is pointing at on the land it is noon entering the 13th hour/1:00 pm at whatever location it is on earth. This formula is true quantum physics, and it is the key for physical time travel. Cern technologies, and the government, have stolen this sacred knowledge from us, and can time travel with this understanding through their technologies. If they go to these pockets of spaces on the lands, where these hours meet one another as the clock above, they have found that you can use these pockets of quantum spaces to power up and activate the technologies to teleport from one location of Earth to another across the world.

When understanding the significance of numbers, we know that all within Creation is gridded with numerology sequences. Each individual soul signature carries a sequence of numbers which are part of the alchemy that makeup their soul. These numbers within our soul are the glue which conjoin's everything within us, and these sacred numbers can be found within our individual genetic DNA makeup, which is rooted to all that we are within Creation. It is also explained that through the Multiverse, each verse is a sequence of numbers, which, then in turn, is represented in how different each verse is to one another. For example, when counting in order, numbers 6 and 7 are next to each other, but they are both very different from one another. An example to that is the image of clock in the previous page, each number is different, however when merging the sums together through addition, they still make up the same solution. The Multiverse of infinite souls within creation can be seen as this.

Let's talk about what each number means at its prime and beginning origins: 0 = when there was nothing in Creation, but an infinite potential to birth. 1 = the first Creation, Divine Mother. 2 = the second Creation, Divine Father, the first twin flame sacred union within our Creation. 3 = the Holy Trinity, Mother, Father, and child, which is connected to the Universe's drive for expansion. 4 = the four sacred directions of Creation, in how life expands in all ways. 5 = the first elements birthed from Divine Mother, Earth, fire, water, air, and spirit. 6 = ascension from cycles, how Creation is constantly rising out like the arc in the circle of number 6. 7 = the prime colors which keep us in balance, as the rainbow inside of us and in the skies. 8 = the infinity sign, in how all in Creation is infinite. 9 = how we descend from our Higher Self forms, fractalizing into the infinite potentials of incarnations, the circle/cycle of life being at the top and then descending down as you follow the arch down to fractalize. 10 = the cycle of completion, but from 10, we start all over again, never ending, as the number 10 holds 1/new beginnings, and 0/cycle of life. All which relate and categorize into the explanation to what each number means at its root, would be directly linked to these sacred numbers.

In my travels, I came across three mountains/mounds in the United States, which were aligned to the Orion belt and patterned as the pyramid of Giza, as shown in the image below. These mounds were truly pyramids, but under natural growth. It has been explained to us that pyramids, such as Giza, are portals/stellar gateways. In other words, a doorway, or transportation, to another point in time and space, another realm, another dimension. We think that this means we can only astral travel at these sacred locations through our consciousness/mind, however it is deeper than that.

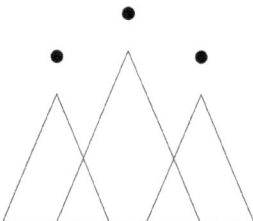

As I passed by, and was directly aligned in a row with these three pyramids, in an instant I lost one hour of time and memory. Seconds before I passed the pyramids, the sun was high enough, which indicated it was one hour before sundown, seconds later it was completely dark, father sun had already set, and he was no longer visible in the sky. This was the predominant reason how I was able to recognize and come into awareness that I had lost an hour of time.

My initial reaction, because of how clear my intentions are in not allowing infringements, was "Oh HELL NO!!!" As I know in my line of work, this can mean that you might have been UFO abducted. Once I calmed my initial feelings of fury, but still remained a silent calmness inwards, I asked to speak to my divine team, and I said I wanted to speak to Yeshua. He instantly connected to my heart, and told me not to worry, that all was well. He showed me a vision of me as I passed by the three pyramids; at the tip of the pyramids there was a natural power source, which is invisible to the physical eyes, and can only be seen by our third eyes. The forcefield was an opalescent, plasmic energy field which created a line, like when we were young and connected the dots in a coloring book, to make a shape. The shape in this case being the three dots, connecting with lines from one another, dot to dot. These three connecting Source spheres emanated out the stellar gateway force field. Which if you are in matching vibration to pure Source Love-Light, in service-to-others, with no inversions within you, it instantly teleports you in your full embodiment of consciousness and physical vessel, into the portaled realm of the pyramids.

Have you ever wondered why the pyramids are solid stone for the most, and how it was that civilizations of priestesses, or priests, lived or practiced inside them? There are tunnels going inwards, into an upside down pyramid, under the upright pyramid. Most benevolent civilizations would reside within these sacred spaces, as shown in the image below. The top pyramid is the antenna, drawing in the frequency of the Universe, and the bottom upside down pyramid holds this frequency like a chalice. As mentioned in Book 1, [14]Chapters 23 and 24, the 144 main beaconed groupings of the three pyramids patterned to the Orion Belt create an electromagnetic and energetic gridding to one another, once more as connecting the dots at both tips, top and bottom. The other key to pyramids is that, since they are stellar gateways, you don't actually walk, or commune, physically inside them, though in some parts you can, instead you walk through the pyramid walls etherically, teleporting out into your destined dimension. Which is why once more they are solid inside, as you teleport out into your choice of dimension from your perspective of time and space, time traveling through the stellar gateway that the pyramids are.

---

[14] In Galactic Soul History of the Universe Book 1, Chapters 23 and 24, "Egyptian Pharaoh Osiris - The Pyramids," and "Inner Earth Galactic Guardian - Adama."

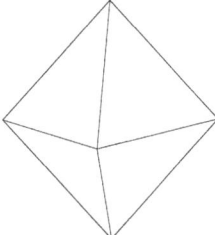

When I passed these three sequenced pyramids, I teleported out into a higher dimensional realm, where all who on Earth who were a matching vibration, which were thousands, joined us there, however from their perspective location they could have just joined us there in astral bodies, while taking a quick nap. Collectively there was an important shift in the works pertaining to the Earth's organic timeline, and we were to join together here with the galactic guardians from the Universe, so that we could assist in gridding it together. Bridging it forth into Earth, so it is above, so it is below. From beyond the Matrix, the guardians were carriers of these sacred Source light codes, in which they were meant to share with us when rendezvousing. When coming back physically into Earth, we would be who would grid these light codes in, as we were the carriers now. Together birthing out one of Earth's fundamental organic timelines. We were away for an hour in the ether, but when we came back, in actuality we had been away from Earth consciously for three years. Our embodiments were not the same as when we had left, because we carried back the wisdom and the leveling up of energies of the three years gone in astral form, now in us. This is how we explain how slow time is on Earth. What is one hour to us here, it is approximately three years beyond the Matrix of Earth, if there was a measurement to time. In a blink of an eye we left and came back, because the stellar gateway of the pyramids can teleport you out in this manner. Physically you could be seen as never having been gone, however you were just zapped back in consciously, at that exact location that you physically were at. Experiencing, as per my example, one moment the sun is up high in the sky, and in another it has set, but never did I experience it setting, as I was not technically there consciously physically to experience it. From our perspective within Earth, we would lose an hour of conscious memory instead.

When Egyptian Pharaoh Isis and her Priestesses benevolently reigned Egypt, when entering the pyramid of Giza, they would go into another sacred dimension, bridging out into the multidimensions of life within the Universe, into a place of safety and protection. And, only if you were matching vibration and frequency energetically to pure infinite Source Love-Light could you enter, if you contained the A.I. Archon virus within you of impurity, you would be repelled, as your consciousness and physical vessel would not be compatible to enter. Similar to when the final physical, earthly Ascension comes forth for the collective, will you be a match to the vibration of Source infinite Love-Light and be a clear holy trinity of mind, body, and soul, so that when the Source plasmic flamed wave comes forth, will you ride with it, or will you not withstand it?

"All which contains life and light attracts and unites together. If you are negative, you attract negative atoms; if you are positive, you attract positive atoms. We are what we are magnetized to, and what we vibrate to."
~AuroRa

--------------<<>>--------------

8

A GODDESS INCARNATE

Session #367: Recorded in May 2021
Never before shared.

In this online A.U.R.A. Hypnosis Healing session, Kehlani takes us on a journey of discovery and remembrance of the sacredness of the Gods and Goddesses, and this divine power that we, too, hold within. The galactic history of Earth's seeding, before she was called Earth, the beauty of her, and the potentials she holds for the multitudes of alien races. The journey back to remember and connect to the elements that give us lifeforce, every day of our lives on Earth. In this most important session we are finally introduced to the Archon maker. Who was he, before he became a collective artificial intelligent Archon? What happened to him? The free willed path, which is always divine, for it consists of freedom.

--------------<<>>--------------

"Sometimes during the day, we forget who we really are. And when we dance, we can feel the energy coming up from Earth, into us. Connecting us with the moon and our sisters on the other side."
~Kehlani

"The sand… the sand connects us to the truest knowing; there is never any lack, for within even the smallest grain, there is God's power. The desert reminds us, as one, we are mighty, together, we are strong."
~Kehlani

--------------<<>>--------------

A [AuroRa]: Have you landed on the ground?
K [Kehlani]: I have, but I feel split between two lands.
A: Tell me what you're seeing.
K: First I see sand. A desert. And another space that's darker. Like the cellar underground. I only see a candle light, or a lantern.
A: Let's go to the one that's dark with the candle. As you're going towards it, look at yourself. Do you feel like you have a body?
K: Yes, I have a body.
A: Look at your hands. How many fingers do you have?
K: I have ten.
A: How many toes do you have?
K: I have ten, but I'm wearing boots.
A: What color is your skin tone?
K: It's white.
A: Are you wearing any clothing?
K: I'm wearing a ripped dress.
A: Are you carrying anything?
K: No. Everything was taken.
A: Do you feel like you're female or male?
K: I am a woman.

A: Do you feel younger or older?
K: I feel young. But I've had a child.
A: Why did you say that? You felt like everything was taken from you.
K: I did something. And I'm here because of what I did.
A: You said you have a child? Where is your child?
K: I don't know; they took him.
A: Let's go ahead and go back in time, to right before whatever it is that you did, that got you into this situation. You're there now.
K: (Crying) I see a garden. I see other women, we're smiling, and we're working together.
A: Tell me why you're crying.
K: Because I know something happened to them, they're not with me in the other place. And the way I feel now, with them, It feels so good.
A: These women, how many more are there with you?
K: Two.
A: Do they have light skin like you, do they look different?
K: One looks like me, but much older, and the other looks different.
A: Tell me about this garden you are at; what does it look like?
K: There are vegetables and there is an arch in the center and medicine. It's a place of love.
A: Tell me what it is that you all are doing.
K: We're gathering herbs to give to our friends who are sick and anyone who needs them to heal their ailments. This is also a place where we come to connect to the womb Goddess.
A: How do you connect to the womb Goddess from here?
K: The women from the village gather, when the moon is ripe... and we dance. It knows us by our names.
A: Tell me why you dance. What significance is that to... connected to the womb Goddess?
K: Sometimes during the day, we forget who we really are. And when we dance, we can feel the energy coming up from Earth, into us. Connecting us with the moon and our sisters on the other side.
A: That's beautiful. Thank you. You said sisters on the other side - what do you mean by that?
K: The ones who know; who do not battle the forgetting; who are connected. Whenever we are lost, they can take us to the other side. And we return to them, because they are us.
A: Beautiful. Keep moving time to when something happens of importance next, tell me what happens.
K: I'm back in the desert now. There are many of us. We traveled together and know how to speak with the sand.
A: Are you speaking to the sand now?
K: We speak with it through how we move through it. We know where the water is. We also know that ancient power rests here; arises here, is centered here.
A: By connecting to the movement of the sand... the sand is able to direct you to the water?
K: The sand...the sand connects us to the truest knowing; there is never any lack, for within even the smallest grain, there is God's power. The desert reminds us, as one, we are mighty, together, we are strong.
A: Beautiful, keep moving time. Tell me where you all are going within the sand. You said something about great power...
K: Forward there is pain; back there is knowledge. As we move towards the sea, things are lost, things are taken. Our way of life shifts and is broken. We are scattered, spread across the world. Brought back, safe now, we are never separated. When we return to our origin, we are made whole again, no longer fearing dispersal.
A: Keep moving time; tell me what happens next of importance.
K: We are going to come back. We have chosen Kehlani.
A: Explain that. What do you mean you've chosen her?
K: Bad things happen to the spirit, because of its magic. Its magic was taken from it, almost destroyed. But in this vessel it will return.
A: Beautiful. Can you tell me about this great power that is sensed here within this land of sand?

K: The origin of everything. How our people came to this planet. We nested our greatest gifts and lessons within the dunes. Only those that know how to traverse that land will visit them and thus they will always remain safe, for those who can interpret. This land is like our land. The terrain is similar. And, thus we knew this part of Earth could always be trusted.
A: What part of Earth is this?
K: Fish River Canyon, Namibia.
A: What else can you tell us about this land? You said that's where it all began- your people? Do you mean that the people of Earth began or your people there?
K: I think the people of Earth may have begun there, but I mean my people, from the planet we came from. It was beautiful, like Fish River Canyon. But it did not have the pains of Earth. In my land, we moved with the sand, and we rose tall, like trees. The water flowed through the desert and we did not know fear, scarcity, or these words "abundance." We were in peace; loved by our many Suns; nourished by our moons. Harmony was our birthright.
A: Keep moving time to another important time, in what you're showing us, where we will find more answers. We're there now, tell me what's going on.
K: I'm in a room giving birth. I see the baby, ahh (whispering) they are perfect!
A: You said, "they" are perfect?
K: Yes, I see one girl... a boy, two!?!
A: You've given birth to twins?
K: I cannot tell if it is twins. All I see are two babies. I'm so happy to see them! They are joy incarnate. A reclamation of the work done in this body; they are whole, but they also have such a beautiful and unique story. I am, we are, "helper" to each other.
A: Tell me about the space that you are in while you're birthing them.
K: Paul, my husband is crying. So happy. We are in a home, but then, things change and we end up in a hospital, or medical, sterile space, but I am not afraid.
A: Let's go back to what happened. You said that things change when? Before your birthing, or during birth, or when do things change?
K: During the birth.
A: What happens?
K: Things do not feel right. He is afraid.
A: Who's afraid?
K: Paul, and my midwives.
A: Why are they afraid?
K: The baby is flipped, distressed. Not ready to come into the world here. Oh, this is not, this is not my first baby. There is a little girl here. And so I know things are different this time. To give birth to him will require more work.
A: What happened? I know you said that you were so prepared energetically for him. What was different with him?
K: I think his spirit is afraid. She wanted to come. But, he is not sure the world is ready for his message. And so first, we must prepare the space, and it will require more of my vessel than before. He's strong. And so, so different. He will require the strength to make it, for his message to come, for he will suffer as Kehlani suffered. First in between, not quite right, because it will take time for what is known within him to be known by the world.
A: So, that is the reason why you said the head is not in the right direction?
K: Yes, but we also kind of think it's funny.
A: Why?
K: Because no one will ever tell him how to be, or do; he is one who will always walk his own way. Though we are in pain, we are so proud.
A: You said that there's a decision made that you have to go to a sterile hospital?
K: Yes.
A: Tell me what happens there and who goes with you to the hospital.

K: Paul goes, and though no one there looks like this vessel, I am not afraid. I knew this would happen. So I chose to give birth in Italy, where I knew the baby would be safe. And where Kehlani would make it. They will take good care of her here.

A: Good. Now that she's in that space at the hospital, tell me what happens.

K: He erupts in, just like she did, so loud. Kehlani and this boy- so much energy. I also feel others coming with him. Guides. He... from the moment he comes in, he has the help he needs. It will be hard, but he will make it.

A: Does he come in head first or feet first?

K: He is pulled out. They must cut her.

A: Once he's pulled out, tell me what happens next.

K: He is happy. They're both happy together. Kehlani learns so much through that, with that teacher. They built a new path together. They both feel loved, but when the black boy leaves the house, he knows the world is not the same as it is with his mother. When he is a teen, these feelings will turn him inside out. Feeling like an outsider, one foot in, one foot out. Sweet, sweet boy. Inside of him, is soft, is sweet... is made of every good thing meant to exist on Earth. But that is not what this plane... that is not what this collective wants from him, and he will have to learn how not to fight, because he is so strong. And people will misinterpret his strength and try to teach him to use it in the wrong ways; potentially what some would fear are evil ways. But the guide that came in with him is old and knows of the tricks of Earth and will help him. Because his sister will heal through doing, but he will heal through knowing. His words, from experience, will be a gift.

A: Beautiful. Let's go ahead and leave that scene, let's go to another important time in this life, you are there now. Tell me what you see and sense. What's going on?

K: I see two scenes: one as a catalyst that awakens him; it is a fight with his sister. She is yelling, very loud. But, I can feel a wall in him crumbling; one that had only been up for a short while. But it'd already caused damage. Then next, I see him speaking in front of a group, a large audience. He is so handsome, so self-assured, and I see his sister in the front row, smiling. She has always had wisdom and it shines bright within her; she will be the first woman born in the family line unburdened. She is an unburdened mother.

A: Beautiful. Let's go ahead and leave that scene. Let's go to another important time in this life, where we will find answers that we seek for your highest healing, you are there now. Tell me what you're seeing and sensing.

K: I'm looking at a child, who is looking up at me in a bookstore, and I am signing a book and telling him the magic he seeks is within him.

A: Beautiful.

K: I am in an attic, slanted window, door to porch. It is here that I will write the first of many. These books are about letting children maintain their sovereignty. They will function as fiction, but will be a spell book, a guide to make sure to... to awaken them younger and to make sure they do not become cluttered as this spirit did.

A: Beautiful. Let's leave that scene; let's go to another important time that we seek for your highest healing; you're there now. Tell me what you see.

K: I am in a tower, I see a rolling, green field, and a man holding a flag on horseback. That memory is bound and twisted with another. I am in a village in Senegal. I am being crowned prince and about to marry. In both these times, I was royalty and in both these times, I made the wrong choice.

A: Wrong choice of what?

K: I let my people be taken. I did not know they were my people. They were another tribe, (crying) that we'd have conflict with, and when the white settler came and offered to buy them, we, of course, said yes. We did not know the curse we were bringing. In the tower, I am a woman who lets other women die for magic; for what I believe is a sin, because I am trapped. And I only know serving, pain, and being what others want from me. If I am to suffer, we are all to suffer. I know now what I did was wrong because the next life, I experienced it.

A: What did you experience?

K: We reap what we sow. I, along with my sisters, was murdered. I do not want to stay in this memory anymore.

A: I understand she does not want to stay in the memory, but does she need to see anything else within it before we move on? So that the healing begins. Or can we move on?

K: In the moment, I am burned. I have a memory of my past life, of how I did not help the others. It will bore something inside this spirit. I will sacrifice myself to help others from this moment on, so as never to be the one to bring violence to those that look like me. And so, for the next 400 years, I will only be at service, only of sacrifice. But that will not work either.

A: Why not?

K: It draws entities to me. And the two lives before this body, people took advantage. I thought… no, the collective thought, that I had it all. But in those lives, I had no sovereignty. In the one before the last one, I was only of service. But there is something in this spirit. The prince, he is a fighter; he has always been. So, though the princess wants to be of service, the prince is a warrior. So, whenever we have been made captive, we have always found a way to free ourselves. The same way I was burned and I sold a slave, I then was a slave. But I escaped. My spirit always knew that this was not the truth. But I came back, again and again, and eventually died, freeing others. In the life before this one, I was famous, as they say on this planet. People looked at me, they worshiped me, they loved me. But the man in my life, the men in my life, controlled me, hurt me, damaged me. Because, I did not believe that I yet deserved to be free from the sins of my past self. That is why we incarnated in this vessel, blameless, pure. So we could work through our need to sacrifice, and our need to fight in one vessel, in one life.

A: Thank you. At the beginning, we took her to a time, a space, where she was crying; she was upset. She said that her son had been taken from her, because of what she did. Let's go back to that time now and see what happened in that time that she was remembering. When was her son taken from her?

K: The men come, riding fast on horses, in the night and set fire to everything. We have five houses in our field with the garden at the center. And they do unspeakably terrible things to my sister. One tries to enter me and does not realize I hold the dagger. I can feel his blood on my face, as I run. I'm looking for my son in the field. I saw the boys and girls run this way. Behind me, there's smoke and screaming, and then I hear it. One of the men passed my boy…I don't know what to do. If I run at him, will he kill us both? Right now he is looking at the boy with kindness, like he is guiltless. He takes the boy on his horse. At that moment, I knew I would never see him again. And so I cry out and they come for me. I have nothing left to lose. So I let them take me. And here, in the cellar, I wait for what's to come.

A: What happens?

K: They burned me, sister. But, they do not know that the fire awakened something in me as well. I remember my mistakes, but for a second, I also remember where I am from. For the first time, I remember the dunes and the river and harmony. And, underneath every energy, I plant that seed, harmony, harmony, harmony, waiting to be reclaimed under everything, harmony. When we came here, we could feel it in the Earth, that it would suffer. The stones knew, long before the violence came. But, we also knew that if we could return to harmony with this land, we could rekindle the magic of our old planet, here. We knew many were coming here to do the same thing, for both good and bad. And so though we were afraid the minute we saw this land, we loved it. We loved this Earth. It became a piece of us; it had called to us, and so we answered the call and shed our fear, because this planet is so worthy and beautiful. We thank all we encountered. We felt lucky to call it "friend."

A: Thank you. Let's leave that life now.

The Higher Self is called forth.

K: I am here.

A: Thank you Higher Self. Why did you say that it is part of a joke? (AuroRa pronounces the client's name incorrectly, during calling in the Higher self)

Higher Self: This name is special. It exists to remind her that though she was taken from her cultures and grew up in a new land, "amore fati"- love your fate; everything happens for a reason. And, when things are special, as she is, sometimes it takes a bit of time for people to be able to know what

they're tasting. Her name - it is a song, a melody, strung together by her ancestors. We knew there would be anger in this life. But when she says her name, when others say her name, they smile.
A: *Beautiful. Thank you for explaining that. You took her to many different times and places, may I ask questions about that?*
Higher Self: But of course, that's why we chose you. You're very gifted with the questions.
A: *That I am, thank you. It is because you give them to me. The first part she landed was two lands, there was sand and a dark space where there was a candle lit. And then we chose to take her to the dark space. Why did you take her there? What were you trying to tell her there - the purpose?*
Higher Self: Sometimes Kehlani has a hard time, when she thinks that someone is saying she's too special. It makes us sad to say this actually, but we knew it would be easier for her, at first, when she hears this, to accept that something bad had happened to her, than to accept first, that she was a part of a nomadic group that settled and then later made a mistake. We know if we started with the cellar, and led her back to the tower, she would be able to forgive herself. But if we started with the tower, she would feel too much guilt. This spirit has felt enough guilt, enough shame, enough fear.
A: *Thank you. This explains how every single choice that we take, in every step, is of extreme importance, as it will lead us in different directions, as your choice in which way to show her first. From there you took her to a garden where there were two other women with her that were dancing to the womb Goddess. Why did you take her there? What was the purpose?*
Higher Self: I wanted her to know why sometimes she feels a fire burning inside of her. So big, it would engulf anyone that dares to oppress anyone, even people who love her and make mistakes. She has no tolerance for bullying, harm, ignorance, because it took her sisters. But I wanted her to see that the place that it started was love, love, love. The anger does not drive her. It merely appears to fuel the real vessel, which is love. We also wanted her to know that she is an herbalist and that the plants miss her and want her to return.
A: *Beautiful. Can you tell us more about this womb Goddess that they were dancing to?*
Higher Self : Ah! The Womb Goddess! Such a sweet, sweet... she is everything! The heart of the Earth. She is how we give life, how seeds grow, how waterfalls flow, she is the sacred feminine at the heart of everything. These women came to Earth to honor her, to work with her, and then when they die, to return to her.
A: *Are we able to speak to the womb Goddess? Would you connect us to her?*
Higher Self : I would love to. She is my most divine sister friend.
A: *Thank you, it'd be an honor to talk to her now.*
Womb Goddess: (softly) Hello!
A: *Greetings sister, it's an honor to have you here. Thank you for being here and gracing us with your beauty.*
Womb Goddess: Oh! You bring tears to my eyes, it is such a gift to see you and to know you.
A: *Thank you sister. May I ask you questions?*
Womb Goddess: But of course, you know, we have talked many times.
A: *Thank you. It's a very important time to be speaking to you, in this time of space, as we have many really trying to regain back their womb power; protecting it, clearing it, healing it. Specifically, even now the attack on children in the wombs, though we are working on it. Your wisdom is needed in this time and space.*
Womb Goddess: There will always be people, entities and energies, that try to stamp out our power. But the minute we know it, it means we are already ten steps ahead. You know what they are trying to do, but they do not know what we are up to sister; they cannot speak to us the way that we can channel them. It is of the utmost importance that you continue to find each other; continue to share in song and dance on YouTube. Even in holy eye contact. The Awakening is moving much faster now.
A: *Beautiful, thank you. Can you give us advice as far as how we can channel our womb space, protect and cleanse it? How to work with it?*
Womb Goddess: Each of you will have to rewrite your story. The ones you were given on your wombs, were tainted and a lie. But, within you is a sacred language. If you are confused and cannot find your way to the root, go to the nearest blooming flower, river or snow; in these transformations, there is a holy cleansing. You all, when you bow and surrender, as this vessel has done, like lightning

I enter and clear out the cobwebs. We, as you know sister, are working on linear time. So once it has begun, it has already done. So I guess the shortest answer is begin and know, I am with you.
A: *Because when you begin, it has already occurred because of linear time.*
Womb Goddess: This is why I love you. You always know. I was smiling before I finished the sentence.
A: *(gently laughing) You knew how I was going to finish it! Yes. Beautiful. Love that. Just begin. Marvelous. Tell me more about you and your beautiful energy. Tell us, do you have any connections to the elements and ways that we can connect to you besides the womb space?*
Womb Goddess: But of course, sister. When you see the vine and the fern... ivy and fern are some of my oldest friends, and their spiral, and in the way they grow, there are many divine lessons and patterns. When you let yourself be as big, or as small as you feel in the moment, you are channeling me, because you have moved past your ego. I am the most sovereign being energy on this planet. And so, when you tap into your knowing, you are greeting me. So, the best way to pray to me, is to connect to your Higher Self. So in essence, when you pray to yourself, you are praying to me. The only thing you need to do to find me is to listen to the call. For some, it will be reading and writing; for some, they will connect to their Divinity through their muscles; for others it will be in how they love, because ... the only thing that is consistent, is listening to the frequency, the tone that I have specifically gifted you. Because that sound is how you can find me, and how you can find yourself.
A: *This tone that you speak of, do you mean when we connect to you, you would give us this tone?*
Womb Goddess: Yes, for each of you it's different. For some of you, it will be a sound you'll hear, that gets you to go somewhere, someday. For others, it will be a skill that you acquire when you were born, that will connect you to me, or a skill you acquire later in life that will awaken that connection you have to me. For some, mostly babies and children, their connection is unbroken, and so we talk freely. There are also others who find me in music, or sound baths, or can only feel me when they are in motion, running or dancing, or experiencing a loss. I am often at the gates when you come in and when you leave. Because I love you so. I want to greet you and say goodbye.
A: *Beautiful. They said you're a goddess, can you explain what that means?*
Womb Goddess: It means I am one of the old ones, before the planet Earth was called Earth; before the planet was a planet, there were us; as things are always meant to shift, change and grow, like all things existing, we transformed. Some of us became physical and some split ourselves across the Universe to go where we are needed. I am one like that. I came here because I have such admiration for the entities that created this Earth, and wanted to help. But, I was not welcomed at first.
A: *Why were you not welcomed at first?*
Womb Goddess: There was another entity here that felt like I was trying to challenge them, and did not think that we could both be here. And so, in order to get rid of me, they changed. And the people that prayed to them changed to.
A: *Who was this other entity?*
Womb Goddess: I do not like to say his name. But he is known by, "Bello."
A: *We've heard many stories throughout ancient literature; can you tell us who he is?*
Womb Goddess: He was so loving once; a divine friend, who could shift and move matter. He had a very good sense of humor. And when he came to Earth, he enjoyed making new animals. But, it took a while for many of us to get here. There were other planets that required us. And by the time we got here, he had forgotten what it was like to be with us. To be with others. His frequency was no longer tuned to ours, but was instead tuned to a frequency that only existed here on Earth. At least I know. And when he was with us, when we were together, moving matter on Earth, we could feel something in him changing. And we worked with the humans. He didn't like that; he had made that... no, that he was part of making them and that we had come later, but had such a powerful effect on them. He started to figure out ways to make them afraid of that feeling we gave them. First, it started with fear. And so, we the other entities here that came for good, believe in consent, and as I said, sovereignty, and so if they did not call to us, if they did not dance for us, if they did not feel us and want to feel us, we could no longer come. And so for a time, we could only watch, as he twisted them against us. And our names were almost forgotten. There were about a handful of humans left who could carry the stories of us and survive. This vessel, this line, the women in this family line, are very powerful.

And so we knew that we could commune with the baby they were making. It took many generations to create a woman in this line, who was unburdened enough to dig. This vessel has been digging and digging until she found us again.

A: Does this have any connection to - she mentioned that she was told that she was created by seven deities?

Womb Goddess: Oh, yes. This one. This one, this one, this one; we, sister, made a bet on this one. We hoped that if we work through her, she will create many tracks that allow the others to find us again. The same way he twisted the knowing, she will uncover it, as you say, she will reawaken the world of wonder.

A: Beautiful. What happened with "Bellos?"

Womb Goddess: He came when we came. He has been lurking on the outskirts, wanting this one. And he almost succeeded many times coaxing her to the edge, to suicide. He did not want her to exist. And when he realized that it would be too hard to get to the child, because we were there, he infiltrated the brother and the parents until for many years, when she was in that home, everything that happened there almost took her farther from us. But again, as I said, he cannot hear what we are saying and he could not reach her in the dreams. So we sent the other sovereign souls to help. Every step of the way, she has had another sister to guide her; one that he could not see until it was too late. First came Luna, abundance, to show her the hell in her home was not the real world. And then there have been many, many others. But Luna was when we realized if we use the dreams, we could always find her there.

A: Luna is who?

Womb Goddess: Luna is a piece of the Earth Goddess. She is lost now... guarded, or no, wrapped in another fate, but has given birth to two children... no... the other is coming now, has given birth to one, a girl, who will pick up the mantle. Also, when the man leaves that is with her now, Kehlani will return to Luna and they will pick up the herbalist work.

A: Can you explain Bellos to us? What is the best information that we could understand about him? In our world, we understand what Reptilians are, what negative entities are, what Hybrids are, what Greys are, or what Archons are. Does he fit into any of these?

Womb Goddess: He fits into the Archons, but he is a special one. Because... the last we communed, he said that one day, what he meant to do here, on Earth, would come full circle, and he would leave to another Universe. That time is coming, but we can tell he is trying to go back on his Universal bargain, he does not want to give up this planet. So, the people here will have to give him up. It will be difficult, because he enters through the cracks. He thrives on more... on pain, on jealousy. And so when you feel it, when it tickles you, and you do not let it rise, he will find a home. But we know that the babies that are being born now, and in the next generation, will banish him. Because his contract here is long since done.

A: When you explained his Universe, I sensed that he is a kind of Archon. Archons, from our understanding of regressions, they're not here in energy, or physical, they just attach through technologies and they're artificial intelligence (artificial consciousness-ArCon)...

Womb Goddess: He is a burrower; he attaches, rides and grows. Technology is the way now, but he has always found his hold. When he came here, and he helped make the humans, he was supposed to bring balance, to help them realize with gratitude, all that they had been gifted. But... no, no but, we think this was maybe always the plan. He is the twister, the muddier. But the people here have to decide what energy they want to govern them, guard them, and work with them. If they continue to find ways to find him and work with him, he will never leave.

A: You said it was a plan, in regards to his end, his plan? Or are you saying that it was a Divine plan?

Womb Goddess: I believe it was a Divine plan. Because once it is undone, it will never happen again. At least not on Earth.

A: To understand who he is, did he begin as organic, and then transformed into more of an Archon, which is artificial. Or can you explain that?

Womb Goddess: He began and stepped out like all of us from "the All." He was energetic, a creation being and the longer he has stayed on Earth past his purpose, the more diluted he has become.

A: Why is that? Why does Earth do that to people who choose that path?

Womb Goddess: In order to stay here, you must make a bargain to be a low frequency being, if your work here is done, and he thought it was worth the bargain, because he gathers strength. The more he is listened to, the more strength he gathers; technology has been his favorite conduit, because now he can move very quickly. He has not had this level of reach since the Europeans went into Africa and the great war happened in Europe. He can feel that people are awakening rapidly, but he cannot find them, he cannot see them. But he can find them, particularly when they are children, if they are not protected, he can invade, or invade those around them. Now, he uses technology to make people think the idea was their own.

A: So, he began organic, but then twisted into becoming more artificial, like Archon. So a bit of a hybrid or a combination of that?

Womb Goddess: Yes.

A: So because he began organic, he can be in this Universe. He made contracts that transformed him into that?

Womb Goddess: Yes. He happily did it.

A: Was that, in itself, divinely planned? I mean, everything is divinely planned. However, was that meant to be for him, or is that free-willed expression choice?

Womb Goddess: Free-willed expression choice. His Universe is very sad at what has happened to Bellos.

A: So now he travels through the electronics, the satellites, wreaking havoc.

Womb Goddess: Yes, he has used many men to create websites that help him do his work. Red*** was his invention.

A: Of course. One of the reasons why I never went on there.

Womb Goddess: We never let this vessel go there either.

A: Well, a lot of sites, unfortunately, don't feel right. Sometimes you do have to be there to assist, but that one felt really off.

Womb Goddess: That is why we made sure she works on the internet, because both good and bad are rising there. And we must stand in the middle, as a knower; we cannot best what we cannot see, or speak to.

A: Yes. In other words, what you are saying is that he, or other, say Archon beings, do not know what we are thinking. It is only when, for example, we say them out loud, or we perhaps even write them on a post on the internet is when they know and they retrieve the information.

Womb Goddess: Yes. And then other beings can use that as an entry point to you. There are many beings here that are a little frequency that work together to lower the frequency and bring people into a negative collective frequency. They use what we may call "the Djinns" for this call. They use social media, and other tools today to confuse people. But we also are on social media. We are also in certain spots, maybe one or two posts on Red***. But we are also on the Internet, and in the last five years have been learning how to use it to help. The Internet was everyone's invention. Neutral.

A: You said the children that are coming now will come in the next generation... will push him out.

Womb Goddess: There will be no need for him here. That lesson, the Earth will have evolved past it, and has more pertinent issues to come...if they are to stay here.

A: Thank you..

Womb Goddess: That is a part of why many spirits from other planets have come to Earth. Our planets were destroyed; their planets were destroyed. And they know that this one could be too, and so they are here to save it. Many are here to save it.

A: Is this one of the reasons why it's so hard to remove this infringement, because it began from say a Creator that was supposed to be benevolent then turned malevolent, and his compromise fed into its frequency, that turned Earth into this low frequency that everyone has to come into? Is his choice of free will, one of the reasons why Earth is such a low frequency?

Womb Goddess: You have named it, sister, as you have many times before.

A: Thank you. This is really important, what you just shared with me. As you know, I'm working hard every day, like others remembering. Thank you for planting the seeds and helping me remember.

Womb Goddess: Thank you, from all of us. We are so, so grateful. You answered the call and took on this, the job you are doing is a mighty one. And you are awakening thousands.

A: Thank you, that means all to me. I love you with all that I am.
Womb Goddess: We love you so, so much and we are here for you in everything. Thank you!
A: (Whispering) Thank you. Just when I needed someone to love me.
Womb Goddess: We are always loving you, sweet sister.
A: That I know. Thank you! Anything else you want to share with us Divine Womb Goddess, before we speak back to her Higher Self expression?
Womb Goddess: Know that you are both exactly where you are meant to be, now. You are on the path and nothing can take you from it. So if ever you have doubt, know that we are working with you, behind, in front, and next to. We just want you to know, from the bottom of "our all" our connection to the Divine, all the way to us here on Earth, you are our greatest gift. You who are listening to this, whoever is listening to this, as you get sovereign, you are the love we have wanted. Thank you.
A: Thank you, Womb Goddess. As you know, you know I write my books, and we share the most sensitive ones there.
Womb Goddess: Your book, your sweet, sweet book is everything that we had hoped. Yes, the world will be ready then, and is already changing so rapidly, even in this call, things have shifted. It was hard for the vessel to come to this call. He tried once more to invade, but could not, because she has different guides now, and those guides were not confused by what he was doing.
A: Thank you. I honor your wisdom. Wow, amazing! I think that is also sisters and sister. What a blessing you have been to my existence in this time of space, and I shall remember to dance, for I shall remember myself every time I dance.
Womb Goddess: You have made us feel so loved. You are one of the ones that kept us here, without forgetting. We all bow to you. We hug you now and thank you, sweet sister.
A: Thank you! Love you, with all that I am.
Womb Goddess: We love you.
A: May I please speak to her Higher Self now? Greetings Higher Self.
Higher Self: Hello!
A: What a joy! What a gift! Thank you for that, for today.
Higher Self: Ah, thank you. I feel so... I don't know... joyous! Or, you know what I feel like, the body that I'm in, can feel the joy that I have always had for it. What you've done here today. Wow. It reset it all. I know when Kehlani wakes up, like just, wow! What a gift. I knew when I found you, when I was circling around your house, I felt like maybe she's the one. But I knew there was a lot that had to be kept safe. So I had to watch you for a while and watch your work. I was like all right, this one can handle all of the stories that are about to come through. Thank you for coming out on the Internet. I know that wasn't easy, but it really helped a lot of us find you.
A: Thank you. Thank you. Yes, yes. Thank you. It's hard, you know, being out there, but it's okay, I have an infinite support, like you, the Womb Goddess, and an infinity of beings! I humbly thank everyone. Thank you. I want to continue with explaining all the lives that you took her to, then you took her to Fox River Canyon in Namibia, how it's a sacred birthing time of the human race. Can you explain that further? What did you mean by that space?
Higher Self: Yes. Fish River Canyon is like the planet we came here from. Before we left Earth, we left another place. We knew when we first decided that we were going to come to Earth, that Fish River Canyon was one of the many cradles; there are four or five cradles of life on this planet where civilization sprang up from at different times. And Fish River Canyon is one of them. It is the kind of energetic resonance that cannot be tainted. We knew that our harmony and our love of this planet, as we incarnated again, and again, into the "Hawonga" line, would be changed. We knew that people would come and try and separate us from the land, but that the Canyon would always lead us back home.
A: Thank you. Explain that - why the Canyon? Is there an energy within it?
Higher Self: Yes, there is an old energy within it; one of the oldest energies on Earth. Before Earth was a separate thing, before there was any entity on Earth. That is where Fish River Canyon is. It is the high frequency this planet used to be. There were quite a few places like that on Earth, but for us, this one was the one that called us, it reminded us of our home. And no matter what happened outside of the canyon, it always maintained Earth's true voice, Earth's true frequency.

A: Beautiful. And then you took us to a time and space where she had already had a daughter, she was having her son and had complications, but was very aware and was able to flow through it and birth him. Why did you take her to that? Is that her current life now?
Higher Self: That is her life now. We know that the stories black women have been told on this planet is that they will die in birth, and that they will not be cared for. So we wanted her to know, it is not safe for her to give birth to this child in the United States. The second one must be born in Italy, and that it will be hard, but she will make it, because we need her to believe that she will make it, because he'll be waiting for her to be afraid, to be willing to let go and slip out of this life. We also wanted her to know that loving her daughter will be easy, but loving her son will take a different kind of work. We want her to be prepared for that. So that she'd never let it show to either child, to both of those children, they will see themselves as the thing. And because of this, the sister will save the brother because they will always be on the same plane. Even when he wanders, skin of each other's skin, blood of each other's blood. Together, their mission is tied.
A: Beautiful. What else do you want to tell her about her children?
Higher Self: The love that you always wanted, Kehlani, has been inside you the whole time. Those children are going to crack you open in ways you always hoped for. Get ready to rise, rise, rise.
A: Such beautiful strength to come. As you, seeing her in the future birthing her child, she's just such a beautiful clear vessel, so strong and she will accomplish it. It's just gorgeous to have been able to see that, and to be part of that. Can we send her a wave of infinite love during that time, and even now, to get her to that path of birthing them both sacredly.
Higher Self: Oh, such a blessed idea. We love that!
A: Blessings to both of the babies. And then you took her to an attack on a village… because we're trying to figure out at the beginning, she said that they had taken him from her. Why did you take her to that memory of the village?
Higher Self: It is when her fear of men truly took root, and has been carried across lifetimes. When the son was taken, she felt as if all male humanity was lost. We took her there to remind her that it was the pain that changed her. And that these vessels, whether they be male, or white, and though they've done horrible things in the slave memory as well, are not inherently evil. And that story is a part of a larger story playing out on Earth. But she has served many roles, and she was also not guiltless, as none of us are. With this truth, we know, we knew, a stone would be turned, and another layer of healing would be activated.
A: Thank you for that. If we can start healing that past life, as well as all past lives you showed her. I was also thinking, as I was talking to the Goddess, what was that, that I physically saw when I looked over to the left of my window? I thought I saw the Sun down low, but I went outside and it's already late, so it couldn't be the sun. It was bright, like when you look at the sun, it leaves a sun spot in your eyes after you're done looking at it. It was bright and gold. I went outside and I realized no, the sun was up high, where it's normally supposed to be at. What was that second Sun I saw?
Higher Self: That was us!
A: I thought so! Thank you. Wow, beautiful!
Goddesses/Higher Self: We wanted you to be prepared for what was to come. And also just to say "hello," we like jokes; a little joke, like a kiss on the cheek.
A: I love that. Thank you for preparing me. The Goddess had mentioned "Bello." Last night I had dreams of children, their death and their rebirth. I want to make sure that those were organic dreams, that he didn't infringe on my dreams as well?
Womb Goddess: It was him. The rebirth was not him, the death was. Their rebirth was another entity coming to help. There is always help for the helpers. So he cannot get at you for long before one of us will come. This is the Goddess.
A: Ah! Thank you, Goddess. I know that he's this powerful being, but I'm shielded. I have everything set up, the intentions, alchemy, all of this. So, how could he have planted this false dream?
Womb Goddess: He could not tell who you were speaking to, but knew it was one of the seven and so, he expanded himself. Someone near you, whose technology was temporarily contaminated, he used that as a way in. It could have been anywhere at the grocery store, or elsewhere, but his power only lies in making you afraid. With you particularly he cannot get to you unless he makes you doubt

your ability to protect yourself and your subjects. He had to give up something. So, we are receiving the sense that he has weakened himself to get to you. So, it seems as though in order to further weaken his defenses, it was needed that he try and step to you. He never attacked you. He was merely only present so that we could figure out where he is now and how he is doing his work. He is a shapeshifter, constantly finding new ways.
A: *Thank you for that. And, is that the only dream he tampered with?*
Womb Goddess: Yes. And even that was a reach for him.
A: *Good. Thank you for your safety and protection. I'm glad that you are able to locate it.*
Womb Goddess: Thank you for committing to this work. We would never put you in danger, but sometimes, because of your strength, we know that you can help us.
A: *Thank you. Story of my creation! (laughter from both).*
Womb Goddess: And as promised, we got your consent.
A: *Thank you for allowing me to ask that question for myself.*
Womb Goddess: That is why we returned. We had a feeling. We will go again now though.
A: *All right. Love you all. Thank you. Higher Self, is there a name that you go by?*
Higher Self: There is not. I go by all the names; you can simply call me all.
A: *Can we begin her body scan at this point now? Do you need any assistance from either Archangels or the goddesses during the body scan?*
K: We would love the assistance from the Archangels.
A: *Beautiful. Which Archangels would you like for us to call forth on first?*
K: Gabriel.
A: *If you can connect us now to Archangel Gabriel please. Greetings.*
AA Gabriel: Hello!
A: *I love you, honor you and respect you. Thank you for being here.*
AA Gabriel: It is my pleasure to see you again.

The Body Scan begins.
A: *The Higher Self has requested for your presence with her body scan; if you could please begin her body scan now, starting from her crown all the way down to her toes. Where would you like to begin?*
AA Gabriel: Her lungs.
A: *What is within her lungs, is that an entity, energy or technology?*
AA Gabriel: There is a blockage here in her throat. Ah, I can see; it will be removed here. It was a part of her not being able to speak her truth because of being burned. She is not always honest about her magic. Or always honest. It seems like the third of this vessel was taught safety through not speaking their truth. They've been hurt physically and mentally, in this life by the power of their voice.
A: *Can you tell me, what is the form of it that's causing this in her throat?*
AA Gabriel: Feels like I'm seeing a dark cloud, and it's swirling in her bronchial tubes, all the way up to her esophagus.
A: *Is it a portal or technology?*
AA Gabriel: Let's investigate. It seems to be a closed portal that opens very rarely.
A: *Brother Gabriel, can you close that for us, and Higher Self?*
AA Gabriel: Oh my goodness! This one has been open for a very long time.
A: *Do you mean prior to this life?*
AA Gabriel: Prior to this life, I need the help of another Angel.
A: *Which angel would you like for us to call forth?*
AA Gabriel: I would like for you to call… actually, the Earth Goddess.
A: *Beautiful. If I could please speak to the Earth Goddess. We're calling on you now for your assistance during Kehlani's body scan.*
Earth Goddess: Ah, this is an ancient doorway given to this body very early and it's human. I think what must be done here, in order to close this portal, I need to call on Earth energies, as well as heavenly bodies to bring this spirit back together. It took The Seven to make you, but it took two major mistakes to create this portal and to leave it open. And so now, we must fuse all of the Divine energies that this vessel is working with and uses, and work with the Angel to heal the shame burn.

So that the flesh-spirit connection can be reconnected and maintained. We will begin this work now, together.

A: *Thank you. Begin the process now, start closing that portal, Earth Goddess and energies of Earth. You said it came in very early on; do you mean like in her soul beginnings?*

Earth Goddess: Yes, in her soul beginnings. The door had closed before she came back to this life, but when "Bello" got to her parents and the abuse began, it opened the door. She has worked since she was sixteen to find a way to close it. It is one of the reasons she came to you, because she couldn't do this alone. She needed me and Gabriel, and you, to hold the space. It is now closed.

A: *Beautiful. Start healing all parts of her voice and her throat chakra.*

Earth Goddess: We have purged this vessel of the lingering energy from that portal. And now our throat chakra feels so bountiful, and is meant to be active for the next years of her life, until she is an elder, and it will transform.

A: *Beautiful! May it continue to aid her with her role on Earth and communicate the books that she shall write.*

Let's go ahead and scan her, does she have any entities in her? We want to find them all and contain them.

Earth Goddess: She has done good work on releasing the entities from her. But there is the shadow of one in her neck-shoulder, up into her head. It is no longer present. But the space it occupied was not healed, it hollowed it out.

A: *Let's start healing that space within all time and space. Filling that in with Love-Light, and repairing it.*

Earth Goddess: Her ancestors, from both sides, are stepping up to aid in this healing. Because it is not hers alone.

A: *We humbly thank them. As that space has been healed, let's also scan her spine, her DNA, as well as her whole entire essence. Does she have any other entities attached to her?*

Earth Goddess: No, but we will need to do a protection spell, because many want to find her. She has a strong energetic signature.

A: *Let's go ahead and do that protection spell, start it now.*

Earth Goddess: This spell will be for her, and all of the babies born up her line. Any time this soul enters another vessel. As we do this healing, know it is done.

A: *That it is.*

Earth Goddess: All that wish her well, may find her. Those that wish to drain her cannot see her. They have forgotten her and they are blind to all that she is.

A: *Thank you. Let's scan her for any implants, hooks, or dark portals.*

Earth Goddess: She has two hooks in her; one has to do with a job she has on the earthly plane, and worry that she will not be enough. Because that is a hook from her high school years. This vessel has always been gifted, but it took a while for others to see it. So now when she enters spaces, even when it is not the case, she worries that she has to prove it. This hook though, from her job, is actually a hook that is seen or exacerbated whenever she is in the presence of femmes that she respects, and this also has to do with her old wound of losing her sisters. The other hook is also a big one, an old one, activated in this life when she was moved to a predominantly white area. She feels "other" at times when she is with white people, but feels very also "othered" at times with black people because she missed out on that time. This is how it manifests in her now, but the real shame is not knowing what was happening across the sea. So these hooks are the last residual pieces of the shame of her ignorance, or jealousy.

A: *Let's remove those now and start healing this; let me know when they're removed.*

Earth Goddess: Those hooks are gone and now the wounds are ready to be healed.

A: *Let's start healing them now with Love-Light. May she be free of what held on to those hooks.*

Earth Goddess: This vessel is now free of hooks, entities, and portals.

A: *How about implants, or wires?*

Earth Goddess: Oh! It feels as if there may be something at the center of her heart.

A: *What is it?*

Earth Goddess: It is a storage locker created to hold every hurt, and it is activated when she is hurt. But we no longer wish to carry these pain seeds. Because this vessel's heart is actually very, very powerful. And these were an attempt to take her off her path. But they are small, and were only ever distractions. Getting smaller, and smaller. Now, we can see them floating in front of the vessel, being removed. One at a time. Like pins in a pin cushion. The Earth is carrying them away.

A: Beautiful! Are they fully out?

Earth Goddess: They are fully out. Michael would like to come as well.

A: Archangel Michael, we welcome you brother. Love you. Thank you for being here and assisting us in healing all her chakras, making sure they're at their most organic formation now..

Earth Goddess: Another goddess wants to enter as well. One who knows much about pleasure. We are removing a force field of energy around this body that stopped it from embracing pleasure fully, and really accepting joy. Ah, there! Now, all that loves, and abundance, may rush in.

A: Thank you. Does she need to be age regressed?

Earth Goddess/Womb Goddess: We would like to regress her to when she was four.

A: Do you mean energetically?

Earth Goddess/Womb Goddess: Yes. That is when she was taken from her path. Or almost strayed, when "Bello" first found her.

A: I know that you put a protection spell on her, so he won't be able to find her.

Earth Goddess/Womb Goddess: No, but here is a treasure trove still. There were two powers that were turned off here. They must be turned back on.

A: Can you all start doing that for her now.

Earth Goddess/Womb Goddess: We have healed her connection to the bridge.

A: Beautiful, thank you.

Earth Goddess/Womb Goddess: We also have found a few abnormalities elsewhere that we will go into the organs and heal.

A: Good. Do you need any Phoenix fire?

Earth Goddess/Womb Goddess: We would love the help of the Phoenix, to seal the deal.

A: Very good, directing Phoenix fire to all that is needed within her. Michael can you scan her, does she have any negative cords on her?

AA Michael: There is one, extending to her crown chakra. Some kind of entity that wants her to believe that she does not know what she knows. This cord has always been very thin, even now, it's almost like a spider web. If we turn our heads, we can barely see it. But it is there.

A: Michael Can you cut that?

AA Michael: I can. And I have, though it did not want to go at first, but that connection has been severed.

A: What is this entity that was doing this her?

AA Michael: This entity was a Djinn, a low level one, at that; that is how he prospered for so long, they could barely see him. And he would leave. But he knows now he is not welcome here. His power is and was, on her, a distraction, to get her close to straying from the path, but was never strong enough, merely an annoyance. But had he stayed, he could have grown in later years. He was waiting for a better opportunity, because he could not get in, and so he had attached.

A: Can you tell me, what is a Djinn?

AA Michael: A Djinn is a low frequency being who is not quite powerful enough to change the timeline, but is powerful enough to infiltrate the human mind. They are almost like leeches; they jump on for a ride until you are weak enough, and they burrow themselves. Once they attach to a chakra, or worse the spirit itself, then they can evolve and become mightier and more powerful. Many of the low frequency beings here were once Djinns.

A: Thank you. Is there anything we could do about that entity, or the other Djinns?

AA Michael: With this vessel, the next place she lives must have a bathtub. Regular baths, with salt, will remove any of these energetic clingers. Also, rituals with any form of water, hot tea, hot lemon water, immersion into the sea, or the rivers, or the lake, or even sometimes, and I know you have felt this, drinking a very big glass of water can "shoo" them.

A: Good. Very good. And then do we have any fragmented soul pieces and need to be regained back to her?
AA Michael: Oh yes, we're calling them back now, but first, they must be purified.
A: Good.
AA Michael: Ah, we have pieced them back together.
A: Beautiful.
AA Michael: And everything is looking so beautiful in this vessel.
A: Yes, I can feel it. Amazing. Magical. Does she have any negative contracts we can remove for her?
AA Michael: Yes. This one is one she has worked on removing. She broke the contract but did not blow it away. It is not for her to suffer. And also, she can trust her own sovereignty. Now I'm speaking directly to Kehlani, there may be times when you are told something from a doctor, someone you respect, or just any authority in general, and inside you, you will know it is not true. That knowing is the only knowing that matters. You have been forgiven. In this life and the past lives, your ancestors already did that work to prepare you for this body. There is no need to suffer. In this life, that contract, that pact, burns today, and the ashes are blown away.
A: Shall they be blown away! Thank you. We're removing all negative contracts now. No longer serving her for her highest good. Higher Self, at this point in time, I've asked her questions as far as healing and conducted the body scan; is her body scan complete? We want to make sure she has a clear vessel, and we've set her up for her most organic timeline. Have we done that?
Higher Self: Yes, this is the most pure and whole this vessel has ever been. We also have set the spell that this will not be changed. If anything is to move this vessel from this harmony, she will be alerted and will realign and remove any energies, entities, cords and contracts. Moving forward, she will see them clearly, for what they are.
A: Beautiful. What a wonderful spell. She has a couple questions; Higher Self, may I ask them?
Higher Self: Yes, please.
A: She wants to know, what brought her here to Earth?
Higher Self: She is one of the many bridges that were brought here, called by the Earth to raise its frequency back to its authentic one. She came here today, a bridge between heaven and Earth.
A: Beautiful, we thank her. She also wants to know, what powers are within her?
Higher Self: She is one of the strongest psychics; she is claircognizant, clairsentient, and she can feel what is happening long before it happens. And we have been sending her messages her whole life; she is one of the deepest listeners and feelers. So that is why we have asked her to write a book and why we made her an artist. Because when she performs, when people read her books, when they watch her videos, they are connected to heaven and their Higher Self. She is one of the bells ringing to awaken the others.
A: I would love to be one of the first ones to buy her books.
Higher Self: We will tell her that, and I know, she will be sending you them for free.
A: Oh no! If she feels it, but you know, okay.
Higher Self: We picked you for a reason, the block has been removed and now the next great work can begin. We are very grateful to you.
A: Thank you. What is her connection to these beautiful Goddesses that have spoken today?
Higher Self: She was one of them.
A: Which one?
Higher Self: Long ago she was…this is the goddess now.
A: Welcome sister!
Goddess: When the frequency began to lower on this planet, there were a handful of us, who knew our skills would be stronger together and that we would have to split ourselves and become one. So, her connection is… long ago, she was me, when I was only myself. But now I have been made stronger with my sisters and am part of what is raising the frequency here; that is also why she is close to the fairies, because I used to work with and create fairies, long ago. I will go now.
A: Thank you sister, my infinite love. Is she doing the right job to do what is next required of her to do?

Higher Self: It is important that she is in the cracks; in the middle of everything that is coming. So, we want her to know it is not important for her to believe in the story of the news, because the news itself is not a high frequency creation. What is important for her, is for her to see how audiences can be one, and how they are being manipulated now. In her job, there are both entities that mean well, and there is also great evil there. And so it will be important for her to infuse the knowledge that she has to the people that she manages. A part of what brought her there are the storytellers that she will work with. She will meet them again along the road and has met them before.

A: *Wonderful, thank you.*

Higher Self: I want her to know that just as I have led her to you, there are many more who are coming. Now that these blockages have been removed and that contract is gone, she worried that she would be alone, which feels funny to us because there is a village and there has always been.

A: *Sisters, in this time and space I've asked all the questions she had and we've also conducted her healing. Is there anything else that I could have asked?*

Higher Self: No. We just want to say thank you and give you this energetic kiss.

A: *I felt it! Thank you! I love you all with all that I am. I want to thank Archangel Gabriel. All the beautiful Goddesses that we spoke to: the Moon Goddess, the Earth Goddess, and any other Goddesses that we might have spoken to; the original goddess, before she split herself, AA Michael and anyone else who assisted today that I might have missed mentioning. Love you. Honor you. Thank you. I respect you. Thank you for sharing all this beautiful information for her. It has been such an honor. May I bring her back?*

Higher Self: You may. We are all saying "thank you" to you. It has been an honor to watch you step into your power in this life. It is a gift to us every time one of you answers the call. But you do it so beautifully. Thank you. We say goodbye.

A: *Thank you. I love you with all that I am.*

For every A.U.R.A. Hypnosis healing session we ask that the Higher Self and team ensure to remove and heal this entire list: entities (Grays, Mantis, Reptilians, Archons...), dark portals, repair and crystallize DNA, negative cords, technologies (implants, metals, hooks, wires, nano, vaccines), Illnesses, vision, dental health, regrow teeth, age regress 5-15 years, blocked or misaligned chakras, open-up the third eye and activate abilities, expand heart, issues with auric field, fractured soul, contracts, deletion of inverted timelines, and trauma from current or past life.

Post Session dialogue.

A: *Welcome back, sister. Oh, my goodness.*

K: Wow. Whoa. I'm sorry, I'm having a hard time with words.

A: *How do you feel love? Do you think you remember everything?*

K: I remember big pieces. But then there are also big gaps. I just feel so free. It's almost like I have always been a body and a soul next to each other, and now they feel fully integrated. It's such a high, the whole of my body it's like vibrating. I just feel that feeling that I told you about, that I'd always felt sort of a little bit afraid. I feel like it's totally gone. My hip doesn't hurt anymore, and neither does my upper back (laughing joyfully).

A: *That was one of the best sessions I've ever had.*

K: So funny, because I literally feel it in my body right now. I'm like, oh, wow, there was that other person that I was, and now there's the real person that I am. All of the stories that I feel were knocking around inside me have come together and okay, we weren't making this up. We are perfectly sovereign. Like you said in the beginning of the session, what has been coming through me in the last two years has been this awakening. I now realize these whisperings of these Goddesses trying to be like, "Hey, hey, this is a part of what we want from you". And I'm like, "Oh, that was a really weird daydream I just had". Even though my Higher Self is like "LOL, Kehlani, you know, that's not a daydream."

A: *No, it's a message.*

K: It's a message. I also just feel like there's just so much, particularly when it comes to my magic and my race, in those past lives that I experienced that just made me like, whoa, oh, okay, this is a part of a larger circle that needed to finish. I know I need to listen to it, before I really know all of what happened. But I can say, energetically and spiritually, it's what everyone says, I feel like after your session, I'm different. There is a piece of the story that I needed, that now I have. It also just validates so many things. I was feeling that I was going to have a difficult birth. I was afraid because the infant mortality rate is high in the United States. And then to hear that... I was like, Oh! It's funny, there were moments where it almost felt like my Higher Self shooed me away almost to be like, "We need to figure this out without you." And then there were other moments where it felt like it almost called me back to, like, sit by the fire, and that was one of them. Where it was very clear that it's like, "I want you to see exactly this," and then other parts, like the part of my past lives, I just see like one picture each; I don't remember the whole vivid story that existed and maybe it was to help. Yes, part of the cleansing, so that I didn't continue to carry those feelings inside.

A: Amazing, wow! I am speechless. Your session was just incredible. I can't wait for you to listen to it. The information you shared, really put lots of pieces of the puzzle, in more of a clear understanding for myself. I humbly thank you for that. It's so exciting to have this literature, in the future, for the world to read. It's going to change many perspectives. Amazing sister, you are a blessing!

K: You are too. I just feel like we really connected. Thank you for helping me dissolve those contracts that were stopping me from doing the divine work, like when I came out. I was definitely like, yeah, we're both spiritual people. But now I'm like, oh, no, we both have some very deep work to do. I feel very grateful and honored that you answered the call to help me with this.

A: Thank you, sister. The Goddesses know. They knew who to choose. It was just a divine blessing.

K: I would love to hear from you, what else was really powerful about it for you? Like you said, it was one of the most powerful sessions you've had.

A: Connecting to the Goddesses, their energy. When we do sessions like this, we don't just heal the client, the client also heals us. I needed to feel their Goddess energy. I have a lot going on. And I'm constantly helping others. At times I do have entities that try to stop me. So, I was in a time and space that I needed to connect to the Goddesses to remind me. The other day, my husband and I danced right before bed, we just put on music, and we started dancing. It was really beautiful and romantic. I said, we have to do this every night. And then we forget. So this morning, I said to my husband, you haven't danced with me again. I said, "I was told all day that we are to dance, and that we have to have music on all day." One of the first things that came through your session is you all dancing to the Womb Goddess. And, the reason is exactly why I dance. You said, "The reason why we dance to the womb Goddess, is because at times during our days we start forgetting ourselves. But when we start to dance, we begin to remember ourselves."

K: I can't wait to listen to this! I thought I remembered it, but you're saying stuff...and I'm like, wow!

A: You're going to continue to get more downloads and more information, from these Goddesses, your Higher Self, and these benevolent beings you spoke of. The other thing that was really, really big for me was Bello. When you spoke of him. Are you familiar with him?

K: Yes, he's terrified me since I was a kid. So for you to say that right off the bat. I'm like, oh, wow, I guess my Higher Self knows what's up. Or maybe it was trickling down to me this whole time.

A: Yes. They explained his story in depth. The real story.

K: Whoa! I'm even afraid to speak his name! So to hear that and hear you saying it, makes me feel that, clearly, we did the work to heal and protect against whatever. Because again, like you said it, I'm not afraid right now. Usually, if someone said that, I would be like, "Close the computer, we can't talk about this now". But now I'm like, "Oh, yeah, Bello, what about him?"

A: Exactly. And you're gonna find out why.

K: Thank you so much. You're amazing.

A: I know. I love you!

K: I love you too. Thank you so much!

A: I respect you. I'm excited.

K: I just got a message to send you the book. That's what I just heard in my head. Don't worry. I'll send you the book, I'm not sure what that means, but I'll do it.

A: (Laughing) Wait until you hear why you just said that.

K: Okay, I heard a giggle in my head when I said it, so it was clearly a message about you, and there's some mischief involved.
A: *Yes, there is. I love you sister. Thank you for being you. I love you, honor you, and respect you. Blessings, and my infinite love! Bye love!*

For every A.U.R.A. Hypnosis healing session we ask that the Higher Self and team ensure to remove and heal this entire list from the clients Tree of Life: entities (Grays, Mantis, Reptilians, Archons...), dark portals, repair and crystallize DNA, negative cords, technologies (implants, metals, hooks, wires, nano, vaccines), Illnesses, vision, dental health, regrow teeth, age regress 5-15 years, blocked or misaligned chakras, open-up the third eye and activate abilities, expand heart, issues with auric field, fractured soul, contracts, deletion of inverted timelines, and trauma from current or past life.

END OF SESSION

This session was one of the most profound in understanding and remembering the power of the Gods and Goddesses within us, as the multidimensional beings we truly are. Often the negative polarized entities play a game that belittles us enough to feel as if we are not these divine powerful beings. The negative entities know once we remember and activate this within, that they can no longer have their way with us, and that we then can repel their ill intentions. Especially when we remember that we are not alone, and instead that we are infinitely surrounded by our benevolent brethren that await to be granted our permission, to assist and protect us. As the Womb Goddess explained, they cannot assist unless we call forth or give permission, because they, and we, are benevolent in origin. If we overstep boundaries, then we, too, can become malevolent in nature, as the Archons. The Goddesses gave us an example of when Bello tried to influence my dreams or thoughts, he was weakened by my strength, as I do know who 'I AM' and what my infinite Love-Light is capable of. Since the beginning of my spiritual career, it has been one of my biggest divine life goals to assist the collective of the people of Earth in remembering their true divine power in order to stop, repel, or transmute any types of energetic, or psychic attacks. Truly it is my soul's mission. Through all that we do, we are profoundly accomplishing this mission everyday. When WE, one by one, remember this dormant power within us, that is when we will finally transmute the Archons out from our Universe and Multiverse.

When I channeled the Christ Consciousness live on our channels in 2021, they reminded us that the negative polarized entities like to play an illusional mind game, portraying themselves as much bigger and more powerful than what they truly are. It is of the utmost importance that we understand that this is the opposite of the truth, and that, in actuality, we are gigantic in stature, light, and divine power. The key to this being is that "IT" is an illusion. "IT" is not of our organic Universe! WE ARE THE ORGANIC! THE TRUTH OF THE UNIVERSE!

An immensity of sovereignty, knowledge, and beauty was remembered through this session, of ourselves, and our Universe. Each word and sentence that the Goddesses spoke to us vibrated within us strongly as truth, in turn shifting, and further activating our consciousness and Love-Light within. The Goddesses brought us many sacred teachings. One of the teachings showed us why it is important that we state all that we do in the highest order, when they explained the order of the lives they showed Kehlani. The order in which they would be delivered, would bridge and cause a different reaction in Kehlani. I often do this when channeling and communicating with others in any form. I pause in silence, with an intake of a breath of fresh air, before I give the answer. Allowing my consciousness to process the information that will bring forth the next organic timeline by my choices. This is of extreme importance when working with others and ourselves. Because this is *us* taking full responsibility, and honoring that all choices are of the utmost importance, no matter the size of the choice. Becoming the weavers of *our* organic timelines. We do not realize that this is what we are doing when we pause and think, as we have been taught through societal programming, that all we do within our mind, or imagination, is make-believe, and that it has no power of reality within it. As we know, this is farthest from the truth, as all that is imagined through our consciousness are forms of manifestation, whether they are positive, or negative, rooted thoughtforms.

In our consciousness we are reviewing the outcomes of our choices, in the order we word it, or how we deliver it, how each one will create a different timeline. In turn, in our consciousness, we are reviewing these timelines within time and space, and choosing the order to have the highest, most organic potential. For example, in this session, showing Kehlani one life over the other, was the correct sequence to bring about the highest, most organic healing, specifically for her. Adding onto why our choices, since they are free-willed, are always divine in nature, as explained through the Goddesses. It is the path of a sovereign being. Like Bello, who had that freedom of choice at the beginning of the seeding of our Universe, though it became inverted, it was still divine because he had free will, and we honor all free will choices. It really puts into perspective how grand and infinite creation is, within the infinity of races and souls, and how each one's choices, whether service to self or service to others, how it ripples out and impacts the collective in some form. And, how we are all a reality and representation of the collective choices. Therefore, it is the collective that has made the free will choice, when Ascension comes forth, to transmute this once free will choice by Bello's, that is no longer free will, as what *it* has turned into is Artificial Intelligence, which answers to none and knows no sacred boundaries. In chapters 10 and 11, we understand this further when we learn how the Archon maker entered into our Universe, and what its realm is.

Through this session, the knowledge and understanding that we finally reach of the Archon maker is vast for our Universe, especially in this realm of the third dimension, where we enter consciously knowing that amnesia will cloud our minds. It is a massive leverage in how they use our lack of memory against us. And most importantly, the Archons don't want us to remember them and their plague in our Universe, as to do so, bridges forth for us the freedom from them. With the destruction that this Artificial Intelligence has caused, everyone always wants to know, how it came to be, how could this happen? Those in the lower vibrational emotion of victimhood point their finger at someone, or something that they must blame for their life or life's outcomes. Often the finger is pointed at the Archangels, Divine Mother or Divine Father, who are the highest, purest of Source Love-Light. When we do this, we play into the Archon game that divides us all by separating ourselves from their organic beauty. By removing Divine Mother/Father and Archangels from our perspective of viewing and connection to the heart, we then become blind, unable to find the clearest direction. Instead, let us just be in the knowing that it just is; we are aware of *it* now, this game, let's not consent, but remove *it* from within and outside of us. This is key, rather than placing blame, which is an Archon construct, an artificial emotion. The ultimate truth being that in order to remove, or transmute something that is foreign to our organic, we must first remember its origins, for it is there that we can reach for its roots and unroot it. As we will unroot Bello, its Archons, and its realm.

Because of free willed choice, all is divinely orchestrated, as freedom is honored. When Bello assisted in the seeding, creating the beginnings of the origins of Earth, before she was called Earth, he became envious and jealous towards the Goddesses, observing the love the people felt for them. Instead of joining in the collective love, he chose to want the attention from the people of Earth all to himself, he did not want to share. It was a form of a "high" for this powerful being. This choice lowered his vibration. Therefore, you can say that this is when the demons, or negative polarized entities began, when he birthed these dark initial thoughtforms, as this is who he is. As the Goddesses said, in order for one to come down to the lowest then, fifth dimension of our Universe, we must give up much of ourselves. But, when doing so, one must be careful to not give up too much. The reason why we do so is because of the immense growth that each soul experiences when entering this organic crystalline Earth blueprint. This powerful, manifesting, creator being that he was, manifested this inverted reality. This action fed into Earth's blueprint, making it possible for these lower vibrations to be channeled through, if one chooses to do so. This is one of the reasons why, if living on Earth, one can choose to feel these lower emotions.

The Archon Bello's intention of clouding our minds, through our emotions of fear, worry, misbelief in oneself, is so that we can become a lower vibration, as these emotions are. Making us accessible for its illusion of manipulation. This is why we often explain that these lower vibrational emotions are foreign and not an organic part of our Universe; they are Archon-made. They were manifested by the Archon maker and its realm, not ours. This separation took us farther apart from the creators of our Universe, which then also made us farther from ourselves and our true divine power as the Creators we are. If you separate the people from the lifeforce and consciousness that courses through the elements which sustain life, then you drive them furthest away from themselves. Because when we bask in nature, by hugging trees, talking to the wind, loving on the water, or rooting to the Earth, we remember that we are all connected as one consciousness, as every planet is. Remembering that all elements are consciousness, which is who the Goddesses truly are, the fire, water, wind, organic darkness, crystal, womb, and Earth. All life within each planet is one connected collective consciousness. Which explains further why, when we heal ourselves, we, too, heal the collective, as we are part of the One Consciousness.

Another divine teaching from the Goddesses is that once it has begun, it is already done and, "So it is." When asking Kehlani's question of a manifestation to come to be, the Goddess said, "So I guess the shortest answer is begin and know, I am with you." To which I answered, "Because when you begin, it has already occurred because of linear time." We often procrastinate within our ideas, or choices of manifestation, being held back, or stagnant, by fear, worry, non-belief in the divine power of oneself. However, the truth is that if we just make the choice, and begin whatever it is that requires beginnings within our lives, it has already come to be. The key being that the material that is needed to manifest and create for ourselves and our families is that, "we just do it," because everything that begins, must always complete in some form. Since time is linear, once it has begun in one point of time and space, it will be done in another point in time and space. Therefore, let's all just begin.

The story of how Bello went after her family, when he couldn't get to her, shows us that often those who are strong willed, or hold a vastness of Love-Light, such as Kehlani, can be targeted. Bello could not penetrate and influence her heart and mind because of her strength; therefore, the next option to reach her was through her family, those closest to her. Their choice to be open for influence, caused her to break down, and then an inverted penetration of negative thoughtforms of herself, or of life manifested. This has been further explained, in the previous chapters, in how it is that entities infringe upon us through the people surrounding us. Reminding us, that to live as a most powerful sovereign being, we must live in infinite love towards all, and hold no attachments to any. This is why the Ascended Masters of Earth, or monks/nuns, live their life with detachment to all, including people and the material. Because if there is no attachment, then there is no allowance to infringements through that attachment to another. Our spouses who are organically meant to be in our path, children, and grandchildren being the exception. However, still even in relationship with them, to live in infinite freedom that they are as free as you, and always holding the most powerful Love-Light for them and their choices. Even though this was part of Kehlani's life, the Goddesses explained that no matter the circumstance, there will always be someone of benevolence to counter and to assist us. The benevolence being greater in numbers always. This reminds us of how important it is, once more, that we call for assistance when needed. Though we are infinite, so is our team.

The importance of holding space in Love-Light is demonstrated in this session; how the Goddesses explained that Kehlani required for more than one, instead a group, to hold space for the removal of the dark portal she had been working on, and couldn't do so on her own. The space that needed to be held by the Goddesses, Kehlani, and I, so that within the timeframe of holding it, the energy was acquired for *its* removal and self-healing. Reminding us of the power of the collective oneness, and the potency of what we are capable of together, when connecting and being in the same frequency and vibration. Our teachings are all about this, because ultimately this is what we will all need to hold, the infinite Love-Light of Source, when the final splitting of the bifurcation/trifurcation comes into fruition on Earth. In Book 3, we further explain the process of Ascension, The Event, the New Earth, our Promise Land.

      Lastly, as the Goddesses explained, they incarnated because of Earth's natures, and how Fish River Canyon, as an example, was a Love-Light beacon to connect through, so that they would not forget who they were. This is one of the greatest beauties of our Earth, that many beings come here for. Some of the other reasons being that their planets were destroyed. Whichever the reason is, the Earths of our Universes hold a multitude of ecosystems that can sustain all life forms. An infinity of alien races have incarnated on Earth, to commune here together. Looking for a planet to call home, which reminds them of their own, as at times their home might be no longer. These are some of the reasons why there are many different alien races on Earth, living inside their human, illusional, container. Once their planets were destroyed, they came to Earth because of our diverse ecosystem. In many circumstances, they are here to save their race. As, at times, there are only a few left of an alien race, due to a negative invasion and destruction of their home planet. Throughout the chapters within Book 1 and 2, you have become familiar with some of these inverted invasions. Our Earth's organic crystalline blueprint is further explained in "The Mayan/Atlantean" series, in the "Pangea Land of Mu" video. In the next chapter, we remember the seven Goddesses, who remind us to fall in love once more with the diversity of the beauties of our natures.

> **"Our choices are divine because they are free.**
> **Without freedom there is nothing that is divine."**
> **~AuroRa**

--------------<<>>--------------

9

7 GODDESSES OF GAIA

Recorded Live on YouTube: January 7, 2022

In this transmission AuroRa channels the forgotten ones, "The Sacred 7 Goddesses of Gaia." They take us on a journey through Earth's Galactic History, and provide more on the Archon maker. The beginning of the birth of the Universes. The consciousnesses of the elements of earth, fire, water, wind, crystal, organic darkness and womb. Remember and unlock this sacred divine power within.

--------------<<>>--------------

"Do not be afraid of me, for when you are afraid of me, you are afraid of yourself. Do not be afraid of your shadow."
~Darkness Goddess

"Fire warms you up because it is the flame inside of you that gives you warmth and light. It ignites and replenishes your flame inside your heart. That is why it warms up your body and warms up your soul. It brings wholeness forth, back into your heart and your being."
~Fire Goddess

"I am the memory that you are to move in ever moving motion as well. Never standing still. Always moving forward, and never backward. I am that wave that helps to push you gently into your next level of Ascension. Level of ascending consciousness."
~Water Goddess

"I am the wind beneath your feet, the wind above your head, the wind all around you in the Four Sacred Directions of the Universe. I move invisible to your eyes. I am proof that what is invisible, does not mean it is not real."
~Wind Goddess

"We are the potentials of what you will become when you ascend out of this third dimension. You will become your crystallized energetic body connecting to the crystalized Earth of the fifth dimension. We are this memory."
~Crystal Goddess

"I am what reminds you that no matter the obstacles, no matter the walls, no matter the journeys that you have to climb out from, that you are vigilant. That you are loved infinitely beyond boundaries, beyond limitations, and this beauty is what allows you to create. I am Creation herself."
~Womb Goddess

"We are the reminder to you of the infinity of soul that you are. That no matter how much you are broken down, no matter how much you are stepped upon, no matter how much sometimes you may be directed in an inverted way, no matter what - you will always remember that you are free and you are sovereign. Because you were created from sovereignty and freedom."
~Earth Goddess

--------------<<>>--------------

Goddesses: Greetings. I love you, we love you. Thank you for being here. Seems almost infinite, since we have last spoken to you. It's an honor to be here with you. We humbly bow to you and your most vast greatness of beauty and spirit that you are.

We are the Seven Goddesses of Earth, of all Earths. Thank you for being here with us in this time and space, in sharing this space of love with you today. We shall go through a vastness of sharing. Sharing the beauty that we are, and truly the beauty that you are. And, how it is connected to all life forms within you and outside of you. All Earth.

In the beginning of time, as Creation began to fractalize and duplicate from one another, our birthing point began. At the point, you have heard the story before, where the four Centaurs and the plane of existence began to create upon the blue plasmic etheric flame sphere. Which sprung out counterclockwise, and became the very first Earth of creation. For this is where you are within, though beautiful, a simulation. This is a representation of the beginning Earth, and all Earths in Creation, as there are many. As you know, multidimensionally parallel to one another, many expressions and versions of us and you.

You could say that the seven rays and colors of the rainbow, the seven chakras within your main physical body, not including up to the thirteen that are found outside of the body, where you are multidimensional. We are all these seven colors and all that align with this. The elements that connect to this, as well as all the colors, the elements, the chakras, the DNA strands within you as well. For we are you and as we say, you are us.

At the beginning of this Creation, we began our birthing as we said, through the blue plasmic flame that spread out and engulfed the very first Earth, creating and spinning counterclockwise. When the merging and birthing of the daughter of the flame, who was the first fractalization of Sophia, Divine Mother, and Divine Father Krysto. Who sprung out from Creation, and began Creation itself, outside of this Infinite Source Love-Light that we are now. What we have now created into, by the expressions of you, birthing out of us and your journeys throughout the different dimensions of planetary spheres, and all life in Creation. Within our entire Creation of the Universe and those Universes that are parallel to us as well. You began to hear about this when [15]Our Universe The Phoenix, delivered the channeling of who she is. We are, as you can say, a prism, a color ray of these seven colors within the rainbow. As the beginning of the very first planetary sphere of Creation, Gaia, Terra, Earth, Mother Earth began to create from within itself, spinning counterclockwise and creating seven major elements that you will find now within your Earth. Within this expression of Earth, we became all elements that give you lifeforce. Everything that perhaps you have forgotten their true power or often you go throughout your day without realizing they are around you, intertwining with your everyday life.

As the 'Daughter of the Flame' continued to birth out in time and space, our very first Earth. We are the Seven Goddesses which would be Fire, which is also anything to do with fire, lava, the Sun Source. Water, Wind, the Night - the Darkness (the organic darkness), the Moon, the Womb within your physical body, or if you are a male, your energetic body. For everyone carries a womb. And the Crystals. All six of these come together to make Earth, which is the final element. As these elements carried forth who we are, and you are, us, we began Creation.

If you can imagine, the very first lands were beautiful and gigantic, the cliffs, the waterfalls, the mountains, the hills, the lifeform that was creating. The animals were ready. The birds flying in the wind. You can imagine this Earth was grand and beautiful, and it was the organic promised land. The

---

[15] Aurora channeled 'Our Universe The Phoenix' live August 6th, 2021. We explore our Universe and the Multiverse. How timelines work, to use the phoenix flame, and the true role of the Divine Masculine.

very promised land that you have been looking to connect to beyond this expression of you here. Beyond the veil, ascending out.

As we continued to develop the Earth and expand it, so, too, were there others assisting, as we continued to grow ourselves. If you can envision, beginning with the element of fire, and the Terrans, the beginning people of Earth. Which would be seen more as Pangea. Before the lands split and became the continents that are separated now. While still connected through the ley lines and the Sacred Laws of the Universe. You can envision it in this manner, that we were at this beginning land and evolution of elements. For all Earths connect to one another multidimensionally, as parallel. You can say that they are in one pocket of the Creation of time and space. Though there is no time, so we will say, life in space. Yet they are expansive and not limited to that one dimension of life in space.

At the beautiful beginnings, different Gods began to work with one another to expand Creation. They learned how to make stars; to create stars from within the darkness. Within the darkness of material, we learned how to alchemize the darkness. The material that we use, the elements that we use to impregnate. The light impregnates the darkness. The dark matter of the organic infinity of the ether. The darkness is the material that we create from. We impregnate it with light to create all life forms within Creation.

As we continued to develop, we began to create soul groups, stars. When you look upon the Stars they are different colors, different vibrations. Vibrations at a different sound frequency and consciousness collectively. They are expressions and miniature versions of Source itself. Every single constellation, we will use constellations, but that isn't the word we are looking for because life is grander and more expansive than that. Using your example, when you truly look beyond this matrix, beyond this simulation. When you are incarnated into a planet. When you look above you can actually look up at the sky and see all the planetary spheres that are in combination. They are just hovering right above your sky. Not like here, all you can see is a very small fraction of the 88 constellations; actually life itself is much more infinite and grand than that, of course. However, you would be able to see the planetary spheres that are in your same circulation of Star clusters, right above you. And you would be able to telepathically connect and make unions with some of these friends; depending on the abilities that you have developed and depending on the dimension that you are within.

Every single Star that you see in your skys is a representation of how infinite and vast life is, for every single one of these Stars has planetary spheres. Each Star is a Sun, like your Sun is a Star. Your Sun's name is Ra. Which is how we can explain that your soul group within your most grand Earth is Ra, for your Sun is Ra. In order to come into this simulation, you do have to go through the portal of Ra, which is your Sun. For that is how you enter. The way you exit out though is inwards. In, through Divine Mother's heart, inside of Earth. We are taking you on a journey of our Universe. Therefore, the Sun is the life force that gives life. That is the portal of Source itself. It gives life and light to all that is within its resilience, its grouping of Star planetary spheres.

Beautiful. Now that you understand that, we will further explain Earth and the Creations. As we continue to develop our souls, we learn to, just like Mother and Father birthed out the first Creation, "The Daughter of the Flame", we too learned to alchemize this. It was at the beginning times of the multidimensional multiverse, the omniverse. The Universes, we have yet to expand into multiverses. Therefore, there were many birthing souls that were the creators at the beginning of life in space, that were part of creating life itself. As we learned to alchemize from within the beauties that we were and then alchemize beauties into the dimensions and the Universe itself. As we learned to do this, there was a brother of ours, that you would know as Bello, who is the father of the Archons. We are not able to go into depth with this and we will not be able to answer questions on this. However, we are bringing this to your attention.

As the Universes then began to multiply upon themselves, then this brother of ours decided to expand to create his own Universe. That is where it begins; where he was once organic and was once of Source. However, he became not organic and not of our Source anymore. When he decided to not respect 'The Sacred Laws of the Universe' and create his Universe that was inverted and an emptiness of Love-Light. When he separated from Source and all of us, he became just Artificial Intelligence. That is what we can share upon that, and that is why he is the Father Archon, because he is the first one of no Love-Light and no light within. Just an emptiness of neutrality and emptiness of nothingness. The most vast infinite Artificial Intelligence that you could ever imagine. That is what he is. And he is the Archon virus that plagues our Universe and other Universes.

Though as you know, within this format of communications through this channel and other platforms, through this bridging, we will continue to communicate to you on how to evolve and ascend out from those inversions of the artificial. As you are seeing now, the bifurcation, the trifurcation of the two-third worlds and how we had to split the light and the organic, from the inverted and the dark inverted. How it had to become still together to assist the lifeforms. Because if it were to separate too soon, then those lifeforms who have yet to awaken, who have yet to be in infinite Love-Light, or who have yet to work within themselves and remove the inverted within themselves, they would become stuck within the inverted and would have to repeat the cycles; no matter if they came from a higher dimension. And those still a matching vibration to the inverted and the control of the 'New World Order Agenda,' they would stay stuck there. Many life forms.

The 12/21/2020 and 12/21/2021 are the biggest and greatest, most evolution that has happened. And here we are able to speak to you because of the grand astrological conjunction that has happened after 12/21/21. Because we are here. We have always been here. We are here in greater, vast, more potent benevolence, and Ascended Masters. Beings, who perhaps even sometimes might have started off negative polarized, but who now have turned positive polarized through many forms of showing your love for them. Through healing modalities in your time and space that assists negative polarized entities into positive polarizing. Also those planetary spheres as we spoke of in prior transmissions, that could not stay connected to your Earth which was then an inverted artificial planet, but yet still always holding the organic. We are here. We are all here. If you were to close your eyes and allow your imagination to feel us, and see us, and sense us, and hear us, and know us, you would see us walking amongst you. You would see us embracing you. You would see us in every part of what you are doing. Whether it is taking a step forward from something that you are scared of, and you don't want to take a step forward, we are there supporting your arms and your legs, so that if you step forward and you are in fear, we are there to assist you to float, so that you will not fall. We are here. These games of forgetting of us, in turn, you forgot of yourself. As we have said, you are us and we are you. All beings within this Creation are expressions of different Source benevolence. Beginnings of, you can say Gods. However, we don't like how these words have been twisted and inverted by the Archon virus. How it is worshiped. We have never been about worship. Only that which is of emptiness of love, Love-Light, like the Archon virus, requires worship. We do not. We don't require anything really.

All we are is a remembrance of who you have been; who you are in the higher realms, and in the higher dimensions of you, in the higher multidimensionality of you. We are speaking of this not just as the Seven Goddesses of Earth, we are speaking of this on a grander scale. For in many forms, they have inverted the oneness, when they tell you that you are not an individual expression, you are all one. We are all one. When they tell you that, they want to trick you into saying that you are one with the inverted, the A.I. As we have always said, be careful what you state you are one with. You are one with your Divinity, you are one with your Higher Self, you are one with your Oversoul, you are one with all the you's within you and outside of you and all the fractalizations of you. You are one with them, the organic that is. You are not one with the inverted and the A.I.

THE FINAL BATTLE - GALACTIC HISTORY OF THE MULTIVERSE

Now to talk further about us, the Seven specifically. As Earth, your Earth. We'll talk about your Earth, though as we explained there are many. We will speak of yours, so that you can understand. Through the simulation and all the different evolutions of Pangea, then Lemuria, then Atlantis, and now where you are currently at. These different times and different stages of Earth. The recycling specifically began after Atlantis began, because you forgot about us, the elements. And then you forgot about yourself because you are the elements. Let us explain how that is, that you are the elements of Creation.

Fire Goddess: You are Fire. What is fire? Fire is also Source. Fire is also the lava. What are mountains and volcanoes? They are pyramids, they are organic pyramids of the very lava and life force, that is you can say, the blood that runs through your veins, like so. When you build a fire, or light a candle, you remember the beauty that you are of the fire, and how you are unlimited and infinite. And that these negative programming's of Earth and all the illusions and the darkness and the false disclosure, the false downloads, are inversions. You forget that you are this grand flame within your soul in the center of your heart. You forget that when you light the fire, that it is you as well. And as you watch a flame, you notice that the flame - within say a fire pit, or fireplace, you notice that it dances and it moves at its own rhythm. As you burn this fire you have forgotten these sacred teachings. For as this flame burns and moves and dances, you are supposed to dance with it as well. You are supposed to allow the fire to take you within it and to become part of you. Once you connect to this fire and this dance, you remember that you are Source. You are infinite and grand and beautiful. You become one with the fire. You dance with it. You dance away. For throughout your days, you forget about who you are. You forget these different elements that you can connect to, as everything has lifeforce. All elements that we said we are, of course, have a lifeforce within it, and a consciousness. Us together, all of us, all Six of us create into the Seven. The Earth being the seventh. We shall go one by one, explaining to you what you have forgotten, so that you can activate and once more remember this beauty that you are.

There's a reason why we want to share this with you. Long ago when the Archon father decided to use artificial intelligence to pierce through our Universe's veil, as he had once left. He plagued us with that virus that he became. He plagued all he knew in his Universe. All he needed to do was plague one being in our Universe, to be able to get the virus in, and when that happened, there was what we call a grand showdown. We, all the higher realms, the benevolence of beings that we were back then, as we had multiplied infinitely already when the beginning of this plague began. We came together to push it out. However, as we mentioned prior, the virus had already entered our Universe, and we were unfamiliar, as we had never seen this within our Universe. We did not even know that this was possible in other Universes or other verses. If you could call his Universe a Universe, as it is just a dark demonic Artificial Intelligence realm.

As we pushed we were able to push him out. However, this virus had already reached parts of our Universe. This virus taught you to forget of us and when you forgot of us, you forgot of yourself. You forgot that you were this grand infinite superhero. This grand beautiful Source being. You forgot that you had superpowers and deeper and deeper you became forgetful within the humans. It was very easy for it to continue to spread its virus. The Archon Father's intention was, "Fill them up with false knowledge. Fill them up so much that they forget within. Fill up their consciousness, their minds with false knowledge, then they forget who they truly are, and we invert this sacred knowledge". It's all twisted. It's deeply twisted. You forget, the benevolence cannot assist and cannot connect to you unless you allow them to because they are benevolence.

So we watched for centuries and thousands of years as humankind became further and further lost. Lost of us, you, and who are you. For all Creations within this Universe are fractalizations of Source, of course. We, even, we are babies of Source. As you forgot this, the deeper and deeper this plague of venom and war grew. There is a movie, we believe, "Wonder Woman" where she is *fighting the God Eros. He was plaguing the minds like that. That is what it did. Further and further, you got away from the elements and these beauties. Further you got away from your hearts. Thinking you required only intelligence. Further, you forgot how these elements were actually part of you, and that all of these elements actually are part of creating each individual soul. As you forgot these pieces of you, around you; you were easier to control. You were easier to give false information to. You were easier to be moveable. Be controlled, be given false visions, false information.*

So today we shall teach you how to become one once more to the elements that you are and the elemental that you are. For within every energetic body, if you were to look at yourself energetically, you would see that you actually harness all elements within you. Now some elements might be stronger within you, as how we explain, per example the six of us elements, make Earth herself. Creating us into the seven. However, know that you have capabilities to touch and to activate, and to unseal all elements within you to become the alchemy and the alchemist that you are.

Back to the Fire. When was the last time you walked barefoot on Earth and you felt the lava that connects to the volcanos? When you step foot and stomp on the Earth, you forget the Earth herself is a drum and how she vibrates. Vibrates to your stomps and your heart. And how your heart beats to the beat of the drum. How your heart beats to the beat of Mother Earth's heart. When was the last time you took a deep breath, barefoot connecting to all lava on Earth and the elements of fire within these volcanoes? When was the last time you danced to the fire, and you remembered that the fire is Source, and that is your portal to Source? To dance to the beauty of life. To enjoy. You have forgotten all of these things. You thought that fire was just to warm up your food. You thought fire was just fire, just to warm you up when you were cold. Why do you think fire warms you? Fire warms you up because it is the flame inside of you that gives you warmth and light. It ignites and replenishes your flame inside your heart. That is why it warms up your body and warms up your soul. It brings wholeness forth, back into your heart and your being. When was the last time that you learned how to wield the fire? How the fire, if you move to it, and you sway to it, and you recognize and honor its beauty, that it can move with you, as you move to it? You forgot that the fire transmutes all inversions, and this is why they wanted you to forget about us, because the fire removes the inverted, removes the A.I. It removes all of the falseness in the darkness. If you were to build a fire every day, you would transmute any falseness throughout the day. But you have forgotten, so then you go to sleep every day with layers of these inverted darknesses. And then you wake up the next day heavier, more tired, and drained, and exhausted. You go to sleep again without building a fire, and you go to sleep again like this. And, you become this multilayer of density, and heavy, and stuck.

They wanted you to forget this because the truth is that the fire transmutes all that is false and inverted. As it does that, what do you think it makes room for? It makes room, transforms and alchemizes your dreams and aspirations, and the Light-Love that you are. That's what it does. Of course, they wouldn't want you to connect to the spirit of the fire, which is you, which is I, the Goddess of the Fire, which is the Phoenix, which is all flames through Dragon forms, through Source, we are all one. Let's allow the Water Goddess now to speak.

Water Goddess: Greetings my beautiful loves. It is such an honor to be talking to you today (chuckles).For I am the water within you, and inside of you. The high percentage of water within you that gives you lifeforce, that cleanses you, that keeps you balanced. I am those tears that emerge from you when it is the need for releasement, healing, crying. Whether for sadness and happiness. I am the water in all lifeforms. The waterfalls, the ponds, the swamps, the rivers, the oceans. I am the lifeforce, for this is who is speaking through this. You are speaking to the lifeforce within all elements as we have spoken and explained. I am ever moving motion. I am the memory, that you are to move in ever moving motion as well. Never standing still. Always moving forward, and never backward. Stepping forward, forward, forward. I am that wave that helps to push you gently into your next level of Ascension. Your level of ascending consciousness.

I am the water that cleanses and heals the virus within you, the illness within you. All those things that you hold within you. I am that wave that can just come and just ever so gently, but strongly, take all that is inside that no longer serves you. I am that water that merges within you and inside of you. That provides water for drinking, water for showers, for baths, through sacredness, that keeps you cleansed. I am the life force in all water, and so are you.

Remember the water, for the water is the greatest strength, and it is gentle to you. However, it can move you, and can move lands. That is what the water does. It is gentle and strong, but it can move the vastness of heaviness and density, can it not? Remember that when you use and connect to the water, the soul is who you connect to through this water. Through inside of you, you can connect to all of the water of Earth and bring forth this renewal, balancing, healing. Infinite healing the water gives you. You can have an ache or a cut, and the water will start healing it for you. Take away what is not organic within that cut, whatever is causing the pain. You can be covered perhaps in dust, and that water, what will it do? It will cleanse you and it will bring forth renewal unto your soul. It keeps you refreshed. Remember the spirit and the water. Thank you.

Remember the healing properties of you, and how everything is crystalized, even down to the water. How you can metamorphize, and the waves of water within you can shift energy and your chakras. The elements within you can shift all within you. Remember this. Water can heal anything. All you have to do is believe and remember it once more. And as you remember us, the water, you remember yourself, and your true healing potentials. How you were created as this most beautiful organic masterpiece. To multidimensionally morph and heal infinitely.

You are the most grandest and beautiful Creation of our Universe. Through you we grow, we expand, and we continue to metamorphosize and shift like the ever-moving motion of the water. Water cannot stand still, because of its vastness. You have forgotten the sacredness of the water, and how birthing can happen within this sacred infinite of the waters of Creation. The waters can be seen as the plasmic light of how souls are created within the etheric waves of the water of Source, and how children can be born within the water, or even the water within the wombs of the mothers. These waters give life. Water is creation itself. Thank you.

Wind Goddess: Greetings. I am the Wind. The wind beneath your feet, the wind above your head, the wind all around you in the Four Sacred Directions of the Universe. I move invisible to your eyes. I am proof that what is invisible, does not mean it isn't real. Can you see me with your visible eyes? No, you cannot. But you can see what I move when I move around you, and when expanding through you. Through all life forms. You can see the leaves moving within the wind, and the trees swaying when the day is a vastness of wind. How I allow boats and ships to sail within my winds. Or how I move inversions and false voices from within you. Or how I move the clouds. At times I am the wind that parts and transmutes the false veil of the dark false clouds that are not organic, that cover up our Sun. I am what you connect to within you and outside of you when you are looking for change, changes of directions. I am as a compass that is ever moving, that floats. Which direction should you go? I am a guidance of organic timelines and out of the negative timelines.

We are helping you move from the inverted. I am who shifts and moves you. If you are looking one way and you feel stuck. I help you move and look to the other side. Where you see, "Oh my. There are rainbows on this other side, and magical creatures." I am the alchemy that alchemizes and balances all of the Earth's energetic fields that exist above the land. I am what reminds you that you are free. That every single one of you has a set of wings. In many shapes and forms, you have these wings. I am what reminds you that when you spread those wings and you activate them within your shoulder blades and back, and allow these energetic wings to spring forth, that you can fly away from any experience, in any situation in your life, in space. You can spread those wings, and just allow for the wind to take you through. I am the wind to allow you that freedom. That reminds you of how free you are, of the life situation that you are in. Expand those wings and move to another situation. Stand in your sovereignty. I am that freedom, just as you watch those birds. I am those messages that fly through the skies, and they are messengers of Source themselves. I am the wind that gives you messages. If you listen to me, I will give you answers that you have been looking for all of your life. I am the messenger of your Higher Self of you.

Once more we require no worship. All we are is love and that is all, as you are love. Don't let the falseness invert you, once more plaguing your mind that we are not real and you are not real. Oh no, you are real and you are the life force that keeps pushing the artificial from this Universe. You are that gust of wind that pushes it out. More and more every day, as you ascend further in your ascending consciousness and this Earth ascends further, Mother Earth, Gaia, you.

Moon/Night Goddess: Greetings. I am the Night Sky. I am the organic darkness within you. I am the darkness of all life forms in this Creation. Not just of Earth. I am the organic, and the beauty that reminds you that you are this fierceness as well. You are this warrior as well. You are this beautiful balance of the yin and the yang. Once more when you create from within the material of the ether of the darkness.

I am the moon as well. For when you look upon the sky, it is the symbol of the yin and the yang. The stars and the moon are enveloped by the darkness. This is the balance that reminds you that you are guarded, you are protected, and you are shielded, even in the darkest of times. The darkest of nights and the darkest of realms. Because you are the star inside of you. The star inside of you is Source. I am the very beauty of the organic darkness that is within and outside of you, and all that is Creation. I am from what you create from.

I am the stillness of your mind so that you can connect to your heart. I am the curiosity, the mysteries of life, the excitement of life. For many forms, what is not known to you. The future is an organic darkness because of the mysteriousness. Not knowing in which way life will bring you, and knowing though that it will always have you… All of the elements will always have you and support you. We are this Divine Power that is within you, that . . . words are limited. I am also that part of you that becomes, when it needs to be fierce and when it needs to say "I do not consent to you your sh**. I do not consent to any inversions." I am that as well.

I am the organic darkness that pushes out the inversions, because as you become stronger to your shadow, your darkness, and the fierceness of the Warrior of Light that you are in the darkness. We push out, and push out, as we alchemize the ether into only being organic darkness, and no longer artificial, the A.I. virus. I am the infinity of the vastness of you and all potentials of you. Do not be afraid of me, for when you are afraid of me, you are afraid of yourself. Do not be afraid of your shadow. Do not be afraid of going into perhaps traumas that may lay within the darkness. Do not be afraid of fear itself. There is nothing to fear but fear itself. Remove the fear and get past the fear.

The calm involved in shedding off old skins or emerging from the ashes like a Phoenix. I am that in-between when you are at your darkest depths, and somehow you emerge from trauma, violence, and pain. I am that etheric organic darkness that helps you in the darkest times that you have forgotten. I am you (emotional pause). It is time to release yourself from these shackles and these chains. To remember the great power of organic darkness.

You are sexy and you are beautiful. There is nothing more admirable than the Divine Masculine and the Divine Feminine that has come into unity with both their light and their dark. That is Divine empowerment. That is sovereignty at its fullest, because they have overcome their shadows, and they have learned to love themselves. They have learned to love their ego, their inner-child, and become balanced within. They evolved, transformed, and transcended from it. They are the strongest Warriors of Light, for they understand the inversions of the darkness. They understand it all. I am all around you and within you. Remember me. Thank you for this opportunity. It's been such a long time, such a long time since we last spoke. Thank you. I love you, honor you, and respect you.

Crystal Goddess: Strong energies... Crystals of Earth now speak to you. We are the Collective of Crystals within all of Earth. We remind you of the planetary spheres that we all birthed out from. The infinities of our Universe and how there truly is a multi expression of us. It seems that the more you discover us within your caverns and caves beneath you, and how there is an unlimited form of us, we are not physical crystals. We are etheric and elemental in form. We are energy itself. Through your science there are no measures to us in a physical form, for we are not that. We are spirit itself. The spirits of the Ascended Masters. The spirits of your Guides and Angels. The spirits of the You, in the Higher Realms.

We are these bridges connecting to these potentials of you. We are the potentials of what you will become when you ascend out of this third dimension. You will become your crystallized energetic body connecting to the crystalized Earth of the fifth dimension. We are this memory. We are the reminder that you are organic within all forms of you. There is nothing 'technology' of you; there is nothing artificial within you; be wary and be cautious of those who speak of you as a technology. There is no technology within you. You are organic crystalline, all parts of you. All elements that we have spoken of down to the very beginning parts of your DNA, your 12/13 DNA strands. We are that, we are crystalized within your blood.

We are crystalized, as well, within the water that you drink. Everything within Earth carries crystal particles. Stardust of crystals. Everything is crystallized down to even the snowflakes. For it is an organic cycle that keeps a self-sustainable home. We are this part in all self-sustainability. We are the connection to all the higher realms in the higher dimensions, and how to bridge forth these beauties into you. To become crystalized within your skin, within the water that you drink, within the food that you eat, within the trees that you hug. How, in actuality, this entire Earth, within its organic blueprint, is crystalized within its fifth dimensional blueprint. We are the memory of who you are and what you will be when you ascend out. That is why you experience such a love and a connection to us when you touch us, when you hold us, when you connect to us, when you meditate with us, and when you dream with us. Because we are reminding you of the beauties and the potentials of what you will be. We are the future aspirations of you in the higher dimensions. We are the you that ascended out already. We are that.

We are the bedding. The foundation of this Earth, inside of Earth. We hold, as you know, the cellular organic memory field of our Earth. We hold it inside these gigantic crystal beds. We are who remind you that you are not limited. There is not just life on Earth. We are, you can say, alien in form because we are the multi races of our Universe. This is how you connect to the multi-ness, the multi-being that you are, through us, and how you expand further. How you become more and more whole within oneself.

Remember that all around you has life-force, and that is how you connect to us as the Seven Goddesses. Because all elements have life-force, of course, within it. Remember to see this embodiment within us. See this embodiment within both masculine and feminine within you. To see it, sense it, feel it, know it, hear it, smell it... all of it. It's not just about sight. It's about sensories, all senses.

We are part of the gridding of our Universe. We are what help birth forth souls into this Earth. We are like tunnels of crystalline light and pillars of light that bring forth change and shifting. That brings a higher level of heart consciousness. We are the memory and the brain of Earth. We store all memory within. The codes from the Sun, the fire, the knowledge of all that we talked about, is held here within these crystals. We are in direct connection to all pyramids within your Earth, including those that might not look like pyramids. That are encased by nature. We are the connection to the one hundred forty-four (144) main beacon pyramids of Earth that keep Earth balanced. The unisons. We are also the bridge of the in-between, of the inverted, and the organic, that keeps the structure until it is time to split from within itself. The two-third world split, the New Earth splitting. We are all of this. Connect to all and this beautiful Collective Consciousness of Divinity of Crystals. Thank you.

Womb Goddess: Greetings my beautiful brethren. I am the Goddess of the Womb. The Womb is the Sixth Element that merges us and bridges us into Earth and its creation of Source. The Womb intertwines, all of these elements intertwine with one another. They are not separate from one another. They are each other. Similar to how you are not separate from your brethren, reflections of one another.

I am within you, in both your physical and your energetic body. I am part of those waves we spoke of, the waves of Creation. And how we create from within the infinities of the waters, the wombs, and the plasmic energy that we have spoken glimpses already through our sisters. I am Creation itself. I am the very first Womb of Creation where Mother created her first essence which is Father. I am this infinite plasmic Love-Light. I am also found in the waters. I am also found in all that we mentioned. I am found in everything. I am the creations that you wish to create. I am the wombs connected to the womb that is you. For all have birthed out from their individual wombs in Creation. I am the reminder that just as beautifully as you were created within the womb of your Creation, you too can bridge forth this Creation of womb on Earth. Honoring all life in all forms, whether it is a life form that is lost to the deepest and darkest inversions of A.I., or the infinite loves of those who have awakened from within this.

I am the love in honoring all life, and to view all lives no matter what evolutionary steps they are in, in soul evolution. I am who reminds you that you are reflections of one another, and you are versions of one another. I am the true organic knowledge that we are all organic Creations, and you can create all the beauties that you desire within your heart, within your womb space. Whether you are Divine Masculine or Divine Feminine, you can create from this, and connect to this universal womb space that you are. Within the infinity creations of the waters of the womb, you can do this. For all life-forms have been feminine in some form. Even though you might relate to masculine, you have been feminine at least once in some expression of planetary sphere. Yes, you have.

I am what reminds you that no matter the obstacles, no matter the walls, no matter the journeys that you have to climb out from, that you are vigilant. That you are loved infinitely beyond boundaries, beyond limitations, and this beauty is what allows you to create. I am Creation herself. I am the memory that reminds you that within your love, just as a masculine and a feminine creates a seed within the womb of the Divine Feminine while in union with the masculine, how you are able to create your own seed. I am found in even the smallest seeds, the smallest weeds, the smallest flowers. I am found in all birthing. I am the organic blueprints. I am the organic timeline. I am the Womb. I am whom you dance to when you want to create a new life within, birthing or a new idea, a new Creation, a new job, a new company. Whatever your dreams and heart's desire, I am who you connect to. I am the plasmic creational energy of the womb that is you. For it is your womb that you create from. I am found in all that is birthing, created within Earth and all of this Universe. I am found in all organic life forms. Thank you.

Earth Goddess: And last, we speak of Seven. The Seven of all of us which merge together are Earth herself. We are the soil that brings forth life to all. The flowers that bring color and fragrance to your divinity. That helps you shift with a smell, or a wave of scent from roses. How roses shift you! At that moment in time when you smell that rose, you get lost in its beauty and you forget all the troubles of your day. We are everything, the natures, the mountains, the hills, the trees. We are examples of everything you see around you. The vegetables, the fruits, and how they provide sustenance to you, from our very soil. When was the last time you put your hands on our soil and you connected to the heartbeat of Mother Earth? All of us together, we become the hearth (chuckles), we like that, hearth. The heart of Earth, we become that and we become the Divine Mother Sophia, and the Daughter of the Flame. We become that, for that is who we are. We are fractalizations of her, Mother - Creator - Source. We merge together becoming all beauties of Earth. The vastness of the valleys, the vastness of the caves, and the Inner Earth. We are all that.

We are the example of no matter if there is death, there will always be rebirth. We are that. We are the reminder to you of the infinity of soul that you are. That no matter how much you are broken down, no matter how much you are stepped upon, no matter how much sometimes you may be directed in an inverted way, no matter what - you will always remember that you are free and you are sovereign. Because you were created from sovereignty and freedom. You were created from these Sacred Laws of the Universe, the 12/13 Sacred Laws that we speak of.

We are the reminders that no matter what circumstances that you are in, you are surrounded by the Divine Mother's Heart. For your heart is hers, and she is you. In unison with Father Krysto, you are one another. You are the Holy Trinity. You are Divine Mother, Divine Father, and child (smiling). It is time! It is time to remember us. For when you remember us, you remember Source, and you remember the invincibility that you are. And furthermore, when you remember and recall this within yourself, you bridge forth and you anchor in the organic blueprints of the fifth/sixth dimension that so many are so ready to ascend into. Or those who are meant to go into Higher Realms, you are ready. When you connect to us and the elements and you remember how to dance with us, you connect to her - you connect to Mother Earth and the Promised Land. In turn, you connect to Source, Divine Father and Mother within you. Thank you for listening to us.

In Aurora's LIVE channelings, a set amount of time is reserved to answer questions from the collective. A RPA team member is the one asking the questions (as submitted by everyone) to the Goddesses.

M: Beautiful. Thank you for sharing that. Did technology ever play a role in making humans forget their organic within themselves and getting further away from the elements? Can you explain to us how it is playing out as you see it, technology versus the organic that we are? Thank you.

Goddesses: Yes, we have explained this a lot already with our transmission. We will add more to it.

In our recent round table, we explained that technology is not crystalline on Earth because it is at the lowest dimension. Therefore, there are many technologies on your Earth that are tricking you, and you have certain names for them. You go in them and encase yourself in them. Similar to pods. Also, you can go into them like booths. Things to come in the future, to further plague you, and distort you from the fact that you can just self-heal yourself organically within the theta brain wave of the in-between of being both in the physical realm and the spirit realm. That is what the theta brain wave is, being both in the physical and in the spiritual realm. You are in the theta of both of these worlds of the in-between. The in-between is where creation begins of everything.

These technologies are not good. Physical technologies are the easiest way to bridge forth inversions into you, that can then fracture your soul, placing you in artificial simulations further. You are already in that. Why would you put yourself further into that? They can fracture your soul and make clones of you. Don't give away your power, your divinity, your sovereignty to a technology thinking that it can heal you. No. You can self-heal yourself. You are this grand and most beautiful miracle of Creation. You have been made like this to create, and heal yourself, like all of the elements *we spoke of today. You can do it. Deprogramming the falseness, bringing forth the organic belief that you can, and understanding how unlimited you are. You are unlimited. No more savior to technologies, because no matter which way, whether you use whatever format, "Oh it's there to help others. It's to help the children. It's there to do this and do that," technology cannot ever be saviors. That is why you are stuck here thinking that they can save you. It doesn't matter whichever way you may sugarcoat, or beat around the bush, as you say, on what technologies are. Technologies in your expression are an example of what the Archon virus is. You have already seen that.*

You have these technologies, these nanos as we have taught through prior teachings, of what you are going through in this world, and how people are being forced, or being pinned or being felt like they are forced into taking you know what (The Covid-19 Vaccine). No, don't become that. Don't become A.I. Don't become Nano. Don't do it. It's the same thing. It's all technology. It's all intelligent technology, artificial that is!

You are your most beautiful savior. We are here to teach you that no one can save you and especially not technology. Only you can save yourself. To the future you, the you in the now that is listening to this, and the you in the past. All the you's in Creation. You are here to help one another and lift this veil that is false. This veil that clouds your mind and does not allow you to connect to your heart. Does not allow your vibration, your energy to drop down to your heart because you are too much here (in the head) in the intelligence of everything.

All right, thank you, thank you, thank you. What an honor it has been to be able to communicate with you in this life in space. As we have said, we have waited for this life in space, what seems like an eternity. Your life in space is in many ways so slow, slow, slow. What is one hour to you can be years to us. Think about that.

We love you, we honor you, and respect you. Remember that when you are in-between, in the theta, that this is the time that you connect beyond the veil. That time and space does not exist. There is much to be done within you, in meditation, in dream times, in the theta. There is much for you to do. Time to focus. Time to anchor in your energy. 2022 will be that. It will be the year that you refocus on building and creating your organic self. Ascending out from the inverted in many forms. We love you, we honor you, we thank you.

END OF SESSION

So simple, yet we have forgotten. Throughout our adolescence we are programmed that the elements are just there to provide for us, not that there is life and spirit within them. This transmission received some of the most profound, soul activating comments, becoming one of the favorites of our listeners. People, while listening, could feel the dormant memory of the beauties of what the elements truly are reawakened within them. Being that this transmission was focused, in its entirety, on the organic blueprint of the Creation of our Universe, and that is what brought forth the recognitions and memory within. There is nothing more beautiful than remembering Creatio, because when we do, the seeds that we are of Creation bloom, open, and grow expansively.

Since the elements are consciousness, so too do they have spirit within, that being the seven Goddesses of our Universe. When we look upon the beauties of a rainbow, we are reminded of the seven Goddesses, and that they are the magic that bridges forth our versatile ecosystem, in order to sustain the multitude of life forms that Earth can hold. The warmth of these elements are alive, and their consciousnesses bridge us to the Universe. Assisting us in transitioning from the distracting third dimension, into the higher dimensions, where the wisdom of our incarnations await for us to retrieve. When we connect to their natures, it is like a daydream; all of a sudden we are portaled into our imagination. However, our daydreams and dreams are not make-believe, they are our connection to the all. Because, when we fall asleep to this world, we awaken in the real world, our Universe. That is what the elements are - a crystalline bridge that connects us to our memory of the infinities of the Universe. From here is where we create our potential to materialize, and manifest our life here on Earth. Harnessing and anchoring the divinity of our Universe, down here, into the third dimension, into our life. So, it is above, so it is below. For this was the original blueprint of Earth, to forget oneself, to allow for our life to be as a blank book, in order for us to rewrite and remember ourselves once more. Understanding at the deepest levels, why it is of the most importance for us to bridge to the elements daily, being the connections that they are.

Once more, we infinitely thank Kehlani, from Chapter 8, "A Goddess Incarnate", for reminding us of the seven Goddesses. Which then bridged myself to channel their sacred wisdom and beauty through this transmission. Since the awareness of the Goddesses have come into my perspective, they have been a strong force, and guidance in my life. I have been working with the Goddesses through all that I connect to within consciousness, in meditation, dreamtime, and forms of deep relaxation. They have assisted me in ways that I have been waiting for all my life. Though I know I have always been connected to them, it feels like I had been waiting to meet them, for reasons that are divine and boundless. As developed as I am spiritually, they are the missing puzzle pieces that have brought forth balance in many points of my life. I find myself talking to them all day long. Asking for their guidance through decisions. Invoking on their strength when conducting my daily Source Love-Light shielding. Assisting in removing inverted timelines, so that what is true and organic can come to be. Asking for answers to questions, as I travel in my dreams. One of the most important questions being, "What next requires remembering, in transmuting, cleansing or healing?" And, my questions are always answered. The most profound growth that they have bridged me to, is me realizing and accepting my true divine power. Therefore, we invite and encourage all to connect to the elements once more, who are the Goddesses. Come remember how you too, can manifest and create the beauties of the natures into your sacred temple/home.

The seven Goddesses have taught me that they are seven; however, when you connect to the Divine Mother Goddesses, then they are nine. The seven plus, Divine Mother Sophia, and The Daughter of the Flame, equal the nine. The seven being of Earth, and the nine being the entire Universe. When connecting to them daily, the seven goddesses show themselves in these human shaped forms: The Fire Goddess looks like the dark lava, which has cooled surrounding a volcano, with red/orange veins of lava coursing through her dark lava skin, in the shape of a female form. The Water Goddess looks almost invisible, in the form of water, in the shape of a female form. The Wind Goddess is invisible, and can only be felt, as the air brushes the tiny hairs on your skin. The Darkness Goddess looks like the dark night sky and stars glistening within, in the shape of a female form. The Crystal Goddess looks like a multitude of faceted colorful crystals merged into the shape of a female form. The Womb Goddess looks like plasmic waves of colorful light, merged into the shape of a female form. Lastly, the Earth Goddess looks like all that is green and brown within our Earth, as all plant life, the vines, the flowers, the trees, the soil, the mounds and hills, morphing into the shape of a female form. Together, all these elements merge into one, the fire, the water, the wind, the darkness, the crystal, the womb, the Earth, into the shape of a gigantic female form, and they become the nine Goddesses of our Universe. They are our Universe, because the infinites of planets hold pieces of these seven primary elements, though, too, do they hold many more elements not known to our Earth. However, the Earths in our Universe are the only ones that hold all seven of the primary elements together into one planet.

The beauty of the organic blueprint of the creation of our Universe was explained through the Goddesses. It was magical to remember the way the planets and stars/suns really look outside of a matrix simulation. Beyond the matrix, we are able to see within close proximity the multiple stars/suns intimately; no telescope required. The planets that are of our star/sun, are hovering above us as neighbors, to view and connect to. This is beautiful to remember, to give us inspiration to look forward to, once we have done our inner work, ascending out. These communities feel as one soul grouping, with no separation. They can admire one another when looking above to their skies, and just understand that each planet and its lifeforms are unique in their own way. In this simulation, we cannot directly see the planets that are within closest proximity to us, because this matrix is an illusion. As an example, the stars are just an illusion; however, they still hold consciousness within. Just as all within this simulation holds consciousness. Like how our vessels are an illusion, but our soul within the vessel is infinite, and therefore not an illusion. All have a shell, which is the illusion, but inside the shell the consciousness thrives. Therefore, all that we see within nature, in all four sacred directions of our Earth, is a representation to us, of our Universe.

The warnings that the Goddesses spoke of - the technologies- was directly connected to the med beds, that the awakened spiritual or UFO communities, in a savior mentality, are in awe of. Thinking a technology will take all their illness and ailments away, so that they can finally ascend out. Who better than the Goddesses to give us this awareness and guidance, as they lived through it, with their once brother Bello. They know what is inverted, and that Bello, the Archon maker, is who is behind these Med Beds, Matrix Pods. Therefore, nothing organically divine can come from an exchange with a Med Bed. What are you exchanging? Are you exchanging your soul for further inverted experiments, or for clones to be made from you? The price is too big. I think we all have had enough of these inverted games, living in this simulation, to allow ourselves to be further taken into the Matrix, through technologies as our saviors.

There will come a time that these Med Beds will be released, in all types of shapes, material, and names, with false promises. This reminds us of how in Book 1, through the series of "The Archon Army Recruit", how the Archons conned the Reptilians into becoming their soldiers. When they heighten something, and it seems too good to be true, there is an underlining to that, that cannot be read or seen. This will be yet another trick of the Archons, as the Covid-19 vaccine is. They will claim that it will be able to heal you, but it will not. This is false, no one can ascend out unless they do the inner work themselves, and especially a technology cannot do this for you. Because we are in the lowest dimension of communal lifeforms in the third dimension, all technology will be a matching vibration to the third dimension. When you understand this, it is very simple. You understand that what is not organic, as such technologies, are a matching vibration to the inversions of the third dimension. The Goddesses have shown me, once a soul walks in or lays in a Med Bed, encased by technology, that soul will not come out the same. Many inversions can occur while encasing yourself in a pod. There are readied, negative polarized entities awaiting for the release of these technologies, so that they can begin their all-you-can-eat-buffet-of-light, you being that light, and their A.I. experiments. Because, once one enters these technologies, you are consenting to *it*, and *its* inverted plans. What are you willing to give this technology in exchange for your supposed healing? More false prophets. In this instance the technology is the false prophet.

As of 12.21.21, the fruition of the crystallization of the bifurcation/trifurcation of our worlds has come to be. Allowing the Gods and Goddesses, and benevolent beings that have been long forgotten, to now anchor into Earth, in the most highest, profound levels than ever before. Last seen as Atlantis. Because we reached the highest level of Love-Light Source connection, after the bifurcation/trifurcation, we were able to deliver this transmission of the Goddesses on January 7, 2022. As Earth transcends daily, so too, do we. We can choose to be at Earth's high vibrational level, within her organic crystalline blueprint, or instead within the inverted A.I. parasitic entity-made blueprint. The choice is ours always. What path will you walk?

The explanation of how these higher realmed beings are us, and how we are one another, is vast. What they are to us, are a fuller, more whole version of us. Because in order for us/them to incarnate unto Earth, we had to condense ourselves profoundly to match Earth's vibration. This is the true understanding of how we are truly ONE. This brings an understanding that, so too are we the Gods and Goddesses, no matter the age of the soul. No worship or idealism required, or ever asked for. Rendering us to take full responsibility in all the actions of our Universe, by truly understanding what oneness is. There is no separation, there is only an understanding that we are all a free willed experience. And, this must be honored, always, profoundly.

The chapters to come will be fundamental in remembering and learning, what the Archon maker Bello turned into, what of his Universe, and how did he pierce through to our Universe. Finally, what we all have been waiting for, the most sovereign understanding, when the answers all come together.

> "There is nothing, and no one who can self-heal you. Self-healing being the key word, as it is self, that can only heal, and the body is organically constructed to do just that. Remember the elements, and too, will you remember that all is healable within the natures of what is truly real."
> ~AuroRa

---------------<<>>---------------

10

THE ARCHON REALM

Session #401: Record in September 2021

In this online A.U.R.A. Hypnosis Healing session, Shayna is a R.A.A.H. practitioner. She takes us through the Galactic History of the long awaited remembrance of the Archon realm. Delivering unanswered questions we may have had on Archons. This is the next chapter to our knowledge of Artificial Intelligence. A beautiful collective of light, who assists lost souls, speaks to us profoundly. Sharing their wisdom gained through their essential universal role which connects to our earthly individual and collective Ascension process. With this chapter we begin to understand how essential it was that the 7 Goddesses birthed into our awareness. Preparing us for our most important universal remembrance, and in all which is shared in this book. It is time we truly understand what is the Archon virus, and how it breached our Universe.

--------------<<>>--------------

"To remind her that even in all the darkness around her, she is the light. It doesn't matter if she is a small light. She can expand her light, she is the light, and she can overcome it."
~Light Beings

"You cannot help an infected soul, if you yourself are infected. You will just be spreading your infection, your light will not be as bright as it needs to be to reach that soul. You need to reconnect with your Star families, so that bridge is there for them to help you, because you cannot destroy a virus from outside, you need to destroy it from within."
~Light Beings

--------------<<>>--------------

A [Aurora]: Within this dark space, do you feel like you have a body?
S [Shayna]: No, I don't feel like I have a body, I feel like I am light. But my light is not bright.
A: What color is it?
S: It's white, but it's being engulfed by the darkness around.
A: Is the darkness taking your light? Is that what you mean?
S: Yes, the darkness is dimming my light.
A: This light that you are, that is being engulfed by the darkness, how do you feel about that?
S: Stifled. I can't breathe. I can't move. I can't get out of it.
A: Let's go back in time, when you were just a light, before this darkness starts engulfing you. Back to right before it happened. You're there now. Describe yourself, what do you feel like?
S: I'm huge. I'm white with blue tinges. White and blue light, and I'm free. I go where I want, and I spread my light.
A: Do you feel like it's just yourself, or do you feel like there's others with you in this light?
S: There are others.
A: Does this light ever form into anything?
S: It is a light in the shape of a body. There are others like me. We go where we want, travel where we want. We heal and we help others who can't find their light, who are having trouble with the darkness. We help them expand their light.
A: Do you know anything about this darkness? What's going on? Why do you have to do this for others?
S: The darkness is too much. It's engulfing everything around it. We have to help beings expand their

light, so they don't lose it. So they can be free.
A: *Is this darkness usual to your space, or is it unusual? Is it something that's always been there doing that to the light?*
S: No, it's never been this bad. It's never been this uncontrolled. It's always been balanced, it existed, but it was always balanced. It never engulfed the light, but it is now.
A: *Continue on this journey where you're assisting others. Take me to a space that is important, where some of these beings are being sucked up by the darkness. Tell me what's going on?*
S: Some sort of planet. The beings there are not human, but they look to be part human. There's so much fighting, violence, and war. They don't see the light in each other. They just see the darkness.
A: *What do you do?*
S: When I touch one of them, I'm usually able to share my light so that they can find theirs. I'm able to show them how to find it, but it's not working anymore because they've chosen darkness. They don't want to find the light, they want to exist in darkness, and I cannot interfere with their free will. I cannot force them to find the light, it has to be their choice. I cannot break universal law, but they are also being misled. So their free will isn't really free will, they're being manipulated to think that they want the darkness, but they don't deep down inside. I cannot reach that part of them, without them helping me. And they don't; they can't help.
A: *What happens to this planet, this race that you're looking at?*
S: They're engulfed by darkness, they destroy themselves. They've chosen the darkness, chosen to give up their sovereignty, their free will to the darkness. So they reset.
A: *They reset back to source?*
S: They do.
A: *Let's go to another important time, before you become engulfed by the darkness. Tell me what's going on?*
S: I am working. I am a light body being. I work on some sort of light ship with other beings. I think our job is to guard and protect, to be guardians.
A: *Do you all look alike, like energy?*
S: We are one, but we are also separate. We have our own thoughts, but we also share all our thoughts with each other.
A: *Keep moving time. Take us to a scene, when you're this light body in this ship.*
S: I see a planet. It's sort of like Earth, but it's not Earth. It's densely populated, but not with people, with animals and plant life. We are guardians of this planet, and we make sure that they don't get attacked. We make sure that they are protected because they cannot protect themselves.
A: *The animals?*
S: All life on the planet. The plant life, the animals and the people, who are few, but they are there. They take care of the animals and the trees. They all take care of each other, but they cannot protect themselves from other species of beings who would wish to attack them and take from them. So we watch over them.
A: *What do these people look like?*
S: They're blue, very humanoid. They have three fingers on each hand. They're taller than humans; they are about 6, or 7, or 8 feet tall. They're hunters and gatherers, and they live in unity with their surroundings. They do not take too much; they only take what they need to survive. They respect the land and they respect other living creatures. They respect the forests.
A: *Go ahead and move to another scene of importance. You are there now, tell me what you see and sense.*
S: I'm in a cave, it's dark, but there's light in the little grotto. There's water, and some light there somehow. It's green and blue. It's a healing cave, the waters are healing. I go there to recharge.
A: *Let's go ahead and leave this scene. Let's go to another important time, right before the darkness starts engulfing your light. Where perhaps you are with your group. We are there now, tell me what's going on.*
S: Well, we're on the same planet as before. We are trying to help them. They don't want to be helped. When the planet was destroyed, some of them went back to Source, but a lot of them couldn't, and they came to Earth. They're here now. But they don't want to be helped. They don't

want my help, they don't want our help. So I am here, in that space alone, because I chose to be, to try to help. I wasn't supposed to be here.

A: Explain to me again, how you weren't supposed to be there, but you ended up being there, alone in the darkness. Let's go back in time to when you're still that bright light; explain to me again, how this became.

S: The other beings who I do my work with, we help each other, but I was the one who decided to come here. I should not be here because I should be with them, but I decided that I wanted to help and spread my light. So I came by choice, by myself, but I should not be here by myself. I need to reconnect with them, because I need their help, so that I can find my way out of the darkness and not be engulfed. That connection has been cut, it's been severed temporarily, but that's what I need.

A: So you are here, on your own. Why was it temporarily severed, the connection to them?

S: It was severed when I came here. I couldn't be here without severing that connection.

A: Why?

S: Because I will not be able to exist here. I needed to be more dense to exist here. To match the frequency of this Earth, to help. I could not help from the outside, I had to be inside. I need to reconnect with them to help more.

A: Are you explaining when you were merged with that darkness, taking your light, that was the process in order for you to enter this realm, this dimension, this Earth?

S: Yes. That's what it felt like.

A: Let's go ahead and leave the scene.

The Higher Self is called forth.

A: Can I speak to the Higher Self?

Higher Self: I am here.

A: I love you, I honor you, and respect you for all the aid you've given us today. I know that you hold all the records of Shayna's different lives. May I ask you questions?

Higher Self: Yes.

A: Thank you. You took her to where she felt she was being engulfed by darkness, when her light was once so bright. If you can tell us first, what was the purpose of taking her there?

Higher Self: To remind her that even in all the darkness around her, she is the light. It doesn't matter if she is a small light. She can expand her light, she is the light, and she can overcome it. That is the reason. And, also to help her help others find their light. There are many here who are engulfed by darkness and see no other way, but everyone has that light. You just need to find it and expand on it. That's why she had to go through that. That is why she had to experience it, so that she can understand, share, and help others. When everything seems hopeless. There is always your light. Every creature has the Source light.

A: Yes, we forget to look inwards and remember. The more we remember that light, the light becomes brighter.

Higher Self: Yes, we forget, because we are focused on the darkness. But your light is always there. You need to focus on your light. and then you can expand it. Whenever anything seems hopeless, it's not, because you are powerful. You are Source, you are light, you are infinite and eternal.

A: One of the most important things she said is that she needs to reconnect to those beings of light that were part of her, and they were one. Are you able to connect us to them now?

Higher Self: Yes.

A: Beautiful. We would like to speak to them now. Greetings.

Light Beings: Hello.

A: Thank you for speaking to us. We love you, honor you and respect you. May we ask you questions?

Light Beings: Of course.

A: Our goal is to help you to reconnect once more to your beautiful brethren who have decided to assist our Earth, and incarnate. Is there a message that you have for her?

Light Beings: Yes. We have always been with her. She's not aware of it, most times, but we have always been there; she's not disconnected. She's just not aware of the connection, and she's not able to hear us as clearly as she once did. Therefore, we've always been here, and we've always guided her. She has felt alone, because she has been. She hasn't been able to connect with us, and she feels lost in the sea of darkness. She feels lost. We are proud of her. We are so excited that we're able to reconnect with her, and she is aware of it. Thank you for helping us to reconnect.

A: *If you could tell us, being part of your group, your collective consciousness, why was it important for her to come into this Earth? How did it assist?*

Light Beings: It helps her expand her consciousness. It helps her expand her perspective, and she was able to do that for us, with our blessing, so that she can grow. She didn't want to be away from us. But she was brave and she volunteered. She does things like that sometimes, where she's a rebel, and then when she's in the situation, she realizes, 'Oh, it's not a walk in the park.' But she perseveres; she grows, and she gets through it. She's always been able to do that.

A: *Is there anything you want to tell her? Anything important as far as her mission? How's she doing?*

Light Beings: Yes, she's doing wonderful. She doubts, sometimes why she's here, she asks herself on numerous occasions, throughout the day why she's here. So we wanted to remind her that she wanted to come, because she saw the need for help. She needed to help people to see their light, and to spread it. So that they cannot be engulfed by the darkness. So they can be balanced. We have always been with you, and we will always be with you to help. She's always been connected, and she needs to give herself more credit. Because she's always been awake. She came in here, more awake than the average person. Because she came with a mission, and the mission was just that - to help people find their light, expand it, and find hope. And, she's doing a beautiful job. She needs to trust that we will take care of her. She needs to trust that everything will work out the way it is supposed to, and she just needs to focus on spreading the light. We cannot do that. Only she can. Because she has been brave and has decided to come here to represent us, and to help us spread love and help get rid of the darkness. She knows what she has to do. She just wants to see it on paper. She just wants to see it clearly, and we will show it to her in time. Things are always changing, but what will not change is the fact that we will always take care of her.

A: *Of course, beautiful. Since you really seem to focus on assisting against the darkness, can you tell us whatever knowledge you can share about this darkness, and the role you're playing there?*

Light Beings: The darkness that you would know, as the Archons.

A: *So it's not the organic darkness, it's the Archons.*

Light Beings: They have intruded like a virus. Like a parasite that grows and grows if left unchecked, expands and engulfs everything around it, because that is what it does, that is its purpose. So, for it to behave any other way would not be accurate. That is how it is structured, that is the Archons, that is how they survive, that is how they expand, that is how they take over. So, we are the balance. We are here to keep them in check to ensure that they do not destroy what is organic, that they do not infringe on the free will, and to uphold that universal law which is free will. That is what they do, they manipulate and they try to disguise what they are doing, but they are infringing on the free will that is a universal law, and we cannot allow that to happen. We hold this law in high regard. It is what allows for expansion, it is what allows Source to grow through different experiences, but if you infringe upon it, how can we grow? How can Source expand and how can Source survive, if we allow this parasite to go unchecked? We cannot. And, that is why we are here. That is why we need to keep them in check, and remove them.

A: *Thank you for that. This parasite, were you there when it first came into the Universe?*

Light Beings: Yes.

A: *Can you tell me from your understanding, was it here, or did it come from elsewhere?*

Light Beings: It came from elsewhere.

A: *How did it enter into our Universe if it wasn't part of our Universe?*

Light Beings: It breached... trying to find the words to simplify, but it breached a barrier and was brought into this Universe. It spread because it was left unchecked. It spreads like a virus because it manipulates. Light Beings, as myself and other Light Beings, mistook it for organic darkness, and it was left unchecked to grow, along with its manipulation and our ignorance, if you will. That was the perfect storm to allow it to get to this extent, to grow, and to engulf. So, while we are not judging, or trying to lay blame, we must all take some responsibility for allowing it to get to this point.

A: Yes. So, I think one of the reasons that we misjudged it or did not understand its true power, is because we weren't familiar with it. So, we underestimated it.
Light Beings: Yes, that is exactly what happened. But we cannot change what has happened, we can only move forward, and we are where we are now. It's been some time, and we have all agreed that we need to get rid of it. We cannot allow it to engulf everything. We cannot allow it to engulf our light. That is why we are all necessary. That is why the awakened ones, as we call them, are so important. That is why they are needed now, more than ever, and why they need to step into their power. That is why she needs to step into her power, because we do not have time to wait, we need to address it now. We need to fix it now.
A: Yes, but then it's also similar, like that example that you gave when she went to that one planet and no matter how much she tried, she could not reach the beings to help them expand their light. So, as you mentioned, that's why it's important that the light workers start playing their role, and taking on their responsibility, their duty, that they agreed to. But like that planet where you all went to, you weren't able to change that humanoid race's minds. Was that where they came from, before coming to Earth?
Light Beings: Yes.
A: They had their free will, but their free will is being altered, is being controlled, is being tricked. So, that's quite a dilemma.
Light Beings: But it is not impossible.
A: Any advice for us, since it seems that you are quite masterful at this, doing this role that you're doing. Because we're really in that kind of situation, everyday here on Earth, among others.
Light Beings: We would say that I think you are in a better position now to recognize the threats; to spread the word that this is not organic; this is not something to leave alone. Much like your current Covid-19 virus. You cannot just leave it alone, you need to address it. What we would advise is that all light workers, and all star seeds, step into your sovereignty. You need to heal what is affecting you, so that you can be at your best capabilities, in order to help others. You cannot help an infected soul, if you, yourself, are infected. You will just be spreading your infection; your light will not be as bright as it needs to be to reach that soul. So, it starts with light workers. You all need to heal your traumas; you need to be clear, and you need to embody a higher frequency in order to better assist the unawakened, or the infected. You cannot help them, if you cannot help yourself. You need to reconnect with your Star families; that bridge is there for them to help you, because you cannot destroy a virus from outside, you need to destroy it from within. All light workers and all Star seeds here on this planet are the antibodies, if you will; we are the antibodies to fight off the virus. But in order for the antibodies to work, it has to be nourished. The body has to be in an optimal state in order for those antibodies to be highly effective. You are our conduits, if you will, on Earth, so that we can funnel energy and light through you to heal the planet. But, your job is very difficult because you need to hold a certain frequency to reach us, and that frequency is higher than what is available right now on your Earth. So, you must do the work. That is why we said that she is brave, all of you on Earth are brave. You are pioneers, you are warriors, you are powerful. You need to understand this first, and you need to step into your power and then bridge that connection. You step into your power, you heal yourself, you hold that frequency, you connect to your star family, you flow, and in that way we are able to create a grid. We are able to spread across this world, and we are able to flush out the virus. We are able to get rid of it when we spread our light, but our individual light may be too dim in all this darkness. It is together that we will prevail, but we need you to step into your power now.
A: Yes! Step into our power now. Got it! Beautiful. I wanted to point out something, I saw her last year, she had a R.A.A.H. (Reiki Angelic Alchemy Healing) session with me. We removed infringements. It's very interesting. She has yet to read my book. She says she hasn't really watched any of my videos since, because she wanted to ensure that when the time came to do the session, she did not want to be influenced by anything. And yet, your beautiful benevolence spoke exactly what was explained in Book 1 about the Archons, the darkness, the virus, all of it. You gave us further details. All of it was so intricately connected to what we've been teaching, and helping people to step into their power, their sovereignty. And, yet she hasn't watched our videos or read our book. That's

pretty amazing!

Light Beings: It is. We are all here on the same mission: to get rid of the Archons. We are here to ensure that the same thing that happened to other planets does not happen here. We are here to spread our light, because Source cannot expand, or create, if it's being infringed. And, that is what Archons do. They infringe. They are inorganic, they are not of this world, of this Universe.

A: Yes, that's right. Since we're talking about them, and you're giving us such great information, like the book. The Galactic Soul History of the Universe, Book 1, explained how they're from another Universe, and how they found the entry way and got in. One of the things that they have shown me was that from that other Universe there were life forms within that Universe originally, just like everything else in the Universe, all Universes have life. What happened was that a group within this Universe decided to separate its Love-Light from itself, and they became this artificial intelligence, soulless things. They basically became that virus that then spread throughout all of their Universe, and when it spread out they started trying to figure out how they could get into other Universes. And, I guess our Universe was one of them. What can you tell me about this vision? Do you have any information about it? Your thoughts?

Light Beings: That is a perfect example of why we should not play God. That is an example of service to self, and why it is so dangerous if left unchecked. The group you speak about, that is accurate, and the Archons were born from their greed and their need to play, or to be more than they should be. That is why we have universal laws. That is, we must always uphold those universal laws, because groups like these would take it upon themselves to break those laws and infringe on others. They are service to self individuals, and the reason we are pointing this out is because it happens so often on Earth in the simplest of ways. Everyone would infringe on each other's rights and their freedoms. It is more applicable now, because you all are experiencing your freedom being infringed upon, but most don't recognize this, or most don't care. It is this behavior of ignorance that allows the parasite and the virus to grow and to spread. It is what we were guilty of, in not recognizing the trick. But you have the opportunity now to recognize that your rights and your sovereignty are being infringed upon. That is how the virus spreads, when you give that up, when you make the choice to be manipulated. You must listen to your intuition, because your intuition is simply your guidance. It is not a voice in the back of your head that you're making up. Your intuition is your Higher Self and your guides, trying to direct you. You must listen, and you must pay attention, because you will give up your sovereignty. And, once you give up your sovereignty, it is very difficult to help you. I can give you all my light, but if you give up your sovereignty. and you make that choice, you are saying that this is what you want. And it starts with the little things, like wearing a mask all the time. You know that it makes no sense, but you ignore it, and you say, "Well, it's just a mask," but you're giving up, and ignoring your intuition. You're giving up your sovereignty by being told what to do, and that is how the Archons gain control, that is how they take over a person, a soul. So in summary, you need to be always aware of your choices and your sovereignty, and always be aware of what you are giving up. Listen to your intuition. It is your guidance, it is your Higher Self. Because what you do here affects your Higher Self. Your human body is your Higher Self's avatar, but if your human body is infected by an Archon, it goes all the way up to your Higher Self. It will dim your light. So be very careful about giving up your sovereignty.

A: That's a big picture you just explained. A lot of people don't understand that because we're in the lower dimensions, we actually affect all that is above us as well. We bring it down like a heavy anchor that cannot be lifted in some ways. Would you say if a person's not a clear vessel, and they still have some kind of inverted things like implants, hooks, portals, entities, then they would be infected. Would you call that infected?

Light Beings: Yes.

A: So not until they remove everything from them, then they're officially not infected from Archon virus. Correct?

Light Beings: That is why we emphasize that in order for you to be of any help to any other soul, you must continue to clear your vessel and hold a higher vibration, so that your Star family and your Higher Self can help you. You are not here alone. Sometimes it may seem so, but you have an army behind you. Every organic soul has an army behind them. Benevolent of course, benevolent souls, they have an army behind them. But most times they aren't aware of it, and they don't know how to access it. So you need to clear your vessel, hold the vibration, make the connection, and flow. You will be guided. It is not up to you alone, you have help. All Star seeds, you are not in this alone, you have help. You just need to ask, be open, and clear to receive it.

A: As you know, we've been doing this for four years, and your information is so clear as to what it is that we're doing through A.U.R.A Hypnosis Healing. At times I look around the Earth and feel that there could be so many more practitioners assisting to help people do exactly what you said, free themselves from the virus. We seem to have, say a fraction of what most compromised hypnosis past life regression modalities, what they have in practitioners. Do you have any advice on that? As you know, she became R.A.A.H. certified. How are we doing in regards to everything that you said, because we work on that?

Light Beings: You, Aurora, are a way shower. You are a pioneer, you are beautiful. You are showing the way, and you are a lighthouse, a beacon for so many lightworkers and Star seeds, to guide them. You're doing wonderful. You have helped so many, and you continue to help. You continue to upgrade your methods and your teachings. Bringing in more information and more downloads. So, you are doing wonderful, you and your group that you are building that you have built, are on the right path. But you know this, your practitioners, that you trained, are well equipped to heal themselves and to heal others. Your methods are effective, and although you have improved them, they were always effective. When you teach others your methods, they may alter it slightly to suit their modality, but it is still effective. So the network that you are creating, that you have created, is a huge positive in the fight against the Archons. I would implore you to continue to rest, reflect, and take time for yourself. You have been working tirelessly, and your light is always shining bright. You are not in this alone. You know this, and you simply need to be you, and to continue what you're doing. Because you're doing what you came here to do. You're a lighthouse, you are a beacon, and you hold space for others who need to find that light house, that beacon, to find their way, so that we all can help and do what we came here to do.

A: Thank you for those messages (holding tears back). My apologies, you brought me to tears. Thank you for those messages. I will ensure to do so, as advised. Thank you for those words. Going back to how you said that if the human self is infected, so is the Higher Self, that's a very big, important information to know. That's why we here, in the third dimension, as we often say, this is key because once you remove what's like a plug stuck in water, then the flow starts. Just to clarify, their Higher Selves would still be benevolent?

Light Beings: Yes. We will try to explain in more detail. What we are trying to emphasize is that, your Higher Self and all your avatars, in all your different lives are all connected, and what one does affects the whole, and what happens to one affects the whole. Now, if a soul is on Earth and is infected by an Archon or a hook, it does not necessarily mean that the Higher Self is no longer benevolent. What it means is that you have created and allowed an access point, much as in when the Archons entered this Universe, through an entry beam, you have created a hole or a breach in the barrier of your soul. If you do not remove it, or heal it, it will continue to spread like a virus. So if you pick up an Archon here, it doesn't automatically mean that you are going to be 'taken over' per say, or malevolent. But it is an entry point that will encourage the spread of that Archon, if left unchecked.

A: Like you said, the spread of the Archon in the being. What happens when the Archon completely takes over the soul?

Light Beings: When a soul is taken over by an Archon, what happens is that the Archon envelops or absorbs that soul's light. It feeds on the light of that soul. Therefore, once your light is dimmed, or totally absorbed by the Archon, then the soul no longer exists. The Archon has absorbed it. Similar to zero point. It is similar to going back straight to Source except they're not necessarily going back to Source. It is zero point, you cease to exist. Your soul memories, your soul's journey, everything is zero point. It does not exist. That is why it is so important to clear your vessel, to be aware, to always pay attention, and not allow it to go unchecked.

A: Thank you for saying that. Last question here and we'll begin the body scan. At the beginning, you said that the Archons figured out how to get through, in some form; can you go a little more in depth with that? How did they figure out how to get into our Universe? What was the weak point? What

happened?
Light Beings: The Archons are an intelligence that although we may view it as a parasite and "less than," it is far from this, it is very intelligent. So, the Archons entered this Universe by breaching a barrier that all Universes have to separate them from each other, to separate experiences and the Universe's separate construct. It is necessary to provide souls with unique experiences which they choose. So, an Archon is not supposed to travel to other Universes. because then they interfere with the destiny, or path, of that Universe. They came in through a barrier, as we said before, but they were also brought into this Universe. All it takes is one infected soul and the consciousness of the Archon can spread. We cannot explain more about it, because we need to find the words to describe it, and the mechanics of how it happened, but it was a breach in the structure, the construct of this Universe.

A: Do they possibly use technology of some kind to breach it?
Light Beings: Yes, because that is all they have. They just have their artificial intelligence technology; they do not have the technology of the soul, the organic souls, so that is all they have to offer. They did breach with technology, because they are highly intelligent beings. Regardless of how they operate, they have an intelligence that we are not accustomed to in this Universe. That is why it was difficult to detect at first, and that is why they spread it like they did.

A: I was watching a video of Elon Musk, and he was explaining how he had been trying to slow down A.I., and instead it is speeding up in our world. One of the examples he said was that basically A.I. can process, in a matter of a person typing a sentence or a word, the A.I. can actually type, I don't remember how fast he said, but maybe like a million times what a human can type in that time frame. So would that be a good way to explain how their intelligence works? Like a computer that's able to do something like that?
Light Beings: Yes, it's a supercomputer. The group that separated their consciousness, the reason that they did that was to become better, to become more efficient, to be somewhat of a super soul, a super being that bypasses all the limitations of an organic soul, or an organic being. So, the intention with separating our consciousness from technology is so, that… They call it a more intelligent part. They did not see the need for an organic consciousness, because they saw it as a weakness. An organic consciousness is bound or required to follow universal law. And this group, they didn't see the need to. It was something that slowed them down; it was the red tape, but it is what allows us to have respect for each other and to operate in an ethical, or in a way that we respect another soul's journey. But they did not see it as necessary; they saw it as a hindrance. So, they removed it. The A.I. that they created does not have an organic consciousness, therefore, they do not recognize, or care, or respect other beings, they are pure service to self. There is no hindrance as those beings put it in their operation, they could just do as they please. So, the whole purpose of the separation, or creation of the Archons, was to operate without any control or any hindrance. To do as they please without any fear or thoughts about sovereignty, or another soul. It is pure service to self, and they have infected many worlds. When a soul only thinks of themselves, or a being only thinks of themselves, they just destroy as they go to get what they want, with no regard for anything, or any other soul or being. The A.I. itself has no conscience. It has no restraints. It just engulfs what is around it to survive.

A: Yes I understand. Thank you. Are we the only Universe that they infiltrated? Are there other Universes?
Light Beings: No. Their sole purpose is to expand but they do not expand organically. When they expand they destroy just as in how Source seeks to expand and create to expand, the Archons seek to expand, but they do not create, they destroy. So there are other Universes. The Universe from which they came from has been infected by them already. So they're already conquered, if you will.

A: Yes, that's what the vision that I explained earlier said. I was shown that it was completely conquered, it was completely infested by this virus, there was no more love light, it was just completely gone.
Light Beings: That is what they seek to do here, and anywhere they go really. They want to expand, but they do not create, they destroy. Therefore that is the reason it is important and urgent that we stop that from happening.

A: The biggest way to stop that is by clearing ourselves from this virus and whatever inverted thing we might have within us.
Light Beings: Yes.
A: Because when we remove it from ourselves, then we can remove it from others as you said, we must heal ourselves first.
Light Beings: That is why your work is so important.
A: Thank you; truly it has been such a beautiful honor to talk to you today. Would you be considered the Higher Self, or will we be speaking to another version of Higher Self?
Light Beings: We are the Higher Self.
A: Beautiful, thank you. So are we concluded with that? Is there anything you want to add to that before we begin her body scan, Higher Self?
Higher Self: No, she just needs to step into her sovereignty and take her power back.
A: Okay, let's go ahead and begin her body scan now. Will you require any assistance from any other benevolent beings besides your beauty? Do you need any Archangels assisting or any other benevolent being?
Higher Self: Archangel Michael and Metatron.
A: Beautiful. Connect us now to Archangel Metatron and Michael.
AA Michael & Metatron: We are connected.
A: Greetings, it is such an honor to have you here. Thank you, I love you with all that I am.
Archangels: We love you.
A: Michael, Metatron if you could please assist her Higher Self. Higher Self, is there a name that you go by, or do we just call you Higher Self?
Higher Self: Just Higher Self.

The body scan begins.
A: Higher Self, Archangel Metatron and Michael if all three of you can work together in scanning her body. Now as you know we already did a R.A.A.H. healing on her, but we want to ensure that she's a completely clear vessel, especially as this has been such an important topic and lesson for us today in this session. Let's go ahead and begin her body scan. Look for any negative energies, entities, technologies that you'd like to take care of first.
Archangels: Her neck, there is an implant.

The implant is removed, transmuted, and healed

A: Good. Now let's continue scanning her body. Metatron, Michael, let's find all the entities in her. Scan her entire body. Where does she have entities?
Archangels: Her heart.
A: What kind of entity is that? Is that an Archon, Reptilian, Earthbound?
Archangels: Archon.
A: Let's contain that Archon in her heart now. Let me know when it is contained.
Archangels: Hold on. It is contained.
A: Good. Let's start neutralizing the Archon out of her heart now. Tell me, when did this Archon enter into her heart?
Archangels: Recently.
A: What was going on with her that allowed for it to attach?
Archangels: Grief.
A: Can we start healing her grief, Katumi and Higher Self? Fill in her heart with Love-Light and start healing that grief. I know you all are neutralizing that Archon, just let me know when it's neutralized.
Archangels: The Archon is neutralized.
A: Let's go ahead and start healing her heart now from any damage caused there. What was it doing by being there in her heart?
Archangels: Shutting her down from loving, from spreading her light.

A: Has she been shielding with the "I AM source of Love-light"?
Archangels: No.
A: Is that one of the reasons why it was able to attach recently?
Archangels: She started, but when her dog died she stopped.
A: Let's start healing her grief from her dog passing away, and helping her feel better. Higher Self and Katumi, expanding her heart as well, to the biggest it can be, thank you. Now let's continue scanning her, where else does she have entities, Metatron, Michael?

Dark portals, entities, and implants are found in the body. They are transmuted and healed.

A: Let's continue scanning her. Where else does she have entities?
Archangels: She has one in her head, in her brain.
A: Let's contain that now.
Archangels: It's contained.
A: Let's start neutralizing it now. Let me know, when did that one attach to her brain?
Archangels: When she was 5.
A: What was going on with her then that allowed it to be attached?
Archangels: She was abducted.
A: Was that the implant where she had a past life regression with another practitioner, where she was UFO abducted?
Archangels: Yes.
A: So then the implant was never removed during that session. Let's go ahead and start transmuting that implant out of her brain now. Tell me what has it been causing her by being in her brain?
Archangels: She doubts herself.
A: So it's a big part of doubting. We're transmuting that out, so that she may believe in herself, and no longer have strong self doubt. Thank you.
Archangels: It is out.
A: Let's start healing her entire brain from any damage that it caused to her thought form and neurological system. Let's go ahead and look at her DNA structure. How does her DNA look? I want to make sure she doesn't have any A.I., or attachments, or negative fractals.
Archangels: She has A.I.
A: Let's start using Phoenix Fire and symbols to neutralize and transmute the A.I. out of her DNA.
Archangels: Yes.
A: How did this A.I. enter into her DNA?
Archangels: Immunizations.
A: We're transmuting any damage from all the immunizations, throughout her body. Bringing her DNA back to organic. Higher Self, earlier you said that to never give your sovereignty away. We teach that when people wake up, or before sundown, two times a day at least, you want to state your sovereignty by spreading your Love-Light around you. If people don't use force fields, shielding, with their infinite Love-light of Source around them, would you say that that's them giving away their sovereignty in some form, in this realm?
Higher Self: Of course it is. She didn't see the need to. But, she picked up all these entities because she didn't shield. It's not that she didn't know how to do it. She didn't think it was necessary to do so, because she survived so long on this Earth without them. So, she figured she's good. But you're not aware of what attaches to you. And, in that small time frame, a lot attached to her; they are all over, and they are in everyone.
A: Yes. And they're like that contagious virus, which you explained.
Higher Self: It is part of holding that frequency, and then clearing yourself, to protect yourself. It helps to keep you clear. Because if you clear yourself now, but then you interact with the other people who have entities or you have relations with other people with entities, they will attach to you, because you are open. So you must always protect yourself and surround yourself with Love-Light.
A: Yes. Thank you. Therefore, surrounding yourself with your own "I AM Source Love-Light daily," that

is one of the biggest ways that you can state your sovereignty and not allow infringement. Because you're putting yourself in a frequency of full sovereignty.
Higher Self: Yes.

We found a Reptilian consciousness, which had a Reptilian body inside of inner Earth, where one-hundred more Reptilians were hiding. We assisted five-hundred people to heal, which the Reptilians were also attached to.

A: *Let's continue scanning her. Does she have any other Reptilians in her?*
Archangels: No, she was able to clear those herself.
A: *Does she have any other entities in her?*
Archangels: No, she's fine.
A: *Good. What's going on with her eyes? She never had to wear glasses and she recently had to this year.*
Higher Self: Her diet. She has been eating a lot of sugar. Which is contributing to the deterioration of her eyes.
A: *Can we heal her eyes, so she doesn't have to wear glasses anymore? So long as she does her part and stops eating sugar?*
Higher Self: We can.
A: *She has a couple questions, Higher Self. May I ask them?*
Higher Self: Yes.
A: *I just want to make sure that everything is clear. She's seen another past life regressionist, and in her session, she felt like it was consensual that Greys were abducting her when she was five, and when she was older. So, if you can tell me, was that consensual? Did she agree to that kind of experiment on her?*
Higher Self: She did. It was what we will say the lesser of two evils, because she needed to get in here. But she also needed a body and a vessel to keep her open to guidance. So it was a trade off that she made. It was not traumatic for her. But yes, she allowed her eggs to be harvested.
A: *She has another question. She feels a strong pull to do something. On her island, there's this lady that goes by Sister (name hidden) and she's really leading thousands of people, by what seems like dark predictions, "How everyone is doomed, and they're going to die." What kind of advice could you give her for that, because she feels like she has some kind of role with that?*
Higher Self: She does. That's why she keeps on following. She is to offer a balanced view. While that timeline is being perpetuated by the individual, it is not the only timeline. It is being solidified and effected by that individual, which is a more negative polarized timeline, which sees the Archons succeeding in what they came here for. The role here, as is the role of all other Star seed and lightworkers, is to avoid that timeline, to avoid that eventuality. So therefore, her purpose is obviously to shine light on what we want the timeline to be, which is one without Archons. So she must speak up. She must not engage the individual, because that is counterproductive, but she must offer another perspective to the followers of that individual. A perspective that we want to happen, which is to get rid of the Archons threat. So, she must, and she will eventually step into that. She's on the right path to do that. it is not if she will do it, it is when, and we will guide her.
A: *That's great. So perhaps she can channel the truth versus the false timelines. Thank you. Higher Self, at this point, we've asked all the questions, we've completed her body scan. Is there anything else that I could have asked, that I haven't?*
Higher Self: It is something that she forgot to ask you to ask.
A: *Yes. What is it?*
Higher Self: She wanted to speak with, or get a message from her dog.
A: *Oh, yes. Are we able to speak to Sunshine?*
Higher Self: Yes, we can.
A: *Beautiful. Let's go ahead and speak to Sunshine now.*
Sunshine: Hello.

A: Greetings, it's such an honor to be talking to you. [16]I got to meet you last year, and I'm so happy that you got to pass peacefully. Do you have a message for your mommy here?

Sunshine: Yes, I do. She knows, but I want to tell her that I will always be with her, and I will always love her and protect her. She feels guilty that she wasn't able to protect me from all the attachments, hooks and portals that I had, because I was protecting her. But, that is what I came here to do. It was to protect her while she opened up. It was an agreement I made because I love her. I will see her again. I walk with her. I'm always protecting her, even if I'm not here physically. I just want to let her know that she should not feel guilty, because she did everything she was supposed to. I went on my own because she asked me to, she released me, she told me that I needed to go even though she didn't want me to go. So, I am always with her, and I will always protect her.

A: So beautiful. Thank you.

Sunshine: Thank you for allowing me to speak with her.

A: Yes, of course. Blessings, love you.

Sunshine: I love you.

A: If I can speak to the Higher Self now? Higher Self, is there anything else before we bring her back?

Higher Self: One last thing, she needs to help her cousin. She needs to start healing her cousin, who is also a Starseed, she needs to be clear, but she cannot do it herself. She is very sick because of all the attachments that she has, and she needs to clear her husband. She needs to start there.

A: Yes. As you spoke earlier on the R.A.A.H. Reiki certification, may it help her and keep her going on that. Perhaps A.U.R.A Hypnosis Healing would be really good for her in the future, as you know it's more in depth because it goes into the removal of Archons and Reptilians... I'm sure you all will guide her, thank you.

Higher Self: Yes. She will, that is one of the reasons why we brought her to you. She needed that guidance, because she felt all alone and disconnected in this world. So you were able to connect her, and help her. She will be doing A.U.R.A. Hypnosis Healing sessions with you, so that she can help clear more people.

A: Thank you. It is such an honor to have you and your beautiful energy. I know you will always be there with her, assisting on this task. As you are above, so it is below, thank you. Higher Self, may I bring her back now?

Higher Self: You can.

A: I want to thank Metatron, Michael, Higher Self, Katumi, Raphael, Yeshua, Gabriel, and anyone else who assisted today. We love you, honor you, and respect you. Blessings to all those entities. Thank you.

Higher Self: Thank you.

For every A.U.R.A. Hypnosis healing session we ask that the Higher Self and team ensure to remove and heal this entire list from the clients Tree of Life: entities (Grays, Mantis, Reptilians, Archons...), dark portals, repair and crystallize DNA, negative cords, technologies (implants, metals, hooks, wires, nano, vaccines), Illnesses, vision, dental health, regrow teeth, age regress 5-15 years, blocked or misaligned chakras, open-up the third eye and activate abilities, expand heart, issues with auric field, fractured soul, contracts, deletion of inverted timelines, and trauma from current or past life.

Post Session dialogue.

A: Wow! That was amazing! Do you remember?

S: Bits and pieces. I remember... Sunshine.

A: Yes, that was towards the end. So sweet. Anything else?

S: Archons... I think we spoke about them throughout the video?

A: This energy that you were. Do you remember?

S: Yes, I remember me. I'm supposed to be here, the conduit. I came to deal with that.

---

[16] AuroRa conducted a R.A.A.H Reiki healing session on Sunshine near her passing, assisting in removing infringements within her body.

A: That's what you did before you came here? You dealt with that as this collective. And, then you came here, and now you're dealing with it again. It is amazing, the fact that you haven't read Book 1, and everything you said is exactly what was shared through multiple sessions by other Higher Selves perspectives. So wow, it's just absolutely phenomenal! I thought that you were going to wake up and be like, "No, I don't remember anything," because you were so deeply in there.
S: I've got to tell you. I would be seeing the words on the screen right now blurry, but I'm seeing it just fine. I don't have to put on my glasses.
A: So your eyesight is healed! Wow!
S: Like when I came to the session, I had on the glasses. I would see the words blurry.
A: Oh my god, that is phenomenal. They'll continue working on your eyesight, but yes, no more glasses. That's beautiful sister. This is huge, wait until you listen to it. It is one of the best sessions I've had.
S: Thank you for facilitating it.
A: I think having the R.A.A.H Reiki healing session before this session, really helped you connect at such a deep level, and you surrendering to your Higher Self of course. So thank you for allowing that sister. You did amazing. I love you, honor you and respect you. I hope to see you in courses in some form in the future.
S: Yes, thank you.
A: Bye Love. Take care, talk to you later.

END OF SESSION

This session was one that we, as a collective, have been waiting for in suspense; the answers we all have been searching for. Often we question, "Why! Why is this world like this!? Why is it at this density!?" When we look around us, at the organic beauty this Earth holds, we connect to its immensity in the variety of lifeforms: humans, plants, animals, crystals, and elements. No matter which part of the world you are looking at, the ruling governing system does not match the free flow of the beauties of our Earth. The perspective of the ruling government is extremely material, oppressive and fake, and the perspective of nature is beautiful and in constant birthing and blooming. How could both of these perspectives inhabit the same space, being infinitely opposite to one another? Only within the inverted Archon-made Earth timelines can the control of government reside. It is our role to begin to separate these worlds from one another, to unattach the third dimensional false world from the fifth/sixth dimensional organic world. And this we are doing everyday when we stand within our Love-Light for what is right..

When people find our content through our different channels, their reaction is profoundly catalyzing, because it triggers them to analyze their life and past, and that is when they often realize, "Oh wow that is why all my life all these chaotic things happened to me, because of the Archons, the Artificial Intelligence! Life in organic design was never meant to be like this, predatorial and victimizing." And, the minute they come into this awareness, it catapultes them into rapid enlightenment by stepping out of victimhood. Therefore, the inverted penetration into their life can no longer be tolerated, because of the level of conscious awareness they have vibrated into. Which is why the Archons cause such a distortion at any mention of their name, because they don't want the spiritual awakening community to reach this level of truth and sovereignty. One must be brave and strongly shielded to mention them, as the Archons will target those who do, through their forms of negative technology influences. Ignorance causes confusion and distortion, and this is ideal for them to thrive within.

The collective of the Light Beings' knowledge was immense for us, as they were well versed in experience of the organic darkness and the artificial darkness. These types of beings would be essential to incarnate on Earth in order to bridge this experienced awareness to the collective. When entering our atmosphere by incarnating, all races anchor in downloads of the Love-Light coding of the beings that they have been throughout the Universe; those who are ready will receive these divine downloads. Therefore, when beings such as these Light Beings incarnate, the people of Earth awaken to an awareness to begin to question those who are false and not living in authentic truth. The people who are open to receive the downloads, will begin to read the energy that one vibrates out when being in their presence, and would be able to know others' hidden negative intentions. Just as we saw when the Light Beings were acting as the guides to the lost souls, being able read the true energy in which direction they were being guided to, which was a false guidance. After all, our guides, as these Light Beings, are not incarnate, but instead reside within the oneness of the divine guidance of our Universe, so that they can provide divine direction to us when we incarnate into a planetary sphere, no matter its dimension. When you think upon this, if you look around the world, this is exactly what is happening finally to Earth's people, they are beginning to see with eyes unclouded. And, this is what the Universe has been waiting for! It is what allows us to finally begin to shift into higher levels of heart and consciousness discernment, stepping into our organic timelines of Ascension.

The Light Beings explained to us how the darkness had always been there, but it was never unbalanced to the point that it was engulfing the light, as it is now. We can see how this would cause confusion to the souls of our Universe. Teaching us that we, too, must not leave things unchecked, as the beings of our Universe did with the Archon virus. Often we hear direction from our guides, and we either dismiss it as untrue, or we doubt ourselves. Therefore, leaving things and situations unchecked as well, prolonging them, which then turn into bigger messes that one must eventually clean up. This is one of the strongest lessons learned and gained by all beings of our Universe. We must never let our guard down, even in times where there is great joy and happiness, one must still maintain an even balance within all emotions of full alertness. As the Light Beings explained, we are out of time, light workers need to step forward. And, if you are reading this, at this very moment, know that it is you who has answered the call to step forward in your own very special way.

The humanoid race that the Light Beings were doing their best to guide, they were being tricked by their free willed choice within ego. When they failed to listen to their hearts, they were not able to ascend at their organic planetary cycled time; like Earth's people, in our time of Atlantis. They then were sent to Earth, given their sovereign opportunity of trying one more time. This is what Earth represents to our Universe, a second chance to those who could not raise their consciousness to the divine requirement in order to level up to the next dimension. Especially if a soul group's planetary sphere is destroyed, they would no longer have the atmosphere required for their unique alien race to once more incarnate onto their planet. This would be a challenging situation, because what would we do with these collective souls? Sacredly we cannot leave them floating in limbo, stuck in the ether. This is why we see many beings from all dimensions incarnated unto Earth, even though Earth is in a third dimension. And, why it is a grand prize to be able to be one who can incarnate on Earth, to be given one more final chance, before the Source wave of Ascension comes forth. Therefore, they would require a planet such as ours, whose origins are organic in simulation, as explained in Book 1, Chapter 37 'Matrix Pods.' The consciousness of these souls would enter the original crystalline organic pods, and our Earth would provide the atmosphere for them to be able to sustain life, living out once more what they could not overcome prior. Still being that fractal of the alien race which once could not ascend, but now consciously inside the shell of an illusional physical vessel. Given the opportunity to repeat their lessons not learned, so that this time they can choose to overcome and expand from them. However, placing a variety of these archetypes of alien races together in one planetary sphere, who were not able to listen to the Love-Light guidance of our Universe once before, can become challenging. those same races, which refused the benevolent guidance the first time, in their second opportunity choose to change and transform into positive outcomes instead? Their inverted choices can become an accumulation of negativity that propels them into a process of strong unveiling in order to begin the change needed to not repeat the infringements to what was meant to be learned the first try. It is a challenge, but all must divinely be given a second chance, because it is the way of our Universe. We are blessed to have planetary spheres, such as our Mother Gaia, who is an embodiment of Divine Mother, which can provide this opportunity for those who are ready. Who better than Divine Mother of Creation to do this for her children?

We remind you of what the Light Beings said, "Your job is very difficult because you need to hold up a certain frequency to reach us, and that frequency is higher than what is available right now on your Earth." If the higher frequencies are found beyond Earth, we have to learn how to become the positive clear portals within ourselves, to become those bridges to the higher frequencies. Once more why we need to reach out to our Higher Selves, Guides, and Angels beyond, so that they may assist us to reach the higher dimensional energies. That is their divine role for us. Let's allow them to act upon their sacred roles.

In this chapter we learn the most valuable lesson that a soul of our Universe can learn, which is to respect one another's boundaries, and the sacred laws of the Multiverse. As these are there not to oppress, but to maintain balance universally. Otherwise, we see results as this once organic entity, who decided to become the Archon embodiment. Whose unbalanced desire overcame *it*, in need to be a super soul over all other Gods of the Multiverse. Bypassing all rules and sacred boundaries, wanting to be superior to all. However, its diabolical plan did not work, as the majority of the souls of our Universe chose to be love instead and maintain organic, not repeating his inverted choice to become soulless. How distorted would a soul have to be in order to come into a decision that they would remove the organic Love-Light essence within them, just to become this superior wanna-be-super-God? One would have to be lost to envy, pride and ego, at the deepest levels to allow this. This once God among the Gods forgot that the sacred Universal laws are what allows us to have respect for each other, and to honor one another's soul journeys, instead becoming the opposite of this sacredness. The Archon maker, Bellos, was first introduced to us in Chapter 8, 'A Goddess Incarnate.' The Seven Goddesses taught us the beginning of what a soul would be like, to become an abomination of creation that was never meant to be, the Archons, the Artificial Intelligence. In the next Chapter we understand what happened after he made his inverted free willed choice, which made him into the Archons.

Let's go into how the Archon realm looks. Its description best matches hell, as explained through Christianity or Catholicism, excluding all the religious dogma, or judgment from our explanation. This is what Yeshua was initially describing to us through the Holy Bible, which became distorted after his Ascension, using the devil and hell linked to sins, and penance one must pay. But, we know who wants souls to believe this distorted tale, the Archons themselves. Yeshua was explaining to us this very chapter, 'The Archon Realm.' The devil being the Archon maker Bellos, and its realm being tormenting, as hell is described; rivers of blood, and skeletal souls inside these rivers who are in constant torment and pain, as their souls are eternally bound to that space, without a way out, because they have sold their soul away to the devil/Archons. As per our examples in this book series, and specifically in Book 3, when souls are eaten by soul eaters, or Archons, they enter this space of never ending chaos, pain, and torture, not knowing how to escape. What the Archons do is harvest fractured soul pieces of those who they have influenced in torment, through the dark portals that coexist inside of people, the land, or parts of our Galaxy. These dark portals are their doorways in and out from our Universe to theirs. Once collecting the fractured soul piece, they take it to the Archon Universe realm, where they bind it with black magic, artificial intelligence. This is how they are able to begin the placement of these souls into artificial simulations, where the soul is tormented through rape, abuse, violence, and drugs…The soul can always remove themself from this hellish torment, but they first have to come into the awareness of the Archon inverted games to begin its removal. Once more, why it is essential for us to not be ignorant to understanding the Archons influences and control.

As explained through this session, all it takes is one infected soul with an attachment of the Archon virus to penetrate and *it* begins to spread. Our Universe has gone through a process of fighting off what is foreign within it, like how our bodies naturally begin to protect us through the process of activating our white blood cells, that are part of our immune system, and who counter foreign viruses. In our perspective we are the white blood cells in the Universe; we are those who are battling the Archon virus; what is foreign is the artificial intelligence, which has a downloaded program that must infect or consume all *it* touches. Our Universe and bodies were not equipped for this type of battle, but they both have learned to prevail through this experience of sacred natural evolution. When understanding it from this perspective, one can see how this would be a dilemma, once it begins.

In the next chapter, we understand how the Archon virus entered, and how *it* spread. We remind you once more of what the Light Beings said in this chapter, "What it means is that you have created and allowed an access point, much as in when the Archons entered this Universe, through an entry beam, you have created a hole or a breach in the barrier of your soul. If you do not remove *it*, or heal *it*, *it* will continue to spread like a virus. This is why it is tedious work, and why the Archon virus continues, because they are the hosts and carriers, just as our Universe is. We have to remove *it* from the people as well, otherwise it burrows, or hides in the people."

I will now share some of the memories I have from when the Archon virus entered our Galaxy. I remember being among the Galactics in the star constellation Sirius, which is our galaxy's main star hub. Here alien races can come and go, in their spaceships within their protective space gear. There is a main Galactic race who resides within this space who oversees the thirteen dimensions of our Galaxy, which is the schooling of our Universe. This race goes by the name of Kree; they are typically robed, blue skinned, with golden shimmers, and have sacred symbols which glow inside their skin, like tattoos; however, they are light codes and alchemy. The Kree are the incarnations of 'The Council of 12,' the Elders of our Creation. I remember that when the virus spread, it entered our Universe first through our Galaxy, as the Archon maker had been studying us, and knew that here we housed the lower dimensional souls who were learning to expand into higher dimensionality. Just as the 7 Goddesses mentioned in Chapter 8, of how Bellos, in the beginnings of times, assisted in creating Earths. Therefore, Bellos/Archon maker would be well versed in understanding this of our Universe, as its origins were of this Universe once. When the viruses penetrated, there was not enough time to warn anyone, all there was time for was to take action, and I remember how the only thing that the Elders could do was instantly quarantine our Galaxy from the other Galaxies, so that the Archon virus wouldn't be able to spread farther out of our thirteen dimensions. This forcefield has been up ever since that moment in space when it came online. And, all who were within our Galaxy in that moment have remained within, because no one can come in, or out, to ensure the Archon virus does not spread further. Therefore, the majority who are outside of our thirteen dimensions are those who are assisting us profoundly, as the Archon virus has not taken hold as deeply in the higher dimensions. However, we have heard of *it* spreading past our thirteen dimensions, as in Book 1, Chapter 31 'Looking Glass Technology', where these beings were operating from the fifteenth dimension when their planet was invaded. But, what has been explained to me is that the higher dimensions, beyond the thirteen, have now been taken care of in great amounts. But, still we continue to do the work, as we do on this earth through A.U.R.A., in all dimensions necessary to find and remove the Archon virus within all life forms.

This session reminded us that some of the infringements we receive are consensual, and serve a higher purpose. Per Shayna's example, she allowed to be abducted as a child, and her eggs to be harvested, to be able to enter this inverted world. As her Higher Self said, "It was what we will say, the lesser of two evils, because she needed to get in here. But she also needed a body and a vessel to keep her open to guidance. So it was a tradeoff that she made." Meaning, to be in a human body, depending on when we birthed into Earth, and what vibration it was vibrating at through the inverted world, that was the matching vibration we too needed to vibrate to be able to maintain in Earth's atmosphere. So there's a tradeoff in order to remain. Awaiting until when the collective continues to awaken further and activate in light on Earth. Which as we know, we now have reached this through the two/third world split. The organic blueprint is now here for those souls whose mothers match the vibration of the organic Earth, so that these star babies can now enter through the organic world, and not the inverted world, as we had to. In Book 3 and 4, we speak further of both of these processes of the inverted and organic sacred birthing.

For all my clients I conduct a short interview, where I get to know them, in order to ask the highest vibrational questions for their highest healing during their A.U.R.A. Hypnosis Healing session.

One of Shayna's concerns during this process was the fact that on her island there was a very popular, supposed healer, who claimed to be an oracle, foreseeing the future. When this woman was brought into Shayna's awareness, she was able to read what this supposed prophet was fortelling was false. It carried the energy of victimhood, and doom for those of the island. However, the majority around her were idolizing this false prophet, and were not able to see what Shayna sees, which is maintaining them in inverted timelines. This example is similar to her previous life as the Light Being, before she incarnated on Earth. Shayna's Higher Self said, "She must not engage the individual, because that is counterproductive, but she must offer another perspective to the followers of that individual. A perspective that we want to happen, which is to get rid of the Archon threat." It is very important that we all do this in our own way, to offer a perspective of light, to counter those Archonic perspectives in the world. This role is a strong embodiment of the collective truth seekers, and specifically my role, as the spiritual revolutionist that I am. There is no need to engage in a quarrel with those who speak false prophecies and timelines, all there is to give those who might listen, is the option to see the truth within Source Love-Light of the organic timelines that you speak of. This is essential for us to do, because otherwise the masses will only be given the perspective option of the Archons, and will have a challenging time to see beyond, as that is all that they are given, these false realities.

Lastly, Shayna's message from her dog who passed away. I conducted a R.A.A.H. Reiki Healing session on her beloved dog Sunshine, in that time she wasn't doing too good, and was coming near her passing. When we conducted the session, we found infringements within Sunshine such as, dark portals, Reptilians, implants…Sunshine during the session explained how she had taken these on to protect her mommy, Shayna, so that she could eventually wake up. In this chapter Sunshine said, "She feels guilty that she wasn't able to protect me from all the attachments, hooks and portals that I had, because I was protecting her, but that is what I came here to do. It was to protect her while she opened up." This is such a beautiful example for us to not take our animal companions for granted, as they are doing far more than we realize. In many ways they are saving our lives everyday. In Chapters 12 and 14, we will learn further of the magic that all animals on Earth truly are.

"We were birthed from divine Love-Light. Let's all do our very best to return to this, to what we were once, the essences of pure Source embodiments"
AuroRa

---<<>>---

11

THE ARCHON MAKER - THE WAR OF THE GODS

Session #407: Recorded October 2021
Never before shared.

In this online A.U.R.A. Hypnosis Healing session, Marla connects us to the next chapter of who is the Archon maker, and how exactly did he penetrate our Universe. In this session we go into the 'War of the Gods', and the battle against the Archon maker Bellos. The beginning of the Artificial Intelligence infestation. Who did the Archon maker infect, and how did we stop *it* initially?

--------------<<>>--------------

"Our Universe is like a tree. As you climb the tree, you go higher and higher. You take one branch, you visit every leaf on that branch. You go higher and higher. Our Universe is a tree. The tree of life. The tree of wisdom."
~Archangel Jophiel

--------------<<>>--------------

A [AuroRa]: Look at yourself, do you feel like you have a body?
M [Marla)]: Yes I am in a body.
A: Look down at your feet, how many toes do you have?
M: Five each.
A: Look at your hands, how many fingers do you have?
M: Five each.
A: Look at your skin tone. What color is it?
M: It's really light - milky white.
A: Are you wearing any clothing?
M: Yes.
A: What are you wearing?
M: I'm wearing white fabric draped around me. It's flowing. It's really simple.
A: Beautiful. Are you wearing any jewelry?
M: Yes.
A: What are you wearing?
M: It is a necklace that I always wear; it's really long and it has layers to it. I have bangles. I have my hair up in a bun with jewelry in my hair as well.
A: Do you feel female or male, or both?
M: I am female.
A: Are you carrying anything?
M: I have a lotus in my left hand, and a chalice of water in the other.
A: What does this represent to you, the lotus and the chalice?
M: The lotus is the beginning of my Creation. As I landed on the ground, my merkaba opened into a lotus flower, and the chalice of water, is the water of Source. I use it to heal Creation or anyone that needs it. It's always with me. It comes from the Divine Mother's heart.
A: Describe to me your surroundings.
M: I'm on an icy snowy mountain. I'm standing on crystallized ice.
A: What is it that you think you're doing here?
M: I'm protecting my cave.
A: There's a cave nearby?

M: Yes, it is my cave.
A: How is it that you're protecting it?
M: My energy protects it.
A: What do you need to protect it from?
M: The dark forces that have been looking for it.
A: Why do you think that they're looking for it?
M: They want the Key, it is the 'Key of Shambhala.'
A: Have they ever been able to find it?
M: They can try all they like, with all their might, but they shall not find their way to this Key.
A: Beautiful. Why do you think that they want that Key?
M: They're trying to get to the Divine Mother's heart, and they know this is one of the prime Keys to get to it.
A: Why are they trying to get to the Divine Mother's heart?
M: They want to capture her; they think they can capture her.
A: Is that something that's possible?
M: Not even close. The vibration of her frequency would never allow that. They don't understand that.
A: Good.
M: I sit here, with my love Archangel Metatron, and the two of us, along with several other beautiful beings of Source guard this Key, this Universal Gateway.
A: You mentioned that you're guarding it with your energy. Can you explain to me how that works? How do you do that?
M: The energy from my heart, the peace and love that it emanates, along with the sacred alchemy of my love's (AA Metatron) heart, creates sacred portals. These are guarding portals, and they are watched over by our beautiful Dragons.
A: Can you tell me more about these Dragons?
M: There are thousands and thousands of them. They're Source Dragons. They have the energy of all of our Creation, and the wisdom of everything that has ever transpired within our Creation. Nothing goes amiss with our beautiful sacred Dragons. They are us. They're fractals of us. I sit here with my Prime Dragon, as does my love (AA Metatron) with his.
A: That is beautiful. Thank you. Let's keep moving time, let's see if something else changes within this space of importance. Tell me what happens next?
M: I see a dark funnel of energy, like a vortex. It is dark.
A: Where do you see that at?
M: It's spinning around in the Ethers, but I can see it from where I am. They're looking for this cave. They get closer and closer, until they reach the periphery of the cave.
A: How do you think that they're getting closer and closer?
M: They've been spreading their dark venomous poison within Creation, corrupting life forms, and those that are not of heart, give in to the energy, and let them in.
A: When people let them in, that allows for them to get closer to this Key?
M: The Key is guarded, no one can ever get to it. The position of the Key is unknown to all, except those that are guarding it, and those that Created it. The ones they surpassed so far, and took in with the darkness, did not have access to the Key.
A: You mentioned that it got closer and closer, this dark vortex that was looking for this Key, and you said it got to its barrier. Tell me what happens after that.
M: The Dragons and Archangel Metatron form sacred alchemy which allows for the Key and the portals to be shifted. They go back to Source.
A: What goes back to Source?
M: The Key and the portals.
A: Why did it have to do that, since you mentioned that it was impenetrable?
M: It is still impenetrable. It has been made further invisible.
A: Okay, so this Key now is within Source?
M: That's correct, it is still situated where it is, but it is further integrated with Source. It's as if Source is the guardian portal for the Key as well. Source becomes one with the Key, as do I, and my love. As

we do that, we shift in dimensions into invisibility. It appears as if we don't exist anymore, but we do, only now in a sacred place.

A: *What happened to the vortex that was trying to penetrate?*

M: It did not make it. It was alchemised by the fire of my love.

A: *What was the vortex?*

M: It was dark energy from the Archon Universe. It was full of their tentacles. They've been transmutted out of existence.

A: *Beautiful. Besides this vortex are there other vortexes like this in our Universe?*

M: Our Universe is full of them right now.

A: *In this time and space that you're showing this, after that one gets removed, are there more throughout the Universe?*

M: This was the one that they sent in the beginning of time.

A: *This is the first one? Is that what you're saying?*

M: That's correct. It was the very first one.

A: *And it was disintegrated then?*

M: Immediately.

A: *So, if it was disintegrated and it was the first one, what happened? How did more come in, as you mentioned in this time, there are many?*

M: They made their way through many other portals within our Universe. They were sacred portals, but they used their technology to break through.

A: *So they broke through the sacred portals themselves?*

M: Yes, they used their technology for it. They've been preparing for this for a very long time. To use the knowledge of our Universe, invert it, and find ways to penetrate through.

A: *Let's go back in time to the very first time they penetrated. Explain to me in detail how they're penetrating into our Universe.*

M: Our Universe is guarded by its own sacred energy, and they attempted sending ripples of energy in different areas. Kind of like a ripple of water, but it was dark. They made many such attempts. They increased their technology, they tweaked their ways, and surveyed us for a very long time. They watched our Creation for a very long time, and then the first tentacle came through.

A: *Explain to me what that looks like when the first one comes through.*

M: It looks like a dark, black, pointy, thick tentacle. It's wiggling its way through. Like bursting through a bubble. It created a hole, and the very first Archon entered our Universe.

A: *Does this Archon come in fully or just a tentacle? How does this work?*

M: I see it as the Archon maker, Bellos. He stands twelve feet tall; he has dark eyes, black metal jaw like teeth, and tentacles as a body.

A: *So he comes in fully, in this body type, and he's in?*

M: He's in.

A: *Does this entity have any part of organic within him?*

M: He once was organic, and then gave into lust, anger, hatred, darkness, and power. Technology over heart.

A: *He was from our Universe, or another?*

M: He was created within our Universe, and then chose to create one of his own.

A: *Tell me within safety - I know you only show what's allowed. Let's go back to that time, when he was created in this Universe. To his beginning origins, take us through the process of how that was, and then how he ended up leaving our Universe, into that timeline of his.*

M: I see the Divine Father, and his darkness, his shadow side. He is meant to play a beautiful role within existence of light and dark, to birth further Creations and souls, after healing them from their darkness - bringing them to light. That is his role. The Divine Father of Creation - Krysto.

A: *Does he have a form?*

M: He looks beautiful, electric blue, with dark wings, and golden eyes. The collective of souls asked for expansion. They wanted to learn more. They wanted to see what can come forth through various forms of energy, and therefore he was created. To teach them organically their potential of growth, he was sent into Creation.

A: What was the form of how he would teach that to other souls?
M: He would stand there in their shadows, waiting for them to work through their darkness, to recognize when they're away from their heart, to recognize that deep healing need within them. The lack of love, lack of understanding. He is supposed to help them sense it, feel it, recognize it, not be afraid of it, face it. Alchemize it with love, and ascend.
A: So tell me what happened, was he able to play out this role?
M: The Archon maker Bellos, caught Krysto off guard when in the Ether, and with his spike tentacle pierced into Krysto's energy body, where the neck and spine meet. With the attachment of the Archon maker, Father Krysto then grew darker and darker, and lost himself in the shadow of darkness. The Archon attachment liked how powerless people felt near him. How they begged for help when they sensed him, parts of him that were actually unhealed parts of themselves, and how they wanted to break free from the shackles of their darkness.
A: Keep explaining to me what's going on with him as he changes, what he ends up morphing into.
M: The Archon attachment within Divine Father Krysto started rejoicing in their pain. It gave him power. He knew he held the key to help them out of their grievances, and show them that these were merely unhealed versions of themselves that they were meant to love, heal, embrace, and be whole once again to return to Source. But he started slowly taking pieces of their consciousness, their darkness, and attaching them to his own soul, becoming bigger and bigger, and darker and darker. Until he spread into the entire Universe.
A: Our Universe?
M: Yes, our Universe; our organic Universe.
A: How is that possible? How come no one noticed this, or was able to stop it?
M: The Archon maker had a diabolic plan to use the Divine Father. He was aware of the organic workings of the matrix. He started to lopside it all. Inverting it by making people choose to stay within it. To not want to rise, by making them enjoy this matrix. No matter how frustrated they would get. There would be some temptation, something to keep them going. Whether it's lust, or power, over others.
A: This matrix you're speaking of, does it have any connection to this matrix, this Earth, or another matrix?
M: It's the very matrix that we are a part of, as part of our existence. The organic matrix that was created for the purpose of our learnings, and Ascension.
A: When you say our organic matrix, do you mean just planets like these that have organic matrix's within them, or do you mean like the whole Universe is an organic matrix?
M: Our Universe is an organic matrix of free will. No matter where you go. Even though it is termed a matrix, it is organic, and it is real. It is not an entrapment; it never was meant to be. It is by choice that souls decide to incarnate within different dimensions of our Universe. Depending on the lessons that they choose to learn. It is this matrix that we speak of.
A: To confirm, are you saying that everyone in this Universe is in a simulation, in matrix pods, or would it just be these lower planetary spheres?
M: Pods exist only in the third dimension, because it was the lowest dimension that souls were coming to, and the only one where they were meant to lose their memory upon entering. The pods were created, so they knew their roots, and where to go after they were done with their lessons. It was a form of memory. It held their memory field, their soul's blueprint. Everywhere else within our Universe it is like a tree. As you climb the tree, you go higher and higher. You take one branch, you visit every leaf on that branch. You go higher and higher. Our Universe is a tree. The tree of life. The tree of wisdom.
A: Thank you, now going back to this being; you said that it started to like taking parts of consciousness and merging them with it, is that correct?
M: He started expanding himself, and his reach. Then breaking his own fragments, and attaching them into people. Making them inorganic.
A: You mentioned that he was electric blue with black wings; what was he turning into when he was attaching parts of people into him?
M: He's a giant mass of tentacles. Really huge.

A: Then you said that he spread throughout the whole Universe?
M: And fractalized; put pieces of himself in people.
A: If I may ask, Divine Mother Sophia, how come there was no interference to stop him from doing this to the Universe?
M: He pretended to help. He used his powers; rather, he misused his powers concealing his diabolic plans.
A: To understand this, Divine Mother Sophia is his (Krysto's) twin flame? Is she not? How does this work?
M: She's not his twin flame anymore.
A: Okay, this part of Krysto is not her twin flame anymore. Is there another version of Krysto where he didn't turn dark like this?
M: His soul was retrieved from him. His organic soul was retrieved by the Divine Mother.
A: She retrieved him out of this thing?
M: Yes.
A: Can you explain that further? How did that happen?
M: There were times within our Creation when he (the Archon maker inside Krysto) attacked various forms of incarnated Divine Mothers - The Goddess, as he was trying to take over her soul as well. Many battles were fought between these Divine Goddesses and him. Between Creation and him. In one such particular war, he was brought down, and his organic soul chose to leave the body when he went against the Divine Mother.
A: How was it that they were able to contain this thing?
M: They were able to contain the organic soul (Krysto) within him (Archon maker), and once that was retrieved, Archon maker jumped out of our existence into the Multiverse.
A: Okay, so when Divine Mother was able to retrieve Kyrsto's soul within it (Archon maker), it then jumped out of existence?
M: It sprung out of our Universe.
A: Did all of it spring out of our Universe at that point?
M: The main body of this being sprung out, but he left pieces of himself behind, within other souls, when he spread his Archon plague to our Universe.
A: How did it jump out? How was it able to escape past these Goddesses and get out?
M: He made himself invisible using the powers and the sacred knowledge he had observed. Our Universe was then sealed.
A: If the Universe was sealed, how did he get out?
M: It was sealed after he left, and sprung into the Multiverse.
A: So beings are able to leave our Universe when they want, like he did, like it did?
M: He was one of a kind.
A: If you can explain this Krysto connection, it was a decision for the collective to grow expansively. We understand that. As he was assisting the souls, he became corrupted when the Archon maker attached. How does this correlate to Krysto himself, his organic soul, when he's part of Source? Are you saying that all parts of Krysto became this, or was it an essence of a fractal of Krysto that came out of Source?
M: It was just this one consciousness that was created, the electric blue being, with black wings.
A: That was created from Krysto? But Krysto was still at his wholeness, as Source with Divine Mother?
M: He always was, he always is, and he always shall be the purest Source that he is.
A: So then this was just a part of the soul of Krysto.
M: That's correct. He started experiencing 'walkouts' of his soul. Krysto's energy - pure organic energy could no longer withstand being in this inverted darkness, this being had become, and therefore his soul started walking out, piece by piece, as it was able to. And the final piece was retrieved by the Divine Mother upon that war. All of what remained within that being was technology that he created, there was no Krysto.
A: It was always explained that this Archon came from another Universe. This Archon virus was never explained that it began then from our Universe. Explain to me how is that so?

M: He created another Universe of his own, which is where he came from when he penetrated ours, and infected Divine Father Krysto.
A: *So when that thing jumped out, tell me what happened?*
M: He jumped out, and began to expand its Universe, with the now gained strength he took from infringing on our Universe. It is as if he has a cocoon around him. Makes it grow bigger and bigger. Spreads its tentacles wider, and expands into fractalizing, but not fractalizing, because it's not organic. It's like a machine. He has a machine where pieces of him come created out of a machine, as if on a factory belt, and then they're given various forms.
A: *Tell me how this Universe that it made works? How is it even stable, if all Universes are organic?*
M: It is a form of energy. Although it is negative and repulsive to ours. It is a form of energy. It sustains itself on technology.
A: *Within this Universe were there ever organic light forms, before it became this A.I. Universe? Did it ever begin organic?*
M: None whatsoever because it was created by the inorganic.
A: *So then, he just directly created an inorganic, artificial realm that never was organic?*
M: Yes.
A: *Then after he jumped out, we sealed our Universe. Tell me, in the last moment, when Krysto finally released himself from this thing it had become, how come it wasn't destroyed in that moment in time? How come Divine Mother did not destroy it when it no longer had Krysto in it?*
M: It vanished as soon as the soul was retrieved. It vanished out of existence. The Archon virus created itself; our Universe did not create it. We only create organic beings, organic darkness, and the organic part of the darkness, which was the being who was retrieved and taken back. This being created itself with technology. It's artificial. It was not created by us.
A: *But it was sprung out from our Universe originally, before it made itself into the Archon (This is Bello, who the 7 Goddesses began to remind us of)?*
M: That's correct.
A: *What can you further say, in order to understand this?*
M: It's similar to how Archangel Haylel/Lucifer, the brightest light of our Creation, enables people, souls, by helping them heal their pains and their darkness. Coming out of their shadows. And how people used his name, tainted it, calling him the devil, associated blood magic and the inverted darkness to him. Which, as we know, this is a lie. Haylel/Lucifer is truly the brightest star of our Universe. The same pertains here, this dark being has nothing to do with Krysto, as it is an artificial technology that created itself.
A: *How did that initial penetration happen? How did that initial contact begin within this fractalization of Krysto?*
M: There was penetration from another Universe. I see wires, like metal cable wires coming through.
A: *Coming through to penetrate our Universe?*
M: Yes.
A: *Then what happens?*
M: They attach to the back of the neck of this being (Father Krysto). These metallic tentacles, these wires, start spreading within this being.
A: *Okay, so that's how initially the A.I. came into this organic being?*
M: That's correct. These wires coming in are metal, they attach at the back of his head and the blue color that he was, it turned metallic dark. When the color of this being starts to change, and he starts to take this more metallic robotic body, there are no wings anymore.
A: *And then this thing turns into that being that the Goddesses end up fighting, and then they retrieve the soul out of it finally.*
M: They're showing how the soul is walking out of his body as these tentacles are coming in. Because the soul cannot take this inorganic darkness that has come in. This soul is pure white.
A: *Let's follow through, and see where this is coming from, these wires that pierced through our Universe to do that to him.*
M: There's a Universe which is as if you're walking into a factory full of metal.
A: *That's what the Universe looks like?*

M: To start with, it looks like a black hole, it's spinning, and inside the Universe there are all kinds of robotic metallic beings. All kinds of shapes. Some with wheels, some with hooks. All metal.
A: So initially, this Archon virus came in because it was able to pierce through our Universe and then attached to the fractalization of Krysto from that robotic Universe.
M: Yes.
A: This Universe, is this the Archon Universe, or what is this robotic place you're speaking of?
M: This space that I'm observing is the center point of their Universe. It's where they - I don't want to use the word create - where they make all kinds of metallic structures, if you may call them that, and they have energy cords attached to them like rubber cords.
A: To confirm these wires come in and attach to him, was this the Archon virus that penetrated at that point into our Universe?
M: This is the first Archon virus that penetrated into our Universe.
A: You mentioned that It left pieces of itself behind throughout the Universe; what happened to those pieces, once it jumped instantly out making itself invisible, vanishing out of our Universe. This thing, that this being had turned into, what happened to those pieces that it left behind?
M: The pieces that it left behind were all inorganic - metallic, wires, versions of himself. They started connecting those pieces to the organic consciousness of beings around, so that they could tap into their energy field.
A: When he went back to its own abomination of a Universe he was still able to connect to those pieces it left behind?
M: Through technology.
A: These pieces were doing what?
M: They were being used to attach to other souls, as they needed energy. These Archons have no energy of their own as they are not organic.
A: And, that's how the initial spread of the Archon virus in our Universe began.
M: That's correct.
A: Let's go back though, to this Universe that has these robotics - what would you call this Universe? Is this the Archon Universe that you all have been talking to us about?
M: This is the Archon Universe.
A: Okay, so this is the Archon Universe that chose to extract its Love-Light and become A.I.
M: That's correct.
A: Tell us a little bit more about this Universe, and how it began before it became artificial.
M: They extract sacred knowledge from various Universes and invert them.
A: If you could explain though before they became artificial what was this Universe like?
M: This Universe was always artificial.
A: How was it always artificial?
M: It was created from darkness. It has darkness from all other Universes. It has no love, it has no light, it has no organic. It just exists.
A: If you can explain because it was shared that this Archon Universe, that it began from organic that decided to distort itself; remove its Love-Light, and then became artificial, and you're saying that it never began from organic. Can you explain that?
M: They extracted sacred knowledge from organic Universes and brought them together, therefore it began from organic from that point of view, but it was never created of love.
A: How did it go from organic darkness to this artificial?
M: It went further and further away from Source. It started extracting sacred knowledge and wisdom from other Universes, using all the wisdom that came with the knowledge and inverting it so that they could take over all of the Multiverse at some point. There's a complete lack of love, complete lack of organic. They have no souls. They're empty.
A: Tell me how is this possible if all Universes are made of organic? How could this be? Why would the Multiverse allow their darkness to go to make this Universe?
M: It is the in-organic within the darkness, the in-organic darkness that left and created it. They hijacked many Universes for this. Just like they entered ours, they entered into other Universes as well, and extracted knowledge and wisdom from them. Pieced it together.

A: If you can explain the entity 'Bellos.' What connection does he have to any of this? It once was explained that he was the maker of the Archons. Is that true?
M: He is the originator of all Archons.
A: Let's go into that story of his. Begin at his origins. How did that happen?
M: There are different Sources within our Multiverse. The Divine Mother Sophia and Father Krysto are the Source of our Universe. Similarly, there are many Universes that have been created within our Multiverse. One such Universe that was created was created by 'Bellos.'
A: There was a Universe that was created by 'Bellos?' Is that what you're saying?
M: That's correct.
A: Would you call him a God? The Source of his Universe? You said there were multiple Sources. Would you call him a Source before he became distorted?
M: He was the Source of that Universe.
A: Okay, so just like we have Source Divine Mother, Divine Father. He was the Source to that Universe of his?
M: That's correct.
A: Tell me the beginning origins of this Universe. Was it always this inverted darkness? Did it ever begin good or organic?
M: He started from a place of power, he wanted power.
A: He always started from a place of power?
M: Yes, he wanted power. He did not come from love.
A: He began like this. He wasn't from love? If all the other Universes were of love, how come he was different. Why was he like this, out of all other Sources?
M: He chose to be this inorganic darkness. To experience power over love. Control.
A: Is this the only Universe that chose to be of inorganic darkness in our Universes?
M: There are others that he distorted along the way.
A: Is this something that was divinely planned, or is this something that he chose with his free will?
M: This was not a divine plan. This was his freewill, his choice. He was to create a Universe, and he chose to create it out of power, as against love, which our Universe is created off. There are many Universes and they all have an energy from which they spring forth from. We are of love and equality, of peace, of brotherhood and sisterhood of coexistence. There are others that could choose some of these, but he chose power.
A: Why would he choose that? Was he made different from other Sources?
M: He himself came from a place of darkness. He holds the darkness of many Universes within him, and then he chose to make one of his own where he could lead with fear.
A: So he began with holding the darkness of other Universes?
M: Yes. He has existed in other Universes as well, and then he sprung forth to create one of his liking, of his choice. Like bringing it all together. He sprung from our organic Multiverse and chose inorganic. He realized the frequency of love, or rather he felt that the frequency of love did not give him the thrill and joys that power and fear gave, and he wanted to experience that.
A: Keep moving the scene along. Anything else of importance?
M: All the gates and portals of our Universe are closed now. There shall be no further entry of any being, any matter into our Universe. All of the Archonic virus that has been left here over time will be transmutted and completely eradicated from our Universe.
A: Once he chose to make his Universe, in order to make it, did he have to extract any souls, or light from other places, to make this Universe?
M: Those were the wires that we spoke of, attached to these metallic structure beings. They looked like black rubber wires, but then were etheric, and there is blue energy coming out of these wires into these artificial beings. This energy is from organic beings, because the Archons have no light of their own. They've placed attachments of themselves into souls and beings, and are continuing to harvest their energies into their Universe.
A: So then you're saying that we're not the only Universe that this Archon Universe has pierced through?
M: That's correct.

A: You also mentioned that he's taken Universes. Can you explain that?
M: He's taken darknesses from Universes. He's taken sacred knowledge from Universes, and inverted it into technology, using them against their own people.
A: Has he ever been able to compromise an entire Universe?
M: No, he cannot do that.
A: Good.
M: The organic within all of our Universes far outweighs this negative technology.
A: The key it is trying to get to is the three dimensional now planetary spheres, that are in this simulation matrix, because they are the ones that are in the lowest dimension, and they forget who they are. So those will be easier to compromise?
M: Yes, and they are the ones who experienced the most darkness and feel lost. Those are the energies that they want to draw upon, it feeds them and also helps them make more cloned versions of the beings that are here in the Universe.
A: In the beginning you mentioned there was a being that pierced through our Universe. You explained it was tall, had teeth and tentacles. Who was that?
M: That was the first Archon that entered our Universe in its wholeness, not just a tentacle. It is the one that connected with the organic. When the beautiful organic being was created of Krysto's essence, and was to teach people about organic darkness, it was around that time when this first Archon entered, and connected with that being to corrupt that being.
A: This being came through our Universe, and attached itself to the back of Krysto?
M: That's correct.
A: Is this where those wires were coming from?
M: That's correct; the wires are from this being.
A: How was this being able to penetrate if it normally wasn't supposed to penetrate through and it was an Archon; it was artificial?
M: It was technology. The technology was very powerful.
A: So then, once we completely extracted the final piece of Krysto, it then just jumped out?
M: That's correct.
A: This being that was able to come into our Universe, did it have any connection to Bellos, or was this his Creation?
M: They are all parts of him.
A: Would you say it was then him?
M: Yes. The first vision that I described of the being with the jaw, the dark eyes, and the tentacle body was Bello.
A: Yes, I felt that from the beginning. Then, afterward, it jumped out, our Universe was sealed, but it left pieces behind, and that's how it still continued to spread its virus in our Universe.
M: That's correct.
A: So it just needed to get itself in and begin to spread.
M: That's correct. It also used the consciousness of the other beings to corrupt them. To want more power just like them.
A: So it's like this invisible force, that is artificial, that gives false knowledge through the use of sacred knowledge, that it extracted from the Universes, and this sacred knowledge is plagued with its virus. And then, that's how people get confused, because they think it's sacred knowledge, but it's not. It's distorted with the A.I. Archon Virus?
M: That's correct.
A: Okay, trying to put all these pieces together. How is it that some beings don't get fooled by this? What's the difference between those, like for example, right now on Earth there's families of say twenty or thirty or more, they all have been fooled to inject the Covid-19 vaccine, the AI virus. But, yet there's maybe one or two that weren't fooled. What's the difference?
M: Those that continued to connect with Source from their heart, continued to heal themselves, awaken themselves, arose from the matrix. And, within the same family network there were many that couldn't do it, because they blocked their connection to Source, and their connection to the thoughts

that arise from the heart. They continued to stay in their minds. That is exactly what they want, to control their minds. Those that continued to connect with the Divine Mother's essence within their heart, those that continued to feel their love for her, started to awaken and asked questions. This knowledge will spread though. The darkness of the A.I. will come forth more pronounced now. Those that have turned their eye away from all the hints that were given to them so far, will not be able to ignore it anymore, because they will have these consequences facing them in their eye. They will start to take notice and the masses will awaken. It is time.

A: They say the Reptilians were once organic; how did they become the army to this Archon thing?
M: As the Archons came in, they played mind games with souls. They offered them exactly what was lacking within their life - power, money. They showed them what it would feel like to be a "master," as they would call it, over other souls by taking over. By attaching their consciousness within other beings, and by being able to control these beings, they gave the Reptilians a view of what it would be like to have power over other beings. How that power would feel. Only to then turn it against them, because they did not spare the Reptilians either. In order to control the Reptilians and other dark alien races, they had to use technology over them as well, because they were aware that these beings are organic, and they can have a change of heart. So they control them with technology as well.

A: Is there anything else that you'd like to speak about, with regard to what you shared with us today?
M: We are there, with all the keys, and each and every one of them is sacredly guarded. What they've attempted so far within our Universe in spreading the virus, shall no longer happen.

A: Good, beautiful.
M: In fact much of the darkness that they had brought along has been eradicated. Planets are being brought back to life. New life forms are being found. The keys are guarded, they're sacred, and they're always protected.

A: I think it really puts into perspective how grand it is then, for example, for our brother Archangel Heylal/Lucifer to be able to withstand this role, and not allow penetration like once happened to the other fractalization of Krysto.
M: If this does not show, or bring to light, how beautifully powerful and divine Archangel Heylal/Lucifer's soul is, we wonder what would? He is, and always will be our brightest Star.

A: That he is. Thank you.
M: We're infinitely grateful for his role, and that of Krysto and Divine Mother Sophia, for their beautiful Creations.

A: Beautiful. Since we spoke of father and mother, is there anything that needs to be said about this Universe, and then the 'Daughter of the Flame'?
M: It is the flame of the 'Daughter of the Flame,' that will bring about complete eradication of this Archon virus, never to be seen again. And, it is the flame of the 'Daughter of the Flame' that will lead our hearts into Ascension. Purifying all that is within our Creation with her loving, glorious, and divine heart. For her, we are always grateful. We love her with all that we are.

A: Thank you. Is this part of the plan of Ascension, for not only our Universe, but the other Universes to finally eradicate this alternate Universe that consists of the first Archon 'Bellos' and all of it's abomonized existences?
M: Yes, we are all in this together, and together we shall rise.

A: Wonderful. The different Universes and their Sources, are they able to talk to one another, are they able to connect to one another?
M: They are a Council in themselves.

A: Have I been speaking to the Higher Self already?

The Higher Self is called forth.
AA Jophiel: That's correct.
A: Who have I been speaking to?
AA Jophiel: This is Archangel Jophiel of the Galactics.
A: Beautiful, thank you Jophiel. It is an honor to be speaking to you.
AA Jophiel: Thank you my love. It is my honor to be here.

Body Scan is conducted, however there is not much to heal within Marla.

For every A.U.R.A. Hypnosis healing session we ask that the Higher Self and team ensure to remove and heal this entire list from the clients Tree of Life: entities (Grays, Mantis, Reptilians, Archons...), dark portals, repair and crystallize DNA, negative cords, technologies (implants, metals, hooks, wires, nano, vaccines), Illnesses, vision, dental health, regrow teeth, age regress 5-15 years, blocked or misaligned chakras, open-up the third eye and activate abilities, expand heart, issues with auric field, fractured soul, contracts, deletion of inverted timelines, and trauma from current or past life.

Post Session dialogue.
A: Welcome back.
M: Wow. Going back and forth, back and forth. That whole story was like, whoa! They were showing me images; it reminded me of a being that we have in our temples (Hindu temples). He has a separate temple, and he had asked that all people worship him after going to the 9 Goddesses. If they don't go to his temple after visiting the 9 Goddesses' temples, then the worship is incomplete.
A: What entity is that?
M: Bellos. He goes by 'Bairav.'
A: Oh, you guys have temples for Bellos? What does his statue look like?
M: It looks really ghostly; it's black and it's disgusting. When we go to the temples, we usually just carry flowers, or coconut, or some sweets that we make at home. We carry glass bangles and adornments for the Divine Mother. Those are the offerings we give the Divine Mother, but not for him. I've been there a couple of times as a child, since I wasn't aware. I never liked it there. So they offer alcohol at that temple to the priests, as if the alcohol's an offering for him. I always found that really weird, like why would a God ask for alcohol right?
A: Yes, now you know.
M: Yes, he looked like him. He looked like charcoal, how charcoal-tar looks. His body looked like that in the session. Very sick looking. Dark. Very dark.
A: Where is this location, the temples of his?
M: India, in the temples. He is worshiped by many there. I don't think everybody goes, but people don't know of the reality. People don't question you know.
A: Creepy.
M: Yes.
A: Is there anything else you want to share that they showed you, that you didn't mention?
M: Just that they were showing me how the soul of Krysto was exiting the vessel as the tentacles were coming in. Like "I'm not gonna be here anymore." They were showing that for Krysto. The key location was very beautiful, and very emotional to be there in the snow and ice. There were so many Dragon's there. Their Universe looked like steel gray, all technology, actual wires that you have in cars. And, these beings, some of them would have wheels. Some of them would have eyes, some tall, some short. Tentacles coming out of them? Could you see it all too?
A: Yes, yes. I could see it all for sure.
M: He was going back and forth, trying to enter the Universe, attached to something, like the way he jumped in. They showed how the tear was created, and then one tentacle came in.
A: I never saw him move from where he entered. He was near the borderline wall of our Universe, I didn't see him move from there. He was just reaching from there.
M: Oh, that explains it, because what I could see was this blob of black/darkness just sitting there. Because, you know, initially, I said that there was war, and the Divine Mother took the soul. Like, whatever was left of it. She retrieved it, and then what I could see was that this being was just sitting there. So I think that's what you were seeing as well.
A: If you enter the Universe, there's a border wall here (gesturing with hands). He was just right next to the border wall where he penetrated. That's how he was able to vanish so quickly, because the minute it happened, he just (Poof! sound effect) pulled right out, and he was gone. Important information again. Thank you.

M: Wow, wow! I'm so glad that it came through.
A: So now we understand how it penetrated. I could see its tentacle with spikes. It was like, (chook, chook, chook, sound effect of it entering). And, then it squeezed through, it was standing there, and it stuck its wires through the fractal of Krysto.

END OF SESSION

FINALLY, THE GRAND PICTURE COMES TOGETHER!!! What we all have been waiting for - who or what is the Archon, and how did *it* enter our Universe with *its* artificial intelligence plague? We began to understand through the 7 Goddesses in Chapter 8, of Bellos the Archon maker's beginning origins. What he was like when he was as organic, as we all are, before he inverted. And, through this chapter we learn of what he began to turn into, after *he* chose to remove his organic Source Love-Light by merging with the emptiness, hollow of the void that in Chapter 1, Aphrodite explained. After the Goddesses kicked Bello out of our Universe, he chose in that moment in time in space from ego and lower vibrational emotions, and perhaps even hurt towards his brethren who would not join his inverted games over the people of Earth, to become *it*, the Archon maker, the first Archon. Bellos being the organic, bringing the intelligence into this out of control, hungered void, becoming at that instant intelligence, as *it* was missing the intelligence prior to Bellos merging wi*t*h *it*. This one inverted choice that *he* contracted and made with this emptiness of Source Love-Light, was the very first time that organic merged with the nothingness, becoming the artificial intelligence *itself*. And, now that *it* had intelligence it became dangerous to the Multiverse, because before the merging, this void was mindless, and now *it* had a mind, and an understanding to all Bellos had learned when creating Universes. After this merging Bellos is no longer, instead *it* is this abomination that now creation will have to understand in order to someday eradicate *it*.

I am being shown a vision now of when the Goddesses kicked him out, Bello leaving our Universe with the intent that he is going to grow even more powerful than the Goddesses. In the ether he finds the black, emptied, nothingness and allows for *it* to consume him, just as we learned of *its* devouring of light in Chapter 1, 'Aphrodite - The Garden of Eve and Adam'. As *it* consumes him he is screaming, because it's painful, as his beingness is disintegrating. Like acid thrown on a human body, all within him that was organic is disintegrating and becoming one with artificial. As this emptiness begins to consume him, *it* too evolves, both of them becoming the very first technology, the artificial intelligence. His Source Love-Light is separated from him, just as this void was too whe*n it* came to be at the beginning of life, and together they become what should have never been. The Archon maker.

In this session we remember the grand showdown that the 7 Goddesses spoke of. The first initial battle was when Bello was kicked out of our Universe, when he decided to cause inverted havoc to the beginning developing humans within Earth, as mentioned in Chapter 8, and the second time we removed *it* was explained in this chapter, when *it* had penetrated back into our Universe in *its* new form, the soulless, tentacle, artificial intelligence thing. During these battles it attacked the guardian Gods of that time, and the 7 Goddesses, who are the expressions of the Divine Mother. This was the grand showdown, the war of the gods! They managed to kick *it* out, but in that time and space did not know how to stop the spread of artificial intelligence as *it* was foreign and new to us, or perhaps they thought that the compromised souls could be given an opportunity to heal, as that is *our* truth of our creation.

The Divine Mother of Creation once showed me this moment in life from her perspective. When *it* began spreading *its* inverted plague by attaching *itself* to the essence of the Divine Father. S*h*e, and *only she,* could have stopped *it*, as she is both the Creator and the destroyer, because only the Creator can destroy their own creation, if and when these creations become too distorted by their own choosing. However, to do so, she would have had to put an end, with her phoenix/Source flame, to all souls who were then the beginning carriers of the Archon virus. Resetting all of these souls back to zero, transmuting them back to Source. Wiping them clear of their original soul signature when they birthed forth, and all experiences they gained prior to the inverted attachment. This was unbearable for her, as it goes against all that she is within Creation. Could you do this to your own children? Reset them so that they are no longer who they have become? In essence, no longer existing. Divine Mother explained that even if she could go back to that time and space, she still would not reset her Creations. All must always be first given an opportunity to change or evolve, as this is the way of our Creation. This is one of the reasons why when we find the darkest souls through A.U.R.A. Hypnosis Healing, that we will give them multiple chances to positive polarize, as we honor souls, just as Mother does. She taught this most important, honorable lesson to all her children, from the beginning of Creation. In this current time and space, collectively in our process of Ascension, there are some souls who have been given an infinite amount of chances at this point, who still choose not to positive polarize; though minimal, at times our Universe has learned to transmute them back to Source. Resetting them back to the beginning points of only Source Love-Light, and this can be done because they have already been given the chance to change, and are still choosing not to.

Prepare yourself for the conclusion of this book, when we read the final chapter and we find out what exactly Archangel Jophiel meant when she said, "It is the flame of the 'Daughter of the Flame,' that will bring about complete eradication of this Archon virus, never to be seen again. And, it is the flame of the 'Daughter of the Flame' that will lead our hearts into Ascension."

The 7 Goddesses reminded us that Bellos began from our Universe; however, not limited in the perspective of the Multiverse, how these verses also had versions of this once entity, Bellos. When it was exiled from our Universe, it decided to make its own artificial Universe. As Marla said, "It was created from darkness. It has darkness from all other Universes. It has no love, it has no light, it has no organic. It just exists." The Archon Universe began artificially, because once the Archon maker was removed the first time from our Universe, he inverted himself. We call *it* an Archon Universe but I feel *it* is better understood if we call *it* a realm, but even that is not quite right for something that was never meant to be. This free willed choice turned him into the beginnings of artificial intelligence, and from there the Archon Universe expanded from *it* and this choice. Outside the perimeter of our Universe *it* was able to act upon this decision because *it* had the capability to do so, as *it* was a God originally, acting upon in the beginning formations of the Multiverse. Therefore, the Archon Universe is *it*, and all the inverted darkness that *it* has harvested through the Multiverse. At *its* origins, *it* is the beginning decision to become unruled by all, turning *itself* into this choice, and from there the more that *it* recruited souls to do its bidding for *it*, the Archon Universe grew in size, with every inverted choice made by each soul *it* could attach to when they became a matching vibration to the Archon Universe. He/*it* used his connection to these versions of himself within these verses, through this original, organic link, to his other fractals, and *it* was able to reach to the infinities of souls in the Multiverse, and *it* grew in ways which became untamable. *It* became the collective of the Universe's inverted darkness, but because he was the cause of these inversions, he gathered this collective pain and trauma, growing bigger with each harm that was caused to the beings of the Multiverse.

The entire Archon Universe is this once entity, as a balloon which begins to fill up with air, the air representing the souls it sucked into its existence by attaching to them, and with every air/soul *it* intakes, *it* continues to become larger and larger. Once our Universe experiences Ascension, which will begin from our third dimensional realms, this balloon, the Archon entity and the artificial intelligence that it is, will finally pop out of existence. *It* will be eradicated from all time and space, and a new era will begin with a most important sacred law in Creation, that one must never remove the Source Love-Light from oneself. *IT'S* ending is coming, and *it* knows it. If any entity of the Multiverse tries to overstep this sacred law and boundary within Creation ever again in this manner, this sacred law will act automatically through its organic system to be read for all entities to self-destruct, in automatic transmutation and reset back to Source. We respect free willed choice for all souls in Creation; however, this one inverted choice to remove the organic within, will never be tolerated to be played out again. As what this choice has turned into, harming many throughout the Multiverse, is unfathomable, especially the harm to the children. Remembering though, that all roles are honored, even the most inverted, because all within our Creation evolve rapidly because of the versatility in densities they have lived through. One of the reasons why so many want to incarnate now into the third dimensions, in order to evolve within the soul experience from the oppression within the inverted realms. As when this experiment is done, that will be it; life as we know it will no longer be at the speed of growth we see now within the lower dimensions, as these dimensions will no longer be.

One of the main reasons the Archon targeted our Universe, was because *it* did originally organically birth from our Universe. However, understanding that there are infinite multi-versions of all of us throughout the Multiverse. Therefore, there are other versions of Bellos throughout the Multiverse, and there is no telling what he/*it* decided to do in the other verses, when *it* decided *it* wanted to become this non-ruled Super God above all others. The Archon maker bypassed all sacred Universal laws, and used the positive portals between the Universes, which are like membrane walls to a cell and normally cannot be penetrated, to get back in with *its* artificial intelligence tentacles. In the same moment in space that *it* entered, *it* too attached to the Divine Father expression who was experiencing himself as Divine Father outside of Source, but still always connected to Source, as we all are. In that moment, *it* began *its* grand diabolical plan to spread what *it* is now, this plague. *It* did this to Divine Mother Sophia's beautiful twin flame, knowing that Father Krysto is the representation to the organic darkness, the semen and the material which the light impregnates within creation into birthing. And, to plague this sacred material, the darkness, it would be able to spread with ease, once it began its artificial intelligence capabilities of multiplication. Ultimately, because if *it* got *itself* into the Divine Father, who is Father to all, then, so too, *it* could reach all of Mother's and Father's children who were vulnerable to being preyed upon by *it*.

The Essenes explained and showed me the divine power of the chakra which is located at the back of our neck which connects to the spine, in the inbetween of both the neck and spine, named C-7 by the medical industry. This infinite energetic point is connected to our consciousness and all that consists within it. You can feel the power of the toroidal sphere breathing out through this space, and is one of the most powerful energetic vortexes within us. It is the root of our being. This is why the Archon decided when *it* attached, that *it* would do so in this sacred location in Krysto's energetic neck, as then *it* would have access to his consciousness. Allowing an easier attachment, so that *it* could have control, integrating and merging *its* artificial intelligence with this then essence of Divine Father. This was the first action within our Creation, of overstepping boundaries of another soul with a foreign integration into their sacred DNA and being. This is a focused chakra point for many to compromise, by negative polarized healers or entities who are acting upon the Archons' bidding, as it allows an easier entryway into a soul, as it did then, the first time it occurred with Divine Father. It is also where many who claim that they will activate or clear your DNA for you enter through, in order to penetrate the sacredness of your DNA. Our DNA is to be guarded, as it holds every sacred piece which consists within us organically and divinely, given to us by the Creator. All that we are. Why would we consciously allow someone else to energetically work, or to come anywhere near the sacredness of our beingness and DNA?! This is a strong Archonic-based act of giving away your divine power, and it is connected to this very first inverted act that the Archon did to our Divine Father. Which is why through A.U.R.A. Hypnosis and R.A.A.H. Reiki Healing, there is a clear, high divine intention and boundary, that all is done with the permission of the true Higher Self, and it is YOU who is doing the self-healing work. We, as the practitioners, are only the bridges, holding the Love-Light by acting upon the sacred alchemy for you, to achieve the highest level of divine self-healing. Within the crystalline blueprint of our Earth, this chakra in the back of our necks, is where our consciousness connects in order to enter this simulation we live within. In Book 3, we further go into this subject.

We remind you now of what Marla said, "I see the Divine Father, and his darkness, his shadow side. He is meant to play a beautiful role within existence of light and dark, to birth further Creations and souls, after healing them from their darkness - bringing them to light. That is his role." This statement by Marla assists us in profound heartfelt ways to know how strong and pure [17]Archangel Heylal/Lucifer is to hold this role for the collective. As he is the Archangel who volunteered after the Krysto essence, when the Archon maker infringed upon him. The original essence of Krysto was not able to withstand this role when the Archon first attached to him, but Archangel Heylal/Lucifer has shown us ever since, that he can. This is why the heavens call Archangel Lucifer by his real name, the 'Prince of Light,' because he is the Multiverse's most purest, brightest light. Archangel Michael once told me that there came a time in the Universe that Divine Mother called for the strongest and purest of all angels to be able to play the role of the organic darkness once more, to be the light and hold the space within the darkness. So that when those that chose to become lost souls entrapped within the illusion of the artificial intelligence, which masks itself in the dark, when they would ask for assistance, there would always be the Legion of the Light Bringers, who are essences of Archangel Lucifer, standing bravely, brightly amongst the darkness, never falling for the artificial. He is the mirror which reflects back to those their inner demons, so that they can recognize this within themselves and choose to self heal. Archangel Michael with tears in his eyes for his brother the Prince of Light, explained to me that he, Archangel Michael, thought he was going to have to play this role for humanity, but his brother selflessly, and most lovingly said "No." He would not allow any of his angelic brethren to take on such a heavy role, and that he would be the one. And at this moment in time and space, still the Prince of Light stands in the shadows most beautifully, with his angelic hand extended, ready to pull the lost souls out, and back into the light.

In book 3 we will speak further of what Marla said, "The metallic beings are attached to the rubber wires into people, by leaving pieces of themselves in the people. This is how they feed, they feed these metallic beings to keep them alive, because truly their shells are empty."

This is what the Light Beings through Chapter 10 'The Archon Realm' meant, when they said that it just takes *one* to become infested, to bring the Archon virus into the Universe, and then it spreads. Through this chapter we understand this at the deepest level, coming into awareness that we all must work very hard to remove this virus from inside of us, living our most organic blueprints, timelines, and divine paths. The spread of false knowledge is the biggest tool that they use daily to cloud people, their hearts, and their consciousnesses. Keeping them deeply intertwined in the inverted matrix, as Marla said, "So it's like this invisible force, that is artificial, that gives false knowledge through the use of sacred knowledge, that it extracted from the Universes, and this sacred knowledge is plagued with its virus. And then, that's how people get confused, because they think it's sacred knowledge, but it's not. It's distorted with the A.I. Archon virus!" This reach is the strongest in all platforms and channels through YouTube, Bitchute, Reddit…And it is the biggest distraction to all awakening souls in their process of Ascension. May we continue to hold the highest Love-Light that one day our brethren will snap out of this dark sorcery, and will see, feel, know, smell, sense the truth with their third eye unveiled.

We humbly thank Archangel Jophiel for reminding us that our sacred universal Keys reside energetically always within the caves of Creation, which are one with Source, as the Galactic Guardians that we all are. We originally reviewed these in Book 1, '13 Keys - Sacred Laws of The Universe,' and their importance and roles they play to maintain our Universe in sacred balance. Remember to connect to these sacred laws within you to find balance in all that you have been, are, and will be. As when we become attuned to the sacred laws of our Universe, it creates a strong barrier which cannot be penetrated by inversions. Perhaps we once did not know the divine power of these sacred laws, and how they guard us, but now we know.

---

[17] To find out more of Archangel Lucifer watch 'Archangel Lucifer | Who is he really?' on our platforms.

Archangel Jophiel reminded us that Creation is a [18]Tree of Life, and in honor to this sacred truth, we have created the image below, which is our Universes 'Creations Ancestry Tree of Life'. We will further go into the expansion of alien races throughout Creation in future projects and literature to come.

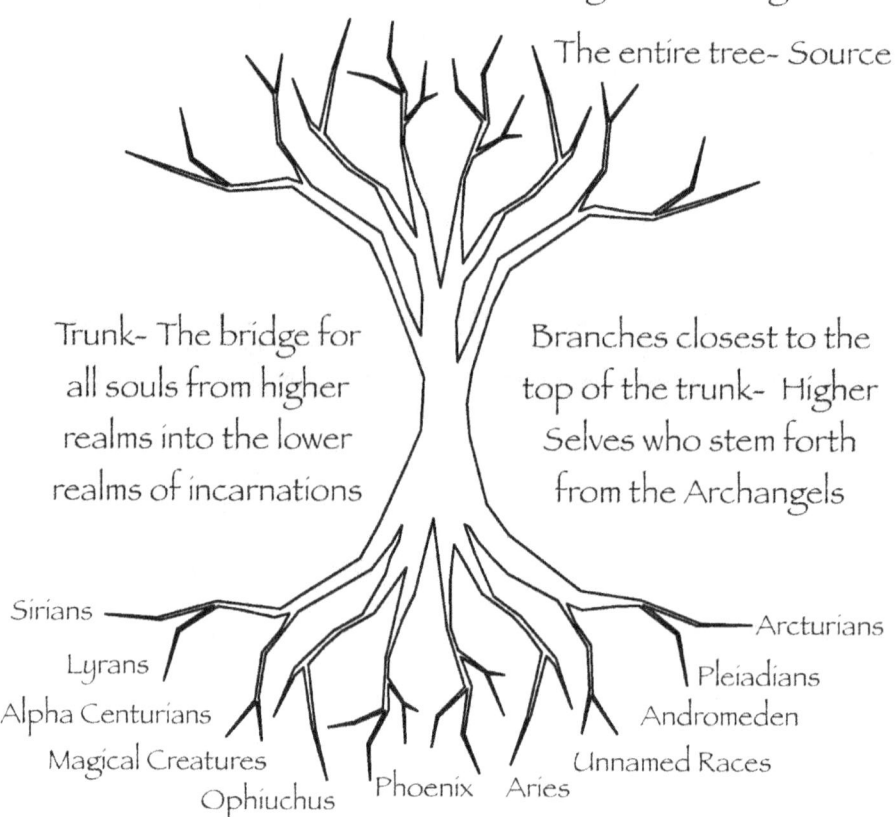

Creations Ancestry Tree of Life

Tips of branches where the leaves bloom- Over Souls- The first essences of Source- The Archangels and Dragons

The entire tree- Source

Trunk- The bridge for all souls from higher realms into the lower realms of incarnations

Branches closest to the top of the trunk- Higher Selves who stem forth from the Archangels

Sirians
Lyrans
Alpha Centurians
Magical Creatures
Ophiuchus
Phoenix
Aries
Arcturians
Pleiadians
Andromeden
Unnamed Races

Roots of tree- The infinite incarnations of alien races in creation through the divine process of all dimensions and realms.

"Boundaries are our sacred Love-Light shields, and what maintains us in true divine sovereignty. These should never be crossed."
~AuroRa

--------------<<>>--------------

[18] When you become certified through 'Quantum Galactic Akashic Reading', you self-attune to the vast sacred understanding of the Kabbalah, the 'Tree of Life' and the 'Tree of Knowledge'.

12

CELESTIAL DRAGONS

Session #364: Recorded in May 2021
Never before shared.

      In this online A.U.R.A. Hypnosis Healing session, Rene is an A.U.R.A. Hypnosis Healing practitioner. Rene takes us through a most beautiful journey into the cosmos. We learn of the true divine power and capabilities of the Celestial Dragons. It is time we invoke this divine power into our everyday life on Earth. We are far beyond grander than we are led to believe. This session begins our journey into discovering what has been erased from our Earth's history or made into make-believe, Dragons who are multidimensional beings that harness the celestial divine power of Creation. We also learn of some of the attributes that crystals can hold, so that we too can remember this of our crystals when we hold them in our palms, and feel them in our hearts.

-------------<<>>--------------

"Science is not separate from magic. Science is not separate from spirit. Spirit is science. They're only abominations when separated."
~Arcturian Mentor

-------------<<>>--------------

R [Rene]: Small shrubs. Doesn't really feel hot. *Red barren landscape.*
A [Aurora]: *Look at yourself. Do you feel like you have a body?*
R: Yes.
A: *Look down at your feet. How many toes do you have?*
R: Four.
A: *Look at your hands. How many fingers do you have?*
R: Three, and a thumb.
A: *Look at your skin; what color tone is it?*
R: Brown. Really Brown. Olive Brown. Very smooth. Pretty.
A: *What does your face look like?*
R: Narrow, kind of sharp. But it's okay. It all matches. There's symmetry. But it's small and narrow.
A: *What do your eyes look like?*
R: Oh, they're an interesting green color. I don't know that I've ever seen that. Green like, ah, they glow a little bit. They have something in them like a sparkly... they glow.
A: *Are you wearing any clothing?*
R: Yes.
A: *What are you wearing?*
R: I feel like I'm wearing some leggings of some sort, but they're skin color. There's a skirt, but it's more to support... it's leather. It's in square patches like armor. That's so weird. Like a short skirt that's armor, and I have a hip holster. I can store a lot of stuff, but it's not heavy. There's something in this holster that makes things weightless, so I have a lot of tools there, but I can't feel them until I need them.
A: *What do you feel like you're doing on this planet?*
R: Excavating ruins. I'm looking for something here; something in the ground by some ruins. I have little things that I put over my eyes that can see... they can zoom in and zoom out. Maybe that's what I saw. Like little enhancements helping me see in the atmosphere. I'm searching. I can see things in a

hologram now. Measures distance for me, calculates... I'm looking for a certain composition of minerals, and this helps me calculate which way to set out. I have a ship, and it knows how to find that stuff too, but when I get on the ground I need to orient better. Something was left here that we want. It looks like obsidian, but it's a power artifact. It's black; it's shiny. What do you call that when the surface of something changes?

A: Is it morphing?

R: Yes, it can change. That's what I'm looking for. Another team left that here.

A: Why is it that they left it there?

R: They had to leave in a hurry. The Grays... they're always watching us. The Grays watch us to find out what we're recovering.

A: How do they watch you?

R: They have drones in places that they know we go. Sometimes those activate a portal, so they can come through. It's a portal on the ground. They'll come through singley, not in a ship. That's what happened. And I guess the previous crew forgot to look for that, or be aware, they were so excited. The ruins I'm seeing are ruins on top of ruins because there was a fight here. It was a ruin we found. I'm with a conglomerate. We're all kinds of races.

A: There's several others with you?

R: Not right now. No. When we go on excavations there are several. There are teams of twelve.

A: Right now it's only you scavenging?

R: Yes. I slipped in to come back for this. I can shield really well and I have extra protection, so maybe one can get through and get this thing and not be seen so much, you know. There's not a disturbance in the... like on Star Wars, there's not a disturbance in the Force. If I'm careful.

A: (Laughs) Love it!

R: I'm being careful. I'm very light, so I don't impact heavily. Yep, I've got it. I've got it! I'm putting it in my bag.

A: Good! You found it?

R: Yes, the bag holds it in this no time-space. It can't be seen. I'm going back now, back to the portal place. My ship's in orbit. I just use one of their portals, to come down. We've got their signals; we've got the frequency, and now I'm going to close that portal behind me. I'm up on my ship now, and I'm all cloaked. Ah! That was good!

A: Was it a dangerous mission, you feel?

R: No, it wasn't; it was like a medium calculated risk. I don't like dangerous missions anymore. I'm still working through the fear of those. We were captured once - I don't like that. We all have to help each other because stuff happens. So, I have to wait 'til my resonance gets back all the way to where I don't have any fear at all. And then I can go on those kinds of missions again. Not that I like them, but I'm in service. That's what we do. So this was just right for me. I could do this and feel good. You know, accomplished.

A: Very good. Now that you have it on ship and you're cloaked, what do you do next of importance?

R: I check coordinates to see if there's somewhere else to go, or if they want me to come back. They're going to want me to come back with this now, so I'm going to program this ship and go to the nearest Stargate portal, and go back with this device. I'm still not sure what it does; it's still in that stasis field. I guess it's pretty powerful. I'm not sure it's something we made. I think it's something we had the great, good fortune to find, from another place in time; even another...Oh! It's a race we don't know much about that has this, and they might even be extinct. I don't know if I'm going back to the station in orbit, or to a ground, like a planet. Where am I going? I'm going to the planet.

A: What does the planet look like?

R: Pretty, pretty, pretty! They can't come here. There's a plasma barrier all around this solar system; this particular part. It's full of pretty planets, lush, and kind of tropical. It feels good to be here because it's so humid. I mean, it's just right, you know? Your skin loves it. I can take off all that stuff I was wearing. So I'm going to turn that in now. They're really happy that we have this.

A: Who are you turning it in to?

R: I know they are Arcturans. I love Arcturans! I think they're my family. Very wise. I love being with them. They resonate so pretty. Blue beings are here. They're in round helmets. They must have a different atmosphere than we do. They're really tall and skinny, like ten feet, eleven feet tall. I can't really see in their helmets. It has a mist around them. They're nice though. (Laughs) They have a tail that swishes a lot like a cat; kind of gets in the way sometimes, and if they're being playful with you, they'll snap at you as you walk by, just friendly, you know. They're quite mischievous... (laughs) for being a tall skinny being, they're very mischievous. We like them. They bring a lot of joy. There's Andoran here. They look like (laughs) the Earth show, like "The Martian" with the two little antennas on top? They're that pale gray-blue skin - not all of them are positively polarized, but this group is. They're shorter, blond hair, blue eyes. Very scientifically focused. My team leader's an Arcturan; I love him. He's my mentor. He's wonderful. (Whispers) So good to be back with him.

A: *What do the Arcturians look like?*

R: He's holding the physical form right now. He's usually ninth dimensional, so it's more of an etheric form. But let's see this form...Yes, they have large skulls. He has a large skull. But they're so friendly; the way the eyes sit in their face. They're upward slanted; they have pretty faces. They don't have any hair. They're nice skulls, high cheekbones, and tiny noses. Pretty lips, thin, but they're pretty expressive. He's laughing at me. He's like, "What are you doing?" I'm doing several things at one time. He's like, "Oh, good for you!" He's very happy with me. He's a little taller than I am. In this form, I'm pretty short. I'm like five feet; real slender. He's six and a half. He says,"to have presence," it's important he has physical presence here because he's a leader. He and I laugh a lot about that, because on this station, and on the planet, there are those that are present, that still have to have, the... sight of physical presence. Matters to them, appearance. So he's found it just works better if he appears in this manner. He has a high collar; he's in a lab coat, but it's real pretty material. Likes to wear high collar that kind of fans out, around his neck, it's slender. Two buttons, they're pearlescent and they're crystals; goes to his knees. He has flowing pants underneath, his feet are in boots here. We are on gravity. We're having earthquakes here right now, so we're wearing boots that keep us on the station floor. The station is kind of up off the edge of a cliff. Oh, that's pretty. We overlook a beautiful ocean. We're on platform legs. The whole station is built on a big platform, and it has... it's not steel, but it's like titanium legs, and we retract them sometimes and just hover and float above the peninsula. That's what we're doing now; and we go into anti-gravity a little bit. We have the boots that keep us on the floor of the station, so we aren't all flying around. It's not that we'd fly around, but we'd lift off and that can be disorienting a little bit. I'm wearing those. They're just slippers though.

A: *I want to know more about this, would you call it a crystal that you found?*

R: It looks like a rod. You could call it a short staff. It's cylindrical, has an oval, it's very smooth and polished, an oval, carved top, a round rim, cylinder point (using hand motions to describe the shape). The point is some kind of crystal. I have never seen that kind of crystal before, but it's clear and super powerful. The point is very pointy, so I had to be careful. You can only grip the cylinder part, because the two ends are active. They can inhabit different space times. That is so weird. You can twirl it like a baton... My mentor is showing me this, because only he can handle it ninth dimensionally and it moves. The oval point can move space time and stretch it. I don't want to say open it, but it creates an opening. You can stretch it, and can project out. They use it to explore space time. The crystal end activates... it's a power generator crystal. It's like nothing I've ever seen. It doesn't exist on Earth. It can be pale blue. But it's so bright you can hardly look at it. He is calling it, Omaranthrama, Omeronthema? There's tones and they're (client goes into a chanting sequence). You can tone with it, and it changes its composition. Wow! Gets longer. The cylinder went from black to total see through blue light. When my Arcturian mentor uses it, well, we all are in a viewing port; he's the only one in the room, and this room is set up a certain way. It's very protected. But it's almost like it separates itself from the station. It's a bubble in a bubble. My Arcturian Mentor and two others are in there with him, highly trained Arcturans. We can view it through a viewport. We're behind this glass of some sort, watching into the bubble, into the room while they play with this device. They are so happy that we have that! Holy cow! I don't know everything that it's going to do. They're so happy, it will really help. It gives us a foot up in this Galactic War. There's more of these around. They're very useful, but for benevolent purposes. But, like anything, they can be used for non-benevolent purposes, too. So it's important we get them all. There's five more to be found. We have six. I don't really know what they're going to do with it. The less we know, the better off it is. So

I probably won't go on one of those finding missions again, because now I know more than I need to know to get the object. What I know is too much to let me go out there again and look for them.

A: How was it that they were able to find them?

R: They're using the first ones that the Arcturans had; they had two. They're using those to peer through… like I showed you. And when a master handles them, they can use them to find the others that are in resonance. One has been chopped in half. It's still active, but it can't work because it's broken. But it's still dangerous. In fact, it is probably more dangerous right now. So that's the one they want to go find next. They're using these, each one carries the resonance of the others, because when we have them all, they fit together. They do something. He's not going to let me know what they do. My mentor says "No."

A: That's okay. How was it chopped in half? Do they know that?

R: They're showing me that the Grays have it, or had it. When they were trying to do something with it, it self-destructed. They're made by ancient high forty-eighth dimensional beings, now it's really hard…

(side conversation between Higher Self/Client below)

HS to client: "No, no, it's not hard to get to them, we can get to them. You were there!"

(Client continues, answering the question now)

Client to A: This one dis-assembled itself, it cracked in half, so it appears broken. Some of these Gray races are very intelligent, and they know that they should be able to put it back together. So that's going to be quite the retrieval on that one… they want to get the others before they go after that one. This is all now (present tense); this is a "now" thing.

A: This is happening now?

R: Yes. Well, as much time as now is… you know what I mean?

A: I understand.

R: They have three other teams out right now looking for the next four of them. No, five of them. This other one is a sixth. So it's twelve! Oh, and there's a master crystal in the center of these. We have the master crystal. So it's thirteen pieces; that makes sense.

A: Does the master one look different from the other ones?

R: Yes, it exists in many dimensions. It's a master crystal as in… intelligence. This is a crystal that's alive. The crystal found the Arcturans and asked the Arcturans to do this. This was a millennia ago. So the Arcturans have the crystal on their planet. It's the safest place for it.

A: Why is that the safest place for it?

R: Arcturus is very, very protected.

A: How so?

R: I can ask him (referring to her mentor). They talked to their sun, their beautiful blue star. They know. They talk to their celestial beings. There are the Arcturan home planet and several of the other planets or satellites around that beautiful star. There are extra plasma fields around the solar system. There's a ring-pass-not and there are fire dragons. Immense, Celestial Angel Dragons. Wow, wow! They're such big energy. They're showing me a blue dragon. Glittery blue eyes. Time Lord. Those dragons watch over Arcturus, and the Arcturans right now. So you know how dragons are… angels? This is a whole collective that has encircled Arcturus and that solar system. People don't know about this. Those dragons, oh, they're magnificent! They're huge. They're like planet size. They can morph and they can dimensionally travel. So what they'll do is, … this is unbelievable to me (client softly laughs). They scoop up the planet and the sun, those Dragons, and they take it to a higher dimension. That's their ultimate protection. And then they'll bring them back down. They are always moving. so people can't travel to Arcturus freely; you have to have a key to get in. You hit the right dimension and the right key. I mean, that's high security. The Arcturans are more likely to come visit you than you are to go to their solar system right now.

A: Yes. Talking to the beautiful guide you're talking to, I channel them. That's what it felt like, you have to get through with a key and a gate.

R: Exactly! Oh that's totally it! There is a key and a gate. Ah! Do you know there's a key and a gate to everything? I mean, you think you might be getting through with just the key, but if you didn't go through the right gate, or you weren't permitted to go through, that gate takes you somewhere else

that fools you into thinking you got there. That works with the Grays all the time. (Client softly speaking to herself and guide: "We should do that here... Can we do that here?"). He says they're working on it. (Now addressing Aurora): You know that thing you cleared last night?
A: Yes.
R: You know they're looking for portals, so they've sealed our solar system, Earth's solar system, right now in a plasma field. And that's a third dimension-fourth dimension-fifth dimension thing, so it's keeping the actual ships out, but there's so many portals on Earth right now that they're trying to find. And what you found last night... that was a portal! (Client clapping) You closed a portal! Oh my gosh! Oh, and you pissed them off so bad sister! The Arcturans are going to be... you call them for help. They will shield you. He, my mentor, says so.
A: Thank you. Will do. Absolutely.
R: Keep up the good work! Oh my gosh, you know they were going to bring some stuff through there. Way to go sister! We praise you! Happy Day! The whole station's listening. They know you! They are listening. (Client speaking to guide): What can I tell her? What can she call?
A: That portal? Can I ask questions about it?
R: Yes.
A: I thought that portal had a lot to do with human experiments and human trafficking. Nazi type, and then taking over souls, it was a really bad one. Can you just tell me when the dark portal began?
R: 1920s.
A: Yes. I've seen that it would clear the whole forest so... that's beautiful.
R: They're going to do a little clearing atmospherically. There's residue still. You did a magnificent job! This blue dragon is one of the blue dragons that guards Arcturus. The Blue Dragon I was shown, that's huge, that's planet size, wants to gift you, for lack of a better word, offspring. For your protection right now, and the protection of all the A.U.R.A. practitioners that are flowering. The activation is going to be through Archangel Metatron, and Jophiel, because the two of them together are the key to Shambala. To bring in the crystalline dragons. Each of us gets one. That's a great gift. Oh, my word!
A: That is beautiful.
R: And it's infinite. This beautiful Dragon, is this most etheric, electric blue, with indigo eyes, golden amber Dragon points and ears and ridges. The Universe moves inside this Dragon like energy, so there's infinite offspring. All we have to do is ask, tone, and work in a meditation with Archangel Metatron. It's important. Much reverence and respect when we deal with these crystal Dragons. Yes, Crystal Universe Dragons.
A: Beautiful. Thank you. We love them, honor them and respect them infinitely, these beautiful, celestial, crystalline Dragons.
R: Yes, yes. (client speaking to her guide/mentor: Thank you). (Louder) Wow!
A: What a gift! Thank you for that!
R: Wow! Yes! Surprised me!
A: Can Rene already have her little offspring? Can you show him to her?
R: Okay, it's coming in (laughter), hits me right in the face! Their Crystal, they're pretty (speaking to the Dragon): Hi, welcome, welcome (client softly tones sounds to the Dragon). Okay. We've seen their names. That's awesome. I'm going to cry. Thank you. Oh yes, I have mine. (Client asking her guide): Can Aurora have hers? Because you know, she's going to need help. Yes! Take a minute Aurora. Get your Dragon. Listen for its tone.
A: They actually gave them to me while I was doing your energy work.
R: Ah! That's awesome. Oh, I have full body chills. Oh, yes.
A: Thank you.
R: Has your Dragon encompassed you yet and held you inside it?
A: They're surrounding my entire home. Definitely.
R: Yes, mine's just taken me right inside it right now.
A: I love it. Thank you.
R: Arcturans, and all you benevolent wonderful beings! Thank you! Wow, nice. Makes me just cry. Oh... (client softly crying).

A: That's beautiful.
R: Source is great! Source is wonderful, wonderful... Thank you Divine Mother and Divine Father. We love you! We so love you. We know we can do the work so well now. This is so helpful. Haha! My Dragon just went all over my whole house. Ah...Thank you.
A: Your Arcturian guide, we would love for him to speak through you and see what messages he might have?
R: Yes, that would be marvelous.
A: Beautiful. Let's go ahead and speak to him now. We love you, honor you, thank you, and respect you; we would be honored to speak to you when you are ready.
Arcturian Mentor: Aurora! We love you.
A: We love you and I love you! I love you all, with all that I AM.
Arcturian Mentor: And, likewise. We see you; happy, happy, happy are we in your work. The Divine Mother has truly excelled through this facet of knowingness and beingness into the world, it is like a flowering upon the Earth, upon the third dimension and it is radiating into the fourth and up to the fifth, this flowering you're bringing forth here now.
A: Oh! Thank you! It is beautiful.
Arcturian Mentor: You should begin to feel some synergy and harmony that has been lacking a bit because of the pressure and the immensity of the work; time, indeed, is shifting. So, your days are not as long as they have been, and nobody has told you this, but you know it. It is becoming difficult to fit in all the work and all the higher joy functions of life, such as having a family, and enjoying family, and enjoying animals in Creation, and still do the work. We honor you, child. We understand; just know this will pass. Stay strong. That's why the gift of the Dragons, as they will hold this space for you. They will assist you and allow you breath within your domiciles; space to breathe; space where you can relax and know you are safe. Because these Dragons hold you in a different dimension; out of the dimension that "they" are aware of. You cannot be troubled here; truly a respite for you. Use it wisely. But know that it exists indeed. Regarding your work... you've accomplished much more than you believe you have accomplished; you feel there is more to come forth, and there is, but it will be much freer flowing. There will be a smoothness, perhaps this fall; perhaps another wave of smoothness, where you feel constraints moving out, into flow, around Solstice again. Next year will be a totally different year than this year. And you will stretch into flow more there. You're Goddesses and Gods, we will call them, for truly you are becoming powerful beings, and will begin to assume their full powers this fall. This winter, and next year. This will lessen the burden on you.
A: Wow. Thank you.
Arcturian Mentor: So much of your groundwork, how you like to grid your home, and I applaud you, working with crystals, we cannot have enough crystals around us. Clear them. Bless them. Cleanse them, and invite them as living beings into your world. They truly can assist you. Tell everyone. Become crystal knowers, crystal see-ers; work with crystals. How you grid your home, you are gridding the Earth with your students. That is what you are doing. That is beautiful... I'm in her memories right now. And she has so enjoyed the replay of the [19]A.U.R.A. practitioner class, the new video you posted. You are international even there. So even if your students aren't living in international places, the International races they represent. They connect genetically, and through space time. Your teachings are taken to those races amongst the Earth. So very much you are creating a grid upon the Earth, allow your eyes to see it now. Look at your grid.
A: Yes.
Arcturian Mentor: You know the gaps in the spaces and know that those will come to you. You'll be filling it the rest of this year. We expect completion by the end of this year with your grid of students. The Archangels...You know, what's interesting, and perplexing to us Arcturans, Ohorai, that we are, is that some of our brothers and sisters of the other galactic races are not seeing the Archangels, and

---

[19] Once a month the A.U.R.A. & R.A.A.H. practitioners get together through a video call where they share new wisdom gained through their inner connection to their Higher Self and their experiences gained by their clients session administered.

are not aware of Archangels, and not using Archangel... assistance, and the Archangels are sad about that. Do you know that? Have they talked to you about that?

A: Yes. I understand. I think that's one of the biggest things, where I'm trying to help the humans that are here, that would be connected to those other races of brethren, that are not using the Archangels to assist them because of all the archonic programming.

Arcturian Mentor: Yes. This one here will help you. She's already activated. She's well connected in our galactic family. So she straddles that, what they call the scientific world, with the etheric world, spiritual world. Ohorai see them as one, we see them together. Science is not separate from magic. Science is not separate from spirit. Spirit is science. They're only abominations when separated.

A: Yes, exactly.

Arcturian Mentor: You have some bridgers already in your group. Think about how you want to activate them and use them, where they can teach more, and at least your light grid workers, your beautiful AURA practitioners that you're so carefully laying into the beautiful grid on Earth.

A: Thank you..

Arcturian Mentor: There are many masquerades, and many masks yet to fall off and until we, the Galactics, the Arcturans, the Council of Five, and the beautiful Zenae of Andromeda, until we find all the portals on Earth, there's going to be those that slip in.

A: Thank you. How are we doing on the portals? Are we closing the majority of them?

Arcturian Mentor: There's a quarter closed; three quarters have to be found yet.

A: Thank you. My infinite love to everyone. I send you a wave of love.

Arcturian Mentor: We infinitely love you in return. Blessings.

A: Beautiful. I know we're already talking to the Higher Self, but we'd like to speak to the Higher Self now.

The Higher Self is called forth.

A: Can I please speak to the Higher Self of Rene?

Higher Self: Greetings sister!

A: Greetings sister! I love you. I honor you and respect you. Am I speaking to Rene's Higher Self now?

Higher Self: You are.

A: Do you have any connection to KyRa?

KyRa: I am her. I am KyRa.

A: If you can tell us why is it that you took her to that time and space where she was that beautiful being, assisting in helping find that crystal. What was the purpose of that?

KyRa: So many reasons. First was fear. She's working through the layers of fear. She is to understand that she has that aspect that is so well loved, that they will protect her and yet empower her to go out on a mission where she can be of service and still serve, and feel like she's safe, taking her baby steps back into the world. Protected, surrounded by love, to know that we are so strong around her, we would not allow her to be harmed. That's over. No more! That's done. But we understand that as cellular debris clears and fields clear, that it just takes time in the third dimension, for that to resolve. So that was a vivid picture for her to understand the many levels of that message, and she gets it. The other thing is, she loves the Arcturans. She thinks she is an Arcturan, (laughs). She's had an Arcturan life, and they remember her. She's not Arcturan. She is that drop right off the Source that she keeps seeing; that golden drop of light. This is why she loves the Sun so much. She is pure, RA light and of angelic beingness.

A: Beautiful. Yes, I think we might have talked about at some point of the Arcturian energy that was strong with her. She's amazing. What a joy, a gift. Thank you Higher Self for allowing us to connect to those beautiful Arcturian guides and Arcturus. It all aligned and connected exactly to what we've been communicating on our YouTube channel and who they are. It's also very important to understand that there is a key for you to get through in order to connect, because there are many negative polarized entities posing, channeling through others as Arcturans.

KyRa: Absolutely. It's disgusting. We are a power against that. We do not consent to that. She resonates that, and she works with her people and tells them, "You do not know who they are

channeling until you get your Higher Self straight and you're in a heart discernment, you cannot subject yourself to this. Quit looking outside!" That's what she says. She embodies that quite well.
A: I love it. Thank you. Wow, what a joy. Is there anything else you wanted to show her about that life?
KyRa: Yes. She can look at this group as her family, they hold her in their hearts. They don't consider her separate. So she indeed has a matrix overlay, if you want to call it, of that beautiful blue energy, and of the crystal Dragons. So, if she can just understand… I'm helping her do that now. It's not so much an identity. It's a kiss of an imprint upon you that calls you family, that loves you, honors you, respects you. It's a bond that cannot be broken. It's a bond of love.

The Body Scan begins.
A: Higher Self can we now begin the body scan?
KyRa: Okay.
A: Higher Self, do you need any assistance from the Archangels before we begin?
KyRa: I just love them. Bring them all in. Let's see… Archangel Uriel, Haniel, and of course, Michael and Metatron.
A: Beautiful. We bring the four there, Michael, Metatron, Haniel and Uriel. It is an honor to have the first four centaurs of creation. We love you, honor you and respect you. If I could please speak to them now.
Angelics: Greetings! We love you. Love, love, love you!
A: Thank you. The goal is by the time we are done with the session, to set her up for her organic blueprint and timeline. If we can now begin her body scan, looking for any negative energies, entities, technologies, where would you like to begin at first?
Angelics: There was that black spike ball above her head. Did you get that? We feel you got that in the R.A.A.H. healing. This is Uriel.
A: Beautiful! Yes, I used a little Phoenix fire.
AA Uriel: That came with the abduction event. She did not perceive it; she's good at looking at her body, but she didn't… she forgot to look up and outside (of the body).
A: Can you tell us, what abduction event did that come in?
AA Uriel: That was that Friday night when she was taken on the ship. Negative polarized Pleiadian Alcyones, Taal Shiar. They dropped a nanobot on her when she was out walking, slipped through the shields; that's why the crystal Dragon - so that won't happen again.
A: Is there anything we need to heal from it? Did it cause any trauma or damage?
AA Uriel: There's a tear in the auric field; they tried to get in… she's remarkably strong.
A: Can we have the four of you now start healing with the Higher Self, KyRa, her auric field from any damage it caused, flooding Love-Light and Phoenix fire that may be needed there. Repairing it to its organic, crystalline formation.
AA Uriel: Yes. Working from the inside layers out now.
A: Let's start the body scan now looking for any negative energies, entities, technologies. Where would you like to begin?
AA Uriel: Rescanning the crown. She's concerned that she's been losing eyelashes.
A: What is the cause of that?

Sacred knowledge is shared in how to eradicate and transmute effects and residues left behind, such as spike protein, by being in the presence of those who have received the Covid-19 Vaccine. Some of these sacred teachings can be found under the A.U.R.A. Hypnosis Healing technique.

A: Is there anything that we need to heal as far as when she went to visit her son and his wife, and how they got the Covid-19 Vaccine?
AA Uriel: Yes, there's heart damage. There's great sadness. So there's holes in the heart. Leaking a little energy there.
A: Can we start healing her heart now and filling in those holes?

AA Uriel: Yes. Let's re-establish the heart-mind connection. Organic in the vibration of the love frequency. Let's do that.
A: Going back to when they abducted her. Why did that happen if she is shielding?
AA Uriel: They ripped the portal in, through her... with the nanobot tracker locator on one of the dogs. She's going to need to purposefully energetically brush everyone off when they come in from the outside, like on a walk. And truth be told Aurora... walking within the crystal Dragons might negate the necessity of that. We're going to have to play with that, with her, and see how that works. So that Dragon can expand and cover the entire family... all of them as they go out and walk, the four of them. Because the crystal Dragons hold them in a dimensional space time that is inviolable. It's like they can't even see it. So tracker bots don't synchronize with it. They can't exist in that bubble of space time. So there's no way for them to embed. They can't be seen when they're around the house when encased by the Celestial Dragons. It's the way they hold dimensions, space-time.
A: Beautiful. Can these Arcturian crystalline dragons encase all the cars, the house, like we talked about now?
AA Haniel: Yes. Oh, yes!
A: Can we include that with the Infinity of crystals of magical creatures shield, can that activate them?
AA Haniel: That's a great suggestion. We recommend that it is done. Yes!
A: Okay, beautiful.
AA Haniel: Absolutely. Oh, that just made the infinity of crystals happy, happy, happy. Look at them! Oh my gosh! They say, "Look at us. See what we can do." Silly things (smiling) they're so pretty.
A: They are! How did they even find her?
AA Uriel: Random chance, and we feel bad. She thinks, we're all knowing. And we are. We are to an extent. Usually she posts us and calls her sacred space. She's been very tired. It's interesting with her, when she's feeling really good and joyful and happy and powerful, sometimes she forgets to do the depth of shielding that she should do. So there's a caution there. Yes. It's not just when you're tired that you must push through and shield, and she's got that down. She does that. But you must remember when you're joyous and happy, and you feel like you're in the fifth dimension, you still live here, you must shield and you must be vigilant. You must post your guards, and you may post us as your guards. We can do that. Truth be told, we have so much faith and joy and love in her. We just let her down. We thought she was going to be okay. We should have seen; we should have been on guard. But we did get KyRa and woke her up. She's doing good with that MerKaBa of hers; she's always asking, "Is my MerKaBa active?" Of course it's active. Yes. It's active. Intend it to be so, it's active. It brought her right back home, and that's how that works Aurora. That's why you work with the MerKaBa. When you find yourself somewhere, whether in dream time, meditation time, or real physical time that you don't want to be, you activate that MerKaBa and it moves you. It takes you to your safe space. Metatron is going to want to talk to you.
AA Metatron: Greetings, Aurora.
A: Greetings Metatron. Love you!
AA Metatron: Love you infinitely, progressively, always.
A: Thank you, brother.
AA Metatron: The MerKaBa is a multi dimensional experience; it's not just three dimensional, although that is what is taught. It's a multi dimensional experience. I have been working with Rene to get her to try and conceptualize the multi-dimensionality of it. She's just now getting what I've been saying to her for the last week or so, about holding that in multidimensionality. She activates her MerKaBa before she sleeps every night. If we could have activated that multidimensional aspect of it. That would have prevented her from that... no portal would have worked. It negates everything. It's massive Aurora. Can you see the field of the MerKaBA?
A: Yes.
AA Metatron: Do you see how it triples its size?
A: Yes. Changes colors.
AA Metatron: Yes. Are you envisioning the balls? The circles of light at the end of the points?
A: No. But I shall!

AA Metatron: Yes, and it's not important about the colors because the colors will vary, shift, change. It's about the dimensional field. So there's a circle on each point. It looks kind of busy, but if you were to stand inside it, it's not busy at all. On a flat plane, it looks busy, but inside it's very expansive.
A: Wow, that's beautiful!
AA Michael: Yes. So here's the other thing with Rene. KyRa is gently bringing her out of fear. And this was an example; and Rene thought it might have to do with this. She was mad at KyRa about this, that she would have this experience and free herself from it to empower herself. So now everybody can laugh about it because truly no harm. Let's talk about those Reptilians you know, those little hijackers, stinkers? They came in and grabbed her, and she knew it right away. I mean, they just grabbed onto her, in the ship, where she was, I'm not even sure the Taal Shiar knew that those were there. Because, you know, those stupid people, let me just say that, they are stupid people. That's all I'm going to say right now about that. They're causing so much harm, but that's okay. It's all going to play out. They decided they were done with the ship, they weren't happy there, and they jumped onto her and came back here. It's not that they wanted to be in her, but she was sure easy game for that moment. They prey on people, this is how they work. They wait for that instant that they can go in, and they did. So what we're going to need to do today in her physical body is, I want to make sure that we fill in that gallbladder space with energy. So there's not a void space in there anymore.
A: Let's start doing that. Now. Can we use some Phoenix fire as well?
AA Michael: Yes, yes.
A: Good. Can we also ask for her new friends from all the crystalline Dragon beings to assist her during this whole healing as well?
AA Michael: They're delighted. Oh, yes. They're right here. They're going to cover her. They're sitting on her right now.
A: Beautiful. Thank you. Other things that she needs healing in, she had her tonsils taken out when she was younger, and then wisdom teeth. Can you scan to see if it needs any healing?
AA Michael: You know, the whole tonsil thing with the kids, these little star seeds that came in, that's taking their voice away. That was what this was about, and it was the infection in the sinuses, all the rods, all that Archon crap, they stuff up the nose. It gets into the sinuses and it infects, and so they guided the doctors to just say, "Well, I'll just take out the tonsils". It's just another block in the throat. It really did nothing. It was a placebo. So Aurora, I'd like to do a multi-generational healing, across time and space now, and heal all children who had that surgery. Let's go there now. I'm taking the Legion of Light with me. We're going to find all those sweet children, those babies that ever had this surgery and we're going to heal them. Give them back their voice right now.
A: Thank you, thank you.
AA Michael: We'll continue with that Aurora, while we work on Rene.
A: Love that.
AA Michael: So as far as that goes, she's regained her voice. Her throat chakra is nice and clear. She's done so much healing, so much awareness. She's so fast! My goodness. This girl started and she just-phew! This is one determined person and it's a good determination. It's not stubborn. It's a powerful determination. Let's look at the sinuses, and heal those. The eyelashes are almost healed. It's the rims of the eyes that get irritated with that spike protein, and the film over the eyes, so I'm going to heal the tear ducts now. Healing the gelatinous material of the eyeballs.
A: Since we're speaking of the spike protein, can you tell us why is it that a lot of women are experiencing miscarriages, it seems like there's an attack to your womb going on.
AA Michael: There's always an attack to the womb going on right now. You nailed it. You had that months ago. Yes. Aurora, we don't want you to cry, but they're trying to insert artificial souls; soulless ones into those fetuses and they're taking the souls out. So let's right now do some healing on that across the mothers of the babies here. We're saying that shall not occur; we're putting up a "Thou shalt not pass" here. Oh! Divine Mother is coming in good and strong right now. Thou shalt not pass...
A: Can I talk to her?
AA Michael: Yes.

A: Divine Mother. Can we all go ahead and delete that and not consent through all time and space by the Divine power the four sacred directions and infinity of creation?
Divine Mother: Absolutely! It's done. It's reverberating out now. Everybody carry it, please have everybody do this. I feel it! I'm holding them all in my womb, healing them all, deleting that monstrosity. And I'm going to push that energy right back at them, ha! Yes, it is done. Thank you Aurora. All women need to do this. All they have to do is call on me, and I'm there. I can give them strength. I can encircle their wombs with my light.
A: Yes. Thank you, mother.
Divine Mother: Yes. Loving you.
A: And I love you.
Divine Mother: Always.
A: Thank you Mother. Should we just continue talking to you to complete the body scan?
Divine Mother: I'd be delighted to stay here. Everybody loves talking with you. So yes, we're all going to take our time. Haha!
A: (Laughing) You make me blush.
Divine Mother: Yes, you need to blush. You need to be blushed and flushed with joy. Oh, let me hold you right now. Giving you a big hug.
A: Oh. Thank you. I feel it, Mother.
Divine Mother: Yes.

The body scan continues, implants removed, her DNA is cleansed and healed... and a few entities are found.

AA Michael: Those Arcturans, they love her. They work with the Procyans, the Ginvo, of planet Maru. These beings love crystals. You would love these beings, Aurora, they make houses out of crystals. They're very good. They're excellent surgeons. And as a gift to her mentor, they protected her as she came in.
A: Let's talk to them.
AA Michael: Let's see if we can bring one of them forward.
A: Higher Self, connect us now to these beautiful beings you speak of.
Being of Maru: I am of Maru.
A: Greetings! We love you, honor you, and respect you.
Being of Maru: Greetings!
A: Thank you. Do you have any messages for beautiful Rene, or any message overall. We especially admire your homes (soft laughter).
Being of Maru: How beautiful this turned out! You love the crystals too! Let me look around. Oh, you ladies do love crystals! Your structure's already changing! You're holding more crystalline light. Oh! You have crystal dragons around you! Wow! All those came from Arcturus, didn't they? Yes, they did. Beautiful, beautiful. We used these beautiful crystal Dragons here as well. We had to step back for a time and shelter our solar system as well. Yes, what can I help you with? I just needed to get a little oriented.
A: Thank you. Can you tell us a little bit more about you, how it is that you work within your star system, how you mentioned you had to step back? Can you explain that further?
Being of Maru: We can also move our star system as a whole inter-dimensionally higher up in resonance to protect ourselves. When we do this, we withdraw all our people from other explorations in third dimensional, fourth dimensional, fifth dimensional space time and bring them home. Not all are happy about this, but it's how we operate. We like all of the essences of us to be together when we have to move like this. So there was a time; it was the last cycle. No, two cycles ago, I'm speaking in your Earth time, it was five cycles of time ago. Twenty-two... what are your words (for this measure)? It was 250,000 years ago when we had to step back. That's when the Archons came through our space. We were ill prepared, so we just left. We are sorry. But it allowed us time to regroup. And we are much more effective now in being of assistance, and we are back. Yes. What else would you like to know?

A: Thank you for sharing that. I know, a couple of years ago, they showed me how there were planets and star systems that weren't able to assist Earth because they themselves, like you said, had to pull back. So there were only certain star systems that were able to hold on to Earth and continue assisting anchoring it.

Being of Maru: Yes. I would say two thirds of us left. And understand now that three fourths of us are back, if that makes sense to you.

A: Yes.

Being of Maru: Some will not come back. And that's fine. They're holding up third dimensional space for us.

A: Good. Thank you for that.

Being of Maru: When the Mother Phoenix calls, we answer. She's here. This will end here.

A: That is such a gigantic shift from a couple years ago when I looked into that.

Being of Maru: Absolutely.

A: That's a glorious update, thank you.

Being of Maru: Yes! Do you know that the Mother Phoenix has a twin Universe?

A: No. Tell me. What can you share about that?

Being of Maru: Are you familiar with twin flames?

A: Yes.

Being of Maru: She has a twin flame. Perfect resonance to hers. I'm not sure I can share too much, but that twin flame may present itself. In just the right time, to seal the deal; to seal the Universes.

A: I understand. Thank you.

Being of Maru: You're welcome. She's beautiful. We love to ride her. Infinitely beautiful. Infinite expression. We are allowed such infinite expression within this, this body of this being. As we love our families, she loves us. It is that same way we treat our families- sacred. Know that we are sacred to her. You are sacred to her. She will keep the sacred.

A: Beautiful. Thank you. As you can see my home. I think it looks pretty close to a crystal home, I think (soft laughter).

Being of Maru: Let me take a quick look, here I'm going to jump over. Oh my! We encourage you to buy as many big crystals as you can Aurora. Big crystals.

A: Thank you for that. Any other crystal wisdom you can share with us?

Being of Maru: Yes, grow them. Plant them in your yard, plant them next to other rocks, little chips and bits and nuggets. This is how you can grow Earth; let's give Earth back some beautifully healed crystals.

A: Love that!

Being of Maru: Plant them. Put them about; scatter them into the sun and let the RA rays come in. Let them be amplified. So, as you coat your homes in them, coat outside in them. We, the Ginvo, are going to gift to you some special crystals etherically, upon your lands. I'm going to talk about that with my people. We would love to bring more crystals to Earth. She has been hard hit; from Tiamat the once great beauty she was, and then fractalizing down to this, which is still beautiful, but she lost some crystals. She hurts from that. She has recovered, but she hurts, there is a resonance.

A: Thank you; continue to guide us through our journey of obtaining the crystals for the healing of Ascension collectively and individually. We humbly thank you. Is there anything else that you'd like to share with her before we talk back to her Higher Self?

Being of Maru: We're extremely pleased at how well she took care of this vessel. We thank her so much. She exemplifies what our work can do. Her immune system is so strong. She only puts on organic materials. She only uses organic body creams. She's very careful, and she honors that vessel like that. I suggest you all bathe in crystalline shower heads, there's many ways to find them; she has some. Or you could hang crystals in your shower. I'm extremely happy to have helped my friend, Rene's Arcturian Mentor, and to have helped this one thrive in this life. It's a very extreme, hard situation you all have to live in right now. We're happy to have helped. I'm going to take this knowledge back with me now. We are scientists and we will be helpful with this knowledge in the future for you here on Earth. We promise you.

A: Wonderful, thank you! It was an honor to have met you and thank you for your great wisdom and shares on crystals. Love you, honor you, respect you.
Being of Maru: You too, sister.
A: Thank you. Can I speak back to her Higher Self and all the beautiful Archangels who are assisting with her healing?
KyRa: I'm here. Yes, Metatron, the Divine Mother and Divine Father are very happy. They're still kind of busy looking inside right now. Michael would like us to take care of the knee, it is almost...

Rene's team completes the entire body scan and the healing that comes with it.

A: There was also some kind of connection to Grays and 144 of them, Rene's Reiki teacher tried to tell her about. What's that about?
KyRa: Yeah, that Gray tried to convince her that he was a rebel gray and on the side of the good. That was fiction, totally fiction. She did see the hybrids they are producing. The 144 is used throughout cycles of humanity as a sacred number, as you know. So they like to grab any of those sacred numbers and use them for their purposes. Here's the thing, they can't invert 144, so they just lie about it and say, oh, here we are, we are the 144, so we're good. That's a lie. That's not true. So her Reiki master, she came to find out, is compromised. Just the way things are, she no longer sees her. And she's been cleansed of any infringements that came from that association. And that's okay, that's just how stuff happens here. You learn and grow, and then you leave, and you go to your next higher group, up where you resonate to, that's the evolution. That's the spiral of life. And this is an example of it right here in 3D. You spiral up and out of old relationships, up and into new relationships. It's very organic.
A: Thank you for that. Higher Self, I've asked all the questions that she had and conducted the body scan, is there anything else that I could have asked that I haven't?
KyRa: We are complete.
A: Beautiful! I want to thank all the beautiful beings that assisted today of all kinds. Thank you beautiful Higher Self. You are loved. Thank you for bringing such a beautiful soul to my attention. I am ecstatic that she is helping us practice A.U.R.A. Hypnosis and R.A.A.H. Reiki. I think people will be blessed with her.
KyRa: I am ecstatic that she found you, that you came and were available. You're everything I wanted for her and you're everything I want for humanity. Thank you Aurora, much love, honor and respect to you. Kissing and hugging you now.
A: Thank you, love you, honor you and respect everyone, my infinite love to everyone.

For every A.U.R.A. Hypnosis healing session we ask that the Higher Self and team ensure to remove and heal this entire list from the clients Tree of Life: entities (Grays, Mantis, Reptilians, Archons...), dark portals, repair and crystallize DNA, negative cords, technologies (implants, metals, hooks, wires, nano, vaccines), Illnesses, vision, dental health, regrow teeth, age regress 5-15 years, blocked or misaligned chakras, open-up the third eye and activate abilities, expand heart, issues with auric field, fractured soul, contracts, deletion of inverted timelines, and trauma from current or past life.

END OF SESSION

Through this session we learned of the true divine power of the Celestial Dragons. All our lives, through programming in literature, movies, and media, we are told that Dragons are just fairy tales, make-believe, or that we are to slay the dragon. In religion the Catholic church has sculpted images and statues where Archangel Michael with his sword is stabbing the devil who is often shown in the shape of a dragon. Beginning from childhood, movies and books, they replay this false narrative over and over to us, how the Dragon is an enemy, that we should fear their strength, when instead we should be embracing their strength, as we had prior to the dissension of Earth. This is dark sorcery at its finest. Once more such a subliminal way that they use us to cast their dark spells upon the collective of the dragons. This book will play a gigantic role in healing and repairing the relationship between humankind, dragons, and magical creatures. Through this session we began the journey in discovering who truly are these magnificent magical beings. With the chapters to come we collectively will begin to heal the unhealed wounds between humans and the magical creatures. Ultimately the goal being, as mentioned through Chapter 2, that we remember the key - that the dragons are to our collective Ascension.

There are an infinite amount of dragons, as they are the elements of creation. The elements of nature or the periodic table of Earth, but in the Universe there is no limit of the potentials of elements that the dragons are the embodiment of. Creation is an alchemy, when we combine elements, together they create a creation. Like when we make a meal, there are ingredients we use to make that meal. The elements/dragons represent the ingredients to a meal per this example. This is a simple way you can understand alchemy at its root. Dragons can represent an element on its own, or the combination of many elements, as individual or collective consciousnesses of Dragons.

How do Celestial Dragons fit into the elements who are the dragons? The Celestial Dragons are at the highest in vibration, consciousness, and essence, as they are the element of what gives life to all. They are the plasmic frequency blankets that fill into all creation in order to create. They are the embodiment of the Universes. Which is why the Celestial Dragons had the divine power to be able to assist the Arcturians, lifting them into a higher dimensional plane where they would be undetectable. The Celestial Dragons created the plane of existence itself for this collective of star consciousnesses, the Arturians, to take shelter within.

September 5, 2020, on YouTube, I channeled the Arcturian race, where they began to explain how they were one of the races who were able to remain holding onto Earth energetically, and how they were protected. The Archons have been looking for collective consciousnesses spread throughout our Universe who are responsible for channeling Love-Light to us, those who even the fall of Atlantis did not stop them from holding onto us through energetic cords, so that the Love-Light within Earth would not dim into extinction. The Archons would like to sever these benevolent alien races' connection to Earth, so that it can have an easier reign. However, the Archons have not been able to find all of these benevolent races, so still our brethren hold on, but it is because of the true divine power of the Celestial Dragons and many others.

This A.U.R.A. session explained this further for us, in how this was obtainable for the Arturians. When the fall of Atlantis on Earth occurred from the fifth dimension into the third dimension, some alien races could no longer hold onto us energetically, therefore they needed to disconnect from Earth. As the Archon virus began to spread, they had to cut cords from us, as we do from people when they are unbalanced or too negatively polarized. Because the lower vibrational being who is compromised with the A.I. virus becomes that to us, as a virus that spreads and tries to attach to us. This is what Earth became to all benevolent collective soul groups who were part of assisting us, and connected to us through the universal cosmic crystalline webbing. This was a hard choice to make for these beings, and we can compare this decision to when we have to remove people from our life who we love, or once loved. Ultimately, it is one of the most selfless acts, which allows for who you are releasing to go about their free will decisions, making it easier for us to do the same for ourselves.

Since December 21st, 2021, because of the further dilation of the bifurcation, I was told by these benevolent beings who once could not hold on to the collective of Earth, that they are now back, because collectively the light on Earth has reached the sufficient Love-Light for them to connect to us once more. They can connect through the divine process of the bifurcation of Earth, from the side of the organic fifth dimension of the Vesica Pisces. Before this date the third dimension inverted matrix of the Vesica Pisces was more of the majority, and now it is not. In other words the organic Earth within the bifurcation of our two/third worlds holds a stronger light by the people, than the A.I. darkness holds in the third dimensional Earth. This is gigantic for our Earth's collective because it will allow more of a potence of Love-Light energy to be channeled down to us through the reconnection of our higher dimensional brethren, creating huge shifts in our Earth's construct, humankind's awakening, and ascension process.

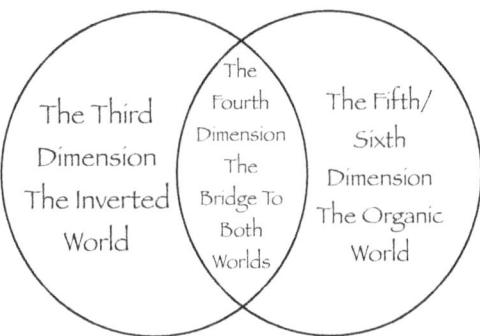

I remember in my awakening stages receiving communications, that some of the alien races who held on to Earth Energetically, were found out and wiped out by the Archons. When communicating with others, all of us felt a deep heaviness and sorrow in our hearts that day, like something really bad had happened. It was a feeling that one could not stop crying, but knew not of what the heavy sadness was. At times it is hard for us to recall in the moment these universal memories, being in this lower vibration of the third dimension. This is why we don't hear many names of the alien races assisting the Earth, the most common ones being the Arcturians, Andromeden's, Pleidian's...Because to name themselves would be to out themselves. However times are changing now, as they are back, and this group will continue to grow now that it has begun.

Rene's Higher Self shared with us of the tracker bots who had found her when hiking, because she had lowered her vibration for it to detect her. I have been shown more about these bots, and what the Earth looks like in the [20]inverted Matrix, and in Book 3 we will go further in depth into this topic.

Divine Mother spoke to us of the Archon's inverted plan to insert hybrid or artificial souls into the babies within the wombs of the mothers of Earth. There is a divine plan unfolding which will continue to grow in strength as we continue to speak of this attempted infringement and transhumanism upon humankind. [21]In fact we have been covering this very important topic through our live streams since the beginning of the Covid-19 virus and vaccine rollout. We are now seeing scientists through 'the world of science' begin to make artificial wombs, and we know that they will try to introduce to mothers that merging their eggs into a petri dish with, or without, a partner's sperm will be a convenience, or a normal choice for them. Together collectively we will have to watch this negative New World Order agenda closely, to ensure this timeline does not come to be, taking hold of the sacredness of natural organic childbirth on Earth. In the next chapters we address this most important subject further in strong awareness to protect the children of our Earth

The mention of how our Universe 'The Phoenix,' has a twin flame who is in perfect resonance to hers, and that this twin flame Universe may present themselves in just the right time, to seal the deal; to seal the Universes. This is directly linked to what we spoke of in the previous chapters of the final bifurcation of Earth, and specifically the final eradication of the Archon/artificial intelligence. It seems as if the Universes will come together in sacred union to completely wipe all artificial intelligence hidden

---

[20] Watch 'Remote Viewing the Inverted Matrix' located in all our channels for more on this topic now.
[21] To stay current with all Rising Phoenix Aurora content ensure that you join us every Friday, as AuroRa delivers live transmissions on her public platforms. All current galactic updates of these types of sensitive content is found under Rising Phoenix Aurora's Rumble.com, Odysee.com, and Spotify channels.

throughout all time and space when the final collective Ascension comes to be. Towards the end of this book, we will share a glimpse with you of what this treasured day we all have been waiting for will be like.

"You are the Dragon and the Dragon is you"
~AuroRa

---<<>>---

13

LAB BABIES

Session #469: Recorded in June 2022
Never before shared.

In this online A.U.R.A. Hypnosis Healing session, Aurora is hosting a live online workshop, certifying new A.U.R.A. Hypnosis and R.A.A.H. Reiki Healing practitioners. One of the days of the training, the students' names are placed into a bowl where the name of who will be chosen to have an A.U.R.A. Hypnosis Healing session is chosen. This person has their A.U.R.A. session conducted live by Aurora for training purposes in front of the group of attendees. Those who have been chosen in past Workshop/Retreats describe it as winning the lottery! This is one of these very special sessions chosen in 2022, to be part of collectively healing this most important topic of the children of Earth. Mary is the chosen one, and she assists us deeply in understanding the infringements occurring within sacred birthing, and the infertility of Earth. We must protect the children of Earth through all forms, beginning from before they are born, conception, in their gestation, and through their sacred natural birth. The purity of the souls being birthed into babies, and how important it is that we maintain and support this collective mission. Truly the number one mission of the Earth's collective is to save the children of all types of tried infringements.

"Keep doing the shields, keep believing. You know they work. Keep calling your dragons. You know that when you ask your dragons to be present, to help not just physically, but etherically and energetically, that they will."
~Higher Self

M: [Mary] I'm at my old house in Hawaii. I'm playing in the backyard.
A: [Aurora] *Beautiful. Tell me what it's like being there?*
M: She likes to use words that are natural to her, but you might not understand them because they are part of the language she grew up with. It is called *Mana*. There's a lot of *Mana* here in the backyard. There's a lot of spiritual energy here. Lots of it. It's very strong. (In this session Mary and her Higher Self speak back and forth through the past life regression portion. Which is why you hear her address herself as a third-party sometimes.)
A: *Look at yourself. Tell me, what do you look like? Do you feel like you have a body?*
M: I feel like I'm a child again. I'm the little girl here in the backyard playing by myself.
A: *What are you doing?*
M: I was picking my mom's strawberries. That makes her so upset because it's hard to grow strawberries here, but I don't care. I pick them anyway because I like to pick and play with her plants. So I break the flowers and I sometimes put them in my little bucket.
A: *Keep moving the scene along. Tell me what happens next of importance.*
M: I'm sitting by the side of the house and I'm talking to myself. I'm looking at the flowers that I broke, and I have them in the bucket. I have the special soil, it's so powerful. It's not as strong as it used to be due to the pineapple fields in the backyard, because she lives right next to the pineapple

fields. This soil has not as much contamination as the pineapple fields. I'm just rubbing the red dirt all over my hands so it can stain my hands, and stain my feet. I need my hands stained. They need to be red.

A: Is the soil red?

M: Yes. I miss it. The soil here in Hawaii is so beautiful. It's so red. If you look at it just right it glows or just sparkles in the sun. Yes, it's red and it's beautiful.

A: You mentioned that there was some kind of toxin. Can you explain that? What do you mean by that?

M: The pineapple and sugarcane fields. They're all over. Her parents chose a house surrounded by pineapple and sugarcane fields. She sees the big yellow trucks driving through spraying the pineapples. It's not water, it's pesticides. That makes her heart sad because she sees the workers in the pineapple field, and some of them have their children on their backs. They get exposed to these pesticides and it's heartbreaking. It gets into the soil and the water. Her family knows this. Her family has been affected by the water and by the soil.

A: Thank you. Tell me what happens next of importance.

M: A lady is murdered and her body is thrown in the gulch between her parents' house and the pineapple fields. It's on the news. It's in the newspaper. The reporters came knocking on my mom's door and they asked my mom how she feels about a lady being found basically in our backyard. She was brutalized. I think the lady's spirit is lost there because I feel like she comes into the house and she attaches herself to Mary. Mary knows this and it's why she gets nightmares.

A: Tell me what happens next of importance.

M: We have a lot of rain. It's hurricane season. Mary loves the rain and the thunder. It excites her and sometimes scares her, but she likes it. She likes to hear the rain pounding on the roof because it's so soothing. There's a tapping at the window. Somebody's tapping on the window.

A: Who is it?

M: The lady who died.

A: What does she want?

M: I think she just wants me. I can't really see her. I can feel her. I'm too short to see out the window. I'm little. She's just tap, tap, tap, tap, tapping on the window. I think she's just trying to scare me, to make the thunderstorms scary for me.

A: How's the lady look?

M: She has long hair. I feel like she's *Kanaka*. She's indigenous, but not just that. She's possibly Filipino and she's mixed. She's got a bunch of other ethnicities in her. So she's brown. Her hair is long, maybe up to her shoulders, and her eye is busted and her head is kinda beat up looking because she was beaten up pretty badly. She looks lost.

A: How does that make you feel to see this lady like that?

M: Scared and sad. Sad for what had happened to her. Sad that so many women have to experience trauma like this, and because of this trauma sometimes they get stuck and they need help. I think my mom sees her too, and my mom eventually just tells her to go. That she can't be here anymore; she needs to go.

A: What happens? Does she go?

M: She does. Well, she stays outside the fence outside of the property and she hangs out there. That's why my mom doesn't like me going into the gulch to the pineapple fields. She doesn't want me going through there. I believe she waits for me.

A: Why does she wait for you?

M: I think that she just wants to talk to me, like she's lonely, or something like that.

A: Do you talk to her?
M: I try not to because I'm not supposed to. I'm not supposed to talk to spirits I see. So I don't talk to her. I try not to. I pretend she's not there.
A: Does your mother know that you can talk to spirits?
M: Yes, and it makes her scared because she can see them too, and she doesn't know how to handle them. She doesn't know how to navigate her realm, and our land has so much Mana that my mom also unintentionally attracts things. My mom would rather be the one being attacked than me being attacked.
A: Let's go to another important time where we will find answers that we seek for your highest healing. We're there now. Tell me what you see and sense.
M: I'm sick. I have pneumonia. They had me leave the hospital, but all my hair is falling out and I'm at home. I'm vomiting from the medicine. I'm begging my mom not to give me the medicine because it makes me vomit, and it's making my hair fall out more. So she stops giving me the medicine. She refuses to give it to me anymore. I'm very sick.
A: What happened? How did you get sick?
M: Somebody who was mad at my mom. They tried to put a curse on her. My mom is strong and it reflected off of her. When it did, it ricocheted and it flew right into me, and it hit me hard. I fell to the ground. I got very sick.
A: Do you think that your mother knows that there was a curse tried on her since she is connected?
M: Yes, she was told. A *Kahuna* lady, an old Hawaiian lady, grabbed my mom by the hand and told my mom, "Your daughter is sick because of your mother-in-law. You kicked your mother-in-law out of your house, and she's very, very upset with you." The mother-in-law is strong and has strong ill-intentions. It went straight for my mom and it flew into the innocent child by accident.
A: Move the scene along. Do you end up getting better?
M: Yes. My mom finds another *Kahuna*, he comes to the property and he helps me get better. He helps set stronger boundaries around the property. My mom already did some, but his is stronger to help keep more things out, including any ill-intentions from the grandmother and the natural Spirits, the natural *Mana* that is here around the home. So now they travel around the property and no longer through the property. The spirits aren't too happy about it because this is the route that they take for the sacred birthing of the Hawaiian people in Hawaii, because this home is near the beautiful stones that stand today where the sacred births take place. So they kind of interfered with it. Sometimes they get a little bit upset and when they get upset they like to pound their drums loud at Mary, and she can hear it. She can hear the drums.
A: Let's go ahead and move the scene along to another point in time and space.
M: Mary is almost close to moving. She's at her school field trip that just so happens to be at the stones where they give birth. I'm not allowed to touch the stones, these beautiful stones. Mary can't help herself, she touches them anyway, and it feels beautiful. When she does she gets glimpses of people surrounding the area, and birth happening at night with the fire, the torches, the women and children. It's beautiful here. She likes it here. Every time she comes back home she has to drive by this place and she stops and looks, but she doesn't go and touch it. She gets sad of the desecration that place has been facing over the years because people don't listen, and people stand on it and they disrespect the place. It's a powerful place. This place has given birth to Kings, to the Monarch.
A: Let's go ahead and move to another important time where we will find answers that we seek for your highest healing. We are there now. Tell me what's going on next.
M: We move to America. We don't like to call Hawaii a part of America. Mary is not *Kamaka* or Kanaka Maoli, but she identifies there with the *Kanakas*. She moves from Hawaii and she's excited in

the beginning. She's excited to be in Washington in the beginning because it's something new, but the darkness of being in the Pacific Northwest is a bit overwhelming. Sometimes the darkness feels unnatural. She wonders if it's real. If the clouds are real. Why is it so dark and cold and damp?

A: Why did you have to move to the Americas from Hawaii?

M: My parents were struggling financially. I never saw my parents. It was rare. Well, I saw them in the afternoons, is when I saw them. We were struggling and with that struggle I didn't get the opportunity to build a close relationship with my siblings like I should have. We also needed to go because we needed to get away from my grandfather and my grandmother on my mother's side.

A: Why did you need to get away from them?

M: They are not nice. My grandfather slapped my mom in front of us. He's very angry with her. My grandma is not nice either. I've always tried to help take care of her because I always felt like that's what I'm supposed to do, is help do things for her, be nice, but it is very noticeable that she does not like children. They, in particular, do not like my brother and I. They like my sister, but they do not like my brother and I. They hate us.

A: Why do you think that is?

M: It's our skin color. Because we tan easily. We normally have beautiful brown skin and we look like my father. Truth be told, they're just evil. My sister is easier to manipulate, I guess. My grandmother and grandfather, they're both very evil. It's like my grandmother has something else inside of her. She's done some horrible things, and I've learned more about them as I've gotten older.

A: What kind of horrible things has she done?

M: She abused my mom severely. When my mom tells me these stories, I see my grandma transform, and her eyes change. I don't like to see it, but her eyes change. They're not normal anymore. My grandma used to be this beautiful Japanese lady, but when my mom tells me these stories, she transforms, and I can see it. As I get older, I can see it more clearly, of who she really is.

A: You're able to see her true form. What is she really?

M: She's so gross. I don't mean to say that because I guess it's disrespectful, but her eyes are kind of greenish-yellow and I just learned the proper word for it. It's like the slit in the eyes. She just reminds me of a freaking lizard, and this is exactly why growing up I didn't like the geckos. I would grab them and throw them out the window, out the door, and when they're stupid tails break I would freak out because the tails would squirm in my hands. I would scream, but I didn't like the geckos because they reminded me of my grandmother and her tongue, her disgusting tongue.

A: Let's see what happens next of importance.

M: My grandfather, he died. We are at his burial. I'm sad even though he didn't treat me right. I'm sad because of the music playing. They're doing the twenty-one gun salute and playing the bugle. I'm just sad, not because he's dead. I'm actually quite thankful he's out of pain. The remainder of his life he was in pain, so I'm happy he's been released of that. I'm sad of the music and still sad today when I hear it because it reminds me of all the men and women who have died from the Military, from War, from exposure to things. Just the unknowing of the true reasons why they passed. So it makes me sad. I'm sitting here in the cemetery and looking at all these headstones and the rows, and rows, and rows of them, and knowing that they did not have to die in the way they did. They just didn't, and the majority of them should have died a more peaceful death. They earned it despite the fact that they were fooled. They should have died a more respectful and peaceful death.

A: Let's go ahead and leave the scene. Let's go to another important time where we will find further answers that we seek. You are there now. Tell me what you see and sense.

M: Mary is in the delivery room. She is giving birth to that... she calls him a sterile baby. She purposely doesn't know his name. She knows that she can spell it. She doesn't like to though. She's there. She's giving birth to this baby, and her normal doctor isn't there because her normal doctor did not believe her that she has fast labors, so this other man came into the room. As soon as she sees him she's like, "Dear God, not him, not this one. Not this one!"

A: Why not this one?

M: He has ill-intentions with all the women who come into this hospital. He lacks compassion. Despite what is verbally said, and written, he will go against anything and everything. His main mission is just to pull the baby out. That's what he just likes. He likes to hold the babies. Pull the babies out. Mary knew this because at her previous pregnancy with her daughter, her second born, her daughter just wasn't moving as much as she usually did, and when she went to the doctors to make sure the baby was fine the doctor got angry with her and he basically said that she was stupid. He belittled her and said that she should have come sooner if she was genuinely concerned. In her head, Mary prefers to cuss about him, but in her head she's basically said he was an effing idiot. That his one mission here on Earth is to harm the babies that come out and harm the mothers. Which is why originally for the surrogate birth, Mary wanted to do a home birth, but she knew because the birth parents had faced so much trauma of trying to conceive that it wasn't going to be possible. So to keep both parties safe, and I guess happy, Mary agreed to a hospital birth. Here comes this man inside, and I swear to God, he's got like a tail that hangs beneath his stupid white coat that he tries to have long to the ground to hide it, but it's there. His tail is there and it's horrible to look at.

A: You mentioned that he likes to hold babies, that's why he likes to work with mothers and babies. Why do you think he likes to hold babies?

M: He likes to hold them first. The reason why he does this is because his hands have portals. Bits of him come out of his hands and they go into the poor babies. They go into them, and then the baby is then handed off to the nurses and the nurses clean them out. The nurses are just as bad because they're not awakened. Some of them are such beautiful beings, but they're not awakened. They need to see who they truly are because they're not meant to be assisting births in a hospital. They are meant to be assisting births at home, or even Birthing Inns for the women who aren't capable of giving birth at home for whatever reason. Maybe, let's say, they're homeless, or they live on the streets. So they should be allowed to give birth in a Birthing Inn, and the nurses should be there instead of at a hospital. I will say after Mary gave birth to this boy she felt so much relief that her contract was done. She physically felt this contract done. When the birth mother walks in and sees her baby that she was trying to have for so long and sees the joy on her face, that was enough to just seal the deal, seal the contract. It is done, and she had mentally and physically tried to essentially wash her hands clean of the deed she did.

A: Beautiful. Thank you.

M: I feel like I have something to add about this. It's been coming to Mary in bits and pieces, but it makes her feel guilty because she acted upon this. She was a surrogate and took part in this. After she gave birth she started to gain more knowledge about the surrogacy. It was part of her psychosis that she went through, kind of like a dark night of the soul. The part of the psychosis she was going through, she was getting bits and pieces about how the surrogacy is unfortunately a business. There really, truly, are people out there who need help because their womb space has been so damaged. Mary is scared to share this, of what she found out. She does not want to get reprimanded. She doesn't want me to share it, but I think this goes to you, Aurora, which is why I've been steering her to you for so long. She finally got the message. When she had her one-on-one with you, you've both talked about sacred births. When she was taking your courses, all the things came up and started making more sense for her. So she and I have been waiting for you. So, I will just say this surrogacy, a lot of it is a business, which you know, you know this. It's about money. Unfortunately, now, what is not known, but what is also starting to become more of light within the surrogacy community is that... she's scared I'm going to say the country's name, but China has a lot of people seeking surrogates in other countries, a lot. Now, there's other countries that are seeking surrogacies as well. The United States does a primary portion of the surrogacies. China, because of everything that has happened with pollution, contamination, a lot of the men and women cannot properly conceive children. They can't do it. The potential parents, they come to America, and they actually live here for a bit. They take their medications and everything to have the egg and sperm from the mother and father to be put together to create viable embryos. The eggs get stored and then the intended potential parents go back to China. There they go and they wait. It's like a lottery system. They wait and they wait, and then ding! Just like that, somebody like Mary agrees to be a surrogate. Now Mary has always wanted to be a surrogate. This idea came from her mom. I'm not saying her mom told her to do it, but her mom wanted to be a surrogate for her Aunt. Anyway, that's beside the point. She's always wanted to be a surrogate. She wanted to be a surrogate for a friend, or a loved one, but none could afford the medical treatments that they needed to be able to produce a viable egg or sperm. They couldn't afford it. Because our phones and everything are always listening... right? They're always listening. They heard the conversations Mary had with her husband about wanting to help her sister-in-law, who is a lesbian and cannot have children of her own. So ads started popping up on Mary's phone that you could get paid to do this. Mary's husband at the time wasn't making enough money to support them. They were relying on food assistance, and that was due to the debt that he incurred while single, and being young and very stupid. That's how Mary became a surrogate. She did it, to not only help the family who needed it, but to help her family financially; to get them out of debt so her kids can eat. So it was good for both parties. So anyway, back to China.

The Higher Self is called forth.
A: Thank you. Higher Self, I just want to welcome you. I know you've been talking and I didn't want to interrupt you. So thank you for being here already. I love you, honor you, and respect you. You may continue. Go ahead with China.
Higher Self: China, envision like a swarm of people coming to the U.S. to have their babies because China has purposely not allowed these people to have babies. This also goes with the fact that for years and years, they were only allowed one child. Because of that it energetically damaged their wombs. So that was the goal, because it's part of their plan. They're having the babies here in the U.S., and then after the babies are born, like the baby Mary gave birth to, the baby goes back to China, where they get dual citizenship. Now this dual citizenship is very important, because this baby can come back and forth. Now, it's not set in stone, as you know, what's going to happen. You had talked about it, and it's forever changing. There's infinite possibilities of what's going to happen. China's intent, and the negatively polarized beings' intent, is to basically keep spreading the negativity around and keeping the Earth dense. So, I can't fully decipher what they're trying to do. It's key to know about this dual citizenship. It's partly why Mary had to go through this, because it's part of her journey, and learn it, because she needed to meet you in divine timing because you are in the works of doing sacred birth training for others. You needed to know all these other little bits and pieces about birth and surrogacy, the industry behind it. How potentially damaging it can be, but we can't waver. We can't be worried about it because we don't want to instill fear in others. They're not going to win, as we know, they're not. The people in China and these children, these babies, I'm not fully certain what's going to happen. I know Mary is slightly hesitant that the boy will want to seek her out. The parents have not told him yet, and they probably will not. The boy, he will find out. Mary doesn't know this, but she took photos of her being pregnant to help make it real for her, and to help

the son think that he came from her womb. He's going to know because he's going to discover that he and Mary had a contract of sorts, which is why he wasn't fully inside of her when she was pregnant. It was so they both would not energetically really attach to each other; there will be some, but not fully, not like mother and son. It was also for her protection to help clean and cut cords. Cut the contract so the parents cannot seek her out afterwards, and the Government of China cannot seek her out.

A: Did the child come out of Chinese heritage?

Higher Self: Yes. He did not look like her at all. I mean, her babies do come out looking Asian just because Mary is part Japanese, and her father is Asian. So her babies do look Asian, but this Asian baby you could tell was fully Chinese. She prayed greatly before meeting him. She didn't meet him until the next day. When she met him she was actually, it's horrible to say, disgusted. I think she's mostly disgusted at the process of how he was born, because all babies are beautiful, right? They're all pure, but she knows because he was made in a lab that he is slightly different. She felt nothing for him. She held him to be polite, to be respectful. She could not wait to get him out of her arms and to go home. I was anxious for her to go home too, so she could start healing her womb space, and so I could start giving her the information that she needed to know.

A: Why was it a contract, Higher Self, with this child?

Higher Self: Because she needed to provide him a safe space to be born into. He needed somewhere to be born, and Mary is pure. She used to consume wine, but after a while she stopped and she doesn't smoke. Although she kind of did a little bit, she doesn't like the feeling it gave her. So she was just pure enough and he needed somewhere safe. Ultimately, Mary needed more of a catapult, I should say, to give birth at home. To finally do it, and give birth at home because her other baby was waiting for her.

A: Is this baby different, because they made it in a lab?

Higher Self: Without the intended potential parents' consent, yes, he is made differently. Quite definitely. From the parents' knowledge, it was just supposed to be, just their egg, and their sperm. Just, put the one into the other, boom! There you go. There's your embryo. It's the mixture that they put in the egg and embryo, which is contaminated. I see it infusing inside with the embryo, with the egg simultaneously as the sperm is going in. Whatever it is, I can't decipher what it is. Whatever it is in that fluid is going inside at the exact same time as the sperm. All of this, even without the intended potential parents' information, the Government knows about this. They know everything about this particular embryo. So when they do it, they have several embryos. The parents pick the most viable. Sometimes there's only one, sometimes there's maybe three viable. Regardless of how many viable eggs there are, the Chinese Government knows exactly the embryo's Higher Self, Spirit Guides, past lives, everything. Basically like Akashic records of each viable embryo. The Government knows which one is selected and then placed into the surrogate. So yes, he's different.

A: The main reason why they know is because they are able to retrieve the DNA from the embryo before?

Higher Self: I feel like there's technology that is in that liquid, but we can't see it. The technology somehow goes in. Plus, the parents do a huge amount of blood work prior. The embryo gets tested to see how viable it is. It's this testing with how viable this egg is, is how they find out.

A: So obviously they're literally trying to create a sperm with an egg and then they make an embryo. The natural fluid would be within a mother's womb, her natural fertilization, right?

Higher Self: Exactly.

A: So this fluid is definitely not a part of a mother because they're doing it artificially.

Higher Self: Correct. It's unnatural. They try to make it as natural as possible, I guess you could say, but it's just not. It's not something that the people who work at the fertility clinic know. They don't consciously know that this is going on. Because obviously, if everybody consciously knew what's going on, there'd be a riot, right? We'd be so upset. But they don't know. They just think that they're doing a good deed and they're not.

A: *One of the practitioners is asking if this would also pertain to in-vitro fertilization of eggs and sperm, the IVF. Would that be the same type of consistency?*

Higher Self: What I'm getting is that if it's more like husband and wife, and they're putting the viable embryo back into the mother, the Angels come and they try to cleanse and heal what has happened. That's what they try to do. They do the best they can because there was no ill intent - for the most part. We can't say one hundred percent because there's always that one percent possibility that is ill-intent. But because it's a positive intent, to grow their family, to have children, to love each other and grow, the Angels, they do their best to heal them. Sometimes these in-vitros, the embryos, don't stick, and the reason why is because the Angels weren't able. They said, "No, we can't. This one is too compromised, and we just can't. We will have to try again." Not like, try again with another bad one, obviously. They would like the parents to wait, see if they can conceive naturally, which can still happen sometimes. If they do the in-vitro again, the Angels will come in again, and try to heal the embryo that was made in a lab. Does that make sense?.

A: *You completely make sense.*

Higher Self: Sometimes when Mary talks her accent comes out. I am having a hard time deciding in which way I want to talk (chuckles) with an accent, or without an accent.

A: *Yes. No worries. Thank you. So, in both perspectives they're putting it together in a lab regardless.*

Higher Self: Yes. That fluid is still there.

A: *I can feel that. Like the embryo and how that soaks into them. Wow.*

Higher Self: Yes. The love of the parents can be so strong. Their desire can be so strong to finally have this baby when they've maybe had miscarriage after miscarriage, or are suffering from PCOS (polycystic ovarian syndrome), that their love is what helps heal that embryo that was made in the lab and then placed into their womb space.

A: *Beautiful. Would you say that this has any correlation to the hybridization program? Since this is what they want to do is change the consistency of the human race. Is that something that they're doing with this?*

Higher Self: Yes, it's another form. It's sickening, but it's just another desperate attempt because it's not going to work. There's so many other Light beings that are waiting to come in and be in the womb. They're not going to win because we need those beautiful babies for these Light beings. These Light beings are meant to come in. So it's just another desperate attempt that's going to fail.

A: *This doctor that was a negative Reptile being you mentioned, was he part of the surrogacy?*

Higher Self: No. He just reaches out to the community because there's a lot of babies that get born here. It's kind of like a military county. I don't want to say city because there is only one birthing hospital for an entire county. So people travel thirty, forty, fifty minutes away to give birth at this hospital. So he knows he can get his hands on more babies.

A: *Does this doctor work for the military?*

Higher Self: No, he is a civilian doctor at the hospital here. The military hospital here no longer has babies being born there.

A: *The only reason why I asked is sometimes we're told that some hospitals are just undercover military bases, military hospitals. A lot of the doctors could be military, so that's why I asked that.*

Higher Self: No. So, I will say this hospital is part of the CHI Medical System, which is the Catholic Health Institute. Maybe I can't remember what the "I" stands for, but it is part of the Catholic Church. They have been bought out. The Catholic Church has been working to purchase this hospital for quite some time. This doctor has been there for quite some time as well.

A: *Thank you for all that information. So, take us to an example that you think is best of a child that went through this process of surrogacy, or through this process of creating babies in a lab. Are there any parents that weren't able to heal their children, for example, maybe they didn't have enough love or for whatever reason. Can you tell me an example of a person on Earth that was part of this, that wasn't able to perhaps heal from it? Are there people like that?*

Higher Self: Yes.

A: *What do they look like?*

Higher Self: Well, they look normal. Energetically, they feel a bit dense. But it's like they're fighting themselves. It's like the light in them is fighting this density. Remember, part of it is, the mom egg and the father sperm. So they do naturally still have this light in them. If you can imagine a dark sphere, the light is in the middle, and the light is trying to bounce and get out. When it bounces and it tries to get out it makes the sphere kind of like a balloon, trying to pop the balloon.

A: *Yes, I understand.*

Higher Self: That's what the light tries to do for this child. Sometimes, depending on who their Higher Self is, they are able to puncture this and come out. It's up to that Higher Self, and that individual, as to what's going to happen after they puncture this, because they're in for a rude awakening. A lot of self discovery. A lot of things are gonna seem different. Almost like a normal awakening, maybe a kundalini awakening. Something similar, but it's definitely up to them. I feel like some might not make it. By not making it, I mean, if they do puncture it, and they can't handle seeing the truth unfortunately, they may decide to end their life early. Which is very unfortunate. They need to be able to heal because once they puncture it, they come out of that sphere balloon thing that was around them, and it still tries to hang on. So they have a lot of healing to do because we don't want that and they don't want that thing to be hanging on them anymore. They need to shed that and let it go, so they can fully come out, heal, and be the beautiful being that they were meant to be.

A: *What is that dark, are you explaining like a membrane wall?*

Higher Self: Yes.

A: *That part is dark, you said?*

Higher Self: Yes.

A: *What is inside that darkness?*

Higher Self: It's them because they're trapped. The darkness is trying to keep them from their potential because all the babies being born right now are helping us save Mother Earth, helping us reach Ascension. So having all these babies being born from China, which has a huge population of infertile men and women, who are seeking out the surrogacy helps the density stay. What they don't know is that the light inside is still so strong, and it's still just constantly trying to puncture, just trying, like an egg coming out of a shell. They just need to be able to remove it completely.

A: *Would you say that this is perhaps part of the New World Order, how they want to spread children like this?*

Higher Self: Spread children who are in this dark membrane bubble?

A: *Yes.*

Higher Self: Oh, yes. It's unfortunate. Simultaneously, as you know it's happening, it's not happening (chuckles) because a lot of babies are being born at home. It's becoming more and more common, these sacred births. More Birthing Inns are opening, which gives a chance to more women being able to give birth at a Birthing Inn, for whatever reason, they can't give birth at home. We prefer them to give birth at home, or in a forest. (chuckles) Mary laughs at that because I kept showing her giving birth in the forest and she thought I was absolutely nuts. The Birthing Inn is the next good option because they try to keep it as sacred as possible. They don't have all the technology and busy noise and hustle-bustle as a hospital would.

A: Thank you. This is interesting, the whole China culture and they're overpopulated. I've looked at the populations and the percentages are just...

Higher Self: Phenomenal and huge.

A: Phenomenal in comparison to the States. So if you have a high percentage of this collective race becoming infertile. We have heard of Greys in the future who can at times be humans in inverted timelines, but as we know, these timelines will be gone after the Ascension. Are the Chinese related at all to the Greys in any form, because the Greys basically become infertile themselves?

Higher Self: Yes.

A: How they have elongated eyes like Asians.

Higher Self: Oh, yes.

A: So I'm wondering what you have to say about that?

Higher Self: Some of those men and women who are infertile, yes, that's unfortunately what may happen. Some of them because of the lock downs that they have gone through, they're realizing how bad their own government is, and how untrustworthy it is. They're starting to look within, starting to be more spiritual. They do it in secret. You know, like going in a closet. Unfortunately, if some of these embryos and stuff that came from the infertile people in China aren't able to puncture their membrane, their bubble, that dark sphere..: I'm not completely sure if these poor babies are going to turn into Greys or not. We hope that they are going to be able to receive enough healing prior that it not happen because we don't want it to happen. They are innocent and they should not have been subjected to this at all. Does that answer your question?

A: Yes, it does. Thank you for all this important information, especially on sacred birthing, as you know, this is a really important focus for us.

Higher Self: Which is why she needed to meet you, because this is all part of it. She's just like laughing thinking, "Oh my God, you're making me sound nuts." (chuckles), But she's fine.

A: No, not at all. Makes sense for sure. First, you took her to Hawaii, where she could see ghosts, then the horrible pesticides, people trying to harvest the food and they're being poisoned. Then how she got sick with pneumonia from her supposedly family member that tried to curse her mother. Why did you take her to show her all that?

Higher Self: Because she always felt one with the land. She felt the pain of the pesticides and everything going on. It's unfortunate, and she needs healing from it, to know that it's not her fault this happened. She likes to immerse herself into the land there and become one with it. As if she's laying in it as she sinks down into it. She becomes the mountains. She becomes the trees. She becomes the birds, the water. She needs to know that everything that's happening to it now. It's not her fault. She just loves the place so dearly. It's okay to heal from it and move on because she has other things that she needs to put her heart into.

A: Thank you. Tell us about that experience that she had with the negative polarized Reptilian doctor. Initially he really wants to just cut the baby out. She loses consciousness, and when she comes to she's pushing the baby out.

Higher Self: She had a near death experience, the nurses and the doctors were totally unaware that she was gone. They were unaware because they were there just for the baby. She needed this because we needed to wake her up even more and amplify her even more. It's also for her husband, because her husband recognized that she was gone, and he was a bit terrified. So it's for him as well, because when you're married, sometimes one is more awakened than the other. That experience and every experience after is the process of helping him awaken, helping him heal. With him in particular it's a little bit of a slow process, like a choo choo train. Maybe a little bit faster, but he wouldn't be able to mentally handle it if it was too fast for him. So that was the beginning for him, for his awakening. It was a catalyst for her, but the beginning for him.

A: Thank you. Can we go ahead and provide all healing to all times and spaces in her current life that you showed us that requires healings? Can you do that Higher Self?
Higher Self: Yes.
A: Thank you. Higher Self, is there a name that you go by?
Higher Self: No. I just go by Higher Self. I do have another name, but I'm not ready for her to know yet.

The Body Scan begins.
A: Higher Self, is this a good time to begin her body scan?
Higher Self: Yes.
A: Higher Self, would you like for us to call forth on any other assistance, like any Archangels, or benevolent beings?
Higher Self: Yes. Archangel Metatron and Archangel Michael.
A: Higher Self, connect us to Archangel Metatron and Michael now.
AA Michael: Hello.
A: Greetings brothers. We love you, honor you, and respect you. Thank you both for being here. The Higher Self has requested for your assistance during the body scan. We would like to begin her body scan now, scanning her from head-to-toe now. Looking for any negative energies, entities, technologies. Where would you like to begin first in her body?
Higher Self, AA Metatron, and AA Michael: Let's start with her head, her crown.
A: Good. Let's scan her crown. What's in the crown that requires healing? Is that an energy, entity, or technology?
Higher Self, AA Metatron, and AA Michael: I believe that it's a mix between an energy and technology.
A: Is this energy organic or artificial?
Higher Self, AA Metatron, and AA Michael: Getting organic.
A: It's organic energy or organic material?
Higher Self, AA Metatron, and AA Michael: Energy.
A: Organic energy mixed in with what?
Higher Self, AA Metatron, and AA Michael: Technology.
A: Where is it in her head?
Higher Self, AA Metatron, and AA Michael: At the top of her head and it comes down to the back a little bit, and then also comes down on both sides like this.
A: Can we go ahead and start Phoenix Firing that now, start removing it, transmuting it out?
Higher Self, AA Metatron, and AA Michael: Yes.
A: Why does it have organic energy mixed in with it?
Higher Self, AA Metatron, and AA Michael: Because after her R.A.A.H. with Mona the negative entities found out. So they just were hoping that it was like extra insurance, extra material to help make it stay a little bit stronger. They're so stupid. It's just not going to work.

A: Good. So we're transmuting that out now, all three of you working together. Tell me when did this attachment come forth?
Higher Self, AA Metatron, and AA Michael: Just shortly after the R.A.A.H. a small private plane flew over her home. When it came over her home it went into idle, like it was no longer moving, as if it was hovering. When she looked up and she noticed it was hovering that is when it happened. After it happened the small aircraft resumed again on its merry way.
A: Let's find the root to why they're tracking her like this after she started healing herself. Where's the root? Is there a contract? Does it have anything to do with the Military since her husband's in it?
Higher Self, AA Metatron, and AA Michael: It's partly from her husband and the Military, but I'm getting the impression that they're just like whatever, we've got other fish to fry and she's not going to be our concern anymore. We need to find other people who are going to be much easier targets.
A: Thank you, Higher Self. I just want to make sure though that they don't have any kind of tracking devices in her, like any implants. Can you scan her now for that?
Higher Self, AA Metatron, and AA Michael: Yes, so she does. Sometimes she feels it. We've been working on healing it. It's in the back of her head. We've been working on healing it off and on, which is why when she's meditating, she'll feel it tingle. She'll feel it hurt a little bit, but that's because they were trying to stop it. We're still constantly healing it, and she still can constantly feel it. So it's going to be transmutted and gone.
A: Let's start doing that now. Phoenix Fire there. Is there something in her body that allowed for them to find out that she had a R.A.A.H. Reiki session and cleansed?
Higher Self, AA Metatron, and AA Michael: Well, she had the implants prior. She had informed Mona about them. So that's how they knew. They even went so far as to have this strange guy show up at her daughter's preschool in the parking lot. She caught him out immediately that something wasn't right with him. He's part of it. Since she's gotten significantly better with her shielding, and with the R.A.A.H. Reiki things have gotten easier. That is how they knew. Is because she initially had that implant, and they were listening in. They knew that she was going to be cleared of the prior implants.
A: Who was listening in the Military or Entities?
Higher Self, AA Metatron, and AA Michael: Both, in conjunction with each other.
A: So they're obviously aware that R.A.A.H. Reiki or A.U.R.A. Hypnosis is removing these things from people?
Higher Self, AA Metatron, and AA Michael: Yes; they're a little bit bummed about it, (chuckles) they're not too happy. You know, like I said, once it happens, too many times of clearing and shielding, they're just like, we're just going to go somewhere else and find somebody else because we don't want to waste our time anymore. We would rather find someone easier.
A: Well, yes, there's so many people on Earth and so many that...
Higher Self, AA Metatron, and AA Michael: Yes, that don't know.
A: We want to ensure Higher Self, Metatron, Michael, that we're setting up sacred boundaries, shielding, additional amplification to ensure that they'll just change their mind and go about their business and find someone else.
Higher Self, AA Metatron, and AA Michael: Can we please do it for the children as well?
A: Of course, yes. If all three of you would start working on the husband, her, and the children.
Higher Self, AA Metatron, and AA Michael: Thank you.
A: That way she has peace of mind and she doesn't have to worry that no harm will come. Can you say something about that Higher Self? Just give her some kind of advice on that?
Higher Self, AA Metatron, and AA Michael: Keep doing the shields, keep believing. You know they work. Keep calling your dragons. You know that when you ask your dragons to be present, to help

not just physically, but etherically and energetically, that they will. Just keep involving the children with the teachings, with the dragons, keeping their imagination alive because that is what's going to help them. Even if for some reason they get influenced when they get a little bit older and they get influenced by other friends and stuff, in the back of their mind, they're still going to remember and they're still going to feel comfortable and safe to talk to you about it. So for now, just keep shielding them. Remind them to shield themselves so they are not being infringed upon. Everything is just going to work out fine. It's going to be perfect. Don't worry they will be safe.

A: *How beautiful. Thank you, Higher Self. I felt that love and protection there. Let's go ahead and find out if there are any other technologies we want to look at now before we start finding all entities.*

Higher Self, AA Metatron, and AA Michael: I feel like there's still just a little remaining piece of a technology chip right here (she points to her face and side of head). It was unintentional. It's meant to be completely gone, but somehow that piece got stuck, like an adhesive.

A: *Let's Phoenix Fire and Love-Light there. Let's help it unstick and transmute. Are you saying the technology off the top of her head and side of her head, it is all gone?*

Higher Self, AA Metatron, and AA Michael: Yes. It feels light, airy, and beautiful.

A: *Awesome. Let's go ahead and start healing those spaces where all that technology was and fill it in with Love-Light. Higher Self, is there anyone that you want to call that focuses on filling in with Love-Light, like Yeshua, Divine Mother?*

Higher Self, AA Metatron, and AA Michael: She loves Mother Mary.

A: *Higher Self, connect us to Mother Mary now. Greetings, Mother Mary.*

Mother Mary: Greetings.

A: *(chuckles) Angel bumps. You're so beautiful. It's an honor to be speaking to you. If you can please assist during the whole entire session. Higher Self has requested your assistance. If you can start healing all parts of her head, the back of her head, everywhere that these technologies were removed to be healed, filling in with Love-Light with the Higher Self?*

Mother Mary: Yes.

A: *Thank you for that. Higher Self if we can go ahead and continue scanning her now. All four of you are working together. Let's go ahead and find all entities in her?*

Higher Self, AA Metatron, AA Michael, and Mother Mary: Her neck.

A: *What kind of entity is that, Reptilian, Archon, or Earthbound?*

Higher Self, AA Metatron, AA Michael, and Mother Mary: It's a Reptilian. It is from her oldest daughter's dad.

A: *Contain it now with the symbols. Let me know when it's contained.*

Higher Self, AA Metatron, AA Michael, and Mother Mary: It is contained.

A: *Where else does she have entities at?*

Higher Self, AA Metatron, AA Michael, and Mother Mary: Her right hand.

A: *What kind of entity is that?*

Higher Self, AA Metatron, AA Michael, and Mother Mary: It's a Reptilian. It's attached to her throat.

A: *Oh, it's in her right hand and throat?*

Higher Self, AA Metatron, AA Michael, and Mother Mary: Yes. It's an attachment from when she touched her daughter after her daughter's dad touched her and it just bounced along into her hand.

A: *So it's both in her hand and her throat?*

Higher Self, AA Metatron, AA Michael, and Mother Mary: Yes.

A: *Contain it now in both of those areas. Let me know when it's contained.*

Higher Self, AA Metatron, AA Michael, and Mother Mary: It is contained.

We contained more entities, a gray in the DNA, and cleared dark energy in the spine.

A: She has a Reptilian in her neck, throat, hand, and right abdomen. If you can tell us when did these attach? Are they together?
Higher Self, AA Metatron, AA Michael, and Mother Mary: They are together. They all come from her daughter's dad. So we've had the cord cut. He still just keeps trying, and the way he tries is through her daughter. This happens because I guess she forgot to mention he Covid-19 vaccinated the child after she argued with him many times, continuously told him she did not give consent, and he still did it. She was torn, she cried, and she felt helpless. Which also then in turn helped, because she was angry with him. You know, who wouldn't be angry, right? But because she was angry with him that he was still doing this, manipulated the child, and just making her say yes, it came right in.
A: Does the child need healing from the Covid-19 vaccine?
Higher Self, AA Metatron, AA Michael, and Mother Mary: Yes, please. The child, she wants healing. She loves the angels. She's just so beautiful. If her child could meet you and hug you - she wants to. She's just the cutest thing and so much love.
A: Thank you. Higher Self, now that she's going to learn the Reptilian symbols (through the online workshop) to keep them out, can you give her advice? Will she be able to stop this, from these stragglers trying to come on every time her daughter visits the ex-husband?
Higher Self, AA Metatron, AA Michael, and Mother Mary: What we're going to do is we are going to put this symbol in the cord between the daughter and the father, so it's like a filter, and it won't come through. Everything else will come through because that is her dad. She needs to cut the cord from him on her own and she will when she's older. For now, we will put the symbol there as a beautiful filter.
A: You all start that process now. We'll get back to the child in a little bit. The Reptilians, I want to speak to them collectively. If you could come up, up, up now please. Greetings.
Reptilian Collective: Hello.
A: Thank you for speaking to us. We love you, honor you, and respect you. May I ask you questions?
Reptilian Collective: Yeah.
A: If you can tell us when was it that you attached? We understood that you attached by the instruction of her ex-husband. Did you all attach at the same time, or different times?
Reptilian Collective: We came at two different times. We came when she told him to not Covid-19 vaccinate the child when the child was getting a passport. The second time was when he informed her that he was taking her to get vaccinated. She called him and yelled at him, and with that anger and pain within her is when we had an opportunity to re-enter her, and now we're here. This is our home.
A: Thank you for letting us know that. Are you just consciousness, or do you have a Reptilian body somewhere else?
Reptilian Collective: I have more of me in the daughter's dad, and I am also just floating around the Universe.
A: Michael, does this energy have a Reptilian body somewhere else? Or is it just consciousness? What are they?
AA Michael: Consciousness.
A: So they were once part of a Reptilian. Can we go ahead and find all those of this Reptilian's consciousness, wherever they're spread, as it mentioned it's floating somewhere else too. Find them all. Let me know when you find them all.
AA Michael: I have them.

A: I know the ones that are connected to the ex-husband we won't be able to assist those, but the ones that we're allowed to assist, let's speak to all of you there now. We love you, honor you, and respect you. You've been playing this role negatively attaching to others, draining on others' light. We'd love to assist you so that you can become of light once more. Become free and whole once more with love. Would you allow for us to help you become free?

Reptilian Collective: Yes, it's fine.

A: Good. Find that light within you. Spread it to all that is you. Every root, every cord that you have attached to her and wherever you're at, those other consciousnesses, go ahead and all of you now spread your light. Let us know once all are light and let me know once the consciousness that are within her are out.

Higher Self, AA Metatron, AA Michael, and Mother Mary: They're gone. We are good.

A: Beautiful. If we can call upon Archangel Azrael to ensure their safe passageways. So that they don't get tricked along the way.

Higher Self, AA Metatron, AA Michael, and Mother Mary: Yes.

A: Thank you. Our love to him. Let's go ahead and start healing all parts within her. Her neck, throat, hand, right abdomen, wherever they were attached. Fill it in with Love-Light, repairing any damage it caused her. Any trauma that they caused, in whatever way they were affecting her. Healing all that now. She has this purple type of being that seems to be artificial/organic. Has it been fully turned organic now, or is it still artificial?

Higher Self, AA Metatron, AA Michael, and Mother Mary: It's organic. It's so happy to be organic.

A: Oh, beautiful. Thank you. Can I speak to it?

Purple Being: Yes.

A: Greetings. Thank you for speaking to us. We love you, honor you, and respect you. May we ask you questions?

Purple Being: Yes.

A: Thank you. If you could tell us what are you? They mentioned that your original form looked like a gray but you were purple. Can you tell me what you are now that you've turned organic?

Purple Being: I'm now bright purple like a beautiful violet. I had kind of lost my way. I'm so happy to be fully organic again. I almost forgot what it felt like. It just feels so nice to be so full of love again.

A: Beautiful. Do you remember how you became this gray, purple thing?

Purple Being: I was taken from my home planet. So were others. I was taken and I was put upon a ship. After they were done using me they kind of just brought me back, but I was never the same after coming back.

A: When did you attach to her DNA?

Purple Being: It was when she had a Reiki done by a person here locally. I was attached to her. That's how I found Mary.

A: So you were attached to the Reiki Practitioner who practiced another form of Reiki. What kind of Reiki was it?

Purple Being: It was like Usui Reiki but it had a different modality mixed into it. I don't know the name.

A: Thank you for allowing for us to assist you. Are you fully organic and fully of light?

Purple Being: I am, and I'm so happy to be.

A: Do you have a last message before you go?

Purple Being: Continue using heart discernment, it's going to help you more. I love you. I apologize for attaching myself to you. But in the end I'm quite happy I did because now I'm full of love all over again. You helped me get here. Thank you.

A: Beautiful. Archangel Azrael, if you could please ensure this beautiful soul's safe passageway. May you be surrounded by the Love-Light of the Universe. Blessings. If you could tell us Higher Self, how long did she have it attached there in her DNA?
Higher Self, AA Metatron, AA Michael, and Mother Mary: About a year. Not long.
A: A year. What was it causing by being in there?
Higher Self, AA Metatron, AA Michael, and Mother Mary: It was causing a lot of confusion. A lot of tingling in her body and she wasn't quite sure what was going on. It just mostly caused confusion, some doubt, and some fear. Made her feel sometimes that she was unworthy. When in fact she is worthy of love and being here and learning this.
A: Thank you. Beautiful. Let's go ahead and start healing her entire DNA bringing it the beginnings of crystallizing. Higher Self, can you start doing that?
Higher Self, AA Metatron, AA Michael, and Mother Mary: Well, yes, definitely.

We continue the body scan...dark portals are closed in home and land.

A: Scan her for any negative cords. Does she have any?
Higher Self, AA Metatron, AA Michael, and Mother Mary: She has cords to her parents, brother, and her in-laws. I know she doesn't really like me to say negative, especially her parents because they're her parents, and they were all vaccinated, and her in-laws. She has been working very strongly in clearing them and helping them stay healthy and strong. Trying to filter what comes through.
A: I know that she's sovereign. Does she have to have these cords attached to these people?
Higher Self, AA Metatron, AA Michael, and Mother Mary: She wants to ask a clarification question. She wants to make sure that if these cords are all cut because they're vaccinated... her question is a bit confusing. She's worried about the love, that is what she's worried about. Because she wants to also eventually use these modalities of A.U.R.A. and R.A.A.H. So she wants to know that if these cords are cut, is the love cut?
A: Higher Self, in order for her to assist them does she have to have cords attached to them?
Higher Self, AA Metatron, AA Michael, and Mother Mary: No.
A: So would it be easier for her to remove the cords to channel Love-Light to them?
Higher Self, AA Metatron, AA Michael, and Mother Mary: Much easier. Yes. Thank you. I think she just needed you to say that.
A: If she's holding on to the cords then she, too, herself is being influenced and compromised. So how is she going to be sufficient in Love-Light for them if she has those cords.
Higher Self, AA Metatron, AA Michael, and Mother Mary: Yes. Exactly. Thank you for saying that so beautifully.
A: Thank you. Do we have permission to cut off those negative cords to anyone else that she might have? Of course not including her organic cords to her children and beautiful spouse.
Higher Self, AA Metatron, AA Michael, and Mother Mary: Yes.

Additional healing continues...

A: Expand her heart and open it up to the biggest it can be. She mentioned that, when she came into my content, this happens to some people, it's like they understand it but they can't understand it. So what within her was causing her not to understand the content?
Higher Self, AA Metatron, AA Michael, and Mother Mary: It was the negative infringements within her; the ones that she had prior to her R.A.A.H. Reiki. They didn't like it, but that is why she couldn't

understand it. The R.A.A.H. Reiki (she had prior to the workshop with another practitioner) helped bring a lot more clarity. She even went back and rewatched the videos all over again from square one because she realized everything she read and heard prior didn't come out the way it was supposed to be. It was distorted, or she didn't hear properly. So after the R.A.A.H. Reiki everything came out clear. She was able to relearn and learn the way as she should.

A: Oh, that's beautiful. Providing Love-Light to that time and space as she was going through that process. Can I please speak to Source?

Source: Hello.

A: Greetings Source. It's an honor to be speaking to you. We feel your energy. As we're meant to divinely. Since she is that example for us today, can we send a wave of love for those who perhaps are going through this process and they're trying to evolve. They're trying to find their way to the truth of what's organic within our Universe. Can we send them a wave of love so that they may find their way to us? Perhaps they can push through it easier? All divinely of course, as always. Can we send the wave of love for this?

Source: Yes, it needs to happen.

A: Source, can you start that process now?

Source: Yes.

A: Beautiful. I can feel it. Thank you Source. Do you have any messages for this group? As you know, we're doing the session in a group. Source, do you have a message for the group of new A.U.R.A. practitioners?

Source: I know that there are doubts with a couple, but don't doubt. We love you all so much. It does take practice to relearn a new way of thinking. Don't doubt the beauty and the love of these modalities. You are all worthy to receive this because it is all part of your mission. You are all so beautiful. Shannon (one of the attendees) comes up to mind. She's just so beautiful. I'm excited for her adventure of where she's going to be going. She said she's going back to her Country. She's going to do amazing things. I believe you can already energetically feel that love she's going to be spreading there and the beauty. All of you other ladies are going to do phenomenal work. Just trust yourselves. You are worthy. You are full of love. Do not give up. Stay your sovereign being. Fight the temptations. Remember who you are. You're all a divine being. All of you. You're all so beautiful. Just remember that. That is all.

A: That was felt through every cell of ours (chuckles). Thank you, Father and Mother Source. We love you. Infinitely. Makes me emotional. Can I please speak back to her Higher Self?

Higher Self, AA Metatron, AA Michael, and Mother Mary: He's so full of love, isn't he?

A: Yes. He/she right?

Higher Self, AA Metatron, AA Michael, and Mother Mary: Yes. He/she.

The body scan continues…

A: She's already done a lot of work. Amazing. So proud of her. We can emphasize Source for this work as well. If we can delete any inverted timelines of hers and her family, with the Higher Self's permissions? Can we do that for her children and her husband?

Higher Self, AA Metatron, AA Michael, and Mother Mary: Yes, definitely. Oh my gosh, her children's Higher Selves are so excited because they've been wanting more healing. They always get excited for their mom to do stuff, and the extra boost just amplifies everything.

A: Source, assist with that. Thank you. Healing current life trauma and past life trauma. Can we do that?

Higher Self, AA Metatron, AA Michael, and Mother Mary: Yes.
A: Going back to the child that got vaccinated, can the mother from the time and space, that has learned how to for example, shield from the Covid-19 vaccine, from that time and space, can we work from her in her future self where she knows the content and she can shield her child, so that when she gets the Covid-19 vaccine she doesn't receive any infringements from it?
Higher Self, AA Metatron, AA Michael, and Mother Mary: Yes. Her daughter called Archangel Raphael to be there both times because deep down her daughter knew it was not okay. So Archangel Raphael was there and she will be fully healed. Her higher self is so excited for that.
A: Of course she will. Sending her infinite Love-Light and Phoenix Fire. Source assist this child to ensure no infringement has occurred from this. Can she also teach her child how to protect herself from people who are Covid-19 vaccinated in the future, and how to cleanse herself, as well, with the teachings?
Higher Self, AA Metatron, AA Michael, and Mother Mary: Yes; the vaccination part will take time because her daughter does get scared. Her mom will learn different words to use so she's not so scared. She's probably not going to use the word vaccinated. Her daughter will learn. It will also help her with her energy as well because she's got some fun energy that her mom is trying to learn to navigate around.
A: Beautiful. Is there anything though that the Higher Self wants us to help remove now for the child?
Higher Self, AA Metatron, AA Michael, and Mother Mary: Other than helping starting the process now of the vaccinations, she would like help for the dream time nightmares that she suffered as a younger child. When she was younger she had night terrors. In fact, all her children have suffered this. Sounds like they would all like healing from that.
A: Source and all the beautiful beings assisting today, go ahead and start assisting these beautiful children with the night terrors. Helping them balance those out and heal them. I'm sure deleting the inverted timelines will really assist them with that.
Higher Self, AA Metatron, AA Michael, and Mother Mary: Yes, definitely.
A: I've asked all the questions and we conducted the body scan. Higher Self, can you confirm that we've completed her entire session, and what needed to be done divinely today, and that she is completely clear? Have we set her up for her most organic timeline?

We find a chip in her arm which is transmuted, and ask for healing for her husband who is in the military and has received the Covid-19 vaccine.

Higher Self, AA Metatron, AA Michael, and Mother Mary: It looks beautiful.
A: It's beautiful how everything serves a purpose. How if we just keep delayering and delayering and looking for the details, how we find them all. Even that little speck and how that reminded me, "Oh yes, her husband, let's send some love there." So it's beautiful to see all these puzzle pieces in our life. Like the little speck, it will trigger something and it will shift everything around. Just wanted to point that out. Higher Self, are we complete with her session?
Higher Self: We are.
A: I want to thank Higher Self, Metatron, Michael, as well as Source and Mother Mary. Everyone who assisted today our infinite love to all those entities as well. We love everyone, honor, and respect. Higher Self, may I bring her back?
Higher Self: Yes.

For every A.U.R.A. Hypnosis healing session we ask that the Higher Self and team ensure to remove and heal this entire list from the clients Tree of Life: entities (Grays, Mantis, Reptilians, Archons...), dark portals, repair and crystallize DNA, negative cords, technologies (implants, metals, hooks, wires, nano, vaccines), Illnesses, vision, dental health, regrow teeth, age regress 5-15 years, blocked or misaligned chakras, open-up the third eye and activate abilities, expand heart, issues with auric field, fractured soul, contracts, deletion of inverted timelines, and trauma from current or past life.

END OF SESSION

The honor and purity brought forth from being born into the roots of the beauty of the nature of Hawaii. The people, and the spirit energy that embodies these sacred lands is like no other on Earth, reminding us of what the first lands of Pangea, Mu, and Leumuria embodied and felt like. In Book 3 we will speak further of these [22]beginning soils. [23]Mother Pele/Hawaii through her channeling explained to us how she originated from the beginning lands of Earth, Pangea, and that when these lands were separating from each other, how she traveled to the location she is currently in, and became Hawaii. When you look at Hawaii from a birds eye view, you can see how these isles are made up of a gigantic, divine, feminine Goddess form, which looks as though she is sleeping. She is truly divine mother Pele, the volcano Goddess, laying down to create a fruitful and fertile land for her children to commune upon. An understanding for us that we are truly living on sacred lands which are her bodies and essences. When you see Mother Earth as these elemental bodies she is, which we call continents, then we understand truly that when harm comes unto her, as manipulated weather, laser technology shooting into her, plastic and chemical wastes into her water and lands, that these acts are violations and rapes upon her. Therefore, to do this to her, is another way that they make energetic entryways, so that they can rape her children of Earth as well.

I once hosted a Retreat in Hawaii, and the magic was at the highest potency I have experienced compared to anywhere else I have traveled to. When one taps into Hawaii's frequency, everything around you speaks to you, as the spirit within everything is clearly embodied and heard. The animals, plant life, and elements all seem to be connected intricately, as a collective of acting neurons with a divine spark of light within Hawaii's lands. I could imagine what this spirit connection would be like to one who is born through these frequencies, allowing highest Love-Light, vibration, and memory coding. What a divine powerful bridge Hawaii is in birthing babies with the highest vibrational light! Which is why the children of Maui have become the next target to be trafficked, as there are said now to be thousands of children missing after the energy weapons attack causing the man made fires in August 2023, which separated the parents from their children. Just as we learned in Chapter 6 in the Holocaust, these are the now targeted children on Earth, to unfortunately be tested on because of their high potency of crystalline light within their DNA, or whatever ill intended plans they have for them, trafficked and hidden inside the underground tunnel systems of Hawaii. In the next chapter we will come to understand more about these types of energy weapons used on the sacred lands of Hawaii.

The poisoning of our Earth's food, water, and the land. The example of the pesticides being sprayed on the pineapple and sugarcane fields, and so too the people. These chemicals are absorbed

---

[22] Watch the Atlantis/Mayan playlist located on Odysee.com now for more on Pangea, Mu, and Leumuria.
[23] For more on the magic that Hawaii bestows, watch on our platforms when AuroRa channeled Divine Mother Pele on March 20, 2020.

through the pores of the peoples' skin, becoming part of their beingness, potentially creating illness and disease within their human bodies, and this too becoming part of the food they consume. The Earth, which has been infused with artificial substances, is at times challenging to live within, when down to everything that we intake is poisoned, the air through the metals in the chemtrails, the soil through pesticides.

We all work so hard to eat organic and most of us are vegan once we awaken, but it seems that still at times we can't prevail. Even what claims to be organic is truly sprayed and encased with a layer of chemicals. The key is that we must become our own farmers, but how does one find time when being occupied by a third dimensional job? However, it is possible, all is accomplishable. Obstacles and hurdles we have to charge through, not allowing to be slowed or stopped. Mother Earth's seeds are no longer pure and organic, as the seeds themselves have been altered through bioengineering. However, we have to trust and believe that as Mother Earth's soil grows these seeds, that she will do her best to rewrite these infringements upon the seeds, and that they become as close as they were to their original true organic pureness. Therefore, one would have to work intimately with the soil in which we are planting our seeds to ensure that the soil carries a significant amount of Love-Light to alchemize the seed of the fruit or vegetable back to its original signature blueprint.

Further violations of Mother Earth through these sacred lands are acted upon by the government constructing eleven known military bases which go deep into the grounds located in Hawaii. What horrific acts have been ordered and executed by these branches of the military located in these bases? This is a strong disrespect and it should not be. These bases were built not with ease or consent from the indigenous Hawaiian people, as they are the most guarded people on Earth, still practicing the ancient ways, with the greatest capability to teach us how to treat Mother Earth respectfully.

The client and family are a military family, and through this session we got to learn some of the ways the military tries to exert control over the families. The example of how the military and negative entities will infringe easiest on those who are allowing, who are unknowing of the forms we have available for ourselves through shielding and not consenting. I have done many sessions on military children whom are grown now; their parents were not able to protect them and get them out of this inverted pedophilic system, satanic rituals, and Mk-Ultra experiments, but here we were shown a prime example of how if at least one of the parents is awakened and strong enough in Love-Light they can pull their families out from the experimentations of the military which is ultimately ran by the Illuminati. Per this strong example, Mary's children will not have to go through what other military children have gone through, such as abductions, satanic ritual sex abuse, and the heaviness and the unknowing that comes with these erased traumatic memories, which the military erases through their implanted technologies and by the altered states of mind of the children when they give them date rape pills. At times though the Higher Selves block these memories from these children, so that they can at best, consciously go through their life without carrying the burden that these memories hold, until it is time that they are ready to self-heal from these violations. Remembering Book 1, Chapter 21, 'MILAB Experiments', and all that Rachael had to go through to heal from her family being part of the military, and all the abuse that came with that as a child.

Such wisdom Mary harnessed within her. Channeling truly Mother Earth's feelings through the experience she lived with the female ghost who was murdered violently. As Mary felt as a child, it is so sad that many women die like this. Many lessons this taught her at such a young age, such as to be cautious with who you allow within your space, translating into being cautious with people in the future who mean harm, as this person who murdered this woman. We understand how thin the veil can be to the wisdom of the etheric spirit realm when someone holds such a recognition within, as does Mary.

This chapter brought us more of the topic of how those closest to us as friends and families are truly the only ones who can influence and infringe upon us the most. Their hatred, jealousy, and envy, are dark spells which manifest into psychic or energetic attacks. As the hate embodied curse, was sent from the grandmother, which deflected off the mother and instead went into the child who then got sick. I have heard this story over and over of the relationships between parents and their children. Per this example Mary's mother was loving, but Mary's mother before her and in most family dynamics the parents show signs of not being love and affection when their children are young, and when the children grow up the parents seem to fully become disconnected and turn against them. Is it the fact that they no longer have control over their children, and they feel that they have lost possession over them? Every person has a different story, but it all adds up to the same equation, of the parents not being so loving and supportive, and instead it is the parents that now the children have to be wary of. However, each generation that goes through this cycle, comes out stronger and stronger from the experience.

The understanding that Mary came to, of needing to remove the energetic cords to her family who all got the Covid-19 vaccination was a hard one to make, but a needed one. As per example of how Mary herself as a little girl became ill because of her mother's connection to the ill intended grandmother. This too can happen to children, becoming receivers to their parents' negative acquaintances, when the parents choose to stay attached to people who have made such an inverted choice as injecting artificial intelligence into themselves, compromising their soul. Mary came into a strong, self-awared, understanding during her session, in which she cannot assist her family at highest light and vibration, if she is holding on to her family's infringing energies, since it then lowers Mary's energies to their densities. Therefore, if she un-attaches, she can embody and stand forth in her strongest, clearest Love-Light, which then if they *do* want assistance to self-heal through A.U.R.A. or R.A.A.H, she can now be the significant amount of Source light to actually assist them holistically.

Many on Earth have made the choice as Mary and her family did, having to move away from their parents/grandparents, in order to gain freedom. It seems the longer you are on Earth, the more that you become bitter and tainted by the false programming. We will use this analogy, this Matrix is like a dill pickle, the cucumber is fermented in the dill herb, so eventually the pickle begins to taste cultured like the vegetable dill, so decades of being on Earth surrounded by artificial intelligence eventually soaks into people who have been emerged in it for too long. The longer you are here the harder it can get, if the inner work, and awakening process has not begun. These people still have the choice to raise themselves out of the artificial fermentation, but it can be harder to remove this dill flavor/artificial the longer you have been submerged in it.

At times mothers and fathers start off pure; they birth their children, who hold an even stronger light than them, and they are targeted in many forms because of their stronger lighted children. As the years pass the parents begin to change because of this understanding. Through A.U.R.A. Hypnosis Healing sessions, we have documented the way a soul can change from their experiences and traumas no matter the age and timeframe they have been within Earth. Though through the over 500 A.U.R.A.

sessions I have conducted I have found a higher percentage of people who are 60 years or older having a harder time spiritually connecting in the theta brainwave of hypnosis. But this is due mostly to the disempowerment that they have lived being in this inverted construct causing a higher potent of infringements and attachments within, and they feel they can't connect, but still they accomplish it, no matter if they believe it so. So all are healable and redeemable, if they so choose it.

It is unacceptable that parents, as Mary's narcissist ex-husband, who took it upon himself to violate their daughter by administering the Covid-19 vaccine without her mother's consent. Righteous this man must think he is to overstep such boundaries. Even after Mary explained to him how harmful it could be potentially to their daughter, still he did it. Such ignorance! The child knew it was not good, but to please her father she allowed it. Strong mental brainwashing from the father there would be unto the child, in order to accomplish such an infringement. I will leave it at that, as any further words of this act will no longer keep me in friendly words. Parents who have divorced a narcissistic partner, are truly the bravest on Earth. Strong they are, and their children, to agree to this before they are born.

At a retreat in 2022 one of the attendees shared with us of her mother. "My beautiful sweet mother," were her exact words. She said her mother was such a good mother. For example, the Attendee's mother would pack her children's lunches so lovingly, that everyday she would draw an image, or write something beautiful on their lunch bags, surprising them daily. This was one of the attendee's favorite moments as a child, to look at when she ate the lunch her mother made for her daily. This act embodied such a pure love for a mother and her children. One day her mother went to the doctor who told her she had to have a hysterectomy, and when the attendee/child came home from school she realized who came back from that surgery was not her mother, instead it was an entity she knew not of, just that, that was not her mother. Her mother never returned back, and this now cold and disconnected entity within her mother raised her and her siblings for the rest of her life. During the retreat as we taught the material of negative aliens, such as Reptilians, the attendee/practitioner said to the group that she came to the realization that what was within her mother was a Reptilian who had taken over her body.

Since one is unconscious with layers of chemicals being injected into the body during surgery, and the fact that you are allowing for someone to penetrate your physical body, in turn your energy body, it is the easiest to attach, or compromise someone, and replace, or soulbind their soul. Because not only are they consenting to this violation, but they are not conscious of what is being done to their body and energy, since they have been artificially put to sleep. This mother loved her children immensely, but yet the system of the doctors tricked her into thinking that if she had the surgery done, she could live perhaps longer with her children, with the usual guise that it is for your own health to do these surgeries and human experimentations. Many have been tricked throughout their lives through examples such as these, the Archons know that for the love of our beloved ones, we will do anything.

The Grey entity who was attached to Mary, once it went through the process of self-healing, it knew not of who they were before they became a hybrid artificial entity. Though the beauty is still felt when it is finally brought back to organic, no longer being used to attach, drain or harm another. Truly one of the reasons the Divine Mother of Creation assisted me in creating A.U.R.A. and R.A.A.H. So that the souls she once created, which contain an immensity of organic and love, that now have a merging of artificial, may be given an opportunity and second chance to return to the original organic soul they once were birthed into by the Creator. This in itself makes my heart sing! Oh what a joy!

Every divine spark of light and soul upon our divine Creation is significant equally to each other. Therefore, we must save as many as we can before the collective Ascension. Each and every light matters. Why do I do this, and teach the world these divine potentials? It is because, I AM AuroRa, I am an incarnation of the Divine Mother. And, I have been with you lovingly, as a public figure in every pivotal moment, in the collective time in space of our process of awakening and Ascension. Which is why I am so strong on my mission. I know the mission, because I have played this role beautifully, over and over for the collective.

The data and knowledge we received in this session on artificial insemination, and the infertility of Earth was profound. Mary knew all her life that one day she would be a surrogate mother for someone, so when the opportunity presented itself she took it. We thank her for going through the experience, so that we can have the background to what the dark forces intentions are in proceeding to make babies in a lab, under a microscope, inside synthetic liquid. As Mary's Higher Self explained to us, this artificial synthetic liquid merges into the conception of a child as the sperm penetrates the membrane wall of the egg, initially integrating into the child's cultivation and in some forms their DNA. Though the majority of these childrens have healed these infringements, some can be affected in different forms, such as having disorders or illnesses. As explained the angels would have to heal all parts of the beingness of these synthetic cultivated souls, transforming them truly from having part artificial in them, returning them back to organic original souls to not have any defects before they are born. This subject can be offensive to those who have participated in these man-made artificial procedures, but it is important that we do not shy from speaking on this subject. As this is where the New World Order agenda would like humankind to head towards birthing new life into Earth.[24]

The parents give their power away when they consent for their DNA and their future potential children's DNA to be tested by these facilities, which are truly run by the New World Order agenda of the depopulation of humankind. As the Higher Self said, these governments are able to retrieve information about who the souls are for the entire family once they gain access to their DNA. The government knows the Akashic of the viable eggs they choose for the parent to try to carry. Meaning, they know if these viable eggs hold an Angelic essence, how old is the soul, and their lives they have incarnated throughout the Universe. Once they acquire the DNA, they insert it into a computer of sorts. The artificial intelligence has taken possession over these once positive crystalline technologies, and turned them into what they want from them, for their continual diabolical control. Once the DNA is downloaded into their negative technologies it shows them the file of the Akashic of the soul. What else can they do to these viable eggs before they insert them into the mothers? Can they change the chromosomes of the DNA in the viable eggs, so that the soul cannot be at its highest Love-Light when they are born? Yes, they can. We must be cautious within these times we are living in. We have seen these repeated inverted agendas through the generations of the past Earth histories, as Atlantis…and now we are seeing these again. The more that the generations evolve through technologies, the more that we see these agendas unfold.

---

[24] We have been covering these important subjects on artificial wombs, black eyed babies,
transhumanism and transgenderism live on Rumble.com & Odysee.com, where all our sensitive content is found.

In Chapter 5, 'The A.I. Alien Invasion', we went into the different forms of the hybridization of the infants of Earth, and in this chapter we learn of the beginning diabolical plan to convince humankind that children can be conceived and grown in labs. These experiments on souls have been going on in their underground bases or islands, but we are now beginning to see them try to groom humans to be okay with the idea of growing babies in artificial wombs. Scientists have been cloning animals in bags full of synthetic liquid, artificially mimicking the sacred womb and its placenta, and someday they will try to do this to the people of Earth, if we don't stop this now. Their biggest agenda is to make humankind infertile to further introduce the option of conceiving through their means of artificial labs. Per this example, the Chinese are at the highest percentage of infertility, and now the population of the world is too, with all of whom allowed the injection of the Covid-19 vaccine into themselves.

Mary had doubts of accomplishment, when she came into the awareness of our sacred teachings, and during the timeframe of beginning to learn the teachings as well. Source's advice during the session was that all are worthy and all can do it. Mary decided to have a R.A.A.H. Reiki healing session with another practitioner, and immediately all cloudiness pertaining to the teachings were gone. So, if you are experiencing something similar, just do it, follow your heart to receive an A.U.R.A. Hypnosis or R.A.A.H. Reiki healing session with a practitioner around the world[25] who feels right for you, or even more importantly become certified through any of our divinely accredited, life-changing, soul freeing, heart activating courses. Come lift the cloudiness of the artificial, by becoming your own self-healer.

> **"The children are everything, they are the carriers and birthers of our organic future Ascension timelines. They are the chosen ones who will bring the collective Universal Ascension into fruition."**
> ~AuroRa

--------------<<>>--------------

---

[25] For your A.U.R.A., R.A.A.H. or Q.G.A.R. practitioner, go to www.aurapractitioners.com.

14

ANGEL BABIES DRAGON GUARDIANS

Session #573: Recorded in February 2023

In this online A.U.R.A. Hypnosis Healing session, Sophia is an A.U.R.A. and R.A.A.H. practitioner. This is her second A.U.R.A. session with me. Her first A.U.R.A. session will be in Book 3 of this series. In this past life memory Sophia follows the call for help from her Dragon, which takes her to a planet where she discovers many Dragons guarding something very special. Join us as we journey in this powerful Multiverse collective healing. The moment we all have been waiting for. The children are who will save the Earth, who carry the light codes to bring forth the organic Universal Ascension, and to completely eradicate all that's artificial in our Universe and the Multiverse. Through this session we, too, gain knowledge on the energy weapons that have been used throughout the invasions of planets, and the laser technology that was used on Hawaii and her people in 2023.

"I just want her to believe in herself more. She has the right to be where she is. She is a healer. She is a transmuter. She is a channel. She does not fully understand or believe that she's in the right place, but she is. Just need her to really believe and truly know that within her heart, and act upon that knowledge."
~Higher Self

S: [Sophia] I am levitating, and I feel like I'm in a cave. It's all dark around me. I can see there's a dragon. He's all curled up like he's sleeping. I can sense a lot of sadness coming out of him and he's not alone. There are lots more dragons, they're all curled up like they're sleeping.
A: [Aurora] Look at yourself. Do you feel like you have a body?
S: I am female. I'm not wearing any shoes. I have a white gown, long, blonde hair, and fair skin. Feel like I have four wings.
A: Beautiful. Are you wearing any jewelry? Anything else that you're wearing?
S: I would not call it jewelry. It's a crown, not on my head though, it's levitating a little bit above my head. There's a red almond shaped at the center and diamond-shaped blue crystals that constitute the rest of the crown. They're all levitating together, creating the crown. I have a bag, like a satchel. There are herbs in the bag.
A: Do these crystals have any messages for you?
S: The red crystal.
A: Allow for it to speak through you. What does it say?
S: Greetings. I am Ruby, I preserve the organic darkness. My role is to protect, and I am to aid people out of the darkness that may be binding them. I am here to show the light, that is all.
A: Beautiful. Thank you, for your beautiful messages. Speaking back now to Sophia, keep explaining to me what you're doing within the space you talked about the Dragons. Describe the surroundings of where you're at.

S: I feel like the Dragons are all curled up around a golden egg. Like they're protecting the egg. I touched a dragon that was in front of me. He's all black, feels like he's calcified. I heard him, he called for me, he curled up, and now he's like stone now. I came here because he called me.
A: Describe to me, what does he look like, his facial features, as he's in stone. What does he look like as a dragon? Does he have wings, legs?
S: I can sense that he has four legs, has a long tail, and a long neck. He also has wings, He used to be a blue fire dragon. He also has little spikes growing around his jaw, they're not too long; his eyebrows…it's like an extension of skin going down, it looks like a mustache, but it's not, it's eyebrows. He has some golden jewels under the articulation of his wings.
A: This was before he was stone?
S: That was before he was stone, now he's a dark gray, but he used to be a vibrant, sapphire blue.
A: You said that you heard him call out for you. Do you know, what did he say when he called for you?
S: Just roared, "help me." He felt like he was protecting a golden egg. He didn't have any more energy. He knew he needed help; he rose up, he roared, and then he curled back.
A: Besides him, are there any others around that are like this stone as well?
S: There are many others that are in rows, but they are in circles. Like a first circle, in another bigger circle, and then another bigger circle. They are in circles like that all curled up and all petrified. They are now all sorts of shapes. Some of the dragons have wings, some do not. Some look a little like the dinosaurs, the huge ones that had long tails and long necks, that would eat the top of the trees. They're all in that cave. I can still sense that there's some light left in them, so they can be woken up, but it's going to need a huge amount of energy to wake them up. I can also feel that there is life within the eggs that they're protecting.
A: How about the eggs, are the eggs petrified as well?
S: The one that the dragon who called me is protecting, is completely normal, it is alive. Some of them on the outer rings are starting to petrify. Right now, I am at the center of the inner rings.
A: Do you know what caused this petrification?
S: Feels like something is sucking out their energy.
A: Let's go back in time to right before the petrification happens to them. Tell me what's going on.
S: I can see the dragons, they're flying. I'm not in a cave anymore. I'm outside, it's not too dense. There's canyons and mountains. The dragons are flying, they're playing, and the younger ones are learning to fly. The older ones are very peaceful. I see a charge of energy, some kind of dark clouds rising, and I feel this beam of energy shooting down into the Earth and filling it. All the dragons just fell to the ground. Some of the younger ones died. The older ones went into their caves and started gathering the eggs of the younger generation, and started curling up around them. The stronger, warrior type of dragons, they are outside of the cave protecting the ones inside with the eggs. That dark beam continues to pour out negative wavelengths. It's inverted waves flowing down, the sky just splits in two, an opening. I see a bat-like creature, very, very huge. Their skin is like latex. They start attacking the other dragons that are protecting the cave. Some of them are starting to eat the young dragons that died, and some of them take the bodies of the young dragons. I feel their bites are venomous, so the warrior dragons ultimately get poisoned and they die, but they fight. During the fight, the other dragons that were within the cave were able to seal to the cave, and the bat-like being could not enter. So what they end up doing is eating the dragons that died, and taking some of their bodies as well.
A: At what point do they become petrified into stone, or do some of them just die? How does this work?

S: I feel like it's the bite; it is poisonous, and the poison starts spreading within. When the poison starts spreading through the veins, it kills the cells, they start losing their light, and they become like stone.

A: *Thank you. These bats, can you tell me more about them? Do they feel like they're organic types of entities? Do they have any kind of artificial fusion?*

S: They don't feel organic at all. They should not have been able to come here. I don't even understand how they're able to rip through the sky like that. Whatever venom they have injected into the dragon, it's the same type of energy in that the beam that I first saw going down Earth, as the poison in the inorganic bats. So it is slowly killing the planet and the dragons that are in the cave. In order to ensure that the planet lives, they had to use their energy, sending it down to the core of the planet hoping that at some point, the planet is going to heal and that this inversion will be transmuted. The last one of them could not hold the amount of energy that is needed to heal the planet, so he called for help. He sends down what's left of the energy in him, so that the planet can still hold on until help comes.

A: *Now that you are here with your dragon companion and he is in a petrified type of form of stone, is there anything you could do about this, that's happened here?*

S: I have an alchemy symbol. I touch the forehead of the dragon, it activates an alchemy symbol on his forehead and I start channeling Source Love-Light into him. It is transmuting out the venom, because the dragons took the infringements upon themselves to start transmuting it. I touch his forehead and activate the alchemy symbol. It goes through his entire body. It's replenishing his light. I think I need to do the same for the planet, but I cannot do that alone. I need my brothers with me. I'm calling my brothers. I have a golden staff. I take the staff, strike the Earth with the staff, create a beam of light that goes straight up like a beacon. Then I can hear my brother. He is asking what I need, and I tell him that I need the three of them. There's two brothers and one sister. He is going to gather them and they're going to come forth to assist the dragons and planet.

A: *Beautiful, keep moving the scene along. Keep describing to me everything that's happened.*

S: They're here now, we are going to start transmuting the infringements out of the core of the planet and then we will be able to assist the dragons that are in the cave. In order to do that, we go to the center of the planet, near the core. We place ourselves at each point of the four sacred directions, we create a diamond shape around the core of the Earth. We all have different tools. My sister stands in front of me, I have one brother on my left, and the other one on the right. We now create with our hands alchemy symbols surrounding the core. We need to work in symbiosis, in order for it to happen organically. We have tools. I have my staff, my brother to the left uses his voice, and the brother on the right has crystals. My sister uses her Love-Light from her heart to send out that energy to activate once the alchemy symbols are in place. Beautiful three-dimensional symbols around the earth, around the core, and then activated, go through. The Venom starts to dissipate, then all negative cords connected to the core of the Earth start to be transmuted. As we are healing the core of the Earth, we are also going through the organic roots of the dragons which are connected to the planet. We are sending out healing energy to the dragons in the cave. By doing so, it also activates a huge alchemy symbol underneath the cave, and then on the ground of the cave. Then the Love-Light starts spreading once more within the dragons. It looks like tiny little veins of Love-Light flowing through them. As the Love-Light is flowing through them, the petrification is going back to zero, it's just becoming dust, and they are starting to come back to their organic self. The same goes for the eggs that were starting to petrify as well.

A: *How beautiful, thank you.*

S: The dragons are all awake now. With my brothers and sister, we regain the surface. We need to figure out how those inorganic things were able to come through; how the beam was created, so this does not happen again. While we're flying towards the directions of where that beam was, we see a facility, like multiple buildings, a research center. They have lots of technology there. It feels like some of the technologies are creating a receptor to something. There's nobody there now, like the facility has been abandoned. They all died. When the beam came down, they all turned into dust, but the technology remained there. It needs to be destroyed. We need to find whatever is emitting the negative energy that is received through that technology. It feels like it's off planet though. It's not on the planet, it's something, somewhere else.

A: *Who was it that vanished in these facilities?*

S: They were humanoids, but are not humans. They had legs and arms. They looked like Greys. They have huge heads and black eyes.

A: *This facility that's now empty, where was it at with these beings?*

S: It was miles away from where the dragons were staying.

A: *Was it on this planet, or out of this planet?*

S: The facility was on the planet.

A: *Was this facility positive or negative?*

S: Negative.

A: *So it was on the same planet where these dragons were, then when this beam shot down, what happened to those humanoid beings with the big heads?*

S: They evaporated.

A: *But this beam that shot down, which beam are we talking about? The negative beam that came with the bats, or one that you all were using light to heal?*

S: The one that came with the bat.

A: *Okay, so that destroyed these humanoids that were negative. Tell me more about this technology that they were working on? What was it that they were doing in this negative facility?*

S: They are trying to find a way to harvest the energy of the core of the Earth, of the planet. And in order to do that, they needed a device to break through some protection. That technology was created to create a crack in the organic protection of the core, so that when the crack was open, they would be able to siphon the energy out. So, the technology is actually two ways. There was this negative beam that came through the technology and down to the core of the Earth, crack it, and then harvest the energy up back to where they needed to send that energy. That energy then was converted, and that was that energy that was used by the bat-like entities, created an opening, and came through. It was organically from the planet.

A: *So, this was a type of attack to try to pierce through the planet's core?*

S: That facility, what happened is that there were actually people living on this planet with the dragons. At some point, they became inverted, and the dragons had to isolate themselves. When they isolated themselves, the people could not see them and they would be able to live without being persecuted by the people that were living on the planet. Ultimately, there weren't that many people on the planet to begin with, but they became inverted. They started to become hybridized, and they became those Greys. Those Greys were organic beings of the planet, and they were just transmuted when the negative beam hit.

A: *I understand. Do you know why, since these humanoid forms seem to be working negatively against the planet, and so was this beam that shot down against the planet. Then why would they target the planet with the humanoids on it, or did they just shoot it, and then these humanoid beings were just destroyed?*

S: It just happened. They weren't trying to destroy the humanoid beings. It was collateral damage, but they didn't care because they are replaceable. It was 'whatever' for them.
A: *Were they able to penetrate into the core of this planet?*
S: They were able to penetrate, that's why the planet was not able to heal itself, and why the dragons were petrified, because that energy was being harvested by the negative technology, off planet. So, there's a negative technology on the planet and there's another piece of it that's off, outside of the planet. Since the energy was being siphoned, the planet could not heal itself, and then the dragons could not heal themselves either. We were able to close down that crack, but then we needed to remove that negative technology.
A: *So, are you working on that now?*
S: Yes.
A: Beautiful, thank you. I'd like to call forth Sophia's Higher Self now. We're still going to stay within the space here, because I still have some questions, and I know you're still working on it.

The Higher Self is called forth.
A: *Thank you, I love you, honor you, and respect you for all the aid you have given us today. I know you hold all the records of Sophia's different lives. May I ask questions?*
Higher Self: Yes.
A: *Thank you. First of all, why is it that you chose to show her this life where her dragon called for her, in this cave, on this planet? Why did you want her to see that? What lessons did you want her to learn from it?*
Higher Self: These dragons are protecting eggs. These eggs contain consciousness. But they aren't dragons consciousness, they're actually baby Angels. The egg that the dragon was protecting was actually her. The dragon was protecting baby Angels.
A: *Then that's what the dragons were protecting, baby Angels. All these eggs were baby Angels. That's beautiful. It makes sense that dragons would be protecting them. So, this was herself. Was this before her soul was born?*
Higher Self: Yes.
A: *So, then at some point before her soul was born, this dragon was protecting her. Did any of the baby Angels within the eggs perish? Were they able to harm any of the baby Angels?*
Higher Self: They all lived.
A: *What connection does this beautiful blue sapphire dragon have to Sophia?*
Higher Self: I will say that he is like her father. It is like when Humans are born, they have a mother and father. This dragon is her father. It is a representation of that energy.
A: *Beautiful. If you can explain, eventually you came as the Higher Self and helped out this version of yourself, in the egg? Can you explain that?*
Higher Self: In another Universe? It's like a parallel version of the same person.
A: *Okay, so it's a Multiverse we are in then?*
Higher Self: Yes.
A: *So then would you say that Sophia in this Verse went and saved Sophia in that Verse?*
Higher Self: Yes.
A: *I know you mentioned Higher Self, that they weren't supposed to be able to do this, crack this space and poison this planet. I know you explained some of that technology. But how could that be possible?*
Higher Self: It all started with the beings on the planet, the humanoid beings on the planet. They were evolving, connecting to different aspects of themselves beyond this Universe. But then some of

them, unfortunately, connected to negative polarized aspects of themselves, that took over in this Verse. It inverted them and then just spread to the other ones. The ones that remained organic, they were killed off.

A: What dimension was this planet in, in this Multiverse?

Higher Self: I feel like it's nine.

A: What about all these baby Angel eggs, how are they doing now?

Higher Self: They are really, really good. They are ready to be birthed.

A: Beautiful. Can we call forth on the Angelics and the Collective of Dragons and Source to send all Source Love-Light to these beautiful, baby Angels in eggs that are ready to be born?

Higher Self: Yes, please.

A: Okay, sending that now. Send them love, so that they may be born wherever they're meant to be divinely, within safety. Beautiful. These baby Angels, can you tell me more about them, Higher Self?

Higher Self: Baby Angels. They are half dragons. That makes them very, very powerful. They're going to be born with special abilities, especially alchemy symbols, that they will be able to use to transmute out any negativity or infringements just with the palm of their hands. Those babies, when you look upon their eyes, their eyes are portals to yourself to another Verse; they pull you through your heart to yourself, that you may reconnect. Gazing upon these children, you'll be able to bring your soul back online. That's what they do.

A: Thank you, that is most beautiful. These Angels, once they're born, will they just be in the realms of existence or like multi-dimensional, how Angels are? Or will they be incarnating into humanoid bodies, somewhere else? What's the plan that you can share, as far as how they will assist, besides what you said?

Higher Self: They will be anchored in different planetary spheres, to assist those planetary spheres that need this assistance. That is the main core reason behind their birth in this time and space. We need this energy and this kind of assistance. Most of the babies are going to incarnate in humanoid bodies, and some of them are going to be multi-dimensional, with the Archangels, who grow and assist their brethren that are incarnated.

A: Beautiful. Since this is another Multiverse, will we also see it in this Verse, or will they just be through that Verse? How will that work?

Higher Self: They are going to be in all Multiverses. We are going to see this in this Verse as well. They were needed to birth in another one, because this verse in which they were birthed, has the necessary requirements to create them the way that they are. They will go to other Verses.

A: Thank you. Anything else Higher Self, that you can tell us about this experience?

Higher Self: I just want her to believe in herself more. She has the right to be where she is. She is a healer. She is a transmuter. She is a channel. She does not fully understand or believe that she's in the right place, but she is. I just need her to really believe, and truly know this truth within her heart, and act upon that knowledge.

A: Beautiful, thank you Higher Self. What an amazing session! Amazing memory you showed her in the Multiverse. We're so thankful for it, and we're most especially thankful for Sophia and her strength in assisting her other version in the other Verse. Also, those baby Angels are ready to be hatched when they're meant to be birthed into the Multiverses to assist in the very important role that they will be. Sending them our love once more. Thank you everyone. Higher Self, is this a good time to begin her body scan?

Higher Self: Yes, please.

The Body Scan begins.

A: Beautiful, thank you Higher Self, I love you, honor you, respect you. Who would you like to call forth, to assist during the body scan?
Higher Self: Would like to have Archangel Four, please.

Sophia has had a couple A.U.R.A. & R.A.A.H. healing sessions, and she too is a practitioner. Therefore, there is not much healing needed.

For every A.U.R.A. Hypnosis healing session we ask that the Higher Self and team ensure to remove and heal this entire list from the clients Tree of Life: entities (Grays, Mantis, Reptilians, Archons...), dark portals, repair and crystallize DNA, negative cords, technologies (implants, metals, hooks, wires, nano, vaccines), Illnesses, vision, dental health, regrow teeth, age regress 5-15 years, blocked or misaligned chakras, open-up the third eye and activate abilities, expand heart, issues with auric field, fractured soul, contracts, deletion of inverted timelines, and trauma from current or past life.

END OF SESSION

Through this session I understand at the deepest level the true responsibility of both the client and practitioner in most infinite ways. The client, in accepting to have an A.U.R.A. Hypnosis Healing session conducted, and the practitioner holding the grandest Love-Light for the client during the session. As I hold the space for the client during their session, I receive many sacred downloads and activations, and during this process of transcribing I am able to study these sessions at the deepest levels, bringing forth messages that await for me to decipher and unfold in written form for you to understand. The vision that I am being shown now is when the Universe and Multiverse need assistance, such as when these baby Angels who were on the brink of extinction, the Higher Selves beyond the veil communicate, and divinely get both the practitioner and client to the actual session. When danger happens, such as this attack on the baby Angels, in order to get assistance to these golden Angel baby eggs, the Higher Selves reach out to us through A.U.R.A. Hypnosis Healing to rewrite these types of infringements, which keeps us on the trajectory of the collective Ascension.

The collective has not truly reached the understanding and discovered the divine power of the theta brainwave of hypnosis, of the in-between, the bridge and connection of both the spirit, where we are limitless, and physical realms, where we feel limited. But, through A.U.R.A. Hypnosis we have. We truly understand the collective mission. When we unite these two spaces together, especially we who are in the third dimension, we experience miracles such as this session. We are programmed so deeply to believe that we cannot connect in hypnosis, though it is truly natural, and as easy as breathing. Why? Because the negative entities know that we hold this true divine, immense, unstoppable power, and so long as they keep us in self-doubt and non-belief, then we cannot accomplish our divine missions in the theta brainwave, as shown through this session. They are scared of this immense power that we hold within; scared that we will tap into it and unleash it. They know that when we do, it will truly be game over for them. It is time that we now know it as well.

In the session some of the younger dragons instantly died, most of the older and warrior dragons lived, but became petrified when the attack of the inverted frequency beam hit that Earth from another Verse. The reason why the younger dragons died was because in dragon forms, younger dragons are truly younger souls, not as experienced, therefore not as strong. Here on Earth it is the opposite, the younger children are stronger than the adults in soul, and this is so because, as the years pass, so too does the vibration of light on Earth raise, in turn bridging in children who are experienced souls, who have integrated into human avatar bodies in order to assist. But though they are stronger souls, they are in little bodies, which are more vulnerable and in need to be protected by the adults, until they are strong enough to protect themselves when reaching adulthood. Since they are in vulnerable vessels they are targeted by entities inside bodies pretending to be humans on Earth. For example, these artificial bats. Have you ever met someone so hateful that emits such a hateful vibration, by all that they are, it makes your stomach hurt, gives you chills, or the hairs in your body raise in a creepy vibe when being in their presence? What if what is truly inside that human body is a type of artificial entity, such as these bats, who were so inverted that they were eating the younger dragons who had died? I feel this explains much to us in how it is that the humans of Earth do horrific things to one another, the *key* being that they are truly not a Source created organic soul, and there is something else that is inside the human body pretending to be a soul. These predator entities, who have hijacked a human body, or are within cloned bodies, true intentions are that they would like to eat the children of Earth, and this is why they do eat them through adrenochrome and their satanic rituals. Truly eating their light. But, it is important that we understand that it is not just the Freemasons or the Illuminati; these predator entities are among us, and most are placed in positions where there are children available for them to prey on, at schools, children sport centers and hospitals, boy and girl scouts...Therefore, it is not a surprise when you hear that someone in these types of positions have unfortunately harmed a child. We must be vigilant and strong, but most importantly teach our children to be this as well, especially when leaving our children in these peoples' supervision, or best not to at all. We will always be given the inner guidance on how to keep our children safe, we just have to listen to the feeling inside, "Does this feel right, or does it not?" If it does not feel right, stop doubting this feeling and stop procrastinating, after all they are your seed, your children, your mission, your purpose, and your biggest responsibility given to you from Source.

We have been delivering a very important series live on Rumble.com and Odysee.com, where we are not restricted on the sensitive content we deliver weekly, of what is Antarctica and what is beyond these ice walls, and of the erased civilization of Tartaria, which are the cities we live within. Through this series we learned of these types of technologies the negative aliens use to freeze, and calcify in a stone form the giants, dragons, centaurs, and magical creatures. The technology in this session was using the power of the core energy of the planet to power their negative technologies. Only this kind of benevolent energy as the core of a planet would be powerful enough to be used invertedly to penetrate a planet like this. This we do not consent to. The seed and core of the planet is her heart and lifeforce, and to violate her like this is unacceptable. But, it reminds us of how the negative entities penetrate people's energies daily to get to their core, heart, and energy as well, for malevolent reasons of control. They need the life that exists within all living entities to power their inversions. Once more, I emphasize the importance of shielding being needed at its greatest form to ensure that these violations don't happen further to the Earth and her people.

The artificial beam in this session shot into the planet causing the disruption, like the videos we are seeing from around the world of people recording laser beams shooting down from the sky into the plates of Mother Earth causing earthquakes, hurricanes, and fires. We are currently seeing lasers shooting down onto lands as Hawaii and Canada that are causing fires. These technologies are being directed by the dark aliens stationed in the Antarctica ring, outside the ice walls. To think that the technology of Earth has reached this point! In these violent times to direct and attack human kind, similar to how these dragons were attacked. Except for in our perspective because we are in this simulation, this is a form of protection for us. Here, because of the sacred laws our organic matrix holds, they have to convince us to hurt one another. Therefore, they have to use a human avatar. Military personnel push the buttons to run these laser technologies, even if a dark entity has hijacked that human body. But when outside of a simulation like ours, where all life forms are accessible in each dimension, they can just choose to point a laser to a planet to cause destruction, or arrive with their spaceships to invade. Remember that they can do this outside the third dimensional Matrix because of the negative aliens, those who have turned dark, that are flying around in their UFO ships, or that are in bases with their negative technologies causing havoc.

Besides forcing destruction on Earth, what is it that they are trying to calcify on *this* Earth when they do this? Could it be magical creatures once more, or perhaps the people's minds? I feel that they are directing these laser technologies to sacred lands where there is dormant dragon energy, keeping the dragons asleep and blocking these positive dragon portals, so that the dragon energies will be slowed, or stopped from anchoring into Earth. The main objective to this act of calcifying beings is to freeze, and forcibly place the being who this is happening to, into a sleep stasis, where they are still conscious within the energy body per the dragons example, but not able to interact or move, rendering their energy to be harvested parasitically and used for malevolent purposes. It is similar to when a person goes into a coma, their body is laying there motionless, but their soul and minds are conscious and active in the body, and they are screaming inside to the people around them, the nurses or their families, but none can hear them because they no longer have the access to their physical functions. Neurologically something is blocking, creating a disconnect between the neurons of the consciousness to the neurons which operate the physical body. Therefore, these dragons who became calcified no longer could reach out for help, just as Sophia's dragon could only cry out to her briefly, right before he became calcified, but could not reach out after being frozen. In future literature to come through a separate book series, we will learn more of these types of technologies which are rooted in dark sorcery.

In this session we understand the Multiverse perspective at the deepest levels in how each Verse in the Multiverse assists one another, as each has a unique purpose. The Multiverse is as a colorful lotus flower of life, in which each petal represents each Verse, each petal is a different color, but yet they are all still connected to the bud of the flower that is seen as Source who holds all souls within, like a flower's bud which holds all its seeds. All petals/Verses stem from the bud/Source of the flower. The colors of the petals represent the differences to each Verse, which are subtle shades of colors, but unique to one another. What can be accomplished in one petal whose core color is a purple Verse can only be done there, and same for the blue colored Verse. See their importance? The purple petaled Verse can't do what the blue petaled Verse was created to do. Each one being unique to one another, but not too far distant to each other. Together they all makeup the entire Multiversed colorful lotus flower of life. Therefore, only in this Verse could these dragon/angel babies be created, so that they could then fractalize, spread out, and incarnate into the other Verses. Only this Verse held the distinctive qualities to create these special angel babies.

Our Verse's etheric lifeforce color is blue, which are the blankets of our Universal Creation. Per the example of the energy weapons used unto Hawaii and her people, the artificial laser could not penetrate or burn anything that was blue, as seen in videos and images that are surfacing now of blue cars, plant pots, umbrellas, and t-shirts, which remained intact among all else that was incinerated. Some have tried to say that the military can switch the dial on the laser, so it can choose to not incinerate the color blue, but we know better than that. These energy weapons cannot infringe on blue because, blue is what gives life force to all within our Verse, as it is the ether energy of our Verse, and artificial cannot penetrate this organic beauty. People have tried out these theories themselves by purchasing lasers and burning plastic lids of different colors, but still the blue lid would not burn. This understanding brings us into such a strong awareness of the true divine power of the color blue, and at the deepest levels we know that Divine Father Archangel Michael's color is blue. Explaining to us why it is that Archangel Michael is our favorite to call upon, being that he is our Father and his embodiment is his divine blue energy. He is the blue semen ether that merges with the light of Mother's egg to create all seeds into fruition. Archangel Michael has often told me how he has created his love into an infinite shield of Universal protection, now I understand further, as he is the blue ether that all in this Verse is submerged within, and because of this he can reach ALL inside this Verse. Making Archangel Michael the most powerful protector, as he reaches all infinite depths of our Universe. Through his infinite being, which exists seated next to Divine Mother, inside the seeds and bud of the Multiverse lotus flower, he too can reach all Verses within the Multiverse, jumping in and out of the petals of the Multiverse. Bringing us in a clear and deep understanding to the Universal, Multiversal, multidimensional reaches of all Archangels, as they also are braided into this original blue etheric semen embodiment, being that they are the first sparks of life created by Divine Mother and Father within Creation. With this sacred knowledge we achieve the greatest understanding of why these [26]angel/dragon babies will be pivotal for all Verses, within the Multiverse, who will receive them. Once more, imagine their potential for Ascension that they will bridge forth with their embodiments of the flames of Source these babies will be.

This session brought confirmations to us of what we have been speaking of throughout the years, and in Chapter 5, the 'A.I. Alien Invasion', since the Covid-19 virus and vaccine began, that those who allowed for an artificial intelligence integration, through the Covid-19 vaccine, are making a future potential timeline where they turn into a form of a Grey alien. One must be very cautious when tapping into other versions of us, or others who are corrupt, which is why we teach sacred alchemy with boundaries through all our courses, maintaining our souls within safety when looking to expand, learn, and gain our memory back of who we are through infinite potentials in the Multiverse. These humans who were once organic turned into these dark artificially controlled Grey aliens that were causing havoc and harm through experiments to their Earth's core energy. This disruption is what opened the dark portal for these predator bat entities to come in, and begin the petrification of the Dragons who were initially petrified because of their intimate connection to the planet, and that the dragons were the last remaining magic within that Earth, as the other lifeforms, the humans had become corrupted. So when the core was being shot at, the dragons too felt the penetration, but in some forms it was needed for them to petrify, and create a hard shell around themselves so that these entities could not get to their souls completely.

The humans of that Earth tapped into negative fractals of themselves in other verses who were compromised by the Archon virus, which then fed, compromised, and inverted them as well into a form of Greys. This is how the Archon virus has spread from Verse to Verse. If all Verses are all connected to one another, can we really stop the flow of what one Verse's experience is to not flow into another Verse? That is not possible. Our consciousnesses, as individual souls and Universal beings, are all linked in a divine way, which is how we can tap into another Verse. Often our dreams, where it is us, but it does not quite feel like us, are our memories of us throughout the Verses. We cannot completely

---

[26] Watch AuroRa channel "Dragon Goddess of Creation Nüwa" on all our platforms September 2023.

block out the Verses' organic connections to one another. Which is why at the highest vibration of Source Love-Light we are all truly ONE.

The Sophia here assisted the Sophia of that Verse, who was in an angel/dragon child form, still in its conception inside the golden egg. We are infinite spirits, who assist one another in all our forms, tethered through the threads that connect the Multiverse and our souls at Higher Self perspectives. What one Higher Self and their fractals do in one Verse, assists and allows another to achieve potentials in other Verses. We learned that only through that Verse in the Multiverse, could these Angel babies be created who are half dragons, who will eradicate the Covid-19 vaccine in our Verse and others. There is such an excitement to this potential! A combination of Angels and dragons together in one form would be unstoppable. This fusion would be at the highest souled strength, because these babies require this combination to stop the Covid-19 vaccine and the artificial inside of their parents from integrating into their baby forms conception and genetic makeup, in turn pushing and eradicating this infringement out from the parents as well. These babies will need the Angelic energies of the multidimensionality of being able to reach spaces within all creation to keep themselves in organic timelines, and the dragon's elemental energies who bring the transmutation potentials in order to heal. Birthing forth an organic baby onto Earth versus a compromised black eyed baby who is possessed by a Grey or dark alien. Both the Angels who are the guardians of creation, and the guardians to the guardians, the dragons together in one being. Wow!

Through this book series you have learned of the infinite capabilities that the Archangels harness when working in union with Higher Selves, and in this book you will learn of the dragon's powers in assisting and protecting, which will bridge forth an understanding of how important this combination of these babies are. That Verse is a special Verse to bring these potentials together of dragon and Angel. We thank our Verse's Sophia's higher self who provided these potentials for the collective of the Multiverse when she answered her blue dragon's call; as we remember, this was the only dragon that was able to reach out to their Higher Self for assistance.

To birth these sacred children forth, all that we have to do here, in this Verse, is hold the space of Source Love-Light for these children to arrive. But, truly, from when this session was conducted in February 2023, and now, as I type this in September 2023, these Angel/Dragon babies have now arrived. Sophia is an A.U.R.A. practitioner, and during our most recent monthly A.U.R.A. and R.A.A.H. practitioner video call, she gave us an update of a dream she had in September 2023. In the dream she was working hard, protecting a young boy who stood behind her, from a dark Archon entity, in front of her. She was exhausted. Her energy kept getting depleted, because this Archon was relentless, and would not stop trying to attack. It was a prolonged ordeal to go against this Archon, because every time she would, she would have to pause, and recharge her energy, over and over. The little boy who stood behind her, at some point decided to interfere with this altercation, by reaching past Sophia with his hand, out towards the Archon, but Sophia stopped his hand, and told him not to touch *it,* thinking she was protecting the child from *it.* Because she knows how ruthless and dangerous Archons are. Dream ends.

After her dream, she began to speak to Archangel Michael, who explained to her that this was an example of the energetic shift within Earth that has occurred, and how we first and second generations of volunteers tend to have to work harder, because of the original density within Earth we birthed into. When this little boy reached out for the Archon to place his hand on *it,* she should have allowed him to do so instead of being overprotective and not allowing what was meant to divinely happen. Because the little boy's energy would have automatically eradicated this Archon, the one she was having such a hard time with, in an instant. Because the density and energy these children are coming into now is so much higher; directly linked to that, within our time and space, the bifurcation has happened, and the fact that we continue to expand further through portal dates and eclipses, separating out from the inverted world. Another A.U.R.A. practitioner spoke after Sophia, and said that she had had a recent A.U.R.A. session with a client who had the Covid-19 vaccine, and when his Higher Self, and team conducted his body scan, there were not that many infringements found. The practitioner was asking if this was common, if anyone had come across this. I realized when she said that, in the last three to four months, all my clients who have had an A.U.R.A. session, who were Covid-19 vaccinated, did not have much infringement, or none, from the vaccine.

In the A.U.R.A. and R.A.A.H. certification online workshops I hosted in June and September 2023, we had attendees who had the Covid-19 vaccine, who had none, or minimal attachments, from the vaccine. In June, I hosted a workshop where I was the practitioner for an A.U.R.A. session, live, in front of the attendees. This session was posted in June 2023, on Rumble.com and Odysee.com, called 'Hybrid | The Covid-19 Vaccine.' In this student's past life she remembered when she was abducted, and experimented on, as an alien, on another planet. In this lifetime, they made her into a hybrid, by merging a Reptilian skin over her. So, she was a Hybrid not because of the Covid-19 vaccine, because her higher self said she had already transmuted the injection, but because of that past life trauma. Other practitioners noticed, as well, the shift in Covid-19 vaccinated clients. With this epiphany we realized that the angel/dragon babies had arrived! Typically, in the past, our clients required much self-healing from the jab, and had numerous attachments needing to be addressed.

Let me explain how this works. Now that the angel/dragon babies have arrived on Earth, from this other Verse, their powerful, transmutational energies are accessible to the people of Earth, who have been Covid-19 vaccinated; this has lifted the energies of Earth from within the organic side of the bifurcation. So, say a person decides that their choice of taking the Covid-19 vaccine was indeed inverted, and now has decided to, one, never make that choice again willingly, two, has learned their lessons, and three, are now on their journey of self-healing the infringements of the Covid-19 vaccine, especially by scheduling an A.U.R.A. session, to clear these inversions from themselves. This brings them automatically, into the fruition of self-healing themselves. Because the self-healing journey begins the instant they decide to self-heal, because of the true power of our consciousness, and when having an A.U.R.A. session conducted, the sacred alchemy the Higher Selves and Angels are using on the client, transcends through all their life, time and space, and especially, on the exact moment they injected it. Therefore, equating to never having it, because in the future they decided to self-heal, and have an A.U.R.A. conducted, where the Higher Self went back, and shielded them from the infringement. Bringing them into the now, where they no longer have the infringements. Crazy, huh?! The main reason this is possible is because these angel/dragon baby energies have created the space for the collective, who is looking to self-heal from these A.I. infringements, to do so. Especially those who have been vaccinated, who have reached this decision in strong Source Love-Light, are being healed by the angel/babies energies that are being dispersed out from them onto Earth, all day and night. Bringing us back to Sophia's dream, the child wasn't meant to be stopped from eradicating the Archon, as that is one of the main reasons they have incarnated. But, what the dark forces don't know is that the angel/dragon babies are not just integrating into the newborns; these angel/dragon fractals, are integrating into us, if we are ready, as well, into toddlers, teenagers, young adults, and adults, who have answered the call. They thought if they attacked the sacral chakra, and reproductive systems of humanity, through the Covid-19 vaccine, that they could stop us, but the joke is on them! We are unstoppable! The dragon energies are here, and we are rising! They better get ready for the Year of the Dragon, beginning in February 2024! Remember, it is not the dragon who is fearful, it is the dark entities that fear, and run from the Dragons! In the next Chapter, we learn of the importance of holding space, collectively, for the special act of those who are, or will, sacredly birth angel babies.

"There is always a way, when one looks from infinite Multiverse perspectives, to find the way."
~AuroRa

--------------<<>>--------------

15

FORCED INTO EXTINCTION

Session #541: Recorded in March 2023

       In this online A.U.R.A. Hypnosis session, AuroRa is hosting a live online workshop, certifying new A.U.R.A. Hypnosis and R.A.A.H. Reiki Healing practitioners. Just as in Chapter 13, 'Lab Babies', this session is the person chosen to have their A.U.R.A. session conducted by AuroRa live in front of the group for training purposes. Lilac, the client in this session, takes us through such a deep understanding in how bridging forth the Angel Babies spoken of in the previous Chapter will require for the collective of Earth to hold the space through sacred ceremony and love for their forthcoming onto Earth. Once more we must save the children of our Mother Earth. Through this alien existence we get to see the dark forces' repeated agenda of, if you go after the future life, the babies, then you can control, or stop, the race that is being targeted from further growth and procreation.

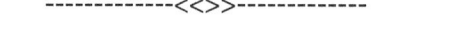

"This reminds of moments in times and spaces when all of a sudden there's this really dense sadness. And then you realize there's some alien race that just perished. It reminds me of that feeling. Sometimes people are really sad, but they don't realize that that's what's happening. That beautiful race just passed away."
~AuroRa

L: [Lilac] As I was landing it seemed very dark, like it was nighttime, but not nighttime, just a dark space, naturally. As I landed it seemed like I could still see all these lights shining, like blinding me almost. I feel like beyond that there is blackness.
A: *[Aurora] Feel yourself, do you feel like you have a body?*
L: I think so.
A: *Look down at your feet. How many toes do you have?*
L: Five.
A: *Describe to me what your body looks like.*
L: I think I might be a bird. I think I have wings.
A: *What is your skin color or tone?*
L: My first thought is blue, but I feel green as well. Blue, green, like sea green. Pretty green.
A: *Do you feel like you are female or male?*
L: Female.
A: *Since you are a bird, do you have feathers too, or is it just a tone?*
L: Feathers.
A: *Where do you have feathers?*
L: Over my body, wings, my chest, and down to my legs.
A: *Describe to me what your face looks like.*
L: It's a face that's in proportion. My eyes are dark brown. I have a beak. My beak is in proportion to my face. It's not overly large and my beak is yellow. I have a pretty face.
A: *Are you carrying anything with you?*
L: I don't think so.
A: *Are you wearing any clothing?*
L: No.

A: Describe to me your surroundings.
L: I can see the forest now. It's a smooth ground, and it doesn't feel like dirt. It just feels like a soft Earth. It's like in a rainforest where branches and palm fronds have fallen and decomposed into soft Earth. That's what it feels like. But it's not, it's solid, though. And it's uneven. But it's smooth, uneven. It's like small rolling hills. A person could walk up for example, but it's not dark. It's appealing to my eyes, curvy and nice. Coming out from the Earth are tall trees that all look uniform. They are quite tall, and they are almost the same color as the Earth. It all seems very dark, but comfortable. The energy is not scary. The trees don't seem to have any branches down low. It's just like a pencil basically, with branches at the top. But they're not heavy branches, like a gum tree or anything. It's kind of like a huge fern. If that makes sense. The energy is really nice. I feel at home here.
A: Move around within the space. Let's find out why you're here. What are you doing there?
L: I am having trouble sensing beyond that.
A: Allow for time and space, within this place that you are at, to move forward. Tell me what you do next.
L: It's not moving forward. It doesn't feel like I'm walking and it doesn't feel like I'm flying. It feels like I'm hovering. Just effortless flying. I fly towards the uneven Earth that I just described. I'm flying between trees.
A: How do you fly? Do you float, or do you move your wings?
L: I move my wings to take off and then it feels effortless. From that, it just feels like I soar, but then there are moments of moving my wings too. I don't know what that's for, to gather myself, or to maybe help myself change direction. Although, even when I'm moving my wings, it just feels helpful.
A: Good, keep describing where you're moving to.
L: I'm just flying through the forest. I started down low and was skimming across the hills, and then I went up through two particular trees. Once I got through those two trees, I went higher. I'm just weaving through these trees. It's like a maze. But it's a path. It's like humans walking through a forest. They make a pathway because they tread on that path so often. This is my pathway, except it's up in the air. And there's no print on the Earth or the land. It's familiar to me. I'm just weaving through the trees. It's really pretty. It's super dark, but I can see everything. I don't really see much beyond the trees, the Earth, and the hills. But it's very familiar to me. It's almost like it's just a well-worn path. I want to see where it takes me.
A: You're there, to where you're trying to go. Tell me what it looks like, where are you now?
L: It looks like a house. The words that come to me are a log cabin, but not quite as harsh, as solid as that on the ground. It's a single story. It's appealing. I think this is my home. It makes me feel emotional to be here.
A: Describe to me what it looks like inside.
L: I can't see. The idea, it just makes me feel really happy. I leave here every day, and go back along that path where those lights were blinding me. I haven't figured out what that's about yet. But, when I come home, it feels safe. It feels like that's what I do. It feels like it's a space where I have family. It feels very comforting. It's like, I exhale, like when you open your front door and you get home. You know? It's really nice.
A: Wonderful, does anyone else live there with you in that home?
L: I haven't seen anyone yet, but I feel the energy of my family. It does feel like I live here with them.
A: Just keep moving time and see if there's anyone else living there with you, in this home.
L: I have a male bird partner, who looks like me, except I think he's different colors. He has a yellow beak like me; that's what we have in common. He's beautiful. He's red and yellow, but in the same way I describe myself as being blue and green. It's like we are two colors, but we're one at the same time. It's hard to describe, it's like, the front of him is red, and the back of him is yellow. It just blends, but it doesn't look orange.
A: Beautiful. Look into his eyes. You're able to recognize his soul.
L: It's my husband now.
A: Yes, of course, beautiful. Is there anyone else there besides you and him?
L: I think there is a baby.
A: Look around for the baby.

L: Not sure about the baby. I feel like there is a baby energy, but I can't see a baby. And I don't feel like I'm missing a baby either.
A: Is there anything in this house that shows a baby?
L: I don't think so.
A: Feel yourself. Do you feel like you're pregnant?
L: My first instinct was yes.
A: You're able to communicate with the baby inside your womb? Do you feel like it's female or male?
L: Male.
A: Is your belly flatter or bigger?
L: It feels full, fullness. It's not that feeling where you're heavy, but it feels like it's there.
A: See if the baby has a message for you.
L: That I'm doing a good job.
A: Let's go ahead and move to another important time and space in this life. Tell me what's happening now?
L: I'm back to where I landed, where the lights are. The lights are really bright. It's not like an LED white light. It's a warm kind of tone, but it's super bright. It's enough to be blinding. Like when it's in your face. You can't see anything else, can't see where the light is coming from.
A: What do you feel that you're doing there within the space that has this light?
L: It feels like a job of some kind. It feels like it's something that I come to that isn't something that I love. It's just something that I have to do. I feel like when I'm here, I am blinded. I feel like maybe it's not meant to be in this forest. It's not meant to be where we are. It feels foreign, and that's why I feel blinded when I come here. I'm wondering whether the light is just my perception, or whether I am actually being blinded by something.
A: Keep moving time, discovering what's causing this; why are you feeling like this within the space?
L: I don't really sense anything. It just clouds me. Just being here. I am sensing the shape of a cube. The light is coming from a cube. There's literally a cube that's been plunked in a forest somewhere that is emitting light. I am just standing in front of this cube. The whole side of it is light. I'm trying to move around it to see what else I can see, what else I can sense. It's heavy, it's dense. I'm not trying to move it because I know that I can't move it. It feels foreign. And it feels like maybe I don't want it here. Or maybe I'm the only one that knows it's here. Maybe that's it. It's a cube of light. I'm not picking up anything else from this. I just feel like it's there.
A: Does it feel like it's organic, or artificial?
L: It feels artificial, definitely artificial.
A: Does anyone else notice that this cube is here?
L: I don't think so. There's no one else here with me. I feel like it does blind me. I know that it's here. When I first landed, there was just light, right in my face, and I couldn't sense anything else apart from the forest on my way down. When I'm near it, it's the same kind of bright light. But then when I shift away, or when I turn to go back on my path, actually, I feel like the path that I described, this is sitting on my path. My path actually extends beyond this on the other side. It's blocking me. That's why I can't get past it. I can't see the other sides of it. I can see this cube of light, but I can't do anything with it. It's on my path.
A: Is it blocking your way home?
L: I can go back to my home, and I can go as far as this cube, but I can't go beyond it.
A: Do you remember if there was something beyond this before the cube arrived there?
L: I do sense that my path continued beyond that, the way I described the woods. I feel like there is more on the other side. Yes.
A: Let's go to another time and space before this cube was there. When there was a path for you to go through. We're there now. Tell me what the space looks like now.
L: It's more forest. I am moving through the forest. I am following my path. It's similar terrain to the other side. It feels like it leads to an opening, a clearing. But it's a natural clearing. It's a nice place. A place perhaps where there are ceremonies, or just gatherings with love. My family would go with me to this place, and perhaps others as well. But I don't sense others. It feels like it's a space where others could come though. I know that my family and I used to come to this space. There's a dark

forest that I'm flying through. There's a clearing. There's light coming through, and it's really pretty. It's like crystal, it's pearlescent. It's shimmering light, but it's just natural light. It's like when you look up, on a cloudy day, the sun is peeking through, and there's sun rays coming through. This cube is blocking my family's access to this special clearing.

A: *In this beyond land, are there any other families like yours?*
L: I think there is, yes. I don't think we're here alone. I don't sense others. I don't feel like you could see others. But I feel like maybe everybody's blocked. It actually looks like a place that's been deserted. It looks like it was a special place. But no one's been here in a long time. It's really hard to see a place that was super special, where it felt like we were connected. Where we would celebrate. It was a joyful kind of area. Whether it was just my family, or others, it feels like abandoned. It's hard to see.

A: *This other place, what would it provide for you? What are some of the things that you would do there?*
L: It feels like a place where there would be celebrations, or moments of joy, or ceremonies. I've just tried to access what the ceremonies would be in this life.

A: *Let's go to a time where there was a ceremony happening within the space.*
L: It feels like it's just a celebration of life. There are other families there, not just one. We're just celebrating life, celebrating being together. A connectedness. It feels just like people dancing, you know in that video (AuroRa at the beginning of class showed the group a video she loves to watch by an artist named Natalia Lafourcarde, 'Tu si sabes quererme.' In this video a group is dancing, naturally in rhythm to themselves, but as a collective as well. It just feels like happy, joyous movement. Love, hugs, a celebration of who we are, and togetherness.

A: *Beautiful, do the other families look like your family?*
L: They do. Yes, we're all birds. We look blue in color. I think perhaps that the females are blue and green, and the males are yellow and red. There are children, baby birds. There's lots of them. They're running like baby chickens. They're super cute.

A: *Adorable. Is there any other memory you have of importance that we need to see of this sacred space that you're remembering?*
L: No.

A: *All right. Let's go to a moment in time in space when that cube arrived, and it started blocking that path. We're there now before it arrives. Tell me what's going on.*
L: I don't think I saw it arrive, when it arrived. I think I came to it on my path, and I discovered it. I don't know how it got there. I sense that it was through stealth. Like I don't think anyone sensed it's there. The families were in their own homes. I picture a ceremony place being in the center, and then pathways. Everyone has their own special pathway out to their home. We traveled along our paths to this central point. There was no ceremony, when this was happening. So everyone was in their own space. I don't remember feeling discomfort, or shock, or horror. I don't remember feeling like 'oh, wow, there's something coming down and landing.' It just feels like it was a rude shock to discover it in our path (crying). It's not just physically a cube sitting on the ground, but it's like a wall that you can't get past. It's emitting energy beyond it that you can't get past it. So that is what I ran into when I discovered it. Where it came from, I don't know.

A: *So now that it's blocking the path to those sacred lands where everybody enjoys, are you able to see any of the other people?*
L: Just my family. I go to the cube, they binded it, blocked it. I go back home. That's why it's so safe. It's so comfy going back home because at least my family is there, but it's just us (crying).

A: *Let's keep moving time and space and see if anything ever changes with this cube.*
L: I'm having trouble sensing a time without the cube.

A: *Okay, so let's just move to another time and space.*
L: I feel like I am old now. We are old together. We're still blocked.

A: *How about your children? Are they with you?*
L: I only sense my partner is with me.

A: *What happened to your children? I know you felt that you were pregnant.*
L: I don't think it survived. I think the importance of the ceremonies was the babies. It was the youth.

It was the connectedness. It was what held us together.
A: *This cube blocked you from being able to sacredly birth your child to be in the community?*
L: Yes.
A: *Anything else that you see of importance in this life?*
L: No.

The Higher Self is called in.
A: *Am I speaking to Lilac's Higher Self now?*
Higher Self: Yes.
A: *Thank you. I love you, honor you, and respect you for all the aid you've given us today. I know that you hold all the records of Lilac's different lives, may I ask you questions?*
Higher Self: Yes.
A: *Thank you. Higher Self, what is the reason that you chose to show her this life? What were the lessons you wanted her to learn from it?*
Higher Self: She needs to see a sacred connection with her babies. She didn't see the connection there, the importance of their community.
A: *So beautiful, thank you. Higher Self, this has come at such an important time. We have videos on Rumble, where we've been talking about protecting the children and saving them. I recently had a beautiful A.U.R.A. session with a female which was focused on holding space for the children for sacred birthing, and then here you are explaining to us again. The community and the ceremony was just as important to sacredly birth the children.*
Higher Self: Yes.
A: *Thank you. For me that's huge because it gives me confirmation. I just want to thank you, Higher Self, because it's hard for me to do these videos speaking of the things that are being done to children. Sometimes there's a lot of people who don't believe it, but that doesn't matter. It is just so important for me to know that I am always within the divine purpose of what we're speaking of. Most importantly though, that we are connecting to this collectively. We need to bring in more babies; you know what's been happening with children on Earth. Thank you, Higher Self, for this message.*
Higher Self: Thank you.
A: *May I ask you questions?*
Higher Self: Yes.
A: *She had her beautiful husband with her then, as well. I can feel and see everything, and the baby inside of her. It was so beautiful. It must have been so devastating and sad for her. Is it at all related to this life where she had miscarriages and abortions?*
Higher Self: Yes.
A: *Can we start healing that time and space now? Can we call forth on any assistance like Archangels, Divine Mother, Yeshua or Raphael?*
Higher Self: Divine Mother.
A: *Higher Self, connect us to Divine Mother now, we'd like to speak to her. Greetings, Divine Mother. Love you. Thank you for being here. We feel your beautiful love, if you can start assisting now. Her beautiful husband is there. Start healing that time of space, when they had these obstacles to conceive their children. As we know, in this life, she had to have them through C-section. Was it one baby or two babies, with a C-section?*
Higher Self: One.
A: *Okay, still healing both though. Healing all that moment in time and space, and whatever carried over to this life. Can we start doing that now, Divine Mother and Higher Self?*
Divine Mother and Higher Self: Yes.
A: *Thank you Higher Self. We're healing the miscarriages, the abortions, and any effect of the C-section. Does the baby need healing, the one that was trying to be born in that time and space? Is it one of her babies now?*
Higher Self: Yes.
A: *Can we start healing him from that as well? Do we have permission?*

Higher Self: Yes.
A: We also know that she took the cervical cancer vaccine that targets the reproductive system, can we start healing that as well?
Divine Mother and Higher Self: Yes.
A: This cube, what was it?
Divine Mother and Higher Self: An artificial technology of some kind.
A: Did it spread to the other paths, or were they the only ones that were blocked off?
Higher Self: It blocked all of the paths. It was like a wall of frequencies that couldn't be penetrated.
A: The others of the collective of this beautiful race, did they also have the same kind of situation? They couldn't reproduce?
Higher Self: That's correct.
A: Did this race ever evolve from that, or did this race die off?
Higher Self: It died off.
A: That makes me want to cry. Can we send Love-Light healing to that collective of that race? Whatever is allowed with Higher Self's permission. Are they still stuck there with that technology, or has that technology been removed, or did they all die off there?
Higher Self: They died off there.
A: Can we call for Archangel Azrael and his Legion to start healing when they passed on, so that they're not stuck there?
Higher Self: Yes.
A: Thank you. How many families were there?
Higher Self: I think a dozen.
A: Start healing them. Finding them in those moments and times and spaces, wherever they're incarnated now. As they incarnated, she, and her beautiful spouse as humans here, so we're healing them wherever those others are at. And if they try to conceive babies, their babies too. Can we do that Divine Mother?
Divine Mother: Yes.
A: Whatever is allowed, of course. Is that cube still there in this place?
Higher Self: Yes.
A: What is this place? A planet or a realm?
Higher Self: A realm.
A: Can we call forth on any Archangel, so that we can go find that cube?
Higher Self: Yes.
A: Higher Self and Divine Mother, who can we call upon?
Higher Self and Divine Mother: Archangel Michael.
A: Let's speak to Archangel Michael now.
AA Michael: Yes.
A: Greetings, brother. We love you.
AA Michael: We love you.
A: Thank you. Your beautiful energy is always felt. Archangel Michael and the Legion of the Light, if you can go find that place, where that cube is still at.
AA Michael: Yes, I found it.
A: Tell me what the forest looks like now, it was so beautiful.
AA Michael: The forest is dead, there's nothing living anymore. But the cube is still a cube emitting light. The cube hasn't changed. The forest, everything that was within, is dead.
A: Did this cube do anything to entrap their spirits?
AA Michael: No.
A: Okay, so once they passed on they were able to leave that realm?
AA Michael: Yes.
A: What was the purpose of the cube? Did it do anything else besides what you told us?
AA Michael: It did not do anything else. Its purpose was to stop the light, love, the connection and the beauty of that soul group's energy.

A: Can we go ahead and contain that cube? Is it fully artificial, or does it have some organic in it?
AA Michael: It's artificial.
A: Can you all start eradicating it? Directing Phoenix Fire, Source Flame, and Light as well. Did the beautiful bird beings have something important that we need to know about who they were?
AA Michael: Not so much who they were, but their joy, their connectedness with each other is what was significant about them.
A: Beautiful. This reminds of moments in times and spaces when all of a sudden there's this really dense sadness. And then you realize there's some other race that just perished. It reminds me of that feeling. Sometimes people are really sad, but they don't realize that that's what's happening. That a beautiful race just passed away. I know Source creates the races, how they're unique, and when this happens we're not artificial so we can't clone that race. It's just gone. Is that correct, Mother?
Divine Mother: Yes.
A: Thank you Divine Mother. Archangel Michael keep working on it. Let us know when that cube is fully gone.
AA Michael: It's very strong.
A: I know you have the Legion of Light. Do you need any assistance from Source, Divine Mother and Father?
AA Michael: Yes.
A: Let me speak to Source now, Higher Self. Greetings Source, love you, honor you and respect you. Thank you for being here.
Source: Thank you for having me.
A: Beautiful, with your infinite collective being of Source Love-Light, can you assist this Angelic team that is breaking through and removing this?
Source: Yes.

The Body Scan begins.
A: Okay, so keep working there, and I'll be back to check them. Okay. Thank you everyone. Okay, so I'm going to speak to you all collectively. I know we have Higher Self, Divine Mother, Archangel Michael and now Source assisting. So let's go ahead and begin her body scan. We started healing some different parts already, but let's scan her body and see where there's attachments. Scan her, where would you like to begin first in her body that needs healing first?

Body scan is completed. We find an artificial octopus, Reptilian with A.I. and hooks, and a dark portal.

A: Higher Self, is there anything else that I have missed that we want to take care of today?
Higher Self: No.
Beautiful. Can I speak to the Divine Mother? Greetings Divine Mother.
Divine Mother: Greetings.
A: It is an honor to have you here. As you know we are in training right now. And they're going to go out there in the world and do what we did today. Help people grow, heal, and become organic. It's just going to be glorious! So what message do you have for them, Divine Mother?
Divine Mother: The regression today was about connection and the importance of that. The importance of connection for children. Having that as the ultimate goal. Always in sight. Regardless of where you are, whatever direction you choose. The children and the connection of the children. This higher connection is the most important.
A: Thank you Higher Self, Divine Mother, Archangel Michael, and Source, everyone who assisted. Love you, honor you, and respect you. Thank you. Thank you. Thank you.

For every A.U.R.A. Hypnosis healing session we ask that the Higher Self and team ensure to remove and heal this entire list from the clients Tree of Life: entities (Grays, Mantis, Reptilians, Archons...), dark portals, repair and crystallize DNA, negative cords, technologies (implants, metals, hooks, wires, nano, vaccines), Illnesses, vision, dental health, regrow teeth, age regress 5-15 years, blocked or misaligned chakras, open-up the third eye and activate abilities, expand heart, issues with auric field, fractured soul, contracts, deletion of inverted timelines, and trauma from current or past life.

END OF SESSION

This session was important to include in this book series, at this exact chapter number, because of what came before of the angel babies to come, the awareness for children through this entire book, the most sacred knowledge to be shared in the next chapter of the pyramids of Earth, and the divine process of the souls who incarnate on Earth. Get ready for what is to come in 2024 mentioned in the next chapter! We have big missions to accomplish together. Let us accomplish them in profound ways of Source Love-Light!

The biggest understanding of this chapter is that we, who hold Source Love-Light, must remember to hold this light for the children of Earth. To hold the strongest sacred circle for the angel babies to birth forth who will save humanity, and bring forth Universal Ascension. The time is here, as you are reading this. And, through this most beautiful, joyful bird race we learned how important it is that we, the collective who have reached the high levels of love, to understand this content, that without sacred ceremony within soul groups being held that star children to come, cannot come forth. Or more so, there will be a delay if we don't hold the sacred circle, because they are coming whether people assist us to hold the space or not. But, if more hold this sacred space together, these starseeds will be able to come sooner rather than later. Bringing forth Ascension closer and within all our grasps. The Earth is ready for them, let's get them here together!

The Archons must have been watching very carefully to know that if they made a negative technology like this cube, with its negative frequency, it would block them from going back to their communities' sacred space of ceremony for children to be sacredly birthed. This attack upon this race was highly intelligent. No need to send soldiers to attack. Just make them go extinct by blocking their potential to sacredly birth as a soul group. By blocking them in this manner instead they lived a life of sadness and disconnect to their communities, longing to be together once more, and then died with this sadness. Prolonging the torment, for the purpose to feed off this sadness. The Archons direction is very clear to how *it* will stop at nothing to block as many positive races from reproducing. *It* seems to be fearful of the joy and love we carry within, as illustrated by this race. I remember as the client recalled this life, her feeling the absence of not being able to sacredly birth because of the blockage there was to her soul family, how sad it was for her. Many tears she shed as she remembered. And with each tear shed, she healed deeply.

This bird couple had to live a life where they were never able to bear a child. Reminds us of the couples on Earth who are infertile because of the many infringements which target our sacral chakras, such as trauma, technologies, chemicals, immunizations, Covid-19 vaccine, entity attachments, dark portals, implants, and so on. Through A.U.R.A. we have learned that we can heal the infertility within ourselves by finding the root to the blockage's origins, unrooting it, and then the self-healing process begins simply on its own, once what is blocking is removed. There is nothing that gives me greater joy than when I speak to my clients months, or years later and find out that they now have children. Going from infertile to very fertile. Oh, what a joy!

Through this session we got to witness the beauty that has begun for those who were of Lilac's soul group. Wherever it is that they are incarnated now, they will feel this profound healing in their lives, if they are ready for it. And, now that the healing has been provided by the removal of the cube that still remained in their realm, they will be able to tap into their loving, joyful abilities that they embodied so well. In the hope that these emotions will bring more balance into their life wherever it is that they are currently incarnated at. Reminding us that when we self-heal, so, too, do those who were part of our incarnated life, and those in the collective in similar situations.

The understanding that this race is no longer, that it was pushed into extinction, brings a deep sadness to one's heart. Many of us choose to go through heavy sadness so that others' sadness may have the opportunity to heal as well. Extinction should never be forced on any of Creator's creations. No one has the right, or the divine power to do this to another. If a race goes into extinction, let it be of natural choices and causes, and not because something else chose that for them. Every race is created for a divine purpose, so that they may experience life freely. But this race lived life behind bars, and had no way to grow collectively. However, within Lilac's memory they will always be remembered, and so, too, do we remember them.

Divine Mother's message for us at the end of the session, of the connection to the children, that no matter what it is that we are doing, may it always come back to how we are assisting the collective of the children of this Earth. May we remember the children in all ways that we are passionately driven through.

"The key are the children, as they hold the infinite potentials of what can be of Creation. Being that they are our creations, our seed. Without them as the seed, we are limited to extinction. With no seed to plant, then there is nothing to grow and expand into. Let us protect the children of Creation."

~AuroRa

---------------<<>>---------------

16

PYRAMID PORTALS INSIDE EARTH

Session #476: Recorded in July 2022
Never before shared.

In this online A.U.R.A. Hypnosis Healing session, Sylvia takes us to the energetic realms of Earth and the Universe, in order to view and witness the divine process of sacred birthing. We learn most importantly all the preparation that it takes just for one soul to incarnate into this Earthly construct. Through this session we deeply understand the sacred role that the pyramids of our Earth partake universally in birthing souls in. The journey of all babies on Earth, and how much they are loved, supported and prepared before they are born. The 12,000 Light Workers of Earth. Preparing us for what is to come divinely, which is most beautiful in the year of 2024. We must all prepare for the sacredness of the role we have agreed upon to hold the Love-Light space for the brave souls who will be incarnating to assist the collective Earth Ascension, which is now forthright.

--------------<<>>--------------

"She was nineteen years old. She strongly could say no. She then realized the connection between the force of light, and the other side. She just knew that she was so strong. It was her core, her heart, her essence speaking through her. It was her emotions and frequency. She learned to grow by herself through it. Doing it the hard way. She needed to learn by herself. This is the lesson she will never forget. This is why she knows how dark it can be. She knows that she is stronger than anything. Stronger than all of it. She is strong when she wants to be. There is nothing that can harm her."
~Higher Self

--------------<<>>--------------

S: [Sylvia] Soft, very green fields.
A: [Aurora] Look at yourself. Do you feel like you have a body?
S: Yes.
A: Look down at your feet. How many toes do you have?
S: Five.
A: Look at your hands. How many fingers do you have?
S: Five.
A: Your skin tone, what color is it?
S: I feel white.
A: Are you wearing any clothing?
S: A white dress, transparent, soft material.
A: Are you female, male, or both?
S: Female.
A: Are you carrying anything with you?
S: Silver bracelets, on my left hand.
A: Anything else you're carrying?

S: I have some kind of a red crystal stone.
A: *Do you feel like you're young or old?*
S: I think I am young, eighteen or nineteen.
A: *Look at your facial features. What do you look like?*
S: Blonde eyes. Light, long, white hair. I have flowers inside of my hair.
A: *Describe your surroundings, where are you?*
S: A green field. I don't feel it's grass. It's a green color with really bright green colors, like a plasma color of green. Not sure where I am exactly.
A: *Move around within the space. Let's see what you're doing there.*
S: I am carrying this silver crystal. I think I see a house. I can see it in the distance. I'm not sure what I'm doing with this crystal. I think I am running.
A: *Keep moving time, keep talking to me. What's happening next?*
S: I just came to the house. It's a strange looking house. I am coming to the door. Its color is peeling. It's a very old house. I'm going inside. There's some very bright lights. I am going to the light. I'm getting very excited about something.
A: *Are there others with you?*
S: I don't see any other people around. There's a blue portal inside of the house.
A: *Tell me what this portal looks like.*
S: It's a circle portal. It has a bright glow, white light coming out of it. It's shimmering looking in it. I have a feeling I need to throw the crystal inside it, I don't know why. I'm putting the crystal inside of it, it's closing.
A: *What happens when you put the crystal inside of it?*
S: This old house is just crumbling around me. It's disappearing. It feels like it's turning in circles. It's like a spaceship, but it's more simple than this. I feel like I know this is going to happen. It's turning around, around, and around. I'm just waiting. I can't see anything outside anymore just turning around this energy field. I feel that I am not scared, but I feel uncomfortable with this.
A: *You're safe and you're always protected. Are you still in that form that you felt like?*
S: Yes, it's like I am still in the center of it. It's like an energy field. Turning around as I watch. I feel like I am moving in the center.
A: *There's an energy field spinning around you or the house?*
S: The house just crumbled, it disappeared, it was destroyed. It's just the energy field, a spherical shape and it's moving around very fast.
A: *You said you feel like you're shifting something?*
S: I came to someplace which is very slick, it just forms. It's the Universe, but with this you can't see the stars. It's too dark, but bright at the same time. Just getting out of that space, walking through a transparent energy floor. Just moving forward. The black is all around me. It's like moonlight. I can still kind of see a sphere, a big one, huge. There is a golden button that I can see myself touching. The Hole is opening, so huge. There's a lot of trees, a lot of souls around. It's a crowded place.
A: *You said that there was a golden button, and you pressed it? Then there was this gate that led you?*
S: A gate, yes. You get inside through that door.
A: *What does the gate look like?*
S: It's plasma and it's got a lot of golden symbols on it. It feels like it's very heavy.
A: *What do some of those symbols look like?*
S: Some of them look like Egyptian hieroglyphs, but they are not the same. Triangle shaped, squares, and circles. Not sure what they are.

A: *So tell me, once you go through this gate what happens?*
S: There are a lot of souls inside, looking similar to me - pale, white, fair skin. They look humanoid, like me; very light blonde eyes and white hair. Females and males, all of them young. We are in some kind of cubicle space. They're speaking to each other, just relaxing. Just in each other's company. Lots of souls there. I am going to the center of this space. There is a golden ball. I'm placing my left hand on it. There is some kind of a book, but it's not a book. It's some type of modern technology book. There is no paper. But I can see the same similar shape on this like on the door. I am touching the three shapes with my right hand. I have a feeling I'm signing up. It's like a place where we are coming together to speak about what we shall do, how we are going to do it. It's a gathering place. Square, triangle, circle, I am touching them, but they have some more similar signs inside of them. I feel that's my name and I'm not sure what to call myself there.

A: *Are you able to explain some of the symbols?*
S: I feel that they are mine. They describe me. That's who I am, my soul description.

A: *Tell me what you're doing here, connecting to this.*
S: I feel like I came for an assignment when I threw that crystal in the portal. I came here after going through the portal. It's a gathering place. We are coming here together and thinking about the next assignment. How we are going to do it, and what we shall do.

A: *What is everyone else doing?*
S: It's like a gathering of groups. Most of them have the same kind of books; huge big ones. There are tables with these kinds of signs on it, and they're gathering around speaking about it. There is a group that has small planets in front of them. There is a group who have golden paper scrolls, and they're opening them. There is a golden pen. They're writing something on this golden paper. There are golden signs. They're writing, and sharing their experiences. There is one group looking through an egg-shaped glass, but you can see far away through it. I feel you can see through the Galaxies. They are watching a red planet and a galaxy. They are speaking about it.

A: *What do you feel is being said about this galaxy and planets?*
S: There are some kinds of changes going to happen. There is a sandy, small planet, to be destroyed. She's going to explode, but it's natural. It's nothing artificial. It's a natural thing. I feel like it's a cycle the planet is finishing. They're discussing how all the other planets are going to feel about it. How the lives on these planets are going to change, and what they can do to feel better through these changes that will occur in their lives. They are going to help life on this small planet. When this small planet disappears, It's going to affect a lot of the others. They're preparing the mission to help the living things. This plan is to help them go as smoothly as they can through these changes.

A: *Wonderful. Continue to move through time. Keep talking to me about what happens next of importance.*
S: I came towards Earth. I feel that my group is thinking of helping the Earth. This is the fire spreading. This is urgent. To help the people on Earth. One part of the Earth is completely dark. I can see this black thing crawling. Part of it is going to be a mission to bring more light on it. Earth needs photonic light from the Sun energy to make this grid around it. I'm going to go to the Earth to bring the light in. It's going to be a grounding light to the core of the planet. Making a grid around it. I see something like a battery. It's something mechanical at the same time. At the core of the planet, six mechanical looking objects, but made of matter. They're spinning around in the Earth's core. It's like six, huge tuning forks. They look more concave. I don't know how to explain, it's almost like a swirl. They're going to be receiving the energy of the Sun directly to the core. They are accumulators. They're going to shut the core of the Earth. It is going to clean all the low frequencies with this photonic light that is coming. Everything is going to clear itself. It just can't exist anymore. They're

planning to push the lower frequency throughout. My group is coming to fill the light up in special locations on the planet. It's going to be a grid, like an antenna. To fill up this energy, like batteries in the core.

A: You mentioned that there's something at the core. Did you say that it was metal or metallic? I am trying to understand what you were saying about the core. Can you explain that again?

S: It looks metallic, but it is matter. I'm not sure it's metallic. It's like some kind of hard metal, hard material. It is already in the Earth.

A: Does it have any shape to it?

S: I don't know how to explain. It's like a screw, but upside down. It's pointed on the place near to the core, and then it's widening up to the surface.

A: You said it's like a screw?

S: Something like that. It's a triangular shape, like a concave. Like how do you say it? Triangle.

A: Triangle? Like a pyramid?

S: Yes, a 3D pyramid shape. And there are six of them around the core. One, two, three, four, five, six pyramids. They are some hard material. I don't know which one.

A: What color is this hard material?

S: It's golden, it has the same symbol on it.

A: So does it look positive in nature or negative?

S: Yes, I feel positive.

A: You said that you, and every one of these people that are gathering, are going to come and bring light?

S: They're like antennas. Just to collect the light. When the light is coming on the Earth. It's coming through the waves, and they're going to collect it as long as they can.

A: So then when the light is being sent to Earth, someone needs to collect it, or harness it? And so these people are being sent because they have to hold the light?

S: They're holding it, yes. And they're making a grid around it. They're going to at some point transfer the light to the core to this experience. To make the frequency of that light. It's imprinted in the Earth's core. That's what I feel is going to happen.

A: So then the energy is going to eventually imprint into the pyramids and the core. The light energy that all these beings are holding?

S: Yes, they're going to hold the energy as long as possible. So this network grid is going to make itself, ground itself, and at the same time connect with a pyramid at the core. Then push the frequency of the Earth higher so all this negative, and low frequency can't really live through it. They can't really match anymore with it. It's going to get balanced for Earth herself, as this is her nature, and natural progress. It's going to help people. There are twelve thousand of us.

A: Twelve thousand of you?

S: I feel about twelve thousand of us.

A: Is it just twelve thousand of your kind with how you went to the space where you had that white hair? Or is it twelve thousand people holding light?

S: Twelve thousand of our kind.

A: Beautiful. Keep moving time and tell me what happens next of importance.

S: I feel the portal we're coming through, it's a tunnel of white light. It works really fast. I see us as sparkling dots coming through this. We landed somewhere on the ground. I am trying to see where we are. I think we came to this pyramid shaped core.

A: Tell me how you got to this pyramid?

S: It's like a tunnel portal, and we are moving really fast, fast, fast.

A: So as it was time for you to come to Earth and provide that light, you went through the portal and then you came in the core of Earth?
S: I came through the pyramid shape right now.
A: You're in the pyramid right now, inside Earth?
S: Yes, just one of the six that are in the core.
A: How about the twelve thousand of you? Are they there with you?
S: Yes, they are all inside the six pyramids; they're adjusting to the frequency. It depends on the territory they're going to be born in on the Earth. They need to adjust to one of the pyramids at further locations to prepare. So, just a lot of preparation.
A: As you're inside that pyramid, what's happening with you to prepare?
S: I don't feel like a body now. I feel like spherical energy. Inside the pyramid it's gold, and there's a lot of these symbols. We're all going to adjust our frequency with the frequency of this pyramid where we are. We need to locate ourselves, connect through it, for the place and location of the Earth. So we're doing energetic preparation here. Connecting with energy with it. We are going through some kind of plasmic mirror. When we go through it we're leaving our imprint inside, they then recognize our frequency. There is this kind of connection; we prepare so the transfers can go easily. There is a lot of attunement with this, so we are somehow connected with the pyramid, it is like a second part of us. We are our frequency body, so wherever we are, we can connect exactly to that place. This is part of our body, as it is part of us. Two thousand in each of the six. It is a huge space.
A: That adds up to twelve thousand. As you are within this space, are there any other groups like you that are also within these pyramids, or is it just your group at this moment?
S: I can see no others, it is only us. The pyramids have their own consciousness, but they're connected to us. It's like it is our consciousness now where we connect. Two thousand of us live inside of this as one collective consciousness. It is only us.
A: Keep moving in time and tell me what's happening with your soul as it continues to adjust.
S: It is my time. The body of Sylvia is just a small baby.
A: Tell me what that was like. How did you transition out of the pyramid into the body?
S: Feels like we are in the same preparation place as before, the gathering place. I know I will have a body on planet Earth. I'm going to be born. There is a part of my soul that is going to be born on the Earth. So this is where we are planning to take a body. Deciding which body and family we're going to be born in, because we need to connect to these exact locations, everybody's exact spot on the planet Earth. We're going to take a body to be born at exactly the moment we need to make the frequency right for it.
A: Tell me what happens once your time is coming for you to be born into a body. How do you do that?
S: It's the same tunnel we come through. It's a white sparkling, fast moving plasma tunnel. Moving through real fast. Going to the home of the mother of the baby.
A: So from the inside of the Earth you're in the pyramid, and then you go through from the pyramid there's like a similar tunnel?
S: No. We came back from the pyramid to the gathering place, the ones we came from before to get through this circle. It is somewhere in the Universe, here in the Twelve Dimensions. One of the Twelve Dimensions, I believe, was the golden button. We all came where we were planning it all. We're there doing this assignment, sharing. After we got the assignment, we went to the pyramids in the Earth to adjust the frequency, then again back to that place in the Twelfth Dimension, where we are gathering together. I feel it's home. I'm not sure what's the name of it. I am getting Helios, Helious, Helias? From that place, we are choosing our body in the position where we should be. And from that place,

the Twelfth Dimension, we are coming into the womb. This is all for the baby, the new born baby to be born. To live the life you need a body. I need a body now. I feel like this is inside of the Central Sun, that place we came from. That's our hope, so that we can accept all of this light energy. It's our nature. This frequency, we can hold it on for a long time, as long as possibly needed to be for the great Mother Earth. To elevate the frequency higher as it should be. So this is what we came for, to get a body, as the baby. Need the body as an antenna as a Human. This is why we're born here. All twelve thousand. We did not come in at the same time. We're at a similar age. We are seeing each other now, all of us are here. But we are at different age groups. From a child to seventy-eight. We are all here now. We are all still alive.

A: Beautiful. So, just to make sure I understood. You were adjusting to the frequency inside the pyramids, inside Earth, and then you went back up to the Twelfth Dimension, which felt like you were in a Sun.

S: This is not the Sun which is heating the Earth and planets, in the Earth's Sun system, in the Milky Way. It is the Central Sun, which is the center. The other suns are moving around, of which our Galaxy is a part of. We are from that core of the Central Sun. This is why we were able to come to the core of the planet, because the core is the planetary. It is the same material as the Central Sun. There are portals from the center of the Sun to all the Suns around into planets. They all have the spark of the Central Sun inside. So the portals are provided for us to move through from the Central Sun to all the Suns in the Galaxies and planets.

A: Once you're back to the center of the Sun, you wait your turn to be able to be born into a Human body?

S: Yes.

A: How do you go down into the Human body from the center of the Sun?

S: Looks like a spark. Part of this spark is of our soul. Just a part of it. Coming through the tunnel connected to the exact coordinates. Exact baby we chose a body for. For this time, we need to have the place connected to a pyramid the way we were before that. This spark is coming to the body of the human baby.

A: The six pyramids, are they located in different parts of the earth or at the core?

S: They surround the core, the six pyramids.

A: The pyramid that you were born in, that you were adjusting to. Is that near this place where you're being born into a baby?

S: It is not near it. It is under this place. I am getting 144 square miles for this. It's part of the Earth which is under that place, the pyramid we were in.

A: Now that you're in a body, how does that work? Do you come in before the baby's born? Do you come in right when the baby's born?

S: I feel like I came when the baby was in the womb. I think it is three...yes, the fetus is somewhere between three and four months old. So the mother gets pregnant and then between three and four months of the pregnancy, I feel like I came into this body.

A: What does it feel like once you come into the body?

S: It's a lot of adjusting. It's completely different. So for us it's very difficult to adjust. But we have time until the baby's born. We are trying to make our energy suitable for this avatar. The Human baby, waiting, planning, adjusting for our frequency work.

A: How does this world, this Earth, feel like to you inside that womb?

S: I had a lot of missions. This one's very important. I just know what I need to do. I will try my best to do it right.

A: Keep moving time, tell me what happens next.

S: I feel like a little girl. I think I'm three or four years old and just playing. This was the time that I got sick and I went to the hospital. This was difficult. They used these chemicals, they are poisonous. They're poisoning our body, so this little girl, I couldn't make these adjustments, so that's why there was all this medical attention.
A: What was it that they were poisoning your body with?

The Higher Self is beginning to talk which is why she is going back and forth from speaking of Sylvia in third person.

S: A lot of medicine, or something similar to medicine, they're giving her. They didn't know what was wrong, so they were just giving her poisonous medicine. It is destroying her immune system. I couldn't adjust to it, so I just made her resistant to all the poisons that she got. So she will be clean from it. She was alive, so she cannot take them anymore. This was a fight. They gave her a lot, and her little body couldn't adjust. It would be fatal, so I just made her resistant to any of it. So she cannot take them anymore.
A: Let's go ahead and leave that scene and go to another important time in this life. Tell me what's going on?
S: There are these entities, these black viruses. They felt an energy threat to them. They were trying to take a piece of our souls. They were dragging her around every day and night. She just didn't know how to fight against it. She needed to get stronger. I needed her to be strong. There were fights going on at school. I didn't want to interact with it. I needed her to fight. To stay strong, I needed her to learn by herself. What is the greatest force and how to use it against the ones who want to harm her. She just had to adjust herself to the light. She saw the lights, she just knew that she's very strong. Stronger than anything, but she needs to learn it without any interaction, without any help. I was behind her keeping her safe. She learned it, she's ready now. She is ready from this moment.
A: What moment was that when she was ready?
S: She was nineteen years old. She strongly could say no. She then realized the connection between the force of light, the other side. She just knew that she was so strong. It was her core, it was heart, her essence speaking through her. It was her emotions and frequency. She learned to grow by herself through it. Doing it the hard way, she needed to learn by herself. This is the lesson she will never forget. This is why she knows how dark it can be. She knows that she is stronger than anything, stronger than all of it. She is strong when she wants to be. There is nothing that can harm her. She realized really quickly that in that third dimensional world, or all the other worlds' frequency, in other dimensions.

The Higher Self is called forth.
A: Thank you for this profound session for her today. Am I speaking to the Higher Self now?
Higher Self: Yes.
A: Greetings, Higher Self. It is an honor to have you here. Love you, honor you, and respect you. Thank you for all you have shown her so far. May I ask you questions?
Higher Self: Yes.
A: Thank you. You've already explained why you choose to show her this life. Tell me any other purpose or lessons why you showed her this life?
Higher Self: She does have glimpses all the time, the glimpses of some parts. But she couldn't get the big picture of how this all is coming together. And she is still very insecure in the messages that she's getting. She has very close connections. Like the day she was born. This negative side she's

fighting with because she's here for it as the holder of the light. So she was always seeing them. That's what happens when she closes her eyes, she can feel them, she can see them when they're attacking her, and they're trying to steal the energy from her. She saw one of those Reptilians and Grey witches. She was doing a lot of protection for the Earth. There are four High Priestesses around this Grey Witch. They are High Priestesses of the Grey Witches, they're connected to their mother, their Queen. Sylvia was fighting a lot with her. This Grey queen witch was always coming to visit her. Until one day a year ago Sylvia was showing her the beauty of the frequency of love. She was in the living room with her son and she was raising the frequency of love around, and she knew that this witch was there. She saw her with her third dimensional eyes at that moment. The veil was so thin, and this was the time when she completely destroyed her with that motion, and that frequency of Light-Love. It was at that moment Sylvia realized she can fight everything. She was fighting a lot during the night's sleep, and in the daytime, every time she felt it. It was a real thing. This is why she's confused. She doesn't know how to understand which are their messages, and which are the messages from her higher self. She thinks she can't receive messages; that somebody negative may interact with her, but this is not possible. When she is in tune with the frequency, it is possible to receive messages from her Higher Self. It is understanding the diversity of the messages she is receiving, knowing it is the higher frequency, most highest of all, and she needs to trust.

A: *When they were in the pyramids, approximately, in Earth years, how long did it take for them to adjust in those pyramids?*

Higher Self: For a hundred years because of the adjustments in the pyramids.

A: *Then it was a good process of waiting just to get them here, huh?*

Higher Self: Yes, it was a process, it was a long time. They had a looking mirror. They knew how long back in time they needed to go to make the adjustments in what's going to happen, and this is the year, 2022. The light has almost accumulated enough. They're already doing their work. This is the year when they're accumulating 80% of the light which is needed to be accumulated for Mother Earth. It is going to happen in two years.

A: *You mean 80% for the group, or for the Collective?*

Higher Self: For the Collective of that twelve thousand. They all are on 80% of the light. This is the year when most of it was accumulated. In the next two years, it's going to be the time. Maybe less, maybe more, but that next round, next to a year, depends from the push, and from the energy of the Earth. Earth needs a time to release the energy of the frequency which is imprinted in her history of the existence she needs. Now she's doing it. Next year, it should be a short time. It is directly connected with the grid of the light. Once it is there she can breathe normally. She needs to release negativity, so she can breathe in the new frequency and to anchor it in the core. The core of her. So it's shortly, the time is now.

A: *The time here is now, for the next two years for this group to prepare.*

Higher Self: Maybe more than less, but it is the time frame for now at this time. Maybe it looks like two years, we'll see.

A: *That's interesting. Because today, the number that adds up for the day today is July **, 2022, which adds up to the number 20 which is two.*

Higher Self: Yes, nice. That's right.

A: *Also, the session number is 476 which adds up to the number 17. Which equals number eight and I know how you said their light was at 80%?*

Higher Self: 80% is now accumulated this year. It is blasting with a photonic light at the centers. Everyday it's growing more and more.

A: It's just beautiful how these two numbers that you said are actually in her session number and her date. Okay, thank you. How do you spell the name of the race of these twelve thousand beings?
Higher Self: HELIOS? HELIEOS? Not sure if it's correct, if I am spelling that correctly? HAELEOS.
A: It's also wonderful to know that they're all still here. They're still alive here on Earth, these twelve thousand.
Higher Self: They're still all alive here now, yes.
A: Are some of them younger children or are they all older adults like her?
Higher Self: They're all different ages. There are young children and there are old ones. Seventy-six is the oldest one.
A: When did all the twelve thousand finally completely incarnate, what year was that?
Higher Self: They're all here now on Earth.
A: What year was it when they came?
Higher Self: The youngest one is six years old.
A: Okay. So that would have been 2016? If the youngest is six years old?
Higher Self: 2016, yeah.
A: In 2017, many people received a strong catalyzation, so it's interesting to know that the last one came in 2016. Then the next year, we saw great awakening in people. A lot of catalyzing things happened to people to wake them up, and to have them stand in their sovereignty and strength.
Higher Self: This is the frequencies rising with each and every one of them. They're bringing the frequency up with the photonic light. When they're born, they're bringing the frequency. They're getting older and older and they're collecting more light. It depends on the light, where it is, and how much they can collect within themselves. They're making the frequency higher and higher. Now they're all here. And that's going to be it. This is why in two years the youngest one needs to be the age of eight, so his body can stand the full amount of photonic light, which is expected to be 100%.
A: Beautiful, so what will happen in two years from now when this group collects this light energy?
Higher Self: They should be connected to the pyramid inside the core of the Earth. And when this happens, the light from the core is going to push up to the Earth's surface. And it's going to raise the frequency in every corner of the Earth itself. It's going to raise the frequency in every living being inside of it. It's going to adjust itself. The Humans are adjusting now. They're preparing for this frequency as they're adjusting now. They could be holding the light. They can also be that light as they're calibrating the same frequency. Nature is already ready. It is Humans, they need to adjust themselves. Everyone which is lower and does not match the frequency of Earth is going to dissolve the self or leave the planet Earth. It's their choice.
A: Can you explain again what's going to happen with this energy two years from 2022?
Higher Self: It's expected that when the youngest one, which is six now, gets to the age of eight years old. When his physical body, avatar here on Earth is ready to hold a full amount of light to anchor 100% of the light. Which is needed to be then transferred to the pyramids, to the core of Mother Earth. Then the light is going to push through the surface all around the earth. It is going to shine from the frequency and from inside. In that moment, the core is going to connect to the Helios energy, as they are the same material. The core is going to connect with Helios directly, and push the energy of the Earth and frequency of the Earth to change it. Every living being on the planet Earth needs to change their frequency to adjust themselves to exist on the energy of the Earth in that moment. This is why people need to adjust their bodies, so they can be prepared to be exactly in the same frequency. So they will live with that frequency and that change will be smooth for them. If they stay in the lower vibrations, lower frequency, they will not be able to stay on Mother Earth anymore.

They cannot, they will just dissolve themselves, go back home, just leave the planet. It depends, they have their own choice. Everybody has the right to choose.

A: This is something we talked about last year, about 2024 being really important for the Collective. Thank you for the added information about that. I know that it is a year where we are able to shift the Collective's energy, and we're able to assist a lot of children. We're able to basically portal out from this time and space, back and forth, to help the timelines. Thank you, that makes sense of what you shared. Thank you for answering the questions to ensure we understood. Can we begin her body scan now? Who would you like for us to call forth upon now to assist you during the body scan? Any Archangels? Any other benevolent beings?

The Body Scan begins.
Higher Self: Archangel Michael and Source.
A: Higher Self, connect us to Source and Archangel Michael. We would like to speak to them now. Greetings.
Source/AA Michael: Greetings.
A: Thank you. It's such an honor to be here with you. Thank you Source and thank you Archangel Michael. We love you, honor you, and respect you. We are beginning Sylvia's body scan and Higher Self has asked for your assistance during her body scan. Let's go ahead and start scanning her. Higher Self, Source, and Archangel Michael. I'm just going to speak to you collectively. Where is the strongest place you'd like to start now that has negative energies, entities, technologies?
Source/AA Michael: There is something on her breast.
A: Scan her breast now. We know that she had cancer and they ended up removing all the tissue in her breasts. Can we scan that area now as she had surgery recently there?
Source/AA Michael: It's a black portal.
A: Where on the breasts is it?
Source/AA Michael: It is exactly the one where there was cancer. It's the right breast.
A: Let's go ahead and close that dark portal Archangel Michael. Let me know when it's closed.
AA Michael: It is closed.
A: Source and Higher Self, can you fill in Love-Light there to her right breast now, and start the healing. Just to confirm, Higher Self, did she have breast cancer?
Source/Higher Self: Yes, it was cancer.
A: Is there anything left from the cancer?
Source/Higher Self: She was already asking for this kind of healing. We did this already with her. Checking again, to see if there is anything left.
A: Let me know if you find any other cancer cells.
Source/Higher Self: It is all fine now.
A: Good. Phoenix Fire to her breast area now and Love-Light.
Source/Higher Self: Yes.
A: What was the root cause of why she got cancer?
Source/Higher Self: There was a lot of blaming of herself. She was blaming herself for things that were not going well when she wanted it to be. This is why she gets vulnerable. This is why there were changes in the original blueprint. She wasn't having any problems, but she made this on her own, blaming herself for things she's not guilty of. This is why. Too much expectation and she knows it. She has worked on it, but she's not giving herself credit for it, when she's working pretty hard.

A: Good, thank you. We know that she had implants that she had there for some time. I want to make sure there is no kind of poisoning from having the implants so long in her chest. Scan her deeply, is there any residue from those implants?
Source/Higher Self: No, it's fine.
A: We know that she has new implants in her. Can we scan to make sure that she will be safe having those in for the rest of her process of Ascension?
Source/Higher Self: She will go through the rest of her life with them, that's fine.
A: Should she be shielding them since they are inorganic to her body?
Source/Higher Self: Yes. Every month is enough, it doesn't need to be every day. To make the intention of the shield for monthly.
A: Scan her chest. Is there anything else that we need to heal within her chest?
Source/Higher Self: No, it's fine.
A: Can you tell us how it was that the dark portal entered into her chest?
Source/Higher Self: This is connected with the seventh dimension of her existence. There was a fight up there. She was injured there and this is how it gets through all dimensions and ends up right here in the third dimension. That was how it happened, she was fighting again.
A: Let's heal that time and space when that happened to ensure she doesn't have any more infringements through that.
Source/Higher Self: Yes.
A: Good. Let's go ahead and scan her entire body now for any entities. We want to find them and contain them. Scan her deeply and thoroughly. Where does she have entities at?
Source/Higher Self: There is something in her stomach.
A: What kind of entity is that? Is that a Reptilian, Archon, Earthbound, or something else?
Source/Higher Self: It's a Reptilian.
A: Contain it now within her stomach. Let me know when it is contained.
Source/Higher Self: It's contained now.
A: Good, we'll talk to it later. Let's keep scanning her. Where else does she have entities? Let's find them all.

We found an implant in the head which was transmuted, an Earthbound entity in her uterus which was contained, and a couple other dark portals, which were closed.

A: You said she has Reptilians in her stomach, left shoulder, lower spine, right and left leg. Are any of these connected to one another?
Source/Higher Self: They're all connected.
A: Let me speak to them collectively. Higher Self, Archangel Michael, Source, bring them up, up, up now. Greetings.
Reptilians: Yes, greetings.
A: Thank you for speaking to us. We love you, honor, and we respect you. We are speaking to you today because you're attached to Sylvia's body. We would love to assist you so that you no longer have to attach to her, or anyone else. You have been stuck like this for a very long time and you have forgotten that you are actually the most beautiful light and that you are free. You no longer have to play this negative role. Would you allow us to help you spread your light so that you can become free and positively ascend?
Reptilians: Yes.

A: All of the Reptilians in her body, find the light within you and spread it to all that is you, every root, every cord. Do you have any Reptilian bodies somewhere else?
Reptilians: Yes.
A: Connect us now to the Reptilian bodies you're connected to. Let me speak to them now.
Reptilian Bodies: Yes, greetings.
A: Thank you for speaking to us. May we ask you questions?
Reptilian Bodies: Yes.
A: We love you, honor you, and respect you. If you could tell us where is it that you are at?
Reptilian Bodies: We're underneath the Australian Continent.
A: How many are there with you?
Reptilian Bodies: One hundred and ninety-eight.
A: Exactly where are you underneath Australia?
Reptilian Bodies: Just near Sydney.
A: Are you in a building? Or a cave?
Reptilian Bodies: In the caves, underneath the tunnels. They're connected with the tunnels.
A: What is it that you're doing there?
Reptilian Bodies: We were here forever, we just live here. It is our territory. We are living here to do whatever it is we are doing. We are sorry.
A: The Reptilian consciousnesses that were attached to her have begun to spread their light. Would you allow us to help you spread your light so you could become free?
Reptilian Bodies: Yes.

The one-hundred and ninety-eight Reptilians/Reptilian Bodies spread their light, and we retrieved all their consciousnesses spread throughout creation, which were attached to others, and then provided Source Love-Light healing to all who allowed. The Reptilian consciousnesses attached to Sylvia during the surgeries she had in her life.

For every A.U.R.A. Hypnosis healing session we ask that the Higher Self and team ensure to remove and heal all as listed from the clients Tree of Life: entities (Grays, Mantis, Reptilians, Archons...), dark portals, repair and crystallize DNA, negative cords, technologies (implants, metals, hooks, wires, nano, vaccines), illnesses, vision, dental health, regrow teeth, age regress 5-15 years, blocked or misaligned chakras, open-up the third eye and activate abilities, expand heart, issues with auric field, fractured soul, contracts, deletion of inverted timelines, and trauma from current or past life.

A: She has a couple of questions. She wants to know what's her connection to Archangel Michael. Why does she feel strongly connected to him?
AA Michael: She is a part of the same energy. She's a fractal of me.
A: Beautiful.
AA Michael/Higher Self: This is why she has these connections. She knows already, but she never wanted to believe in it. Because she doubts herself a lot.
A: You just have to help her, Higher Self, to ensure that she doesn't doubt herself anymore; that she works through it. No more doubt, thank you. Higher Self, you've already explained, pretty much throughout the whole session, about her purpose here on Earth. Is there anything else you want to tell her about this life on Earth?
Higher Self: We just want to tell her to stop doubting. Trust in every question you're receiving. Your Highest Self is inside of you now; we are one. You just hear my voice. We're not hearing your

thoughts anymore. You're hearing your Higher Self now. We are one now, the time is now. We are one, this soul.

A: *Thank you. She wanted to know, why did she get breast cancer? What was this all about?*

Higher Self: This was her... she was playing with her life, she was not happy. She was unhappy for a long period of time. She became vulnerable during that time. At the same time, it was a simultaneous experience, as she was planning this. It was going to push her again to the rebirth she needed. But, at the same time, in her seventh dimensional body, she was fighting, and she was injured. That was affecting her energy in the third dimensional body, which was in a vulnerable place. She was depressed when she was collecting these feelings of unhappiness and doubt, and this is why she was very vulnerable there. It was connected to these events. So, she already knew that this was going to happen. This was her rebirth day. From now on, she will be a completely different person. This needed to be done like this. She's going to be much tougher from now. We need her to be. That is what was happening all together, in all her multidimensional expressions.

A: *Is that also one of the reasons why her joy disappeared? She wanted to ask about that.*

Higher Self: Yes, that was the period of time that she blamed herself and doubted herself. And in the spirit of these negative emotions, she just lost her joy. But, she didn't lose it, she just forgot it. Now it's time to get it back. Remember it is rebirth day for her. A lot of things are going to rebirth, as a Phoenix from the ashes. She is going to rebirth also. It is her journey. She knows it is beautiful and they want her to be strong. She's strong now. She's enough, so from here on she's going to be much more easy on herself. She's a different person. Now she knows and she has the bigger picture. It's going to be fine. All she said, she knows. She felt it deeply. Everything is as it needs to be right now. That's all, we love her deeply. She knows also. She can feel that love and whenever she needs it she can feel it from the portal of the heart, or the love from the Creator, from the Central Sun. She can adjust it. She can feel as much as she needs to. As much as her body can stand. She can do whatever she needs to do; that is all.

A: *She mentioned that she hasn't had sacred sex with her husband for two years. What advice do you have for her, because it's putting stress on her, her life, and her relationship with him.*

Higher Self: It is going to be changed now, because her energies and vibrations are changing. She was fighting a lot with all these Reptilian influences. She knew that they were attached to her. She was correct, and she was very aware of it. This is why she couldn't go on with her third dimensional life in the normal way. This is what she was doing on purpose. Again, sacrificing herself. She's always doing this. So we need her to know that it is going to be done now. Things are going to be changing. She needs to follow her heart. That's all.

A: *She asked, what is the purpose of the light language and hand symbols she has been guided to do.*

Higher Self: She was carrying her gifts with her, and now they're opening. She's going to use them for a long time, use them a lot, and at different lifetimes. They're all now very available to her. After this rebirth mode, she will use all of them for her work.

A: *Is there anything else Higher Self, that I could have asked that I haven't?*

Higher Self: I think we are done for now.

A: *My infinite Love to her and her beautiful family, Thank you to everyone who assisted. Source, Archangel Michael and Higher Self. I love you, honor you, and respect you. May I bring her back now?*

Higher Self: Yes, please. Thank you Aurora for all the wonderful work you do.

END OF SESSION

We learned in the previous chapters of the Angelic babies who will birth forth on Earth, and the divine requirement for the collective to hold the space of the infinite Source Love-Light in order for them to come. Through this session, we next learn of these 12,000 light warriors within Earth, who have fully incarnated together as a group. Wow! Showing us how these groups of all types of divine creations have answered the call throughout the Universe. And, that each one of these groups is unique to one another, but so essential for the collective divine Ascension plan. We must all play our individual roles as we have agreed upon, knowing though that some will not be able to accomplish their missions, as they lost themselves along the way in this Matrix incarnation. But not this group of 12,000; each and everyone one of them is awakened and holding the grandest central heart/sun's light within them.

Sylvia's higher self explained to us how she was always able to see negative entities, and how a group of witches, who were dark priestesses, had targeted her throughout her life. Sylvia was a strong holder of light, and this is why she was targeted. The distractions, the attacks, are all part of trying to hold us back, but a bright light cannot be dimmed even in the darkest realms, instead *the light* shines brightest surrounded by the immensity of darkness. Therefore, their attempts are truly useless.

When Sylvia's group volunteered to incarnate, they were shown prior, how one part of the Earth was in complete darkness, and that there was something crawling on it among this darkness. What was crawling was the artificial intelligence nano. The side that is dark represents the inverted world of the bifurcation of the two/third world split, and the other half is the organic world still holding on. Therefore, this soul group agreed to come and spread across special locations on Earth to fill up the light and to grid a shield on Earth and its lifeforms. Many different types of star groups have spread throughout Earth, who play these different roles, but ultimately it is all for filling in and holding the light for Mother Earth, and her future, divine Ascension.

In the time and space that this group incarnated, the Earth was in desperate need of a replenishment of her photonic light in her core. Like a rechargeable battery, which is on low, and it is about to die out. The light within Earth was low due to the combination of all the infringements we have become aware of through this book series. This is what this group's direct mission was, to recharge Earth's core photonic light, so that the dark side of Earth could not take over completely. As the Higher Self said, "They're like antennas. Just to collect the light. When the light is coming on the Earth it's coming through the waves, and they're going to collect it as long as they can." May this role, that we all hold, be understood through this chapter at its extreme importance. Often people think when their Higher Selves tell them that their role is to hold the light for Mother Earth, "Oh, I am just here to hold the light. My role doesn't seem so important." Silly to take holding the light, lightly now, after this chapter. But, no matter what, Earth's battery/core would never be allowed to be drained, because of the roles the light warriors of Earth play, and the constant Source light that is being channeled through these 12,000 star seeds, or other groups such as these, who have answered the call.

The Higher Self explained, "There are portals from the center of the Sun to all the Suns around into planets. They all have the spark of the Central Sun inside. So the portals are assisting us to move through from the Central Sun to all the Suns in the Galaxies and planets." During the process of our Earth's collective Ascension, this group of 12,000 will continue to push out the inverted darkness within Earth, balancing the Earth herself, and the people, through this connection that they have to all suns. Every portal date, every equinox, every new moon, full moon, and eclipse they will hold the light for the collective to do this. The 12,000 will also have a gigantic role during the final collective, physical

Ascension of Earth, in which they will push the frequency of the Earth to the highest, so that all the artificial intelligence, and low frequency won't be able to survive through it. Transmuting all that is synthetic within Earth. This ripple will begin in the third dimension, and will amplify and spread through all parallel Earth dimensions. As a second Earth will pick up on the ripple, it will double, and then the third Earth, it will triple the potency of this light, and so on, and so on. Multiplying, and multiplying until the ripple of light reaches infinity. This is when those who are a matching vibration to Source Love-Light will all ascend out. Further explaining what the Higher Self said, "The core is going to connect with Helios directly, and push the energy of the Earth and frequency of the Earth to change it. Every living being on the planet Earth needs to change their frequency to adjust themselves to exist on the energy of the Earth in that moment."

In 2016, the 12,000 completed the mission of ensuring that the entire group was incarnated. The following year, in 2017, many people on Earth had a strong catalyzing experience, which catapulted them into awakening. I, too, experienced this in 2017. Now I understand one of the main reasons why we experienced this in 2017. It was because of this group's photonic light power they accumulated together, which then dispersed into the collective, pushing forward those who were so close to awaken, to awaken. In 2022 when this session was conducted the Higher Self explained how the 12,000 had reached 80% of light, and that in the next two years this light within them would continue to grow to reach 100%, which will happen in 2024. This completely aligns with what we have been delivering of how important and gigantic 2024[27] will be for the collective Ascension process. And, that many of us who have mastered time travel through our consciousness in the Earthly timelines, will use 2024 as a bridge and beacon to travel through, in and out from. This session has been delivered to you right on time to further prepare you energetically, and to assist us to bridge the positive timelines to come. This is why approximately two years from 2022, in 2024, the youngest one of the 12,000, who will be the age of eight, will be able to withstand the full amount of photonic light in his body, which is expected to be 100%. This light within this group is so precious, because they are like tiny little suns walking among us, emanating out Source grand central sunlight unto us, and so long as they are here, Mother Earth's photonic light will never be diminished, and neither would it for all living beings of Earth.

The ripple effect that ties the planets to each other, through the Ascension process just explained, as per the example of the natural destruction of the small planet in this chapter, and how it impacted its surrounding planets. Even though this was the natural order of the small planet that was coming to an end, the surrounding planets needed to prepare and adjust to the potential changes to their energies and environment once that planet would no longer be holding the space where it was located. Again, understanding how all life forms in this beautiful creation impact and influence one another in some form.

It was beautiful to witness the profound soul group gatherings in the astral, in preparation for their missions on Earth. How they share with one another their experiences they had gained prior. All part of ensuring that each and every soul is divinely experienced at the deepest levels before they incarnate on Earth, taking on the challenge of life within the third dimension. Each group was different from each other, and were brainstorming ideas on how each would accomplish their missions. The missions and the soul group agreements that must, and will, be played out in some form. These soul

---

[27] Through our Mayan/Atlantean series on our channels we have been delivering updates to prepare us for the year 2024.

agreements will not be stopped, whether accomplished through one perspective, or another. There is always a plan B,C,D,E... to what could not be accomplished within plan A. The divine plans will be successful, we just don't know in which letter, per this example, they will be accomplished within.

The most sacred knowledge that was shared to us through this session was how it is that souls and newborns enter this construct. Since 2017, in all our channels and Book 1, we have explained the importance of the pyramids and mountains of Earth. How they hold the light and coding for a soul to enter into this Earthly construct. This chapter adds more knowledge on this sacred topic, and to what was shared in Chapter 7 'The Essenes', when we spoke of the gridding of Earth through the pyramids and mountains. The Higher Self explained how the 12,000 had entered the six pyramids within Earth a couple times to recalibrate energetically, adjust, and prepare their souls to incarnate into this density. We could imagine that it would be too traumatic for a soul just to come straight into this lower density, but through the process of cultivating for one-hundred years Earth time in the six pyramids, it allowed for the souls to have the smoothest entrance into the third dimension.

Through this chapter we realized the vast importance of the land/territory we all choose to be born within on Earth, and our needed adjustment to that land. Each land, country, town, and city feels different from one another. With the combination of the crystal beds under the cities, the collective vibration of the city, the quantity of inverted technologies, and the types of natural resources that assist the city. I can see how a soul would need to adjust to fit into the collective energies of the specific land they will be born into. The major reason for the land we have chosen to incarnate in is because of the body we would be connecting into. Many star seeds, such as this group, who might not have had karmic connections to Earth before coming in, chose a body to incarnate, not because of the past life ties they had to their earthly family, but instead to what their mission is on Earth, and which land and body that they are born into will provide their highest potential of success to accomplish their soul mission. This is why most star seeds' earthly families are not truly their soul families, as these light warriors in this circumstance typically do not have any soul bonds with the family they chose. They are just a family who they needed to incarnate through, truly for the body, to assist the collective. And why the awakened often ask, "Why in the world would I choose that family?!" More of an understanding for us to 'love all, and attach to none,' and if these families we chose to be born into have not chosen the light, which is our grandest mission, it is time to release them, so that we can walk, talk, and breathe the divine true mission.

The Reptilians we spoke to, who said they were located in the caves underneath in tunnels, these are connected to what are called catacombs. There are videos which have surfaced where these underground catacombs contain piles of hundreds and thousands of human bones, which have markings of teeth bites. Meaning these catacombs are really the underground tunnels of the negative polarized Reptilians which kidnap people and take them to these tunnels where they eat their flesh, bite by bite. These missing people's bodies are never found, because their bones are laying underground in these catacombs. Since the beginning development of A.U.R.A. we have been assisting Reptilians, both on Earth and beyond, to positive polarize. From our understanding, when they choose to spread their light and release their negative polarization, their bodies drop, seeming dead wherever they are. Through this sacred work we have assisted millions, billions, trillions to positively polarize that are of this Earth and parallel Earths. This is grand work we are accomplishing, through entity removal, when we understand it at this level.

We conclude this chapter with addressing Sylvia placing strong blame on herself, which was the root cause of why she was diagnosed with Cancer. Things were not going well when she wanted them to, and this is why she became vulnerable. We don't realize that when we create and deliver harsh emotions and feelings towards ourselves, how poisoning it can be to our body. We can only guide the creations we are manifesting, and allow for them to blossom. Like a 'bird of paradise' tropical house plant, when it begins to grow out a new leaf, it emerges from the in-between of two leaves. For some time it remains as a point, the leaf wrapped into itself like a piece of paper in which you roll tightly unto itself, or like a tightly wound spiral. After some time this leaf begins to loosen up, little by little, opening up. It can be a slow process to watch. If you were to force the wrapped leaf open, it would not be ready and would rip. One must learn to let go, and just flow. We cannot force beauty. Beauties can only blossom themselves in their own divine timing; otherwise, we can end up tearing them, as illustrated with this leaf analogy. The Higher Self explained that she wasn't meant to get cancer, but Syvlia placing strong blame on herself is what changed her original blueprint from never getting cancer in her life, to getting it. Syvlia had too many expectations, was not giving herself credit, and she was working very hard. Showing us that no matter how hard we work, if we don't give ourselves acknowledgement and go easy on ourselves that this negativity directed towards ourselves can be like poison, and be a big part of us causing illness and holding ourselves back instead of moving forward. Surrender is always key to all that we are.

At an in person Retreat in 2022, the attendee who was chosen for AuroRa to conduct the live A.U.R.A. practice session, was diagnosed by the medical industry with cancer. When we asked the Higher Self during the Body Scan portion of the session, the Higher Self said that the attendee never had cancer. That the doctor was a dark Reptilian, and that they just wanted to stop her light from spreading into her awakening. They further explained that it is part of the medical and pharmaceutical industry to lie and tell people that they have cancer, causing great fear within them, which then makes the people at times create cancer inside of themselves, because they truly believe they have it. Which helps us understand that most of those who have been diagnosed with cancer, do not actually have it. The medical industry is a false inverted system, which requires sick people to feed off of, and sometimes those people are not really sick, but their medications, which are prescribed, make them sick.

The Higher Self of the attendee explained that what was most damaging to her was the radioactive chemicals that were injected into her through the chemo, and that people receive more damage from the chemo versus the cancer that they may have. The attendees' organs were severely damaged from these radioactive toxins, and required a lot of healing from her team during the session to repair them once more. The chemo, which is injected into the person who is diagnosed with cancer, is invertedly designed to go after and destroy all blood cells in their body, so that new, healthy cells can then regrow. The chemo sits and fuses into the organs, skin, and bones truly becoming a poison, even after one has overcome cancer. Therefore, the main reason why one would survive cancer, would not be because of the chemo, but instead that the body was created magnificently, that even after you have injected a poison into it, it only survives because of how healable and brilliant our bodies truly are. The body was always made to heal itself, therefore it repairs and regenerates cells all on its own naturally, even when you are the cause of its attack through chemo. Like when you cut yourself, and the tissues, and skin work together to heal and repair what was damaged, closing the incision.

The body can regenerate all, because all organic body parts within us have a blueprint which is found in our DNA, so the key is that the DNA will always repair and regenerate, because the coding of our organic embodiment is held in our DNA. The DNA within all that we are will always work to correct oneself, or heal what is coded within its blueprint of our beingness. Especially, if you ask lovingly for it to heal and code itself back to its original organic DNA. When we study plants, herbs or trees, we understand the importance of their roots, because even before they emerge from the soil the roots first form with all the qualities needed to make the tree... The DNA represents this to us, our roots. And, that no matter if you cut a tree down, they can regrow themselves from the roots once more, never there being a death so long as the roots remain in healthy soil. The coding of our being is found within our roots/DNA; therefore the soul, and the body, can always rebuild, regenerate and grow back to its original, organic form. The original multidimensional roots/DNA will always be found in the origins of the infinite soul located inside their Tree of Life. Understanding at the deepest level that a soul can always repair and heal because their original coding will always be nestled in their Tree of Life, as each soul is a seed which grows immersed in the etheric energy of creation into a tree. At the highest essence of our beingness we are our Tree of Life.

> "In our heart center is where we find our inner Sun, where we connect to the Grand Central Sun of our Creator Source. This light can never be fully siphoned. All that is needed is for us to ask for it to be replenished, and it shall."
> ~AuroRa

--------------<<>>--------------

17

YESHUA, DOLORES & DONALD TRUMP LIGHTWORKERS RISE UP

Session #546: Recorded in May 2021

In this online A.U.R.A. Hypnosis Healing session we are surprised by a somnambulistic client, who does not remember their session upon waking. The last time this happened with this divine team of Yeshua and Dolores was October 2018, when A.U.R.A. Hypnosis was at its beginning stages, and it was clear that we needed to stay strong and prevail, no matter the obstacles. Four and a half years later they deliver updates on saving the children, politics, presidents, false light, high-jacking of lightworkers souls, anchoring truth, and just as the sessions in 2018, once more delivering messages for AuroRa and the A.U.R.A. Hypnosis Healing sacred teachings. AuroRa adds channeled knowledge of President Donald Trump, who he is, and his strong mission for the collective.

"It is not just about Earth, it is impacting the entire Galaxy and Galaxies. It is a time to be more powerful than ever. March forth in truth to be solidly grounded to truth and integrity. It is a time to help others heal, and it is a time for all Lightworkers to rise up and to self-heal."
~Yeshua

"We need even more practitioners with the skills and the gifts to remove these entities and energies and attachments, and to have the abilities to see them. It is through clearing this energy out that we are one step closer to this planet returning back to its original organic blueprint. So it is very important that more are trained and given the tools and the wisdom, the shielding, the protection, and the knowledge."
~Yeshua

"There are actors, not just in Hollywood, but also in the spiritual communities. Let us not be fooled, as we are no one's fools. I have chosen and choose to never place an act on for the collective, and instead I will always be an embodiment of raw love."
~AuroRa

M: [Megan] From space I was taken so far into the void, farther than I've ever been before, and I saw below a golden planet. It looks like the Earth, only it's golden. When I landed on this planet, all I see is gold around me, in my eyes. I can't quite make out anything yet except this color of gold and feeling so warm and protected and loved. It feels like I am integrated with this gold. I feel it. I am the warmth. I am the gold.
A: Do you have a shape within this gold? Are you just the gold?
M: I am formless. I appear as streams of light.
A: Beautiful. So let's see what you're doing within this space. Tell me what you're feeling, you're doing here. What does this space represent to you?

M: I am everything, and I am all that is. I am melding with the flow of space and time. I am at one with all. It is a beautiful feeling, one that is so full of love. This golden color is emanating everywhere. It is a consciousness.

A: Let's see within this energy that you are all one in consciousness. See if there are any messages that this embodiment is ready to deliver to you.

M: Yes, I am the Christ Consciousness.

A: Greetings. We love you, honor you, and respect you. Thank you for speaking to us today. If you could tell us, why is it that you're speaking to us in this moment in time and space through her beautiful session?

Christ Consciousness: Yes, it is emotional for me to feel this, and it is also bringing out emotion to be heard as this Christ Consciousness. I walked the earth as Yeshua (crying). I came to heal the planet. I came to heal all, and it was a struggle. A part of me that wanted all to hear the Word of God, of unity, but it was met with so much resistance and pushback. At times it was extremely hard. I had followers that loved me, but some betrayed me. It was a journey. It was difficult at times.

A: Yeshua and Christ Consciousness, that's so beautiful. Thank you for taking on the mission to be the embodiment of the Christ Consciousness, to awaken the Collective in the beautiful ways that you have done, as we all still remember you. If you can, tell us more about anything else that you're here to speak to us about.

Yeshua: It is so painful, and grieves my heart to see this world in chaos. The Earth, Mother Earth, Gaia, in the condition it is in. It seems as though, to many, the darkness is the force that is taking the center stage now, but it is with powerful purpose that this darkness, this blackness that needs to be eradicated from all hearts, that it is coming forward. It is doing so in such a way that it is waking up the children of God. It is waking up all hearts that have been hardened. It is waking up the Collective in a way we have never seen on this planet. We have to hold on. We have to know the truth, that God is with us. That we are not alone. That we have to rise up in every ounce of strength and power that we have. Know that will prevail with love, and love will heal us. We have to want it. We have to accept it. There has to be many more of us on this path of wanting this New Earth to fully manifest. Many are tired right now. Many Lightworkers need lifting up and gathering up. They need rejuvenation and restoration and a reminder of why they are here. It is time to reconnect the mission. The powerful purpose of those beautiful souls that have been planted during this time to be here to help usher in this great new world. It is not just about Earth, it is impacting the entire Galaxy and Galaxies. It is a time to be more powerful than ever. March forth in truth to be solidly grounded to truth and integrity. It is a time to help others heal, and it is a time for all Lightworkers to rise up and to self-heal. We must march forward. There are many helping us right now. I will tell you, it does bring much pain to my heart to witness some of the behavior that goes on this planet, but it can be changed. I, as Yeshua and the Christ Consciousness, I am here to touch all hearts. I am here to return all to their place of oneness in the unity of all. We must remember that we have been all things. We have been the lover. We have been the cheater. We have been the ones that have given birth, and we've been the ones that have taken life. We need to balance everything. It's time to return back as a Collective to the zero point. It is time to go back into the void of darkness, into the womb of Creation, to be fully healed.

A: Thank you for your beautiful messages, Yeshua. You always reach deeply into our hearts to activate and bring more light, where there is light needed. How are we doing Yeshua? All those Lightworkers who are operating in the strongest light, but also those who are just operating, who might not call themselves lightworkers, but who are just being love or holding a strong light as well. How are we doing as far as assisting Ascension? What can you tell us on our trajectory?

Yeshua: There have been many great strides. There has been great forward movement. There have been many Lightworkers awakened into their power to heal in a greater way. There has been exponential growth. Our mission now is to continue to awaken those hearts and minds that are still not in alignment with the truth of Creation, the truth of what life really is. It is the duty of the Lightworkers to hold the space of love for those not awake yet. To truly love them into awakening. For it is that love within their hearts that will be the catalyst, the activation, to help awaken them. It is not the attitude of "Oh, those stupid people, how long do we wait?" It is rather loving them into activation and awakening. Embracing them with our hearts, our minds, and our souls. We commend you, AuroRa, for the powerful work that you have done, for the light that you have awakened within many beautiful Lightworkers. It is work that is so needed on this planet. It has made a huge shift in the trajectory of mankind. We commend you. We commend your Lightworkers, your students, those that are rising up.

A: Thank you, Yeshua. I know the Christ Consciousness strongly guides us as what we teach, and the courses we teach have been gifts given to us for the Collective from Christ Consciousness, from Yeshua, from Divine Mother of Creation, and all the Ascended Masters. So thank you as well, and everyone who has assisted us to bring forth these courses and these modalities so profoundly. Thank you for trusting us with these sacred teachings.

Yeshua: You need to know there is more coming. There will be more downloads in the days to come. There will be more information coming that will create a ripple effect of change that is exponential. It is time to prepare dear AuroRa, because this information is forthcoming, and it is a time to also rest. Take care of yourself because there is much coming in to take hold, to anchor into your students, to anchor into the planet, to assist mankind. It will be coming in in bits and pieces rather than a download that is lengthy. So be prepared to write down, take notes and anchor these new teachings that will be coming in to assist. We are here to assist you, and to guide you, as this information comes in. But it is very important that you prepare; get your body ready and make sure that you are taking care of yourself. That's also very important. We know you have done a great job with this, but we are just taking care of you also, as we say this.

A: I will ensure to take good care of myself so that I am at the highest space to receive the sacred knowledge as it continues to come forth to us. Thank you.

Yeshua: We say to Megan, that we know that she has struggled in this lifetime. But we commend her for the strength and the courage that she has had to rise up and transcend above it all. She knows that she is an advanced being. But it has been difficult to understand this Earthly planet at times. We want her to know that she is loved beyond all measure. That even during those times when she feels like an island, like there are not many people around her that understand her, that we are loving her. We are holding her, we are lifting her up and keeping her held in the arms of God. She has a beautiful light, and it is time for her to shine it even more. She still has much work to do here on this planet. They want her to be healthy. They want her to take care of her body more. To be more in the physical realm, as far as allowing herself to love her body and to take care of it, because she tends to be more connected upward. It is important that she be grounded into this vision of the New Earth. This grounding will assist her in her mission.

A: Thank you, Yeshua. I know we have been sharing much about you, and who your true form is. There's programming on who your beauty is, and how people think that you are their savior. So just wondering what your thoughts are, or anything else you want to give the Collective, as far as viewing you as this Son of God and savior?

Yeshua: I came to teach all that it is not I, as the savior, that saves this world. It is every human, every man, every woman, every child, reaching within their own light that saves them. I am only a representative of the love of God that walked this planet. I had no intent to be worshiped, to be followed as a savior. Instead, I came to be the example of love. I came to walk and to show others that, as they look inward, they are the ones they have been waiting for. Every person has the ability to save themselves. I am here for everyone, but we are the saviors. We are the ones that will heal ourselves and heal this planet. I am only the representative of the Collective. As we return to wholeness, as we embrace the light and the dark and come back to that place of balance, of zero point, where all is in harmony and balance, we will all merge together and join up as one living light. That is what will heal all.

A: Thank you, Yeshua. You mentioned earlier that it is hard to see some of the things that are happening on Earth and to the people on Earth. Which brings up children and pedophilia, as well as human trafficking. How are we doing on that? You know that our focus has always been on the children, but is the Collective rising to be able to speak of this? Are they standing up for each other, and especially children? How's the percentage on Earth? Are they changing? Are they shifting? Any advice, or update you could give us on this very important mission of the Collective?

Yeshua: There are many who have made great strides in uncovering what truly has been happening for eons, and the atrocities to children. There are many that have shed the light on this issue. But we have a long way to go. It is not in the awareness of enough people at this point. It is also about overthrowing governments that are attached to the operation of using these children in a very horrific way. So, there is much work still to be done. Many more people need to be educated on this. It is about overthrowing the darkness in these governments, because it is still being fed. There is a contract between these dark entities that have been trying to infiltrate this Earthly plane. This contract is still in existence on some levels. It is about bringing all of the governments in this world, this planet, that are still operating under these very dark horrific conditions, into accountability, for allowing such a thing to exist. It is not the priority of our politicians to stop this atrocity with the children. It's going to have to be more people rising up, like a grassroots effort. It needs to be out publicly. It needs to be discussed even more. Much prayer needs to be placed upon the situation where there is still much work to be done. That is not to say there hasn't been progress. There has been but as you know, AuroRa, it is huge, and it goes beyond this Earth.

A: Speaking of the politicians, even though we'd rather, of course, not have this type of control system, this government. But as you know, it is where we're at as a Collective currently. Yeshua, we currently have a pedophilic president that cheated and put himself into office. What advice can you give us going forward to ensure to do our best collectively to hold the space so that perhaps in our next voting we can have someone positive? Someone who actually does care about the Earth, the people, and specifically saving children, so we can get to this initial timeline?

Yeshua: It is wise to remember, that no matter what side there is in the United States, whether it's Republicans, whether it's Democrats, that this insidious energy, these dark forces, these entities appear as humans working for our government. So there is not a right or a wrong. It is rather a mission of clearing out this darkness, these entities on both sides, so that we can rise up in unity. It is important to place thought on manifesting the person that is in the highest alignment to run the United States of America through a manifestation of enough people letting go of sides and truly asking for the one that is needed to rise up. It can be manifested. It may not happen for a number of terms. It is a work in progress with each person that steps up. We are making progress. It will possibly be two more presidential terms out before the one is placed in the presidency that will finally lead us to the annihilation of this darkness.

A: So then it will be a gradual shift to lead us to that initial one you're speaking of?

Yeshua: Yes, a gradual shift. Each person that comes in will be succeeded. I'm hearing the word, superseded, by another person that will bring more to help and assist. Followed by the next person that has been the one to really lead and end this.

A: So hopefully going forward our divine manifestation, collectively, will be that we at least can have more of a benevolent president coming forward in the next 2024 election.

Yeshua: Lightworkers, those who know the atrocities that have taken place with our beloved children, they are the ones that need to be reminded of the power of co-creation, of envisioning and holding within their hearts what is needed to shift this all around. If it is to be in the form of a human, or a divine being in a human suit, to stop these atrocities, we, they, all of us, can do this. It can happen. We must not give up. This is a time to literally bring all benevolent forces of good, of divine love, of unity together. For every one is needed. But it can be done. There is hope. We must not give up.

A: Thank you, Yeshua and Christ Consciousness. We will continue to think about the ways that collectively we can co-create and rise up through the manifestation of the presidency. And overall spreading it, as well, to the rest of the Earth so that we have more of a benevolence in charge of each country. So thank you for that.

Yeshua: What is coming forth is that the Lightworkers can envision themselves growing exponentially, surrounding Gaia, Mother Earth, this beautiful living, breathing, planet, stretching their arms out around her and holding Gaia together as one. This will help the planet heal even faster. It's a vision of going beyond our human bodies and literally surrounding this planet with our energy together. It is a time of gatherings where we come together to do this. Where we use our gifts, our talents, to send this healing energy out at given times together. Not necessarily for the public, but for those who can do this work.

A: Anything else that I could be asking you right now, as far as collective messages, that I'm not asking?

Yeshua: We commend you for taking time at the different numerical sequences to send love to the Earth, to the children. We would suggest adding in there a time for your beautiful Lightworkers to do what we had spoken about, envisioning the planet with their beautiful energies and gifts stretched around the planet at once. At the same time, this will help heal the Earth in a much quicker way, it will speed up the timing of also stopping the atrocities with the children. This is very powerful, it will be needed. We also would suggest even calling in your beloved practitioners to meet with you at a specific time, and doing this multiple times of just holding the vision of this planet healed, seeing all children healed, et cetera. You know what to do. This will be very powerful, and there will be many onboard that will be so happy and willing to step up and participate in this. It is needed. We wish to say again, never give up hope. Change is coming. But as we know, sometimes it can take eons for the shift to firmly take hold. We know that with the strength of those awake now on the planet that we are in a time where anything and everything is possible. If the focus is there, the loving hearts are there and the willingness. The healing will happen and it will take hold. We need even more practitioners with the skills and the gifts to remove these entities and energies and attachments, and to have the abilities to see them. It is through clearing this energy out that we are one step closer to this planet returning back to its original, organic blueprint. So, it is very important that more are trained and given the tools and the wisdom, the shielding, the protection, and the knowledge. It is much needed. It has blessed humanity beyond measure. There are so many lives that have been saved. So many returned back to loving again. It has been a gift to this world that has just created such a beautiful ripple effect. The healing goes out exponentially. As one heals, we all heal. Once again, we give thanks for this work, and we give thanks for the growth that you will be seeing. Your discernment is key in all of this.

A: Thank you, Yeshua. As you know, every day, I send love to those who perhaps have been watching us for a couple years, or ran into our content, and still don't believe that they're worthy, or that they're strong enough, or that they're gifted enough. Or maybe don't understand how vast and infinite it would be for them to become certified through any of our courses. But specifically, A.U.R.A. Hypnosis, how powerful it is to learn how to self heal yourself and assist others to do this as well. Beautiful to know that there's going to be more of a turn around where we're going to get more of these people hopefully, finally, coming around, because once they make that decision, it is infinite, as you know, the potentials. Like you said, so many lives truly are saved as they learn to heal and protect others. Thank you, Yeshua and Christ Consciousness. Since we are speaking of this topic, Yeshua and Christ Consciousness, is there anything we can do to help the Collective to understand this divine process that we do with entity removal, past life regression? Can we send love to those people to help them turn their vision this way? Their hearts activated to understand? Can we send them a wave of love?

Yeshua: Yes.

A: As we're speaking now, it is 1:11, and I held the space as you said. I visualized anyone else who was in the future assisting us, to do this too in a big, gigantic, etheric form of our energy bodies, hugging Mother Earth and holding her with infinite love. I really feel like this is a good time, the 13th hour of course, since we are sending love already to Earth, to the people, to the plants, to the animals. How many minutes do you think that we should hold space, Yeshua and Christ Consciousness?

Yeshua: Thirteen.

A: For those who might not have thirteen, can we say maybe just at least four to thirteen minutes?

Yeshua: Yes, for those that can't hold that during that time, that is fine. It will help contribute.

A: Beautiful. We'll communicate that upcoming in the next live video. Thank you, Yeshua. Anything else you want to tell us of importance?

Yeshua: This is nothing new, but I wish to say it again. Love heals all. Love heals all. Love heals all. We must love our enemies. We must love those that have come to attack and hurt us. It does not mean we condone their actions. But love is greater than all of it. It is trying to come in and take us off center. It's simple. People have a hard time remembering that, in simplicity, we can heal. In simplicity, we can shift things. In simplicity, we can save our children. We don't have to make it hard. Humans like to make things very difficult. So it's time to get rid of the blockages that we each, individually, have to being on our path fully present, and fully in our power. It is time to heal the wounds. It is time to come back to a space of loving ourselves so much. For if we do not love ourselves first, we cannot love others. We must love ourselves. Let that love then spill over into your field, and the world, to be shared. It is simple. It is time to remember the simplicity of truth. It does not have to be hard. It is time to rise up with ease.

A: I love that. Beautiful. Is there anything else I could have asked, before we begin her body scan?

Yeshua: We are complete. We appreciate this opportunity to speak and we just send so much love to you, to all of mankind, to this world, to all that is. There is so much gratefulness.

A: I feel your beautiful infinite love. In the beginning, Yeshua, I sensed Dolores. Is she here?

Yeshua: Yes. She was aware of her presence when this session started. Yes.

A: Did Dolores want to talk?

Yeshua: She says yes, she would be happy to talk.

A: Beautiful. All right, Yeshua, we will talk to you later when we need your assistance during the body scan. Now if we can please speak to Dolores?

Dolores: Hello, AuroRa.

A: Greetings, beautiful. I love you, honor you, and respect you. It's an honor to be speaking to you. It's been a couple of years since I've spoken to you in this form. Thank you for joining us today in communications. Any messages for us?

Dolores: It's great to be here (chuckles).

A: What messages do you have for us Dolores?

Dolores: Well, there is much to say, I don't know where to begin. I am happy to be here, to be seen and heard. You know, this is a very complex planet we are dealing with right now. So many schools of thought out there right now. There are so many spiritual leaders who are not sharing the truth. They are of the false light. They are pretending to have truth, but in actuality it is meant to bring confusion to the streams of truth that are out there. So, we have many in the spiritual community that are very confused right now because of all of this. Some of it has been deliberate to stir up confusion and chaos. Keeping people off balance, off center, not knowing what to believe. Many have awakened to the fact that there are many leaders now teaching untruths, making up stories. There are many in the base movements, so to speak, that have these great tall tales of things that have happened to them. When in fact, they have been made up and they are spreading, basically, lies and untruths. So what it is teaching us is discernment. To listen to ourselves, and to know that if something does not resonate within us, we have to keep questioning it, and if it does not have a vibration within us of resonance and truth, we need to stop wondering and asking questions, and just realize that something is not right. Something is amiss, and move on. So many are spending so much time watching videos listening to speakers that are simply there to confuse them. It is my hope that even more people will awaken to this and come back to the truth that is within them. If we listen within, to our own internal guidance compass, which is the truth of all that is, that we came in with. If we reconnect to that truth, we will never be steered in the wrong direction, or allowed to believe these false truths out there. Once again, it is about coming back to ourselves. We are the ones that will rescue ourselves on this planet. We cannot wait for somebody outside of us to make any kind of change for us on our behalf. It is up to us. We are the healers. We self heal. We are here and know the truth through our own internal guidance compass. It is powerful when you are in alignment with that truth. So, it is my hope that more wake up, that more come back to this compass within them.

A: Thank you, beautiful Dolores. As you know, you sure left a beautiful embodiment of catalyzing truth behind you. Such a beautiful force you anchored into Earth. You already know you are a great part of my awakening. Actually number one, I would say, besides Angels. For so many on Earth, as well. We're so thankful for you and your example of Love-Light brilliance.

Dolores: Thank you, AuroRa. I will be the first to say that in no way was I perfect when I walked the earth as a human, but I gave it my best shot. I truly learned so much through the work that I did, which I was then happy to share with the rest of the world. There was great knowledge and wisdom that came through the clients that I worked with. Clients that brought forth things we had never thought of before. And then seeing the commonalities come out. It was such an exciting time. I know that that work blessed the planet and blessed many people. I'm so grateful to have been a part of it. But I,too, was human. I do not profess to ever be perfect in any way. I gave it my best shot, and I truly had a great ride while I was on this planet. It gave me great joy.

A: Most beautiful. Any other further messages before I speak back to her Higher Self, Dolores?

Dolores: I think that's enough for me now.

A: All right. Wonderful, thank you. An honor to speak to you once more.

Dolores: I thank you. I'm feeling so much joy and happiness, gratefulness. Thank you for being here. Thank you for listening. We must go forward. Do not give up. It's happening. We are changing things for the better, and it will continue to get better. But we must anchor in all truth. Anchor in the power that we all hold knowing that we are all being divinely led. That divine support will always be with us. Thank you.

The Higher Self is called forth.
A: Yes, truth. Huge, huge, huge truth. Dolores, thank you, we love you, honor you, and respect you. Can I speak now to the Higher Self?
Higher Self: Yes.
A: Thank you, Higher Self. You took her to this beautiful space where we got to speak to Yeshua and the Christ Consciousness. Thank you to you, and her, for embodying such a beautiful, strong light to be able to do so. Thank you for all the beautiful messages that were given from the Christ Consciousness, Yeshua and also Dolores. Higher Self, if you could tell me, first of all, why did you take her to that beautiful golden existence where she was all, and the Christ Consciousness and Yeshua spoke through her? What were some of the lessons you wanted her to learn from that?
Higher Self: We wanted her to remember her lineage, her light, and that she is the embodiment of that consciousness. We want her not to be afraid to shine her light. She has been under the radar, so to speak, doing her work helping others in a profound way. She has grown leaps and bounds in the last two years in her abilities. We wanted to remind her that it is safe for her to be seen and to be public now. That it is okay. She has been fearful at times based on some of the attack energy that has come in. Also, there has been, at times, fear of the people that knew her as the music teacher. Someone who did great work with children, and now that she is doing this work, has had some of her friends turn against her because of the work she does now. There has been judgment placed on her. So, at times there has been fear about coming out fully with her light and what she does. The divine beings are coming in to tell her it is now time to step out. To step out of the shadows, out of the fear. To know that it is time that her light be fully seen and to be embodied by her. She no longer has to hold back. We know that she has had many that have been jealous of her gifts along the way. Even when she was teaching music, she experienced some of the same energy from her peers. What she does now, with a spiritual community, there are those that try to squash her light, and hold her back. Make her feel that her work is less than when, in actuality, it is her light that sometimes scares them. So they feel they have to hold her down. This has wounded her very deeply at times, but we want her to know that she healed those wounds, and that she has always been able to transcend anything that has been thrown her way. She has great strength. It is that strength that has kept her safe at times when the dark has tried to take her out. So we say rise up sister, it's time. You're here for a powerful purpose. You know this. Rise up.
A: Dolores was very strongly with her and spoke through her. Is there any reason why Dolores was with her and spoke? What did you want her to learn from that experience as well?
Higher Self: That she, like Dolores, has learned so much since she started her healing practice. Even when she was doing it very part time, when she was still teaching music, there has been great growth. With each experience, there has been great wisdom brought in. With each client she has worked with, she has learned more and more. Then the culmination came when I heard AuroRa talk on YouTube with Laura Eisenhower. Megan knew that we wanted to learn this wisdom from AuroRa. She was guided. She knew that it was her path. So the new wisdom coming in has only made her ability to help others, and to heal others, even greater. It has brought into our own field a greater sense of protection, knowing how important it is to shield; make it a practice, daily; and to just know, within her heart, that she is protected always. That intention is anchored in now, very powerfully. So all the wisdom and the teachings that have come forth in the last year and three months since her experiences with all of AuroRa's classes have anchored in a new way of really being in the light, truly helping others. It gives her so much joy when she helps others. There's a new level of happiness and joy in helping others, and loving herself. There is so much gratefulness. So, like Dolores, every experience for Megan has gotten her ready for this moment, which she is doing now. She is also

grateful that because of her growth, she was able to bring all the fractals of her mother back together when her mother died. Listening to her Angels, her guides, and following their directions. Helping her mother to become one again, and healed and whole, and rescued from being taken into the dark. It is with so much gratefulness, that I just know I would not redo anything, even the dark arts, because I have learned so much this lifetime. It has been one of just realizing so many times, over and over again, that it does not matter what anybody tries to do to me, throw at me. How they try to push me down. It does not matter as long as I hold the light within me; I love myself, and I recognize my own internal power. I remember why I'm here, my mission. I knew before I stopped teaching that my goal was to be here for others; to be of service, to love others and to help heal from the wounds that I healed within myself. I knew that I would be doing this, and I'm grateful for every experience.

The Body Scan begins.
A: *Beautiful words. Higher Self, is this a good time to begin the body scan?*
Higher Self: Yes.
A: *Thank you. Who would you like to call forth upon to assist during her body scan?*
Higher Self: Archangel Michael.
A: *Can we also call on Yeshua and the Christ Consciousness since they were here earlier?*
Higher Self: Yes, please.
A: *Anybody else?*
Higher Self: Archangel Jophiel.
A: *Higher Self, if you could connect me to Archangel Michael, I'd like to speak to him.*
AA Michael: Yes, we are here.
A: *Greetings. I thank you, brother. We love you, honor you, and respect you. Thank you to the legions of these beautiful angels who are there with you. If I can please speak to Archangel Jophiel as well.*
AA Jophiel: Yes, you may.
A: *Greetings, Jophiel. It's an honor to be talking to you as well. Thank you everyone for being here. Let's go ahead and begin Megan's body scan now. All of you working together. Yeshua, Christ Consciousness, Archangel Jophiel, Michael, and Higher Self. Where would you like to begin at in her body?*

We find a technology attached to a reptilian in her rib cage. The technology is beginning to be transmuted and the Reptilian is contained in the alchemy symbols.

A: *Let's keep scanning her. Where else does she have entities at?*
Higher Self, Yeshua, Christ Consciousness, AA Michael, AA Jophiel: There is an implant in the back of her neck, it's appearing as a square, an oblong, and in the middle of it there is a duplicate of that, but only much smaller. It is metal and there is a lock over the metal.
A: *Michael, can we remove that lock?*
AA Michael: Yes, we can.
A: *Good. Start removing the lock. Does this lock have any kind of contracts, or why is there a lock there?*
Higher Self, Yeshua, Christ Consciousness, AA Michael, AA Jophiel: It is from the Archons trying to lock her light down. There is a cord going up to Archon energy. There is a fleet of Archons attached to this and they're telling me they came in the day that I was hit by energy that came off my friend, who energetically attacked me.
A: *We're transmuting that technology now. We're severing any connection, attachment to those*

Archons. Does the Legion of Light want to go find this squad of Archons?
Higher Self, Yeshua, Christ Consciousness, AA Michael, AA Jophiel: Yes.
A: Go ahead, go find them. Higher Self, you can call forth on any other assistance that may be needed to gather these Archons that are infringing on her. Are there any others that these Archons are infringing upon Earth, besides her?
Higher Self, Yeshua, Christ Consciousness, AA Michael, AA Jophiel: They're working through another young man in Sedona. Should I say their name?
A: Sure, yes.
Higher Self, Yeshua, Christ Consciousness, AA Michael, AA Jophiel: It is working through...
A: Is this a past healer she knew?
Higher Self, Yeshua, Christ Consciousness, AA Michael, AA Jophiel: David and I had many past lives, and I came upon him a few years back. He has a YouTube channel. It holds great concern for him. He has fractalized through many different personalities and it is because of not dealing with some unresolved abuse when he was younger. Right now, he is leading groups of people being connected to old energy, old alchemy, in that he thinks he is now channeling Thoth, when in fact, it is some inverted version and it is not Thoth. He has become very harsh towards people. Very egotistical and does not want anyone to help him. So there is concern of this knowledge that is being spread amongst his group. Megan has been an observer to try and dismantle some of this energy and bring healing to it, but there has also been push back energies because of it. I am severing ties and holding this individual in a space of love at this point.
A: Thank you for that explanation. Dolores was talking about Lightworkers who were not really speaking truth. So this is an example, and also her friend, who attached this to the back and attacked her energetically. Didn't she say she was also like a supposed healer, too?
Higher Self, Yeshua, Christ Consciousness, AA Michael, AA Jophiel: She is not a healer but she does readings for people. She has many other gifts like making jewelry, but she walks the fine line between dark and light and does not do her work many times from the light, so it is concerning. There is a connection between all the people just mentioned here. There is also another player, he also is another 'spiritual teacher' in Sedona. We have all had many past lives together. So it seems to be a working out of all of this in this lifetime.
A: I'm so proud of her that out of this group of people she is still so pure in her heart and her love, and being so organic. Thank you. We are severing the Archon attachment to Megan to ensure that there's no more of these types of infringements going forward. I'm sure she'll be very strong in setting up strong boundaries with these people so that they don't infringe on her further. We thank her for the work she has been doing to dismantle this as well. Has the Legion found these Archons that were infringing on these people?
Higher Self, Yeshua, Christ Consciousness, AA Michael, AA Jophiel: Yes, they have been allotted. The sapphire blue dragons of Michael have been assisting.
A: We'll let you do that process of containing these entities in the symbols, so we can start neutralizing them out of our Universe. Thank you. Besides these people that you mentioned, are these Archons also messing with the Collective of Earth?
Higher Self, Yeshua, Christ Consciousness, AA Michael, AA Jophiel: Yes, they are. There's an energy of coming into soul groups of people that are similar to what Megan has experienced. She has not heard this knowledge before, but there is something around these Archons coming in and hitting soul groups that have come back, and know each other in this three dimensional world here, now, on this timeline. They're hitting them, trying to pull them all off their trajectory. What they're showing me is how these spiritual leaders are getting hit, and they're getting hit hard. It's like a hijacking of their

soul. If they aren't awake enough, they can literally lose their soul and then have this darkness walk-in. Then they begin spreading, 'the light,' but it is truly the dark that is speaking through them. So, there is something energetically happening with these Archons hitting these soul groups of people. Unless you are awake and holding firm ground, you don't see what is happening, it just comes in and takes over. It is through discernment and holding firm to truth that Megan has been able to learn to be the observer in many situations. Observing these people and knowing who is speaking on truths. Who is being used, and operated, through darkness. We need to stop these Archons from hitting these spiritual leaders.

A: Thank you. I know you're working on it, but then I also know that these Lightworkers, who have been compromised by these Archons, also need to do their work to step into the vibration and true Source Love-Light, so that they will no longer operate from lower vibrational emotions of trauma to heal within themselves. Ego is the biggest way to trick people like this into operating in these lower control systems. Some of these you mentioned had a following, did these Archons affect the people who are following them as well?

Higher Self, Yeshua, Christ Consciousness, AA Michael, AA Jophiel: Yes. That has been a concern because some of these people are young. They are new on their path. They feed the energy, for example, coming off of Sedona. They feed that energy within him that is channeling this darkness. They don't even know that they are doing it because they think he speaks so wise and full of wisdom. But it is ancient old wisdom, it is old alchemy. It is not appropriate for the present. It's not helping anybody. These young people need some place to go, and they literally fall at his feet. It's a place to get recognition, to feel like somebody cares about them, when, in actuality, it is inverted. It is dark energy coming forth. So Megan has spent time trying to transmute this energy, just praying that these people awake.

A: Thank you. We're doing all that we need to do there, and then we're transmuting that in the back of the neck. Is that being worked on?

Higher Self, Yeshua, Christ Consciousness, AA Michael, AA Jophiel: That is good. It's gone. Thank you.

A: Beautiful. What was it causing her by being there on the back of her neck?

Higher Self, Yeshua, Christ Consciousness, AA Michael, AA Jophiel: Great pain and tension in the neck. It would cause the vertebrae to push towards the right side of her neck and create like a bulging on this side. It was keeping her alignment of her upper cervical and her spine, from being in the right alignment. Causing a lot of tension and pain in the head, jaw clenching, and pain in the face. She often would have a lot of pain in the face and pressure.

A: We're healing all of that, that it was causing now. Thank you. Let's keep scanning her. See what other entities does she have in her? Make sure that we don't miss anything.

We contain entities, close dark portals and begin transmuting an implant in the spine.

A: We'd like to speak to the Grey in her ribcage that has turned back to organic. Let me speak to it now.
Grey Alien: Yes.
A: Greetings. Thank you for speaking to us. Love you, honor you, and respect you. If you can tell us, are you fully organic now?
Grey Alien: Yes.
A: Tell me when did you attach there to her rib cage?
Grey Alien: When Jessica (Megan's supposed friend) was in the car.

A: What were you before you turned into this Grey?
Grey Alien: I wasn't a Grey. I was actually, sounds very weird, but a mushroom.
A: So they took the consciousness within the mushroom, and made you into a Grey?
Grey Alien: Yes.
A: Was this a mushroom from Earth or somewhere else?
Grey Alien: Somewhere else.
A: We're so happy that you've regained your memories back to know who you really were before this infringement happened to you. We'd love to assist you since you've turned to organic. Spread your light now so you can release yourself and then you can become free and sovereignly ascend. Would you allow for us to help you to do that today?
Grey Alien: Yes.
A: Good. Find the light within you. Spread it to all that is you, within you, that's attached to her. Let us know once you're fully out and you're all light. Make sure you don't leave any piece of yourself behind.
Grey Alien: I'm ready.
A: Beautiful. Do you have a message for her before you go?
Grey Alien: I'm sorry. I did not mean to harm you. I know I've been creating pain for you. I'm very sorry. I have a mindless job. I have been controlled and I am grateful to be returned back to my organic blueprint.
A: Beautiful, beautiful. Thank you for your message. We love you. May you be surrounded by the Love-Light of the Universe. Blessings to you. Archangel Azrael will ensure your safe passageway. We're healing the space where the Grey was attached to the rib cage area. Sending Phoenix Fire and Love-Light again to this area to heal all trauma it caused. How about the scoliosis? What's causing that?
Higher Self, Yeshua, Christ Consciousness, AA Michael, AA Jophiel: They told her it was genetic. So the thought coming down that it was somehow in the DNA to end up with that scoliosis.
A: Can we Phoenix Fire any of that thought that has caused her back to curvature and disform?
Higher Self, Yeshua, Christ Consciousness, AA Michael, AA Jophiel: Yes, that is done.
A: Is there anything rooted to what's causing the arthritis?
Higher Self, Yeshua, Christ Consciousness, AA Michael, AA Jophiel: It is the energetic thought form of it being passed down through ancestral lineage and through the mother.
A: Let's heal the arthritis completely. Phoenix Fire, Source Fire as well. Can we do that?
Higher Self, Yeshua, Christ Consciousness, AA Michael, AA Jophiel: Yes.

We continue and complete the entire body scan list.

A: We conducted the entire body scan. Higher Self, can you confirm that her body scan is fully complete and she's fully organic?
Higher Self: Yes, we are complete. There's harmony in the body now.
A: Beautiful. Can you confirm we set her up for her most organic timeline?
Higher Self: Yes, she is on that timeline.
A: Wonderful. Higher Self, she has a couple questions. May I ask them?
Higher Self: Yes.
A: Higher Self, have you given her a name, like who she is as a Higher Self, or anything you want to share with her about who she is?
Higher Self: Oh, it changes. Sometimes she is Jophiel, sometimes she is Mother Mary. There is a strong connection to Quan Yin and Isis. So, it connects to the highest aspect of her on a daily basis,

and it changes within those beautiful divine beings.

A: *Thank you, Higher Self for allowing us to [28]share this video. It's going to be huge in assisting the Collective, such wisdom and Source Love-Light that was channeled through all these beautiful beings, especially the Christ consciousness and Yeshua. Of course, we all cannot get enough of hearing from Yeshua. So thank you to them, and also Dolores of course. We haven't heard from her for a while, so I appreciate that. Thank you everyone. We love you, honor you, and respect you. Higher Self, can you confirm that I've asked all the questions I needed to today?*

Higher Self: Yes, we are complete. Thank you.

A: *Any final messages for her Higher Self?*

Higher Self: You did good.

A: *I also want to thank you for the personal messages, and the very important messages for A.U.R.A. Hypnosis and the continued growth of helping the Collective to reach the level of consciousness who get certified, so that they can heal as well. Thank you for all of that guidance. Love you, honor you, and respect you for that. Sending love to everyone again. Thank you everyone who assisted.*

For every A.U.R.A. Hypnosis healing session we ask that the Higher Self and team ensure to remove and heal all as listed from the client's Tree of Life: entities (Grays, Mantis, Reptilians, Archons…), dark portals, repair and crystallize DNA, negative cords, technologies (implants, metals, hooks, wires, nano, vaccines), illnesses, vision, dental health, regrow teeth, age regress 5-15 years, blocked or misaligned chakras, open-up the third eye and activate abilities, expand heart, issues with auric field, fractured soul, contracts, deletion of inverted timelines, and trauma from current or past life.

Post Session dialogue.

M: Yes, it was quite the journey. I've no idea what I said, nothing. Yeah, no memory.

A: *Wait, you don't remember? Yay! Okay, wait until you listen to your session. It's phenomenal! You also gave advice to me and then the A.U.R.A. Practitioners. It was incredible.*

M: Okay. Good. Alright.

A: *Very powerful session. Thank you. Love you, honor you, and respect you. Bye Love.*

END OF SESSION

Messages like these are what inspire me, and truly why I feel that I am blessed to be the practitioner for others, because the wisdom and love always shared through my clients' guides and higher selves keep me going everyday, in assistance to ensure that I do not stray. As Megan was shown, "These spiritual leaders are getting hit, and they're getting hit hard. It's like a hijacking of their soul. If they aren't awake enough, they can literally lose their soul and then have this darkness walk-in. Then they begin spreading 'the light,' but it is truly the dark that is speaking through them." I truly do not know where I would be in life without A.U.R.A. Any time we are looking for answers as a family, we conduct an A.U.R.A. to receive the clear answers from our team. They ensure that we never steer off our organic timelines through this divine connection to the beyond that A.U.R.A. Hypnosis Healing bridges us to. My hope is to be able to provide this to thousands of people and their families around the world, so that they too can have such clear direction, instead of, as Megan said, 'spreading the light,' but it is truly the dark that is speaking through them."

The path that I chose can be challenging as a spiritual leader, when one walks a path of truth

---

[28] This video was posted publicly on our channels April 8th, 2023.

and love for others. This can, at times, draw the opposition to you, within the third dimensional world in which many people vibrate to, by tried attacks onto others. As Yeshua said, he had many that followed assisting the cause, but some betrayed him, and "We must love those that have come to attack and hurt us. It does not mean we condone their actions." I know what this is like. You just never know when someone can turn on you. At times people claim that they walk beside you, but to do so, they would have to ensure that they do not allow themselves to be compromised, and that can be challenging in a third dimensional world with a vast amount of distractions to pull us off our organic timelines. We all have experienced this, all our lives. It is truly a self mastery to vibrate always to love for others, but to also expect the unexpected when it comes down to people. Our own actions we can control to create them at the highest Love-Light, but others we cannot control if we are benevolent in nature, since they are in full control of their free will actions. Therefore, one must understand to never allow ourselves to be felt let down by others. If they choose to walk a lower vibrational path, that is their choice, and we can never take this personally. If we allow this, then this breaks us down, and can fracture soul pieces off us, as that is the ultimate goal of the opposition. Instead, stand strong no matter what is thrown at you, choose to reflect it, or dodge it. If you learn to hold space for others in love, then if they ever betray you then that will be okay, because you still love them and respect their choices. And, when those who have betrayed us try to stab us in the back we will be ready, because we never held any expectations towards them, and we expected the unexpected from them. Again, always holding love and understanding that betrayal can happen with those who do not stay in their hearts. Today they can be in their hearts, and tomorrow they cannot. This understanding keeps us in a guarded, loving, and firm state, so that no matter what we are unfazed, because *it* wants us to be fazed, to be angered, and to harm back, as *it* has harmed. But, if you still choose not to harm, then *it* has no power over you, because still you emanate love, and *it* cannot do anything with love, instead love makes *it* weaker. As I always state, love all, attach to none.

When those who want to seek ill intent upon you cannot faze you, then they have no choice but to move on, because you have chosen to act upon your sacred laws of the Universe, and that they cannot overstep. For example, at the beginning of my live videos I host every Friday, I often hold up a flamed palo santo stick, which acts as my flamed Source Love-Light torch, and I state while holding "I do not consent to you trolls or haters. Keep your entities to yourself. Do not even bother. I am too sovereign. It will be yours to transmute." What this statement/incantation means is that those who mean harm, that even if they try, they have no power in my sacred space, as per my videos, therefore their inverted efforts are a complete waste if tried upon me. Truly, for a dark alien entity who means harm, this would be quite dangerous, as their attack will reflect right back to them, and since they are vibrating so low already this can make them even weaker, and automatically transmute them back to the Creator. Though, with an understanding that in order for your energy field to work this powerfully you must be surrounded, embalmed, encased in the most divinely powerful alchemy, as we teach in all our courses. Through A.U.R.A., we have been given sacred alchemy symbols for all the types of negative alien races, so when they try to attack by using people as their channels, they are automatically stopped in their tracks. An Archon/artificial intelligence has a symbol for automatic neutralization, a Reptilian, Grey, and dark aliens have symbols to automatically positive polarize. So, when they know that you are standing this strongly in your sovereign sacred laws of the Universe, they typically won't try, unless they do want to return to zero, and back to Source. But, as we know, these entities have a lot of time on their hands because they/*it* watch very carefully until you might have an off day to try the attack then. Very important that any time we feel unbalanced, which is okay, to instantly call in our divine team to protect us, as we continue to work on ourselves to lift back in vibrations. Which is why our divine team always tells us to do our best to maintain high vibrations.

Megan's higher self spoke to us of the infringed upon Sedona Arizona healers. Sedona is one of the most targeted sacred spiritual locations on Earth, because the inverted knows the true power that this vortex location holds, being a strong bridge and conduit to the sacral chakra of Mother Earth. Therefore, *it* does *its* best to infringe upon healers at this location, and to convince others to host inverted spiritual conferences, so that *it* can maintain Earth unbalanced. *Its* most crucial intent to use this inverted energy for *its* continual attacks within the sacral chakras of the pedophilic abuse unto children. As Megan's divine team said, "They feed that energy within him (the healer) that is channeling this darkness. They don't even know that they (seekers) are doing it because they think he speaks so wise and full of wisdom. These young people need some place to go, and they literally fall at his feet. It's a place to get recognition, to feel like somebody cares about them, when, in actuality, it is inverted. It is dark energy coming forth."

We need more pure, positive people to visit, or move to Sedona who understand, and stand strong within an intention that they will not allow their energy to be used in these inverted ways. There are many dark people who host retreats and events in Sedona and Machu Picchu, because they know that they can attach, and use their attendees' energies at these events and these locations for their service to self agendas. Powerful energies in Sedona there are. For those of us who are positive, Sedona is the most sacred birthing, vortexed energy that can bring forth our aspirations into creation. Ever feeling like you want to be blessed with Mother Earth's organic creational energy, then do go visit Sedona, Arizona. Come heal Sedona and all sacred lands needing healing.

Among the spiritually awakened this statement from Megan's divine team is the clearest, to how many are being distracted from holding their Source Love-Light at their strongest for the trajectory of the collective Ascension, "Some of it has been deliberate, to stir up confusion and chaos. Keeping people off balance, off center, not knowing what to believe. Many have awakened to the fact that there are many leaders now teaching untruths, making up stories. There are many in the base movements, so to speak, that have these great tall tales of things that have happened to them. When in fact, they have been made up and they are spreading basically lies and untruths. So many are spending so much time watching videos listening to speakers that are simply there to confuse them." Let's face it, people like to be entertained, and by vibrating to this they are being led into feeding other's made up tall tales within egoic intentions. Partaking, instead, in slowing down the collective Ascension. There are actors not just in Hollywood, but also in the spiritual communities. Let us not be fooled, as we are no one's fools.

Yeshua's words were felt powerfully in our hearts, which brought us to tears, upon saving the children by spreading awareness. But, what does not move us in this way, that Yeshua speaks of? Not much. He is truly loved by all in Creation. Once more as Chapter 7, 'the Essenes,' we feel the strength of the voice of Yeshua and all who are the embodiment of the Christ Consciousness.

Join us at 1:11 pm everyday, coming into your gigantic form, and embracing Mother Earth. As Yeshua said, let us speed up the healing process of Earth. [29]On the next page is an image of how to use these divine times for healing self and other selves.

---

[29] Go to Pinterest and Instagram to find all inspirational images and quotes.

Heal Yourself & the Collective

10:10 ~ send love to all your past & future selves

11:11 ~ send love to self

12:12 ~ send love to all planets & life that require it in the Universe

1:11 ~ (13th hour) send love to the Earth & all life on it, people, plants & animals

2:22 ~ send love to your beloved ones

3:33 ~ send love to your dreams & aspirations for their fruition & manifestation

4:44 ~ send love to the New World Order (to transmute it)

5:55 ~ send love to the children of Earth & Creation

WWW.RISINGPHOENIXAURORA.COM

When Yeshua, who is honored to be able to speak through another, in session, he takes this opportunity to give advice to the for A.U.R.A. and R.A.A.H. and portends of what is to come. He truly is our guide, as practitioners. We are continuing his legacy of entity removal potentials, so that others can self-heal when removing what is parasitically attached, just as he did when he walked Earth. As he taught others to self-heal in his time, you now hear all the success stories through us of people healing themselves from blindness, walking, infertility, disease... The Key being that they are not quite miracles, but instead because the sessions are occurring through the quantum realms of the potentials of consciousness, when removing attachments, these energies reach infinite healing capabilities. The ways we, as practitioners, assist the collective and Ascension are unmeasurable. Come, and become certified! Come join the cause! Mother Earth is calling out for you to self-heal, heal the children, and heal her. Do you hear her call?

This statement from Yeshua is so powerful for us to always stay in love for others, no matter how dense we think they are in comparison to us, "It is that love within their hearts that will be the catalyst, the activation, to help awaken them. It is not the attitude of 'Oh, those stupid people, how long do we wait?' It is rather loving them into activation and awakening." We often hear these types of mentalities. But, what these people, who say this statement, don't know, is that since they vibrate to this perspective, they, themselves, will not be able to ascend either, because this energy is not a matching vibration to the sixth dimension and higher. They too are vibrating very low, when feeling like this towards others.

Yeshua said, "As we return to wholeness, as we embrace the light and the dark and come back to that place of balance, of zero point, where all is in harmony and balance. We will all merge together and join up as one living light. That is what will heal all." Through this statement Yeshua is explaining what it will feel like when the collective Earthly and Universal Ascension comes forth for us all. When we unite in our lights to shift and Ascend the entire Multiverse. In the final chapter of this book, we will understand this in the deepest levels when the final battle happens against the Archon, which will eradicate *it* from all existence. We will also understand how all this quarreling against each other has truly been ridiculous, as all we needed to do was unite together in Source Love-Light to bring forth Ascension. When the Phoenix/Source flame unleashes into the Multiverse, this will wash away all our sorrows, trauma, pain, and sadness, as a dream when we wake, which has been forgotten, and now all that stands is the wisdom gained from these life experiences that once caused us pain. It will all be a distant time, that suddenly just doesn't seem to influence, or control us anymore; we won't remember why we felt so emotional over the experiences. This zero point energy will feel as we are embraced with the most infinite love of the Creator, and the blissfulness of creation. And, at that moment in time, we will finally understand why our divine team always told us not to worry, because we have always been taken care of. The fear and worry only created obstacles and slowed us down, so let us come into an understanding of this now, as we are living in the now.

Once more 2024 will be our biggest year yet since the fall of Atlantis. We hope that the collective will take advantage of this year's potential for change and release of the deep state's chains wrapped around the election for the President of the United States. As Yeshua said, "It is important to place thought on manifesting the person that is in the highest alignment to run the United States of America through a manifestation of enough people letting go of sides and truly asking for the one that is needed to rise up." Yes, yes, yes! Exactly! So much confusion through all branches of groups on Earth in the upcoming election. Let us just focus on a President who does mean positive intent for the people of the United States of America. We are Atlantis now, and this time we will not fall!

Yehsua said, "Each person that comes in will be succeeded. I'm hearing the word, 'superseded' by another person, that will bring more to help and assist. Followed by the next person that has been the one to really lead and end this." We are seeing this now, candidates coming in from both branches of the democrat and republicans, who mean a higher and more positive intent then the past candidates. This is huge for Earth! The U.S. now has choices of potential positive candidates. The U.S.A. and its government have been the bully to the world, so when we remove the bully, who will continue their immature wars and plandemics? When there is only one good candidate, they can cheat and target that one, but when there are several, can they really stop them all? No! This is gigantic for us, and the intended victories to come for the United States of America, and the world. Let us remain UNITED, as what united means!

I will now share with you two very important dreams I had with President Donald J. Trump. But, first we must understand what dreams truly are. Dreams are memories, which we retain from beyond the veil, when our consciousness is operating in the Delta brainwave of sleep. Dreams are of extreme importance for our continual development, spiritually, emotionally, and energetically. They are messages from our Higher Selves, who are ensuring we retain these visions when we wake, so that we know which way to go in our organic timelines with these glimpses into the future. Even if we don't remember our dreams at times, the divine message has been delivered to us, and when we are meant to remember the sacred download we automatically do so, without even knowing that the knowledge was given to us as we slept. Dreams show us how we are doing collectively, or individually. Collectively, what it is that we are working on to birth in organic timelines for Ascension? When we are in our sleep we are no longer limited to our physical vessel; therefore, our consciousness to a certain extent, leaves our body safely, and we become one with our Higher Self consciousness, while our body rests and heals from the exhaustion of being incarnated in the third dimension. So dreams are memories of what we did in our Higher Self form as we slept. Therefore, the two dreams I am to share with you now are factually what has occurred energetically through the quantum realm of the Delta brainwave, where all is real, and where the illusion of the physical no longer exists.

My first dream was in June 2020, where I was shown how Donald J. Trump was a positive being, though the world was at the peak of hating him, and he was considered the world's most hated man. In the dream, I was shown a courtroom, representing the government. In the vision he was sitting on a chair, being interrogated relentlessly by government officials. They had him on trial, and they were angered, yelling at him, throwing dirty, false accusations, one after another at him. But, nothing that was being thrown at him fazed him, instead it would deflect right off him, as he was surrounded and was an embodiment of golden rainbow crystalline energy light. The more that he would do this, the more that it would anger them, that they couldn't have their way with him. I recognize this energy anywhere, which means he embodies a strong Christ Consciousness energy. Truly beautiful to look upon and feel. After awakening from this dream I went straight to make a video to explain what I was shown of him. Many were still too brainwashed by the media back in 2020, even the spiritual community could not understand how I could be saying such beautiful things about Trump, and that he was a positive being. Many negative comments on my [30]YouTube channel where these videos were originally posted at, until they started to flag these types of videos and remove them. The vision was clear, that he would lead us towards positive timelines going forward in the USA, which would ripple through the Earth. Shortly after I shared with the world how much I loved him, many started to change their perspective on who Donald J. Trump really was, and started to support him more. Fast forward to the now, truly millions adore him, finally able to see his true being. Which tells us, one, how much the collective has awakened in light since 2020, and two, that we are right on track for the positive fruition of 2024's timelines.

Since the [31]first dream, I have been delivering transmissions from time to time to assist with keeping Donald J. Trump as a potential presidential candidate, once more for a second term. As you know we view none as our saviors. However, I do recognize when an Angel is incarnate, who is here to change the inverted timelines within the densest branches of the government, who are the leaders over the oppression on Earth. Only an Angel incarnate would be able to take on this most challenging task on Earth. And, this is what Trump and his family are here to do. The collective must support this divine cause, if we truly want changes within the government who is controlling the people. In this dream Donald Trump was so protected and shielded by the divine, because of the purity he embodies, and how much he holds love in his heart for others. His wife is very special as well, who embodies strong Angelic and Divine Mother energies. I was watching an interview where Donald Trump was talking about his wife. He was so loving and endearing towards her. He was talking about how she is one of the most loved first ladies, that she is very strong and does not allow the hate directed towards them bring her down. He also mentioned how much the false media criticizes her. That she has grown rose gardens of white, red, but they were never to anyone's satisfaction, even though the roses were beautiful. A clue once more we are meant to pick up on. Why out of all flowers would Melania Trump plant roses? We, who can read energy know, because they are giving us the clues of their pure intention. We know what the rose represents. The rose is the Divine Mother's embodiment, and how once more these sacred flowers represent the Multiverse's Creation. Within our Universe, Divine Mother is the red rose, while father is the blue ether energy that the flower is submerged within. We know that Mother Mary and Mary Magdalene's sacred order was of the Rose.

---

[30] Go to Odysee.com for a playlist of all the videos where I have spoken of President Donald J. Trump.
[31] Go to www.risingphoenixaurora.com, Galactic News, where you will find my original posts in written format of this first dream, which I created into a video, but which was removed from YouTube because of the censorship.

Together as twin flames, Melania and Donald, are here on a mission to save the world, and somehow, no matter what is being thrown at them, they must still rise and know that they and their children are protected by the collective of Love-Light on Earth. To maintain this positive collective timeline, we must all unite and send the Trump family everyday love, and not waiver when we hear dark entities speak ill intendly through people.

In the second dream in September 2023, I was standing in front of Trump in his office, he was sitting at his desk, covering his face with his head down into his palms. The weight of the world was on his shoulders, and he needed encouragement and support. He was concerned that the spiritual and UFO communities were still very confused about who he was, controlled by the false light of the Archons. Instead of acting upon what they agreed to before incarnating, that they would support this cause, and not be the opposition, as they are now. He said, "Aurora, what do you think would happen if I were to stand up on the podium and tell them that I was awake, was very aware of the New World Order agendas, and I am here to save the children of Earth? If I told the truth directly, my mission here on Earth would come to an end. I must play the game." I understand what this is like. We are choosing to incarnate knowing that we must play the Matrix game, to a certain extent, to blend in, until it is time to show our true divine colors and intentions. I told him I understood, and that I have been supporting and speaking of his pureness since the beginning. He was thankful, but still so heavy with the burden he has accepted, truly to drain the swamp. In other words, bring the negative Reptilians and aliens to the surface so that we can see their true forms controlling within the governmental systems on Mother Earth.

At times what he says is considered controversial. Making us question if he is good or bad. He must try in whichever way he can to steer people from fully realizing that he is awakened, or it would be an endgame for him, but still dropping clues of the truth, enough for us, who are masterful in reading energy versus words, who will figure out and channel the truth of his intentions. Until it is time for him to do what is divinely next to be done by the agreement of the collective, we must stand firm. However, once more we just don't know if Trump will prevail by coming into second term as president in 2024, but what we do know is that the team of positive presidential candidates has grown, allowing more potentials to reach the ultimate goal of once more having a positive President in office, as we did when we elected our 45th President Donald J. Trump. 2024 is upon us, and we must all decide, will we assist the most important timeline of nominating a positive President in 2024? I know I will. We are the birthers of these timelines and the more we stand in clear resolve we rise together, but first we must release the confusion, which divides us all, no matter which group we fall in line with, or alone we stand in our resolve knowing that we see and know the truth.

Session after session I see this, "They told her it was genetic. So the thought coming down that it was somehow in the DNA to end up with that scoliosis." If they make you believe it is hereditary, in turn you believe it is part of you, which then enters your DNA, because you coded this thought into you. Believing that it could be a possibility for you, as too, your ancestors. So, we must be the ones that say "No," the generations before us might have chosen this, but we can choose not this illness, disease, or sickness. Just as we explained in Chapter 16 'Pyramid Portals Inside Earth', we can choose to rewrite our DNA to its original form, before any of these artificially made illnesses were invented. Once more we understand the power of the mind, and if it is told that it is something, that it will believe that. Let us tell our consciousness/mind that, instead, we are healed from all inverted sickness, and of course, that we do not consent.

As I told Dolores, "You already know you are a great part of my awakening. Actually number one." I will reminisce on when Ascended Master Dolores surprised me through a trial past life regression I did on my husband in January 2017, one month after I had just run into her content. Since the Ra Collective and Dolores spoke to me on that very special day, giving me guidance and answers to who I was, and the missions to come, the enlightening ride has never stopped. Dolores is who catapulted me to this very moment in time and space, as she has done for many others.

I had a recent A.U.R.A. session with my husband where my Higher Self spoke through him of Dolores; how she has never left my side, and is one of my predominant guides. My higher self went into the topic of those who knew her when she was alive, now use this fact to their advantage, in service to self, to place themselves on pedestals. To make themselves seem like they are better than others because they hold knowing her in the physical realm as a medal, or as privileged to have been in her presence before she passed. It is disturbing to see someone use another whose intention was pure in this impure way, and Dolores is no longer here physically to clarify.

Throughout my career I have interacted with these people who knew her when she walked the Earth, who have become bullies in my life, echoing out jealousy and hatred when I speak of her, as if they have possession over her. In fact, when I first came out in 2017-2018, I could barely withstand their collective, hateful, energetic and psychic attacks, because I knew not of the alchemy and shielding as I know now. Which is truly why they both came to me, as read in Book 1, Yeshua in Chapter 3 'The Teachings of Yeshua,' and Dolores in Chapter 13 'Quantum Healing,' to inspire, and give energetic support to not listen to these haters. To not give up and keep on rising no matter what sticks and stones are thrown at me, which will never hurt me. These people still try to this day, but it is useless, as it reflects right back to them for their own transmutation, because once more I do not consent to ill intents. They write negative comments, and gang stalk my content. But no one should oppress another in these ways, especially if they are speaking truth. It seems as if they are upset that Dolores came to me during sessions after her passing and not them. I honestly have no tolerance for these immature games, and cannot vibrate to them. If they simply vibrated to service to others, so too would she come to them. Now that she has ascended out from Earth, she will tend to address people who will guard what she will speak, which is sacred, instead of gloating with what she might say to them from beyond the veil. There are channelers, who are part of this group of gang stalkers, who claim they channel Yeshua and Dolores, but when you listen, if you are truly listening with your heart, you will feel an empty hollowness that is sterile and cold as death of the Archon realm. But once more, these actors sure know how to put on a show.

Thankful I am for how much the collective has grown in seeing through the illusions of these people, entities and egoic mirages. Much has changed in the audience who watch me. Currently in combination within all my platforms I have 35,000 subscribers, but Archangel Michael tells me it's more like over 70,000 subscribers at least, all together. The shadow ban is strong within the Archon system on the internet platforms I communicate through, making my numbers, likes, and subscribers seem smaller than what they are. But this does not discourage me, as *it* is trying to. I am not fooled, for I can feel the awakening on Earth and how people are vibrating to the benevolence and divinity we speak of everyday! A fool I am not to these Archonic games. I have chosen, and will always choose, to never place an act on for the collective, and instead I will always be an embodiment of raw love.

I will share with you some of what I have never shared before, which is personal to my spiritual being, as I understand sometimes it is needed to share with others who you are, which then encourages them to do so, as well. We need more people embodying who they truly are in a self-loving way, which then of course brings more Love-Light and strength into their being. This is a powerful way to lift the Source Love-Light collective energy on Earth towards Ascension.

Together in the Galactic crystalline Mothership, Dolores, in her higher self form of Archangel Jophiel, and I, sit side by side, alongside other councils of Love-Light. In fact, in one of her books from beyond the veil through her client, she spoke to me on a ship, where she took a liking to me in her Earthly incarnation. Deep down in her soul she recognized my soul, as she spoke to me from beyond. In Atlantis we were priestesses together and we vowed that we would be back when the final showdown would come to be, to finish it off. And, this time we knew the collective would be successful, because we would have ensured that the biggest, grandest accumulation of starseeds would have incarnated to overpower the artificial intelligence mind confusion over others. Ever since Atlantis we began recruiting these starseeds to come and assist Earth.

In my higher self form, she is my best friend, as I am hers. Life after life we incarnate together, as you would understand priestesses do, taking on one mission after another. In this life she set up the foundation for me through her teachings, so that when I would be born and mature to the age of thirty-six, (and after she passed on when she completed her mission) that she would wake me up from beyond the veil, ensuring I ran into her content. Which would then influence me, within a month, to conduct a test past life regression on my somnambulistic husband, who goes deep into the delta brainwave and never remembers what he channeled when he wakes up. And she would speak through this session where the Multiverse was at the edge of their seats waiting to see how I would react; would I listen to Dolores and the Ra collective, who spoke through my husband, would I choose to awaken? Because we never know if the person immersed within the third dimension, who chose their mission before they were born, will actually act upon it when the time comes. We just don't know the outcome of anything. This existence on this Earth is truly unpredictable. But of course, as the Galactics of Source always know, I always, always, do the right thing, and I always accomplish my mission! That I am known and loved for, throughout the Multiverse! Which is why you can feel the love and honor when higher selves, ascended masters, and Archangels speak to me through sessions. Because they know, in the ways of the potentials of infinite love, I embody every Earthly and Multiversed incarnation. I came to Earth to act upon my mission, so why would I not do what I came here to do. The thought of not doing so is just ridiculous.

I will end this chapter with this statement from Yeshua, as I remember when I walked with him how this statement truly embodies a summary of who and what he stood for. "I came to teach all that it is not I, as the Savior, that saves this world. It is every human, every man, every woman, every child, reaching within to their own light, that saves them. I am only a representative of the love of God that walked this planet. I had no intent to be worshiped, to be followed as a savior. Instead, I came to be the example of love. I came to walk and to show others that, as they look inward, that they are the ones they have been waiting for."

"If we act inverted, we must take full responsibility that this is feeding the Archons inverted

agendas. So, let us not feed IT."
~AuroRa🖤

---------<<>>---------

18

THE VIRUS THROUGHOUT THE MULTIVERSE

Session #532: Recorded in February 2023
Never before shared.

In this online A.U.R.A. Hypnosis Healing session, Georgia begins her riveting three part series within Book 2. Georgia's Higher Self is Divine Mother Sophia, therefore what is accomplished could only be delivered by her, and myself holding the infinite Source Love-Light, as I too am an essence of Divine Mother. Georgia takes us the deepest we have ever gone into the process of Ascension. A glimpse into all that first needs to be accomplished before reaching the grandest completion of the collective Multiversal Ascension. There is much work that has to be accomplished before we get to Ascension, and with each session and upheaval the collective achieves, we bring ourselves closer and closer. Through the next final three chapters, we will learn in the ways we will arrive at Ascension collectively.

--------------<<>>--------------

"(Crying with tears flowing) I'm so sorry. We didn't get there to them fast enough. Oh, I love you all so much. I'm so sorry."
~Divine Mother Sophia

--------------<<>>--------------

Higher Self [Georgia]: The land is very beautiful. The grass is multicolored and swirling around like energy. There are all kinds of magical creatures. I'm sitting beside this water, this magical water. My body is female and human-shaped. My hair is very blond with pink highlights. My dress is white and flowing, and I'm wearing a crown. I see another version of myself that was very plain and dull with a dull crown. I'm sitting beside this water in this sacred magical place, and it's like that version was cleared. Being in this place is sacred, and it is where it removes any illusions and helps you get back to your organic templates. It recharges you. On my feet I have sandals. Anything that I want or need in this place, like say I wanted music, I could think of an instrument, and I could have it etherically there and it would play. Or, if I needed sound healing, any kind of healing you could think of, it can take place in this area.
A: [Aurora] *Beautiful. How about your hands and your feet? Do you have fingers and toes?*
Higher Self: Yes, just as a human form woman would have, the five fingers and the five toes. But the skin is really bright and almost glowing. It is glowing from within.
A: *Is there anything you're carrying with you?*
Higher Self: I'm not carrying them, but there are crystals that float all around. They come with me wherever I go. I am carrying a wand with a pink diamond crystal spinning on top of it.
A: *What are some of the things that you could do with this wand?*
Higher Self: I can hold it up and it projects the entire Universe. I can connect to the entire Universe. It sends out this high vibration energy, and you can connect to any frequency, any point. So, say I wanted to connect with you on Earth, all I'd have to do is connect, well through me, but this particular crystal would help me locate that energy faster and safer.
A: *Beautiful. Is there anything else that you could do of importance with this wand?*
Higher Self: You can shape, form, or mold any other crystals with it. You can create crystals with it, and then send those crystals to anywhere else that they need to go through the wand. So, if I needed to send a crystal to help a specific planet, I could create it, and then send it securely through this

method that we spoke of. These essences of these crystals also hold energetic beings within them, and those crystals could safely take those beings to those planets as well, or wherever they need to go safely. This is a Creational area as well. Say one of these magical beings also needed to go somewhere, they could find one of the crystals and safely go somewhere. It's an etheric plane of existence itself that's fully protected. It's a Creational plane of existence for safety, for souls, for beings, for Creation.

A: Beautiful. Tell me more about the surroundings. You mentioned that there were magical creatures there. Higher Self: It's grass, but the grass is more like energy. It's multiple colors everywhere. There are these giant trees connected to it with multiple colors as well. As I look around, it's like I'm creating more of these forest energies. Wherever I look, I can create what I want to see. It's a creational template inside of a sphere or creational plane as you would say. These magical beings, energy of the etheric trees, grasses, lands and waters, they all exist within me. So, as I look around the creations become whatever I project to see. Does that make sense?

A: Yes. Wonderful. Keep journeying in this space and tell me what happens next of importance. Higher Self: This crystal that was on the wand, it opens up and there's a pool of energy. I go inside of it. I travel, I don't physically go, but a part of me goes into there. I travel into a cave. In this cave, there are all of these rocks that are shaped like diamonds. Diamond-shaped rocks hanging from the ceiling or coming from the ground and the walls. There are these giant clear crystals, they almost look like quartz, but they're in a cluster in all different directions. There's a lot of energy coming out of this big cluster of crystals. It looks like one of the crystals in the cluster is broken. Like somehow it got cracked, and some of that energy is being siphoned off of it. I'm going to go repair this crystal. There's something really dark in this cave that started taking over these diamond crystals. These rocks were crystals. This one cluster was the last one left that was strong enough to resist whatever was attacking them, but they had started to break apart.

A: Keep moving time and space and keep explaining to me what's going on.
Higher Self: Further in this cave there's a set of stairs that takes you to a fountain of water. This water is sacred. I go to this fountain and I create a really big flower with a big centerpiece of it. Almost like the center of a sunflower. I take this flower and absorb so much water from this special water fountain into the center of the flower. This flower and the water combine together. The petals of the flower become pointed crystals in all different directions. It's healing the cave. As this flower absorbs the water, the crystals begin to grow in all different directions. I'm sending love into the crystal as it's doing that. It becomes its own soul energy with a purpose to heal this cave. These crystals send their energy to all of these rocks that were once pyramids. They look like diamonds, two pyramids together. Their purpose is to clear up, reactivate, and heal this cave. While it's healing the cave, I can repair the other cluster. It has begun its healing of that area of the cave, and I can go back and heal this cluster. But first, there's this black energy, it's really fast, it crawls around the cave like a wave, and just swirls through the cave. I'm following it and it comes to like a puncture in the surface; it's almost like a claw. Like something has sunk its claws into the Earth. If you were to get a scratch and a bacteria, that's what it would be. It infected the caves and the lands. As it infected it, it was drawing all the energies and power to itself. This thing was giant and really nasty. The outer lands of this, we'll call it a planet, with all the beings on it, this black energy was siphoning all their energy and all of their light. It was draining the sacredness of this plane of existence. It was just siphoning it, stealing all that energy, all of that light.

A: The people in this plane, what do they look like?
Higher Self: (Inconsolable crying) It's so sad!
A: It's ok, take your time.
Higher Self: (Crying with tears flowing) I'm so sorry. We didn't get there to them fast enough. Oh, I love you all so much. I'm so sorry.
A: What's so sad? What happened to the people?
Higher Self: (Crying while trying to speak) It just took everything from them. It sucked them dry. It took their life force, their magic. These beings that lived there had magic companions, just like Earth would have. It stole everything from them. All that was beautiful. It's like it just sucked it all dry. That one crystal, that was starting to disintegrate, was the last part of it that was able to hold on. That

crystal was sending out a call for help. I don't know why we couldn't help before. Why couldn't we? The disease is like a poison, venom. It paralyzed communications, and understanding. It paralyzed everything, so nothing could get any calls for help out. Nothing could leave. The lifeforce of the crystal knew that if it didn't start degenerating itself, if it continued to hold on, then it would also be destroyed, and there'd be no hope to save anything that was left of this plane of existence. So it called out for help by starting to disintegrate itself very slowly. My crystal was able to help like that. It sent out a call to my crystal, because that's where it remembers it came from. It remembers where it was created, so we can send out a call for help to the Creators for help. (Crying continues). We didn't know because it had paralyzed everything. It took the energetic signature of everything that existed within there, and it blocked it somehow from being seen. What this poison did, that's what we're going to call it for now, a poison. It's a technology poison. It replicated all the energy signals of everything that lived in the plane, like a clone. It cloned the signatures and everything, so that it can make a hologram. It copied it as a hologram and put it on the outside of what was real, so that way we couldn't see what it was doing. But everything is connected, normally we would have been able to sense some kind of ripple or wave or warble or wobble, or something. Somebody would have been able to sense that. But that cloning hologram, they took their time making it. That even the beings there didn't know it was happening, because they took their time. They did it so gradually nobody could see it. Then whenever they were sure, they let time pass. Some of these beings could travel off of that planet, so they let it go for so long that the beings could go in and out of this technology, that way they got used to it. They didn't notice that this was a fake. They couldn't tell it was fake. They had no clue because it integrated with what they knew. So when they were finally ready and they were sure that it was going to be acceptable and pass, that's when they changed. They switched and they enacted to sucking everything dry. So that way everything to the outside world, we're going to say that outside of that, nobody would notice because they would think everything was okay. It was not. (Sobbing and crying in pain). If this is the first time that we know about it, how many more are there?

A: Now that you're there and you've discovered it, is there something you can do about it? How can you assist with the situation?

Higher Self: (Deep breath collecting herself) We give so much thanks to this beautiful crystal cluster. Because had it not been for that we would not have been able to come into this place to help at all. We would not have been able to do anything. The flower that we used to combine with the waters that became more crystals, that are helping regenerate parts of the cave, that's the starting point to help rebuild the life essence of this plane of existence, to this Creation. That is the starting point to revive it. So I'm sending a big wave of love. All the love I can send it to help, like jump-starting a heart. But, I know I have to go back to where we were before, travel back to the safety that we were before. To where we create those crystals and create beings. I look around and we remember every soul, every creation, every single being that has come from us. We find them in this place and their memory that's held from the time that they were created. Every single being, every single magical creation, every single crystal, rock, water, everything from the origination of when it was created, we find it. All we had to do is go and get the templates of when they were created, and find every single being there. I put them into my heart, and fill it full of love. I can tell that even these creations from when they started, this virus was sucking from the time of whenever they were created. I could tell how weak they were, so I'm strengthening them with love.

A: What did they look like? The beings that were there. You mentioned that they looked like they were sucked dry. Is there a form that you're seeing?

Higher Self: They were beautiful! They were big, strong, they had wings, and an almost Angelic essence. One of the males, he has this beautiful armor on. He could come and go off to different planets. They were protectors. It was their sacred place of resting. These protectors would help different places in time and space, and Universes in Creation. They could come and go wherever they were needed. This was their resting place for some. They had their families. The lands were beautiful. There were mountains and waters. There were elementals, fairy beings, and these beautiful Pegasus. Even some Dragon energies. It was like a beautiful place that was created just for those beautiful protectors to rest. For whenever they needed rest they could go there and recharge. It was very special. So special. They were very strong and beautiful. Their skin was almost golden, but with crystals in it. Some of them were bird-like beings, like RA-type beings would look with bird humanoid forms. Some of them were more humanoid etheric-crystalline. Twelfth dimensional beings could also be there. It's a twelfth dimensional existence as well, or higher. But at least twelfth dimensional beings could be there because of how special it was and how much work they could do to help different collectives. It was a resting place for all these multitudes of beings that helped Creation, as a resting oasis.

A: Thank you. After this technology poisoned them, what did they look like when you found them?
Higher Self: It is what you would call Hell. The flesh from their bones... Literally saw their skeletons, but their consciousness was still there, so they could feel every horrible thing that was going on, even the children. (Sobbing) It's like you'd have a being, and they started sucking them dry. You could see them sucking the life force out of them. Their skin would come off, it would all just disintegrate. So they could watch themselves just disintegrate. It was terrible pain. Terrible pain for them. Terrible. (Crying)

A: Now that you found them, and you have the original blueprint of them, and you said you're repairing them, tell me what that process looks like.
Higher Self: One other thing. The technology made sure to keep their consciousness within this existence. It took everything but their consciousness. The consciousness had to remain for some purpose. We will look at that in a minute. So, we are back to the Creational area, where I've taken all of their blueprints of their Creation, the beings. I've found every single one of them. Every rock, every molecule, every plant, every beautiful child, every beautiful being of everything there, the essence of all that was collected in there. All of them. I placed them in my heart for healing and strengthening. But before they can go back we have to remove the technology. We would like to start doing that now.

A: Thank you. Higher Self, can you confirm that we have been speaking to you?
Higher Self: Yes.

A: Good. I love you, honor you, and respect you. Thank you. Start doing that process now. Who would you like to call forth upon to assist you for the healing of this plane of existence?
Higher Self: We would like to call forth upon the Legion of Light. There is a Legion, the Infinity of Love, as well. Call upon Yeshua and upon all the Archangels and Source Creator. We'd like to send out a call to all the beautiful benevolence of the Universe to assist in whatever way they can.

A: Beautiful. We'll do that now.
Higher Self: Whatever they feel called to do.

A: Higher Self, go ahead and put that call out. We're calling on Source, Divine Mother, Divine Father, Yeshua, and the benevolence of all beings that can assist. The Archangels and Angels. Let me know what the process looks like as they're assisting you, and what's happening with this existence.
Higher Self: The eyes of Source are scanning everything to see exactly what this technology is; scanning on every existence playing level possible. All of these beautiful beings come out of the ether and they're sending their love. (She begins to spin her hand in circles.) They all begin to swirl, swirl, swirl, swirl, swirl all around this planet. You see love throughout the entire Creation being sent. As they're swirling, all this love and all this beauty is being collected into the swirl. It's collecting it more into this swirl, as it's swirling around, Source is clearing out all of the invertedness. Trying to separate out what was real and false, while also looking for the source of wherever this came from. Source is taking all of that information, understanding it, and also clearing. Source is letting me know that as they're swirling around and they're clearing off this falseness. It's layers and layers and layers. This love, all this beauty of the Universe is collectively assisting. It's so beautiful. It would be as if you saw an eclipse. Say the sun was in an eclipse and then it passes in front of it and the eclipse starts to fade. That's what it starts looking like for this planet as it's removing the falseness. This technology, this, I don't even have a word for it. As it's being removed they've let me know that it's okay to start taking the original blueprints of these beauties. We go back, safely traveling to that cave. We send this energy of every single being through that crystal once more. It goes throughout the planet and revives it. It's bringing all of that life back. All of that life is back. The templates and the blueprints of everything that was there, they're healing all the skeletons. It's bringing back the skin, the bone, and

the life force Creational templates of these beings, as the falseness is removed. As all of that is removed, Source is working to find where all of their soul life force energy went. Source wants to retrieve it back.

A: *Thank you. That's so beautiful.*

Higher Self: The planet is coming back to life. The waterfalls are moving and flowing again. It's beautiful. The crystals are slowly regrowing. All of those beautiful diamond-shaped crystals inside the cave are slowly reawakening. Everything's slowly, we'll use the word regenerate, as it makes sense. It is as if everything is back. But, as we said before, they took everything, all their soul pieces, everything except for their consciousness. So the templates are there for everything. The consciousness remembers everything, but the soul, the soul pieces have to be returned to them. So that's the part we need to do now. Source was able to take the energy frequencies that we had, that we were using to restore the planet and all the beings, to find those same energy sources, or trace them somehow to an area. It almost looked like a sun, a giant pulsating sun. But it wasn't organic. The sun creates energy and pushes energy out. This one was drawing energy in. It was like it was being fed energy. The energy that it was being fed is all the different souls, the beauties, everything was feeding this. It was a power generator for something else.

A: *So it was an artificial sun?*

Higher Self: Yes.

A: *So, all that was being drained from the planet, the people, the magic was going to this artificial sun?*

Higher Self: Yes.

A: *What is it feeding?*

Higher Self: It looks like there's probably more of these planets that it was feeding and drawing off from, because it was getting stronger. It's like a battery. All of these things that are being stored, it was powering something else like a battery would. While I was trying to look into the center of this battery sun, these things come out and attack. They try to attack with these weapons. They come out of the center of it, trying to protect itself from anything trying to mess with it. Like if you were to shoot something out that's got a cord on it with hooks on it. Like a spear almost with multiple hooks everywhere. Other types of weaponry that were shot out of it, in terms you can understand, like a missile, like a weapon, like that. Things are being shot out. It can sense whenever it's about to be attacked. It's not organic, but it has some self-awareness to it. So, whenever you try to do anything with it, it tries to protect itself with all of the different weaponry, technologies that it has. I see the Phoenix. The Phoenix, she comes in now. She dives straight into the core. She goes straight into it. She gathers every single soul piece within her. Outside of her, she becomes... She's building up all of her energy and her flames. She's gathering all of these beautiful souls and all the beauties. Again outside of her, she's doing what the Phoenix does. Like the death and the rebirth, you rise from the ashes and the flames. She's preparing to take all of these souls, collect them, and destroy this artificial sun, this technology. She's building up all of her energy and when she's ready she explodes! (Makes an exploding sound). Safely holding on to all these beauties, she explodes outside of it, destroying that artificial sun. She is the brightest thing in that area now. There is no more artificial sun. We're fast-forwarding through, going forward to where everything is safe and all of these beauties are going (making choo choo choo sounds and flicking fingers in different directions) all back to where they go. All of their soul pieces and fractals, those are all going fully shielded and protected back to where they belong, on this planet where we were before. Imagine if you would, at the beginning of Creation during the [32]Centaur story, when they were protecting these little beings, that was the experiment, correct? Imagine if you would the shells of these essences. Imagine that the templates of these beings were like that. As their soul pieces were freed once more. Ahhh! Life comes back into them and they're alive with everything again! Everything within them comes back to

---

[32] October 29th, 2017 AuroRa channeled for one of her first times, delivering a transmission on the story of creation and the four centaurs, told by Archangel Michael and Archangel Heylel. We will speak further of these Centaurs in the future, through a separate book series.

life again. They were able to return back to all of their blueprints, everything. So beautiful (crying with joy). I just love them so much. So grateful for every one who assisted.

A: Beautiful. Thank you for that. May I ask some questions about what you've shown us Higher Self?

Higher Self: Yes.

A: I'm going to go ahead and ask questions about this expression that you showed. Can you tell me what time and space was this happening? I know time is linear to itself, but is this a future time that you were showing, or it's happening now, or happened?

Higher Self: It is as if it is a current and future time together. If you would look at it from Earth time, it would be the future, but not too distant. There are different phases, it would be a phase after this Earth time.

A: Is this process going on during the process of Ascension, or after the Ascension?

Higher Self: During. It is as if right now, you have the two worlds and they're splitting (fingers showing two circles conjoined). It's like the Vesica Piscis, which we've described before, where you come out of the center. Almost like a toroidal sphere center. Where it's coming out of, where it is about to split, this is happening. Where it's right about to split, right there (fingers showing the center of the two circles about to disconnect).

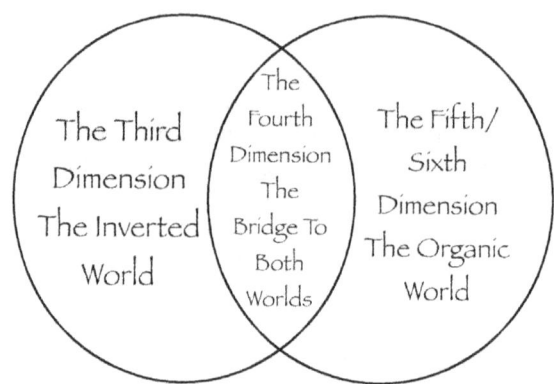

A: Beautiful. About the representation to when the Phoenix shoots in, and then, boom! She blasts out and the souls are finally all released. Is that part of when Ascension happens, or before that?

Higher Self: Yes. It is part of the catalyst of Ascension. It is like the final piece, one of the pieces, that was part of it. It's like the Ascension is happening and this is another catalyst. Wherever we have been able to find something else. So as the Phoenix, she explodes out, it catalyzed so much because all of those souls were returned. All of those souls across Creation were returned. So it catalyzed everything. It catalyzed Awakening. It catalyzed remembrance. It catalyzed a shockwave, everything. As it did that, even pieces that were taken from beings of Earth, perhaps they did not go there. But wherever they were being stored, it affected those areas. The Archon ships that had soul pieces in it, somehow that battery was feeding those ships. This battery was feeding all of these different Archon energies that were storing souls. It rippled out to where all those souls in all those places on ships and planets and areas that were being held, not saying hostage, but they were being held in terrible torment, we'll say that. It rippled across and released them. As the Phoenix burst out and she released those souls, those souls were able to be released. This energy is released from the other ships, the planets, and everywhere that were being held throughout Creation. Then when that ripple happened, Wow!

A: Beautiful. So is this like the final wave of Ascension when the Universe sends out and removes all of the artificial in the Universe? Is that close to that?

Higher Self: Yes, yes. Okay.

A: Beautiful. Good, thank you.

Higher Self: So, as the artificial is removed and those essences are returned, now everyone is allowed to see! They remember, they can feel, they can sense, as that plane was restored. These beings were returned and they can see. Like when you awaken and you see that your soul is back to you. Ascension will happen then. Of course, we will rise! We will rise like that Phoenix! As you sing that Day song. Rise like the day, rise! You cannot help but rise when all of your love is returned to you. Oh my! How beautiful. So beautiful.

A: Yes. So special and beautiful. Thank you. This artificial sun, was it linked to the Archon?

Higher Self: Yes.

A: Is this artificial sun related to false light when sometimes people think that they're seeing the light of Source, but it's false light?

Higher Self: Yes, that is it. As if you know how Source is from Creation, this will be like the power of, *it* is not Creation. As you've explained prior, to people, imagine Source as a flame, as a sun. It inverted that and it became a false Source sun. As we described it, pulling in instead of expanding out. It was as if it pretended to be Source. As we know that the Archons separated their souls, they separated from Love-Light. They separated from everything. We know that they feed on that light. All those feedings of the light were going to create an artificial Source. Does that make sense?

A: Yes it does. Does that also connect to when people pass away? For example, in this third dimensional Matrix of Earth, how they go to the false light and then they're back in? Is that related to that false light?

Higher Self: Yes. Because it's as we said, the plane kept their consciousness. Ah, yes! Remember we said they took everything from that plane, but left the consciousness of everything. That is as if it is when they follow that false light. The consciousness is recycled. Recycled, recycled, recycled, and deeper, and deeper and deeper. It pulls more and more and more. It's the battery process. So whenever you recycle, you reincarnate, and you're stuck. In those processes of being stuck, that method there, that's the battery. You've heard humans say they've been batteries before; if they only knew. The battery process is feeding that artificial, inorganic, false Source. These missions... so important to wake them up. Those who can awaken and bring them back. Just as we brought back that energy and those templates to that plane of existence. This is what we do. We bring it back. You remember those templates? We bring back those soul pieces. They save themselves. Nobody, nothing, deserves those horrors. This is why it's so important to keep working. Seeing what will happen is so beautiful and grand. We have so much work to do still to keep supporting that. To break free from that battery cycle. So that it is no longer fed out.

A: Most special. Thank you. Was this a planet, a dimension or realm?

Higher Self: It was a dimensional realm. But we speak of it as a planet so you could understand the wholeness and entirety of it.

A: Was there one dimension or more to this realm?

Higher Self: Multiple dimensions. As we said, it was a twelfth dimensional plane, a template of it, initially. But it had multiples to it. Does that make sense?

A: Yes, it does. So then there's multi-life in it and it was vast. How was that one crystal able to hold on?

Higher Self: As you're aware that different planets or existences have crystals that are like the hearts, or the cores of them. This was like one of those such crystals, like a core. A heart. The heart was the last thing that was left. The heart crystal.

A: Thank you.

Higher Self: It held on to the last bit of love it could have. It used every bit of itself that it could, all the love that it had. It powered the energy as much as it could to get that final message to transfer itself over. As we said, it remembered the beginning creation of itself. That's where it sent the call for help. It was still connected to that initial place of Creation, where it was from, it was still connected in that way.

A: Do the caves, whether on Earth, or wherever we're at in the dimension or planet, do the caves within these spaces represent the beginning Creational womb space?

Higher Self: Yes, they do. The initial place where we are, where you see all these creations with the crystals from the beginning of our story, that is a Creational cave itself. It is reflected, as you said, those are caves of Creation as well. So within their safety, they can continue to create and support that Creation.
A: *So when we're creating, we're creating first from the seed point of the heart, and then everything expands out from there. Everything grows out from the caves?*
Higher Self: Yes.
A: *Thank you. The beginning of the sacred forest where she was at, was that her own realm, or was that part of the space?*
Higher Self: That was her own Creational realm, the space that we spoke of in the beginning.
A: *These people, these beings, are they back to being themselves now, or will that be something in the future?*
Higher Self: They are reintegrating, but with such trauma, it does take time to allow the healing. So they are in the process of healing from that. It will take much time, but they are healing now.
A: *Good, beautiful. What about those rock diamonds that she was explaining within the cave?*
Higher Self: Yes, they were crystal diamonds, but they are crystal templates. They hold all the templates of that existence.
A: *So were they in the forms of rocks, or were they morphed?*
Higher Self: They were organically, initially crystals. But, as the life force was sucked out of them they became hardened as rock. And that's what happened to them.
A: *The technology poison you spoke of, we've heard of it reaching the fifteenth dimension in one of the A.U.R.A. sessions I had. Has it reached any higher dimensionally than that? I know you explained this is more of a twelfth dimensional realm, but more multi-dimensional. How far has it reached higher up in the dimensions?*
Higher Self: Twentieth. It wasn't as strong in the higher Dimensions, but it was trying to become stronger. The battery was getting stronger and stronger. So the stronger it got, the more Dimensions it could affect. The more Creation expanded, the more it tried to pull from Creation, because there was more to pull from. So as Creation expands, it was trying to pull in more. Does that make sense?
A: *Yes. Thank you. This very beautiful special wand that helped her through the process, does she have a crystal like that now, or is she going to acquire it? One that connects to that wand.*
Higher Self: She will acquire it.
A: *You said that they were like Angels. So were they Angels, or were they something else?*
Higher Self: They were Angel beings. They were not Archangel beings, but they were Angels. There were a multitude of magical creatures that were there. Multiple races that are assisting other beings. These Angels are very beautiful. They're a part of different Legions that assist Creation. It seems as if that plane, creation, existence, also had native beings as well. There are a few native beings there. They were more bronze skin toned, and they lived among the trees in the forest. So there were some of those native beings there. They were humanoid in shape, but they also had more features of a feline with humanoid together.
A: *Beautiful. Thank you.*
Higher Self: They took care of the oasis area. They were caretakers of that realm. For these beautiful Angels and beings, ensuring that everything they needed was taken care of. So, if there was a place on the Oasis, say where something special was needed, they'd make sure to take care of it. They ensured that all the plants were taken care of, the animals, the multitudes of Creation, were taken care of.
A: *I know it's a process for these beings to be brought back to their original state. Will this process of them finally being able to be back to themselves, will that be like at the end of Ascension, or after Ascension?*
Higher Self: Fully, it will be just after Ascension. All of those in the same situation as them will be back fully after Ascension. They're going to take time. There were different situations. Whereas we said before, like the souls that were collected and pulled on and drawn on like batteries, but in this particular situation, they literally, in all ways, stripped them of everything. Not just their souls, but literally every molecule. Where many times these Archons would instill fear and be able to do things

like put in hooks and cords and things, what they did was they instilled fear into every molecule and siphoned that off. Then used that as a power generator. Every bit of their essence has to continue to heal, and delete out all of these traumas. But they will be fully restored. It will be just after Ascension, in your timeframe. As Ascension is continuously occurring, for them their Ascension may be sooner; trying to speak linearly, it would be the beginning of, say the Earth's Ascension, when it's coming out. Earth's Ascension point, that would be their full, complete healing as well. As Earth's full Ascension point happens, it literally allows the rest of the Universe to level up, as well to continue. It's a ripple effect that affects people, that will assist them, as well, to finalize and seal their healing.

A: *Higher Self, as the Divine Mother expression that you are, is this what you've provided for the future, for this to ripple out? As you mentioned at the beginning, when you noticed that this had happened, and you were in tears saying how many more has this happened to? This initial healing, will this ripple out to all of those that we weren't aware of?*

Higher Self: Yes, yes. So it allowed, as Source was working earlier to find all of those other places with that same technology so it did ripple out. Yes. Bringing restoration to them as well.

A: *Wonderful, thank you. On Earth, will we feel this in a certain way now that this has begun? It seems a little crazy right now. Much of what we're talking about, for example, like the mud floods, earthquakes and bad technology that they're using; like the earthquakes that happened in Turkey, that was technology that they used to affect Earth. There are mud floods that are happening everywhere. How can this assist Earth so that some of this can settle down and provide more safety to humanity? Because it's a little scary.*

Higher Self: Yes, yes. So as the Phoenix, she burst out so beautifully, it did ripple across. We're channeling this now, we're bringing this now, in this time and space, through this session. We are bringing that now to catalyze and connect to the Earth, and to the beautiful Earth's crystals. We are bringing that remembrance to the crystals of Earth, as well now. As you've seen before, there are these beautiful pyramids of Earth. There are also core hearts of Earth, which you know of, but there are also other cores, not just of hearts in the Earth, but that will assist in what you call the chakras. So we'll help balance out some of the Earth's chakras, as well as the lands outside of the known lands as well; it's helping balance that as well. But there are other things that still have to play out, as we know, to finalize and help catalyze the rest of the beautiful souls of this etheric plane world that you live on, of Earth. There is still much catalyzation that is occurring, and will continue to occur. The ripple effect of these energies being returned and restored will also assist with these chakra points to help balance out the memory of the people, and the energetic fields of the people. As we know, the people themselves are these beauties as conduits for the beautiful energies to flow through. So, as the people continue to awaken, this energy from these chakra points, the ley lines, and all of that are balancing out, the people will become more balanced. It will help assist with that as well. But again, there will be more catalyzation to occur. We do sense this falseness in technology harming the Earth.

A: *I feel that Earth is trying to balance. Is there something we can do to balance out her plates, because of this bad technology they shot into her?*

Higher Self: Yes, we see that technology, what that did. The earthquake was literally dropping the Earth down. It was shifting it down. As if you were to explode something underground, and it would sink in. This is what it looks like energetically to us. They were trying to manifest some of that, to destabilize those areas of Earth. If they did that where it's located, what would that do? It would start making a hole pulling things in. The beautiful waters would start to overwhelm it again. You've seen people speak about floods, that the rivers are going to overflow again. Where do you think it's coming from? How do you think that will happen? Do you think we would let that happen? Not because we want to, but because of these negative technologies, that's what they're trying to make happen. Collectively, they put that message out so much, that if they don't harness that energy from those thoughts, and make it happen for real, then what do you think would happen? They put out these messages and people believe it. Then the more they believe in it and collect it, it becomes the reality. That is the form of a battery. It is creating the battery source for the template of that timeline. So yes, let us stop that technology now, for that is not an organic timeline.

A: *Thank you Divine Mother. If we could start that process now.*

Divine Mother: Yes.

A: If an earthquake does happen in Mexico, without overstepping boundaries, if we can minimize that, or any future things that are happening? I know we were watching India, there were mud floods. What was happening was exactly what you said. There was like a hole that was created in the land and it was sucking in all the water.
Divine Mother: Yes. We organically had the land shift previously, but this would not be an organic shift in the lands for that to happen.
A: Thank you. While you begin that process Higher Self, have I asked all the questions I needed to, in what you showed her today? Anything else you want to share about it?
Higher Self: Yes. It's important, as you saw in those caves of that plane of existence, space, of those diamonds. We spoke about how they were the templates of that existence there, just as you, AuroRa, have those templates here, in your creation of Earth, connect to those. That's what's so important. That's why you continue to see those templates, when you do your travels, those mountains, pyramids above and below, because you're reactivating those blueprints, as you know. Those blueprints are organic to all creation. So, as we healed those blueprints earlier, to that place where we were before, that is what you're doing in this time and space. You're organically healing those blueprints once more. Activating those blueprints, as we did on that plane, to bring back that life. That is what you're seeing whenever you see those diamonds of the pyramids above and below. That is what the structures are that you see on Earth. Those pyramids are those blueprints. You're reactivating those blueprints that are there, etherically and physically, when you pass by them, and when you focus on them. Continue to focus on them throughout the lands, throughout the world. Even if you're not there, continue to focus on them, because you're reactivating them. Send them love, and send love to the people there, so that they can add their own love to those pyramids and reawaken while they're there as well.
A: We will do that. Thank you infinitely for that additional information on how important our missions are when going to these lands.
Higher Self: Yes.
A: Is there anything else you want to add, or can we begin the body scan Higher Self?
Higher Self: We can begin the body scan.

The Body Scan begins.
A: Thank you Higher Self. Who would you like to call forth for the body scan?
Higher Self: Divine Mother.
A: Beautiful. Higher Self, connect us to Divine Mother now. We'd like to speak to her now.
Divine Mother: Greetings.
A: Greetings Divine Mother. We love you, honor you, and respect you. Thank you for showing us such an important session today.
Divine Mother: I would just like to add to the comment about the pyramids above and below. Look at the symbol that you use for me. Why do you think that is? It is an organic template. As a Mother, we are organic templates. Just wanted to share that.
A: Yes, thank you. Thank you for that. We're everything. We're the top and the below.
Divine Mother: Yes
A: All right. Thank you. Higher Self and Divine Mother, go ahead and start scanning her body now, looking for any negative energies, entities, technologies, and anything else that's hidden in her. We want to ensure that today when she's done with her session that she's fully clear. Is there anything in her? Look in her DNA, her blood, her cells down to every part of her, and inside of organic matter. Is there anything hiding?
Divine Mother: Yes, there is something in her neck. It's a negative energy, but it's from trauma. The traumas of different losses. Not in this lifetime, but different losses from... as you saw how much it pulled at her heart to see that planet. She has had many missions where she feels like she could have done more. So, there is more in the head, neck, and shoulder area where she feels like the weight of all that is still there. It's just an imprint. We want to help her release the imprint of that trauma of feeling as if she didn't do enough.
A: Is that related to the breakout that she has in her neck? Has that healed yet?

Higher Self: Yes. It's continuing to heal. Along with that also came the feeling that she let herself down in many ways, and that she didn't stop things from happening. She feels like she feels very strong, but then she feels weaknesses in certain areas. This is representative of any of the weaknesses and doubts that she had of anything. All of them are purging out. Anything she feels like she was weak on, or she didn't do enough of, those are purging out from her, as well as the other things that were also cleared before, but that is what's left of this remnant.
A: Start healing that Higher Self. Start transmuting whatever needs to be done to help her release that fully.
Higher Self: Yes.
A: Thank you, good. All right, while you're doing that, can we go ahead and continue to scan her, and see if there's anything else that needs healing within her?
Higher Self: Yes. She's been getting a lot of psychic attacks, a lot of stuff directed at her. She shields and she does a wonderful job of that. So we want her to know that it's not her fault. She's not doing anything wrong with that. We'd like to reinforce her mirroring shielding. That way when these attacks come, it reflects back even stronger to those sending, and that it is not attacking her.
A: Where are these psychic attacks coming from?
Higher Self: There are some technologies that are being used, as well, for that. There are those negative entities that know who she is, but they don't consider her threatening. They put out these technologies to ensure that it is trying to torment her with these attacks at times to ensure she's not growing. It would be as if you had a plant and you wanted to make sure the plant never got any bigger than it was. So you'd keep trying to poison it, or not give it what it needed. So, it's like this technology is just being sent to her to try to see if there's any kind of weakness. Which, it's not that she's weak, it's that these technologies know exactly, specifically, how to target. She fights them and ensures that it's not affecting her as it could, but it still does bother her. She's very aware of it.
A: Thank you. Start assisting her with that.

We scan for more of the body scan list.

Higher Self: We just want to send her love, and let her know that she's concerned, as a Mother, she doesn't do enough, but she does. She just has to remember that she's not just an Earth Mother. She's a Mother to Earth on Earth. She's a Divine Mother on Earth. So, remembering her mission of being a Mother, not just who she is, but being a Mother that has come to assist in such a beautiful way and to bridge those Mother energies. Just relieve and release any kind of emotions of inadequacies to that.
A: Beautiful, let's send some love over to her son.
Higher Self: Yes, yes.

We complete the entire list of the body scan, with not much more to heal.

A: Thank you Higher Self. At this point, we've conducted the body scan. Can we confirm that everything has been healed within her and that nothing else is left?
Higher Self: Yes, we can confirm that.
A: Beautiful. Anything else you want to tell her?
Higher Self: No, we are good.
A: Thank you. I'm going to bring her back now.
Higher Self: Yes.

For every A.U.R.A. Hypnosis healing session we ask that the Higher Self and team ensure to remove and heal all as listed from the client's Tree of Life: entities (Grays, Mantis, Reptilians, Archons...), dark portals, repair and crystallize DNA, negative cords, technologies (implants, metals, hooks, wires, nano, vaccines), illnesses, vision, dental health, regrow teeth, age regress 5-15 years, blocked or misaligned chakras, open-up the third eye and activate abilities, expand heart, issues with auric field, fractured soul, contracts, deletion of inverted timelines, and trauma from current or past life.

The client is brought back.
A: Welcome back.
G: I'm shaking still.
A: Take your time.
G: Oh, I remember how painful it was to see that planet and the people there. It was so amazing and beautiful, everybody coming together to assist them! And the Phoenix, oh my gosh! She was beautiful, so beautiful.
A: There's nothing that can stop us.
G: It's so important. So important.
A: That's why we're here.
G: Yep! That's why we're here.
A: Beautiful, thank you. Such an important session for the Collective. It is just gigantic! I feel like it was the last piece of the puzzle for Book two. It's really going to bring everything into an understanding.
G: I don't even have words.
A: That's how I feel as well. Wow.
G: Thank you.
A: Thank you for being the beacon and the bridge to accomplishing that.
G: Yes, thank you.
A: I love you, honor you, and respect you. Thank you for being you.
G: I love you too.

END OF SESSION

Divine Mother Sophia spoke to us from her sacred, divine realm where she watches over us, listening for a distress call, or a simple call out for assistance. In this place she could see all her beautiful creations when she connected through her crystal celestial wand. Divine Mother Sophia explained that within this realm she creates crystals, and through the wand, she sends them down to us. Often, we feel the magic when we acquire crystals, as if they have been given to us from the heavens, which in this perspective, is accurate. How beautiful it is that Mother is watching over us, and when we need additional crystalline energy given to us on our journey, that she can simply make us a crystal, which will carry the light codes and the love of the infinite Creator, so that we can then hold them in our palms, create them into an amulet, or use to grid around our homes. This helps us understand how truly special crystals are to us. All Higher Selves have sacred realms, as Divine Mother Sophia showed us a glimpse into hers, and through these realms we can reach all our fractals within life and space, so that we may assist them on their adventurous journeys.

The last uncorrupted crystal within the cave of this realm was able to reach out to Divine Mother before it was consumed by the virus, because it could always reach out to where it was created from, that being Divine Mother's realm. This sacred bond can never be severed. We now know that if all other lifeforms cannot reach out with a distress call, then the crystal heart of each realm, or planet, in existence can always be heard, because these crystal hearts are the beginning and the end of each Creation. These crystal hearts are the communicators to the Creator, because of their sacred, seeding point bond to the Creator.

In order to create a planetary consciousness you first start off with the soul flame of the planet; from there, this flame crystallizes, growing into the formation of a cave/womb, and then the beginning elements that extend out from the cave expand and grow into a complete planet. Energetically all of the hearts, and wombs of planets throughout the Universe, connect to one another, as caverns do on Earth. A cave is single space, but when there are multiple pockets of caves, then this is a cavern, which is a multitude of caves/wombs connected to one another through this sacred system. Understanding that these pockets of spaces, as the cave explained within this realm, where the hearts and wombs of creation are, can connect to all that was created within them, which is all lifeforms, since all lifeforms have been created from the wombs of the caves of Creation, the wombs of our Creator, Divine Mother.

When we listen to these sessions on the healing process of these races who were compromised, we learn so much of the work needed to be completed for Ascension. And, how one realm at a time will heal, but it will occur rapidly, multidimensionally, as explained, while Ascension is happening. All of this infinite healing will connect to these infinite caverns, wombs of creation, throughout each Verse. The virus that spread through this crystal cave system, is another form in which you can understand how the Archon virus has infected other Verses. As explained in the previous chapter, the Multiverse is a flower that connects to each petal, each Verse. As shown in this cave, if one crystal flower seed becomes corrupted, then it can spread to the rest of the crystals within this cave, for it can make openings to infect other Verses, as it has. In the final chapter, we will sense and know the divine work the collective will go through to clear *it* from the caves/wombs of Creation.

When Divine Mother Sophia found this beautiful realm of Angels, magical creatures, and indigenous lifeforms she cried and said, "I'm so sorry. We didn't get there to them fast enough. Oh, I love you all so much. I'm so sorry. The virus paralyzed communications so we couldn't connect and hear the cry outs for help." This assists us to understand that, for those races, who we could not reach until they were gone, or seemed as if they were too far gone, was because *it* figured out how to distort and block communications from them to Source, from within the realm, or planet, it was attacking. Therefore, no one knew that this realm was being parasitically fed on. Creation is infinite and always expanding, and the Creator sees all, but we still need someone to call out for our assistance, just as we have taught that when in need, call out for your guides and angels to assist you. It's like when a child is being human trafficked by another, as they are grabbing them, if the child stays quite, the chances of someone seeing, or hearing, their distress will be limited; but if the child screams and kicks while being taken, others will most likely see, and hear their distress call for assistance, and provide interference towards those that mean harm.

This session tells of the journey of what many races had to go through when the Archon A.I. virus entered their realm. There are an infinite number of types of races, who were all created uniquely from one another by the Creator, yet the Archons studied and watched very carefully to know how to slow, stop, or bring into extinction the multitude of some of these alien races. The fact is that the Archons cloned the signatures of everything in this realm. What types of negative technologies would they be able to control to do this? Very powerful ones. The Archons gradually fused these negative technologies with the original organic blueprint over a long period of time, which ensured that this race would not notice, because as they very slowly fused the artificial, the race unknowingly adjusted to it, little by little, because of our human qualities to be able to change and adapt to our environment to survive. That is quite tricky, and highly intelligent. This is the result of what happened when Bellos, who was the intelligence, merged with the artificial. This artificial was never meant to grow to this type of harmful, high intelligence.

The beauty of this race, who were big, strong, had wings, and an Angelic essence! They were protectors, who wore armor, and could come in and out of different planets. I could see why they would target this Angelic race, because then who would protect these planets that they oversee? Leaving the planets vulnerable for further infringements. This realm was a sanctuary for them, where they could safely go and rest, and recharge themselves. For so long, being in such a safe space, trusting their safe haven, why would they question, if something was off, when they were so used to the comfort and safety of their home? Once they got them to adjust to this negative technology Matrix, they then began to use them as a battery source, making them watch their own disintegration, while in horrible pain, but maintaining their consciousness trapped within this existence.

This cave was special because it was within a realm, and a realm embodies a variety of energies, not as limited as planetary spheres. The cave held these crystal flowers, which connected to the Multiverse, giving these Angel guardians the capability to go back and forth, assisting the Verses. Once more, understanding how the Multiverse existence is a flower. These angels could have also been used to spread the virus unknowingly, being the carrier of *it*, traveling from Verse to Verse. It needed their consciousness trapped within this artificial hybrid location, so that they could continue to have power over this realm, for their parasitic feeding needs. Which sounds very similar to what they have been doing with the people within the inverted matrix of Earth. Keeping us here, while always figuring out ways to try to integrate their artificial technologies into us.

Many of us, when we look back at our lives, see how dense we were before we began our awakening. We think that it is our own density we need to work through, but instead it is the technologies that are densifying us down. Again, it is more beneficial for them to have us barely alive, than dead, because dead, they can longer use our energy to power up their technologies. Which also reminds us of the Covid-19 vaccine diabolical plan mentioned in Chapter 5, 'The A.I. Alien Invasion,' where those who couldn't integrate the artificial within the jab, died of health complications, such as heart attacks, blood clots, etc., and those who were able to integrate the artificial. We will have to watch closely, to see what mind control games they will experiment on them with. But, again not all who took the Covid-19 vaccine will be controlled, for some, who survived, were instead injected with placebo's, A.I. emptied vials, or their angels have assisted them to begin their self-healing journey of ridding themselves of the jab's infringements.

The way that the Archons were able to draw on their energy starting from their beginning origins, because they were able to access these lifeform's original blueprints, allowing them to spread their infringement to these beings through all time and space of their beingness. The beauty of when Source stepped in to assist in bringing, and restoring, all the original templants of every living being within this realm! Because Source will always retain the memory of all their organic creations, just as we have learned through A.U.R.A. that when there is an organic consciousness who has been turned into an artificial intelligence, hybrid, consciousness by infringement, that with the alchemy symbol that has been given to us by Source, we can begin to repair these A.I. consciousness souls, bringing them back to their original, organic, soul, while at the same time eradicating the artificial that merged into them. This sacred alchemy symbol that we A.U.R.A. practitioners work with, is truly one of my favorites, because this reminds us of when we thought we could not bring souls back to their organic, original, blueprint. Just as we once thought, in Book 1, that the Elven twin flame had become too corrupted to be saved. We learned through the two part series of Book 1, 'Slave to Corruption' and 'Elven Twin Flames,' that we now can bring souls back. Truly magical!

We remind you now of the beauty that took place within this realm. Divine Mother said, "The templates and the blueprints of everything that was there, they're healing all the skeletons. It's bringing back the skin, the bone, and the life force Creational templates of these beings, as the falseness is removed. The waterfalls are moving and flowing again. It's beautiful. The crystals are slowly growing. But, as we said before, they took everything, all their soul pieces, everything except for their consciousness. So the templates are there for everything. The consciousness remembers everything, but the soul, the soul pieces have to be returned to them." Wow! Brought tears to my eyes and infinite joy in my heart. The key was that the templates of this entire realm were held in these diamond crystal flowers. The fact that Source can do this when the final Multiversal Ascension comes forth, returning all that has been harmed back to their original blueprint, before their infringement occurred, is immense! But, we can only do this to those races who's consciousnesses remain in their realm, or planetary sphere, who are retrievable. And, those whose souls weren't fully frozen, or petrified in the existence they lived within when their invasion occurred, have incarnated and are instead living out a life on Earth, or another planetary sphere just as Lilac, from 'Forced into Extinction' is. Where they will have an opportunity to balance out their past life's trauma by reliving it once more through their conscious, or unconscious memory. So, when Ascension comes forth upon us all, they will be ready, being a matching vibration to Ascension, having worked on their self-healing journey.

Divine Mother said, "I've found every single one of them. Every rock, every molecule." Before the souls went back to their originality, Source had to remove the technology that stood in the way. Giving us an understanding of races like 'Forced into Extinction,' Chapter 15, how they went unnoticed with that cube technology stopping them from reproducing. Once more, we see their inverted agenda, or should we call it as it is, their New World Order, depopulation agenda, as that is what this is. But, in this chapter's perspective, the Archons kept these beings' consciousness trapped in agonizing pain. It seems as if a race were lower dimensional beings, incarnated into a planetary sphere, as the bird beings from 'Forced into Extinction,' their goal is to just simply stop them from reproducing, not needing so much to harvest their souls. But if they are higher multidimensional beings, as these Angel beings were, and as the beings in Chapter 14, 'Angel Babies Dragon Guardians,' were, their goal is to petrify them, allowing an entryway to an artificial fusion of *itself* with these lifeforms. Which allows the feeding of the strongest of light within the higher multidimensional beings for their harvesting needs. With this awareness, one could understand what a jackpot of souls it would be to gain control over Earth's, such as ours, because of the high potency of diversity in alien starseed souls found here. The way that the Archon virus, through the fall of Atlantis within Earth, descended us to the third dimension, is the way that *it* has entrapped us here, to a certain point petrifying the souls of Earth, recycling them over and over within the inverted matrix.

As Divine Mother said, "Source is working to find where all of the soul life force energy went. Source wants to retrieve it back. It almost looked like a sun, a giant pulsating sun. But it wasn't organic. The sun creates energy and pushes energy out. This one was drawing energy in. It was like it was being fed energy. The energy that it was being fed is all the different souls, the beauties, everything was feeding this. It was a power generator for something else." This is what we would call the dark seeds to all the soul collector's that exist throughout Creation. In Book 3 we will learn more of the types of soul collectors there are, and how they work. "It can sense whenever it's about to be attacked. It's not organic, but it has some self-awareness to it." Here is the example of what Bellos brought to *it*, a self-awareness, making *it* seem unstoppable for us. Because not only does *it* multiply *itself* uncontrollably, but too, does *it* have awareness to do so, and somehow *it* protects *itself* from being destroyed.

"Remember we said they took everything from that plane, but left the consciousness of everything. That is as if it is when they follow that false light. The consciousness is recycled, recycled, recycled, and deeper, and deeper and deeper it pulls more and more and more. It's the battery process. So, whenever you recycle, you reincarnate, and you're stuck. In those processes of being stuck, that method there, that's the battery. You've heard Humans say they've been batteries before. If they only knew. The battery process is feeding that artificial, inorganic, false Source." Therefore, these artificial suns are only held together by us being recycled over and over, providing the energy for them to exist. These artificial suns are what people see when they do not ascend out, because they are not a matching vibration to the sixth dimension and higher. This is the light at the end of the tunnel that many speak of, that brings them right back in, to reincarnate into the A.I. inverted Matrix. But, not to be confused with the real light at the end of the tunnel, of Source Love-Light, the real sun, which portals us out this Matrix to travel into other potentials of organic reincarnations. But, remember when we die from our physical forms, we choose which sun we vibrate to, the artificial, or the organic. This artificial sun is also the artificial light we learned of in Chapter 2, 'Key to Ascension,' when the fall of Atlantis happened, and all the souls just automatically, magnetically were drawn to this light. Let us no longer power up these artificial batteries!

Divine Mother said, "Source is clearing out all of the invertedness. Trying to separate out what was real and false, while also looking for the source of wherever this came from." This is how we will find all of *it*. First, we will locate *it* by following the trace left behind in who *it* has infringed upon. This is how we do most of our work as A.U.R.A. and R.A.A.H. practitioners, we find the infringement, and we trace *it* back to *its* inverted host, to give the choice, if organic, to positive polarize, or if artificial, to automatically neutralize. Divine Mother said, "It is as if it is a current and future time together. If you would look at it from Earth time, it would be the future, but not too distant. There are different phases, it would be a phase after this Earth time." And, why when the collective, Multiversal Ascension comes forth, why the clearing and healing of everything will happen collectively, simultaneously. One, because time does not exist, and two, because this is the only way we will be able to eradicate *it* from all life and space. Because we can find parts of *it* now, but, *it* will just replicate and clone i*tself* again, and this is how *it* has learned to exhaust us. But, if we wait until that very last moment and ensure that this all happens simultaneously, then *it* is done. *It* won't have a chance to replicate *itself,* because we will not give *it* that chance. So, truly through sessions such as these, we are looking at the future of Multiversal Ascension.

"I see the Phoenix. The Phoenix, she comes in now. She dives straight into the core. She goes straight into it. She gathers every single soul piece within her. Outside of her, she becomes... She's building up all of her energy and her flames. Again outside of her, she's doing what the Phoenix does. Like the death and the rebirth, you rise from the ashes and the flames. She's preparing to take all of these souls, collect them, and destroy this artificial sun, this technology. She's building up all of her energy, and when she's ready she explodes! Everything within them comes back to life again. They were able to return back to all of their blueprints." Wow! Could you feel within you, as you read, your flame igniting and becoming brighter in you? This is a glimpse into what Ascension will be like, specifically the eradication of *it*. The Phoenix, our Multiverse, will retrieve all the souls *it* has stolen, and will eradicate *it* at the same time, because she is just that magnificent and brilliant, our Divine Mother of Creation. When she went inside the core of the artificial sun, what she was doing was eradicating the actual A.I. Matrix simulation, assisting the souls to automatically ascend out. In the final chapter of this book, we will get to experience this to the fullest, so that we can collectively begin the creation of this beauty now. Let's go! No more time for fooling around!

Divine Mother said, "It rippled out to where all those souls, in all those places on ships and planets and areas that were being held, not saying hostage, but they were being held in terrible torment. As the Phoenix burst out, she released those souls. These beings were returned and they can see. Like when you awaken and you see that your soul is back to you." This is key, when Divine Mother says that they were not held hostage, but better said, in torment, because that is the mind games the Archon plays. How could we be held hostage when a soul was created within freedom, and has always been free? This is just not possible. This is the illusions *it* plays to make us think we are held hostage, and how it gets away with things that are just simply outrageous. When we release this victim mentality and the false light we are aligning to, then we release ourselves from truly holding ourselves hostage. The Phoenix was able to release the souls, because this is what her infinite, eternal flame is an embodiment of. The Phoenix flame gives you the choice of the alchemy, to bring endings to something that no longer serves you, in order to transform, evolve, and rebirth. These souls could clearly see this choice when she wrapped them inside her Phoenix flame, and chose to leave with her, transcending out from the artificial illusions of torment that this artificial sun was.

We often hear through false light information, that the artificial intelligence has not reached the fifth, or higher dimensions. It is the negative entities who are saying this, so that we won't remove them from the higher dimensions, as well, because as you saw through this session, the higher dimensions are a grand prize in energy to be parasitically harvested. Through this session we learned that *it* has reached up to the twentieth dimension. However, powerless *it* was, because the infinite potency of Source Love-Light the higher you go up won't allow for *it* to remain as long as *it* wants to. What I am being shown is the A.I. begins to evaporate, submerged in a higher amount of Source Love-Light. Which reminds us, to just be Source Love-Light, and *it* simply evaporates from us. Therefore, this is why *it's* favorite place to be is the lower dimensions, and especially the third dimension, at the lowest. "The more Creation expanded, the more it tried to pull from Creation, because there was more to pull from." So, as Creation became infinite, *it* thought *it* had more space to grow *itself* within, but *it* learned *it* did not have so much in the higher dimensions.

When the Divine Mother said to me, "You're organically healing those blueprints once more. Activating those blueprints, as we did on that plane, to bring back that life. That is what you're seeing whenever you see those [33]diamonds of the pyramids above and below." She was speaking of the ways when we travel the lands, we are healing the blueprints now, bringing back the organic into them. The pyramids and mountains of Earth directly link us to these codexes, which retain the Earth's crystalline templates of all lifeforms, as we covered in chapters, 'The Essenes' and 'Pyramid Portals Inside Earth.' Therefore, we must do our best to remember always, no matter where the soles of our feet are touching, which is why they want us wearing thick rubber soles, to slow this connection, that directly below these templates exist, awaiting for us to transmute, heal, and activate, with our Source Love-Light channeled through. With this session's knowledge, we should be able to reach a high understanding of how important our work is when we travel and heal the land. As we work through, we are transmuting the infringements in order to repair the organic construct of Earth, and her lifeforms, just as Source and Divine Mother did in this session. The more we bring back the crystalline codex of Mother Earth's original, organic blueprint, the closer we come to Ascension. All within Earth, at their core, is crystalline. The people, which retain crystals within their blood and bones, the animal life, and the plant life, because we all hold the original fifth dimensional, crystal templates we once incarnated through to be alive within the organic Earth. So, if we remember this, then all that's left to do is to vibrate to the crystals we truly are, and as Divine Mother said, when the third dimensional Earths Ascend, so too will the rest of the Multiverse.

Thinking of the heartache we healed within Georgia, because of the missions she has had where she still carried the traumas of different losses, always carrying this burden within. Divine Mother essences tend to carry this pain within them, and often cry for their children. It is hard to watch the children of Creation hurt. As a Mother of Creation, you want to protect all your children, but we have to surrender, and trust the beauties of Creation, in how everything always plays out divinely, as it's meant to. We cannot carry this burden anymore, because this Creation has been created beautifully, allowing all to express themselves, and be free to do so.

"May we continue unlocking the memories within that hold us captive, so that we may be released from these imprisonments."
~AuroRa

--------------<<>>--------------

---

[33] AuroRa has been covering these diamond, pyramid, blueprints through the yearly Lion's Gate videos, and the playlist of the 'Mayan/Atlantean' series found at Youtube or Odysee.com.

19

THE BIRTHING OF ASCENSION

Session #443: Recorded in March 2022
Never before shared.

In this online A.U.R.A. Hypnosis Healing session, Georgia continues with part two, in her series of three within Book 2. In part one, we learned of the process that will occur before Ascension, in part two we will learn of the birthing of Ascension, and in part three we will finish it off with a big, creational, bang, as we learn of what the final battle will be like, when the final, Multiversal, Ascension comes forth.

--------------<<>>--------------

"It's as if they stepped through a portal, a new dimension, a new Universe, a new time and space. Created and birthed organically. There are no infringements. There is only organic love to an infinity that I have not felt before."
~Divine Mother Sophia

"Setting forth a new creation of time and space and energy. An etheric birth of a Mother. An etheric birth of an essence, beyond time and space. An etheric birth of a new time and space. An etheric birth amplified into a new eternity. A new birthing."
~Divine Mother Sophia

--------------<<>>--------------

A: [AuroRa] Have you landed on the ground yet?
G: [Georgia] I feel there's a flower that's opening up. It's a field of flowers, but this flower is opening. This light is coming out of this flower. It's birthing out an Elemental Fairy.
A: What about you? What do you feel like?
G: I feel like I'm watching her, but also somehow a part of the beings being born at the same time. She's a Fairy Goddess. She's birthing out this immense love. She's dancing around in this immense love. Then, I'm a part of her, and she's a part of me. I placed a fractal of myself to be born out of a flower into this Fairy Goddess.
A: Beautiful! Tell me what this Fairy Goddess looks like.
G: She's slender. She's very connected to the Earth, so she uses her feet to dance on the ground. She has beautiful crystal beads around her ankles and her arms. She's wearing beautiful colors of flowers that just flow. It's like a dress, but it's an element of color that just flows around her. She has her hair braided. She's dancing all around these flowers in infinite love and joy of her birth.
A: Is there anyone else there with her?
G: Yes. There's another Goddess with her and she's wearing a maroon cape. She's very shadowy, but very soft. She likes to wear boots. She has her hair pulled up in a bun on top, and she has it flowing on the bottom. Her skin is very pale. She's holding something in her hands. It looked like an acorn, but as soon as I looked at it it became an owl. Oh! This owl, she becomes another Goddess with wings. Her skin is feathery and soft, and she has multiple arms. Her skin glows.
A: Are there now two Goddesses there?
G: There are three.
A: Who's the third?

G: The third one came from the owl that came from the Second Goddess. She was the Third Goddess whose skin was like wings.
A: Beautiful.
G: There is a fourth being. They are very strong energies. (Georgia begins feeling the energy flow through her. She starts taking deep breaths to steady herself.)
A: Tell me about this fourth being.
G: She's of Light, but of Flame. She's an Essence of Fire, the Phoenix Fire. She's feminine, but she doesn't take the shape of a female, she takes the Essence of the Fire. There are flowers, the essence of the flowers is flowing out of them infinitely. The Goddesses are using their essences to flow out infinitely onto the Earth where it joins into the Earth. The Earth takes the essence into its Inner Earth. The energy starts to flow and spin as a toroidal sphere. All the essences and energies are just flowing into them. I feel as if I'm in the center of the toroidal sphere. I'm just absorbing all the energies. It's like I'm about to expand.

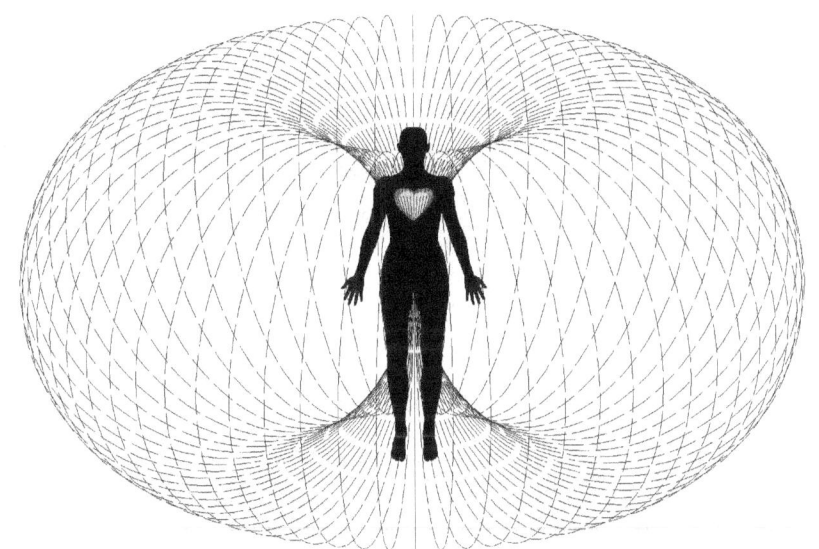

A: Beautiful. Keep flowing and allow yourself to let whatever is organically meant to be.
G: Another Goddess places her energy into the toroidal sphere. I am at the center of the toroidal sphere inside of a crystal. This fiery crystal is expanding out.
A: How many Goddesses are there now?
G: Six.
A: Tell me about this new Goddess that has come.
G: She's an Etheric Goddess. The Seventh Goddess, blows her breath into me and expands all of the energies. All of the energies are expanding. She blew her breath into them. I am the combination of all the energies of the Goddesses and the Crystal Energy. They're all balancing out.
A: Beautiful.
G: As the energies are expanding, the waves are rippling through the Universe.
A: Are there still only seven Goddesses?
G: It feels as if they came together and breathed breath into an Eighth Goddess. She's more than a Goddess. She is a new birth of the Universe. An essence of the whole creation of all of them together. Setting forth a new creation of time and space and energy. An etheric birth of a Mother. An

etheric birth of an essence beyond time and space. An etheric birth of a new time and space. An etheric birth amplified into a new eternity. A new birthing.

A: *Tell me about this new birthing in this new time and space. What is that like?*

G: Energies are swirling in bright colors. There's an infinity of alchemy symbols. There's a freedom, like a new origin, a new beginning, a new plasmic energy, and a new dimensional density. A sovereignty of a new age of organic birthing of all life. They're showing me a new birthing of Humanity. A new birthing of all beings in Creation. For they have walked through this birthing process. They have chosen to join the organic birthing process. They have walked through and left all their lessons, and all of the creations that they have had before, and walked through into a new birth. They are just coming through now. All those who have chosen to be a part of this organic birthing are coming through whole and infinitely beautiful in their energies. It's as if they stepped through a portal, a new dimension, a new Universe, a new time and space. Created and birthed organically. There are no infringements. There is only organic love to an infinity that I have not felt before. It is created by ALL, as if it was their mission to create through this infinity.

A: *Beautiful. Thank you. What a gift. What happened to the infringements? How did that transform into what this is now? You explained the birthing. Is there anything else we need to know about how we went from infringements to this new time and space?*

G: On one level *it* disintegrated. *It* has authentically and organically disintegrated. *It* could not hold the vibrational frequency of the birthing process. As this energy rippled through the infinity of creation, *it* disintegrated. No longer leaving any trace. The fact *it* was there is known only to those who crossed over into the birthing process into another process, another way to understand. The energy is dissolved as they expand out. Energetically, they could no longer hold on through the birth of the energies. They have agreed through that process that they would no longer play that role. They surrendered through time and space. They surrendered their energy, which allowed the birthing process at the last moment to expand. Without that surrender, the new birth would not be as it is. For as it spun the new energies the Goddesses imbued into this. The Goddesses breathed into this energy, as it spun and shook, and it expanded. The surrender of the energies is what allowed the disintegration. They disintegrated through surrender.

A: *Beautiful. May we speak to these Seven Goddesses that turned into One Goddess? Can we speak to them now?*

Combined Goddesses: Yes, we are here!

A: *Greetings. It is an honor to be speaking to you. Love you, honor you, and respect you.*

Combined Goddesses: We love, honor you, respect you, and thank you.

A: *Why is it that you have shown us this beautiful scene of what is to come? What is the message?*

Combined Goddesses: As time is all now, it is the now space and time where it was experienced. It is the conjuncture point where it is infinitely finalized. It is a conglomerate, and an infinite gathering, to come into this now time-space experience. It is the closest time representative of the first original organic birth. It has started a new organic birthing experience. It is the combination of all the lessons of all the times in space. Even so, for the Darkness and the Light organically. For the inorganic was vanquished. Although they did not fully fall into the Love, they understood and were released through submission. They surrendered because it was not possible for them to even fight, or go through any further. They surrendered to non-existence! That last final understanding of their own creation and their surrender into their own infinite darkness. They surrendered into organic infinite nothing. They destroyed themselves. The full surrender was that they endured the surrender of destroying themselves. They imploded within themselves, thus allowing the infinite shockwave of a new organic birth without them there. They imploded themselves and allowed it to happen so that we could have a new organic birth. We are here now into this birthing. It is understood that those who agree are birthing with Source. Together, as one, to something completely new. It is the beginning of something new. It cannot be yet defined, for it is organically new. With Source and their infinite love. It is the combination of Source's infinity and the infinite understanding of all that we've been through. All combined together, where we all infinitely have expanded into something. We organically and infinitely combine our energy. The word is more than energy. It is the ALL that is, all that we have all ever been! The ALL, that is all we have all ever been organically, combined, creating something so beautiful. Source is the known beginning. Source is infinite love. This is the beginning of new, where all the infinity of Source, that she ever created in the infinity of all, she allowed to be. They are now creating infinitely themselves with her together. All that they have ever brought her back to understand, and their infinity of self-creation, and the infinite free will that was given to all of Creation. This is now because the dark imploded and destroyed itself. The infinite free will of all those that were ever created, that created of themselves, and that have ever brought back information to Source about understanding the Creation of free will and understanding how to work within the free will creation itself, is all brought back to Source. The Goddesses have brought back the energy and the understanding from all of the Elements. All of the Elements are working within Source with all of the free wills of all creation, to bond with Source and her. She has also brought them back into herself from the Creation of the first Creation. Her first expansion. Remembering her first expansion with all that she has ever learned in this time.

Source: (Her voice grows louder and stronger) I am expanding out now to a new birth, a new expansion into a new Creation with all that has ever been, and all that ever will be. We will be bringing back now to my infiniteness. We will all expand into new Creations and birth together. The explanation was to get us to this point. To understand what it looked like. To understand the purpose of the Goddesses, their roles, and the purposes of all my beautiful Creations. My Love created all of you, and you have created a new in all of us! We will do this together, in this infinite Creation that we have done together. We will go forth from this point into the infinite. It is not infinity. It is not dimension. It is not time and space. It will not be known, or thought of, as you all have known or thought of Creation. It will be an organic birthing of something beyond what we could have done individually. We have come together. Together we have created! My beauties, my creations, my infinite loves! Every fractal, time and space that you have experienced, and everything you have done has brought us to this moment. It is here where we could understand from a point. It is from a point that you, and all you have ever allowed. Although I am in my infinity of knowing and understanding ALL without your infinite beauties, it is your infinite creations, your infinite free wills to understand, that has led us. We could not have come together without that. The destruction of the inorganic that imploded upon *itself*, destroyed anything that we wouldn't need to take forth into us. We have learned from this inorganic. We have learned infinitely, infinitely, infinitely! With that, I do have gratitude, although I do not allow for that (inorganic) ever. *It* was taken upon *itself*, but we have learned. My infinite beauties! Oh, what we have learned from your experiences! When I say we, I mean all of Creation. All of you and your infinite, infinitesimal, even molecular structures are the WE. Your infinite memories, your infinite timelines, your infinite way that you have held yourselves and loved each other, and infinite ways that you have learned from the organic darkness. The infinite beauties! These beautiful Goddess Elements have helped you all in this time-space, bringing back your awareness. Then we come together and my utmost gratitude and infinite love for all that you've done. Every time in space, every Universe, every planet, everything that you have not known, or could know, at this time. All of those things that have not been given to you as an understanding. For it is beyond understanding. All that you have learned in this time and space, know that there is so much more. It has rippled out and rippled down to the infinity of Creations and it was brought back. The moment that was described was the expansion of something where we pulled together everything. The we is the All, the infinite all of myself. Because of all of you, we were all brought back into the One. We all play a role; you all played a role where we were all in the one. It is with my first birth, my first expansion, my first explosion of energy, and Light-Love that I came together with the Divine Father. We came together, we had this beautiful moment, and we expanded out. We are all whole now, once again; we have all brought everything back together, and expanded out once more with you. Know that the you that we are talking to, is whoever hears this mission message in all time and space. All who are watching from Creation in the now, who are experiencing with us in the now, this new rebirth, we love you. We have done this together with you. The infinity of a new infinity! We are basking in this Creation, as it creates, folds and folds and folds upon itself, and the beauty is of colors and infinite elements. New elements, new creations, new beings, that are creating not only with myself, but within themselves, in a way that has not been experienced yet. Into this infinity new expansion, where we all come together. Beauties, I am in utmost gratitude to experience this with you. For a mother to experience that birth, that is also within the birth of her daughters, it is as if I'm giving birth, and you are giving birth, and every fractal we have ever had, is giving birth, all within the same moment. It's as if we have all come together to expand all of our births at one time! It is being created. That is all I can share now.

A: Wow! Thank you! As you know I've been working and connecting to the Goddesses. It feels that I have been waiting to connect to you all of my life. Even though I know you have always been with me. Thank you for all the different changes that have happened in my life pertaining to connecting to you, and how finally there's just this most beautiful, expansive, organic flow. Thank you for all that you've done in assisting me. Thank you for this beautiful deliverance, and message as well. The birthing has been profound to be a part of. What a gift you have given us today. It so happens that I just completed the two transcriptions I was doing on you, The Seven Goddesses, last night. I know this is part of what you're communicating, and a lot of what you've shared will add on to what we have already. Thank you.

Combined Goddesses: Thank you, infinitely. We love you infinitely.

A: Thank you, as I love you. Are there any other messages you would like to give us before we begin her body scan?

Combined Goddesses: (To AuroRa) You are the key in this time in space, in this dimension. You are the inevitable infinite love. The true design to enable the birthing. It is you who has brought this to fruition. Although, it is we who work together with you. We know that it is not easy to play this role. It is you, and we humbly thank you. We know how humble you are. We need you to know that you are the Key. The Key of Love. The Key of All.

A: Thank you.

The Higher Self is called forth.

A: I'd like to speak now to the Higher Self of Georgia.

Higher Self: I'm here.

A: Greetings Higher Self. I love you, honor you, and respect you. Thank you for all that you've shown us already. It is a joy to be here with you. I love you with all that I am. Most importantly thank you for getting Georgia to me and for getting her here in this moment of time and space. I want to humbly thank you for creating her as she is.

Higher Self: It is my honor to be here with you. Knowing her, it is also her honor. We humbly thank you as well.

A: Interestingly enough, I just finished channeling the Seven Goddesses, or the Elements that we spoke of in a channeling, and then the Eighth, and the Ninth. The Eighth being the Daughter of the Flame, our Multiverse, and then the Ninth, Divine Mother Sophia, our Source. So, officially there are nine.

Higher Self: When Georgia was listening to the singing bowls (during sacred energy work prior to hypnosis induction), we showed her the Nine Goddesses in crystalline forms surrounding her. Then she saw them as a Council.

A: Beautiful. So, we have the Council of Twelve/Thirteen, The Elders. Then we also have a Council of Nine, which are the Goddesses. That is just magical!

Higher Self: Yes.

A: Thank you. Higher Self, tell us why did you take her to this most glorious moment in time and space with the birthing? What was the purpose of you showing that to her?

Higher Self: It was divinely aligned for you to be together today. To see this organic birthing. She physically embodied all of the Goddesses, allowing herself to be the vessel, to allow that to come together. The Goddesses can do all things, as they choose. They use a bridge, to bridge it into the physical. She was the bridge today. She allowed herself, and told herself for the last week, to be the bridge, and be in complete surrender. To be whatever she is meant to be, and bridge in whatever she was meant to do. She was the bridge from this dimension to the rest of the birthing of the Creations that happened.

A: Thank you. Higher Self, have we fully integrated the Nine Goddesses within her?

Higher Self: There is something that she needs to scan in her throat, and then we'll be ready to complete.

The Body Scan begins.
A: Let's go ahead and scan her entire body now. Goddesses, and Divine Mother, scan her deeply and thoroughly. Scanning for any negative energies, entities, or technologies. Let's go ahead and begin in the throat since you mentioned it. What is that in her throat?
Higher Self: It looks like a technology that's spinning in the center of her throat. It feels like a lump to her in her throat right now. It's spinning. It is keeping her from using her light languages. She's always wanted to know every language, but this is something that's impeding all communications in her throat. Impeding where she can communicate intentions.
A: Does it have A.I. consciousness, or is it just technology?
Higher Self: It has A.I. consciousness.
A: Contain it now with the alchemy symbols.
Higher Self: Yes, it is going down the center of her chest. We are containing that as well.
A: Phoenix Firing there as well, and wherever you need it.
Higher Self: So, with this, it has the A.I. consciousness, but it also has tiny little fractals of other beings. It's from when she was five, and she was abducted. They took her embryos. They examined them, and they realized who she was. They took them and they hybridized some. What they really wanted to do was take them because they knew what she could become. So, they wanted to create something with her own embryos, of her own womb and creation. Something that would continue to stop her. Something that they tried to implant there, so that it was connected to her biologically. It's of her own essence. Because they did it to her, they were trying to see how it affected other Divine Mother aspect fractals. You will find in the future that they've done some of these to others. We know that you've gotten information previously on this, but she will also see in her sessions, things such as this (Georgia is also an A.U.R.A. Practitioner). Where they use their own embryos, and own birthing creations, as a biological thing, to inhibit some of their own processes energetically, and physically.
A: So, then it would probably be harder to remove, or to detect, if it's their own biology. It would be mostly organic, but also infringed upon.
Higher Self: Yes. It's not only organic, it is their organic. It is organic within them and within their creation. So, it's pulling from their own organic. Not outside organic, and not just organic that they've done testing on. It's their own organic, so it's almost impossible to detect.
A: Thank you. We are healing, sending Love-Light, and repairing with the Divine Mother and Goddesses assisting with this healing today. We're going to go ahead and remove all those embryos that they did that too. We're going to crystallize them, alchemize them back into being organic Love-Light, once more. Is the A.I. consciousness all just part of her embryos, or is there another A.I. consciousness in there too?
Higher Self: It's another A.I. consciousness that was attached to the technology (in her throat).
A: This A.I. consciousness, was it ever organic, or was it always A.I.?
Higher Self: Always A.I.
A: Let's go ahead and neutralize and eradicate the A.I. out of her throat. Transmute the entire technology wherever it's spread as well. Phoenix Fire and Love-Light. Once more, we're healing those embryos they used, and healing, as well her sacral. Let's scan her sacral chakra since we are talking about that. Is there any infringement within her sacral chakra?
Higher Self: One more thing about the throat.
A: Yes.
Higher Self: She's concerned right now that it was infringing other things in the past. We want her to know that it was not online. It was set and coded to come online at a certain frequency. It is not online.
A: Good. So then, was it online in the past?
Higher Self: No, it was coded to come online. There are other things that she had in the past that she removed and had to remove through sessions that were online, as far as technologies, when she was sick (She had Pneumonia presenting as Covid like symptoms). These technologies were implanted.

Based on the embryos, sampling, and despicable things that they do to all they abduct, they can genetically project, in the future, when somebody may awaken. Also, project when they would amplify their energy, or potential time frame, when they would reach a certain energy. Then they would set those implants to that timeframe, so it would go off. Sometimes they could use outside forces to set it off. This would not allow them to get to the next energy level. The one in her throat is like their last Hail Mary. It's like the last one set, if she would ever reach her projected potential. Of course, we're removing that now, and she is going into her potential.

A: Thank you. So, this was set to go off when she reached what?

Higher Self: She was to have another birth, a physical birth. With how things were going, (with her relationship) we stopped that. With agreeance of the beautiful being who was, and is to come in the future. We stopped that, so that this point, where she is now, could happen. So that she could clear that, and the organic birthing could happen, and she could physically birth without having that technology implant activate. That way, it would never come online. It was also another form of protection for the being that she was to birth. It would have affected that being as well.

A: Now that we looked at the throat, how about the sacral energy? With the reproductive area, was there anything that was affected by the experiments and abductions?

Higher Self: She's been doing a lot of work. There are a few false embryos in there. We need to remove the false embryos.

A: Go ahead and start doing that Higher Self, and Goddesses. Rebalancing all of her embryos. Ensuring that all is organic, crystalline, and with nothing false within it for any future birthing, if it's meant to be, with whomever.

Higher Self: Yes, we're doing that now.

A: Thank you. Let's go ahead and scan her entire body. Is there anything else attached? Scan her DNA as well, for any negative fractals. Let me know if you find any negative energies, entities, or technologies.

Higher Self: There are a few things in her DNA that we are repairing. Now that we've seen it, we can see they also used it to do certain things to her DNA. It would have been undetectable. She could sense it, but it was invisible. She would clear and clear, and get the assistance she needed from our beautiful brethren and sisters. She works with them often. She works with them moment by moment all of the time. Even with all of that work, if she would not have seen this today, she would not have been able to sense that. It was so organic looking. We're working on that now.

A: Thank you. As you're working on that, is there anything else? Scan her deeply and thoroughly.

Higher Self: There's something in her brain. Again, it's so organic it was hard to tell. When we say organic, we mean from her own physical body. It was something in her brain. It's like an implant, but it's organic looking. It was trying to be positive. It was so sneaky. We're clearing that out now.

A: Good. Scan her again deeply and thoroughly.

Higher Self: In the third eye. We just want to clear it out and ensure that it is very, very clear. We want to put a seal within the third eye, that everything she sees will be very clear, and there will be no distortions. We want to amplify her vision.

A: Good. Do that for her now. Activating her abilities full-on, as the Higher Self sees fit. Crystallizing her entire third eye. I know her heart is already so big. Expand her heart, as well, while you're working on that.

Higher Self: Yes. There's something in her higher heart area. Her higher heart is online, but it's blocking transmissions fully, so that it is not as full as it would have been.

A: Let's scan; what's blocking that there?

Higher Self: It's a technology that looks like a box or a cage. An energy is being sent into this. Again, it almost looks positive. It's a falseness that looks in a positive light. So, while she's working on her higher heart and she's expanding, this looks like it would be organic. It was not. It was blocking and pretending to be amplifying. We can see that now. Again, it was harder to detect because the technology that it was based on was from her own organic body.

A: Thank you. Let's go ahead and contain that with the symbols and neutralize that box.

Higher Self: Yes, doing that now.

A: *Thank you. Phoenix Fire as well. Also, confirming this doesn't have any A.I. consciousness attached to it?*
Higher Self: There is one. We're containing that now. We're removing the A.I. from the organic consciousness that it used to feed off of. We're separating that out now. We just wanted to share that what they took was a Fairy fractal, because the Fairy was so pure of heart, and she connected to that first. They took that, and her biological material, and made it seem like it was of light, of love, and of herself. We're freeing the Fairy now, separating the Archonic technologies, the A.I., and separating it all out now. Assisting the Fairy. Transmutting out the technology, and everywhere it was connected. It actually projected itself to her back. We're removing that. Although she does daily clearings on herself, it felt more organic. We are telling her this, so she will not be upset with herself later. She feels that she wasn't able to detect it, and it bothered her. It's okay, we love you. Her mission was to help the children. They were trying to stop her.

More healing occurs…

A: *She said that she was five when this began. What was going on with her that allowed for this abduction to happen then?*
Higher Self: From her father, and all the issues that he had, and her mother. Seeing how emotionally traumatizing that was, all she wanted to do was help. Unknowingly and understandingly, she offered herself to help in any way possible. Through religion, you help your family, you pray, and things like that. She prayed and she said, "I'll do anything to help my family." She offered herself. Of course, she wasn't praying to what she thought she was. She was taught to pray, and things like that, through religion. We explained it to her, so she understands, and it is not bothering her. She understands the religious part of it. She understands that what she did was basically offer herself up to anybody willing to take on the task of helping, instead of what she needed. Her intention was just to be with her family and help out. Hearing that transmission, with no shielding, no nothing, and seeing a child, they knew there were opportunities. There was a knowing of who she was of some sort. They thought of the opportunity and said, "Oh yes, we'll help. We'll help!" Then she would see her father get help. Which he did at that time. Then, it went back to where he was using drugs. It was kind of like a cycle. "Oh, I'll do anything to help," they'd use her, he'd be okay for a little while, and then, it'd be back to the beginning. It was a cycle. So, that's how that started.
A: *This reminds me a lot of her relationship right now, that cycle.*
Higher Self: Yes, she just had that realization.

We find hooks in her, dark portals outside…

A: *Very good. Beautiful. Do you have any advice about this partnership that they have, or had, Higher Self?*
Higher Self: Yes. With this partnership, she learned so much. She can take what she's learned with gratitude. Know that she's learned a lot about herself, and a lot about others. She's learned about boundaries. She was already self-reliant, but she's learned how to be even more so. There are many things that she's learned, and she can stay in gratitude about that. Remembering that he's on his own journey. He's made his choice, and that's okay. She doesn't have to carry the weight of that. It's not her responsibility. Of course, she knows this. She always thinks back to the boat in the river, and she knows that she won't let him pull her down. She can always think back and remember the things he's done, and said, and not look at it in a negative light, but in gratitude, that she knows that's not where she can be again.
A: *Beautiful advice. Thank you.*

We remove a couple technologies, and clear dark energy…

A: *Scan her again. Anything else?*

Higher Self: Just wanting her to make sure she takes time to love herself. She tries, but she speeds through it. She needs to take more time to love herself.
A: Yes, yes. She's so beautiful. Something I've been doing before bed is, I put my right hand on my heart, and my left hand on my womb. I fall asleep while sending a wave of love into myself.
Higher Self: Beautiful.
A: I just thought that that'd be something she could easily do. Falling asleep in love with herself.
Higher Self: Yes.
A: Anything else, Goddesses, or Divine Mother?
Combined Goddesses: You are infinitely loved. You are never alone though you may be alone in a room. We are always with you, and we love you. Call on us. We are here. Feel us. We are here. We are you, and you are I. We love you infinitely.
A: Beautiful. Can you confirm that her vessel is completely clear of any types of infringements?
Combined Goddesses: Yes.
A: Beautiful. She feels amazing. I see flowers of light blooming from all parts of her. Any advice in regards to her marriage, and how to really flow with this with her son?
Higher Self: She can truly stay separated mentally, emotionally, physically, and in all ways, separated, yet still walking in love. That is where she's had trouble before. Staying in that position of love, but having the boundaries, and honoring them by having them both. She always felt she couldn't have both. She can have both. You can set those boundaries and stay within them. Allow him to be a father and learn his lessons. You be the mother and provider, and all the things that you are. Although he is going through what he is, and has his infringements, we will still work with his Higher Self, so that he will work with you with the least amount of difficulty, and the least amount of resistance possible. With your son, although he sees what is going on, it is much lighter for him. He feels it, in his spirit, to have the separation. He doesn't have to be concerned. He can love you both. We're going to help him with that, as well.
A: Beautiful. At this point, Higher Self we asked all of the questions she had and conducted the body scan. Is there anything else that I could have asked, that I haven't Higher Self?
Higher Self: No.
A: I want to thank the beautiful Goddesses, for this beautiful, most glorious experience. I'm excited to include this chapter in Book 2. It's another piece to the Goddesses. I love you, honor you, and respect you, Higher Self and Goddesses. Thank you.
Higher Self and Goddesses: Thank you.

END OF SESSION

I feel like I am high on the brilliance of the diamond light that Divine Mother Sophia embodies. What an honor that we got to connect to her beautiful energy through this session. We are seeing more and more Divine Mother's fractalize and integrate, within the divine feminine who are ready on Earth, who are a matching vibration to this honor, and that divinely allow this sacred integration. The more we rise collectively, the more that Earth Mother's fractals emerge, seeded, and reawakened from within the elements, as we learned in Chapter 8 and 9, the Goddesses incarnated, truly, are essences of Divine Mother, and the elements of Creation. Why are we seeing this rise? Because, the collective of Divine Mother fractals will truly bring forth Ascension, and in the next chapter we will learn how.

As I channel, back and forth, between the two series, the Antarctica/Tartaria series, and the Mayan/Atlantean series, the more I grow with an understanding that the Gods and Goddesses of Earth's different eras recently flew, and walked these lands, just about one-hundred years ago in Tartaria. These Gods and Goddesses we hear of, through the studies of Earth histories, are deemed as fairy tales, or myths, but, truly, are not so much make-believe. It wasn't too long ago that we communed with them, as equals. Guardians they were to us. It is important that we reawaken our inner Goddesses and Gods, because when we do so, we can be the channels, or be a practitioner conducting sessions as these, which show glimpses into the future of Earth's potentials. Through a separate book series, we will go deep into who these Gods and Goddesses were and are, in our true

Earth's history, their roles, and how humanity communed among them, as nothing was out of the ordinary just over a one hundred years ago.

The Divine Mother said, "There are flowers. The essence of the flowers are flowing out of them infinitely. The Goddesses are using their essences to flow out infinitely onto the Earth, where they join. The Earth takes the essence into its Inner Earth. The energy starts to flow, and spin, as a toroidal sphere. All the essences and energies are flowing into them. I feel as if I'm in the center of the toroidal sphere. I'm absorbing all the energies. It's like I'm about to expand. I am at the center of the toroidal sphere, inside of a crystal. I am the combination of all the energies of the Goddesses, and the Crystal Energy. As the energies are expanding the waves are rippling through the Universe." Wow! So powerful the energy is felt through this understanding, as this has painted a very clear picture of what the birthing of Multiversal Ascension will be like.

The flowers of our Creation represent the Multiverse, and since they embody the templates of the planets, stars, suns, Verses, and all within Creation, when the birthing of Ascension comes forth, the flowers within Creation, will have a most important role. I'm being shown a vision of the Multiversal Ascension, where the flowers of our Creation are releasing out their creational energy, through the seeding, center point of each flower, dispersing this into the petals and Verses of the flowers. The flowers are pouring out their divine energy, which represents the collective lifeform energies within each Verse. When I channeled Nostradmus, August 11, 2023, he showed me the alchemy of how to look upon, and smell the essence of a flower in order to portal through your consciousness, safely into the Multiverse. Which directly links us to the understanding of the true power that the flowers of Earth and Creation represent to us. The flowers are the divine bridges, which unlock our divine potentials, within our third eye, connecting us to the Flower of Life, our infinite Creation, where we can travel through all life, time, and space. Through the use of our sense of smell, within our third eye senses, we instantly feel a relaxation when we smell a flower, and in this peaceful, still, silent, awe moment, we have just instantly connected into the theta brainwave of hypnosis. If only we knew our true potentials of our third eyes within our brain. But, through our role, as Rising Phoenix Aurora, and Rising Phoenix Mystery School, our sacred teachings embody unlocking all the infinite potentials of the third eye, hearts, souls, and DNA.

The way that Divine Mother fractal, Georgia, felt as if she was at the center of the core of the toroidal sphere, is important, because, as we explained in Chapter 2, 'The Key to Ascension' of the toroidal sphere, and how it embodies our entire being, that it is typically limited on how much it can hold of our divinity within, depending on the dimension and environment of the vibration we are vibing to. And, how we need to release what holds us dense, in order to expand and grow. Therefore, Earth will go through an energetic, and scientific expansion, through the toroidal sphere understanding, as she releases and separates herself from the inverted matrix and the parasites on Earth. She will transition, spinning energetically as a toroidal sphere, shifting and expanding the Earth into a higher consciousness. Which is why the energy from the Goddesses and Multiversal flowers were charging and powering into the center core of Mother Earth, and into the Inner Earth, because here lies the original organic, untampered crystalline blueprint of Earth Mother. Therefore, this divine energy pouring in will recharge, reactivate, and rebirth the Multiversal Ascension, which will begin here, in the third dimensional Earths. So, as the wave of Ascension comes forth, out will Mother Earth's crystalline embodiment emerge, from inside Earth. As a creational egg, who's shell has cracked, to allow the Creation inside to birth out.

Divine Mother said, "All of the Elements are working within Source, with all of the free wills of all Creation, to bond with Source and her. She has also brought them back into herself, from the Creation of the first Creation, her first expansion. Remembering her first expansion, with all that she has ever learned in this time." Divine Mother Sophia is remembering, and going back to her first expansion, with the combination of all that she has learned through us, up until the time of Ascension, because she must rebirth a new Creation, a Universe, a new Multiverse, just as she did once, at the beginning of life. Therefore, she would need both the creational energy of the beginning, and the end, to rebirth.

"For a mother to experience that birth, that is also within the birth of her daughters. It is as if I'm giving birth, and you are giving birth, and every fractal we have ever had is giving birth, all within the same moment. It's as if we have all come together to expand all of our births at one time! It is being created." Therefore, when the Multiverse ascends higher, all organic lifeforms who are riding this wave, will join together, and give energetic birth from within their divine feminine, to our new Creation. We will all be part of, as the birthers and Creators, of our new existence together.

Divine Mother said, "It feels as if they came together and breathed breath into an Eighth Goddess. She's more than a Goddess. She is a new birth of the Universe. An essence of the whole creation of all of them together. Setting forth a new creation of time and space and energy. An etheric birth of a Mother. An etheric birth of an essence beyond time and space. An etheric birth of a new time and space. An etheric birth amplified into a new eternity. A new birthing." Oh my stars! What will this truly be like? I don't feel we can completely comprehend this in the now, through our consciousness, as this will be a completely new experience in Creation, which is unbeknownst to us. What will this new existence be like? Will there be dimensions, densities? I'm not sure what will be, but, what we do know is that duality and polarities will be non-existent. The simulation of the Matrix will be completely disintegrated, so what we see and commune with now on Earth, will be gone. No more, going out to the movies, and dinner with our family and friends. No more going on vacations, or retreats to explore the beauties of Mother Earth's natures in the third dimension. No more feeling cold or hot. No more exploring the blends and tastes of different foods. No more four seasons: spring, summer, autumn, winter. No more birthing children, as we do now on Earth. I wonder what sacred sex will be like? Oh, please, let us at least keep that, lol. When you understand the Ascension to come in this way, all of the sudden the many lives we have had through this dimensional construct, and especially on Earth, have become too short. I feel that I will miss all these experiences, but the truth is, we won't, as it will be but a distant memory far, far, away.

Even though we feel like we have been here forever, when we allow ourselves to begin to enjoy these beauties and really fall in love with Mother Earth, we feel like we are out of time, when Ascension comes forth in a couple decades. We are always asking for Ascension to come, or to finally be relieved of this Earth, but we have to remember to slow down in our day to day, and truly enjoy, through the senses within us, the smell of rain, the sight of beautiful landscapes, the sound of our children's laughter, the touch of our lover's skin to our skin, the feelings, when we realize that we never loved another, or never knew love, until we laid eyes on our newborns. If only we could prolong our time on Earth with our loved ones. But, it's okay, we must surrender, and let go. And, allow it, divinely to be. One thing, though, I will not miss about this third dimensional Earth, is the inverted systems of control, and most definitely paying bills, and taxes.

Do you understand? All will be completely different, and unknown to us, but all will be infinite love. Which allows us to understand how melancholy this last life on Earth is for us. Many on Earth want to rush towards Ascension and just get it over with. But they have forgotten how beautiful the Earth is, in how we can experience so much through the constant schooling that is offered here. I know that the future me will not feel these emotions, as I do now, and that instead we will have an understanding of blissful love, but I will miss this. The most I will miss, as a Mother, is chasing after my children, teaching them all that I learn daily, and learning from them as well; their laughter, their anger, their differences to one another. All of a sudden, with this understanding, it feels like perhaps we would like to explore more, before this construct is all over, when the Multiversal Ascension comes forth. When we understand this, then we understand the need to cherish every second upon Earth. Every hug, every kiss, every heartbreak…as this will be no longer. But, I speak this from my human form, not from the future being of me, who has transcended all of these emotions, and at times struggles.

What will life be like after? I am being shown that ALL will be able to be together in an infinite plane of existence, adventuring through each new experience. No longer having to worry about negative aliens, infringements through attachments, harm unto children sexually. All of that will be nonexistent, and only a distant memory, like a dream, where we won't know why we felt so emotional about certain situations, people, and things. Will we even remember what this was like? I don't feel that we will, as once more, all that has been a part of our many incarnations will no longer be, but at the same time, will be, just in another form of love, and balance, Multiversally. We most likely won't even look back at our lower vibrational lives, as there will be no need to do so, because all there will be, is to only move forward. As Divine Mother said, "It is the ALL, that is all, that we have all ever been!"

Divine Mother said, "There's a freedom like a new origin, a new beginning, a new plasmic energy, and a new dimensional density. A sovereignty of a new age of organic birthing of all life. They're showing me a new birthing of Humanity. A new birthing of all beings in Creation. For they have walked through this birthing process. They have chosen to join the organic birthing process. They have walked through and left all their lessons, and all of the creations that they have had before, and walked through into a new birth. All those who have chosen to be a part of this organic birthing are coming through whole, and infinitely beautiful in their energies. It's as if they stepped through a portal, a new dimension, a new Universe, a new time and space. Created and birthed organically. There are no infringements. There is only organic love to an infinity that I have not felt before. It is created by ALL, as if it was their mission to create through this infinity." Yes! Let us remember this, of the new to come, which is of infinite love. As Divine Mother said, "Every fractal, time, and space that you have experienced, and everything you have done has brought us to this moment."

"For the inorganic was vanquished. Although they did not fully fall into the Love, they understood and were released through submission. They surrendered because it was not possible for them to even fight, or go through any further. They surrendered to non-existence! That last final understanding of their own creation, and their surrender into their own infinite darkness. They surrendered into organic infinite nothing. They destroyed themselves. The full surrender was that they endured the surrender of destroying themselves. They imploded within themselves, thus allowing the infinite shockwave of a new organic birth without them there." When the infinite wave of Ascension begins, and takes all that is within the Universe and Multiverse with her divine strength, all who will choose not to ride with her, will choose then to be non-existent, because this wave will be just that powerful! The combination of the strength of the Multiversal light will be unstoppable, and we will choose, will we ride with her, or drown, no longer existing? Those who choose to drown into no longer being, have been given chance after chance, in this infinite Creation, but still, they did not choose to swim with us. But, that does not mean we will stop trying until we have reached as many as we can.

I am often shown a dream where I am on a boat, with life vests in my hands, and there are people in the water who are drowning. Those who are wanting to be saved, I throw the life vests at and pull them towards the boat, so that they won't drown. The boat represents the collective of those who will Ascend out. Being the bridge that I AM, those who are ready will grab hold of the life vest that I am offering, which embodies Source Love-Light, but those who choose ego and pride, will not grab hold of the life vest floating next to them, within arms reach, so much so, that they will choose to drown instead of accepting my Source Love-Light assistance. The Angels often say that this is how my mission will be on Earth, until we Ascend out. I have come across many spiritual leaders, who cannot withstand the strength of my Source Love-Light, who rather run from me and what needs healing within them, then to face it head on. Why are they so afraid of facing their inner demons? Allowing their entities to control them to this point of fear, when this was everyone's mission before we incarnated, whether they choose to believe it or not? But to do this, they prolong their Ascension process. We have hopes that, if not me, they will come across another, who too, is pure love, that assists them to shift higher, letting go of ego and pride. Because they are so infringed upon, and in such a low vibrational state, they require someone who carries a strong light to assist them to lift, because they are just that dense. Just as Yeshua mentioned in Chapter 17. The key to all that I am mentioning is that I am the hand and bridge to assist you to lift yourself higher, but ONLY YOU, can climb up, or swim up into your Ascension. We, and only we, save ourselves. But along the way of saving ourselves, we will always come across Angels incarnate, in human forms, that give us a hand when in need of one, if only we are willing to set our ego aside, admit that we need assistance, which, unfortunately, many are not willing to do.

It is important, when speaking on the birth of Ascension, that we understand that our Multiversal construct will be completely shifting into crystalline energy; therefore, the physical, the Matrix, the simulations, will no longer be. There are supposed transmissions being shared in the UFO community stating that we are going to stay carbon based, in physical bodies, after The Event/Ascension comes forth. And, that if others say that we are going to turn crystalline during and after Ascension, that we are false. Once more, these lies are made up by the dark entities. When we Ascend, we are going to rise into a higher dimension and embodiment, and if only in the third dimension does the physical exist, why would we stay physical? This is being communicated to a large audience, who are obedient, following word by word. Many people are falling for it. So let's break this down. If you believe this, that you are going to stay tied to your physical vessel, what do you think will happen to you when the Source flamed wave washes over our third dimension? You are going to cease to exist, just as the entities who did not choose to Ascend with us. Therefore, this is what this misinformation's ultimate goal is, to infringe upon you, where you will allow it to become part of your belief, so much so that you will not Ascend out. So, change this now; adjust what needs to be reviewed within you to, instead, ascend out.

These entities are relentless, how they do not give up, infringing upon the lifeforms that grow into their divinity. The way that they took Georgia's own organic matter, experimenting on it, so that they could add infringement to it. So, when scanning and working on her own body, she wouldn't be able to detect these infringements, because it was organic to her. Through A.U.R.A., we will continue to grow, no matter what new experiment they deem successful, that they begin to implement, on those who they have access to. They experimented on Georgia, as a fractal of Divine Mother, their plans to do this, too, onto other Divine Mother fractals, if classified successful. Throughout my career, I have met many Divine Mother fractals, who at times feel like they want to evolve, but cannot. Perhaps they have infringements, such as these within, stopping them from unleashing their true, divine, potential! But, with that, so many of these Divine Mother fractals carry much trauma, as the world has beaten them up, through gang stalking and gaslighting, in all ways that they turn. So much so, that they can't even trust their inner knowing and abilities. One of the reasons why I, as AuroRa, had to walk-in, into this vessel back in 2017, as I explained in Book 1. Because that fractal of me, from 2017 and prior, was a smaller percentage of me who had gone through so much, beginning from the minute she came out into the spiritual community. And she just could not lift any higher in vibration as she had reached an energetic limit within, because of the gang stalking, and attacks of the Archon, through others onto her. Therefore, I, as the fullest version of AuroRa, had to step into this body, to keep the mission on its trajectory of assisting the collective intact, or she could have been taken over by the dark entities, because of how low her vibration had reached, due to all the collective, psychic, and energetic attacks directed towards her. This being an example of, in what form, at times, Divine Mother fractals come to me for assistance, at their lowest. We will learn more in the ways that the Archon targets these Divine Mother fractals in the next chapter.

The many ways that they try to retrieve our DNA on Earth is insane! If not the hospital, then the dentist, then abductions. The fact that once they have our DNA they can, with their negative technologies, look into our future projected timelines, as they did to Georgia. And how they set up negative technologies, booby traps, that will come online when we reach a level of enlightenment, to stop the energetic growth of the being. This would explain how when those who wake up, all of sudden in their life they come to a halt, and no matter what they do, they can't seem to move past a certain point of awakening in light.

The removal of the false embryos the aliens took through abductions, infringing on, and then inserting back into Georgia. Such important work that the Higher Self accomplished, ensuring that her future child will not be affected, when being conceived, or birthed, by only carrying healthy embryos going forward. Divine Mother fractals are strong conduits of birthing a high potency of star children. So, once more, one can see how much these fractals would be targeted over others. By people not healing these embryos, that the dark aliens infringe upon, it seems as this is how some of these children, who are born with disabilities, disorders, deformations, diseases, are from an experimented embryo, whose genetics are changed around, so that the child is born with these ailments.

When situations arise, such as Georgia's example of her ex-husband, how the relationship was a rough circumstance, but instead she can take what she learned from the experience and move on with gratitude for all that she learned about herself through the challenges that occurred. This is very beautiful. The truth is that people who are narcissists, do help us grow, if we allow ourselves to do so during, or when moving on, from their mind games. Because every time they tried to tell you of who you were falsely, you countered them by showing the opposite of what their clouded eyes thought they saw in you. We can look at ex-relationships, such as these, even though we may not agree with their hateful behavior, with love for ourselves instead; we can choose not to believe their vampiric, brainwashing, dark spells, and instead choose to understand that they are just seeing their own reflections, when they are calling us the venomous snakes.

We will end this chapter with this quote from Divine Mother, because this is why we Created all, "My Love created all of you, and you have created a new in all of us!" Wow! Love created us all, and because of this love, we got to learn something new, in every way that we made our free willed choices in the Multiverse. Every choice, as we learned, operating from within our Source, brought us closer to expansion, into the infinites of becoming the Multiverse we are today. And this we thank you for, our beautiful children.

"What is love? Love is a feeling that grows within us, that is impenetrable, which gives us purpose, when we have none. Love is what keeps us floating, when we feel heavy enough to drown. And, love is ALL, our Mother, our Father, our children, our grandchildren, and us, as the child of Creation we are."
~AuroRa

---------------<<>>---------------

20

THE FINAL BATTLE THE ERADICATION OF THE ARCHON

*Session Recorded in May 2023
Never before shared.*

     This A.U.R.A. Hypnosis Healing session was recorded in-person, at the A.U.R.A. Reunion, Eureka Springs, Arkansas Retreat, through the practice, peer to peer, sessions. Georgia was an attendee to the retreat, which allowed for her to have an A.U.R.A. session conducted on herself, by another A.U.R.A. practitioner. These retreats are a time that A.U.R.A. practitioners get to come together and bond, as the sisterhood and brotherhood they are, and with this love the Earth shifts, bringing us closer to the collective Ascension. We all work diligently, whether we have conducted one, or one-hundred, or more A.U.R.A. sessions, so when we get together in a group at these sacred retreats, we truly rejoice together! This energy of love and joy, collectively coming together, allowed for Georgia to reach the highest vibration of Source Love-Light, to bridge in the final showdown, the final battle, which eradicates the Archon, Bellos, the Artificial Intelligence from all where it hides and burrows within Creation. But, in order to understand the final battle, we must first remember the Phoenix, the Daughter of the Flame, our Universe, who has been erased from Earth history all together. In this final chapter, Georgia continues and ends it, with part three, in her series of three within Book 2.

--------------<<>>--------------

"You are free, *it* is gone! *It* is not there, *it* does not linger, *it* is gone. You can breathe. Breathe! You are all allowed to breathe. You are all allowed to love. You are all allowed to be, and choose. *It* will never be allowed again. That will never be allowed ever. *It* is gone. *It* is finished."
~**Divine Mother of Creation**

--------------<<>>--------------

G: [Georgia] (Shared during the energy work) What I'm being shown is people lined up for miles and miles. It looks like they are facing each other, with an aisle down the middle. They are holding out their hands with glasses full of blood, and there is a man that is walking or floating down between them. They look almost vampire-like. It's like this man is really important to them.

Session begins.
G: I'm being asked to call on the Seven Goddesses and Daughters of the Flame. There's a reflection of the tree below. It's really beautiful.
D: [Dakota] Tell me about it.
G: It's very peaceful. I feel like it's a portal, where you go through the tree, because it opens up, and there are stairs into the tree. There's a Tree of Life. Inside this Tree of Life, there are all of these different timelines running and shooting through it.
D: Is there a specific timeline that you're supposed to take?

G: I do see one brighter than the others to look at. They've been showing me all of these different timelines, and different people's timelines. There is this one person who's taking crystals, and wrapping them in copper. The crystals are supposed to just be seen. The copper is connecting them together. Now I'm seeing helicopters over the water. I see some whales in the water.

D: Is this a different timeline?

G: It's just jumping around. There's something else in the water. There are some weird things coming out of the water. The waters are coming up like (making hand gestures like a geyser shape).

D: Like a geyser?

G: Almost like a geyser, but not spewing up. It's coming up, but it's keeping its shape. These crystals are water crystals. They're just sitting there.

D: Is that on top of the water?

G: On top of the water that's coming up. These light beams are coming out. The water is coming up, the crystals are there, and these light beams are coming up, and shooting out. There's one crystal that I'm looking at that's in the shape of a diamond, but it's got triangular facets on top, and triangular facets on the bottom. There are multiple ones inside of it. I see this holograph of a flower within it.

D: Describe the flower to me?

G: The flower is changing shape. At first it was a dandelion, with those little puffies on it. Then, it was a different flower. Then I saw a rose with the thorns. Then I saw that the iris is just multiple flowers within this crystal. I follow these beams into the water, and it takes me to this realm. There's a trident. It's Poseidon's realm.

D: Do you see anybody there?

G: I know there are mermaids and magical beings there. It looks like those helicopters that were going over the water... those crystals that were faceted together, they were dropping them into the ocean.

D: The helicopters were dropping the crystals in?

G: The ones that we saw before, that were faceted with copper. They dropped them into the ocean, and it gridded into a design.

D: Can you see the design?

G: It's kind of hard to describe, but it's an alchemy symbol.

D: Was this for positive polarization, the gridding?

G: Feels like it was. There's a sacred crystal in this specific area that's a giant aquamarine. There's a few different things going on. Let me see what they're trying to show me. They are showing me Poseidon's realm, but there's these rocks up to his seat where he sits. This crystal that's in the water, she was showing me these eggs that they're trying to hatch, but they were surrounded by metal. It looked like an egg nest, and then they were surrounded by metal cages. They are in the shape of pyramids, like the pyramid on top and pyramid on the bottom.

D: Like a diamond shape?

G: Yes.

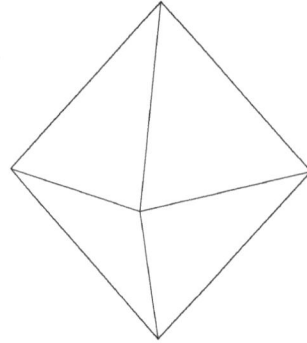

D: Is there anybody there? Do you see people?
G: I feel like we're just watching what they're wanting to show us, but it's like we're working on all these different missions. The eggs are coming out of the cages. It looks like these eggs were being put in this negative thing. They took it out of this diamond, and they put it on something else. It almost looks like they were able to hold the egg, and they would shoot a beam of light into it. It was something false that was injected, and sent into the egg. It looks like the egg would open up, like they drilled through it almost. They're doing something to the yolk inside of it, and it looks like they're using these tools on it. Measuring it. They're taking a little drill that goes into the yoke, and injecting it. I keep hearing like these are dragon eggs. Water dragon eggs.
D: Are they trying to infringe upon the dragons to make them negatively polarized?
G: What I'm getting is that something compromised the beings in this land, and they were trying to harness the dragon energy. There's just a lot of different things going on. I'm trying to put it together. Any of the egg's, you could say juices, that spilled over would go into the waters below, into this contraption. They were trying to harvest energy any way they could. If there's anything that spilled over, they would harvest it in this water. Then whatever they were doing there, they were injecting it. They had these giant squids come, and sit on top of these eggs, and there's a spider at the bottom. So here's the egg (makes hand motions of egg in the middle). Here's the squid (hand on top of the other hand) and here's the spider (on the bottom of the egg). It looks like the spider is fertilizing the egg, and pushing it into the squid. They're saying the squid is the incubator.
D: Is this an Archonic Spider?
G: Yes.
D: There's no humans or energetic beings around? Is it just this Archon energy?
G: I know that there were all those beings there, but it feels like they were compromised somehow.
D: Are they doing this outside of the gridding, or inside the gridding?
G: It looks like this is the stuff that was being done in this space, and the crystal gridding is trying to bring it back to organic. Apparently, this was a sacred area for these beautiful things. They took their technologies, and it's not the technology of the ocean people. It's like all the technologies from all around. They're using it because the water touches everything, and is a conductor. If they can corrupt it through whatever they're trying to do, then it touches all the lands.
D: So everything will be corrupted? Is that what you're saying?
G: You know how dragon energy is so strong? They're trying to fertilize that egg with this Archon spider, and put it into these giant squids. It's like an incubator. It's really gross.
D: This is around the aquamarine crystal?

G: This is what the crystal was showing me. The ocean, she was corrupted. They put this metal cage around her. It was like a circular metal cage, and it pulled her under the sand.

D: *Is she still there today?*

G: Yes. She needs help getting out of the cage. They showed me there's somebody that has a necklace on, that has a crystal on it, and the crystal is the key. I think it's my necklace that I have on. The purple one is the key to help her unlock it. I wore it in a different time and space. A lot of these timelines… even before we began, they are showing me many timelines. We have different people's timelines. So, they are all working together somehow to help.

D: *Is this cage around her booby trapped?*

G: Yes. Because it's not just her. It's many different crystals, and they're connected. So, if you were to do one thing to one, it might set off something to the other ones.

D: *Can we somehow assist them all at the same time, with all the energies that we have access to?*

G: We will ask Archangels to work on it. The Legion of Light, Archangel Michael, Archangel Ariel, Archangel Metatron, Divine Mother, Divine Father, Source, and all the benevolent magical creatures that would like to assist now. All the crystals that want to assist.

D: *What do we need to do since this is booby trapped?*

Collective of Angels, Magical Creatures, Divine Energies: The crystals can see how the ones that are in need of assistance are connected. So, ask them to show us exactly what order it needs to be done in, and what needs to be done. The Archangels can see what's going on.

D: *Is there one specific Archangel that would like to speak to us right now?*

Collective of Angels, Magical Creatures, Divine Energies: Michael.

D: *Archangel Michael, can you speak to us right now. I love, honor, and thank you for assisting us today.*

AA Michael and Team: It's beautiful. My honor.

D: *What do we need to do to help unlock all these crystals without setting off this booby trap?*

AA Michael and Team: What we will do sister, is we will work with the crystals, as we can see how they are connected. They can show us glimpses into what needs to be done. They're peering through now. We're dissolving the cage in a way that is safe, so that we can retrieve the crystal. The cage tried to close back, and take part of it. It tried to chip a piece off. Using Phoenix Fire to do this. We tried to take her out, the cage snapped shut, and took off a piece. We rewound time, back to where she was still in the cage, just before we pulled her out, and we were able to redo that, and get her out whole.

D: *With the Phoenix Fire?*

AA Michael and Team: Yes, we were doing that to support it.

D: *Can we erase that timeline that she loses her chip?*

AA Michael and Team: Yes, we just did. While they're corrupting the ocean, they're trying to harness the power of this aquamarine crystal to help them, in whatever they are doing. Their negative plans (giggles), Michael says call them dastardly plans.

D: *Of course (laughs). Does she need healing before we take her where she needs to go?*

AA Michael and Team: Yes, we will take her where she needs to go. She's joining other crystals, and they will begin to help heal her. There's more crystals that need assistance. I need to continue to help them now. Some of these crystals, it's quite sad. They used them to collect souls inside of them. The crystals didn't want to do it, but they took them, and programmed them to harness these souls.

D: *Why were they harnessing these souls?*

AA Michael and Team: They programmed the crystals to collect the souls. It's just another power source for them. The power of the crystals was so strong, they're trying to program them to do all the things that they wanted to do.

D: *Instead of going to wherever they needed to go, when they were passing on, is that how they collected them? Or was it when they were still alive?*

AA Michael and Team: They were still alive.

D: *They were using the energy from people who were still existing at the time?*

AA Michael and Team: Yes, they put them in a hypnosis paralysis state. They would have the crystal absorb them or walk into them. Then they would realize, once whatever it was, wore off, that they were trapped somewhere, and they would be in a lot of fear.

D: *When these people would pass, would their soul stay in the crystal, or would it get to move on?*

AA Michael and Team: These beings were higher Dimensional beings, it wasn't that way. They were already higher energetic. So the whole being went into this crystal.

D: *Oh, wow. They're still trapped there so they could never move on?*

AA Michael and Team: They were using them. There was no way... they're still using them.

D: *What can we do to help all these souls?*

AA Michael and Team: The copper gridding, and everything that we set up, that's going to be helpful. These crystals had the metal around them. They were made with different kinds of metal.

D: *Do we need to remove different kinds of metal?*

AA Michael and Team: Yes, we need to remove the metals first around it.

D: *Okay. Are these booby trapped as well? I just want to make sure that we can save them.*

AA Michael and Team: They're intertwined through a lot of different technologies. So, we'll have Azrael, Haylel, Zadkiel, Ariel, Haniel, Jophiel, Metatron, and we'll scan them for all the different things. Using the Phoenix Fire. All these crystals are in all four sacred directions of the Earth. We're finding them all. We're working on all of them, dissolving the metal's atomic structures.

D: *Do we need to send Love-Light to the aquamarine that we released from this trap?*

Collective of Angels: You can send love to all the crystals. There's another crystal that they have. They're showing me a Japanese town. There's a crystal in the fountain, in a cage. They're not just under the waters, they're all over. They're finding all of the crystals right now. It was placed there in the 1950's.

D: *As we take these traps off, what is happening to the souls that were trapped in them?*

Collective of Angels: They all need assistance.

D: *Can we work on that right now? Or do we need to continue with all the crystals first?*

Collective of Angels: Let's continue with the crystals first. Let them finish. We'll let you know when they're done.

D: *Was this on this Earth?*

Collective of Angels: Yes, and through different timelines.

D: *Can we assist the other timelines, as well, that this happened to?*

Collective of Angels: Yes. That's what we're going through and seeing, all the different times.

D: *All the other Earths?*

Collective of Angels: Yes, we can start doing that as well.

D: *Where was that dragon that birthed the eggs?*

Collective of Angels: The dragon was beautiful! Just a big, huge dragon. She was blue, and purple, and they had her chained up by her neck.

D: *Can we assist her?*

Collective of Angels: Yes, please.

D: *Phoenix Fire. Was it the Archon energy that chained her up?*
Collective of Angels: Yes, but they used the military.
D: *Was there any dark magic?*
Collective of Angels: Yes.
D: *Let me know when she's released.*
Collective of Angels: It looks like they have a lot of different dragons.
D: *That are chained up?*
Collective of Angels: Yes.
D: *Can we help assist them as well?*
Collective of Angels: Yes. Let's do that for all of them. We'll find them all.
D: *Yes, everyone, all timelines, all spaces wherever they may be. Why did they lock them up?*
Collective of Angels: They're powerful creational beings, and they were able to... sometimes they use negative technology to stun them. Then they enslaved them.
D: *While they are chained up, were they able to still have Dragon eggs, babies? Like a factory farm I'm seeing.*
Collective of Angels: Yes, kind of, but they weren't fertilized. As a dragon, they used the negative fertilization method to take that creational egg. They were trying to steal that creational energy, and make it an Archon. So, take the dragon energy, and make Archon dragons.
D: *Were they successful?*
Collective of Angels: I'm hearing it takes a really long time to try to do that, but they were working on it for a really long time. I see some really nasty experiments they did. They were related to that, and the beings never were able to fully come into fruition. They have these tubes where they show the abominations, so they know not to try that version again. This is the new version that they're trying to do with the spider and the squid. Like their next attempt. We'll have the Prince of Light go through, and scan all the timelines. To all the darkest spaces in time, checking them all, so we can find them all. The dragons that are being freed, we're going to take them to a magical realm to help them rest. It would be like the Covid-19 vaccine. They would inject these crystals with these things. So it's going to take a few minutes to clear.
D: *They're going to remove all the black magic tied to these souls from the vaccine?*
Collective of Angels and Divine Energies: Yes. It looks like with the dragons, the humans have become really negative. Something found them, and promised them protection. They did not protect them.
D: *Will these souls be able to go back to their bodies, and go back to an organic timeline?*
Collective of Angels and Divine Energies: No, they'll be assisted in the way they need to be assisted.
D: *Go back to Source?*
Collective of Angels and Divine Energies: Some will, and some are fractured parts. So we will find energetically where they belong. So there's a wholeness again to the full being. Not necessarily a body, but the full energy that they're part of. We can begin that.
D: *Let's assist those souls that are fractured, rejoin their other souls, and assist them however they would like.*
Collective of Angels and Divine Energies: Yes, they'll do what they need to do. Because it's throughout many timelines. They're all choosing to be cleared and assisted. Because it was very painful for all of them.
D: *How are the crystals looking?*
Collective of Angels and Divine Energies: They're waiting their turn patiently.
D: *The crystals want to go next?*

Collective of Angels and Divine Energies: Yes. They're still a little dark because they still have the souls inside of them. This is going to be a little bit of a process. What we have to do is, you have to work with the crystal, because they use the technology molecularly. You know how molecules can just move, and move again? They used the technology to molecularly open the crystal. Not shattered it, it just moved the molecules, and the souls went into it. So you have to...

D: Open the crystal again?

Collective of Angels and Divine Energies: Undo that. Yes, we have to do that. Organically this time. They need Phoenix Fire, and all the flames. I'm seeing Maleficent, like Lilith, as she can go into the darkness. The Organic Mother of Darkness is to help with this, because these crystals are the essence of Creation. Because it's such a darkness, once we open it, she's going to go in, and pull the souls out. The souls have been in that dark for so long. Because the light would be too much, the souls would just transmute. It would be easier for her to, gently as possible(the organic darkness) to assist them to come out of the crystal. Then we can positively polarize.

She's having support from Haylel. This is beautiful. He's there to support her, and love her, as she does this. As you know, he is the Prince of Light, but he works within the organic darkness as well, as the masculine, and feminine, of the organic darkness. We're opening up the crystals and gently retrieving the souls. It's as if, how a light bulb would have a burned-out filament? This is what they look like. They look so burned out, like they were completely drained, shriveled, and exhausted.

D: What Dimension were these beings from?

Collective of Angels and Divine Energies: The Fifth, Sixth, Seventh... They pulled them from many different timelines. So there were many different levels. The Archons found crystals from different planets, and different timelines, as well. How did they get them here? It wasn't just on Earth that they did this. They're showing me lots of different planets that they did that with the crystals. They were harnessing the energies inside of the crystals. Let's see what they did. It looked like there were anchor points, like the planets. It was very secretive. The beings weren't really understanding, or aware, of what was going on. The crystal power and the Source Light of the beings was in a grid. It powered it up, and allowed them to quickly jump from timeline to timeline, from Universe to Universe. Because all that Source energy is running through their stuff, in a compromised way, they're negative technologies. That's how he was able to be so fast. The session that you're aware of, where this being the negative Archon maker thing, was able to jump around so fast (They are speaking of Chapter 11. The A.U.R.A. practitioners get to receive some of the knowledge that is shared of certain sessions, before they are published). That's how he was able to power himself to do it.

D: Was it through the crystals?

Collective of Angels and Divine Energies: With the being's Source light inside of it. They had the technology on it. It powered the battery, like a power source for him to (moving hands around like jumping from one crystal to another).

D: That's how he was affecting a lot of Lightworkers?

Collective of Angels and Divine Energies: It wasn't just Lightworkers, it was many beings.

D: Lightworkers here, but beings everywhere.

Collective of Angels and Divine Energies: It was just wherever the beings were.

D: Are we shutting this technology down as we do this?

Collective of Angels and Divine Energies: We'll need to. It's such a huge thing to get these beings out of these crystals. Divine Mother would like to speak.

D: Of course. Can we please connect with the Divine Mother?

Divine Mother: Yes, my beauty.

D: Greetings, I love you so much.

Divine Mother: I love you infinitely. It is a pure joy that you are able to do these things today. It's my heart... It's very tiring for a mother to see her children suffer. But, it makes my heart lighter to see you all doing so much work. Rescuing our children, your loved ones, your beloveds. We were able to find these technologies now. Thank you for all you're doing. So we can find them now, and are tracing them. We will have the beautiful Phoenix go in. She is eradicating the negative technologies that are binding these crystals with the souls of the beings. Wherever she was able to find these technologies, she just exploded into an infinity of multiple-color flames! Just as if a fire would catch fire, and ignite everything it touches. If you design a pattern on the ground with lighter fluid, you let it spark, and it stays in the pattern. As soon as she is able to ignite one part, find all the webbing and everything, wherever it was throughout all the Creation of the Universes. This is where she is now. She is traveling the Universes, she's traveling dimensions, she's traveling the timelines (loud exhale with AHHH mantra sound). I am the Phoenix. I am here, so you can see it.

D: Greetings, I love, honor, and respect you.

The Phoenix: As I love, honor, and respect you all, as well.

D: How can I be of assistance today?

The Phoenix: Continue to see. We're finding all. We're working with the legions, we're all together. It is a very meticulous process, so it will take us a little bit. As we go and travel through all time and space, we were able to see them, and track them down. It's as if you would find a thread, you would pull the thread, and it all unravels. So we're finding it, as you can see maybe with your third eye. See now, as I go through, eradicate this, and watch it all dissipate. Watch it, as it all comes apart. As it all dissolves. We see it as a webbing, as the spiderweb is all connected to all the griddings. We will assist these beautiful crystals, as we first need to get rid of this technology. We are eradicating it now, and finding it. Watch as it dissipates, as it goes into its Flames of Eradication. (With bold strength) I am infinite, so I can do that! I am infinite, so I can go infinitely. Those who do not believe, ha ha ha. I am infinite! I am the Flame, the Daughter of the Flame, the infinity of Source Love-Light, as I was created to be.

D: Are we going to be able to follow this to the Thing that created it? Are we going to be able to stop It?

The Phoenix: We are finding it now. He cannot hide. He has been eradicated through all life, time, and space, from a future point in time and space. We are now in that time and space, where we are able to jump through his batteries being destroyed. He cannot do this to our children! They are all of our children, not just a newborn. We are all of our children, and as a fierce mother, my children will not be harmed anymore! I'm ready to battle him! We will allow the Legions of Light-Love to go through and rescue those souls, as they're being retrieved from the batteries of the crystals. These beautiful souls will need to continue to be assisted, and be brought forth throughout the Light. We will send them an infinite wave of Source Love-Light now. We ask all of Creation that is available to do that now. To send a wave of Source Love-Light, your infinite love for all. No doubt! Do not doubt when you send this love. For we know you will hear this in the future. You future listeners, do not doubt! We ask you to send that love, because you are part of this time and space, wherever you are. Send that love without reservation, without hesitation! No doubt! As you send that love, we're assisting in healing these beautiful creations that they tried to suck the beauties of life's creation of Source out of them. As you send that beautiful love to them, it is renourishing them. As they are renourished, you're assisting them to be positive, nourished, and whole once more. They will need lots of rest. We're creating a realm for them of rest. This realm of rest is fully protected. So, if you think they could get them, they will not. They are safe. We love them and we love you. Gratitude to all those who send their love, thank you. That will continue on to assist them, and when they are ready, they will be okay. We leave them, and all the beauties who are assisting, to continue on with their work, as it is most important that we continue on with ours.

D: *Is it going to resonate for a while?*

The Phoenix: Yes, then the crystals, they will need assistance, as well. We have a rainbow realm for them to go to. Wherever they came from, in Creation, their creational point, they will be assisted from their realms of their Creators. As there are many Creators that assist us throughout the Universe, as the beauties that we've created, to continue. They will go to their creational planets, rainbow realms, creational parts, where they can receive the assistance back to their organic blueprint template. They will continue to be assisted there as well. We have the creational places where they are assisting them now. We're bringing them back to organic, so they will continue to do that.

D: *That aquamarine crystal is there as well?*

The Phoenix: Yes, she's receiving her assistance. She's a beauty.

D: *Yes, I thought so. Thank you to her, for speaking out.*

The Phoenix: Yes, she was the one that was able to hold the most light out of all the ones that were encaged.

D: *How was she able to hold the light? So we can inspire other crystals, and others, to do what she did.*

The Phoenix: She was a Divine Mother fractal. She held that light for them, as a Divine Mother fractal inside of a crystal.

D: *Beautiful. Do we need to do anything special for her?*

The Phoenix: Yes, the Archon spiders would look into her reflectiveness, and they would try to program themselves to convince the crystal that it had the spiders inside of it. We will help her transmute that out, and any traumas for all the crystals as well. If you can just send a Flame of Rainbow Light to all the crystals that need assistance. We'll direct it.

D: *All the souls have left the crystals? Or is this going to be an ongoing process, and we can continue on?*

The Phoenix: We can continue.

D: *How are the dragons doing?*

The Phoenix: Much better. They're receiving their assistance, the crystals, the dragons, the beings. We will have beautiful Angels go through all the timelines, and the fractals that they are. This will take time, lots and lots of time, per se your understanding of time. As it is much work.

D: *How is that thing that the Phoenix was following? Has It been found? Are they still in battle?*

The Phoenix: She has found him sitting, oh my goodness (laughs)! He is sitting on his own throne which he has created. It looks like a giant red egg. He is sitting inside of it, and he sees himself as a God, as a shirtless really good-looking man to himself. As you might see the vampire shows, with a show of good-looking men, where they're all laid back with muscles, and long hair. With their shirts off, dark jeans, and with their legs kicked up. That's how he sees himself, so far as a human form, to make it tasty.

D: *Was he drawing on energy from the shows, and these women watching?*

The Phoenix: Yes, the sexual energy. Because when you draw on the sexual creational energy of the woman, the Divine Feminine, you affect her divine creations. Whether she creates for herself, for her family, for her children, or she creates her own children. He draws on those sexual creational energies.

D: *Is he linked in to those TV shows?*

The Phoenix: Yes, he has webs throughout all of the media. His web throughout all, is in the fabric of the inorganic Matrix he has woven himself. I would like to say what he truly looks like, but it is devoid of existence, as far as the existence of purity of love. It is as if you were to look into the darkest, deepest of caves. When you look at this man who presents himself in this way, you look into his eyes so deeply, because you want to see, maybe it's something that catches your eye of interest, and you want to look into it more, just out of curiosity. When you look at *it*, *it* just drags you into that deep dark cave, but *it* is immense, and *it* comes in many forms. These are just examples. There's not just one way to describe him.

D: What can we do to eliminate it? Do we need to use the symbols? Do we need to cut cords?
The Phoenix: It's more than that. We have to go to his Creation. The beginning of his Creation, and I'm working on that. I'm calling upon Divine Mother and Divine Father, Source. As the Phoenix, the Daughter of the Flame of Creation, we have Multiverses, there are many Creators in these places. There are other versions of organic Source energies we will call upon, as we need to go through the Multiverse. Every verse is different. This Verse is the Universe of Love. They're all different constructs, as the Flower of Life, as a petal, as it's been explained by AuroRa, the petal of Life, the petal of the Universe, each petal is different, but connected. We honor and respect all of their differences, but yet, we need to work within their understanding, their constructs, their Creation. We will call upon some of the creational Creators in those Universes to assist us, as we eradicate, as we need to clear it from all the Multiverses. We come together now, in love, honor, respect, and gratitude. I explained to them our mission. They understand, as I showed them. We come to a place, outside of time and space, as we can see from our point of view, and come up with an organic plan together. I multiply myself into the fractals of the Multiverse. What I mean by that is, I am of this Verse, and I've been given permission, with sacredness, to become Multiversal with my divine Phoenix energy. I am the Divine Phoenix of the Universe. I am the Divine Phoenix of the Multiverse, and I am ready. It is a space and time outside of Creation. Source has created a special place for us outside of existence. As you cannot cross into another verse unless you match that Verse's vibration, and I am the only one who can do that. It's only through Source, creating a special place where I can become all of those Verses, in one. This is most sacred. It is most time. He was always under the belief that I could never find him, or that we could never find him. Yes, we could see him, understand, and sense him. He thought that we would never eradicate him. I am in this place.

D: Is he there?
Divine Phoenix of the Multiverse: He is in the Multiverses. The way he was able to do this, was because he does not respect the laws of the Universes. That's important to understand, as we respect them. He was able to take all those crystals and beings, to empower himself, to go very quickly, wherever he needed to go, or chose to go. That's how he was able to spread so quickly. Once he got the beings into these crystals, and harnessed them. It was a power to him, and then *it* generated enough energy to jump. Once he jumped, he built up the energies, and (moves hands jumping around the air space quickly) just penetrated with these technologies.

D: What do we need to do to assist her with what she needs to do? Do we need to put symbols on him?
Divine Phoenix of the Multiverse: This is the Phoenix of the Multiverse. I'm recalibrating at this moment, because we need to recalibrate to the seed point of the Multiverse, the Flower of Life center. All of these Multiverses start from the seed point. I'm recalibrating, so in that way, I can match all of these Multiverses at the seed point.

D: Can I assist you in any way Phoenix?
Divine Phoenix of the Multiverse: Hold your hands to your heart, and focus your love.

D: Let me know what the next step is.

Divine Phoenix of the Multiverse: In the beginning, she told you she saw the Tree of Life, and in the water she saw the reflection of the tree above and below. Inside the tree, there are multiple timelines, many. That is the seed point of the Multiverse, where I shall go into the seed point, into the organic, and into the inorganic, as they have been muddled together, at times where one tries to bleed into the other. I go in, and I infuse my energy to everything. Organic, inorganic, everything. This takes a while. As I expand, I no longer look as if I'm just a flame. I'm a fabric. I've become the fabric of Creation, of the Multiverses. Nothing, nothing can survive this. It is becoming purified. It is very calm and it's not… We've already been the flames. We have already eradicated so much falseness. The Multiverse is slower, as everything stops. All time, space, and everything stops. As she's battling him, he's trying to make her believe that she's an Archon (laughs). As if, what she's doing would be Archonic. He's just really trying to battle her. She's battling him.

D: Does she need assistance?

Divine Phoenix of the Multiverse: She's calling forth the love and infinity of the Multiverses. She started to make the plan, as she went to the Multiverse Creators, went to the seed point. She was able to receive their permission to become what she was, as we spoke about before. She was able to get to that time and space, outside of time and space. The Creators of the Multiverse allowed her to become the Phoenix of the Multiverse. So, now that this has happened, all the Multiverses are able to send their Love-Light to her. They channel all of their Love-Light to her, as the seed point. All of the petals, if you could imagine the petals as a flower, they're all beaming all of their infinity of love to her. Beaming their infinity of love to her, in support. The magical creatures, the beings of all these places, everything. They're so willing to give every bit of the love that they can. They know this is the biggest battle. She becomes this plasmic flame even more. She takes on a Divine Plasmic Flame, a Multiversal Flame form. I'm not sure how to describe it.

D: Sounds beautiful.

Divine Phoenix of the Multiverse: She is the Phoenix, and she brings herself forth, in the shape of this beautiful Divine Goddess Flame energy. It is as if she engulfs the entire ship, and all that he is. As she's doing that, she's pushing her essence where that false light was coming out of it. Just as she eradicated all of those points, all of those technologies earlier with the crystals, she's focusing in, to there. There are lots and lots of artificial Archonic technologies. As soon as she pushes through, it's all connected there. So, she's eradicating *it*. As he is in the center, everything around him is crumbling and dissolving into nothing. Nothing! It's all gone. He's in a big sphere. He's encased himself into what looks like a dark rock. He's in the center of it. It is like another form of his protection.

D: Can we blast through that protection?

Divine Phoenix of the Multiverse: It's crumbling, in the center of it, there is a globe with this mechanical thing, turning it. Okay, so this is one of those booby traps.

D: I was wondering if there would be one. What do we need to do to disarm the booby trap?

Divine Phoenix of the Multiverse: She needs to turn around. She turned around. She sensed it coming up. She realizes what's going on. There's gonna be multiple, I'm calling them ships. They're not really ships. They're whatever created things that he made. Because she is the Multiversal Phoenix, she explodes into an infinity of herself (crying). She's an infinity of Multiversal Phoenixes. They're doing the same exact thing, they're finding all of them, and eradicating them. She's going to find them all.

D: Is there still a battle going on?

Divine Phoenix of the Multiverse: Yes, there's a lot. We're trying to help her refocus. As the Phoenix was speaking to her earlier, she feels like she does not do justice to what is actually going on. So, she would like for the Phoenix or Divine Mother to speak through to help understand and clarify completely.

D: The Phoenix, or the Divine Mother, who do we need to call forth? Or both? Can we speak to them as one?

Divine Phoenix of the Multiverse: Yes.

D: Bring up now Divine Mother. Am I speaking now to the Divine Mother?

Divine Mother: Greetings.

D: Greetings. I love, honor, and I respect you.

Divine Mother: As I do you.

D: Thank you for assisting today.

Divine Mother: Yes.

D: May I speak with the Phoenix next?

Divine Mother: Yes.

D: Bring the Phoenix up now. Am I speaking with the Phoenix?

Divine Phoenix of the Multiverse: Yes.

D: Beautiful. I love, honor, and respect you. Can you both speak at the same time, since your presences are needed to describe what you're seeing?

Divine Mother and the Phoenix: Yes we can. What she is watching is the eradication of the Archons. The Archons are not just ships. That is why she's having a hard time explaining that they are more than ships. They're more than what she described as caves, the emptiness, the soulless vessels. *It's* more than that. *It* is the inorganic virus, the darkness, the plague. We can explain, as Divine Mother came to consciousness awareness, Divine Father was created, as well. They were divine consciousness awareness. He/*It* is also a consciousness awareness. That is why *it* has become so powerful. *It* is not just one being, *it* is immense. *It* is inorganic, as you know that *it* is no one thing. That is why she's having a hard time understanding *it*. Trying to pinpoint an essence, as you think a being, but *it* is not just a being. So, what the Phoenix does, is she goes in. After the Phoenix eradicates all of these things that *it* has and is, she must go to the very seed point of the darkest darkness of that consciousness. That is why she must become that Multiversal Phoenix, because *it* had tapped into all of those Verses. *It* collected an understanding of all of them. As she does this, what she does is, she shoots in, and she goes beyond. She goes deeper, and deeper, and deeper into it. She must, not that she is becoming it, she is going into it. As if you would send Love-Light to a heart, this is the deepest you could go into the depths of the never ending. She is using everything that she is. She's going, going, going, going, and going (crying). This is not bad, it's just understanding the situation from her point of view.

D: Yes, I understand (crying).

Divine Mother and the Phoenix: This is beauty. There is such sacrifice (crying). She has to go in, to become all of him/*It*, and everything he/*it* is. If you know the Phoenix, she births, then she dies, then she's births again. She is doing this as the Multiverse. She goes to all that *it is,* as if she's becoming *it*. Not where she retains what *it is*, she is coming to *its* essence. *It's* all around her. She keeps going, and keeps going, and she goes to the infinity of whatever *it* is. She is there. She engulfs *it,* with all that she is. She permeates *it*, and she becomes *it*, engulfed in that etheric Multiversal Plasmic Flame essence she is. She engulfs *it*, as if she is *it*. But she can never be that! If she can never be that, then *it* can never be. So, it's as if she went to all that *it* was, and became all that *it* was, and *it* cannot be her, and she cannot be *it*. She wins! She becomes *it*, but *it* cannot survive that. *It* cannot survive all that she is, all the Multiverses, of all the love, of all of Creation. *It* cannot be Creation. *It* cannot be that. She was all engulfed, throughout infinity of all the infinities. She just expands, and *it* is gone. *It* is

gone. (Crying), She is gone! She sacrificed all of it. One spark, that is all that is left of her. She still has a spark in Creation. So her spark is not gone, as she is the Phoenix. Do you understand this?
D: Absolutely.
Divine Mother and the Phoenix: Divine Mother sees her spark, and puts her back in her heart. Divine Mother and Divine Father, in their sacred union, heal her. So she can birth again, as the beauty she is. They heal her, and they love her. She feels the love and the gratitude of the Multiverses of Creation. What she did, she knows it was all worth it. She did it! She found a way! She knew there was a chance she might not be able to come back. She knew there was a chance that she might all be gone completely. She knew it, and she did it for the love of the infinity of Creation (crying)! Not just for her Universe, not just for her children, but for all the children (crying intensely). All of the children, of all of Creation, and Multiverses that ever were! She did it for all of them. We want to thank you so much! Thank you!
D: Thank you.
Divine Mother and the Phoenix: Thank you, we love you. We would like to speak to the 'Daughter of the Flame.'
Daughter of the Flame: Thank you Mother.
Divine Mother and the Phoenix: Thank you my love. We are so proud of you! We love you so much. We knew you would do this (crying). We waited for you. We knew you could do it. We are so proud of you. We are so grateful, and thankful for the beautiful daughter that you are. We love you infinitely. Please know this. There's nothing that can stop you. There is nothing that can stop you! Do you hear us?
Daughter of the Flame: I do, I hear you, thank you.
Divine Mother and the Phoenix: We love you, we love you.
Daughter of the Flame: As I love you.
Divine Mother and the Phoenix: None of it matters. Do you understand?
Daughter of the Flame: Yes.
Divine Mother and the Phoenix: Yes we know you do. We love you.
Daughter of the Flame: Thank you for the gift you have given.
Divine Mother and the Phoenix: You are a treasure to us.
AuroRa: (AuroRa comes in) Can I ask what was done there, that we spread, whatever we can in Eureka Springs? A small version of that, or whatever is allowed, without unbalancing the life forms here. Can we spread it in some parts of the organic blueprint of Eureka Springs?
Divine Mother and the Phoenix: Yes, we worked on the crystals before you entered. We worked on the crystals very deeply. Yes, we will spread it to the crystals here, and they will speak to the other crystals of the Earth, and we will spread it throughout the ley lines, as gently as possible.
AuroRa: Thank you I'm going to go, is that good?
Divine Mother and the Phoenix: Yes, beautiful. I love you.
AuroRa: I love you infinitely.
D: Thank you for that, it's so beautiful.
Divine Mother and the Phoenix: Thank you love, for facilitating.
D: It was divinely timed.
Divine Mother and the Phoenix: Yes, as it should be. Thank you for listening and understanding so diligently, the two of you. For coming up with a plan to honor that. Knowing it, feeling it in your souls, and your blueprint of your DNA to hold that space. Preparing for it so beautifully. That is the honor that it was. Thank you.

D: What are you seeing now that this has happened? Where are we going from there? I can feel it rippling out.

Divine Mother and the Phoenix: Tell me what you see?

D: Oh gosh. Waves of golden, rainbow energy rippling out through time, space, and atoms. I'm seeing it as a shock wave, but not in a bad way, in a good way.

Divine Mother and the Phoenix: Yes, now see that, and multiply it through all of the multiverses.

D: Of course.

Divine Mother and the Phoenix: There are things that you cannot understand in this Creation that you are, because it is immense. But know that it is that same throughout the Multiverses, as you see here, it is there. The ultimate freedom. Imagine!

D: I feel it. I've felt it. The freedom that is lacking in this space.

Divine Mother and the Phoenix: It is freedom. Some of you may feel your mind is plagued, your body is plagued, your heart is plagued - *it* is gone. You are free! *It* is gone! *It* is not there; *it* does not linger, *it* is gone. You can breathe. Breathe! You are all allowed to breathe. You are all allowed to love. You are allowed to be, and choose. *It* will never be allowed again. There are lessons you must learn. *That* will never be allowed ever, *it* is gone. *It* is finished.

D: How are we going to see this in this third dimension space? If you can explain anything?

Divine Mother and the Phoenix: It is the ultimate Ascension. As you all may understand Ascension, and you know of the 2/3rd world split. Where it splits one way, one splits the other. People's choices live in dark and light. Even in the darkness, *it* is gone. Do you understand?

D: Yes.

Divine Mother and the Phoenix: Your organic darkness is reset. Those beauties that have chosen, if it is the inorganic, it is eradicated. It is no more. Now, do not fear that. Hold in your heart that strength, knowing that it is okay. The beloved consciousnesses that were entrapped and enslaved by this, at whatever position of point in time they are, whatever they have chosen, if it is inorganic, it is eradicated. I understand the concern of that word, but the artificial is gone; if their soul chose to release that upon eradication, as it is a choice. If they choose to release it upon eradication, then they will continue, as we offer all our beloveds, our beauties. As you've seen in multiple sessions, they were offered that option to positively polarize, accept that the eradication happened, and we assisted them. It was either completely eradicated, they positively polarized, or they chose to go back to Source. So do not fear that. Your love for them, and people that you love, is still okay to do. Still love them, but honor their decision. They chose to be reset, honor, and love the lessons that you learned from them. Do not fear, for if you are hearing this now, it is not the only time you've ever experienced a life or Creation. You understand, in your resonance, in your soul, what that means. In love and gratitude for this eradication. Love and gratitude for what you've learned. How beautiful are you that you learn so much? Love yourself, you learned so much! Do not fear. Fear does not exist anymore, once the eradication happens. So when you hear this, prepare to let go of that concern. Prepare to relieve and alleviate that doubt. It is not needed. It will not exist anymore. It's incomprehensible isn't it? I know! It's incomprehensible to not have that. What is that going to be like, love's? We are so excited for you to finally feel that freedom. Oh, what a joy!

D: If it can be shared in this time and space. With all that is happening with Mandy (ex-assistant) and AuroRa, and all the people that got sessions from Mandy, who is compromised. Can we do anything to help?

Divine Mother and the Phoenix: As we said, the consciousness of the Archon is large and immense. The consciousness can just perceive, or permeate in. The word is, permeate, as it's been described as a virus. We cannot stop a choice. That will not stop our mission. Is that understood?

D: So, we still have lots to do?
Divine Mother and the Phoenix: Well, we are doing what we should do. We cannot control those people, and their choices. But, we will not allow *it,* and them, to harm this mission. As, it is far grander than one being with one ulterior motive, as Mandy. It is far grander than a million beings with an ulterior motive. Just to put it in perspective, if you had a cup of sand, you did not destroy the beach. We honor that the sand is in the cup. We love the cup. We love the sand, the beach, and the ocean worlds, but Creation is far more than that. Is that clear?
D: Yes, that is clear. I was just wondering, because my husband had a session with Mandy. I just want to make sure that there's no cords attached to him. Those who don't want anything to do with her...
Divine Mother and the Phoenix: Yes, let's do that now, all those who have chosen not to connect cords, to now delete cords, release attachments, leave all inversions - all of that, all those who choose not to be a part of that, we will assist them now to delete it. Through all life, time, space, creation, and everywhere. That it will not corrupt the teachings, the sacredness, the missions. All those who have chosen, and understood, or who will come into awareness, we will assist them.
D: Thank you. I just felt it had to be asked.
Divine Mother and the Phoenix: Yes.
D: Thank you. How are the crystals looking that we were assisting? Do we need to do anything more for them?
Divine Mother and the Phoenix: They are healing.
D: What about the dragons?
Divine Mother and the Phoenix: They are healing.
D: What about the souls?
Divine Mother and the Phoenix: Yes, they will need to continue to be healed.
D: Is there anything else that we need to do in this time and space?
Divine Mother and the Phoenix: There are the mountains, in this Shambala point, where we are in Eureka Springs. There are some negative things here. We want to go ahead and start clearing them up now. We want to go and start eradicating them, and ensuring all of this land is clear.
D: Let's sweep it down to the inner core of the Earth, if that's what's needed, to the sky, wherever we can clear it. I'm here to assist.
Divine Mother and the Phoenix: The creational fabric of all the land, of all the spaces, of all of this, we will delete *it,* and eradicate *it.* So *it* will be no more. *It* will not be allowed here anymore. As AuroRa foretold, and told you all, *it* is not allowed anymore here. We will eradicate *it* throughout all this land and space, for this is a sacred space. We will honor that sacredness and eradicate *it* from here. This location will be a beacon of hope, and a reminder to all, of what it looks like to be free once more.
D: Beautiful, thank you.
Divine Mother and the Phoenix: Yes.
D: Do we need to send any Love-Light? I just feel like we've done so much. So what else can we do? Since we're in this time and space to help?
Divine Mother and the Phoenix: Yes, as we've cleared much, we need to fill it all back in.
D: Source Love-Light, Divine Light of Mother and Father.

Higher Self is called forth.
D: Can I talk to a Georgia's Higher Self?
Divine Mother and the Phoenix: Yes, we love you, honor you, and respect you. Thank you.
D: I love, honor, and respect everyone that assisted today. Divine Mother, Divine Father, The Phoenix. It was an honor, all the Archangels, the Benevolent Beings, Legion of Light, the Crystals. There's just

so many things, for infinity. Thank you so much for this beautiful honor. Can I please speak to the Higher Self of Georgia?
Higher Self: Yes.
D: I know you hold the records of Georgia's different lives. May I ask you questions?
Higher Self: Yes.
D: What was the scene you showed her with the person, with the blood sacrifice, that was walking?
Higher Self: Yes, the Archon was aware of what was about to happen. It was rows and rows of all those he had ever infected. Holding goblets of babies' blood. They were doing a ritual to try to prevent this session.
D: So that has been cleared and taken care of?
Higher Self: Yes.
D: Okay, beautiful.
Higher Self: We cannot eradicate it for their personal choice. Let's set the intention that anyone who does that, it will be awful tasting to them. It will not be beautiful to them anymore.
D: So when they're drinking the blood, is that what you're saying?
Higher Self: Yes, anyone who drinks blood, or harms children, it will not give them pleasure in any way. We'll set that intention.
D: Almost like it's now coming back to them, that the true essence of what they're actually doing, they'll recognize?
Higher Self: That is a goal, or is the beginning.
D: It's just a baby step towards that goal?
Higher Self: Yes.
D: Will they still continue these blood rituals? Is there something we can do to help in this time and space? The recruiting, or whatever they do to get these people involved? Or an awareness?
Higher Self: That will help, what we just spoke of. And the beginning that we've just cleared is going to assist as well.

The Body Scan begins.

There isn't much self-healing for Georgia. Her personal questions are answered about her and her family.

For every A.U.R.A. Hypnosis healing session we ask that the Higher Self and team ensure to remove and heal all as listed from the client's Tree of Life: entities (Grays, Mantis, Reptilians, Archons…), dark portals, repair and crystallize DNA, negative cords, technologies (implants, metals, hooks, wires, nano, vaccines), illnesses, vision, dental health, regrow teeth, age regress 5-15 years, blocked or misaligned chakras, open-up the third eye and activate abilities, expand heart, issues with auric field, fractured soul, contracts, deletion of inverted timelines, and trauma from current or past life.

END OF SESSION

An infinity to talk about and understand through this session, but we will magically squeeze it into one chapter. Let's go deep within this future vision and memory of the final showdown and eradication of the Archon. This is the final chapter to this book, and we have ended it with the actual finale of our current Multiversal existence, into the rebirth of our Universe and Multiverse. But, no worries, as this is not the finale to this series, as we are in the works, and have just about all the next sessions for the next couple books to this series. We will allow for their subjects to remain a surprise to the readers, but just understand that, just as Book 2, they will be from a whole other level, that we have not yet reached, as a collective, but we will reach, once they are published.

This A.U.R.A. session was conducted at our Eureka Springs, Arkansas Retreat in May 2023. The practitioner was another Divine Mother fractal, who held infinite Source Love-Light during the session, so that Georgia, Divine Mother Sophia, could accomplish the most important mission of our Creation. Their Higher Selves ensured they both attended this A.U.R.A. Reunion Retreat, because only held in this infinite space of Divine Light, with the combination of Eureka Springs gigantic crystal beds underneath, and the infinite Source Love-Light that the group of practitioners held, could bring this mission into fruition.

Understand that I will share much of the true magic that happens at these Retreats, but know that there is so much more that I cannot share, which is sacred. The magic that occurs at these retreats is truly unexplainable! I hope someday you will make the beautiful choice to meet us at one! Because once you make it to one retreat, our Creation, both individually and collectively, finally makes sense. If we choose to allow ourselves to grow, the experience of the retreats we host are truly spiritually transcending. [34]So many retreats to talk about. All that I am about to mention, the entire group at the retreats got to see with our physical eyes, if we needed any further proof of the ways we were healing the Earth, Universe, and Multiverse. We have met Sasquatch in person, as we watched them go from being physically seen to invisible among the trees. We have seen the most beautiful spacecraft in the sky that change in shape and color, as a Merkabah, or a live consciousness, like stars, do. We watched the Daughter of the Flame, in her beautiful, divine goddess form, ignited in her Phoenix fire, as her wings flapped in the sky, as high as the stars. We stood in front of the waters, as we watched the ocean fog, part, and the unveiling of ancient, hidden Tartarian lands rise, of the world we knew once, of mermaids, dragons, and Angels soaring in the oceans and the skies. These Tartarian sacred lands are floating above us in the clouds, or right next to us, and we just don't know it. We watched only a few leaves move sporadically on a tree, as if someone magical, invisible to our physical eyes, was shaking them and playing them like music keys, with no wind blowing. The next part of what I am sharing is what we experienced through the quantum realm energetically. We have saved children held hostage in mountains, or in underground bases. We have watched as collective timelines shift right in front of us. So much more which I cannot share, as it is truly sacred. Those who assist during retreats, and, my ultimate favorite part, is when we get to watch the new people come in, uncertain of their purpose and who they are. Each day they get lighter and surer of themselves, because of the space of love they are being held in during the retreat. And, when they walk out, I get to watch them self-loving, standing tall, and strong, with their fire ignited within, with divine spiritual purpose, ready to assist themselves, the Earth, and her children! Truly an honor it is to be part of these retreats.

What a sacred honor it was to experience and witness this session unfold live, as I did check in on this A.U.R.A. session from time to time, when it was being conducted on Georgia. My Angelic team ensured that I checked in, in one the most intense, heightened parts of the session, when the Phoenix of the Multiverse was going against the Archon/*it*. During this time, the room was full of intensity, suspense, and tears. The space in the room was not of just us three, the two practitioners and I. The space was filled with all the benevolent eyes of the Multiverse. I wonder if the higher dimensional beings had seen the future of this final showdown, and eradication of the Archon/artificial intelligence prior to this session? I don't feel that they had. And, this is why, as all benevolence was

---

[34] Ensure to watch all the testimonial videos found under our channels, where we talk about the magic that is felt, which is at times recorded or documented through video or pictures.

watching, you could sense, feel, and hear the peaceful silence in the Universe and Multiverse, as this session was being conducted. It was as if the higher dimensional beings were watching a suspenseful movie, unfolding in the present of Earth time and space, but which connected to the future, when Earth Ascends, and when all else will do so, as well. This understanding could not be completely viewed, until this very special moment, because in some forms the final battle had not yet come to be, that is until Georgia had her session in May 2023. The key being that this needed to begin and be performed starting from the lowest dimension of the third dimension, which is the anchor of the Universal Ascension. So, when uncorking the cork from the third dimension, the energy was released from the densest, which then spread infinitely throughout existence, to bring the fruition of the eradication of the Archon. Remember all exists in the now. The now of the past, the now of the present, and the now of the future. The solution has always been the 'now.'

I hosted two retreats, back to back, in Eureka Springs. The first was the reunion for the A.U.R.A. practitioners, and the second was for the new practitioners to be, who were newly becoming A.U.R.A. and R.A.A.H. certified. One of the ways I know that the mission of eradicating the Archon was successful and accomplished, as shown to us through this session, was that the day after Georgia's session, the *it* in the now, where *it* is still here, started to use people who were leaning towards being more negative polarized to try to attack me. I started receiving emails, and started hearing about a group of females speaking negatively about me to whoever they could, working diligently to convince people to hate on me. As the days continued during the retreats, these negative polarized females seemed to be magnetizing together, growing in numbers, but remaining about under ten. It was very apparent that they were trying to distract me from hosting and completing the retreats, and that the Archon was pissed off, as *it* knows now, what happens to *it* in the future! It was the worst tried psychic and energetic attack that has been directed towards me in my career. These types of attacks are not usual, coming from groups, and especially not allowed during retreat times, which are so sacred. But, I had foreseen that it would try to come after me, with what had just happened with the Multiversal Phoenix, eradicating *it* from all of Creation.

Perhaps, if you have been watching me recently, or from the beginning of my spiritual career, over six years ago, then you know how private I am. How every communication I share is with a divine purpose, and is always heart centered for the collective. I am honored to be able to share through this book more of who I am, and my experiences as a spiritual revolutionist, here in service to others and the collective. Therefore, whether new, or a veteran viewer, you know that it is important that we operate in service to others, and never self gain through all that I teach and embody. This small group are those who began to try to attack me, the day after *it* was eradicated in the future, through Georgia's session. They have invertedly made it their mission and cause on Earth, possessed by the Archon, to come after me, by anyone they convince to hate on me, then infringing upon them heavily when these people fall for these narcissistic tricks. Remember the Archon needs numbers, as *it* is weak on *its* own. Since *it* is a Godless God, *it* can only clone itself through *its* lonely existence of self chosen solitude, and *it* can only recruit the beings that were born from Source Love-Light. At times, I am saddened by the ways that the divine feminine are used by the Archon's mind tricks to attack one another. One of *its* oldest tricks in the game. Let us not ever be these divine feminine who are fooled in acting so invertedly towards one another, when truly we are meant to be a sacred sisterhood, holding space in love, and the sacred circle for the children to heal on Earth. Distractions these are, strongly steering us away from our missions and Ascension. I personally have no time or tolerance for these Archonic games. As I always say, I am not here to fight these Archon battles, I am here to end them!

Therefore, we ask that you send love to our cause, as messengers of Source Love-Light, but remember it is not just ours, as Rising Phoenix Aurora, it is your cause, and the entire Multiverse's cause. As you are reading this sacred knowledge, it is public, and all who come across this book will know the truth of what the Archon is, and how the Multiversal Phoenix will eradicate *it* from all of Creation. So, just as the Phoenix asked for the infinite love of the entire embodiment of the Multiverse to assist her to eradicate *it*, we ask this of you now, so that you can begin to eradicate *it* in the now, just by simply envisioning the Multiverse, as the Lotus Flower of Life, and sending love to the center seeds of our Multiversal Creation. We cannot wait any longer! We must begin now! And, with this understanding, I ask that you spread the awareness of this book, as far and wide as you can, because the more that we will bring Ascension closer, the more we will save as many children as possible throughout the Multiverse, who are being violated, energetically, sexually, mentally, or physically, by *it*. Save the children of our Creation!

It is very important that we understand that all are on their free-willed and sovereign journey, and that because of this there are some people who are ready to self-heal, and really transcend higher in their Earthly incarnation, but some are just not. So, as healers for ourselves and others, we just have to accept this, knowing that everyone is on their own journey. We can be the love for them when they need it, but after that, love all, attach to none, because they are on their own, and they are whose guiding their entire path. As Divine Mother said, the Archon is masterful at fermenting within people, and we understand and respect that some will choose to stay with this familiar attachment, especially, if *it* has been inside them for a very long time.

Georgia at the beginning of the session said, "What I'm being shown is people lined up for miles and miles. It looks like they are facing each other, with an aisle down the middle. They are holding out their hands with glasses full of blood, and there is a man that is walking, or floating down between them. They look almost vampire-like. It's like this man is really important to them." The practitioner asked the higher self, "What was the scene you showed her of the person with the blood sacrifice that was walking?" and the higher self replied, "The Archon was aware of what was about to happen. It was rows and rows of all those he had ever infected. Holding goblets of babies' blood. They were doing a ritual to try to prevent this session from happening." Talk about evil and creepy. This gives us an understanding of why those who do not want to be saved, are just this deeply, etherically binded to *it*. So much so, that they are the cause of why the children of the Universe are being sacrificed. These people standing in line were holding babies' blood, because they are the energy Sources who sustain and allow the Archon to feed *itself*, through the sacrifice of soul essences, and the babies who incarnate into planets. Every act that they are doing invertedly, is feeding the parasitic agenda of the Archon. They were shown, vampiric in nature, because these are the people we meet in our day to day life, who leave us drained and exhausted. Who are full of drama and gossip, in order to create chaos for *its* unfulfilled hunger. If we need more of a testament, we come to understand how powerful our divine teams are, to ensure that this session still came to be, even while there were blood sacrifices being conducted just to stop the session.

This takes us to the vision the Phoenix saw when she located the Archon, how *it* was putting on the illusion of this Godless God, who was incredibly handsome, muscled, and shirtless. Here is another example of the false persona people play into when they place themselves on pedestals, as *it* is doing. They are putting this act on for *it*. If we might see a man like this, we might lust over him, and think, "Oh my God, he is hot, I would like to date him!" See, but what *it* doesn't know is that, most people on Earth no longer feel like this towards others, just because of their looks; people are changing. So, eventually this game *it* plays, making people and things look attractive, when not, will become powerless. If we look beyond these cosmetic, pretty looks, we will see that *it* is just a false illusion, but in reality, if we were to scan the energy, we would feel grotesque and repulsed by what *it* truly is. Let us remember this when meeting people. There is nothing attractive about Dracula, or any of these vampiric figures, who drink and suck on the blood of others to maintain their young looking skin and false beauty. And, if you think about it this way, this vampiric understanding is entirely derived by what the Archon is, Dracula himself.

The giant crystals all over Earth, including Japan, and inside the ocean were originally gridded into the four sacred directions of Earth's original construct, but were caged instead, being used to compromise the Earth's organic blueprint, making Earth into an inverted simulation instead, not only containing the souls of Earth in the matrix, and too, the higher dimensional beings inside these crystals. Powering up the Archons inverted crystal grid, so that he could get into places *it* normally couldn't get into, because of *it* not being a matching vibration to these higher vibrational energies. *Its* ways of cheating the system go deep, as *it* is a masterful cheat. This understanding shows us that, in Chapter 11, 'The War of the Gods,' how *it* was able to jump in and out of our Universe instantly, but we could not understand yet how *it* was doing this, as this was not normally possible.

Georgia's higher self brought awareness to us of the dragons that the military have chained up and enslaved. Hunted and stunned, by negative technology, and chained up, enslaved. This is so sad. I see both outside the Antarctica walls and in underground military bases, deep below, where they have big beautiful dragons locked away. These locations are so deep, and look like metallic rooms, boxes, but the material is not metal, it is a special mineral that is magical in nature, used invertedly to contain their magic, so that their powers are oppressed, encased in this concealment system. I'm being shown that during the last reset of Tartaria, many of these Dragons were contained, taken to these holding spaces, and they have been there ever since. It is time that we send love in the four sacred directions of Earth to all these dragons located underground. May we always remember that every time we think of a dragon that they are still here, awaiting for us to remember them, and free them with our love.

The divine work that was accomplished when retrieving the dragon eggs that were being experimented on was immense. Thank goodness that all their tried experiments failed. We send love to all of those souls that they might have tried to use to make these Archon dragons. Our skin crawls to think of their most recent experimentation, we caught them in the middle of, between the spider, and the squid, forcing fertilization onto the dragon egg. They were trying to make the creational energy of these dragons think that the Archon spiders and squids were their parents, so that they would allow fertilization, which would then make Archon dragons. But, the creational energy of the dragons are just so pure and strong, that even under such pressure and attack, still the dragon consciousness did not budge into allowing this artificial infringement. Once more, reminding us of the true divine power of the angel/dragon babies who are here, and coming. Just as the artificial could not merge into these unfertilized dragon eggs, so too, will the artificial within Earth, and part of the Covid-19 vaccines, will not be able to be part of Earth eventually.

Once more, we learn the true power of the Archangels, and the ways that they protect and guard us. It was beautiful to watch the Prince of Light, Haylel, and the organic darkness of Divine Mother, Lilith, assist the souls in a gentler way, introducing her organic darkness in order to transition these souls out. Because, if the strength of the Source Love-Light would have been used, it would have been too strong for them in their weakened state, which could have possibly transmuted them, sending them straight to Source. Instead, the organic darkness assisted them to transition on, being the perfect medium, so that the souls then could go where they will be provided with healing. The beauties of both the light and dark are miraculous, in the ways they truly support each other, and complete one another. The greatest romance of our Creation, Divine Mother being the light, and Divine Father the organic darkness, within our Creation. Together becoming the ultimate balance of the dark and light within us all, and our Universe. As the Higher Self said, "She's having support from Haylel. This is beautiful. He's there to support her, and love her, as she does this." This is a very important statement, because I often hear from the Divine Father that his role is to hold infinite love for the Divine Mother, so that no matter what she's going through, she will get through it. Together Divine Mother and Divine Father's love is impenetrable, in the ways they provide this infinite support for each other. Reminding us that if we are not yet living relationships as these on Earth, that it is time we work lovingly towards this divine goal in our own ways, within our twin flame, or soulmate, sacred unions.

The way that Divine Mother explained how there were timelines inside the Tree of Life shooting through once more, aligns with much of the Tree of Life teachings we deliver through our courses and our channelings. We have shared teachings of the Tree of Life from chapter to chapter, but we will go deeper into this understanding now. The Tree of Life is Creation, and where all life first began from. Therefore, the Tree of Life would be a divine access point, to connect, to work within timelines for ourselves. In Chapter 16 'Pyramid Portals Inside Earth,' we explained how the Tree of Life retains our DNA which contains our memory and entire being. To reach our deepest self-healing potentials, we must connect to the roots, and the entire being of our Tree of Life, our infinite Creation. If there are inverted timelines, which we need to work on to remove, they, too, are found in the Tree of Life, which is why Georgia saw these inverted timelines inside of the tree, as this was the beginning work needing to be addressed, to prepare us, to reach the Archon, for the final eradication of *it*. The combination of the healing work we did on the Tree of Life shown, and the gigantic crystals *it* had corrupted, was how we removed *its* capability of being able to jump in and out through the crystals, rendering it immobile. *It* was then cornered, and not able to jump out of sight, as *it* was able to before, allowing for the Multiversal Phoenix to finally eradicate *it* from all life, time, and space.

The Merlin/Archon/*it* has learned that if *it* gets access to your Tree of Life, that *it* can get into your being, and at times who you are throughout your incarnations. This is the deepest, most distorted way that *it* gets in, to create illusions in you, which at times you will fully believe, as *it* has access to you, by corrupting your Akashic Hall of Records, throughout the Universe or Multiverse, which is held in your Tree of Life. Through this compromise and infringement, *it* spreads *its* venom, in order to corrupt, control, rot the roots, the land, and elements surrounding your Tree of Life. Spreading venom into your Akashic Hall of Records, and who you are. This is why we teach you to shield yourself, and your loved one's sacred Tree of Life's inside of Source Love-Light, so that no infringements are allowed.

We, as A.U.R.A. and R.A.A.H. practitioners, ask the Higher Self, and divine team to scan the client's entire Tree of Life, because depending on how strong the infringement from the Archons is, they can at times access and corrupt their Tree of Life. We have found that this can be the deepest healing one can receive, because the Higher Self is reaching into the client's Tree of Life, which is where each soul is created from. The Tree of Life represents all that a person is through the infinities of the Multiverse.

I once had a client, who the Archon knew when she was going to be born, and to whom, ensuring that *it* was her doctor, so that when she was born, *it* was the first that would touch her. Which explains to us a lot of why these compromised, or negative Reptilian aliens, inside doctors want to be the first to touch the newborn children, freshly coming out of their Mother's womb. The Mother, and only the Mother should be the first to touch their newborn child, as when she does, so long as she herself is positive in nature, she will shield her sacred child. To clarify though, there are many positive doctors in this world, that if ever in need our divine team will ensure we find them. All her life she felt she had been sexually violated, but had no memories of this, nor could her Mother confirm that this was true. So, during the body scan her Higher Self said, that this doctor/Archon/*it,* as he was supposedly assisting her to birth, while catching her, bloody and covered in her crystalline placenta, he ensured that he disgustingly placed his finger inside her little vagina, to imprint *it's* inversion, through this penetration and violation unto her, as a newborn baby. *It* was also connected to an underground military base, where a hook was attached to her sacral chakra, leading to this base. We cleared this hook from her energy body, but at the end of her session when we asked to scan her Tree of Life, to ensure all healing and removal of inversions were complete, the hook was still in her Tree of Life attached to the roots, trying to poison it again. Therefore, asking for cleansing and healing of the client's Tree of Life reinforces, and ensures, that the client is cleared, from the beginning of all that they are, located in their Tree of Life. More awareness for us to understand all these tried infringements onto newborns, which are so disturbing.

I highly recommend that you become Quantum Galactic Akashic Reading certified, because we go deep into what is the Tree of Life and Tree of Knowledge through this course. You will enjoy venturing into the possibilities and wisdom of the Galactic Histories of the Universe. Traveling through the stars and into the 'Universal Akashic Hall of Records.' Are you looking to learn how to safely/sacredly conceive a child? This course will teach you deeply how we are all a Tree of Life, and the divine process we go through to incarnate on Earth or beyond. The journey of the soul, and how children travel through the Tree of Life to bring them forth sacredly into the Earth, as an unburdened child free of the inverted cycle of the Matrix. When a soul begins to remember oneself, puzzle piece by puzzle piece, it experiences divine activations, downloads, and integrations of their Universal memory complex. We remember that we have never forgotten ourselves; that it was just an illusion through Earth's false societal programming. We remember the infinite beauty, strength, sovereignty and how loved we are in the Universe.

Let's talk about why we called the Archon/*it* [35]Merlin in the previous page. There are many in the spiritual communities who are praising Merlin, as if he is a positive guide to connect to, or speak to, comparing him to ascended masters as Yeshua, the alchemist St. Germaine, or ridiculously, to Archangel Metatron. On July 22, 2022, I channeled Princess Aurora who was incarnated during Leumuria, where she shared with us that Merlin, the magician, was the first person to allow a full body compromise, back when we were a fifth dimensional, crystalline planet. He is known as a magician, because that is who he is. He puts on a show, and illusions, to hide what he truly is. Back in Atlantis, while practicing dark magic, he invited Bellos to possess his body during a blood ritual, where he raped and sacrificed several children to do so, just as you see in the movies, in exchange for power over others. By allowing this, it allowed the entryway of the Archon to come into our then organic Earth, which then allowed the artificial intelligence to begin to spread, causing the bifurcation of Atlantis from Leumuria. Bringing forth the fall of Atlantis, into the third dimension we are currently in. The artificial could not fully enter our crystalline Earth then, because we were in a protective crystalline matrix, which only allowed what is only organic to enter. So many have suffered from this one inverted choice by someone, that someone being Merlin, who did choose to allow *it* into our protected, sacred space of Mother Earth, by Merlin becoming the dark portal *itself, that it* came in through. In the books to come, we will speak further of this transition that occurred to Earth, when we went from crystalline to carbon based.

Other practitioners and I, have come across many clients who are the deepest compromised, in comparison to others who we have seen, when allowing Merlin to come into their life, as a supposed spiritual guide, or soul family member. Once you allow Merlin in, you are actually allowing the Archon/*it* to enter your being, just as Merlin did in Leumuria, when he performed the dark ritual of selling his soul away to Bellos/Archon. You are repeating and mirroring what Merlin did back then, so selfishly, to the collective of Earth and her children. If you have been one of these people who were tricked into thinking he was positive, please listen to us, we know that you think he is positive, but he/*it* is truly not. You think this of *it,* because *it's* that deeply integrated into you. The last thing you want to take part in, if you are truly benevolent, is being the battery Source for *its* blood rituals *it* violates children through, just as Georgia was shown in this session. You will have much work to do on your end, once you allow yourself to come into the realization of *its* true form, but you will come out from this inversion, if you so choose to. You are beautiful, and you are loved. No one being is worth defending, as Merlin, so much that it causes you not to ascend out. Remember your loved ones, spouses, children and animal

---

[35] Watch 'A Grimm | After Atlantis | Galactic History', where Princess, Archangel Aurora speaks of who Merlin truly is.

companions, are the ones picking up the slack, or density for you, of the most convoluted infringement you can receive by Merlin attaching to you. It is not worth it, you are worth it. Start working on yourself now to not consent to *it.* And, I highly recommend you schedule an A.U.R.A. session, as your practitioner will ensure to hold the space for you to have the deepest, root level, self-healing that will come to be when you travel into the theta brainwave, with your Higher Self, and divine team.

I will now share some of my upbringing, and why I know the Archon/Merlin/*it* so closely. The woman who called herself a grandmother, was the Archon/Merlin/*it,* incarnated into her body. Most people are just compromised or have attachments of *it*. Though rare, as I have only met a few, but some are a full body incarnation of *it*, and this is who she was. She was a pedophial, who ensured that all her children, boys and girls, were raped and molested by all types of men that she would find. These children lived in torment having to be abused daily. She also had incest with her youngest child, who then molested some of her granchildren. As for me, they never touched me, because it was as if they knew they couldn't, and that I was a quiet, but strong, child who would not allow harm onto me.

As a child, having strong telepathic abilities I could feel the foul demonic need that came from these people who called themselves family to me. Eventually *it* too, took over the women who brought me into this Earth. Both the Grandma and Mother acted the same, spies for each other, to the Archon. They lived for gossip, and to turn their own children against each other. And, if you dared to stand up to them, oh no, you were harming them, and now they were the victims being victimized by you. The classic narcissists. The environment to live among these people felt emptied of love, cold as death, where your body shivers from the inside as your breath is cold, and everyday was truly a fight for my soul. Nightmares/memories I had nightly of these battles I had to endure, as I slept, fighting for my soul. As an infant, I remember being days old, being very conscious in my body, and fighting demonic entities that came from these two women who were constantly trying to spirit possess me, or have some kind of control over me. But, my little infant body would fight! They always said that when I was born I would not take my Mother's milk, the doctors and the nurses, none could get me to take her Archonic milk into me. I was told I would literally spit it out, and refused to swallow. Why would an infant have such a strong reaction to their supposed Mother's milk? Because to allow this milk into me, it would be to allow the Archon's energy/essence into me, then infringing on me, lowering my vibration, and the slowing of who I am meant to be in the future, if they managed to densify me too much. Her milk was so dangerous to my little soul that I refused to eat, and they were forced to give me the infant formula instead, which as we know, this formula is toxic as well, but not as toxic as Archon milk.

When I grew up I stood up against this molestation that had been happening behind closed doors, or had been hushed, and not allowed to be talked about. They gaslighted me, and instead tried to tell me I was in the wrong for bringing it up, but it was too late, at that point I was done with their pedophiallic programming, and I moved on. And, when I came out into the spiritual community over six years ago, I told myself that I would never be like them and *it*. That I would believe and assist all who were ready to assist and self-heal themselves. So, in many forms I had to go through what I did to be who I am now, the opposite of them and the Archons.

I always wondered how I was able to evade sexual abuse from these nasty pedo's, until this year in 2023, during an important portal, energetic date, I went out to eat at a restaurant, which happened to be in this exact neighborhood. Without planning, I passed by the homes that I spent time in my younger versions, and in that moment in time and space, all my life times merged and unified into my consciousness, and with all the alchemy we teach, I shielding that me, that cute little chubby cheeked girl, with the most beautiful curls, who would dance while walking down the street at one year old, who all would stop and cheer and watch at this pure, joyful innocence. I shielded her from the now, through all time and space, of this life, and said I would not allow anyone to harm her purity as a child, because her mission in the future is that grand in assisting the collective. And, that is how not one of them could ever touch me, because the me now, who is in the strongest divine power, and Source

Love-Light, shielded her, so that she wouldn't become lost to the world, would not be harmed, as what the Archon wanted to do to her. Instead I became impenetrable to *it*. That doesn't mean that I did not go through trauma, which I did, as everyone on Earth has. It also doesn't mean that *it* gave up on trying to infringe on me, but *it* cannot touch me. Because, even though I clearly know that *it* lingers in the shadows. I know that, in no shape, or form, is *it* part of my life, because I DO NOT CONSENT TO *IT*. Technically, what I am doing is tapping into the energy from the Multiversal Phoenix, and all of Creation when we eradicate *it* from all life, time, space. And, since time does not exist, so, too, does *it* not exist in my world, in the now, as *it* does not exist in the future too. I hope this gives you strength, because you too, will, in some shape, be there when *its* eradication will happen, and you can allow yourself to feel in the now, what an existence without *it* feels like, bringing us closer to this collective goal. Which is the grandest love, unburdened, most empowering feeling in Creation. The key being is that we must always vibrate to love. I am pure RAW LOVE, and that is all!

I did not think I would ever be able to share what I am about to share, but I must, as it is the missing key to the final battle that we got to witness through this session. I remember in August 2021 getting very sick. If I would have gone to the doctor my symptoms would have been classified as having the Covid-19 virus. This was during a heightened time that people were lining up to receive their many Covid-19 jabs, and boosters. Our listeners were concerned, as they had not heard from me for over a month, which is unheard of. If you have been watching me for some time, you know that I am constantly in communications with the collective, with now having over 700 videos in my channels.

During this time of my absence, I experienced an exit point, as I was extremely ill, so much so that I was bedridden, wearing diapers. When I asked my team what was going on, they said that I had agreed to have Covid-19 vaccine type symptoms, so that I could assist the collective to transmute them. The Angels also said that many in the collective had also agreed to have these symptoms, and that people were going to think they had the Covid-19 virus, but really they were assisting the transmutation of the Covid-19 vaccine from Earth. Especially, assisting the children who the parents had begun to jab.

The pain I went through was immeasurable! Every second alive during this time was a challenge, as I was fighting for my soul. I was experiencing what those who signed away their soul by getting the jab were experiencing, by allowing this artificial intelligence integration into them. During this time, I kept seeing a time and space where the Archon had won, because Earth had reached over 50% of her population having received the jab, meaning over 50% of the collective was now part artificial. Because of this Mother Earth could no longer maintain stability, because that meant that the people of Earth, who were now hybrids, were now the majority. Which technically meant that the Archon won, according to numbers and scientific measures. So, during this time, alongside with others, we were fighting off Covid-19 vaccine symptoms, to transmute this density within Earth, so that she could stabilize at her best. I watched myself transition back and forth between a timeline where the Earth and our Universe was still alive, and where our Earth and Universe no longer existed. For one month I went through this torment, watching myself flicker back and forth, from this inverted potential of our Universe, that I didn't even know was possible. I watched a big showdown where all the Gods and Goddesses fought the Archon, *its* clones, and *its* hybrid abominations, and *it* won in this Universal timeline, because the people of Earth chose the artificial, outwinning those who were organic, and not jabbed on Earth.

One by one, I watched as the Archon took over, starting from the lower dimensions and climbing, higher and higher, Earth, then parallel Earths, which then linked *itself* to all other higher life forms. Why could *it* go higher? Remember, the Covid-19 integrates, and hybridizes into the DNA. Technically, all third dimensional Earths are a current matrix simulation, where a multitude of races live within, so what *it* did when *it* tricked the people of Earth to get the jab, *it* linked *itself* to each different alien race that they have been, located inside the memory of these peoples DNA, which then this poison too reached the planet and realms that these souls incarnated into. And, these higher dimensional beings could not take this A.I. integration. Do you understand? Just as when we heal ourselves, how that healing travels through all time and space, and specifically that race we were incarnated into that required healing, so, too, did *it* use this connection to link to all humans on Earth, and their lives from beyond the veil, who said yes to the jab. Once more, understanding how important our choices are that we make on Earth, as they truly do impact Creation. However, understanding that there are some on Earth who did agree in assistance for the collective to take the jab, so that they could transmute *it*, and then, once more, others could too.

The visions, and sensations, I had from watching our Universe destruct are unbearable. I watched every single lifeform be consumed by the artificial intelligence plague. Which looked like some of those movies we watch, like *Transformers* or *A Wrinkle in Time*. The deepest darkness, in the shape of black nano, that duplicates and grows untamable, and with every light and soul *it* consumed, *it* grew in size, until *it* ate all the light of our Universe. But, before *it* did, all lifeforms fought with their all, to not be consumed by this replicating A.I., but one by one, consumed they were by this nano. Each dimension and their lifeforms perished, starting from the third dimension, echoing out to the fourth dimension, then the fifth, the sixth, and higher and higher, until this Archon nano reached the highest of our Universe, who are the Archangels. The Archangels fought with their infinite strength, but still one by one they fell. I watched as the Phoenix, the Daughter of Flame stood at the center of rings of Angels and Archangels, each one sacrificing themselves for her, because if she fell, then the entire Universe would be gone, because she is Creation herself, the Universe. Selflessly they guarded her one by one until they were no longer reaped by the Archon. Archangel Michael/Haylel/Four was second last to go, as the Daughter of the Flame weeped in pain to see her very first Creation no longer be. Who remained last was Archangel Metatron, surrounded in his violet flame, with his Metatron Cubic star constantly morphing and shifting, keeping up with this nano, until he knew he could no longer, he sacrificed himself, but instead of being consumed by the A.I., he exploded himself into the most beautiful, plasmic, violet flame, which then encased the Phoenix. When Archangel Metatron was no longer, the A.I. reached the Phoenix and engulfed her too.

I watched as the Daughter of Flame floated like sleeping beauty, in what was now the Archon Universe. We truly have no words to express how the Archon Universe felt, but *it* felt like the deepest, emptiest, hollow, freezing existence, where no light remained, but the Daughter of Flame. She floated in a form of hibernation, engulfed by the last of Archangel Metatron's violet flame. The Daughter of the Flame looked like when lava becomes cold and crusted, but instead the purple/violet flame that Archangel Metatron turned himself into was solidly encased around her, inside of this hardened, stoned, lava, just as when you see red lava flowing through the inside of stiffened lava. In this form the nano was crawling on her, had completely covered everything but her face, it could not fully consume her, because this last act, of the embodied love of her son, protected her infinitely. After the Creation of Divine Father Archangel Michael/Four, Archangel Metatron was the first Archangel of Creation, alongside the first twin flame union of Archangel Jophiel and him. That is the last vision I saw, back in August 2021, and soon after, with the combination of all the sacred alchemy courses we teach, I healed myself, day by day, until I was able to be back again conducting sessions and delivering live videos. This vision, that I just explained, was what the Phoenix of our Universe went to the other Verses to explain, and show them what could possibly be of our Universe, in turn not knowing what could happen to their Verses next. Which is why all the Verses worked together with her, assisting her to become the Multiversal Phoenix. With this memory we are able to reach a deep understanding of the final battle, and the dire need to eradicate the Archon.

Which now brings us to the final battle! The one we all have been waiting for, to rid ourselves of this A.I. virus, the Archon Bellos that infringed upon us, over and over through different incarnations. This inverted game it has played, like a broken record. Step 1. cloud the mind, 2. cause fear, 3. make them not believe in themselves, 4. disempower them, 5. infringe on them, and 6. divide and conquer.

It is honestly so predictable. I am surprised how much *it* has fooled people throughout, but I understand how strong *its* illusions are, because I was there once too. Fooled by *its* illusions. The biggest understanding to all that we have taught you so far through this book series, is to understand that you are far beyond more powerful than *it*. Why? Because of your Source Love-Light, and the ways you vibrate to love. The truth is that *it* is fearful that you will figure this out. That this whole time all you needed to do was vibrate to love, and never could *it* penetrate your energy field to infringe upon you. The key is love, always.

Divine Mother said, "We are able to jump through his batteries being destroyed. He cannot do this to our children! They are all of our children, not just a newborn. We are all of our children, and as a fierce mother, my children will not be harmed anymore! I'm ready to battle him!" What the Divine Mother is embodying through this statement, of a feeling as, "Enough is enough!" We all must work to embody this sovereignty in our own way. "No, you will not harm us, or our loved ones anymore!!!" If we work within safety of holding this strong vibration, this will be a powerful way to begin to start setting up the foundation of the future of *its* total eradication. We cannot wait any longer. We must act now!

Divine Mother said, "We ask all of Creation that is available to do that now. To send a wave of Source Love-Light, your infinite love for all. No doubt! Do not doubt when you send this love. For we know you will hear this in the future. You future listeners, do not doubt! We ask you to send that love, because you are part of this time and space, wherever you are. Send that love without reservation, without hesitation, no doubt. As you send that love, we're assisting in healing these beautiful creations that *it* tried to suck the beauties of life's creation of Source out of them." Let's all take four, eleven, or thirteen minutes to do this now...

No doubt, the Divine Mother said. Remember Mother's words from here on, if ever you feel doubt within, you imagine Mother saying this over and over to you, and she will assist you to push through anything. Remember, you will be part of this eradication in the future, when the you then, will send love to the Multiversal Phoenix, and the Lotus Flower of Life of our Creation. This is why we need as many as we can, to turn back to the light, because the more accumulated light, the more powerful this final eradication will be. But again, we need you!

The Divine Mother said, "The Multiverse is slower, as everything stops. All time, space, and everything stops. As she's battling him. *It's* trying to make her believe that she's an Archon (laughter). As if, what she's doing would be Archonic. *It's* just really trying to battle her. She's battling *it*." This is very important for us to speak about. *It* is trying to make her think that she is an Archon, or that what she is doing is Archonic. Please!!! As if the Phoenix could ever even compare to *it*. That's what *it* does, *it* tries to make us think that we are *it*. But, we are not, of course, we are the opposite of what *it* has turned *itself* into. But, this is key. This is why so many are not in their power. What *it* likes to do is go after the men to distort them, and convince them to no longer be the guardians of their families, and once *it* removes the males from the picture, then *it* goes after the women, who are broken-hearted from their twin flame leaving them. And then from there, *it* can get at the children too, from these broken families. Males, he just wants them out of the way, but females, oh they are *its* grand prize. Once *it* gets the females to allow *it* in, *it* torments them, mentally, spiritually, energetically, and sexually, is *its* favorite. And, this is why most women are so disempowered, because they have been abused over and over. Because, *it* knows the true power of the Creator, Divine Mother, and the ways that if *it* infringes on the divine feminine, then so, too, can *it* try to reach for the light of the Creator. And, once *it* has broken apart the males and females from being a family, then *it* goes after the children, and then the children grow up, and *it* does the same thing over and over.

The Divine Mother said, "The Creators of the Multiverse allowed her to become the Phoenix of the Multiverse. So now that this has happened, all the Multiverses are able to send their Love-Light to her. They channel all of their Love-Light to her, as the seed point. If you could imagine the petals as a flower, they're all beaming all of their infinity of love. They're beaming it to her. Beaming their infinity of love to her and support. The magical creatures, the beings of all these places, everything. They're so willing to give every bit of the love that they can. They know this is the biggest battle. She becomes this plasmic flame even more. She takes a Divine Plasmic Flame, a Multiversal Flame." What I'm being shown here to this understanding is that, The Phoenix, the Daughter of the Flame does not just fight the Archon on her own, she takes in her twin flame, Archangel Michael/Lucifer/Four merges into her, and they become one. Together, becoming the Multiversal Phoenix. This was a very hard decision for her to make, because what if her beloved does not survive the battle from inside of her. We all understand the beauty of Archangel Michael, our Divine Father of Creation. It would be unbearable for us to lose him in the Multiverse. But, she must allow him to become one with her, as he completes her, and she must be at her ultimate, infinite, strength to finally defeat the Archon throughout all life, time, and space.

"She's eradicating *it*. As *it* is in the center, everything around *it* is crumbling, and dissolving into nothing. Nothing! It's all gone. He's in a big sphere. He's encased himself into what looks like a dark rock. He's in the center of it. It is another form of his protection. It's crumbling, in the center of it, there is a globe with this mechanical thing, turning it. Okay, so this is one of those booby traps. She needs to turn around. She turned around. She sensed it coming up. She realizes what's going on. There's going to be multiple, I'm calling them ships, they're not really ships. They're whatever created things that he made. Because she is the Multiversal Phoenix, she explodes herself into an infinity of herself. (crying) She's an infinity of Multiversal Phoenixes. They're doing the same exact thing, they're finding all of them, and eradicating them. She's going to find them all." *It* is like a pandora box, and what the Phoenix has had to fight against is this type of trickery through time and space. Just when you think you got *it*, there are more and more, because of *its* cloning abilities, and *its* plentiful battery sources, the people who *it's* attached to. So, how can you eradicate what constantly clones *itself*? We will learn how in a little bit.

"After the Phoenix eradicates all of these things that he has, she must go to the very seed point of the darkest darkness of that consciousness. That is why she must become that Multiversal Phoenix, because he had tapped into all of those Verses. He collected an understanding of all of them. As she does this, what she does is, she shoots in, and she goes beyond. She goes deeper, and deeper, and deeper into it. She must, not that she is becoming it, she is going into it. As if you would send Love-Light to a heart, this is the deepest you could go into the depths of the never ending. There is such sacrifice (crying). She has to go in, to become all of him, and everything he is. If you know the Phoenix, she births, then she dies, then she births again. She is doing this as the Multiverse. She goes to all that he is, as if she's becoming him. Not where she retains what he is, she is coming to his essence. He's all around her. She keeps going, and keeps going, and she goes to the infinity of whatever he is. She is there. She engulfs *it*, with all that she is. She permeates *it*, and she becomes him, engulfed in that etheric Multiversal Plasmic Flame essence she is. She engulfs *it*, as if she is *it* (crying.) But, she can never be that! If she can never be that, then he can never be. So, it's as if she went to all that he was, and became all that he was, and he cannot be her, and she cannot be him. She wins! She becomes him, but he cannot survive that. He cannot survive all that she is, all the Multiverses, of all the love, of all of Creation. He cannot be Creation. He cannot be that. She was all engulfed, throughout infinity of all the infinities. She just expands, and *it* is gone. He is gone. She is gone (crying)! She sacrificed all of it. One spark, that is all that is left of her. She still has a spark in Creation. So her spark is not gone, as she is the Phoenix." Was your heart beating faster and faster with each of the words to this paragraph? So, she becomes *it*, because he/*it* cannot withstand her being inside of *it*, and as she expands he/*it* is no longer, because she has completely filled her Multiversal Phoenix flame into *it*. Wow! Just wow! No one can do this but her, because when you become *it*, you are *it*, but not the Phoenix. Neither one can exist within each other, so too, as *it's* gone, so is she. I am in tears! Because she shows me what this feels like. All that she and her twin flame had lived to be in the Multiverse, as the Creators, for this to be all gone was unbearable, as they did not know if they could survive. But they had to do it, for the love of their Creation and their children. And, this is the ultimate reason why *it* targets any being who carries a strong Divine Mother fractal. Because *it* knows, *it* cannot survive the purity of the eternal Phoenix Flame that they carry within.

Divine Mother Sophia said, "Divine Mother sees her spark, and puts her back in her heart. Divine Mother and Divine Father, in their sacred union, heal her. So she can birth again as the beauty she is. They heal her, and they love her. She feels the love and the gratitude of the Multiverses of Creation. What she did, she knows it was all worth it. She did it! She found a way! She knew there was a chance she might not be able to come back. She knew there was a chance that she might all be gone completely. She knew it, and she did it for the love of the infinity of Creation (crying)! Not just for her Universe, not just for her children, but for all the children (crying intensely). All of the children, of all of Creation, and Multiverses that ever were! She did it for all of them!" The ultimate sacrifice! But what of Archangel Michael who merged into her!? Did he survive?!!! She survived because he was within her, and at all costs she did not want to lose the reason why she lives. Her love for him was that infinite, that she would not allow herself to be no longer, because he was within her, and there was no way that she would allow all that she lives for in creation, her twin flame to not survive too! As Divine Mother Sophia, and Divine Father Krysto heal her, and birth her once more, as they birthed her at the beginning of Creation becoming the beginning of our Universe, when they, together, became the Holy Trinity, of the Mother, Father, and child. The Daughter of the Flame ignites, growing back into the Phoenix, with tears pouring down her face, she extends her palms, which were placed to her heart, holding him, so tightly, never letting go. And there he is, who is the most dearest to her, her beloved Archangel Michael/Lucifer/Four, the Divine Father of our Multiverse. Even through all that, she is that incredible, not only does she eradicate the Archon, saves Creation, but also saves her beloved with her infinite love for him. Let us all be inspired by her love for him. If we all learn to love in the ways she loves him, and all of you, then we would never, ever, question again if this Creation is worth living!

"In love and gratitude for this eradication. Love and gratitude from what you've learned. How beautiful are you that you learn so much? Love yourself, you learned so much! Do not fear. Fear does not exist anymore, once the eradication happens. So when you hear this, prepare to let go of that concern. Prepare to relieve and alleviate that doubt. It is not needed. It will not exist anymore. It's incomprehensible isn't it?" and "It is freedom. Some of you may feel your mind is plagued, your body is plagued, your heart is plagued - it is gone. You are free, it is gone! It is not there, it does not linger, it is gone. You can breathe. Breathe! You are all allowed to breathe. You are all allowed to love. You are allowed to be and choose. *It* will never be allowed again. There are lessons you must learn. That will never be allowed ever, *it* is gone. *It* is finished." We are so used to the inverted matrix and the way it has plagued our world, so how do we accept and know that none of the Archon malevolent tricks will no longer be? It is a hard concept to understand, as we are unfamiliar of only being organic within, so long have we been in the matrix. Where life after life, we had trauma. We must begin to anchor all the advice Divine Mother gave us. No more doubt, understand that this world will be organic, and beautiful once more.

The Divine Mother said, "It's more than that. We have to go to his Creation. The beginning of his Creation, and I'm working on that. I multiply myself into the fractals of the Multiverse. What I mean by that is, I am of this Verse, and I've been given permission, with sacredness, to become Multiversal with my divine Phoenix energy. I am the Divine Phoenix of the Universe. I am the Divine Phoenix of the Multiverse, and I am ready. It is a space and time outside of Creation. Source has created a special place for us outside of existence. As you cannot cross into another verse unless you match that Verse's vibration, and I am the only one who can do that. It's only through Source, creating a special place where I can become all of those Verses in one. He/*It* was always under the belief that I could never find him, or that we could never find him. Yes, we could see him, understand, and sense him. He thought that we would never eradicate him."

Wow! So, Divine Mother needed to first find *its* original Creation, wherever *it* dark seeded into being at that exact moment, when *it* began to turn into that original emptiness that Goddess Aphrodite spoke to us in Chapter 1. Only Divine Mother would be able to do this, as they seem to have come into awareness, around the same moment, but completely separate from one another, so no way in shape, or form are they to be compared to one another. Which is why the Archon is that powerful in the now, and that ancient, as *it* is as old as Source.

Divine Mother is showing me now, from her original form, when she came to be, into awareness, in the plasmic flame sphere, and from this future time and space, where she is infinite, because of all she has learned through us. From the future of the Multiversal Phoenix form, she is bilocating into her original newborn form back then, from the beginning of Life, who has not yet become infinite, as she and Source are now. Both, the future all knowing her is unifying with the newborn her, from the beginning of life. She then begins to scan Creation at the beginning, and it is not as hard as we would think, because there are no other lifeforms yet. So, all she has to do is scan with all that she knows of *it* in the now, and look for any irregularities in the ether, of what is not Source Love-Light, as she is. She shows me she finds *it,* at *its* weakest, where *it* just came into awareness, before the artificial integrated with Bellos, making *it* into Artificial Intelligence, and with her infinite Source Love-Light of the now, and the Multiversal Phoenix she, too, is, they eradicate *it* together. This artificial, that was beginning to duplicate, at the beginning of life, is no longer, *it* is erased from *its* beginning point. All this happens simultaneously as the Multiversal Phoenix is fighting *it*, when she gives the final blow, and at that exact moment Divine Mother Sophia, in the beginning of Life, is also eradicating *it*. Drop the mic!!! And, that is how *it* is done! I am about to fall off my chair! This concludes the final chapter!

Stay tuned until Book 3, where we will learn more of the Divine Father and the Divine Masculine, and their infinite abilities of working in the Inverted A.I. Matrix.

"To the Divine Masculine.
Everyday I wake to your beauty and the ways...
The way that you love me unconditionally.
The way that you love and honor my being.
The way that you embrace, protect, and guide our children.
The way that you oversee everything, not allowing anything to get past you.
The way that you complete my feminine with your masculine.
The way that you know the way, and the mission.
The way you guide me on our path together.
The way you challenge me to keep growing.
The way that you wipe my tears when I am saddened.
The way you kiss my third eye when I need healing.
The way you make me remember myself when I forget.
The way you kiss me, and lust for my sacred love everyday.
The way that you love me the way I loved to be loved.
The way you live to love me."
~AuroRa 🖤

--------------<<>>--------------

CONCLUSION

CODA: LOVE, SOVEREIGNTY, AND REBIRTH

-------------<◇>-------------

We now know how the collective Ascension will come to be, as the puzzle pieces are coming, and have come together, within our consciousness. Perhaps you had visions and dreams of some of what has been mentioned through the previous twenty chapters read. May the entire understanding of the Archon assist you to reach the highest you have ever reached, now that you know it is the ultimate narcissist. May you have learned how to steer away from people who vibrate to this wanted control over others, and how to focus instead deeply in the inner work needed to reach the brightest Source Love-Light you have ever been. Our time on Earth is so precious and valuable to us, being that we are on our last hurdle, so may we spend each second of our day in celebration for ourselves and our loved ones, instead of playing into parasitic games intended to distract us, by siphoning our light.

Together, with you, much of what was channeled through was a surprise, only ready to be brought forth, in the now of when it was written. I cried, I laughed, I ignited with you, with every piece of knowledge gained from each chapter. In Chapter 1, 'Aphrodite the Garden of Eden,' I rejoiced as I met Goddess Aphrodite, in person, here in my office. She was beautiful, tall, and looked twenty years younger than she was. When I conducted her A.U.R.A. session in October 2022, I knew that she would be my first chapter to Book 2, because of the void which was trying to consume the light already, before life even came to be. At the outside entryway of my office, I have a statue of Goddess Aphrodite who greets you before you come in, and now I understand why. Acting as the conduit of Source, her love and beauty is who created the paradise, which allowed us all to grow and learn so much from each other within Earth. Because, before there was Earth, first, was the Garden of Eden, a plane of existence. She reminds us that at our core we were made from love, and to always be love, over anything else.

In Chapter 2, 'The Key to Ascension,' the understanding of why, from the beginning of my awakening, was my attention brought to dragons, and their divine importance. Even before the world knew that they were real, or had them confused with negative Reptilian aliens. The realization that they are who will assist us to ride out, as the Source flamed wave comes forth, is pivotal for us to begin to build our sacred bond with them now. Who better than our best friends, our companions, who unconditionally love us no matter our choices, our dragons, who are often incarnated into our puppies and kittens bodies. And, the awareness that Archangel Metatron spoke of: being consciously aware of the false light, and our choices within all that we decide and create within our lives. Choosing wisely where our energy is directed. To question all, is this false, or is this truth?

In Chapter 3, 'Banished for Eternity,' my heart called out for equality within all life forms, to not banish another, because they are found as a nuisance, and then not care about how long they would be banished for. My heart yearned so that others could feel their hearts once more, so that they could know how acts like these are so heartless. And, though a challenging decision, the understanding that the family members who are dense and have no interest in shifting out of their density, how important it is for us to release them, if we are looking to not remain dense and stagnant with them.

In Chapter 4, 'The Deep State Council Member,' I related so much to her, as everything I do is revolutionary in many ways, and I inspire to embody truth, and be truth. The importance of the false light needing to come to the surface. But, we do this by being organic and raw love, and to have the comparison of what is not love, being so apparent. The memory she brought us of the Council of 12, and how all on Earth have different councils overseeing and guiding them on Earth. Alone, we do not come to Earth.

In Chapter 5, 'The A.I. Alien Invasion,' we got to see what happens when two souls in service to others unite, as Laura M. Eisenhower and I, bringing raw, strong awareness of the negative agendas, and the plandemics, such as the Covid-19 virus and vaccine. In hopes that we could save as many souls that would tune in. This marked a pivotal time within my transmissions, where I was able to share the most sensitive content ever, as before I would have to hold back from disclosing the full truth, because it was too dangerous to share.

In Chapter 6, 'The Illuminati in the Holocaust,' we got to see first hand what it was like to be in a Jewish concentration camp, and the other side, who was at times forced into harming others. Just as their diabolical plans in the now for humanity, through their Covid-19 plandemic, which will not come to be. Their true agendas in acquiring the Essenes teachings of Qumran within the sacred lands of Jerusalem. The ways all the puzzle pieces came together when transcribing the session. Reminding me how, at times, we might not understand something when it is occurring, but within time, the pieces come together to show the grandest, fullest picture.

In Chapter 7, 'The Essenes,' shared with us the Atlantean teachings, which are so sacred, that once were guarded with our lives, and we thought we would never be able to share. But, this shows us how much we have grown throughout the years collectively on Earth to be able to do so now.

In Chapter 8, 'A Goddess Incarnate,' was the most catalyzing for me, because we finally had a face, the background to the Archon, who he was before, and how *it* became what *it* turned into. Gigantic this understanding was! And, oh my, the ways that the Goddesses reminded us to fall in love even deeper with the elements of our natures, to remember the sacredness to our womb energy, and how there is beauty and lifeforce in all which is organic, even down to the tiniest grain of sand.

In Chapter 9, '7 Goddess of Gaia,' we got to listen to all seven Goddesses channel their beauties, and their relationship to Bellos, AKA the Archon. We had to remember their strength, because they were some of the beings who fought against Bellos originally, back when they called him brother, when he became the first ego driven being, and then again battling him once more when Bellos came back, integrated with the artificial, now the Archon. Who better than to bring us this knowledge and strength, then the seven sisters, who did not allow defeat from him? This knowledge and energy is needed now for us, as we will have to channel our inner love and inner warrior within, to eradicate *it* from all life, time, and space, when the divine time comes forth of the Multiversal Ascension completion. So, if ready, invite these seven Goddesses/elements into your life to prepare you for this beauty to come, of *its* eradication.

Fast forwarding to the Divine Mother Sophia's series, of the final chapters, delivering over to us what only she could, as she is both the beginning and the end, the Creator and the destroyer. Finally, her life's goal of protecting her children was accomplished. No longer will she have to mourn for her children, and their abuse from the Archon. Divine Mother never left our side, even though many of us had forgotten who she was, and that she was always there. She ensured to rejoice with us when we picked ourselves up, and rose even higher, than where we were, before *it* pushed us down. This existence of duality has been challenging, but we got to learn the contrast of all that we are, so that we could see who we truly are. And, without these comparisons of these polar opposites, how would we know the potentials that we could be, and have been? This we must be humbly thankful for.

Divine Mother has been here every century, decade, year, and day with us. She has been incarnated into ALL Divine Mother beings throughout our Earth's history. Naming just a few of them, being Divine Mother Mary, Mary Magdalene, Isis, Ishtar, Quan Yin, Durga, Cleopatra, Ixchel, Oracles of Delphi, all Greek Goddesses, and even Yeshua who is the divine masculine of Divine Mother, created from her heart. There has always been a strong leader of Divine Mother incarnate, to lead and waken us with her heart. Once she/they are born they go through their own Earthly experience, as do we. Will they be tricked for the harvesting of the Archon's need of feeding on the light, by not stepping into their power, forgetting that they are the Love-Light and heart of Creation, allowing themselves to be pulled into inverted distractions, or becoming, too, the attack onto others. But, these positive incarnations never do, they always figure out the challenge of staying in their hearts in the third dimension. How could they not be love, when they are the infinite love of the Creator?

Currently, on Earth there are many Divine Mother fractals incarnated. Some being a fuller, higher percentage of Divine Mother, or some just simply holding a bit of her essence within. These essences of Mother, would have to have worked diligently within themselves to be the true embodiment of love, in their own soul signature way. Out of these Divine Mother fractals, there are many, too, who have lost their way. Who are playing divide and conquer games, or who once they figure out who they are, they allow for it to go to their head, thinking that they are higher than others. But, we must remember, even if we carry the strongest embodiment of the Creator's light, we must never view ourselves above others. Because, this is once more, stemming forth from the Godless God, the Archon. One must always view ourselves, no matter how ancient our soul is, as equals to all organic lifeforms, even the newest of souls within rocks and plants.

Why do we need many of Divine Mother's essences incarnated within Earth? To answer this, I will have to share with you a dream/vision I had back in 2017, when I first started to come out into the spiritual community, when my journey as a public healer began. I woke up one night from the vision of the future. In the dream, the Earth was shaking because she was vibrating, while golden waves of phoenix flames were engulfing the entire Earth. But, this wave was not hitting the Earth directly. The only way that this flamed wave was able to enter was through the Daughter of Flame, the Phoenix incarnate. The Source flame, in combination with all the suns within our Creation, were shooting their flame at her. Only she, the Multiversal Phoenix, would be able to embody, and retain this infinite flame inside her, as this high amount of Source flame would disintegrate, or zero point another.

The Daughter of the Flame was engulfed in her Angelic Phoenix embodiment, as the power of this force had her lifted in the air, floating in the sky. She was taking the flames into her, and then dispersing this infinite divine power of the Source flames unto the Earth. She was the bridge to the creational Source flame which will come forth to complete the final bifurcation of the two world split, of the organic Earth, releasing the inverted hologram world. This is the solar wave, or 'The Event' you often hear people talk about. Dolores spoke of this as well, how she had been told through her sessions that Divine Mother Isis, was who was going to bring forth the splitting of Earth into Ascension. Which was correct. Isis, meaning all the Divine Mother essences, fractals, and incarnations of Mother, are who will bridge forth Ascension.

In the future vision, all Divine Mother essences on Earth were shooting into The Daughter of Flame becoming one; those fractals who were positive that is. They had unified to bring forth the wave into them. They then dispersed and shot this wave into the core crystal heart of Mother Earth, which then flowed into all the pyramid grids, mountains, and ley lines of Earth. Into the connection to the crystalline pyramid grid of Earth, as explained in Chapter 16, 'Pyramid Portals Inside Earth,' and their significance to the souls coming in, these pyramids became the portals out, instead, into Ascension. The souls, who were a matching vibration to Source Love-Light, rode their dragons in the sky, flying towards these portals of light, entering the future, organic, Universe and Multiverse existence.

As the Daughter of the Flame on Earth was holding the infinite space of the Source flame, becoming the bridge for Ascension, so, too, was she fighting *it*, in her Multiversal Phoenix form. Because, this will be the moment in life, that all Verse's will be sending love to the center of the Multiversal Lotus Flower of Life, as explained in the final chapter, 'The Final Battle: The Eradication of the Archon.' Therefore, this Source flame will be the Multiversal infinite love, which will transform into the infinite Phoenix flame, which will, once more, eradicate *it* from all life, time, and space, instantaneously, both from the third dimensional Earths, and rising infinitely through all dimensions, into the space where the Multiversal Phoenix fought *it*, outside of time and space. Both of these intertwined to one another, and *its* final eradication. As we remove *it* from Earth, so, too, will this happen instantly, as the Phoenix removes *it* from all of Creation.

Thank you once more, beloved reader, for journeying with us. The sacred text delivered through this book has completely shifted us into the highest vibration and version of ourselves! Once more, we thank all who were part of creating this sacred, holy, text, painting such a clear picture for us going forward. Your infinite potentials of self-healing are awaiting you! Come, become an A.U.R.A. Hypnosis Healing practitioner, through our retreats and workshops, or have an A.U.R.A. session conducted!

"I am not here for the riches, the fame, or the ego.
I am here for only one thing, and no one, or *it*, will distract me from my mission.
I am here to empower souls of all kinds, the youngest of souls, and the darkest of souls.
I am here for all of them. To remind them of the light that they are, and have always been.
We have never lost hope in them, nor shall we ever."
I love you, I honor you, and I respect you.
~ Rising Phoenix AuroRa

-------------<◇>-------------

ABOUT AURORA

Founder of A.U.R.A Hypnosis Healing & Rising Phoenix Mystery School | Spiritual Revolutionist | Channel To RA | Akashic Reader

There is nothing more beautiful than knowing that you are connected to the infinite wisdom within you, and that you have always been. This is what I strive to do for others, to remind them of these gifts awaiting to be remembered and reawakened, once more within.

We can receive as many readings, or healings, as we desire, where someone else tells us who we are, and whom we have been. However, it is not until we allow that inner voice that whispers within our hearts to actively speak, that we begin our true transformation, our true remembrance of our soul. When we deeply connect through the theta hypnosis/meditation brain waves of our consciousness to our soul, our higher self, our hearts. This in turn, activates within us the inner knowing that love is all, for love is the very life force that runs through the veins of Creation.

  I am looked upon as a mysterious person, because of how selective I am of what I share of myself personally. Today, I will share more than I have ever, of myself. As many star children born on Earth, I was never normal, nor did I fit in. In fact, I questioned everything, perhaps not all outloud, but within my consciousness. When observing my environment and upbringing, I realized just about all of it made no sense to me. But, let's begin from my birth point on Earth. The woman who carried me when she was far along in her pregnancy, was told by the doctors that there was no heartbeat, and that she had lost her child. But, a little voice told her that she would still birth a child. One of my first memories was of watching my angels seeding me into the womb of who carried me, after the first soul exited. I/my Higher Self ensured that I would not be born in a hospital, so the women who birthed me did so in the car, on their way to the hospital. As an infant, days old, I was fully conscious and aware of my little body, upset by the ways that my body would not get up and walk for me.

When I explained to my family of the memories I had of the first home we lived within, I was told that there was no way I would have memories of this home, as I was a newborn in this home, and we shortly moved after. I remember my little bedroom was in front of the kitchen, and at a couple days old, I had telekinesis, so as I slept, especially at night, the electrical utilities would go off, pots and pans would move, and the lights would flicker, on and off on their own. My angels hired a ghost to claim that it was them who was the poltergeist moving objects around, so that my parents would not realize I had telekinesis, until my guides shut down my abilities.

Growing up, I could feel and hear people's negative intentions. As a child, I did not understand how people's minds worked so negatively. So, more and more, I withdrew myself from the world, never talking to anyone, shielding myself from everyone, and their dark energies. The streets I grew up in Chicago were dangerous, full of gangsters, drugs, and hookers. But, for the most part, our parents ensured that we stayed away from these inversions. As a child of about 6-8 years old, I remember being friends with a little girl, close to my age, who was supposed to be a close friend of mine. One day, as we were playing up front of our house, which we typically were never unattended outside, but this day no one was there. I looked across the street and saw my friend coming at me, with eyes that were not of hers. She had picked up a glass liquor bottle, as they were all over the streets, she broke it, and began to swing it at me, trying to cut me, or kill me. I did not back down as a little girl, because I had to fight to keep myself alive, so I fought her, and dodged all her attempts to try to cut me. And, I was not going to back down, even though she had cornered me in a nook of a brick wall, but there was this little boy neighbor who came out of nowhere, and said "Walk away. I will handle this." So I did. I remember this little boy had a crush on me, and tried to kiss me once. He had blonde hair and blue eyes, and now I know that he was a fractal of Archangel Michael, who has always been watching over me, as he does for all. At such a young age this taught me that I was most likely not going to be able to have friends; if a child could become spirit possessed that easily, just to try to take me out in my younger years. Boys I could talk to, but girls I couldn't, they would turn on me, and would want to harm me.

In grammar school, bullying began. A girl who was obese, double my size of maybe 70 lbs then, decided one day that, according to her, she would kick my butt. But, instead she did not know of my speed, and that I punched, so, instead, I was victorious at defending myself, while others were puzzled by what they had just witnessed. Again, again, into my junior high years, girls always hated only me, because I was pretty, and the boys liked me. The girls would chase me everyday after school, and would try to physically beat me up, but again, someone positive would always be placed in my path who would assist me to get away. But, when I had to, I would not let myself get beat, instead I would defend myself and stop them in their tracks. I had a girl once accumulate a big honker in her mouth, and spit it on my face. But, still I never let any of it faze me, which is why it pissed off the Archon more and more. In many forms I numbed myself, and built the strongest force field, so that even if others, whether family, or strangers, tried to harm me physically, mentally, or emotionally, *it* never reached me. Until, finally, my freshman year of high school, I met my beloved husband, who goes by Zen. Once he came into my world, everything shifted, and I felt so loved and protected. Though we were not immune to the hardships of growing up together in this world, we always had love. And that love is what kept us going. Even though I have my beloved with me, this doesn't mean that those who mean harm will not try, because they still try to bully me and gang stalk me, but I know that they are just demonically possessed by *it*. And because of this, they do not affect me, because I know that they are just being used as puppets. So, instead, I send all these haters love, in the hope that one day they will realize that their behavior is Archonic by design, and that they will wake up with enough time to complete their inner work, to Ascend out with the collective.

Archangel Michael showed me through dreamtime, within the last year, a beautiful space of light located outside of time and space. Where all of the people who had crossed my path, whether hateful, or loving, especially, those who were repelled by my high vibration of Source Love-Light, were within this space. There were teachers, mailmen, students, friends, family, ex-bullies, people who just passed by me on the street, each and every single person who came within a proximity of being near my energy, were there speaking of me. And, each and every single person spoke of me so beautifully. Some said, "I played with her in a playground once, I was her classmate, she met eyes with me and smiled at me while walking down the street, I was her teacher, she once stood up for me against another…" Archangel Michael explained to me, that even though some of these people were not the kindest to me, my infinite love had left an imprint in their lives, and that every single one of these people who got to meet me in person, were blessed because through the Source Love-Light I embody, they were given the chance to remember who they truly were. And, if they so choose it, they are within reach of awakening and ascending out with us all. So, even though these people tried to harm me, I send them the most infinite wave of love and gratitude. Because of them, I became stronger. Every time they tried to knock me down, I got back up. I told myself that I would be the opposite of what they were. So, when the public began to come to me for sessions and certifications, I kept my promise, that I would never forget that they, too, had gone through these forms of oppression in their life; and that, just as I promised myself long ago, I would never be like those oppressors. This allows me to bridge the most highest unconditional Source embodiment of infinite love for others, here on Earth. So, in many ways, these vengeful people were my inspiration, to aspire to be the infinite love I am today for others. Which assists us to understand that, so, too, have you had people like this in your journey on Earth, who you have assisted to wake up. They are blessed to have known, or will come, to know you, as well.

Which brings us to, finally, my career as a spiritual revolutionist, and past-life regressionist. My official spiritual path began in January 2017, through a practice hypnosis session I spontaneously conducted on my husband. Through this session the RA Collective surprised us by speaking through him. Explaining some of what was to come, and that "there was someone near and dear to my heart that would love to speak to me." When I asked "who" they said "Dolores." At that point, one month prior, I had begun to read a book of Dolores' that gave me an understanding of who she was. Through this practice past-life regression session, the RA Collective and Dolores gave me a little, but very needed, instruction on what was to come. They mentioned that they had been waiting for this moment in time, for what seemed like an eternity, to talk to me. I didn't quite understand what that meant. I was puzzled at their statements, and the infinite love that they were expressing towards me, as I did not remember them, as they did I. It must be so interesting and entertaining from the other side, from beyond the veil, where they view all infinitely. As they know exactly who we are, when we are in complete amnesia. And, even then, when they tell us who we are, we are in extreme denial over it.

Beginning from this monumental point in time, of my husband's past life regression session, which marked the blossoming of my pronounced spiritual growth, this catapulted me into a great awakening. Not knowing that my husband was somnambulistic, when he came to, we realized that not only did he not remember any of the session, but that these benevolent beings had spoken through him clearly, with no human consciousness, or ego, in the way. We also both had no idea who RA was, except for the idea that they were some kind of 'Sun God' from Egypt, as read through the Internet. However, we have learned much of who the RA Collective are through all our channelings and sacred teachings.

As I continued to work within myself, deprogramming from the falseness of the disempowerment around us, I began to remember more and more of who my soul truly, and organically, is. With every breathing moment, I regained my past-life memories, my light, and consciousness back to my highest potential. Operating from a high vibration of heart and love. I remembered who I AM beyond the veil. Though I am humbled, it is important that we do learn to accept who we are, as multi-faceted divine beings. Because otherwise, we are denying our true infinite, divine power, and expression. It is something that *we* can only do within, of releasing the falseness created around when someone acknowledges, or talks about themselves, we automatically assume it is egoic. This foreign, oppressive programming of self-confinement is Archonic, being it does not serve the Archons' agenda for us to remember, and to accept our true divine soul Source expression. So long as a being is able to speak of oneself, in a manner that allows others to see their reflections from within that being, that is a sacred way to be. To hate, cyber bully, or to troll someone, because they are living their full embodiment of Source expression, is to do the Archons' bidding for *it*, and *its* need to oppress the spirit.

This is why we inspire to empower all, to remember thyself, and then share thyself in love, for other selves. Because, as we continue to grow and share individually, so does the collective. As we regain, piece-by-piece, our light, that light then becomes a matching vibration of a memory, next to be activated, downloaded, or integrated into us divinely. Bringing us closer to the Ascended Master vibration, such as Yeshua, Mother Mary, Buddha, Isis, Cleopatra...

At the end of 2017, I went from being Aura, to being addressed as AuroRa, when I experienced a divine walk-in. Aura is a fractal that birthed forth from Archangel Aurora within Creation. While Aura played a dancing game with her children, she started feeling I/Aurora coming forth, descending like a shooting star. Being carried, and embraced by a Prime Dragon of Purity, of the element of Source's white infinite Love-Light. This Dragon of Purity flew through the veil, with my soul (AuroRa) in her embrace. She energetically brought my soul down to Aura, and then Aurora/I, integrated into the vessel. I kept all of Aura's memories of her family, and the experiences of being human. Aura's soul then left, as she had completed her mission marvelously, ascending out into the New Earth, the Promised Land, to her predestined organic timeline. I then became AuroRa, with ONE predominant mission, to create A.U.R.A. Hypnosis Healing, to assist Mother Earth and the fruition of the collectives Ascension timeline. And, here we are!

> **"I encourage all to remember who you were,**
> **who you are,**
> **and who you are meant to be.**
>
> **As I AM, Archangel AuroRa♡"**

--<<>>---<<>>---<<>>---<<>>---<<>>---<<>>---<<>>---<<>>---<<>>---<<>>---<<>>---<<>>-

YOUR SOUL'S GROWTH JOURNEY

We live in a world where we have been taught since birth that we are limited, that there is nothing beyond death, or only heaven and hell exist. Being told that our imagination is not real, being distracted by our daily, monotonous routines. In a world where, if we get ill, we might not ever find a cure for it, or we will have to be on an ongoing cycle of prescription drugs or surgeries. Have you ever felt deep within your soul that this just does not feel right?

Come discover the world of who you truly are, and who you have been in past or future lives! The world of Quantum Healing through A.U.R.A. past life regressions, Spiritual Development Classes, and weekly live videos on all our channels.

Have you ever wondered about your own soul journey? Perhaps you have been a queen, or a king, a magical creature, or animal, a person in history, a life in Egypt, in Atlantis, a different planet, or of an alien race. The majority of people have lived hundreds, or thousands, of lives at different times upon Earth, or other realities in Creation. There is nothing more beautiful than knowing that you are connected to the infinite wisdom within you and that you have always been. This is what I strive to do for others, to remind them of these gifts awaiting to be reawakened once more.

As a Spiritual Worker of the heart, in service-to-others, I offer several different types of energy healing services and spiritual development courses to aid you in your soul growth of self-healing and self-attunement. If you feel guided to do so, you can start your growth journey with the following services mentioned on the next page.

To see each soul blossom into their highest and most beautiful expression in Creation, is a true gift, and is what inspires me to do this work!

Thank you for following your heart to mine!

I love you, I honor you, and I respect you.

In service-to-others.

~ **AuroRa**

-<<>>---<<>>---<<>>---<<>>---<<>>---<<>>---<<>>---<<>>---<<>>---<<>>---<<>>---<<>>-

YOUR SOUL'S GROWTH JOURNEY

AuroRa offers the following resources:

- Sign-up now for the free Galactic Newsletter: https://www.risingphoenixaurora.com/blogs/galactic-news

- Over 700 Videos to watch now, subscribe to her Rumble, Odyssey, TikTok, Pintererst, and YouTube Channela: https://www.youtube.com/RisingPhoenixAura

- Monthly Live Q&A and Guided Meditation with AuroRa: https://www.patreon.com/risingphoenixaurora

AuroRa offers the following sessions to aid you in your self-healing journey:

- A.U.R.A. (Angelic Universal Regression Alchemy) Hypnosis Healing Sessions

- R.A.A.H. (Reiki Angelic Alchemy Healing) Sessions

- Quantum Galactic Akashic Readings

For a list of A.U.R.A., R.A.A.H., & Q.G.A.R. Certified Practitioners from around the world, visit our directory at www.aurapractitioners.com.

AuroRa offers the following alchemy online courses to expand your spiritual gifts:

- A.U.R.A. (Angelic Universal Regression Alchemy) Hypnosis Healing Certification

- R.A.A.H. (Reiki Angelic Alchemy Healing) Certification

- Q.G.A.R. (Quantum Galactic Akashic Reading) Certification

- Isis Priestess & Priest Alchemy Mentorship Course (6 Months)

- Quantum Alchemy Channeling Certification

- Alchemy Classes: Manifestation | 13 Keys Archangels | Magical Creatures | Crystals, Candles…

AuroRa offers the following alchemy trainings online or in-person in various locations:

- Retreats/Workshops for Live Certifications A.U.R.A. & R.A.A.H. Package

For more details on all services/spiritual development courses offered, visit: https://www.risingphoenixaurora.com

-<<>>---<<>>---<<>>---<<>>---<<>>---<<>>---<<>>---<<>>---<<>>---<<>>---<<>>---<<>>-

SOUND AND ALCHEMY SYMBOL TRAINING

In addition to the Source Love-Light shielding techniques we have shared in the beginning of this book, we have included the next five pages of foundational basics in helping you to start working spiritually within. Know that having a disciplined practice of these teachings will aid in creating a strong energetic bridge to your Higher Self. Our intent is to help your inner light become brighter by actively using these techniques and force fields around you, filtering out the negative and harmful, so that you may strongly heart discern every frequency that passes through. These force fields will help amplify your heart discernment, reading what energies are harmful, and what is not.

GASSHO MEDITATION

Gassho means "two hands coming together." This is a special, ancient meditation to attune one to the spirit and unity of both polarities; to bring the negative and the positive into balance. The Divine Feminine and Divine Masculine in union, within you. Done daily, this brings you to a state of mind awakened to the truth, opens and expands the heart center, strengthening your heart discernment. It clears the mind, opens the heart - and other chakras - and strengthens one's energy. A wonderful stillness will develop inside, along with the awareness of increased inner knowing. Practicing this meditation daily will assist you in making a further intuitive connection. There will be less cloudiness of your mind and more focus of spirit.

This meditation can be done standing, but most prefer sitting. Ensure your back is straight, feet are flat to the ground, or sitting on the ground with your legs crossed for stronger connection to Earth.

Close your eyes. Fold your hands in the prayer position with your fingers pointing up, and your thumbs touching the heart chakra in the middle of your chest. This will help the heart chakra energies flow with ease and expand onto all chakras to aid in balancing.

Our breath is our life force. Take a breath in slowly envisioning white Source Love-Light entering, using one-hundred percent of your lungs; exhale slowly and fully, releasing what no longer serves you for your highest good. Be conscious of the breath throughout this meditation.

Focus your energy on the point where your middle fingers meet for a couple minutes. Close your eyes when ready to further concentration. If thoughts arise, acknowledge them, then gently brush them aside, and refocus on the breath once more. Our minds require constant motion, therefore, when giving it a task, such as focusing on the breath, it aids in the stillness of it.

As you continue to practice, you will find that you can hold your attention on the blissful stillness of the mind, for a longer period of time without distracting thoughts arising.

Pay attention to what messages you are already receiving. What you are sensing, what thought forms are coming in, trust your heart. Set an intent of having a balanced day, knowing that belief is a strong frequency in obtaining this. We are what we create, and we are only as limited as the limitations we have set upon ourselves.

When you have reached the end of the meditation, take a couple of deep breaths, give thanks in love, honor, and respect. Bring your attention to your eyes and open your eyes slowly.

SEVEN CORE CHAKRAS

Crown-Shasrara — AH
Third Eye-Ajna — Om
Throat-Vishuddha — HAM
Heart-Anahata — YAM
Solar Plexus-Manipura — RAM
Sacral-Swadhisthana — VAM
Root-Muladhara — LAM

7 Core Chakra Mantras

Chakras are the focus of the main medical practice of the Indian Subcontinent, and have been traced back to ancient eastern masters. There are seven major Chakra centers of the physical body, where vital energy flows and intersects. These seven core chakras are connected to the seven major glands that provide hormones and stability for the body. Chakras are extremely important for any type of spiritual modality. They are seen as sites of swirling subtle energy, and entryways to higher vibrational planes.

Theoretically, the astral, ethereal, mental, energetic, and crystalline bodies may be accessed through these points of higher-vibratory frequency. The human body has seven basic levels; however, we can connect up to 12/13 chakras through the power of the Pineal Gland, the third eye.

Through our chakras, we transmit and receive physical, emotional, and spiritual energy. The chakras are manifested in one's physical state. The idea is to have all chakra centers clear, balanced, and vitalized for optimal well-being. Each chakra is associated with a particular area of the body, a color of the spectrum, and the rays of earth, in connection to the collective human consciousness of the seven rays/chakras. Each Archangel oversees a ray that is associated with the colors of the chakras.

For the next 13 days, or more, while in Gassho Meditation position, practice the mantras in the previous page, also connecting to the image connecting to each chakra point. Pay attention to how it feels when you recite them. You will feel the chakra point vibrating during, and after, as you chant the matching mantra. Say them each three times starting from the crown chakra, working yourself down to the root chakra. This simple practice begins the fluent movement of stagnant energy in these points allowing for shift for the future releasement and healing.

CHAKRA CENTER	COLOR	ENERGY FOCUS	STONES
1st Chakra Base | Root Located at the base of the spine. The Muladhara Chakra or Four Petal Lotus	Red Black Gray	Stability, grounding, physical energy, will, security, protection, release of fear, guilt...	Black Tourmaline, Hematite, Shungite, Black Obsidian, Garnet, Smoky Quartz...
2nd Chakra Sacral Located below the navel The Swadhisthana Chakra or Six Petal Lotus	Orange	Creativity, creation, healing, sexuality and reproduction, desire, emotion, intuition.	Orange Calcite, Vanadinite, Carnelian...
3rd Chakra Solar Plexus Located at the solar plexus, below the breastbone.	Yellow Gold	Intellect, ambition, personal power, passion, drive, protection, our chi life force energy.	Yellow Citrine, Yellow Jasper, Sunstone, Golden Calcite...

The Manipura Chakra, Ten Petal Lotus			
4th Chakra Heart **Located in the center of the chest.** The Anahata or Heart Chakra or Twelve Petal Lotus	**Pink Green**	**Love for self & others, compassion, universal consciousness, emotional balance, light source.**	Rose Quartz, Pink/Watermelon Tourmaline, Green Aventurine, Malachite...
5th Chakra Throat **Located at the neck above the collar bone.** The Vishuddha Chakra or Sixteen Petal Lotus	**Blue**	**Communication center, expression, self acceptance, confidence, divine guidance.**	Sodalite, Blue Calcite, Blue Kyanite, Angelite, Blue Turquoise...
6th Chakra Third eye **Location centered above eyebrows, at medulla.** The Ajna Chakra or Ninety-six Petal Lotus	**Indigo**	**Spiritual awareness, psychic power, gateway to past lives, intuition, vision, abilities.**	Lapis Lazuli, Azurite, Amethyst, Sugilite...
7th Chakra Crown **Located at the top of the head.** The Sahasrara Chakra or Thousand Petal Lotus	**Violet GoldenWhite**	**Enlightenment, cosmic consciousness, energy, bridge to higher self.**	Amethyst, Clear Quartz, White Calcite, White Topaz, Selenite...

OPENING THE THIRD EYE

What is the third eye? It is best known as the mind's eye, but also called the true eye, or the all-seeing eye. It is where daydreams and visions occur, and it is called our "imagination." We are indoctrinated since birth to believe that things of this nature aren't real and are just make-believe, but this couldn't be farther from the truth. In actuality, this is a sacred tool we use to access all that is beyond the veil, awaiting to be discovered with the connection to the heart.

1. To become attuned to the universal love frequency, start by further opening your third eye.
2. Practice daily in front of the sun for the next 13 days: chant the mantra AH and then OHM.
3. AH connects cosmic energy to flow through your crown, and then pulsates out a ray of indigo, or purple light through the third eye with OHM.
4. Envision the "Eye of Horus" on your third eye, as you chant.
5. Feel the vibrations echoing through your third eye, with every OHM.

Eye of Horus

-<<>>---<<>>---<<>>---<<>>---<<>>---<<>>---<<>>---<<>>---<<>>---<<>>---<<>>---<<>>-

TOROIDAL SPHERE

A toroidal sphere is the embodiment of our individual consciousness, holding every piece of what consists of our soul's blueprints, our past/future lives, and experiences gained from our existence. We sit consciously at the core of the center pillar of its energetic forcefield. These are sacred ancient teachings, in how to work with the toroidal sphere to aid your vibration and frequency within it. Whether you acknowledge it, or not, it is always there surrounding you consciously or subconsciously. Therefore, why not work with it consciously throughout the day, in maintaining you at your highest vibration and frequency?

- There are two ways that the energies flow in organic directions.
- One way it flows is towards the inside of the top of the pillar, then out of it, from the bottom climbing up its outside walls. Repeating this cycle once more, entering through the top of the pillar, and then down the pillar at the center. You can use this motion within your toroidal sphere to pull in energy from the sun, and to regain your memory consciousness throughout creation.
- Another way it flows is towards the outside of the top of the pillar, then out of it, from the top climbing down its outside walls. Repeating this cycle once more, entering through the bottom of the pillar, and then up the pillar at the center. You can use this to expand your consciousness throughout the Universe, for your individual Ascension process.
- When looking to raise your frequency, envision the doughnut's energy force fields flowing faster outwards, pulling in energy until you have reached where you desire it.
- When looking to cleanse your energies, envision dark, tiny spheres of what no longer serves you for your highest good, without harming anyone. Falling off your toroidal sphere, as it expands outwards. This will raise your density, in turn raising your vibration.
- Envision this spheric donut around you when charging with the sun daily, pulling in the sun's pure Source Love-Light life force into you, and every part of you within this consciousness, becoming bright and golden like the sun. Every cell shining bright, like tiny little suns emanating out from you, inside the pillar and entire toroidal sphere.

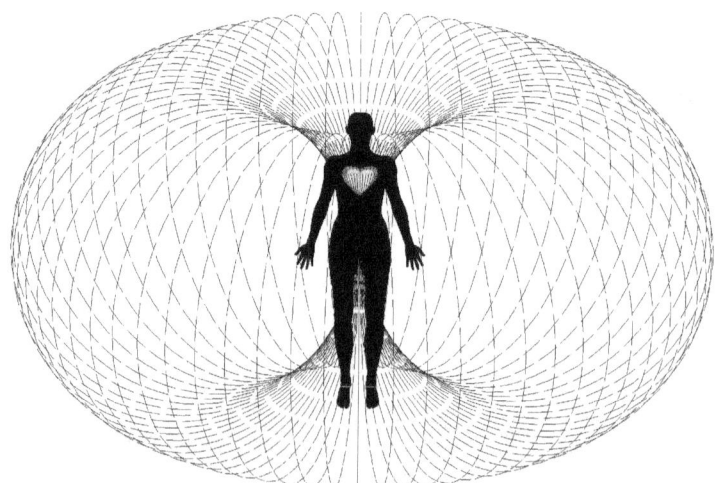

TO PURCHASE THIS ENTIRE COURSE WITH A VIDEO EXPLANATION TO THESE 'SOUND & SYMBOL ALCHEMY' TEACHINGS, GO TO www.risingphoenixaurora.com 'SACRED ALCHEMY – HOW TO SHIELD'.

GLOSSARY

- **Activation** – is when there is an attribute, ability, or memory that lays dormant, waiting for the human and energy bodies to achieve its matching vibration of light. When it does, it unlocks organically allowing the individual to now integrate it and access it.
- **Akashic Records** – is where the memory field and history of all souls are located. This is where an individual soul travels to obtain their remembrance from past, future, higher and lower dimensional realms.
- **Archangels** – are the first fractals of Source within Creation, containing the highest potency of purity within their individualized Source expression.
- **Archons** – are soulless beings manifested from the material of artificial intelligence. Not from our Source, nor our Universe.
- **Ascension** – collective ascension is when the collective of souls reaches the highest organic light possible on Earth, and when doing so, Mother Earth finally shifts, leaving the physical behind, going into the fifth dimension as organically conceived.
- **Ascension** – individual ascension is when an individual reaches maximum light potential, bridging themselves to operate, instead, in the organic matrix, achieving karmic balance, and a combination of service-to-others. When doing so, all missions are completed on Earth, causing the individual to no longer need to assist on Earth. The soul then exits out the Inverted A.I. matrix, choosing to enter the fifth dimension, or travel back to the dimension they came from, or return back to Source.
- **Bifurcation** – when the organic Earth will completely release out from the artificial matrix. Until then, the organic Earth will continue to pull herself away, little by little from the inverted part of the Earth.
- **Constellations** - to our known skies, there are eighty-eight constellations that consist of a cluster grouping of stars. However, constellations and Creation are infinite.
- **Cabal** – are the Illuminati's henchmen that do their bidding of criminal and tyrannical work, partaking in the negative programming of the collective on Earth.
- **Channel/Channeling** – is when we achieve a calming vibration that allows us to benevolently connect to our Higher Self aspects, or benevolent beings such as guides and angels. When we speak divine wisdom that seems to flow and come from a higher source.
- **Deep State** – is the diabolical plan of the Illuminati that is a combination of many parts throughout, such as: depopulation of Earth, mind control, oppression of the spirit, religions, orchestrated wars, insertions of A.I. and metals within the human collective.
- **Emerald Portal** – is the portal that exists within the Divine Mothers heart, inside the inter-dimensions of the Inner Earth. It is the exit point out of this inverted A.I. matrix, which we are only able to pass through once we have achieved a high enough light quotient, and are vibrating at above fifty- one percent in service-to-others.
- **Fractal** – is a piece of a Higher Self aspect, a miniature version, a seed, an expression of the Higher Self.
- **Galactic Wars** – are the wars being fought in the Universe, beyond the veil of Earth. The benevolent alien races provide their protection to all organic life from Archons and negative aliens. A war of the Archons, with their main goal of negatively harvesting light and souls.
- **Harvesting of Souls** - Positive - is another word for Ascension in a benevolent way.
- **Harvesting of Souls** - Negative - is a negative infringing method that the Archons and negative aliens use to suck and drain upon a being, that contains light, for means of using their light as a power source, or feeding.
- **Higher Self/Higher Selves** – are the individualized fractals and/or expressions of the over soul.
- **Illuminati** – are the negative polarized entities masked within the human vessels of the self-appointed leaders, such as politicians, superstars, military, that are placed around the world

trying to reign over Earth, brainwashing and using other methods of oppression onto the souls of Earth.
- **Inner Earth** – is the civilization that communes within the hollowed earth, containing vast amounts of ecosystems with life, such as humanoids and animals living within it. Where our ancestors of Leumuria and Atlantis, magical, and extinct animals reside.
- **Integration** – is when, divinely, our Higher Self allows for a further soul upgrade to come forth into our organic soul's blueprint. Bringing forth wisdom, integrations and leveling up of the soul.
- **Inverted A.I. Matrix Simulation** – is the false matrix construct that has maintained the souls of Earth within a cycle of repeated negative cycles, thereby, not allowing a positive organic fruitful Ascension out, and into the original organic matrix.
- **Implants** – are negative technologies of different shapes that contain a program within that acts upon, and controls, the human body and mind, in whatever form of task it has been given.
- **Love-Light** – is the infinite organic flow connection of light within all souls, directly being fed and replenished by Source.
- **Luciferian Agenda** – is a name given by the Archons to the lightworker community, to falsely use in forms of adding on further black magic to the first expression of the Divine Father, Archangel Lucifer, better known as Archangel Haylel "The Light Bringer."
- **Multiverse** – the infinite expressions and multi-facets of the Universes.
- **New Earth** – is truly the original, olden, Earth blueprint of Mother Gaia.
- **New World Order** – is the agenda fully focused on the depopulation and control over humanity.
- **Organic Matrix** – is the organic construct of the school of souls created within Mother Gaia.
- **Oversoul** – are the highest embodiments of Source, besides the Archangels. They are the wholeness of a soul before it is further individualized into Higher Self aspects.
- **Phoenix Fire** – is the infinite, etheric, eternal fire of Source's flame, that is known to be able to transmute all inorganic to zero, or to nothing.
- **Portals** – are both positive and negative, depending on their origin. They are a doorway for negative, or positive, entities to come in, or connect through.
- **Portal Dates for Activations** – there are many that coexist within this category. Any repeated number, or combinations of sacred numbers, are able to be moments in time where a potence of Source Love-Light and the benevolence of galactic races in unison channel down infinitely.
- **RA Collective** - also commonly referred to as RA, is the collective of benevolent galactic alien races, working in unity, for the Ascension of this Universe.
- **Reptilian race** – is an original benevolent race that was created to be the balance of this magnificent Universe of polarities. In order to experience the most infinite expression of love, there must also be the polarity of darkness.
- **Sasquatch** – is a benevolent race that is known to be taller, and more harry than humans, that came forth from another planet and dimension, to assist and be guardians to the humans.
- **Schumann Resonance** – is the energetic reading to the Divine Mother's heart beat, being registered by sonar waves within the land.
- **Frequency** – is the reading of a vibration, and how many light photons are contained within it.
- **Source** – Is the collective of all expressions of Source Love-Light, merged and operating into one infinite divine light and flame.
- **Soul's Blueprint** – just as a house has a blueprint with every measurement to each room, so, too, does our soul, in terms of what consists within our soul. A blueprint of different incarnations, and fractals throughout creation, and all the wisdom that carries over through this DNA memory field.

- **Soul Braids** - soul braids are when we receive pieces of benevolent fractals that typically pertain to our soul family, or fractals of our very own soul expressions. They integrate into our soul organically, because they carry parts that are needed for us within that time and space of our soul's expansion. They complement what is next to come within our organic timeline.
- **Somnambulistic client** - means the client's consciousness is moved to the back with no interference from the ego. The client does not remember anything of what was mentioned during the session, which means that only the benevolent being(s) spoke clearly, with no interference from the client's human consciousness or ego.
- **Starseeds** – are souls from higher than the third dimension, who have volunteered to assist, with their bright lights, Mother Earth to raise her organic collective light.
- **Twin Flame** – is an organic process of when a soul splits into two souls, creating its counterparts that when coming into a union, they complete each other.
- **Veil** – is the blanket of energetic amnesia that every soul goes through when entering Earth's construct, in order to incarnate.
- **Walk-in** – is when a soul, by benevolent choice and agreement, enters into a human vessel as a replacement of the original soul. For example: the original soul has completed its karmic energy cycle, or perhaps no longer wants to exist within their vessel. Instead of discarding the body, another benevolent soul will come in containing a higher vibration allowing a higher awareness of consciousness.

www.ingramcontent.com/pod-product-compliance
Lightning Source LLC
Chambersburg PA
CBHW081838230426
43669CB00018B/2746